A GAZETTEER

OF

THE COUNTRIES ADJACENT TO INDIA

ON

THE NORTH-WEST;

INCLUDING

SINDE, AFGHANISTAN, BELOOCHISTAN,

THE PUNJAB,

AND THE NEIGHBOURING STATES.

COMPILED BY THE AUTHORITY OF
THE HON. COURT OF DIRECTORS OF THE EAST-INDIA COMPANY,
AND
CHIEFLY FROM DOCUMENTS IN THEIR POSSESSION,

BY

EDWARD THORNTON, Esq.

Author of the "History of the British Empire in India."

IN TWO VOLUMES.
VOL. II.

LONDON:
Wm. H. ALLEN AND CO.

1844.

COX, BROTHERS, (LATE COX & SONS,)
PRINTERS TO THE HONOURABLE EAST INDIA COMPANY,
74 & 75, Great Queen Street, Lincoln's-Inn Fields.

A GAZETTEER,

&c.

LADAKH.

LADAKH, or MIDDLE TIBET, a very elevated and rugged country north of the Punjab. It is bounded on the north by the unexplored region south of Chinese Turkistan, and the Chinese territory of Khoten; on the east, by the Chinese territory of Khoten, and Chan-than and Rodokh, districts of Great Tibet; on the south, by Koonawur, Kulu, Lahoul, Kishtewar, Chumba, and Kashmir; and on the west, by Kashmir and Bultistan.[1] Moorcroft reports as to its extent as follows:—"The precise extent of Ladakh can scarcely be stated without an actual survey, but our different excursions, and the information we collected, enabled us to form an estimate, which is probably not far wide of the truth. From north to south, or from the foot of the Karakoram mountains to the fort of Trankar, in Piti, the distance is rather more than two hundred miles; and from east to west, or from La Ganskiel Pass to that of Zoje La, it cannot be less than two hundred and fifty. The outline, however, is irregular, being contracted on the north-west and south-west, and the whole area may not much exceed thirty thousand square miles."[2] The information obtained by Vigne justifies us in placing the northern boundary a little farther north, and stating the position of Ladakh as being between lat. 32°—35°, long. 75° 30'—79° 30'. The most important feature in the physical aspect of Ladakh is the great valley of the Indus, which traverses the country through its whole length from south-east to north-west, and divides the great northern range, called variously Kouenlun, Mooz Taugh, or Karakorum, from the stupendous mountains of Rupshu, Spiti, and Zanskar.

[1] Elph. Acc. of Caubul, 510; Ritter, Erdkunde von Asien, iii. 616; Gerard, Koonawur, 152; Moorcr. Punj. Bokh. ii. 258; Baber, Mem. Introd. xxvii.; P. Von Hugel, Kaschmir, iv. 140; Wilford, on Mount Caucasus, As. Res. vi. 459; Zimmerman, Karte Inner Asien's; Burnes' Bokh. ii. 221.

[2] Moorcr. ii. 258, 259.

Into this main valley others of less dimensions open, being drained by the rivers which discharge themselves into the Indus. Of these, the principal are the Shy Yok on the north, the Zanskar on the south. There is a general though very irregular slope of the country from the south-east, lying about the upper course of the Indus, to the north-west, where that great river crosses the frontier into Bultistan. The whole of Ladakh is included within the drainage system of the Indus, with the exception of Spiti, which is drained by the river of the same name, a tributary of the Sutlej;[3] and the small basins drained into the respective lakes of Chamorreril and Pangking. The most elevated mountains are in the east and south-east, where some rise to heights probably superior to those of any summits on the face of the globe. Lloyd, describing the mountains of Spiti, on the left bank of the Indus, observes:—"The summits of this highest range have been estimated, upon good grounds, by the Gerards, who alone have explored many portions of these wild recesses, to rise to the enormous elevation of 30,000 feet."[4] To the east, at no great distance from the frontier of Ladakh, rises the celebrated Kangree, or Kylas, also having the estimated height of 30,000 feet.[5] In the south of Zanskar are the vast peaks Mer and Ser, considered by Hügel[6] the highest summits from the Sutlej to the Indus. The mountains of Karakorum or Mooz Taugh, on the north side of the valley of the Indus, are believed by the natives to be of much less height than those just mentioned. Vigne, who has done much more than any other European towards exploring them, learned from native report that, at the pass into Yarkund, they are without snow for the greater part of the year, and he concludes their height to be somewhat under 15,000 feet.[7] A little farther west, however, this enterprising traveller ascended to the height of 16,000 feet.[8] Moorcroft[9] states the confluence of the Zanskar river and the Indus, near the western frontier, to be nearly 12,000 feet above the sea, and we may safely conclude that the elevation of no part of Ladakh is less than 10,000, that of few parts less than 15,000, and that a few summits approach the enormous height of 30,000 feet. At the eastern extremity, is the very elevated and dreary plain or table-land through which the upper part of the Indus holds its course, and which, terminated to the east by the colossal Kylas, stretches to the north-east into

[3] Lloyd and Gerard, ii. 146; Gerard, Koonawur, 29.

[4] Lloyd and Gerard, Himalaya, i. 143.
[5] Gerard, Koonawur, 141.
[6] Kaschmir, i. 194; ii. 166.

[7] Kashmir, ii. 364.
[8] Vigne, Kashmir, ii. 358.
[9] i. 417.

the unexplored regions of Chinese Tartary. These plains consist generally of sand or gravel, the disintegrated relics of the granite, quartz, slate, sandstone, and limestone of the mountains.[9] Occasionally low round hills may be observed, all as bleak and barren as the plain, and apparently incapable of sustaining animal life. "Yet such, and even loftier situations," observes Gerard,[1] "are the pasturing regions of innumerable flocks, where it is difficult for the eye to detect any nutritious vestige." In such tracts only do the shawl-goats attain perfection. "The deserts of Tibet are their natural soil, where they feed upon a prickly stubble or heathy-like grass scarce visible to the eye. Yet myriads of these beautiful animals chequer the almost barren slopes of the mountains to which they seem destined."[2]

[9] Moorcr. i. 266, 439.

[1] As. Research. xviii. 253.

[2] Gerard, ut supra, 246.

The great mountain ranges of Ladakh in general are of primary formation — granite, quartz, slate, and gneiss.[3] In one place, Vigne[4] mentions the occurrence of trap. The geology of the south-eastern part presents the singular phenomena of enormously lofty mountains of recent formations, such as stratified and conglomerate limestone, siliceo-calcareous rock, consisting in a great measure of shells, fossilized bones, and other animal exuviæ.[5] In some places mountains, consisting almost entirely of fossilized animal exuviæ, have a height of 17,000 feet, and overtop the ranges of primary formation.[6] From his own observation and the reports of the natives, Gerard concludes that "the mountain ridges and the plains of the interior, from the skirt of Ladakh, and even the limit of Turkestan, to the table-land of the Brahmaputra at Teshu Lumpu, abound with fosil relics, the living prototypes of which have disappeared from the earth." Notwithstanding that a large portion of the mountains of Ladakh are composed of formations usually metalliferous, the mineral deposits, as far as hitherto explored, are singularly poor. Gold has been found in the sands of the river Shy Yok, but its collection is discouraged by the authorities, apparently from combined motives of policy and superstition. Some lama predicted that unless the pursuit were discontinued, the grain harvest would fail, and there is also a belief that gold lying in the soil belongs to local deities, who would inevitably inflict dreadful misfortunes on such as should sacrilegiously seize it.[7] Lead, copper, and iron ores have been discovered, but these are too bulky and heavy for transport through so difficult a country, and as

[3] Moorcr. i. 266, 439; Vigne, Kashmir, ii. 263.

[4] ii. 358.

[5] Gerard, Obs. on the Valley of Spiti, As. Res. 264, 277.

[6] Id. ib.

[7] Moorcr. i. 314.

fuel is excessively scarce, they will, probably, continue for ever valueless, unless coal should be brought to light in quantities sufficient for their extensive reduction. Sulphur may be obtained in many places, and soda is abundant. Borax,[8] which is here an article of commerce, does not appear to be a native product, but to be procured by means of barter, from Chinese Tartary or Great Tibet.

[8] As. Jour. N.S., Sept. Dec. 1835, p. 178, Golaum Hyder Khan, Acc. of Moorcroft's Journey.

The climate is characterized by cold and excessive aridity. The snow-line, or lowest limit at which snow is perpetual, is so unusually high in Spiti and Rupshu, at the south-eastern extremity of Ladakh, as to shew the utter futility of attempting to theorize respecting the so-called isothermal lines, in the present scanty and imperfect state of our information as to the data from which they should be determined. Gerard observes respecting Spiti, in lat. 32°,—" The marginal limit of the snow, which upon the sides of Chimborazo occurs at fifteen thousand seven hundred feet, is scarcely permanent in Thibet at nineteen thousand, and upon the southward aspect has no well-defined boundary at twenty-one thousand feet;" and one summit, twenty-two thousand feet high, was seen by him to be free of snow on the last day in August.[9] This absence of snow probably results in part from the very small quantity of moisture kept suspended in the highly rarefied atmosphere, in part from the intense heat of the direct rays of the sun, the latter cause being in some degree dependant on the former. " Wherever we go," observes Gerard, "we find the sun's rays oppressive." In one instance, in the beginning of September, at an elevation of fifteen thousand five hundred feet, a thermometer, resting upon the rocks, marked 158°; in another, at fourteen thousand five hundred feet, the instrument, placed on sand, marked 130°; and in a small tent, at an elevation of thirteen thousand, it indicated 110°. These phenomena Gerrard attributes to the rarefaction and tenuity of the atmosphere, from elevation, and the absence of moisture,—circumstances which allow of such immediate radiation of heat, that at the same moment there will be a difference of more than a hundred degrees between places only a few hundred yards asunder, occasioned by the one receiving and the other being excluded from the direct rays of the sun. He justly adds, "These facts, and their effects upon the constitution of men, animals, and vegetation, are not properly understood in Europe, or, if known, are explained upon theoretical assumptions

[9] As. Res. xviii. 256, Obs. on Spiti.

which have no grounds of existence in nature."[1] At Rupshu, at the elevation of sixteen thousand feet, it freezes every night even at midsummer; but the heat of the day so far countervails the cold of night, that the lake Chamoreril, fifty miles in circumference, is free from ice during the summer months.[2] At Le, considerably lower, having an elevation of about ten thousand feet,[3] frost, with snow and sleet, commences early in September, and continues until May, and the thermometer, from the middle of December to February, ranges from 10° to 20°;[4] even in June, the rivulets are often, at night, coated with ice. Notwithstanding this general low temperature, as the heat of the sun's rays, during the day, in the summer months, is very great, and scarcely ever intercepted by a cloud. Tartarian oats, and other crops requiring a high temperature but during only a short period, succeed here, though they have been found to fail when tried on the mountains of Europe having a much higher mean temperature.[5] Moorcroft found the thermometer, when exposed to the sun's rays at midday in July, to range from 134° to 144°.

The atmosphere is in general dry in all parts of the country, nearly all the moisture which the soil receives being from snow. Moorcroft,[6] who lived in the country above a year, says— "During our stay, rain fell but on ten days, and then in very small quantities, between the end of April and the middle of September, and this, we were informed, much exceeded the average fall." In the very elevated tracts the parching effects of the attenuated and dry air are represented as greater than in the most sultry wastes of the torrid zone. Gerard[7] states, "The dryness was quite withering; every thing flexible is converted into a coriaceous hardness." Butchers' meat is dried up and preserved from putrefaction at a temperature of 66° or 68°. Things do not rot, they merely fall into dust in a long course of ages; the argillaceous roofs of the houses are actually baked by the sun's rays till they become like tile; timber is nearly indestructible, insomuch that in ruined buildings it remains unchanged for centuries, while the walls crumble away.[8] The vegetation, consisting of a short spiky grass, or of furze and other thorns, a few inches high, is never green, having at all seasons a brown and scorched appearance. This is the only food of the indigenous sheep, remarkable for size, the quality of the flesh and wool, and for strength, activity, and endurance,

[1] Id. xviii. 251.
[2] Id. 259; Moorcr. ii. 51.
[3] Vigne, ii. 341.
[4] Moorcr. i. 267; As. Jour. N.S., 1835, Sept. Dec. p. 179.
[5] Gerard, As. Res. xviii. 251.
[6] i. 260.
[7] As. Res. xviii. 260.
[8] Gerard, ut supra, 256.

in consequence of which they are the principal and almost the only beasts of burthen in many parts of Tibet.[9] From the influence of food and climate, the goat, the yak, the deer, the dog, and even the horse, acquire, under the ordinary hair, a wonderfully fine and downy wool, which they lose when removed to more luxuriant pastures, and climates of greater moisture and warmth.[1] Men appear to be alone proof against this influence, "being denied all beard, while their black bushy heads seem to be insensible to thermal changes."[2] This is the more remarkable, as the lamas never wear any head-dress.

The rivers of Ladakh are the Indus, or Sin-Kha-bab, and its feeders, the Shy Yok on the right side, on the left the Zanskar river, and lower down the river of Dras. This last receives a considerable feeder called the Pushkyum.[3] The Spiti river, as already mentioned, discharges itself into the Sutlej. There are two small isolated systems of drainage, one in the south-east, into Lake Chamoreril,[4] the other in the north-east, into Lake Pangkung. Both these are considerable pieces of water: the former about fifty miles in circuit, and brackish, the latter about twice that size, and extremely salt.[5] Thog-ji Chenmo is a small lake a few miles north-west of Chamoreril.[6] These lakes and streams are mentioned under their names in the alphabetical arrangement. The rivers receive numerous torrents, generally during summer subject to regular diurnal increase, from the heat of the sun in the daytime thawing the snow on the neighbouring mountains. From this cause, a stream, quite inconsiderable in the morning, becomes often towards evening rapid, deep, and powerful.

The scantiness of vegetation necessarily restricts the range of animal life. The carnivorous quadrupeds are bears, leopards, lynxes, ounces, wolves, foxes, and various musteline quadrupeds.[7] The natives informed Moorcroft[8] that the mountains are infested with a sort of tiger. This is probably the panther not uncommon in Kashmir. According to Vigne, there are yaks in a state of nature in the more secluded wilds, where also roams the kiang, an equine quadruped, respecting the zoological character of which Moorcroft[9] leaves us more in the dark than might be expected from his professional pursuits. He says "it is perhaps more of an ass than a horse, but its ears are shorter, and it is certainly not the gurkhor, or wild ass of Sindh." These

[9] Gerard, ut supra, 247.
[1] Id. 245-247.
[2] Id. 245.
[3] Moorcr. i. 264.
[4] Id. ii. 51; As. Res. xviii., Gerard, 259.
[5] Moorcr. i. 434.
[6] Id. ii. 47.
[7] Gholaum Hyder Khan, 177.
[8] i. 312.
[9] i. 312.

animals are speckled, fawn colour and white; they are wonderfully active and fleet, and utterly untameable.[1]* Though placed under physical circumstances so widely different, they seem to have much resemblance to the quagga which frequents the burning wastes of Southern Africa. There are also various quadrupeds vaguely described: wild goats, wild deer, ibexes, and wild sheep; and besides these, marmots, and a few murine quadrupeds. Birds are not numerous. Ravens are large, fierce, and powerful. The large chakor is a bird resembling a partridge, but of the size of a guinea-hen. There are sparrows, linnets, redbreasts, and larks. Waterfowl abound in the lakes. The rivers teem with fish, which the superstition of the natives does not allow them to molest. The domestic quadrupeds are horses, yaks, cows, asses, sheep, goats, and dogs. The *zho* is a hybrid between the male yak and the cow, and is very valuable both for draught and burthen. Though prolific, its progeny degenerates. The dogs of Ladakh resemble the Newfoundland breed, are of a dark colour, large, fierce, and sagacious. The Purik sheep is domesticated in every cottage, where it like a dog watches the meals of the family for fragments of food. It is very diminutive, not being larger than a common lamb of six months old, but has a bulky carcase in proportion to its height. The flesh is excellent, and the wool, which is clipped twice a year, is very fine. The ewe produces twice a year. Moorcroft[2] considers that it would be a valuable addition to the cottage economy of Britain, where three could be more easily maintained than one cur dog.

[1] As. Res. xviii. 247.

[2] Jour. Roy. As. Soc. 1824, p. 51, Moorcr. on the Purik Sheep.

Ladakh has little timber; willows and poplars are planted about every village, but there do not appear to be any trees of wild growth. The *sarsink*, which appears to be identical with the *sanjit* of Kashmir, the *elæagnus*[3] of botanical classification, is

[3] Royle, Bot. of Himalaya, 30.

* Our information respecting wild equine quadrupeds is very uncertain and confused, probably in some measure because hybrids may have been mistaken by travellers for unadulterated varieties. In a note on Hodgson's "Mammals of Tibet," and signed "Cur. As. Soc.," in Journ. As. Soc. Beng. 1842, p. 286, an opinion is set forth that the kiang is essentially a mountain animal, and distinct from the wild ass so often met with in the waste plains of Asia. Abbott, whose party chased and killed a wild ass in Khaurism, gives a description of it very different from that of the kiang of Gerard and Moorcroft. It was sluggish and slow, and instead of escaping by its speed, stood at bay, and attacked the pursuers with its teeth and hoofs. He observes, "the quarry just killed was a veritable donkey."

Heraut and Khiva, i. 227.

a tree, attaining a height of forty feet and a diameter of a foot, with leaves like those of the myrtle, minute flowers of exquisite fragrance, and fruit the size of an olive, of a cream colour, passing into yellow or orange from exposure to the sun, and containing a stone enveloped in a mealy pulp, palatable and wholesome. This pulp, when fermented, yields by distillation a spirituous liquor, generally preferred to brandy.[4] There are ten varieties of apricot, some of very fine flavour, others unpalatable except when dried in the sun; in which state they continue unchanged for years, and are considered an acceptable article of diet. Apple-trees abound and bear large quantities of fine fruit. A prickly bush grows wild in a great many places, and bears a profusion of small acid berries. The rhubarb of medicine grows in vast profusion and of the finest quality. Dr. Royle mentions it in the following terms:[5]—" Mr. Moorcroft sent some rhubarb, which for compactness of texture, colour, and properties, was as fine as any I have ever seen." Its botanical character has not been strictly determined, though mentioned by writers under the name of *Rheum Moorcroftianum*. Dr. Royle distinguishes it from both *R. Emodi* and *R. spiciforme*. However luxuriant the vegetation of the plant, the root is always found partially decayed, without the medicinal qualities of the sound part being from this cause in any respect impaired.[6] The western part of Ladakh produces an umbelliferous plant, called by the natives prangos (*Prangos pabularia*), and considered by Moorcroft superior for fodder to almost any other used for the purpose in any part of the world. The root is perennial, the leaves two feet long, and the stem five or six feet high. The whole of these are cut, dried, and used as fodder, which, though heating, is highly nutritious and strengthening. It grows on the barrenest and bleakest ground, and yields the enormous quantity of nine tons of fodder to the acre.[7] The Longma, or sand-grass of Ladakh, rises from six to twelve inches above the ground, and forming an intricate network of stalks and fibres above and below the sandy surface, thus protects itself from being blown away by the violent winds which prevail. It has a long root, which strikes downward so deep, that its lower extremity cannot be reached by digging. The leaf is stiff and harsh, with sharp edges, and though not relished by cattle as long as other food is procurable, proves highly invigorating when they are compelled by necessity to resort to it. This appears to be the principal food of the

[4] Moorcr. i. 209.

[5] Bot. of Himalaya, 315.

[6] Moorcr. i. 305.

[7] Id. i. 288, 292; Royle, 230; As. Jour. June, 1825, p. 708, Lindley, on the Prangos Hay Plant.

yak, the shawl-goat, and other quadrupeds indigenous in the wilds of Tibet.[8] Lucerne is extensively cultivated for fodder. The people of Ladakh are industrious and skilful agriculturists, forming the sloping surfaces into terraces, irrigated by means of water-channels conducted from the higher ground. The kinds of grain cultivated are wheat, barley, and buck-wheat, and Moorcroft mentions that some of the crops were superior to any that he had before beheld. Carraway, mustard, linseed, and tobacco are cultivated to a slight extent. The esculent vegetables are carrots, turnips, onions, cabbages, radishes.

The manufactures of Ladakh are few, rude, unimportant, and adapted for home consumption. The principal are woollen cloths, which are made thick, soft, and strong, and, from the cheapness of labour and of the material, are of very low price.[9] Commerce is principally in transit, as Ladakh, from its situation, is the great thoroughfare for commercial intercourse between Chinese Tartary and Great Tibet on the one hand, and the Punjab on the other. The most important article of trade is shawl wool, a small portion of which is produced in the country, but much more imported from Chanthan, and forwarded to Kashmir. The other imports from Tibet, or from Chinese Tartary, are musk, borax, drugs, salt, tea, sugar, gold, silver, silks, velvets, camlets, furs, felts.[1] Russian goods, such as broad-cloth, leather, hardware, and drugs, find their way through the same channel. The more valuable of these imports are destined to the Punjab. The imports from Kashmir and the Punjab are shawls, chintzes and other cottons, copper and tin utensils, shields, dye-stuffs, spices, drugs, pearls, butter, honey, and grain. It is obvious that very little of these can be intended for consumption in Ladakh, as there being no manufacturing industry, little but wool can be given in return. Moorcroft supposes the collection of gold, if allowed by the government, would form a very great source of national wealth. The beds of the rivers, he states, "abound with gold, in oblong grains and laminæ, detached from their matrix, and bruised, broken, and flattened in their journey down their stony channels."[2]

The population is of that variety of the human race called the Mongolian by Blumenbach and his followers, and are classed under the general denomination Tibetan. The amount is estimated by Moorcroft[3] at between 150,000 and 180,000 persons.

[8] Moorcr. i. 295.

[9] Id. i. 325.

[1] Id. i. 356; Vigne, ii. 344.

[2] Jour. Roy. As. Soc. i. 52.

[3] Punj. Bokh. i. 330.

They have the usual features of the Mongolians, but improved by intermixture with the Kashmirian; the women especially, according to Gholaum Hyder,[4] are pretty and fair, with rosy cheeks. In moral character they are mild, good-humoured, peaceable, and honest, but timid, indolent, excessively dirty, addicted to intoxication[5] and sexual immorality.[6] Gholaum Hyder[6] observes:—"They are the most peaceable race of beings in the world, very quiet, honest, and hospitable." In consequence of this disposition, crimes of violence are scarcely known. Polyandry is common among the lower orders, and, according to the last-quoted authority, under peculiarly disgusting circumstances. "In a family of two or more brothers who are poor, only one of them marries, and the wife is common to all, and no jealousies or quarrels ensue."[7] Primogeniture here has such high privileges, that on the marriage of the eldest son, the property of the parents passes to him, and they become dependant on him for maintenance, while the younger brothers are little better than servants. The men wear close dresses of woollen cloth and large mantles, which, for the rich, are made of European broad-cloth, for the poor of sheepskin, with the wool inwards. The dress of the grand lama or priest is yellow; that of other lamas of superior rank red; and as these dignitaries wear broad-brimmed hats, they closely resemble cardinals in costume.[8] The dress of the women consists of a jacket and petticoat of enormous dimensions, and a sheepskin mantle. When rich, they are loaded with a variety of fantastic ornaments and uncouth jewellery. "A Ladakhi female, in full costume," observes Moorcroft, "would cause no small sensation amongst the fashionable dames of a European capital."[9]

The diet of the Ladakhis in easy circumstances consists of the flesh of yaks, sheep, or goats, with vegetables, rice, and wheaten bread; that of the poorer classes, of barley, porridge, vegetables, and a very small quantity of bread. Tea is taken three times a day by such as can afford it. It is prepared by boiling the leaf with soda, then straining off the liquor, and mixing it well with butter and salt. They also drink *chang*, a weak fermented beverage, made from barley. They are fond of dancing, singing, horse-racing, and the *polo* or *chaugan*, a sort of game which may not inaptly be described as cricket played on horseback.

The language is Tibetan, according to Klaproth,[1] the primitive dialect of the aboriginal people inhabiting the vast mountain region between Hindostan and Tartary. It is very rough, and abounds in harsh combinations of consonants, unutterable even by those accustomed to the most rugged tongues of northern Europe. It has many roots in common with Chinese, and not a few with the language of the Samoeides, Ostiaks, and other tribes of Arctic Asia. Some consider that it has an affinity with the dialects of Turkestan and Kashmir.* Adelung[2] knew little of this language, though he gives the names of perhaps a dozen who have treated of it. Whatever may be the value of Tibetan literature, it has been cultivated by native scholars to considerable extent and with much industry. Csoma Körösi †[3] mentions one compilation in one hundred and thirty-six printed volumes, consisting of treatises "*de omni scibili, et in quovis ente*," theology, logic, grammar, rhetoric, prosody, astronomy, astrology, ethics, medicine, mechanics. The religion is Lamaism, a form of Bhuddhism,[5] resembling apparently in its moral and spiritual tenets those entertained by the early ascetics and by the quietists of later date.‡ In the existence of monastic establishments for both sexes, the acknowledgment of a supreme infallible head of the whole religious community, and the adoption of pageantry in public worship, some seeming resemblance has been traced to the characteristics of the Romish church.§

Moorcroft[6] describes Lamaism as "a strange mixture of meta-

[2] Mithridates, i. 69-71.

[3] As. Res. xviii. 509.

[5] Jour. As Soc. 1834, p. 654, Csoma Körösi, Pref. to his Dict.

[6] ii. 340.

* "The language of Tibet has much in common with the dialects of Turkestan and Cashmir. It abounds with nasals like the latter, whilst in articulation and accent it resembles Turkish." This position may be considered to have received the sanction of Professor Wilson, the translator and annotator of Izzet Ullah. — Oriental Mag. 1825, March, 111, Izzet Ullah, Travels beyond the Himalaya.

† This Transylvanian left his country in search of knowledge, and without funds traversed Persia, Turkestan, and Afghanistan, and made his way to Calcutta.[1] He subsequently explored Great Tibet, and gave the results of his researches into its literature and philology in a Tibetan grammar and dictionary, 2 vols. 4to., published in Calcutta. He, however, has abstained from tracing the affinity between this language and others.[2] He also gave publicity in various other forms to a vast mass of information on Tibetan literature and religion. Csoma Körösi died of fever at Darjeeling, in Nepal, in 1842,[3] apparently a victim to his zeal for knowledge.

[1] Jour. Roy. As. Soc. 1834, p. 128.
[2] Jour. As. Soc. 1834, p. 653.
[3] Id. 1842, p. 303.

‡ An extraordinary proof of this will be found in the summary of the spirit of Lamaism given by Csoma Körösi. — Jour. As. Soc. 1838, p. 147.

§ This view is supported by Wiseman, as quoted in Vigne, vol. ii. 251—256.

physics, mysticism, morality, juggling, and idolatry." The transmigration of souls is received as a prominent tenet. The Deity is worshipped in the character of a trinity, but adoration is paid to a great number of inferior beings, represented by a variety of curious idols. The general character of Lamaism appears to be more gentle than that of many other superstitions, and under its influence the terrific Moguls and other Tartars have become a comparatively mild and peaceable race. In Tibet all set aside for the service of religion profess celibacy, whether they be *lamas*, who may be considered the secular clergy, *gelums*, or monks, or *anis*, or nuns. The number of these persons bears an enormous proportion to the bulk of the community, perhaps because, in such a climate, the demand for food and raiment countervails in a great many individuals the other animal desires. Moorcroft[7] states that nearly two-thirds of the productive lands are appropriated to the support of the priesthood. Such a state of society may be supposed to operate as a powerful preventive check to the rapid increase of population in the narrow and barren territory of Ladakh.

[7] Trans. Roy. As. Soc. 1824, p. 52.

Previously to the conquest of this country by the Sikhs, the government was a simple despotism, which, during Moorcroft's residence, was administered by the Khalum, or prime minister of the Rajah, who was himself but a mere pageant: at all times the sovereign was liable to be deposed by the intrigues of the influential lamas, and his place supplied by the next in hereditary succession.[8] The revenue was not paid in money, the people being bound to support the Rajah and his officers, not only by furnishing provisions and all other things requisite for subsistence, but serving as domestic as well as agricultural labourers. They were likewise bound to take the field in case of collision with neighbouring states. Gholaum Hyder[9] says, the " troops are mostly horsemen, armed with a few matchlocks, bows and arrows, and swords, and may amount in all to 2,000 men; the infantry may be about 1,200 men, armed with matchlocks, bows and arrows, and swords." They are incredibly cowardly, and so ill armed that, according to Moorcroft,[1] on occasion of a war with their neighbours of Bultistan, the infantry had but one matchlock for ten men and one sword for six. It is not therefore surprising that Ladakh made no resistance to the troops of Gulab

[8] Moorcr. i. 332.

[9] As. Jour. 1835, Sept. Dec. 177.

[1] i. 336.

Singh, the Sikh chieftain of Jamu, who took possession of it in 1835,[2] and retained his acquisition up to the time of the latest intelligence from that quarter.

[2] F. Von Hugel, Kaschmir, iv. 140.

The *parganahs*, or principal divisions, of Ladakh are—Nobra in the north, Rupshu in the east, Spiti in the south-east, Zanskar in the south, Ladakh Proper, or Le, in the west and middle.[3]

[3] Moorcr. i. 315.

LAH, in Sinde, a small town on the route from Mughribee to Mahomed Khan-ka-Tanda. Lat. 24° 38′, long. 68° 30′.

E.I.C. Ms. Doc.

LAH, in Sinde, a small post, which was maintained by the Ameers for levying the customs, on the route from Cutch to Hyderabad. Lat. 23° 58′, long. 68° 40′.

Burnes (James), Mission to Sinde, 32.

LAHORE,[1] in the Punjab, a large city, generally the residence of the ruler of the Sikhs, is situate on an offset or small stream flowing from the Ravee, and about two miles east of the main stream. It is surrounded with a substantial brick wall twenty-five feet high, broad enough for a gun to traverse it, and strengthened by many circular towers and angular bastions at regular intervals. Runjeet Singh ran a good trench around the walls, and beyond this constructed a line of strong works and redoubts round the entire circumference, mounted them with heavy artillery, and cleared away such ruins and other objects as might yield shelter to assailants. The circuit of this line of fortifications exceeds seven miles.[2] The fort or citadel occupies the north-west angle of the city, and contains extensive magazines and manufactories of warlike stores, as well as the residence of the Maharajah. There are several large and handsome mosques. The Padshah mosque, said to have been built by Aurungzebe,* is a massive, lofty structure of red sandstone, of great size, and ornamented with spacious cupolas. It was converted into a barrack by Runjeet Singh. The Vizier Khan mosque is also a fine edifice, ornamented with lofty minarets, and covered with varnished tiles inscribed with Arabic sentences, which are popularly supposed to comprise the entire of the Koran. These splendid structures have been desecrated by the Sikhs, who killed swine in them, and converted their courts into stables.[3] The Sonara mosque is another splendid building. There are besides many handsome mosques and Hindoo temples, but they for the most part exhibit striking symptoms of the decay into which the city has fallen. One of the greatest ornaments of

[1] Masson, Bal. Afg. Panj. i. 411.

[2] Moorcr. Punj. Rekh. i. 104.

[3] Hugel, iii. 220.

* It is attributed to Jehangir by Hügel (Kaschmir, iii. 211).

Lahore is the Shah dura, or tomb of the Mogul emperor Jehangir.[4] It is very extensive and beautiful, of a quadrangular figure, with a minaret at each corner, rising to the height of seventy feet.[5] The principal material is red sandstone, but there is a profusion of ornaments executed in marble, arranged in elegant mosaics, representing flowers, and texts of the Koran in Arabic and Persian.[6] These texts consist of a hundred repetitions of the name of God in different modes of expression. There is a tradition that Aurungzebe demolished a dome that formerly covered this mausoleum, in order that the rain might fall on the tomb of his grandfather, in reprobation of his licentious conduct; but Moorcroft[7] supposes that the building was never finished. This beautiful monument is about three miles west of Lahore. It is separated from the town by the river Ravee, which has lately swept away part of the wall inclosing the tomb, and threatens speedily to engulf the structure itself.[8] The Maharajah gave it as a residence to a French officer of the name of Amise, who caused it to be cleared out and put in repair, but died shortly afterwards. His fate was considered by the Mahometans as retributive of his impiety in desecrating the sacred pile, which has since been closed up. Another of these huge ornamental tombs is styled that of Anarkalli, a youth, according to tradition, a favourite of one of the emperors, who, instigated by jealousy, having seen him smile at a lady of the imperial zenana, caused him to be put to death, by being built up in a brick cell, and this splendid mausoleum to be raised over him. Unfortunately, the tone of Mahometan morals is not such as to render the story incredible. Three miles north-east of Lahore is the garden of Shah Jehan,[9] the Shalimar, or "House of Joy." It is about half a mile long,* with three successive terraces, rising one above the other, and contains four hundred and fifty fountains, which throw up water, subsequently received into marble tanks. Runjeet Sing[1] barbarously defaced this superb monument of oriental magnificence, by removing a large portion of the marble embellishments to his new capital, Amritsir.

The streets of Lahore, which are very narrow and filthy,[2] contain numbers of lofty but gloomy houses, inclosed within extensive dead walls. The bazaars, though numerous, and

[4] Moorcr. i. 109.
[5] Von Hugel, iii. 161.
[6] Burnes, iii. 160.
[7] i. 109.
[8] Masson, i. 412.
[9] Burnes, iii. 160.
[1] Masson, i. 415.
[2] Jacquémont, Voy. v. 97.

* Hügel assigns much greater dimensions:—" Der ganze Garten der 1½ Meile lang and ¼ breit seyn mag" (iii. 258).

LAHORE.

stocked with profusion of costly wares, are in general contracted and mean. There is an abundant supply of water from wells in the town, independent of the branch of the Ravee which washes the wall.[3] The vicinity is fertile and well cultivated, being covered with the most luxuriant gardens and orchards. The great extent and size of the ruins scattered over the adjacent country bear evidence of the former greatness of the city. Von Hügel[4] describes the scene as a huge mass of serais, palaces, and ruins, which must be seen, to form any notion of their multitude and extent. The population is still considerable, the streets being crowded in an extraordinary degree;[5] yet in this respect, as well as in regard to trade, Lahore is greatly excelled by Amritsir,[6] which has recently grown up into a successful rival; for though Runjeet Singh resided much at Lahore,* where he delighted to shew his state, Amritsir was both the spiritual and commercial capital of his dominions. Still Lahore, even in its decay, is a great city. Von Hügel[7] says, that it stretches in a semicircular form four or five miles along the branch of the Ravee, and yet that if we judge from the ruins, it is not one-tenth part the size of what it once was. It is very difficult to make even any safe guess at its population, but from its extent and the multitudes which throng it, the number can scarcely be less than from 100,000 to 120,000. This indeed is a great declension from the amount in the time when it was the residence of the Mogul emperors,[8] and was nine miles in length; the population then, probably, was eight or ten times the present number.

Lahore appears to have fallen into the hands of Mahmood of Ghiznee in 1009[9] on his advance to destroy Naugracut, and in 1152 it became the capital of the Gaznevide dynasty. In 1186 it was captured from the last Gaznevide by Sahub-ud-dein, the Gourian monarch. In 1523 it was taken by Sultan Baber,[1] whose posterity made it a favourite residence, and raised it to its greatest splendour. In 1748[2] it fell into the hands of Ahmed Shah, the first Durani emperor. In 1799[3]† Runjeet Singh was, by

[3] Burnes, iii. 160; Masson, i. 411.
[4] iii. 256.
[5] Moorer, i. 105.
[6] Burnes, iii. 172.
[7] iii. 259.
[8] Rennell, 69.
[9] Price, Mahomedan Retros. i. 285.
[1] Id. iii. 675.
[2] Elph. 546.
[3] Von Hugel, iii. 163; Masson, i. 417, 427; Prinsep, Life of Runjeet Singh, 52.

* Our limits do not allow us to give even a brief abstract of Von Hügel's description of Runjeet Singh's magnificence. This (iii. 206—384) will well repay perusal.

† Jacquemont[1] states this to have taken place in 1801, and quotes Elphinstone, whose words however are, that Shah Zeman set out from the Punjab

[1] Voyage, v. 286.

Zeman Shah, invested with the government of Lahore, with the title of Rajah. He immediately manifested his determination to possess the substance as well as the ensigns of power, by expelling three Sikh sirdars, who attempted to retain possession, and he thenceforward made it one of his favourite places of residence. Lahore is in lat. 31° 36′, long. 74° 14′.

LAHOREE BUNDER,[1] in Sinde, a village on the south or left bank of the Buggaur, or western branch of the Indus, twenty miles from the Pittee mouth. When visited by Alexander Hamilton,[2] in 1699, it was the principal port of Sinde, being accessible for ships of 200 tons burthen, and at the close of the last century it was the seat of an English factory. It has since fallen to decay, in consequence of the contiguous channel having ceased to be navigable. Lat. 24° 31′, long. 67° 24′.

[1] Burnes' Rep. of Ports on the Indus, 2.
[2] A New Acc. of the East-Indies, i. 114.

LAHOUL, or LAWUR, in the north-east of the Punjab, is a small territory bounded on the north by Ladakh, east by Kulu, south by Burmawur, and west by Kishtawar. It is about sixty miles in length, and forty in breadth, and probably contains two thousand square miles. It is situate in lat. 32° 35′—33° 20′, long. 76° 30′—77° 30′. This territory is surrounded by lofty mountains, the Ritanka Pass on the south, having an elevation of thirteen thousand three hundred feet,[1] and the Bara Lacha Pass, on the north-west, sixteen thousand five hundred;[2] some peaks in the vicinity rising a thousand feet higher, and being covered with perpetual snow. Lahoul is traversed by innumerable torrents, the feeders of the Surajbhaga and the Chandrabhaga, the junction of which forms the river Chenaub. The elevation of the whole territory must be very great, as Kishtawar, above a hundred miles lower down the course of the rapid Chenaub, is more than five thousand feet above the level of the sea.[3] There are no towns in this secluded tract, the only collections of habitations being two small hamlets, one called Gosha, the other Tandi, both situate close to the confluence of the Surajbhaga and Chandrabhaga. Notwithstanding the elevation of the surface, good crops of grain are produced. The inhabitants, a Tartar race, are

[1] Moorcr. Punj. Bokh. i. 191; Vigne, Kashmir, i. 164.
[2] As. Research, xviii. 275, Gerard, J. G., Obs. on the Spiti Valley.
[3] Vigne, Kashmir, i. 203.

on his return to Peshawur, which he reached on the 30th of January, 1799. His guns were lost in the Hydaspes, on his return, by a sudden rising of the river; but they were afterwards dug out, and restored by Runjeet Singh and Saheb Singh.[2]

[2] Acc. of Caubul, 572.

much employed as carriers between Chumba Kulu and Ladak, and in this avocation generally transport goods on the backs of ponies, of which they possess a good hardy race, about thirteen hands high. The dress of both men and women consists of woollens, as well in summer as in winter. The cloth, which is thick, warm, soft, and smooth, is made in the country. The men wear coats, trowsers, blankets, woollen caps, and grass sandals. They have also coats of sheepskin, with the wool shorn short, and worn next the skin. A woman in easy circumstances is generally loaded with coarse trinkets of silver, mother of pearl, amber, turquoises, coral, glass beads, and small bells, the tinkling of which may be heard at a considerable distance.[4] The men, too, wear a profusion of earrings, armlets, and necklaces. Both sexes carry round their necks little leather bags containing amulets, given by their lamas or priests, for they are generally votaries of lamaism. The women carry leather pouches containing needle-cases, and other implements of female industry. The men bear about with them knives, steels, pieces of quartz, and tinder for striking light. Their hamlets contain in general from ten to twenty houses built of stone, two or three stories high, and with flat roofs well stored with faggots of willow or fir. The lowest story is a place of shelter for cattle, and access is obtained to the upper parts of the house by climbing up a notched stem of pine. These houses are built row above row on the steep sides of the mountains, each lower row serving as a step to the next above it.

[4] Moorcr. i. 201.

The indigenous vegetation is scanty, as might be expected from the great general elevation. Moorcroft[5] observes—"there was little herbage, except stinking hyssop, abrotanum, artemisia, pimpernel, chenopodium, and sorrel. The dog-rose was abundant with a rich crop of scarlet hips." Gooseberries, currants, and apples are produced, of small size, and sour, austere taste. There are juniper bushes, dwarf tamarisks, firs, and willows. The traveller just quoted saw occasionally[6] the red-billed and red-footed crow, and a bird which he calls "the large Tartar raven." The inhabitants of Lahoul are subject to the ruler of Kulu, who is regarded as owner of the lands, and who receives from the cultivators a rent paid in grain.

[5] i. 204.

[6] i. 209.

LAIGPOOR, in Sinde, a town near the left or eastern bank

Burnes (James), Mission to Sinde, 38.

of the Indus, and on the route from Cutch to Hyderabad. Lat. 24° 34′, long. 68° 28′.

E.I.C. Ms. Doc.

LAKAHURRAH, in the Punjab, a village on the route from Lahore to Mooltan, fifty miles north-east of the latter city. It is situate on the left bank of the Ravee, about thirty miles above its confluence with the Chenaub. Lat. 30° 30′, long. 72° 3′.

Map of Sinde.

LAKA-KA-TURR, in the Great Desert of Sinde, a village on the route from Jessulmair to Wadole. Lat. 26° 6′, long. 70° 7′.

Outram, Rough Notes, 256; Ms. Survey Map.

LAKOORA, in Beloochistan, a village situate on the route from Kelat, by way of Nal, to Sonmeanee, seventy miles south-west of Kelat. The surrounding country, which is rather fertile, is cultivated to a limited extent, and the road in this part of the route is good. Lat. 28° 5′, long. 66° 2′.

Walker's Map of N.W. Frontier.

LAL KANYO, in the Punjab, a village situate in the Doab of the two rivers Chenaub and Jailum, and very near their junction. Lat. 31° 9′, long. 72° 7′.

E.I.C. Ms. Doc.; Moorcr. Punj. Bokh. ii. 350; Masson, Bal. Afg. Panj. i. 157; Hough, Narr. Exp. in Afg. 311; Ritter, Erdkunde von Asien, v. 296.

LALABEG.—A small expansion or valley in the Khyber Pass, nearly half-way between its extremities. It is remarkable for a tope, or artificial mound, of great dimensions and high antiquity; the dilapidation of which so far exposes its structure, as to shew that it is solid and built of unburnt bricks laid in mortar. There are two square platforms, one rising above the other and displaying some attempts at architectural ornament. These are surmounted by a solid dome-shaped building, one hundred and ten yards in circumference and fifty feet high, the base being accessible by a flight of steps. Its origin and the date of its erection are unknown, but it has been supposed to be a *dhagope* or Budhist monument, intended to preserve the remains of some eminent person of that persuasion; and at the same time to enshrine some relic connected with the same belief. Lat. 34° 8′, long. 71° 17′.

LALLEE, in the Punjab, a town in the Doab of Jinhut, and nearly equidistant from the Chenaub and the Jailum. It is situate in a level desert tract, and at the base of an inconsiderable eminence, the summit of which is occupied by a station of fakirs, and is also a much frequented place of pilgrimage. The population of the town is about 5,000. Lat. 31° 49′, long. 72° 33′.

LALLOO, in Sinde, a village on the road from Bukkur to Hyderabad, sixty miles south of the former town. Lat. 26° 52', long. 68° 46'.

Ms. Survey Map.

LALPOOR.—A town on the north or left bank of the Kabool river, at the eastern extremity of the plain of Jelalabad. Here, the Caroppa route crosses by a ferry to the main road from the Khyber Pass to Jelalabad. The river at this point is sometimes fordable, and in April, 1842, was actually forded by a detachment of the British army, sent to expel the Afghan chief of the town and district. The elevation above the sea is 1,404 feet. Lat. 34° 17', long. 71° 4'.

E.I.C. Ms. Map; Mil. Op. in Afg. 233; Jour. As. Soc. 1842, p. 78, Grif. Bar. and Ther. Obs. in Afg; Hough, Narr. of Exp. in Afg. 306; Leech, Khyber Pass, 11.

LANDEE KHANA,[1] the most difficult part of Khyber Pass, lying about twenty-three miles from Kadam, the eastern entrance, and seven from the western entrance.* The pass here descends very steeply to the west, and is both narrow and rugged, so as to be with difficulty practicable for wheel-carriages. It is in one place a mere gallery, twelve feet wide, with the lofty rock rising like a wall on the north side, and a deep precipice on the south.[2] In April, 1842, the British army, under General Pollock, when forcing the Khyber Pass, encamped near this spot.[3] The elevation above the sea is 2,488 feet. Landee Khana is in lat. 34° 10', long. 71° 13'.

[1] E.I.C. Ms. Map; Id. Khyber Pass, 10; Jour. As. Soc. 1842, p. 78, Grif. Bar. and Ther. Meas. in Afg.; Hough, Exp. in Afg. 310.

[2] Havelock, War in Afg. ii. 189.

[3] Mil. Op. in Afg. 210.

LARAM MOUNTAINS, in Northern Afghanistan, a range dividing the valley of Suwat from that of Panjkora. Very little is known respecting it, except that it extends about sixty miles in a direction from north-east to south-west. Lat. 35° 20', long. 72°.

Jour. As. Soc. 1839, p. 312, Alexander's Exploits on the Western Bank of the Indus, by M. A. Court, Map.

LARGEBUR KAHREEZ, in Western Afghanistan, a village on the route from Kandahar to Herat, and two hundred miles north-west of the former place. It lies in a valley, bounded on both sides by very lofty mountains, estimated to have an altitude of ten thousand feet above the level of the sea. There is an abundant supply of good water from a Kahreez, or subterraneous aqueduct, and some cultivation is observable in the neighbourhood. Lat. 32° 32', long. 62° 54'.

E.I.C. Ms. Doc.; Conolly, Jour. to India, ii. 68.

LARGEE, in Afghanistan, a dreary valley north of the Derajat, and separated from the Indus by a prolongation of the

Elph. Acc. of Caubul, 35.

* Some consider this celebrated defile to terminate about a mile and a half westward of Landee Khana, whilst others extend it nearly to Duka, about seven miles farther in that direction.

Salt range of mountains. It is about forty miles in length and eight or ten in breadth, arid, barren, and desert, being visited merely because the great route from north to south, along the western side of the Indus, passes through it. The middle part is in lat. 32° 20′, long. 71° 15′.

Burnes' Pers. Narr. 44; Leech, Rep. on Sindian Army, 65; Kennedy, ii. 180; Outram, 50; Masson, i. 461; Burnes, Rep. on Commerce of Shikarpore, 29.

LARKHANA, in Sinde, a town fourteen miles west of the Indus, situate on a great canal, which leaves the main stream of that river near Sukkur, and communicates with the Narra, or great western branch. The surrounding country, which is fertile, populous, and highly cultivated, is probably the finest tract in Sinde. The town is rudely fortified, and has a citadel at its western end, which, during the rule of the Talpoor dynasty, was the head depôt of the artillery of the Ameers of Hyderabad. Larkhana is one of the principal grain marts of Sinde, and has a good bazaar, containing three hundred and seventy shops, well supplied with wares. The principal manufactures are the weaving of silk and cotton, which are of the yearly value of 6,000*l*.; and the place derives some commercial advantages from being situate on the great route from Southern Sinde to Cutch Gundava, Beloochistan, and Kandahar, through the Bolan Pass. The population, estimated at 10,000 or 12,000, bear a character of great profligacy. Near the town, on the banks of the Narra, is a large ruined fortress, called Maihota, built on a huge mound. Larkhana is in lat. 27° 30′, long. 68° 16′.

LARKHARA.—See LARKHANA.

Jour. As. Soc. 1839, p. 312, Alexander's Exploits on the Western Bank of the Indus, by M. A. Court. Map.

LASPISSOR MOUNTAINS, in Northern Afghanistan, a range subordinate to Hindoo Koosh, and south of it. They have been very slightly explored, but are represented to extend about fifty miles, in a direction generally from east to west. Lat. 36°, long. 70°.

Jour. As. Soc. 1841, p. 332, Conolly (E.), Jour. of Travel in Seistan.

LAUSH, in Afghanistan, in the province of Seistan, is an ancient fort, belonging to a local chief of the Ishaukzye tribe of Afghans. It is, as the name vernacularly implies, built on a cliff. The cliff is four hundred feet high; the Furrah river flows at its eastern base, and is undermining the weak and friable mass so rapidly, that in a few years it must fall with the superincumbent buildings. There are many caves excavated in the cliff, having access and communication with each other by subterraneous passages, and intended as places of refuge for the inhabitants in cases of extreme danger. The people of the country consider this fort impregnable, it being inaccessible on the side of the cliff, and rendered difficult of approach on the north and west by deep ravines. It could, however, be stormed from the south, and is so slenderly built that it might easily be destroyed by shells; or the whole might be overthrown by exploding a mine under the cliff. Shah Pussund, the Ishaukzye chief, obtained this fort by stratagem from Shah Kamran, of Herat, who has made repeated attempts to regain possession of it; these have hitherto been fruitless, but the failure of native attacks affords no ground for concluding it to be proof against the resources of European skill and science. The surrounding district, called Hak, is remarkably fertile and well watered, but has been miserably devastated by the frequent inroads made by the troops of Herat. Laush is in lat. 31° 51′, long. 61° 46′.

LAVOR, in Afghanistan, a village in the district of Booneere, twenty miles north of the junction of the Kabool river with the Indus, in lat. 34° 12′, long. 72° 18′.

E.I.C. Ms. Doc.

LE,[1] in Ladakh, or Middle Tibet, of which it is the capital, is situated about two miles from the right or northern bank of the Indus, here called Sin-kha-bab. A narrow sandy plain stretches between the river and a chain of mountains, which rise on the north about two thousand feet, and on this level space the town is built. It is enclosed by a wall surmounted at intervals with conical or square towers, and extending on each side to the summit of the mountains. The streets are very irregular and intricate; in many places they are covered over. The houses varying in height from one to three stories, and in some instances extending to more, are built partly of stone, partly of unburned brick; being whitewashed, they have a lively appearance. They generally have wooden balconies in front. The roofs are flat and ill-constructed of the trunks of poplars, covered with a layer of willow twigs, and this with another of straw, a coat of mud overlaying the whole, which at last constitutes a very insufficient defence against rain. The walls taper as they rise, so that the outer surface slopes inwards. The rain and cold are very imperfectly excluded by wooden shutters, or strong curtains drawn across the windows. There are no chimneys, and the wood-smoke is consequently offensive and suffocating, often producing severe and permanent injury to the eyes. The furniture is very rude, and withal very scanty. The floor sometimes serves for bed, chair, and table, while sheep, goats,

[1] Vigne, Kashmir, ii. 340; Quarterly Oriental Mag. March, 1825, p. 107, Izzet Ullah, Travels beyond the Himalaya; Moorcr. Punj. Bokh. i. 315; As. Jour. Sept. Dec. 1835, i. 175, Gholaum Hyder.

and other stock, not unfrequently lodge in the same room with the family. The palace of the Raja, though simple in construction, and rude in finish, yet being several stories high, and having a front of two hundred and fifty feet, is a conspicuous object. There are several temples as rudely built as the houses. The hereditary Raja, a votary of Lamaism, was deposed by Guolab Singh, the powerful Sikh chieftain of Jamu, who now holds the country.

Le is important as the great rendezvous for the intercourse between the Punjab and Chinese Tartary, and the principal mart for the sale of shawl-wool brought from the latter region. It has above five hundred * houses, and probably four thousand inhabitants. Its elevation above the sea is stated by Moorcroft[2] to be more than 11,000 feet, and by Vigne[3] to be about 10,000. Lat. 34° 11′, long. 72° 14′.

[2] i. 259.
[3] ii. 341.

LEHREE,[1] in Beloochistan, a town of Cutch Gundava, is situate near the southern base of the mountains, connecting the Suliman range with the Hala. Pottinger[2] describes it as having from a thousand to fifteen hundred houses, and surrounded by a mud rampart, strengthened with bastions. Here, in the beginning of 1841, Nusseer Khan, the son of the slain Mehrab Khan of Kelat, assembled an army of about four thousand men, attempting to maintain a post among the neighbouring hills; but being attacked by a British force, consisting of nine hundred sepoys, sixty irregular cavalry, and two field pieces, commanded by Lieutenant-colonel Marshal, he was utterly routed and fled, accompanied by only two men.[3] Lehree is in lat. 29° 14′, long. 68° 24′.

[1] E.I.C. Ms. Doc.; Masson, Kalat, 382.
[2] Belooch, 310.
[3] Jackson, Views in Afg. 18.

LEIA,[1] in the Punjab, an important commercial town, situate on a small branch of the Indus, about three miles eastward of the main stream. It is a place of great business, not only in direct but in transit trade, as it lies on the main road from Hindostan to the west by the Kaheree ferry, and is, besides, the mart for the abundant and rich produce of the surrounding fertile country. The principal articles of sale are indigo, madder, sugar, silk, cotton, wool, iron, copper, groceries of various kinds, ghee, or clarified butter, and grain. It yields a revenue of a hundred and twenty-seven thousand rupees. The population is 15,000, and

[1] Leech, on Leia, 89; Burnes, on the Derajat, 98.

* So states Moorcroft,[1] but Gholaum Hyder[2] gives the number at fifteen hundred.

[1] Punj. Bokh. i. 316.
[2] As. Jour. 1835, i. 175.

must have greatly increased from the time of Elphinstone,[2] who describes it as a poor place, containing five hundred houses. Lat. 30° 59', long. 70° 59'.

[2] Acc. of Caubul, 27.

LIDUR, a river of Kashmir, is one of the feeders of the Behut or Jailum, and by some considered the principal of the streams which unite to form its volume. It rises on the southern slope of the mountain bounding Kashmir on the north-east, in lat. 34° 10', long. 75° 35', and at an elevation of probably not less than 14,000 feet. Its current is in consequence very rapid until it reaches the alluvial tract in the bottom of the valley, where it becomes a dull and muddy stream. After a course of about forty-five miles in a south-westerly direction, it falls into the Jailum, about five miles below Islamabad, in lat. 33° 40', long. 75° 3'. At the confluence, the volume of water of the Lidur is scarcely inferior to that of the Jailum.

Vigne, Kashmir, ii. 22; F. Von Hugel, Kaschmir, iv. 288; Moorcr. Punj. Bokh. ii. 110, 246.

LILLEAH, in Sinde, a village situate near the left bank of the Indus. Lat. 26° 42', long. 67° 59'.

Walker's Map of Sinde.

LODHU, in Sinde, a village on the route from Bukkur to Hyderabad, and thirty-two miles south of the former place. Lat. 27° 16', long. 68° 54'.

Ms. Survey Map.

LOGURH, in Afghanistan, a district of considerable extent, south of the city of Kabool. It extends up the northern slope of the high land of Ghuznee, and, as its elevation in all parts exceeds six thousand feet, the climate is very severe in winter. The Logurh river with its various feeders intersects and drains this district, which, being fertile, well watered, and cultivated with much care, is one of the most productive parts of the country. Lat. 34° 20', long. 69°.

E.I.C. Ms. Doc.; Elph. Acc. of Caubul, 434; Baber, Mem. 148.

LOGURH, a river of Afghanistan, rises south-west of the city of Kabool, in a volcanic district of singular conformation and appearance, and which is also called Logurh. After a course of about eighty miles, it falls, about ten miles north-east of Kabool, into the river of the same name, in lat. 34° 32', long. 69° 8'. It is superior to the Kabool river in length, and perhaps equal in volume of water.

E.I.C. Ms. Doc.; Masson, Bal. Afg. Panj. ii. 207, 358; Baber, Mem. 148.

LOLAB.—A long narrow valley, embosomed in the Green Mountains, forming the northern boundary of Kashmir. It in one place has a large level circular expansion about five and a half miles in diameter, described by Vigne as realizing all that the imagination can picture of quietude and retirement. In the

Vigne, Kashmir, ii. 169.

centre is a morass which appears to have been once a lake; the sides are verdant, and overgrown in many places with jungle. It seems to be a sort of *Nephelococcygia*, or metropolis for the birds of Kashmir, which every evening congregate here in vast numbers. Ravens, crows, and jackdaws appear in great flocks in the air above the tops of the enclosing mountain, and all moving towards Lolab. As soon as they are sufficiently near their resting place, they dart down with surprising rapidity, and alight in such countless numbers as literally to blacken the ground. Lolab valley is drained by a small river of the same name, which, rising in the expansion just mentioned, holds a circuitous course, first in a westerly, and then in a south-easterly direction, and at the distance of about thirty-five miles from its source falls into the Jailum, in lat. 34° 13′, long. 74° 17′. The singular place of concourse for birds is in lat. 33° 34′, long. 74° 52′.

E.I.C. Ms. Doc.

LOLUM, or more properly Lolur, in Kashmir, a village thirty-two miles north of the town of Sirinagur. Lat. 34° 26′, long. 74° 24′.

Vigne, Kashmir, ii. 160.

LOODHUN, in the Punjab, a village situate on a watercourse connected with the river Ghara, from the right bank of which it is distant about four miles, and sixty miles south-east of Mooltan. Lat. 29° 51′, long. 72° 27′.

E.I.C. Ms. Doc.

LOONEE, in Afghanistan, a village on the route from Ghuznee to Dera Ismael Khan, about thirty-five miles west of the latter town. It is situate on the Gomul river. Lat. 31° 54′, long. 70° 20′.

E.I.C. Ms. Doc.; Masson, Bal. Afg. Panj. i. 321, 325; Atkinson, Exp. into Afg. 189; Hough, Narr. of Exp. in Afg. 77.

LORA, a river of Southern Afghanistan, rises about fifty miles north-east of Quetta, or Shawl, in lat. 30° 49′, long. 67° 20′, and, after flowing south-west for a distance of about eighty miles, is lost in the sands of the desert of Khorasan. Its water is briny. The Rogani Pass, from Sewestan to Shorawuck, winds along its course. It is crossed, five miles north of Hykulzie, by the route from Shawl to Kandahar, and has there a channel between forty and fifty feet deep. In April, the water was found to be only seven or eight yards wide and two feet deep. The name is generic, signifying " river," in the language of the natives.

E.I.C. Ms. Doc.

LORA, in Afghanistan, on the route from Ghuznee to Kabool, and nineteen miles north-east of the former place, is a district containing some walled villages, and abounding in streams, which render the road through it difficult. Lat. 33° 46′, long. 68° 27′.

LORGURKARA, in Bhawlpoor, a village on the route from Khanpoor to Subzulcote, and twenty-six miles north-east of the latter place. Lat. 28° 22′, long. 70° 5′. E.I.C. Ms. Doc.

LOSUR,[1] in Ladakh, a village of Spiti, is situate near the confluence of the Losur river with the river of Peeno. It is the last inhabited spot which travellers find in ascending the course of the latter river, and has an elevation of about 13,400 feet.[2] Above this part of the valley, through which the river flows, the mountains rise in mural cliffs so steep that no snow can rest on their faces, though it lies deeply on their tops, which are for the most part flattened, forming table-lands. The general character of the soil and atmosphere is excessive aridity, but in some places patches of fertility, at the bases of the declivities, are rendered productive by means of irrigation. On one of these slips is situated the village of Losur, and the appearance of this singularly secluded place, as described by Gerard,[3] is far from repulsive. "Lofty as the level of Losur is, there is little in the landscape to betray its position, when viewed in summer, embosomed in flourishing crops, and herds of shawl-wool goats. Yaks and horses meet the eye upon the high acclivities of the mountains, and an ardent sunshine keeps the air looming from the effects of mirage." The inhabitants are Tibetans or Tartars of the Mongolian type, and their complexions are darker than in the low and sultry plains. When the ground is covered with snow, their black figures contrast strikingly and somewhat grotesquely with the dazzling whiteness of the surface on which they move. Losur is in lat. 32° 8′, long. 78° 5′.

[1] Moorcr. Punj. Bokh. ii. 55.
[2] As. Res. xviii. 241, Gerard (J. G.), Observations on the Spiti Valley.
[3] As. Res. xviii. 270.

LOSUR, a small river of Ladakh, is formed by the junction of two streams, the one flowing in a south-easterly direction from the Parang La Pass, the other north-easterly, from the range which, on its farther or western side, sends numerous feeders to the Chinab. Lower down, the Losur river receives, near the village of Losur, a stream called the Pin, or Peeno, and thenceforwards is generally known by the name of the river of Spiti, which, after a further course of about fifty miles, generally in a south-easterly direction, falls into the Sutlej close to Numgeea, in lat. 31° 48′, long. 78° 38′. Moorcr. Punj. Bokh. ii. 58.

LUGGAREE, in Sinde, a village on the route from Hydera- E.I.C. Ms. Doc.

bad to Omercote, and sixty miles west of the latter place. It is situate on the right bank of the Poorana river. Lat. 25° 22′, long. 68° 51′.

LUGHMAN,[1] in Afghanistan, a district north of Jelalabad, and bounded on the north by Hindoo Koosh; on the east, by the river of Kama; on the south, by the river of Kabool; and on the west, by the river Alishang. It forms part of the province of Jelalabad, and thither the ruthless Mahomed Akbar Khan conveyed the British prisoners reserved from the massacre at Khoord Kabool. It is forty miles long, thirty miles broad, and, though having a rugged surface, is fertile, well watered, and populous. Its name is said to be correctly Lamghan; acquired, according to Baber,[2] from its containing the tomb of Lam, or Lamech, the father of Noah. The inhabitants are Tajiks, and speak a patois called Lughmani, compounded principally of Persian and Pushtoo.[3] The district yielded annually Rs. 113,000 under Dost Mahomed Khan. It lies between lat. 34° 25′—35°, long. 70°—70° 40′.

[1] Masson, Bal. Afg. Panj. iii. 291.

[2] Memoirs, 142; As. Res. vi., Welford on Mount Caucasus.

[3] Jour. As. Soc. 1838, p. 780, Leech, Vocabulary of the Laghmini Dialect.

LUK BAWUN, in Kashmir, a village situate at the north-western extremity of a long ridge of green hills, which, extending from the Snowy Panjal, gradually diminish in height and size, till they terminate on the plain. Though now scarcely containing half a dozen houses, Luk Bawun was once a considerable place. Here, are the ruins of a large bath and an extensive stone-built tank. Lat. 33° 36′, long. 75° 6′.

E.I.C. Ms. Doc.; Vigne, Kashmir, i. 323.

LUKA, in the Punjab, a town on the route from Ferozpoor to Mooltan. It is situate in the Doab between the Ghara and the Chinab. Lat. 29° 50′, long. 72° 20′.

Vigne, Ghuznee, 13.

LUKH, in Beloochistan, a pass twenty miles west of Belah, on the route from that town to Kedje. The word means a Pass. Lat. 26° 10′, long. 66° 9′.

E.I.C. Ms. Doc.

LUKHOKI, in the Punjab, a small town in the Doab between the Ghara and the Ravee, is situate about three miles from the right or west bank of the former river, and on the route from Ferozpoor to Mooltan. Lat. 30°, long. 72° 41′.

Vigne, Ghuznee, 13.

LUKHSUR, in Beloochistan, a village on the route from Belah to Kedje, and forty miles west of the former town. Lat. 26° 14′, long. 65° 52′.

E.I.C. Ms. Doc.

LUKKEE MOUNTAINS, in Sinde, are a considerable range connected with the Hala, or Brabooic mountains of Beloochistan.

With the Jutteel, the Keertar, the Pubb, and some other ranges less known, the Lukkee contributes to give character to the singularly wild tract constituting the western part of Sinde, extending between Beloochistan and the alluvial tract on the Indus, and also between the desert of Shikarpore and Kurrachee. The Lukkee is the most eastern of these ranges, and runs from the Jutteel[1] south-eastward, towards the high lands opposite Hyderabad, being known in different parts by the various appellations of the Eeree Lukkee, Daran Lukkee, and Hallar Lukkee. These mountains are in general of recent formation, containing a vast profusion of marine exuviæ. "The organic remains of former ages," observes Burnes,[2] "are innumerable; the asteroid, the cockle, the oyster, the nummulite, and almost all kinds of sea-shells, may be collected on the Lukkee range." Huge fissures, apparently produced by earthquakes, traverse this range, which, in the frequent occurrence of hot springs and sulphureous exhalations, exhibit signs of volcanic action. Some parts appear to be of more ancient formation, as they produce lead, antimony, and copper. The elevation of the highest part of this dreary and sterile range is estimated at from 1,500 to 2,000 feet. Between the town of Lukkee and that of Sehwan, the mountain has a nearly perpendicular face, about six hundred feet high towards the Indus, between which and the precipice, there was at one time a road, though in some places so narrow, that only a single camel could pass at a time. In 1839, this defile was washed away by the turbulent river, which now sweeps along the base of the cliff.[3] The length of the Lukkee range is about fifty miles. Lat. 25° 30′, long. 67° 50′.

[1] De La Hoste, on the Country between Sehwan and Kurrachee, in Jour. As. Soc. 1840, p. 311.

[2] Pers. Narr. 40; Kennedy, I. 164; Westmacott, Acc. of Khyrpoor, in Jour. As. Soc. 1840, p. 1208.

[3] Kennedy, ii. 208; Outram, 42.

LUKKEE, NORTHERN, in Sinde, a large town in ruins, on the route from Shikarpore to Lukkur, and twelve miles south-east of the former place. Under the Durani sway, it was wealthy and populous, but since it passed into the power of the Ameers of Sinde, it has fallen into utter decay. It has now scarcely an inhabitant, and as its abandonment has been recent and sudden, the appearance is singular, the houses being entire and habitable, yet untenanted, or affording shelter only to a few marauders. In the time of its prosperity, it yielded an annual revenue of a hundred thousand rupees. It is ten miles from the right bank of the Indus. Lat. 27° 48′, long. 68° 46′. Another

E.I.C. Ms. Doc.; Masson, Bal. Afg. Punj. I. 359.

town of the same name is situated a hundred and twenty miles farther south, for an account of which see LUKKEE, SOUTHERN.

Burnes' Pers. Narr. 41; Kennedy, Sinde and Kanbool, I. 161; Outram, Rough Notes, 40.

LUKKEE, SOUTHERN, in Sinde, a town situate a short distance south of Sehwan, close to the west bank of the Indus, and adjacent to the entrance of the Lukkee Pass. Its site is picturesque, being near a lake a mile wide, and several miles in length, which appears to have been at one time a reach of the Indus. The Lukkee mountains, sloping down to the west of the town, and a little to the north, abut on that river, which sweeps along their rocky base. Close to the town is a spring of sulphureous water, which has a temperature of 102°, and flows from the base of a calcareous precipice six hundred feet high. Lat. 26° 14′, long. 68° 1′. This town must be distinguished from another of the same name, situate a hundred and twenty miles farther north, for an account of which see LUKKEE, NORTHERN.

E.I.C. Ms. Doc.

LULLEEANA, in the Punjab, a village twenty-six miles south of Lahore. Lat. 31° 16′, long. 74° 24′.

Jour. As. Soc. 1839, p. 307, Court, on Alexander's Exploits on the Western Banks of the Indus; Macartney, in Elph. Acc. of Caubul, 656.

LUNDYE, or, RIVER OF PANJKORA, in Afghanistan, one of the principal tributaries of the Kabool river, rises on the southern declivity of Hindoo Koosh, in the unexplored region north of Panjkora. It flows from north-east to south-west, and having received the Sewat river from the east, and some others of less size, falls into the Kabool river between the Khyber mountains and the Indus, and in lat. 34° 10′, long. 71° 47′.

Walker's Map of N.W. Frontier.

LUNGUR, in North-western Afghanistan, a village thirty-two miles south-east of the town of Siri Pool. Lat. 35° 50′, long. 66° 13′.

E.I.C. Ms. Doc.

LUR, in Western Afghanistan, a village with a deserted fort on the route from Kandahar to Herat, and one hundred miles north-west of the former place. It is well supplied with water from subterraneous aqueducts, and there is considerable cultivation in the vicinity. Forage also can be obtained, the spontaneous growth of shrubs and grasses. Lat. 32° 9′, long. 64° 11′.

Walker's Map of N.W. Frontier.

LUREE, in the Punjab, a village situate on the left bank of the Swan river, on the route from Attock to Julalpoor, and fifty miles south-east of the former town. Lat. 33° 30′, long. 73° 1′.

E.I.C. Ms. Doc.

LURGE, in Afghanistan, a village forty-eight miles south-west of Ghuznee. Lat. 33° 3′, long. 67° 44′.

LURROO,[1] or DURROO, in Kashmir, on the route from the Banihal Pass to Islamabad, and about eight miles south of the latter place. At the time of Forster's visit, it was a small but very populous town. It does not appear to be mentioned by Vigne or other late travellers, and it is not improbable that it may have been completely ruined in the dreadful depopulation which, within the last few years, has afflicted Kashmir. Wilson[2] conjectures it to be identical with Lolora or Looloo, mentioned in the Ayeen Akbery[3] to have had eighty crore of houses. Abulfazel,[4] however, states that Looloo was in Kamraj, or the western division of Kashmir, and Lurroo is, according to Forster's account, in the south-eastern part of the valley. Lat. 33° 36', long. 75° 6'.

[1] Forster, Jour. Beng. Eng. ii. 5.
[2] As. Res. xv. 17, Wilson on the Hist. of Kashmir.
[3] ii. 158.
[4] ii. 159.

LUS,[1] or LUSSA, a province of Beloochistan, bounded on the north by Jhalawan; on the east by Sinde, from which, along its whole course, it is separated by the Hubb river; on the south by the Indian Ocean; and on the west by Mekran. It lies between lat. 24° 50'—26° 15', long. 65° 28'—67° 18', is sixty miles in breadth from north to south, one hundred and ten miles in length from east to west, and five thousand two hundred square miles in superficial extent. It is in general rather level, especially towards the sea-coast (where the soil is impregnated with salt), and along the shore rises into sand-hills of moderate height.[2] In the eastern part a range of mountains extends from north to south, being the continuation of the Hala range, known by the names of the Pubb or Brahooie mountains, and terminating at the sea in Cape Monze. Across this range, in lat. 25° 23', is an important pass, leading from Sinde to Sonmeeanee, and the route by which, proceeding westward, forms the prolonged sea-coast line of communication with Persia.[3] In the western part of the province is another mountain range, similarly running north and south. The country between these is level, or slightly broken by low hills, having an unproductive soil covered with stunted woods, or scanty pasture, grazed by horned cattle, goats, sheep, and numerous herds of camels. There are two rivers or torrents, the Poorally and the Hubb. The Poorally rises in Jhalawan, crosses the northern frontier, and, taking a course nearly due south, falls into the sea a few miles west of Sonmeeanee. It is in general a shallow stream, rolling over a wide and rugged bed, but, when swollen with rain, it becomes a

[1] E.I.C. Ms. Doc.; Pott. Belooch. 298.
[2] Jour. As. Soc. 1840, p. 151, Hart, Acc. of a Jour. from Kurrachee to Hinglaj.
[3] Masson, Kalat, 297.

furious torrent. The total length of its course is about a hundred miles. The Hubb rises in the north-east angle of the province, and runs along a rocky channel among the ravines and valleys of the Brahooic mountains, with so small a body of water, that, in the dry season, the current does not reach the sea. In the wet season it falls into the Indian Ocean a little to the left of Cape Monze, after a course of a hundred and ten miles. Such a country must of necessity be pastoral, the scanty population that exists being confined to the course of the Poorally, and producing only a little grain, pulse, and tobacco. The people are supported almost entirely on the produce of their flocks and herds, pasturing great numbers of goats, cows, buffaloes, and camels. They consume but a small quantity of grain, and most of that is imported. The inhabitants are called Lumris or Numaris, and speak a dialect similar to that of Sinde. They are governed by a chief, called the *Jam*,[4] whose residence is at the little town of Bela, hence considered as the capital. He is a vassal of the Khan of Kelat, to whom, in time of war, he supplies a contingent of troops, which, on the last occasion, amounted to four thousand men. His annual revenue is computed to be 25,000 rupees, derived almost exclusively from custom duties. The only places which can properly be called towns are Bela, Sonmeeanee, and Lyaree. Bela, the capital, has, according to Carless, eight hundred houses, and a population of about 5,000. Sonmeeanee has a population of about 5,000, and one thousand houses. Lyaree is very small and inconsiderable. The population of the whole province is probably 60,000.

[4] Jour. As. Soc. 1839, p. 190, Carless, Acc. of Jour. to Beylah.

LUTTABUND PASS, in Afghanistan, is the most northern of the four collateral passes through the Kurkutcha range. It is about six miles long, and little frequented; the caravans generally travelling by the Huft Kotal pass farther south, especially in winter, as then the Luttabund is blocked up by snow. It is probably about 7,000 feet high. On arriving at the highest part of this pass from the eastward, the traveller has a view of the city of Kabool, twenty-five miles distant, to the west. Lat. 34° 21′, long. 69° 28′.

E.I.C. Ms. Map; Wood, Khyber Pass, 3; Burnes' Bokh. i. 129.

LYAREE, in Beloochistan, a town or rather hamlet in the province of Lus, at the head of the estuary of the river Poorally, and twenty-five miles from its mouth. Pottinger[1] states it to contain from sixteen hundred to eighteen hundred houses, which

[1] Belooch. 300.

unquestionably is an exaggerated estimate. Outram[2] styles it a "paltry little village," and Masson[3] says that it contains "about twenty mud houses, inhabited by Hindoos, and eighty huts, the abode of Mahometans." This statement, though sufficiently accordant with Outram's account, is quite at variance with that of Pottinger, but is in all probability far nearer the fact. There is an insignificant manufactory of salt here. Lat. 25° 37', long. 66° 25'.

[2] Rough Notes, 188.
[3] Bal. Afg. Panj. ii. 25.

M.

MACHEE, in Beloochistan, a village of Cutch Gundava, situate a little to the west of the road from the town of Gundava to Larkhana, forty miles south of the former, and fifty north-west of the latter place. Lat. 27° 54', long. 67° 38'.

E.I.C. Ms. Doc.

MADDEHJEE, in Sinde, a considerable village on the route from Sukkur to Larkhana, and twenty-eight miles west of the former place. It contains about one hundred and fifty houses and twenty shops. A plentiful supply of water is procurable from six wells, lined with burned brick, and there is convenient encamping ground on the south-west of the village. Forage for both camels and horses is in abundance. The road in this part of the route runs through thin jungle. Lat. 27° 36', long. 68° 34'.

E.I.C. Ms. Doc.

MAGAR TALAO[1] (Alligator's pool),* in Sinde, a collection of hot springs nine miles north-east of Kurrachee, and swarming with alligators. De la Hoste states that there are two hundred of those animals in a small space not exceeding a hundred and twenty yards in diameter. Some of them are very large, and their appearance, basking in the sun, is not unlike a dry date-tree. They belong to several fakirs, who have attached themselves to the tomb of a Mahometan considered by his countrymen to have been a character of peculiar sanctity. Hence is the name *Muggee Peer*, by which the place is popularly known among Europeans,

[1] E.I.C. Ms. Doc.; Jour. As. Soc. 1840, p. 914. De La Hoste, Rep. of Country between Kurrachee and Sehwan; Vigne, Kashmir, ii. 414.

* From مگر an alligator, and تالاو a pool.

32 MAG—MAH.

being a corruption of *Magar Peer* or *Pir*, "the alligator's saint." These thermal springs are situate amidst rocky and very barren hills, and spring out of the bottom of a small fertile valley, thickly wooded with date-trees and acacias, over which the white dome of the shrine is visible. Adjacent to the shrine are a few highly ornamented tombs, the architectural style of which resembles that of some English structures of the age of Elizabeth. Allen[2] says, "The devices were principally scroll and diamond work; the carving, though not very bold, was elaborate in design and neatly executed." The principal spring issues from the rock on which the shrine is built, and has a temperature of about 98°, the water being perfectly clear, and of a sulphureous smell. Another spring, about half a mile distant, has a temperature of 130°. The water, received into tanks, forms a grateful retreat for the alligators. On occasion of a stranger's visit, the fakirs regale these animals with a carcase of a goat, and their struggles and contests to secure the prey constitute a scene at once ludicrous and disgusting.[3] They are very tame, and never seek to injure human beings. It is remarkable that they are genuine alligators, and totally distinct from the *guryal*, or long-snouted crocodile, which abounds in the Indus, a short distance to the east. The fakirs live in a few mud huts, the only human habitations in this vicinity. Lat. 25° 2', long. 67° 5'.

[2] March through Sinde and Afg. 26.

[3] Wood, Oxus, 26.

MAGHRIBEE, in Sinde, a town situated on the Piniaree, a branch of the Indus. Below the town a dam has been thrown across the Piniaree about fifty miles from its mouth. It is forty feet broad, and of proportionable height, but the water in the swell makes its way through numerous small openings to the channel below, called the Goongra, which is navigable to the sea, discharging itself by the Sir mouth. The Piniaree is also navigable from the town upwards to the Indus. The traffic is almost exclusively in rice, which being produced abundantly in Sinde, is exported down this channel to Cutch. Population 5,000. Lat. 24° 11', long. 68° 17'.

Burnes' Bokh. iii. 238, 239; Pott. Belooch. 358; Burnes, Rep. on Commerce of Hyderabad, 17.

MAHER PEER, in Sinde, a village on the middle route from Roree to Hyderabad, and forty miles south-west of the former town. Lat. 27° 21', long. 68° 32'.

Ms. Survey Map.

MAHOMED AGA, in Afghanistan, a village situate on the route from Kabool to Shawl, twenty miles south of the former town, in lat. 34° 11', long. 69°.

E.I.C. Ms. Doc.

MAHOMED ALI, in Sinde, a village on the route from Sehwan to Larkhana, and sixty-three miles north of the former place. It is situate on the right bank of a great offset of the Indus. Lat. 27° 12′, long. 68° 6′. E.I.C. Ms. Doc.

MAHOMED AMROO, in Sinde, a village on the route from Sehwan to Larkhana, and five miles south of the last-mentioned town. The road in this part of the route lies over a level alluvial country, in general waste, but having occasional spots of cultivation, and intersected by watercourses, rendering the passage of wheel carriages difficult. Lat. 27° 26′, long. 68° 16′. E.I.C. Ms. Doc.

MAHOMED KHAN KA TANDA, in Sinde, a town on the route from Hyderabad to Cutch, and thirty miles south-east of the former place. It is situate on the bank of the Fulailee branch of the Indus, and the neighbouring country, though near the border of the desert, is fertile and well cultivated. It is one of the most thriving places in Sinde, in consequence of its manufactures and of the transit trade from Cutch. During the Talpoor sway in Sinde, it was usually the residence of one of the subordinate Ameers. Lat. 25° 5′, long. 68° 40′. E.I.C. Ms. Doc.; Pott. Belooch. 375; Burnes, Commerce of Hyderabad, 17, 20.

MAHOMED KHAN NOHUR, in Sinde, a village situate on the left bank of the Indus. Lat. 28° 19′, long. 69° 34′. Map of Sinde.

MAHOMED KHAN TANDA, in Sinde, a village on the route from Sehwan to Kurrachee, and seventy miles north-east of the latter place. Neither forage nor supplies for human subsistence can be procured. Lat. 25° 28′, long. 67° 55′. E.I.C. Ms. Doc.

MAHOMED SAYUD-JA-GOTE, in Sinde, a village situate on the left bank of the Eastern Narra river, on the route from Bukkur to Omercote, and forty miles north-west of the latter place. Lat. 25° 46′, long. 69° 22′. E.I.C. Ms. Doc.

MAIDAN, in Afghanistan, a beautiful and fertile valley through which the route from Kandahar to Kabool passes. The village of Maidan, the principal in the valley, is situate on the left or north bank of the Kabool river, and twenty-two miles south-west of the city of that name. Here, in September, 1842, the British army under General Nott, in the advance on Kabool, defeated a superior Afghan force. Lat. 34° 21′, long. 68° 44′. ¹ E.I.C. Ms.Doc.; Leech, Rep. on Sindh. Army, 89; Hough, Narr.Exp. in Afg. 245; Outram, Rough Notes, 118; Havelock, War in Afg. ii. 100; Mil. Op. in Afg. 401; Allen, 289.

MAIMOKE GHAT (or FERRY), in the Punjab, situate on the Ghara river. By this ferry the route from Hindostan passes to the town of Pauk Petten, where is a celebrated shrine of a Mahometan saint. In consequence of this, the ferry is much Jour. As. Soc. 1837, p. 192, 212. Mackeson, Voyage down the Sutlej.

frequented at the time appointed for his festival. Lat. 30° 16', long. 73° 11'.

<small>Walker's Map of N.W. Frontier.</small> MAIMOODDA, in Bhawlpoor, situate on the left bank of the river Ghara. Lat. 30°, long. 72° 48'.

<small>E.I.C. Ms. Doc.</small> MAIMUND, in Western Afghanistan, a small town near the route from Herat to Kandahar, and thirty-four miles west of the latter place. It is situate at the opening into a well-cultivated valley, inclosed by eminences of moderate height. Lat. 31° 42', long. 64° 51'.

<small>E.I.C. Ms. Doc.</small> MAJGURRA, in Afghanistan, a village on the route from Dera Ismael Khan to Ghuznee, by the Golairee Pass, and twenty-nine miles north-west of Dera Ismael Khan. It is situate at the foot of a pass across the Suliman mountains, through which the road is difficult to within a short distance of the village. There is water from a subterraneous aqueduct. Lat. 32° 2', long. 70° 8'.

<small>[1] Burnes' Bokh. iii. 264.</small> MAJINDA,[1] in Sinde, a town on the route from Hyderabad to Sehwan, and forty-five miles south-east of the latter place. It is situate two miles from the right or western bank of the Indus, in an alluvial plain, but indifferently cultivated. Its population is 2,000. Majinda[2] has an extensive bazaar and a good supply of water. The road in this part of the route is good. Lat. 25° 51', long. 68° 19'.

<small>[2] E.I.C. Ms. Doc.</small>

<small>E.I.C. Ms. Doc.</small> MAJU, in Sinde, a village situate on the route from Tattah to Sehwan, near the right bank of the Indus, and sixty miles north of the former town. Lat. 25° 33', long. 68° 20'.

<small>E.I.C. Ms. Doc.</small> MAKAM, in Afghanistan, a halting-place on the route from Kandahar to Shawl, and sixty miles south-east of the former town, in lat. 31° 5', long. 66° 5'.

MAL.—See MULL.

MALEEA, in the Punjab, a village situate on the route from Ramnuggur to Ferozpoor, and a hundred and twenty miles south-east of the former town. Lat. 31° 46', long. 73° 55'.

<small>Walker's Map of N.W. Frontier.</small> MALEKPUR, in Kashmir, a village twenty miles north-west of the town of Baramula, in lat. 34° 20', long. 73° 59'.

<small>Vigne, Kashmir, i. 140.</small> MALEKRA, in the north-east of the Punjab, a town in the southern range of the Himalaya, and close to the celebrated fort Kot Kangra. Here is an idol called Bawun, an object of great veneration to the superstitious Hindoos. It is without its head, which is supposed to be at Jewala Muki, and to breathe forth

the perpetual fire issuing from the rock there. Malekra is a neat clean-looking place, built on the side of a hill, traversed by the road from Nadaun to Kot Kangra. Lat. 31° 57′, long. 76° 4′.

MALGEERK, in Afghanistan, a village situate on the right bank of the Helmund river, three miles south of the town of Giriskh. Lat. 31° 45′, long. 64° 19′. E.I.C. Ms. Doc.

MALLA-JA-GOTE, in Sinde, a village situate on the Goongroo branch of the Indus, a short distance from its confluence with the Piniaree. Lat. 24° 30′, long. 68° 20′. Ms. Map. of Sinde.

MALLOODIE, in Sinde, a village on the route from Subzulcote to Shikarpoor, and thirty-five miles south-west of the former place. The road in this part of the route lies through the jungle overspreading the low alluvial ground forming the left bank of the Indus. Lat. 28° 6′, long. 69° 10′. E.I.C. Ms. Doc.

MAMADPOOR, in Sinde, a village on the route from Subzulcote to Shikarpoor, and twenty-two miles south-west of the former town. The adjacent country is low, level, alluvial, overrun with jungle, and containing numerous watercourses and ponds, replenished during the inundation of the Indus, at which time this tract is extensively flooded. Lat. 28° 10′, long. 69° 20′. E.I.C. Ms. Doc.

MAMOO KHAIL, in Afghanistan, a fort close to Gundamuk, on the road from Jelalabad to Kabool, and about sixty miles east of the latter place. Here the British under General Pollock, in their advance on Kabool in 1842, defeated the Afghans, and destroyed the fort. Lat. 34° 17′, long. 70° 4′. E.I.C. Ms. Doc.; Mil. Op. in Afg. 377.

MANASA BUL, in Kashmir, a beautiful lake, which discharges its water into the Jailum on the right or north side. It is a mile and a half long, three-quarters of a mile wide, and very deep; bounded on the west by picturesque hills, while on the north and east the successive ranges of the northern Kashmirian mountains rise in great grandeur, and on the south a fertile and verdant plain stretches to the Jailum. It is altogether, according to Von Hügel, one of the most beautiful spots in existence. On the northern bank are the remains of a palace built by Nur Jehan, the celebrated Queen of Jehangir, the Mogul emperor. Here the substratum of the soil is of limestone, which is reduced to lime in a large kiln belonging to the government. Lat. 34° 13′, long. 74° 35′. i. 359; Vigne, Kashmir, ii. 147.

MANCHAR,[1] in Sinde, a lake formed by the expansion of [1] Burnes' Pers. Narr. 41; Outram,

47; Leech, Rep. on the Sindian Army, 68; Masson, Bal. Afg. Panj. i. 461; Burnes, Bokh. iii. 270.

the Narra, a branch proceeding from the Indus, on the western side. The Narra flows into the lake on the north, the redundant water being discharged on the south-east by the river Arul, which has a course of about twelve miles, and, flowing by Schwan, falls into the Indus about four miles below that town. The lake is nearly of a circular form when the water is low, and is then about ten miles in diameter. During the inundation, it expands so as to be twenty miles long, the breadth remaining much as before. The space left uncovered by the receding water is sown with grain, especially wheat, which yields very heavy crops. Though shallow at the sides, the lake has a considerable depth of water in the middle, and so great is the abundance of fine fish, according to Burnes, that a thousand boats are employed in the fishery. They are taken by spearing, the great quantity of weeds preventing the employment of nets. In the season when the lotus is in blossom,[2] the lake presents a very beautiful appearance, as its surface, farther than the eye can reach, is covered with an unbroken succession of bloom and leaves. Lat. 26° 15′, long. 67° 40′.

[2] Westmacott, Acc. of Khyrpoor, Jour. As. Soc. 1840, p. 1207.

Masson, Bal. Afg. Panj. i. 447.

MANGA, in the Punjab, a small town on the left or east bank of the Ravee. Lat. 31° 17′, long. 73° 46′.

E.I.C. Ms. Doc.

MANGEEGURA, in Afghanistan, a village of the Daman, close to the route from Ghuznee to Dera Ismael Khan, and fifty miles north-west of the latter town. It is situate on the Gomul river. Lat. 32° 3′, long. 70° 10′.

MANGEEGURD.—See MAJGURRA.

E.I.C. Ms. Doc.

MANIHALA, in the Punjab, a village situate about eleven miles south-east of Lahore, on the road to Loodianah. Lat. 31° 35′, long. 74° 27′.

MANIKYALA, in the Punjab, a village remarkable on account of an antique monument, or tope (as such objects are called by the natives), of great dimensions, said by the people of the neighbourhood to have been built by a prince of the name of Manik.[1]* According to Elphinstone,[2] the height from the summit of the artificial mound on which the tope is situated to the summit of the tope itself, is about seventy feet, and the circumference is one hundred and fifty paces; but Court[3] states the height to be eighty feet, and the circumference from three hundred and ten to three hundred and twenty feet. There

[1] Moorcr. ii. 311; Hough, 341.
[2] 79; Jour. As. Soc. 1834, p. 557, Court, on the Topes of Manikyala.
[3] Wilson, Ariana Antiqua, 38.

* According to Vigne (ii. 190), it is Muni-Kyala, "the city of rubies."

does not appear to be anywhere so complete a description of this monument as that given by Elphinstone[4] in the following words:—"The plan of the whole could, however, be easily discovered. Some broad steps (now mostly ruined) lead to the base of the pile round the base to a moulding on which are pilasters about four feet high and six feet asunder; these have plain capitals, and support a cornice marked with parallel lines and beadings. The whole of this may be seven or eight feet high, from the uppermost step to the top of the cornice. The building then retires, leaving a ledge of a foot or two broad, from which rises a perpendicular wall about six feet high; about a foot above the ledge is a fillet formed by stones projecting a very little from the wall, and at the top of the wall is a more projecting cornice."[5] Above this complex basement, which may be taken to be from sixteen to twenty feet high, rises a dome approaching in shape to a hemisphere, but truncated and flat near the summit. "It was built of large pieces of a hard stone common in the neighbourhood (which appeared to be composed of petrified vegetable matter), mixed with smaller pieces of a sandy stone. The greater part of the outside was cased with the forementioned stone cut quite smooth." These stones are about three feet and a half long,* and one and a half broad, and are so placed that the ends only are exposed. Elphinstone and his party considered it decidedly Grecian. Moorcroft, on the contrary, is of opinion that "it has not at all the character of a Grecian edifice. It has a much greater resemblance to the monumental structures of the Tibetans." Erskine, as quoted by Wilson,[6] observes of it: "Although its origin is unknown, yet, in its hemispherical form and whole appearance, it carries with it a sufficient proof that it was a magnificent dahgope or Buddha shrine, constructed at a remote period by persons of the Buddhist faith." In 1830, General Ventura,[7] in the service of Runjeet Sing, sank a perpendicular shaft in the centre of the platform on the summit, and at various depths found repositories, one below another, at the intervals of several feet. These contained

[4] Acc. of Caubul, 79.

[5] F. Von Hugel, iii. 120.

[6] Ariana Antiq. 32.

[7] Burnes' Bokh. i. 66; Jour. As. Soc. 1834, p. 314, Prinsep, Coins and Relics discovered by Ventura.

---

* Hough remarks: "The difficulty in the execution of this work consists in the great size of the stones, which it would be difficult to remove from a quarry." Moorcroft observes, "They were, however, but pebbles, compared with the blocks we had seen in the ruined buildings of Kashmir, and the workmanship was equally inferior." (ii. 311.)

38　　　　　　　　MAN.

coins of gold, silver, and copper, boxes and vessels of iron, brass, copper, and gold. The copper coins were considered to be some of those struck by the Indo-Scythian kings, Kadphises or Kanerkes, who are thought to have reigned[8] about the latter part of the first and the commencement of the second century. There are fifteen other topes in this neighbourhood. One of these opened by Court, another officer in the service of Runjeet Sing* was found to contain a coin of Julius Cæsar,[9] one of Marc Antony, the Triumvir, and none of a much later date. The country around[1] bears traces of having been formerly very populous, and the inhabitants assert that it was the site of an immense city. Burnes[2] and Wilson[3] consider it the site of the Taxila[4] of the Greeks, the Taksha-sila of the Hindoos, the greatest city between the Indus and the Hydaspes (the Jailum). North-east of this place is a mausoleum surmounted by a dome, the burial-place of the Ghikar chiefs, who formerly held this country. Lat. 33° 32′, long. 73° 9′.

[marginal notes: [8] Wilson, Ariana Antiq. 35, 353. [9] Wilson, 36; Ritter, Erdkunde von Asien, v. 107. [1] Moorcr. ii. 311. [2] i. 67. [3] 196. [4] Arrian, v. cviii.]

MANJA, in Sinde, a village situate on the road from Bukkur to Omercote, near the right bank of the river Narra. Lat. 26° 38′, long. 69° 2′.

[margin: Ms. Map of Sinde.]

MANJAI, in Afghanistan, a large village on the route from Kandahar to Ghuznee, and twenty-four miles north-east from the former place. It is situate near the right bank of the river Turnak, the valley of which is here fertile and well cultivated. Lat. 31° 40′, long. 65° 40′.

[margin: E.I.C. Ms. Doc.]

MANJAWAL, in Afghanistan, in the Derajat, a halting-place on the gun-road from Sangad to Raknee, by the Buzdar, or Sangad Pass. There is a stream of water here, and a few habitations of shepherds are scattered over the neighbourhood. Lat. 29° 56′, long. 71° 3′.

[margin: E.I.C. Ms. Doc.]

MANJAWAL, in Afghanistan, a village situate in the Derajat, ten miles south-east of Raknee. Lat. 29° 55′, long. 70° 2′.

[margin: E.I.C. Ms. Doc.]

MANSA (contracted for Manasa Sarovara), in the north of the Punjab, a small lake in the southern range of the Himalaya, a mile in length, half a mile in breadth, and very deep. Forster[2] styles it " a delicious spot." It is considered sacred by

[margin: Vigne, Kashmir, i. 178. [2] Jour. Beng. Eng. i. 277. [1] Jour. As. Soc. 1834, p. 566, Note on the Coins discovered at Manikyala. [2] In Jour. of same year, 636.]

* Prinsep[1] considered that this tope was constructed about the middle of the fourth century; but Cunningham[2] maintains that its construction is probably to be dated about the commencement of the Christian era.

the Hindoos, who visit it in pilgrimage, regarding it as a meritorious act to make the circuit of it to propitiate the Devi, or presiding spirit. Lat. 32° 30′, long. 75° 8′.

MAPA, in Afghanistan, a village on the route from Ghuznee to Shawl, and a hundred and fifty miles north of the latter place. Lat. 32° 12′, long. 67° 34′. E.I.C. Ms. Doc.

MARAGOND, in Kashmir, a village fifteen miles north-east of the town of Sirinagur, or Kashmir, in lat. 34° 14′, long. 74° 47′. Walker's Map of N.W. Frontier.

MAREE, in the Punjab, a village situate on the left bank of the Indus, about three miles higher up the river than the town of Kala-Bagh. Lat. 32° 57,′ long. 71° 41′. E.I.C. Ms. Doc.

MAREE, in Afghanistan, a village situate on the road from Dera Ismael Khan to Mooltan, and near the right bank of the Indus. Lat. 31° 31′, long. 70° 54′. Walker's Map of Afg.

MAREHI, in Afghanistan, a village thirty miles south-west of Peshawur, and twelve miles north-west of Kohat. Lat. 33° 41′, long. 71° 21′. E.I.C. Ms. Doc.

MAROOF, in Afghanistan, is a district in the hilly country north of the Kojuk Pass. Here was a fort, described by Outram[1] as "the strongest fortress we had yet seen in the country, being constructed with double gates, a ditch, faussebraye, and towers of solid masonry." It had been evacuated by the Afghans, and the British completely demolished it. This demolition took place to avenge a frightful massacre perpetrated here in 1839 by the Afghans, on a large body of the camp followers of the army of the Indus. Above two hundred of the natives of Hindostan, who had accompanied the invading force, joined a caravan proceeding from Herat to the Derajat, and being treacherously induced at Maroof by the Kafilabashee, or head of the caravan, to deliver up their arms to his safe keeping, were, with the assistance of the natives, all massacred.[2] Maroof is in lat. 31° 38′, long. 67° 5′. [1] Rough Notes, 154; Kennedy, Sinde and Kabool, ii. 128. [2] Atkinson, Exp. into Afg. 175.

MAROOJABUR, in Sinde, a village on the route from Hyderabad to Bukkur, and fifty-five miles north of the former town. Lat. 26° 6′, long. 68° 32′. Ms. Map of Sinde.

MAROOT, in Bhawlpoor, a town in the desert extending through the eastern part of that state, is situate on the route from the town of Bhawlpoor to Bhutneer, and seventy miles east of the former place. It is surrounded with a mud wall of considerable extent, having numerous bastions. The adjacent country Boileau, Rajwara, Map; Conolly, Jour Eng. Ind. ii. 201; Masson, Bal. Afg. Panj. i. 2, 25.

is a tract of hard clay, producing coarse grass, except where occasionally overspread with loose sandhills. Here is a considerable mart for grain, brought from the fertile parts of Bhawlpoor to meet the demands of the dealers, who purchase and convey it to the desert tracts eastward. The garrison stationed here by the Khan of Bhawlpoor usually consists of a regiment with six guns. Maroot is in lat. 29° 13′, long. 72° 43′.

Ms. Survey Map. MAROW, in Beloochistan, a village situate near the western extremity of the Bolan Pass, on the route from Kelat, and fourteen miles east of the town of Moostung. Lat. 29° 48′, long. 67° 1′.

E.I.C. Ms. Doc. MARREH, in the Punjab, a village situate in the Doab, between the Indus and Chenaub rivers, eight miles east of the former and ten miles west of the latter. Lat. 29° 41′, long. 71° 3′.

Moorcr. Punj. Bokh. i. 239. MARSILLA, in Ladakh or Middle Tibet, a small town, the residence of a lama of high dignity, who is the principal municipal officer in that part of the country. It is situate on the south or left bank of the Indus, in a well-cultivated district, and is a neat and well-built little town. Lat. 33° 52′, long. 77° 40′.

E.I.C. Ms. Doc.; Leech, on Trade of Shikarpoor, 70. MARTEE KHAN KA TANDA, in Sinde, a town on the route from Khyerpoor to Hyderabad, and sixteen miles south-west of the former place. It is important on account of its having a brisk direct trade with Marwar, from which it annually imports cottons to the value of 4,000*l.*, and other articles to the value of 6,000*l.* Lat. 27° 24′, long. 68° 34′.

Moorcr. Punj. Bokh. ii. 269; Vigne, Kashmir, ii. 308-310. MASTUCH, the capital of Chitral, is situate between the Hindoo Koosh and the Laspissor mountains, and near the left bank of the Kooner river. It consists of about four hundred houses, defended by a fort, and standing in a plain of moderate extent, from whence roads proceed to Peshawur, Badakshan, and Yarkund. The climate is in general temperate, though much snow falls on the neighbouring mountains, which are rocky, bare, and lofty. There is some trade here, which appears to be principally in the hands of the rajah, who receives from Yarkund chintzes and other cottons, boots and shoes, metals, coral, pearls, tea, sugar, and horses. The return is principally made in slaves, and this unscrupulous ruler, if he cannot kidnap a sufficient number from the neighbouring states, does not hesitate to seize and sell his own subjects. The men are tall and athletic, but very cowardly; the women coarse and profligate. The heads of these people are conical, in consequence of a custom which prevails of moulding them into that shape by tying a strong band round the head of the infant shortly after birth. The grain cultivated is generally wheat or barley. Grapes are produced in great abundance and excellence, but rarely made into wine, as the people are Mahometans, principally of the Shia persuasion, though the rajah is a Sunni. Mastuch is in lat. 36° 12′, long. 72° 31′.

MASTUNG.—See MUSTUNG.

MATAN, in Kashmir, a Karywa, or table-land, extending from the town of Islamabad to the base of the range inclosing the valley on the east. Notwithstanding its situation below those vast mountain masses, it is devoid of streams or other natural means of irrigation,[1] but consisting almost entirely of very fertile alluvial earth, it bears, where cultivated, abundant crops of wheat, barley, and most kinds of grain, excepting rice. The great depopulation of Kashmir, however, has rendered it, for the most part, a waste, presenting a surface of the finest verdure, unbroken by tree, shrub, or human habitation. With the exception of a fakir's dwelling, recently fallen in ruins, " There is not a vestige of a human habitation upon the green waste. A solitary villager may be seen passing from one district to another; a few cattle may be grazing in the distance, and a shepherd or two may be seen collecting their flocks for the night, whilst the bleating of their charge only breaks in upon the silence without disturbing the extraordinary tranquillity of the scene."[2] * Moorcroft seems greatly to underrate its extent in stating it to be " commonly a mile in breadth."[3] Hügel assigns to it a breadth of four or five miles in every direction, and adds, that it appeared almost inter-

[1] Jacquemont, Voyage, v. 246.

[2] Vigne, Kashmir, i. 405.

[3] Moorcr. Punj. Bokh. ii. 254.

* Hügel[1] also mentions the solitude and unbroken silence of this fertile plain, which formerly was irrigated by means of a great aqueduct now completely ruined. " Das Plateau ist, wie mit der Hand geebnet völlig baum- und strauchlos, kein Feld, keine Hütte ist auf demselben. Spuren früherer Bebauung sind jedoch durch die noch bestehende Abtheilung in Felder sichtbar; sie wurden vormals durch eine grosse, nun zerstörte Wasserleitung bewässert." Jacquemont, on the contrary, states that it was almost entirely under corn crops:—" Le plateau de Motonne est presque entièrement cultivé en céréales diverses." The discrepancy, however, is explainable by the supposition that the desolating change took place between 1831, the time of Jacquemont's visit, and 1835, when the Karywa was surveyed by Hügel,[2] and probably by Vigne.

[1] Kaschmir, ii.455.

[2] Id. i. 305.

minable from an optical illusion frequently occurring from the state of the atmosphere in the valley. This table-land is elevated from 250 to 300 feet above the great alluvial plain of Kashmír.[4] On a slight eminence at its western extremity, are situated the ruins of a very ancient building, which excites in all spectators, feelings of admiration approaching to awe, by the elaborate skill displayed in its construction, and the simple, massive, and sublime character of its architecture. It is built of huge blocks of hard compact limestone, the black colour of which adds to its gloomy grandeur. The blocks * are generally from six to nine feet in length, having proportionate breadth and thickness.[5] This extraordinary monument of early civilization consists of an outer colonnade, inclosing an area in which stands the principal building detached. The shape of this inclosure is rectangular; the length being two hundred and forty-four feet, the breadth a hundred and fifty.† The longer sides face north and south. Within each of the four sides a row of pillars is carried along the entire extent of the building. Each pillar has a shaft seven feet long and a foot and a half in diameter: a pedestal two feet and a half high; a capital four feet high: the whole height of the inclosing peristyle is about fifteen feet. The pillars, which are fluted, are six feet and a half distant from each other, and a foot and a quarter from the wall. In each interval between the pillars is an entrance seven feet high and four feet wide, into a small chamber or recess six feet deep from front to back, and constructed in the body of the wall, which, exclusive of the chambers, is six feet thick. Stone blocks of regular dimensions, eight feet long and two feet wide, form the roof of all. The workmanship throughout is excellent, and in an elaborate yet chaste style. There are four great gateways; one in the middle of each side, and facing the four cardinal points; those facing east and west being much finer than the others. Within the inclosure made by this peristyle, and equidistant from the side walls, but much nearer the eastern than the western end, is a mag-

[4] F. Von Hugel, ii. 453.

[5] Vigne, i. 386.

* Vigne[1] states that these stones are cemented "with an excellent mortar." Jacquemont,[2] on the contrary,—"Il est construit dans toute son étendue de tranches posées successivement les unes au-dessus des autres sans ciment." The general character of architecture of this description renders the statement of Jacquemont more probable, but " non nostrum tantas componere lites."

† These dimensions are taken from the plan given by Jacquemont. Pl. 66.

[1] i. 386.
[2] Voyage, v. 247.

nificent temple, of a rectangular outline, seventy feet long, sixty feet wide, and in its present ruined state about forty feet high.[6] [6 Vigne, i 301.] The great thickness of the walls diminishes the interior space. The whole character of the building, like that of the inclosing colonnade, is massive, simple, and severe, yet in excellent taste. Some notion of the style of architecture may be formed by imagining a combination of the Egyptian, Tuscan, and Saxon. The temple is at present roofless; Hügel supposes it to have been always so, and to have been left in an unfinished state. He considers its plan to have been in some degree akin to that of the cave temples at Ellora and other places. The ground within and without is strewed with great quantities of vast blocks of stone, which may have been displaced either by the violence of earthquakes, which are frequent here, or by that of hostile superstition; but the former may be regarded as the more probable. There are a few mutilated and time-worn images and sculptures in bas-relief, but nothing to determine with any approach to certainty by whom the building was raised, or what was the period and purport of its erection. The tradition of the Kashmirian Pundits assigns it an antiquity of about two thousand five hundred years. With them it bears the name Korau Pandau, and is attributed to Kaura and Pandu,[7] two kings who figure in [7 P. Von Hügel, Kaschmir, ii. 463.] the remote legends of Hindoo mythology. It is also known by the name of the temple of Martund,[8]* or the Sun and Srinagur,[9]† or the City of the Sun. Vigne[1] thinks that a resemblance may be traced between this structure and the first temple of Jerusalem as described in scripture.[2] Hügel[3] supposes that it was dedicated to the worship of the *linga*, and assigns the date of its erection to the period intervening between the waning of Buddhism and the establishment of Brahminism. In common with others who have visited these ruins, he regrets the weakness of language to express the feelings to which they give rise. "My[4] description unfortunately gives little conception of the impression produced by this simple majestic structure, which I class amongst the finest ruins of the world. The forms are throughout noble, and the embellishments often tasteful; but it is peculiarly characterized by the huge masses of which it is constructed, and the effect of these is heightened by the dark hue of the marble, and

[8 Vigne, Kashmir, i. 315. 9 Jacquemont, 248. 1 i. 395. 2 1 Kings, vi. 3 Kaschmir, ii. 463.]

[4 Id. ii. 463, 464.]

* مارتند． † سوریه sun, and نگر city.

the desolation in which it stands in the most fruitful valley in the world." These ruins are situate in lat. 33° 45′, long. 75° 8′.

E.I.C. Ms. Doc.

MATCHIE, in Afghanistan, a village situate on the right bank of the Indus, thirty miles north of Mittunkote. Lat. 29° 16′, long. 70° 48′.

MATINEE.—See MITTANI.

Walker's Map of N.W. Frontier.

MATISTAN, in Afghanistan, a village ten miles from the left bank of the Helmund river, in lat. 33° 14′, long. 66° 58′.

E.I.C. Ms. Doc.

MATUM, in the Punjab, a village situate on the route from Lahore to Mooltan, and fifty miles south-west of the former town. Lat. 31° 10′, long. 73° 35′.

E.I.C. Ms. Doc.; Prinsep, Life of Runjeet Singh, 129.

MAUNKAIRA, or MUNKERE, in the Punjab, a town situate in the Doab, between the Jailum and Indus. It is surrounded by a mud wall, and has a citadel, built of burnt brick; but its principal defence is considered to be its position amidst arid sandhills, which afford no water to invaders. Runjeet Sing, when he invested it, at the close of 1821, supplied his troops at first with water carried for a considerable distance by beasts of burthen, and then without delay proceeded to dig an adequate number of wells. The siege was pressed with so much vigour and success, that the Nawab, Hafiz Ahmed, surrendered to the Sikh ruler, on condition of being indemnified by a jaghire in the Derajat. Maunkaira is in lat. 31° 23′, long. 71° 30′.

Map of Afg.

MAYAR, in Afghanistan, a village situate near the right bank of a feeder of the Lundye river, and about six miles from the confluence. Lat. 34° 59′, long. 71° 47′.

E.I.C. Ms. Doc.; Mil. Op. in Afg. 361.

MAZEENA, in Afghanistan, a fort situate in Nungnehar, fifteen miles south-west of Jelalabad. Here the British troops, in July, 1842, defeated the Afghans, and destroyed thirty-five forts in the vicinity. Lat. 34° 13′, long. 70° 34′.

Vigne, Kashmir, ii. 183; Von Hügel, Kaschmir, iii. 25.

MAZUFURABAD, in the Punjab, a town at the confluence of the Jailum and its great tributary, the Kishengunga. It is a small place,* and apparently only worth notice on account of

---

* The statements of travellers as to the size and population of this place are widely different. According to Vigne it has from 150 to 200 flat-roofed houses. Moorcroft (ii. 307) states it to contain about 3,000 houses; while Hügel gives it a population of only 2,100 inhabitants. There can be no doubt that Moorcroft's account is greatly exaggerated, and probably Hügel's estimate of the population is so too.

its commanding position at the entrance of the Baramula Pass into Kashmir. There are ferries here over both the Kishengunga and the Jailum. Lat. 34° 12′, long. 73° 24′.

MAZYE, in Afghanistan, a large village in the Pisheen valley, close to the route from Shawl to Kandahar, and distant forty miles north of the former place. The surrounding country is cultivated to a considerable extent. Lat. 30° 39′, long. 66° 39′. _{E.I.C. Ms. Doc.}

MEEALEE, in the Punjab, a thriving town thirty-seven miles east of Kala Bagh, on the Indus. Here are indications of coal, represented to be of fine quality. Lat. 32° 52′, long. 72° 6′. _{Wood, Rep. on the Coal of the Indus, 80.}

MEEANEE, in the Punjab, a small town on the right or west bank of the Ravee, which is here, when fullest, five hundred and thirteen yards wide and twelve feet deep. It is on the great route from Loodianah, by Amritsir, to Attock, and the Ravee is crossed at this place by a much-frequented ferry. In the cold season, when the river is lowest, it can be forded. Lat. 31° 49′, long. 74° 27′. _{Macartney, in Elph. Acc. of Caubul, 661.}

MEEANEE, in Afghanistan, a village situate in the south of the Derajat, on the right bank of the Indus. Lat. 29° 21′, long. 70° 40′. _{Map of Afg.}

MEEANEE, in Sinde, a village on the route from Hyderabad to Cutch, and six miles south of the former place, is situate on the left or eastern bank of the Indus. The word Meeanee,* in the Sindian language, means a fishing-station, and hence there are several places of that name. This village is in lat. 25° 20′, long. 68° 20′. _{Jour. As. Soc. 1840, p. 138, Hart, Jour. to Hinglaj; Wood, Oxus, 45; Burnes (James), Mission to Sinde, 33.}

MEEANEE, in Sinde, a village on the left of the route from Sehwan to Larkhana, and five miles north of the former place. It is situate on the northern bank of a considerable *dund* or piece of stagnant water, and is inhabited by fishermen. Lat. 26° 24′, long. 67° 55′. _{E.I.C. Ms. Doc.}

MEEANEE,[1] in Sinde, a village on the banks of the Fulailee branch of the Indus, and six miles north of Hyderabad. It will long be celebrated as the scene of a great victory obtained here by the Anglo-Indian army, under Sir Charles Napier, over a much more numerous force of the Belooches, headed by the Ameers of Sinde. The British general, having ascertained by _{[1] E.I.C. Ms. Doc.; Corresp. relative to Sinde, presented to Parliament by command of her Majesty, 1844.}

* From مِنْ *min*, a fish.

his emissaries that between twenty and thirty thousand men, the finest troops of the Belooche nation, were drawn up on the banks of the Fulailee in his front, and that the lapse of another day would place nearly thirty thousand more in his rear and on his left flank, moved forward to extricate himself from this threatening situation, and gave the enemy battle, on February 17th, 1843, though his own force amounted to but two thousand eight hundred men of all arms, and twelve pieces of artillery. The Belooche force actually on the ground amounted to twenty-two thousand men, with fifteen pieces of artillery. After a close and obstinate engagement for above three hours, during which those brave barbarians shewed desperate valour, the right of their position was carried by the Anglo-Indian cavalry, and their army totally routed, losing "artillery, ammunition, standards, and camp, with considerable stores, and some treasure."[2] The British lost two hundred and fifty-six men killed and wounded, the enemy about five thousand. Six of the principal members of the Talpoor dynasty immediately surrendered themselves. Meeanee is in lat. 25° 26′, long. 68° 24′.

[2] Napier, in his Despatch.

E.I.C. Ms. Map.

MEEANEE, in Sinde, a village situate near the right bank of the Indus, eight miles south-west of Hyderabad. Lat. 25° 18′, long. 68° 19′.

Walker, Map of Afg.

MEEAN POOSHTEH, in Afghanistan, a village situate on the left bank of the Helmund river. Lat. 30° 53′, long. 63° 26′.

MEEA ROZAN, in Sinde, a village situate on the right bank of the Indus, thirty miles south-west of the town of Mittunkote. Lat. 28° 41′, long. 70° 3′.

E.I.C. Ms. Doc.

MEEAWUL, in the Punjab, a village twenty miles south of the town of Julalpoor, and twenty-five west of Ramnuggur. Lat. 32° 26′, long. 73° 15′.

MEEMUNA.—See MEIMUNA.

MEENGANA, in the Punjab, a thriving manufacturing town three or four miles from the left or eastern bank of the Chenaub. Here as well as at Jung, and some other towns in the same tract, are manufactured great quantities of white cotton cloth for the Afghan market. Burnes states that 1,800,000 yards are made annually for this purpose. Lat. 31° 10′, long. 72° 12′.

On the Commerce of the Derajat.

MEENISMAJERA, in the Punjab, a village situate ten miles from the right bank of the Chenaub river, in lat. 31° 49′, long. 72° 47′.

Walker's Map of N.W. Frontier.

MEER ALI.—See MIR ALLAH.

MEERANPOOR, in the Punjab, a village situate on the route from Mooltan to Bhawlpoor, and thirty miles south of the former town. Lat. 29° 41′, long. 71° 32′. E.I.C. Ms. Doc.

MEERBUR, in the Punjab, a village situate on the right bank of the river Chenaub, twenty-five miles north of its confluence with the Ghara river. Lat. 29° 43′, long. 71° 12′. Map of N.W. Frontier.

MEER DOUD SERAI.—See MIR DAOUD.

MEERGURH, in Bhawlpoor, a town in the desert, extending through the eastern part of that state. The adjacent country, though barren from want of water, consists, in most places, of a firm earth, which is in many parts overspread with grassy jungle, yielding sustenance to cattle, especially after rain. In some places, however, it is covered with loose sandhills. The town consists of several dwelling-houses and a few shops, defended by a small brick-built fort. There is a good supply of water from wells, to which the cattle from a large tract of the surrounding desert have recourse. Meergurh is in lat. 29° 10′, long. 72° 52′. Boileau, Rajwara, Map; Conolly Jour. Eng. Ind. ii. 291; Masson, Bal. Afg. Panj. i. 2, 25.

MEERJEE, in Afghanistan, a village situate on the route from Kabool to Peshawur, and fourteen miles south-east of Jelalabad. Lat. 34° 15′, long. 70° 36′. E.I.C. Ms. Doc.

MEERKAN, in Sinde, a village situate near the right bank of the Poorana river, twenty-two miles south-east of Hyderabad. Lat. 25° 17′, long. 68° 39′. Ms. Map of Sinde.

MEERKHAN, in Bhawlpoor, a village situate on the left bank of the Ghara river, ten miles east of the city of Bhawlpoor. Lat. 29° 27′, long. 71° 45′. E.I.C. Ms. Doc.

MEERKHAN TANA, in Sinde, a village on the route from Sehwan to Kurrachee, and seventy-five miles north-east of the latter place. It contains two or three shops, and is situate on the banks of the Murraie, a torrent which often ceases to flow; but water can at all times be obtained by digging in its sandy bed. Lat. 25° 30′, long. 67° 57′.

MEERPOOR, in Beloochistan, a small village of Cutch Gundava, on the great route from Sinde to Ghuznee and Kandahar. It is situate on the river, or rather torrent of the Nari, but, in the dry season, has no water but what is obtained by digging in the bed of the channel, and that is brackish and unwholesome. Lat. 28° 36′, long. 67° 56′. E.I.C. Ms. Doc.; Hough, 46; Havelock, War in Afg. i. 188.

48 MEE—MEI.

MEERPOOR,[1] in Sinde, a flourishing town near the left, or eastern bank of the Pinyaree, a great branch of the Indus, and on the route from Cutch to Hyderabad. The surrounding country, which is fertile, well cultivated, and productive, yielded annually a revenue equal to £50,000 to the Ameer of Meerpoor, the least important and wealthy of the Ameers of Sinde. This town is of importance as commanding the line of communication between Cutch and Sinde. Population 10,000.[2] Lat. 24° 45′, long. 68° 20′.

MEERPOOR, in Sinde, a village ten miles east of Garrah or Gharry-kote. Close to it is Moujdurria, a ruined city, exhibiting abundant evidence of former population and wealth. Lat. 24° 40′, long. 67° 49′.

MEERPOOR, in Sinde, a village of the Delta, is situate near the right bank of the channel of the Buggaur, formerly the great western outlet of the Indus. Lat. 24° 30′, long. 67° 36′.

MEERPOOR, in Sinde, a village on the route from Hyderabad to Omercote, and fifty-two miles west of the latter place. Lat. 25° 24′, long. 69°.

MEETEE, in Beloochistan, a village of Cutch Gundava, situate on the route from Kotree to Dadur, and sixty miles south of the latter town. Lat. 28° 39′, long. 67° 30′.

MEETLA, in Sinde, a village situate on the left bank of the Western Narra river, on the route from Larkhana to Sehwan, ten miles south of the former town. Lat. 27° 23′, long. 68°. 11′.

MEHR, in Sinde, a village on the left or eastern bank of the Indus, opposite to the decayed town of Lukkee. Lat. 26° 14′, long. 68° 3′.

MEHY BONDEE, in Beloochistan, a halting-place in the province of Lus, is situate on a torrent falling into the river Hubb. Lat. 25° 23′, long. 67°.

MEIGHRA, in Bhawlpoor, a village situate on the left bank of the Ghara river, twenty-five miles north-east of the town of Khyrpoor. Lat. 29° 46′, long. 72° 28′.

MEIMUNA, in Afghanistan, a town with a district of the same name at the western extremity of Hindoo Koosh, in the Huzareh country. The country, though elevated and mountainous, is tolerably fertile and well cultivated. The chief, who has an income of about Rs. 150,000, generally professes allegiance

---

[1] Burnes (Alex.), Bokhara, iii. 213, 224; Burnes (J.), Mission to Sinde, 38, 62.

[2] Burnes' Bokh. iii. 227.

Outram, Rough Notes, 8.

Ms. Survey Map.

E.I.C. Ms. Doc.

Ms. Survey Map.

E.I.C. Ms. Doc.

Kennedy, Sinde and Kabool, ii. 207.

E.I.C. Ms. Doc.

E.I.C. Ms. Doc.

Jour. As. Soc. 1841, p. 126, Conolly (Arthur), Extracts from Demi-official Rep. on Khorasan; Burnes, on Herat, 42; Moorer. Punj. Bokh. ii. 497.

MEKRAN.

either to the rulers of Kabool or those of Herat. Conolly, probably the only European who had visited it, does not give its exact locality, but calculating from the statement of his marches, it is probably in lat. 35° 50′, long. 64° 35′.

MEKRAN,[1] in Beloochistan, the most extensive and westerly province of that country. It is bounded on the north by Afghanistan and the province of Sarawan, on the east by the provinces of Jhalawan and of Lus, on the south by the Arabian Sea, and on the west by Persia. It extends about five hundred miles in length from east to west, two hundred in breadth from north to south, is situate between lat. 25° 28°, long. 58° 66°, and has a superficial extent of about one hundred thousand square miles.

[1] Pott. Belooch. 297-307; Jour. Roy. As. Soc. 1839, p. 328-340; Jour. of a Route through the Western Parts of Makran, by Capt. N. P. Grant.

All the knowledge concerning this wild and barbarous country possessed by Europeans is derived from Pottinger and his companion, Christie, and from Grant, who preceded the former two in the career of discovery, having passed through the country the year before their visit. The north-western part is traversed by considerable mountain ranges, which rise to the north into the elevated tract known by the name of Kohistan or Highlands. The mountains of the Kohistan extend easterly until they join an offset of the Hala range, so that the general character of the whole of the north of this country is that of a hilly, uneven, and rather elevated district. The two more remarkable ranges of northern Mekram extend east and west, and in some degree parallel to each other, the Wushutee range (the more northern) being the greater. Between them lies the district of Punjgoor, of very inferior elevation. The long, narrow tract extending along the sea-shore is low and level, except at the eastern extremity, where a range of hills, styled by Hart[2] the Hara, separates this province from Lus. During rainy weather, numerous torrents flowing from north to south discharge themselves into the sea. Pottinger,[3] describing them, says—"They all usually have a broad and deep channel from the coast, until they reach the mountains or stony hills, where they become contracted into narrow and intricate watercourses, that are quite dry the greater part of the fair season, and in the wet one swelled to terrific torrents, which run off in the course of a few hours after the rain that has filled them ceases." The beds of those

[2] Jour. As. Soc. 1840, p. 151, Hart, Acc. of a Jour. from Kurrachee to Hinglaj.
[3] 301.

torrents are filled with dense jungle, harbouring numerous wild animals.

There are two wet seasons, the one in February and March, the other in June, July, and August. In the early wet season, the prevailing wind is from the north-west, and the rains continue three or four weeks. The latter wet season, according to Pottinger,[4] "comprises all the fury of the south-west monsoon." The hot season, which begins in March, lasts till October, and the heat is so great during the *khoormu puz*, or "date ripening," in the beginning of August, that none can venture out. Along the sea-coast there is scarcely any winter. In the high lands the weather is cool during November, December, January, and February. The winds during the hot weather destroy every sign of vegetation, and scorch the skin in the most painful manner. The population, as might be expected, are in a great measure pastoral, deriving subsistence from their sheep, goats, and camels; kine seem not to thrive, the country being too rugged and barren. A little grain is cultivated in a few fertile and watered valleys, and in the hottest parts the date-palm thrives remarkably, yielding an important article of food.[5] In some places grapes are produced, of good quality. There is scarcely any trade. The scanty exports consist of wool, felt, hides, butter, dates; the imports of raw cotton, coarse cotton cloths, iron, and sugar. Fish is caught in considerable quantities, and forms the principal support of the inhabitants along the sea-coast, who thus retain the habits of their ancestors, the *Icthyophagi*, mentioned by the historians of Alexander.

The most powerful tribe of Mekran is the Narroi Belooches, who, in their predatory excursions, mounted on fleet camels, have been known to traverse, in three days, two hundred miles of country, with the design of enslaving the inhabitants and driving off their cattle. Part of the north-west territory is held by Kurd tribes, who have established themselves there as offsets from that branch of their nation settled in Laristan. The inhabitants of the sea-coast have a large admixture of African blood, in consequence of their intercourse with the countries lying to the south-west; and hence they are of larger and more robust form and blacker hue than the other Mekranis, who are described by Pottinger[6] as "a puny, delicate race of men." All classes

[4] 320.

[5] Masson, Kalat, 291.

[6] 306.

MEKRAN. 51

of the population are much addicted to intoxication, produced by the use of a fermented beverage obtained from dates. The women are represented as very ugly; they are also very dissolute in their habits, and both sexes impair their constitutions and abridge their lives by excesses. The arms generally in use are the matchlock, sword, shield, and knife. The number of men bearing arms is computed by Grant[7] at 25,000, and if they be assumed to be in the proportion of one to eight to the entire population, an estimate thus obtained will make the total number of inhabitants 200,000, being at the rate of two to the square mile.

[7] 359.

Mekran is divided into a great number of petty districts, the fluctuating extent and limits of which depend altogether on the comparative power of the respective tribes to maintain their possessions. Those in the south-west are partially subject to the Imam of Muscat; those in the north-west, to Persia. The rest of Mekran had been under the influence of the Khans of Kelat for above two hundred years[8] previously to the accession of Nusseer Khan, who, about the middle of the eighteenth century, in consequence of a treaty with Ahmed Shah Durani,[9] obtained undisputed possession of it. The Khans of Kelat have made scarcely an effort to maintain their claim to sovereignty,[1] and the country is in a state of independence—consequently in a state of confusion, which is thus described by Pottinger:[2]— "All is now anarchy and bloodshed; each district has its own system of revenge, and travellers or merchants can only move from one part of the country to another when accompanied by an armed party sufficiently strong to repel attack."

[8] Malcolm, Persia, ii. 238.
[9] Elph. Acc. of Caubul, 551.
[1] Masson, Kalat, 203.
[2] 307.

Mekran is important in a military point of view, as containing two routes practicable for the march of an army from Persia to India. The more northern lies among the mountains, at the distance of about a hundred miles from the coast. It is well supplied with water, and abundance of dates and cattle may be obtained, but the road is in many places impassable for artillery. The other road lies along the sea-coast, by Jask and Chobar, to Kurrachee, over the level country between the sea and the mountains. Grant[3] says, "In the part of it that I travelled I experienced no want of water, except in a small tract of forty miles, between Shirahan and Serik, where the water is soon dried up in the wells; but this is of less consequence, as they are numerous.

[3] 338.

Little or no rain had fallen this year, and yet the nullas always afforded a large supply of water." This road is passable both for cavalry and artillery, sufficient forage may be obtained for horses, and, as on the more northern road, dates and cattle are procurable, but no other supplies; so that it would be requisite to have depôts of provisions at suitable intervals. It is, perhaps, scarcely necessary to observe, that this was the route taken by Alexander in his return from India.

E.I.C. Ms. Doc.; Hough, Narr. Exp. in Afg. 93.

MELEMANDA, in Afghanistan, a halting-place on the route from Shawl to Kandahar, and forty miles south-west of the latter city. Here are several villages situate on a small stream, a feeder of the Doree, and containing many wells. The country to the east is very rocky and uneven, that to the west rather level and well cultivated. Lat. 31° 16′, long. 65° 58′.

E.I.C. Ms. Doc.

MENEEKA, in Sinde, a village situate on the western route from Larkhana to Sehwan, and forty miles north of the last-mentioned place. Lat. 26° 52′, long. 67° 51′.

E.I.C. Ms. Doc.

MENOTEE, in Beloochistan, a village of Cutch Gundava, on the route from Sukkur to Shahpoor, and eighteen miles south of the latter town. Lat. 28° 30′, long. 68° 30′.

[1] F. Von Hügel, Kaschmir, i. 193; ii. 166.

MER and SER,[1] in the north of the Punjab, two mountain summits, which rise to great height and with sublime effect, fifty or sixty miles east of the eastern boundary of Kashmir. In their regular conical form they as closely resemble each other as though they had been cast in the same mould, but they differ in hue, one being completely white, the other as uniformly black. They seem to be situate close together, and if this be the case, they must be nearly of the same height. No explanation appears to have been given of the singular fact that, being of the same height and situate in the same latitude, one is covered with perpetual snow, the other quite bare. Hügel considers them identical with the Kantal mountain of the early maps of Kashmir;

[2] Kashmir, ii. 395.

but Vigne[2] is of opinion that the Kantal is the lofty mountain south of the Bultul Pass. They are probably, with the exception of the mountains in Rupshu, the highest summits between the Sutlej and the Indus. Hügel clearly viewed them at Vizirabad, in the plain of the Punjab, overtopping the Panjals of Kashmir, and many other intervening mountains, though the distance is not less than a hundred and forty miles. Mer and Ser may be considered situate about lat. 34°, long. 76°.

MERAUB LUKIA, in Sinde, a village on the route from Sehwan to Larkhana, and sixty miles north of the former place. The surrounding country is low, alluvial, and well cultivated. The road is intersected at a short distance from the village by a watercourse, causing difficulty to the passage of carriages. Lat. 27° 10′, long. 68° 6′. — E.I.C. Ms. Doc.

METAEE, in Afghanistan, a town in the Derajat, on the route from Ghuznee to Dera Ismael Khan, and distant ten miles west from the latter town. The road is good in this part of the route, and there is a supply of water. Lat. 31° 50′, long. 70° 44′. — E.I.C. Ms. Doc.

METRAO, in Sinde, a mud fort situate on the route from Roree to Jessulmair, and twenty-six miles south-east of the former place. There are five good wells, but scarcely any supplies can be procured, in consequence of the barren nature of the adjacent country, exhibiting only stunted jungle and naked sand-hills. The road is deep and very heavy in both directions from the fort. Lat. 27° 23′, long. 69° 46′. — E.I.C. Ms. Doc.

METRIE, in Sinde, a halting-place on the route from Roree to Jessulmair, and twenty-five miles south-east of the former place. Lat. 27° 30′, long. 69° 13′. — E.I.C. Ms. Doc.

MEYLMUNJ, in Afghanistan, a village situate on the Moorghab river. Lat. 34° 52′, long. 64° 22′. — Walker's Map of Afg.

MHELA-MAUNDA.—See MELEMANDA.

MIANEE, in the Punjab, a village situate near the right bank of the river Ravee, twenty miles north-east of Lahore, on the road to Kashmir. Lat. 31° 49′, long. 74° 29′. — Walker's Map of N.W. Frontier.

MIHEE, in Afghanistan, a village among the Murree mountains, which separate the north of Cutch Gundava from Sewestan. It is situate on the circuitous route from Bagh to Kahun. Lat. 29° 19′, long. 68° 49′. — E.I.C. Ms. Doc.

MILLEE, in the Punjab, a village ten miles from the right bank of the river Jailum. Lat. 31° 59′, long. 71° 56′. — Walker's Map of N.W. Frontier.

MINKRAVORA, in Afghanistan, a village in the valley of Suwat, and situate near the left bank of the river of the same name. Lat. 34° 53′, long. 72° 19′. — Jour. As. Soc. 1839, p. 312, Court, Alexander's Exploits on the Western Bank of Indus. Map.

MIR ALLAH, in Afghanistan, a ruined caravanserai on the route from Herat to Kandahar, and forty-two miles south of the former city. It is surrounded by cultivation, and a fine stream of water runs under the walls. Lat. 33° 50′, long. 62° 14′. — E.I.C. Ms. Doc.

MIRBUL.—A pass over the Snowy Panjal mountain, bound- — Vigne, Kashmir, i. 342.

ing Kashmir on the east. By it the road proceeds from the valley of Burengo on the west, to Kishtewar on the east. Elevation above the sea 11,500 feet. Lat. 33° 20′, long. 75° 28′.

E.I.C. Ms. Doc.

MIR DAOUD.—A caravanserai in Western Afghanistan, on the route from Herat to Kandahar, and distant eighteen miles south from the former place. It has a fine stream of clear water from a subterraneous aqueduct. Lat. 34° 7′, long. 62° 10′.

MIRZA AWLUNG, in Afghanistan, a halting-place in the Huzareh country, and fifteen miles south of Siripool. Lat. 35° 56′, long. 65° 37′.

E.I.C. Ms. Doc.

MIRZAPOOR, in the Punjab, a village situate on the left bank of the Chenaub river, twenty miles south of Mooltan. Lat. 29° 54′, long. 71° 16′.

E.I.C. Ms. Doc.

MISHKINYA, in Afghanistan, a village situate among the Suliman mountains, and on the route from Dera Ismael Khan through the Gomul Pass to Ghuznee. Lat. 32° 2′, long. 70° 1′.

E.I.C. Ms. Doc.

MISKHEL, in Afghanistan, a village situate forty miles south-east of Ghuznee. Lat. 33° 7′, long. 68° 36′.

MITENDA KAT.—See MITTUN KOTE.

Masson, Bal. Afg. Panj. i. 123.

MITTANI.—A town in Afghanistan in the plain of Peshawer, lying south of the city of that name. Lat. 33° 51′, long. 71° 35′.

[1] Burnes' Bokh. iii. 89; Id. Trade of the Derajat, 110; Id. Pers. Narr. 72; Lord, Med. Mem. on Indus, 59; Wood, Oxus, 76; Boileau, Rajwara, 37.

MITTUN KOTE.[1]—A town near the western bank of the Indus, close to the confluence of the Punjnud, or stream conveying into it the united waters of the Punjab. Burnes found the Indus here, at the latter end of May, before the swell attained its height, 2,000 yards wide. Later in the season, the adjacent country, to a great extent, is overflowed, and becomes one uninterrupted expanse of water, as the land is, for a considerable distance on each side of the river, on a low level. At this time of year the climate is unhealthy. Mittun Kote is admirably situated for commanding the trade of the Indus throughout its whole extent; and hence, has by some been recommended as the best site of an annual fair, where the traders of Afghanistan and of Central Asia might be supplied with Indian and British goods, but its insalubrity is a great objection to such a selection. It is surrounded with flourishing date groves, from which the Sikhs, who now possess it, derive a good revenue. Elevation above the sea, 220 feet.[2] Population 4,000. It is four hundred and sixty miles from the sea, in lat. 28° 54′, long. 70° 25′.

[2] Burnes' Bokh. iii. 209.

MOCHARA, in Sinde, a village situate on the right bank of the Indus, ten miles south-east of Tattah, and near the divergence of the Buggaur branch from the main river. Lat. 24° 40′, long. 68° 1′. Ms. Survey Map.

MODRA, in Sinde, a village situate five miles west of Nuggur Parkur, in lat. 24° 21′, long. 70° 41′. Walker's Map of Sinde.

MOGHUMDEE, in the Punjab, a village situate three miles from the left bank of the river Chenaub. Lat. 31° 37′, long. 72° 48′. Walker, Map of N.W. Frontier.

MOHAVEE, in Afghanistan, a fort of the Derajat, thirty miles west of the Indus, situate at the eastern entrance of a pass across the Suliman mountains, through which the route from Dera Ghazee Khan to Boree, and thence to Kandahar, proceeds. Hence this route is called generally the Boree route (which see). Mohavee is in lat. 30° 30′, long. 70° 24′. Leech, App. 40.

MOHUMBAH, in Sinde, a village situate on the northern border of the Great Western Rinn, in lat. 24° 20′, long. 70° 15′. Ms. Map of Sinde.

MOHUNKOT, in the north of the Punjab, a village among the mountains of the southern part of the Himalaya, and on the route from Chumba to Jamu. It formerly had a fort, well situated on a sandstone rock, overlooking the town; but when the rajah fell beneath the power of Runjeet Singh, the latter chief caused it to be demolished. It is situated at a short distance to the east of Manasa, a small lake, considered sacred by the Hindoos, and visited by them in pilgrimage. Lat. 32° 30′, long. 75° 12′. Vigne, Kashmir, i. 178.

MOHUNKOTE, in Sinde, a fort amidst the Lukkee mountains. During the Talpoor dynasty it belonged to the Ameers of Hyderabad. Lat. 25° 50′, long. 67° 57′. E.I.C. Ms. Doc.

MOHUNSA.—See MONSUR.

MOJGURH, in Bhawlpoor, a town on the route from the city of Bhawlpoor to Jodhpoor, and forty-five miles south-east of the former. It is situate in the desert extending through the eastern part of the state of Bhawlpoor, which has generally a soil of hard tenacious earth, covered in most places with grassy jungle and stunted shrubs, but in some overspread with hills of loose shifting sand. The site of Mojgurh is of firm ground, with low sandy eminences on every side, but at such a distance that light guns cannot command it. The walls are built of brick; they are Elph. Acc. of Caubul, 14; Masson, Bal. Afg. Panj. i. 2, 24; Boileau, Rajwara, 75.

56   MOK—MOO.

about fifty feet high (including the parapet, of about seven feet), and two and a half feet thick, with a terreplain four feet broad. On the north side they are in many places perforated with cannon-balls discharged during the siege carried on by the first Khan of Bhawlpoor. The place is half a furlong square, with numerous bastions, and an outwork on the east side to cover the entrance. A mosque conspicuously surmounts the gateway, and a little to the north is a Mahometan tomb, with a cupola profusely ornamented with coloured glazed tiles. There is a large tank outside the walls, and within are several wells containing abundance of good water at the depth of fifty-eight cubits. Mojgurh is in lat. 29° 1', long. 72° 11'.

Map of N.W. Frontier.

MOKULMUSSEED, in the Punjab, a village situate fifteen miles south-east of the city of Mooltan. Lat. 30° 3', long. 71° 39'.

[1] Von Hugel, Kaschmir, iii. 48.

MONSUR,[1] in the Punjab, a small town near the east or left bank of the Indus and the northern frontier of the Sikh dominion. It is a poor place, with a weak and rudely built fort. Vigne[2] mentions it by the name of Mansa. Lat. 34° 14', long. 73° 11'.

[2] ii. 185.

MONZE CAPE, or RAS MOOAREE, a sharply projecting headland, forming the western extremity of the coast of Sinde, is the termination seawards of the high lands known in different parts by the names of the Hala, Brahooic, and Pubb mountains. Pottinger[1] states that "it springs abruptly to a conspicuous height and grandeur out of the sea," but Horsburgh[2] describes it as of moderate height, and in this he is borne out by the outline given in Dalrymple's charts of the coast of Sinde. On the north-west of it is the island of Chilney, or Churna, the channel of separation being four miles wide, and six or seven fathoms deep in the middle. Lat. 24° 46, long. 66° 38'.

[1] Belooch. 251.
[2] Ind. Dir. i. 403.

E.I.C. Ms. Doc.

MOOBAREKPOOR, in Bhawlpoor, a village situate eight miles from the left bank of the Ghara river, and thirty miles north-east of Khyrpoor. Lat. 29° 45', long. 72° 33'.

E.I.C. Ms. Doc.

MOOKASHRUK, in Afghanistan, a village four miles south of Ghuznee, on the road from thence to Kandahar. Lat. 33° 29', long. 68° 13'.

Walker's Afg.

MOOKHTA, a village in Afghanistan, situate on the river Helmund, on the route from Kandahar to Seistan. Lat. 31° 35', long. 64° 12'.

MOOKR, in Afghanistan, a village situate on the circuitous route from Giriskh to Bamian. Lat. 32° 13′, long. 65° 35′. [E.I.C. Ms. Doc.]

MOOKUR.—See MUKUR.

MOOLA, a river of Beloochistan, rises a few miles south of Kelat, and flows south-east a distance of about eighty miles; it then turns north-east, and subsequently east, and after a course of about a hundred and fifty miles, is ultimately absorbed by the parched soil of the *Rinn*, *Pat*, or desert of Shikarpoor, in lat. 28°, long. 68°. The Moola or Gundava Pass winds along its course. [Leech, on Sind. Army, 86; Masson, Kalat, 331.]

MOOLA or GUNDAVA PASS, in Beloochistan, generally follows the course of the Moola river, and conducts, by a circuitous route, from the elevated region of Kelat to the plain of Cutch Gundava. It commences near the source of the Moola, close to Angeera, in lat. 28° 10′, long. 66° 12′, and at an elevation of 5,250 feet; for about fifty miles it proceeds in a direction generally south-easterly, along the bottom of the valley, or rather through a succession of deep and in general rocky gorges, down which the stream flows, thus cross-cutting the eastern brow of the Hala mountains. At Nurd, in lat. 27° 52′, long. 66° 57′, and having an elevation of 2,850 feet, the valley, and the stream flowing through it, takes an abrupt turn to the north-east, and continues to hold that direction, for about fifty miles, to its termination near Kotree, in Cutch Gundava, at an elevation of 600 feet above the sea, and in lat. 28° 24′, long. 67° 27′. As the route generally follows the course of the stream to within a short distance of the north-eastern or lower extremity of the pass, there is always abundance of good water. The descent being four thousand six hundred and fifty feet in about a hundred miles, the average fall is forty-six feet in a mile. At Paesht Khana, about forty miles below the upper extremity of the pass, the river Moola receives a considerable stream, flowing from the north. Through the valley along which this stream flows, a route proceeds direct from Kelat to this part of the Moola Pass, but is not practicable for artillery or carriages. This direct route is called the Panduran Pass, from a village of that name situate on it. In the close of 1839, the Anglo-Indian detachment under the command of General Willshire, after storming Kelat, marched to Sinde through the Moola Pass, and a brief notice of the marches and halting-places on the route will, perhaps, best shew its character. To Bapow, a [1 E.I.C. Ms. Doc.]

distance of twelve miles, the descent was considerable, amounting to 1,250 feet, the difference between its elevation and that of Angeera. The river in some places disappeared, sinking, probably, in its gravelly bed; where it came to light, the depth nowhere exceeded a few inches. On every side very steep and high mountains were visible. The next march was of twelve miles, to Peesee Bhent, elevation 4,600 feet, the bed of the river still in many places dry, and in general constituting the road. In one place precipices, 500 feet high, were so close to each other, that the passage between them was not more than thirty or forty feet wide. An enemy might here effectually prevent the progress of troops by merely rolling down a few blocks of stone, and there are no means of turning the defile. The march to Putkee, distant twelve miles, and of the elevation of 4,250 feet, lay through a wide part of the valley, displaying considerable cultivation; the road in some instances diverged from the channel of the river, but crossed it several times. To Paesht Khana, a distance of ten miles and a half, and at an elevation of 3,500 feet, the road was at first very difficult, lying over the stony bed of the river; it afterwards became better, crossing a considerable plain, in which the direct road from Kelat by Panduran, lying to the north, joined the Moola Pass. The next march was twelve miles, to Nurd, elevation 2,850 feet, and the most southern point of the pass. The road several times crossed the river, which receives from the south a stream, along the course of which a cross road proceeds to Khozdar. On the right of the road the two peaks, Dodaudan (two teeth), towered to a great height. In the succeeding march, to Jungi Kooshta, distant twelve miles, and of the elevation of 2,150 feet, the character of the valley and inclosing hills improved, as they afforded good pasture. For the next march, to Bent-i-jah, distant ten miles and a half, and of the elevation of 1,850 feet, the road scarcely deviated from the course of the river, and was in general good. In the following march to Kohow, distant above eleven miles, and of the elevation of 1,250 feet, the road had a slight ascent and descent. The next march brought the detachment to Kullar, distance ten miles, elevation 750 feet. This is probably the termination of the pass, though the route proceeds thirteen miles farther, to Kotree, in the plain of Cutch Gundava. In a military point of view, it is preferable to the Bolan Pass, as the road is better, the ascent easier and more regular, water abundant, and some supplies obtainable. The guns brought through the pass by the British were light field-pieces of the horse artillery. Masson,[2] who appears to have carefully explored the pass, gives its character in the following words:—"In a military point of view, the route, presenting a succession of open spaces connected by narrow passages or defiles, is very defensible, at the same time affording convenient spots for encampment, abundance of excellent water, fuel, and more or less of forage. It is level throughout the road, either tracing the bed of the stream or leading near to its left bank."

[2] Bal. Afg. Panj. ii. 124.

MOOLA GOORI, in Afghanistan, a village situate on the right bank of the Lundye river, twenty miles south of its confluence with the river Surat. Lat. 34° 31′, long. 71° 38′.

E.I.C. Ms. Doc.

MOOLAKADEE, in Afghanistan, a village on the route from Ghuznee to Kandahar, and a hundred miles south-west of the former city. Lat. 32° 33′, long. 67° 15′.

E.I.C. Ms. Doc.

MOOLA KHAN, in Afghanistan, a village on the route from Kandahar to Ghuznee, and ninety miles south-west of the latter town. Lat. 32° 46′, long. 67° 28′.

E.I.C. Ms. Doc.

MOOLA KURME, in Afghanistan, a village situate on the route from Ghuznee to Shawl, and sixty miles south of Lake Ab-istada. Lat. 31° 49′, long. 67° 21′.

E.I.C. Ms. Doc.

MOOLANA, in Beloochistan, a village of Cutch Gundava, situate on the road from Gundava to Shikarpoor, twenty-five miles east of the former town. Lat. 28° 27′, long. 67° 55′.

E.I.C. Ms. Doc.

MOOLANOH, in Sinde, a village in the Great Desert, extending between that state and Rajwara. Lat. 26° 26′, long. 70° 9′.

Walker's Map of Sinde.

MOOLEANEE RIVER.—See DUSTEE.

MOOLTAN[1] in the Punjab, a great and ancient city, which, since the pre-eminence of the Sikh power, takes an important part in the commercial and monetary transactions of Western India, outstripping Shikarpoor, and being inferior in this respect only to Amritsir. It is situate three miles east of the Chenaub,[2] the inundations of which reach it. Elphinstone,[3] who saw this city in 1809, before it had been stormed by the Sikhs, describes it as "surrounded with a fine wall between forty and fifty feet high." This is now dilapidated, but the citadel continues a place of strength, being more regular in construction than pro-

[1] Leech, Rep. on Commerce of Mooltan, 79.
[2] Masson, Bal. Afg. Panj. i. 396.
[3] 21.

MOOLTAN.

bably any other place laid down in India by native engineers, though some of the ravages of the late siege have not yet been repaired. It stands on a mound, and is an irregular hexagon, with its longest side, which measures six hundred yards, to the north-west.[5] The wall, substantially built of burnt brick, is about forty feet high outside, but only four or five feet from the ground inside, in consequence of the accumulation of the materials of older buildings. It is surmounted by thirty towers and protected by a ditch, faced with masonry.* The only buildings within it of any importance, are the battered palace of the former Khan, and a lofty Mahometan shrine. It was stormed in 1818 by Runjeet Sing,[6] who cut to pieces the Afghan garrison of three thousand, with the exception of five hundred admitted to quarter. The booty on that occasion is said to have amounted to four millions sterling.† The army of the besiegers consisted of 25,000, of whom 1,900 were slain.

Mooltan is the largest town in the Sikh territory after Lahore and Amritsir. The present town is built on a mound of considerable height, formed of the ruins of more ancient cities. The bazaars are extensive, and are well supplied with all articles of traffic and consumption, and the shops amount altogether in number to four thousand six hundred.[7] Its principal manufactures are silks, cottons, shawls, loongees, brocades, tissues. Its merchants are considered rich, and about fifteen of them are computed collectively to possess a million and a half of rupees. Banking constitutes a large proportion of the business of Mooltan, in which it has in some measure supplanted Shikarpoor; and the prosperity of the town is in all respects considered on the increase. It yields a revenue of 575,000 rupees.

The vicinity is covered with an amazing quantity of ruins of tombs, mosques, and shrines, which shew the former extent and antiquity of the city. North[8] of the place is the magnificent shrine of Sham Tabrezi, who, according to tradition, was flayed alive here

---

* Such is Masson's account (i. 396). Burnes (Bokhara, iii. 112) says, "The fortress of Mooltan has no ditch; the nature of the country will not admit of one."

† Prinsep states, that Runjeet Sing compelled his troops to disgorge their booty, which he appropriated to his own treasury. This, however, is at variance with the account given by the Maharajah himself to Moorcroft; but his highness might not, perhaps, regard a slight sacrifice of truth to the honour of his liberality.

---

[4] Masson, i. 395.
[5] Burnes' Bokh. iii. 112.
[6] Id. 113; Moorcr. Punj. Bokh. i. 101.
[7] Leech, Com. of Mooltan, 80.
[8] Malcolm, Hist. of Persia, ii. 402; Vigne, Ghuznee, 16.
Life of Runjeet Singh, 117.

as a martyr, and at whose prayer the sun descended from the heavens, and produced the intense heat from which Mooltan suffers, and for which it is proverbial. The adjacent country watered by the inundations of the Chenaub, produces fruits, esculent vegetables, grain, and other crops, in great abundance and perfection. Mooltan is said by Burnes[9] to be to this day styled "Mallithan," which he translates *the place of the Malli*, and thence infers it to have been that capital of the Malli taken by Alexander. But Arrian[1] mentions several such cities, and his brevity and the slender acquaintance which he had of the localities, must render any decision on such points at the present day hazardous and uncertain. Mooltan was taken by the Mahometans, under Mahomed Ben Kasim, at the close of the eighth century; by Mahmood of Ghiznee at the commencement of the eleventh; by Tamerlane at the close of the fourteenth.[2] Since its capture by Runjeet Sing, it has been garrisoned by Sikhs, who, though only amounting to five or six hundred, keep in severe subjection the Mahometans, supposed to amount to forty thousand persons.[3] The number of the entire population is estimated to be about 80,000.[4] Lat. 30° 8′, long. 71° 28′.

[9] iii. 114.
[1] Arrian, vi. 8.
[2] Price, Mahomedan Hist. iii. 251.
[3] Burnes' Bokh. iii. 116.
[4] Leech, Com. of Mooltan, 79.

MOONDEESHEHUR, in Afghanistan, a village on the left bank of the Turnak, and on the northern route from Kandahar to Shawl, being twelve miles south-east of the former town. Lat. 31° 33′, long. 65° 39′. E.I.C. Ms. Doc.

MOONDER, or MOONDRA, in Sinde, a village on the route from Sehwan to Larkhana, and thirty miles north of the former. It is a considerable place, and has, in watercourses and wells, a supply of water sufficient for a large body of persons. The surrounding country is level, fertile, and well cultivated. Lat. 26° 47′, long. 67° 54′. E.I.C. Ms. Doc.

MOONEE, in Afghanistan, a village on the route from Dera Ghazee Khan to Kahun, through Hurrund, and twelve miles south-west of the latter place. Lat. 29° 21′, long. 70° 2′. Walker's Map of Afg.

MOONGWUD, in the Punjab, a village on the route from Ferozpoor to Mooltan, and thirteen miles north-east of the latter town. Lat. 30° 10′, long. 71° 41′. E.I.C. Ms. Doc.

MOORGHAN KEHCHUR, in Afghanistan, a village situate on the left bank of the river Turnak, twenty-three miles east of Kandahar, in lat. 31° 37′, long. 65° 51′. E.I.C. Ms. Doc.

MOORGHAUB, in Afghanistan, a considerable river, rising Jour. As. Soc. 1841, p. 127, Conolly (Arthur).

in the Huzzareh country, about lat. 35°, long. 66°. It receives numerous streams in this mountainous region, and, taking a north-westerly course, flows by Merve, and is lost in the sands of Khorasan, after running about two hundred and fifty miles.

<small>Extracts from Demi-Official Rep.; also, 1834, p.10, Mohun Lal, Brief Descrip. of Herat; Fraser, Jour. Khorasan, App. 57; Burnes' Bokh. ii. 35; Abbott, Heraut and Khiva, i. 20.</small>

<small>Walker's Map of N.W. Frontier.</small>

MOOSA KORESHEE, in the Punjab, a village situate on the right bank of the Ravee river, in lat. 30° 51', long. 72° 59'.

<small>E.I.C. Ms. Doc.; Jour. As. Soc. 1842, p. 61, Grif. Bar. and Ther. Meas. in Afg.; Hough, Narr. Exp. in Afg. 157.</small>

MOOSHAKEE, in Afghanistan, on the route from Ghuznee to Kandahar, and twenty-nine miles south-west of the former place. It is a collection of eight forts, in a fertile, populous, and well-cultivated country, inhabited principally by Huzarehs. There is an abundant supply of water from subterraneous aqueducts. Elevation above the sea, 7,309 feet. Lat. 33° 18', long. 68° 3'.

MOOSTUNG.—See MUSTUNG.

<small>E.I.C. Ms. Doc.</small>

MOOTAKHALA, in Afghanistan, a village on the route from Ghuznee to Shawl, and sixty-five miles south of the former place. Lat. 32° 52', long. 67° 43'.

<small>E.I.C. Ms. Doc.</small>

MOOTIAH, in Afghanistan, a village situate on the upper course of the river of Kunduz, and four miles south-east of Bamian, in lat. 34° 48', long. 67° 49'.

<small>Walker's Map of N.W. Frontier.</small>

MORADPOOR, in the Punjab, a village situate twelve miles from the right bank of the Ghara river. Lat. 29° 43', long. 71° 53'.

<small>Ms. Map of Sinde.</small>

MORAH, in Sinde, a village on the western route from Bukkur to Hyderabad, and ninety miles south-west of the former place. Lat. 26° 46', long. 68°.

<small>E.I.C. Ms. Doc.</small>

MOREED KA KOTE, a village in Bhawlpoor, situate on the route from Khanpoor to Jessulmair, twenty-five miles south of the former town, in lat. 28° 20', long. 70° 54'.

<small>F. Von Hugel, Kaschmir, iii. 112.</small>

MORI, in the north-east of the Punjab, a lofty mountain, is one of the southern ranges of the Himalaya, stretching south-east of Kashmir, in lat. 32° 10', and about long. 75° 50'.

<small>E.I.C. Ms. Doc.</small>

MORODANEE, in Sinde, a village situate on the road from Bander Vikker to Tattah, and twenty-six miles south-west of the latter place, in lat. 24° 30', long. 67° 43'.

<small>E.I.C. Ms. Doc.</small>

MOROO, in Afghanistan, a village on the road from Kabool to Ghuznee, twenty-five miles north-east of the latter place. Lat. 33° 50', long. 68° 28'.

MORUL, in Ladakh, a village on the right bank of the Indus, opposite the confluence of the river of Dras, which discharges a body of water little inferior to that of the principal stream, in lat. 34° 43′, long. 76° 9′. Vigne, Kashmir, ii. 390; Moorer. Punj. Bokh. i. 264.

MOTA MAR, in Sinde, a village on the route from Subzulcote to Shikarpoor, and fifteen miles east of the last-mentioned town. The road in this part of the route lies through a low, muddy, alluvial tract, extending along the right bank of the Indus, overspread with jungle and intersected by watercourses. Lat. 27° 54′, long. 68° 57′. E.I.C. Ms. Doc.

MOTCH, in the Punjab, a village situate on the left bank of the Indus, eighteen miles south of Kala-Bagh. Lat. 32° 47′, long. 71° 29′. Walker's Map of N.W. Frontier.

MOUJDURRIA, in Sinde, a ruined town ten miles east of Garrah or Gharry-Kote, shewing by the remains yet existing of houses and defences that it was formerly a place of considerable importance. Lat. 24° 40′, long. 67° 49′. E.I.C. Ms. Doc.; Outram, Rough Notes, 8.

MOURDALIE, in Sinde, a village on the route from Roree to Jessulmair, and a hundred miles south-east of the former place. It consists of a few shepherds' huts, supplied with water from a small muddy tank. The road for some distance in the direction of Roree is heavy, winding among or over sand-hills. Towards Jessulmair it is better, as it passes over a surface of hard clay. Nothing available for the support of animal life can be obtained, except a little coarse grass. Lat. 27° 23′, long. 70° 30′. E.I.C. Ms. Doc.

MOUTNEE, in Sinde, is an offset on the left or eastern side of the great Sata branch of the Indus. Though once a large stream, it has now become a mere shallow rivulet, discharging its water into the sea by the unnavigable Kaheer mouth, in lat. 23° 51′, long. 67° 38′. Carless, Official Rep. on the Indus, 1; Burnes' Bokh. iii. 237.

MOYUMBUB, in the Punjab, a village situate on the right bank of the Ravee river, in lat. 30° 33′, long. 72° 23′. Walker's Map of N.W. Frontier.

MRITTEH.—See MUTTEH.

MUCHNEE, in Afghanistan, a ferry over the Kabool river, at the place where it enters the plain of Peshawur from the Khyber mountains. The river here, two hundred and fifty yards wide, is crossed by those who take the Abkhana route, which lies from east to west, and north of the Tatara and Khyber passes. So boisterous is the current, that the passage can be made only on inflated skins. Lat. 34° 12′, long. 71° 30′. Leech, Khyber Pass, 12; Burnes' Bokh. i. 114; Masson, Bal. Afg. Panj. iii. 238; Macartney, in Elph. 656.

MUD—MUK.

E.I.C. Ms. Doc. MUD, in Sinde, a village situate near the left bank of the Indus, on the route from Roree to Mittun-kote, twenty-two miles north-east of the former place. Lat. 27° 57′, long. 69° 3′.

E.I.C. Ms. Doc. MUDAREE, in Afghanistan, a village situate on the right bank of the river Indus, seven miles south of Attock. Lat. 33° 49′, long. 72° 16′.

Walker's Map of N.W. Frontier. MUDUDA, in the Punjab, a village situate on the right bank of the Ravee river, fifty miles south-west of Lahore. Lat. 31° 11′, long. 73° 35′.

E.I.C. Ms. Doc. MUGDOOM, in the Punjab, a village situate on the left bank of the Chenaub river, about twenty-four miles north of its confluence with the river Ghara. Lat. 29° 41′, long. 71° 15′.

MUGGEO PEER.—See MAGAR TALAO.

E.I.C. Ms. Doc. MUGGER PEERKE, in the Punjab, a village near the route from Ferozpoor to Mooltan, and a hundred and twenty miles north-east of the latter town. Lat. 30° 30′, long. 73° 19′.

MUGGUR TALAO.—See MAGAR TALAO.

Walker's Map of N.W. Frontier. MUHAR, in the Punjab, a village situate about eleven miles from the left bank of the Chenaub river, in lat. 31°, long. 72° 21′.

E.I.C. Ms. Doc. MUHIDPOOR, in the Punjab, a village situate on the left bank of the Chenaub river, about twelve miles north of its confluence with the Ghara. Lat. 29° 30′, long. 71° 8′.

Walker's Map of N.W. Frontier. MUHOTAI, in the Punjab, a village situate on the left bank of the Chenaub river, twelve miles north of the city of Mooltan. Lat. 30° 17′, long. 71° 31′.

Wood, Oxus, 16, 17; Kennedy, Sinde and Kabool, i. 76; Burnes' Pers. Narr. 10, 18; Outram, Rough Notes, 16. MUKALI, in the Delta of Sinde, a range of low hills extending twenty miles, from near Tattah on the north, to Peer Putta on the south. The height of these hills does not exceed one hundred feet. They consist of coral or limestone, abounding in remains of shells, and have a rugged surface devoid of all vegetation, excepting a few stunted shrubs. Lat. 24° 40′, long. 68° 55′.

E.I.C. Ms. Doc. MUKAM, in Afghanistan, a halting-place in the Pisheen valley. It is situate on the road from Kandahar to Quetta, forty miles north-west of the latter town. Lat. 30° 46′, long. 66° 46′.

Vigne, Ghuznee, 13. MUKDAMRAM, in the Punjab, on the route from Ferozpoor to Mooltan, and twenty miles east of the latter town. Lat. 30° 15′, long. 71° 46′.

Elph. Acc. of Caubul, 38. MUKKUD, in the Punjab, a town on the eastern bank of the Indus, near the base of the Salt range. Lat. 33° 8′, long. 71° 48′.

MUKUR, in Afghanistan, a district with a village on the route from Kandahar to Ghuznee, and one hundred and sixty miles north-east of the former city. The village is situate in a populous, fertile, and well-cultivated country near the source of the Turnak, which rises in numerous springs from the base of a mountain having an elevation of 2,000 feet above the plain. Mukur has an elevation of 7,091 feet above the sea. Lat. 32° 52′, long. 67° 41′. E.I.C. Ms. Doc.; Journ. As. Soc. Beng. 1842, p. 60, Grif.Bar.and Ther. Meas.; Hough, Narr. Exp. in Afg. 154.

MUKWAR, in Bhawlpoor, a village situate on the left bank of the Ghara river, eighteen miles west of the town of Bhawlpoor, and twenty miles from the confluence of the Chenaub and Ghara rivers. Lat. 29° 24′, long. 71° 21′. E.I.C. Ms. Doc.

MUKWUL, in Afghanistan, a village situate near the right bank of the Indus, and thirty-five miles north of Dera Ghazee Khan, in lat. 30° 35′, long. 70° 50′. E.I.C. Ms. Doc.

MULKA, in the Punjab, a village situate about twenty miles from the right bank of the Ghara river. Lat. 30° 28′, long. 73° 4′. Walker's Map of N.W. Frontier.

MULKABAD, in Afghanistan, a village situate on the eastern route from Kabool to Shawl, and about fifty miles south of the former town, in lat. 33° 53′, long. 68° 51′. E.I.C. Ms. Doc.

MULL, in Sinde, an offset on the left or eastern side of the Sata, or great eastern branch of the Indus. Though once a large stream, it has now become a shallow rivulet, discharging a scanty body of water through the Mull mouth, in lat. 23° 56′, long. 67° 48′. The Mull is navigable for boats of twenty-five tons as far as Shahbunder, about eighteen miles from the mouth. Carless, Official Rep. on the Indus, 1; Burnes' Bokh. iii. 237.

MULLEEREE RIVER.—See GOORBAN RIVER.

MULLOH RIVER.—See MOOLA.

MULLUHPOOR, in the Punjab, a village on the route from Ramnegurh to Ferozpoor, and sixty miles south-east of the former town. Lat. 31° 30′, long. 74° 2′. Walker's Map of N.W. Frontier.

MULLYAN, in the Punjab, a small town on the route from Ramnegurh to Lahore, and twenty-five miles north-west of the latter. Lat. 31° 47′, long. 74° 54′. Hough, Narr. Exp. in Afg. 357.

MUMMOO,[1] in the desert between Afghanistan and Mekran, a halting-place situate on the route from Nooshky to Seistan, and a hundred and twenty miles west of the former place. It received its name from being the burial-place of Mulick Mummoo, a Pir or saint, at whose tomb the Mahometans offer prayers [1] E.I.C. Ms. Doc.

and distribute alms.² The water here is brackish, and no good supply can be had nearer than Kulchee, seven miles farther west. Mummoo is in lat. 29° 55', long. 63° 9'.

_{² Christie, in App. to Pott. Belooch. 405.}

_{Ms. Map of Sinde.}
MUMSEE, in Sinde, a village situate near the left bank of the Western Narra. Lat. 68°, long. 27° 7'.

_{E.I.C. Ms. Doc.}
MUMUKE, in Afghanistan, a village situate on the left bank of the Kabool river, and on the route from Kabool to Bamian, thirty miles west of the former city, in lat. 34° 23', long. 68° 36'.

_{Moorcr. Punj. Bokh. i. 172; Vigne, Kashmir, i. 80.}
MUNDI, north-east of the Punjab, is a small territory, comprising several valleys with their inclosing ridges, on the southern slope of the Himalaya. The capital, which is also called Mundi, is situate at the confluence of the Sukyt river with the Beas, which is here two hundred yards wide, very deep, and crossed by a ferry. These rivers have, every twenty-four hours, a periodical rise and fall, in consequence of the melting of snow by the heat of the sun, so that they rise towards evening and continue to do so throughout the greater part of the night, decreasing towards morning and throughout the forenoon. The Rajah's palace is an extensive building, with whitened walls, and covered with slate. It is surrounded by a beautiful garden, containing a profusion of the finest fruit-trees and flowers. The bazaar is large and well stocked. Mundi seems to be peculiarly under the influence of Hindoo superstition, and the horrible rite of *suttee*, or burning the *sati* or widow, with the corpse of her husband, is frightfully prevalent. When the Rajah dies, between twenty and thirty women invariably perish in this dreadful manner, and the number who suffer among the humbler classes is proportionate to the rank of the departed. In the vicinity, are productive mines of iron and salt, and the greater part of the revenue of the prince is derived from these sources. The Rajah is tributary to the Sikhs, and is treated with much oppression and contumely by them. Mundi is in lat. 31° 40', long. 76° 53'.

_{Walker's Map of Afg.}
MUNDUI, in Afghanistan, a village of Sewestan, in the road from Dadur to Dera Ghazee Khan. Lat. 29° 48', long. 68° 26'.

_{E.I.C. Ms. Doc.}
MUNEEARA, in the Punjab, a village on the route from Ramnegurh to Ferozpoor, and seventy miles south-east of the former town. It is situate near the right bank of the river Ravee, twenty miles south-west of Lahore. Lat. 31° 27', long. 74° 2'.

MUNEJAH.—See WANGANEE.

MUNKERE.—See MAUNKAIRA.

MUNOORA, in Sinde, a fort on a bluff head-land at the eastern extremity of the spit which landlocks the harbour of Kurrachee on the south. Lat. 24° 48′, long. 67°. (See also KURRACHEE.)

MUNSOOR KAREEZ, in Afghanistan, a collection of hamlets on the route from Ghuznee to Shawl, and eighty-three miles south from the former place. It is situate in a barren country on the western shore of Lake Ab-istada, at the place where a small river discharges itself. Lat. 32° 33′, long. 67° 50′. E.I.C. Ms. Doc.; Outram, Rough Notes, 149; Kennedy, Sinde Kabool, ii. 120.

MUNSOOR KHAN GOONDEE, in Afghanistan, a village situate on the right bank of the river Doree, twenty miles south of Kandahar. Lat. 31° 22′, long. 65° 23′. E.I.C. Ms. Doc.

MUNSUR, in the north-east of the Punjab, a village situate on the left bank of the river Chenaub, five miles west of the town of Doda. Lat. 33°, long. 75° 15′. Walker's Map of N.W. Frontier.

MUREE, in Sinde, a village situate on the left bank of the Indus. Lat. 28° 10′, long. 69° 17′. Map of Sinde.

MURR.—See MEHR.

MURRAIE, a river, or rather torrent, of Sinde, rises in the Keertar range of mountains, lat. 25° 30′, long. 67° 45′, and after a course of about twenty-five miles, generally in an easterly direction, falls into the Dhurwal river, a feeder of the Indus. The Murraie, where crossed by the route from Sehwan to Kurrachee, has a wide sandy channel, often destitute of water, which, however, can at all times be obtained from pits in the bed. E.I.C. Ms. Doc.

MURRAIE MUKAM, in Sinde, a village on the route from Sehwan to Kurrachee, and seventy-five miles south of the former place. Water is procurable at all times from pits in the bed of the Murraie river. The road in this part of the route is rather good. Lat. 25° 30′, long. 67° 53′. E.I.C. Ms. Doc.

MURRA KHARRA, properly MURRA KHAIL, in Afghanistan, a village situate on the route by Kurkutcha, from Kabool to Peshawur, and fifty-five miles east of the former city. Lat. 34° 19′, long. 69° 51′. E.I.C. Ms. Doc.

MURROW KOOSTUK, in Beloochistan, a village in Cutch Gundava, on the route from Poolajee to Deyrah, and thirty miles east of the former place. It is situate close to the north-eastern E.I.C. Ms. Doc.

frontier, in a fine grassy plain at the southern base of the mountains surrounding Kahun. Lat. 29° 1′, long. 68° 58′.

Vigne, Kashmir, i. 212.

MURU WURDWUN, in the north of the Punjab, a long, deep valley, with sides of gneiss and mica slate. Down this valley a river of the same name flows and joins the Chenaub at Kishtawar. The valley contains a village, also bearing the same name, opposite which the Nabog Nye Pass, twelve thousand feet high, leads into Kashmir. Lat. 33° 50′, long. 75° 26′.

Burnes, Pol. Power of the Sikhs, 4; Masson, Bal. Afg. Panj. i. 85.

MURWUT, in Afghanistan, an extensive, beautiful, and fertile valley, on the west side of the Indus, and south of the valley of Bannoo. It has on the west the lofty Suliman range, and on the north the snow-clad peaks of Sufaid Koh. Though exposed to the incursions of the marauders of the neighbouring mountains, it is so productive of grain and other necessaries of life, that it is thickly peopled. Society is here in a singularly primitive state, as the people have no general government, each village being under its own independent chief, and acknowledging no other authority. The valley is sometimes visited by an expedition of the Sikhs from the Derajat, who levy an enforced tribute from the inhabitants. Murwut, the chief place, is little more than a village. Lat. 33° 10′, long. 71° 15′.

E.I.C. Ms. Doc.

MUSTOEE, in Afghanistan, a village in the Daman, situate on an offset of the Indus, three miles from the main stream, and about fifty miles south of Dera Ghazee Khan. Lat. 29° 29′, long. 70° 48′.

[1] E.I.C. Ms. Doc.; Masson, Kalat, 314; Bal. Afg. Panj. ii. 68.

MUSTUNG,[1] in Beloochistan, a town on the great route from Kelat to Shawl, and seventy miles north of the former town. It contains about four hundred houses, surrounded with a crenated mud wall. The neighbouring country is probably the richest part of Beloochistan, having in summer a mild and salubrious climate and producing the finest fruits in abundance, besides grain, madder, and tobacco. Winter, however, brings considerable cold, and on this account the wealthier inhabitants, at the approach of that season, emigrate to the warm district of Cutch Gundava. The present town has replaced a more ancient one, the citadel of which was destroyed by Ahmed Shah; the ruins are observable on a mound close to the wall. The height above the sea cannot be less than 5,700 feet, as there is a slight ascent in travelling to this place from Shawl,[2] which has an elevation of 5,563 feet. Lat. 29° 48′, long. 66° 47′.

[2] Jour. As. Soc. 1842, Grif. Bar. and Ther. Obs. in Afg.

MUTON, in Sinde, a village situate on the left bank of the Indus. Lat. 27° 5′, long. 68° 8′. *Walker's Map of Sinde.*

MUTTA, in the Punjab, a small town on the route from Ramnegurh to Lahore, and forty miles north-west of the latter place. Lat. 31° 58′, long. 73° 48′. *Hough, Narr. of Exp. in Afg. 356.*

MUTTAREE, in Sinde, a town on the left or east bank of the Indus, fifteen miles north of Hyderabad. Population 4,000. Lat. 25° 35′, long. 68° 26′. *E.I.C. Ms. Doc.; Burnes' Bokh. iii. 264.*

MUTTEH, in Afghanistan, a village situate on an offset of the Indus, about a mile from the right bank of the main stream and ten miles north from Dera Ghazee Khan. Lat. 30° 14′, long. 70° 51′. *E.I.C. Ms. Doc.*

MUZAREE, in Sinde, a village on the route from Larkhana to Sukkur, and seven miles west of the latter place. It is situate on the right bank of the Indus. Lat. 27° 44′, long. 68° 47′. *Ms. Survey Map.*

MUZIFFERABAD.—See MAZUFURABAD.

MYDAN, in Afghanistan, a small valley, with a village, in the south of the Huzareh country. Lat. 33° 44′, long. 65° 56′. *Walker's Map of Afg.*

MYE OTTA, in Sinde, a village situate on the road from Sehwan to Larkhana, ten miles north of the former place, and near the right bank of the river Indus. Lat. 26° 28′, long. 67° 54′. *E.I.C. Ms. Doc.*

MYESUR, in Beloochistan, a village of Cutch Gundava, on the great route from Sinde to Kandahar and Ghuznee, by the Bolan Pass. It is situate on the Bolan river, which, issuing from the pass of the same name, falls into the Nari. Lat. 29° 8′, long. 67° 42′. *E.I.C. Ms. Doc. Hough, Narr. Exp. into Afg.; Havelock, War in Afg. i. 193.*

MYMUNUH.—See MEIMUNA.

N.

NAA BALA, in Afghanistan, a village of the Derajat, situate about twenty miles south of the town of Dera Ismail Khan, near the right bank of the Indus. Lat. 31° 35′, long. 70° 55′. *E.I.C. Ms. Doc.*

NAAGHI, in Afghanistan, a village situate about twenty miles south-west of the town of Bajour. Some have supposed it *Vigne, Kashmir, i. 121.*

to be the Aornus of the historians of Alexander, the capture of which was one of the most arduous exploits of that conqueror. Lat. 34° 49′, long. 71° 15′.

Vigne, i. 212.

NABOG NYH, or NABOG NYE, a pass over the mountain-range, bounding Kashmir on the east and dividing it from the valley of Muru Wurdwun. It is formed of gneiss and mica slate, and thus differs in structure from most of the mountains bounding Kashmir, which consist principally of basalt, trap, or other description of rock, generally regarded as of volcanic origin. The height of the pass is 12,000 feet. Lat. 33° 43′, long. 75° 20′.

E.I.C. Ms. Doc.

NADALI, in Afghanistan, a village about twenty miles southwest of the town of Girishk, in lat. 31° 37′, long. 64° 3′.

[1] Vigne, i. 132; Moorcroft, i. 69-79, 124; Forster, Jour. Beng. Eng. i. 258.

NADAUN,[1] in the north of the Punjab, a small town on the left or south bank of the Beas, here a deep, rapid, and clear stream, a hundred and fifty yards wide, and running at the rate of three miles and a half an hour. The right bank is of sandstone, lofty and abrupt; the left of mould, lower and shelving. Here is a ferry much frequented, being on the route from British India to Kashmir. Nadaun was formerly a flourishing place, and was held by an independent raja, but the prince was expelled by Runjeet Singh, and since that event the town has fallen into decay. Near Nadaun is Jewala Muki, a celebrated Hindoo temple, surmounted with a richly gilded roof, and inclosing a fissure in the rock, from which issue jets of inflammable gas, which, when lighted, are considered the breath of the tutelary deity.—(See JEWALA MUKI.) The assessment of the land revenue here payable to the Sikh government is regulated by a curious contrivance, which, according to Moorcroft,[2] "without diminishing the amount, was likely to be satisfactory to the peasantry.—This was by a rough analysis of the soil. A given quantity of the earth was put into a fine muslin sieve and washed with water until all the mould was carried through and nothing but the sand left, and according to its proportion to the whole, a deduction was made from the assessment." The rate for rich soil was about five shillings an acre.

[2] i. 121.

The site of Nadaun is delightful, and during its prosperity it was celebrated for fine gardens and various other attractions. Vigne[3] mentions a popular proverb—"Who will come to Nadaun, and then leave it?" It is in lat. 31° 46′, long. 76° 18′.

[3] Kashmir, i. 133.

NAD—NAG. 71

NADIR DEH, in Afghanistan, a village situate about four miles to the right of the road from Ghuznee to Shawl, in lat. 31° 40', long. 67° 20'. E.I.C. Ms. Doc.

NAEEWALLA, in the Punjab, a town on the route from Ramnegurh to Lahore, and fifty-five miles north-west of the latter place. It is situate in an extensive plain of great fertility and well cultivated, producing abundant crops of grain, especially wheat. Lat. 32° 17', long. 73° 41'. Hough, Exp. in Afg. i. 353.

NAGAR, or NAGYR, north of the Punjab, a small town or village, the principal place of a petty state also called Nagar. This is situate north-west of Bultistan, and south of Pamir. It consists chiefly of a valley of about three days' journey in length, and six or eight miles broad, and is intersected and drained by a stream, which falls into the Gilgit river. Fuel is scarce, and this deficiency is felt severely, as much snow falls in winter; the summers, however, are sufficiently warm to mature grapes, melons, and crops of wheat and barley. Gold dust is obtained by searching the sands of the river. The inhabitants are known among the neighbouring tribes by the name of Dungars, and are governed by an independent raja. The female sex in this region are remarkable for their attractions. Vigne, who takes a great interest in such topics, adduces the following singular testimony to their charms:—"The women are famous for their beauty, and Nazim Khan used to assure me, that their complexions were so fair, delicate, and transparent, that when they drank, the water was perceivable in their throats." The chief place, Nagar, stands on the banks of the river, and is defended by a fort. The name is generic, and signifies *town*,* but, by no unusual appropriation of such terms, it is used in this instance to designate a particular place. Nagar lies in lat. 35° 47', long. 74° 22'. Moorcr. Punj. Bokh. ii. 265.

NAGGAR, in Afghanistan, a considerable walled town in the plain of Bannoo, westward of the Indus, and at the foot of the Salt or Kala Bagh range of mountains. It is a commercial place, and has a good bazaar, but the walls have been allowed to fall into great decay. The surrounding country is fertile and well cultivated, but suffers much from the incessant intestine wars of the inhabitants, and the inroads of the Vizeree freebooters from Masson, Bal. Afg. Panj. i. 89.

---

* نگر town.

the neighbouring mountains, to guard against whose attacks, every dwelling is fortified. Lat. 33° 10′, long. 71° 5′.

<small>Forster, Jour. Beng. Eng. i. 344.</small>
NAGROLAH, in the north-east of the Punjab, a village on the route from Chumba to Kashmir, by the Banihal Pass. It is situate thirty miles north-west of Chumba, in a rugged country between the upper course of the Ravee and that of the Chinab. Lat. 32° 47′, long. 75° 35′.

<small>E.I.C. Ms. Doc.</small>
NAKODUR, in the Punjab, a village on the route from Lahore to Loodeana, and eighty miles south-east of the former town. Lat. 31° 7′, long. 75° 30′.

<small>Masson, Bal. Afg. Panj. ii. 38; Pott. Belooch. 261; Outram, Rough Notes, 177.</small>
NAL, in Beloochistan, a small walled town in a fertile and well-watered valley of the same name. It is considered to be a place of much antiquity, and has a fort, the stronghold of the Bizunja tribe of Belooches. The western route from Soumeeanee to Kelat passes through it, but is little frequented on account of the bad character of the Bizunjas. Lat. 27° 39′, long. 65° 59′.

<small>Ms. Map of Sinde.</small>
NALJEE MAENEE, in Sinde, a village situate on the left bank of the western Narra river, and on the road from Sehwan to Larkhana. Lat. 26° 43′, long. 67° 50′.

<small>E.I.C. Ms. Doc.</small>
NAMOOSA, in Beloochistan, a village on the route from Shawl to Kelat, and ten miles west of the former town. Lat. 30° 10′, long. 66° 50′.

<small>Walker's Map of Afg.</small>
NAMUTZYE, in Afghanistan, a village thirty miles south-east of Ghuznee. Lat. 33° 12′, long. 68° 21′.

<small>[1] Vigne, Kashmir, i. 254.</small>
NANDAN SAR,[1] in Kashmir, a small lake situate, with four others, on the northern side of the Pir Panjal mountain, and a little north of the pass of the same name, which also is sometimes called the Nandan Sar pass. The collective waters of these form the source of the Dumdum or Huripur river. Ac-
<small>[2] Kaschmir, i. 184.</small>
cording to Hugel,[2] the Perhamgalla river flows from Nandan Sar to the south-west, and the Dumdum to the north-east, but this double efflux seems very improbable. Nandan Sar is held in high reverence by the Hindoos, and is visited by them in pilgrimage. Lat. 33° 31′, long. 74° 26′.

<small>E.I.C. Ms. Doc.; Jour. As. Soc. Beng. 1842, p. 61, Grif. Bar. and Ther. Meas. in Afg.; Hough, Narr. Exp. in Afg. 159.</small>
NANEE, in Afghanistan, a small town on the route from Kandahar to Ghuznee, and ten miles south of the latter place. It is situate near the western extremity of the extensive plain of Shelgurh, on the bank of a feeder of the river of Ghuznee. There are abundant supplies to be had here. The elevation above the sea is 7,502 feet. Lat. 33° 25′, long. 68° 12′.

NANGA PURBUT, or PARWUT.—See DIARMUL.

NANUNDUR KOT, in the Punjab, a village situate on the right bank of the river Ravee, in lat. 32° 5′, long. 74° 57′.

NAO DEH, in Afghanistan, a village situate on the left bank of the river of Furrah. Lat. 32° 20′, long. 62° 2′. _{E.I.C. Ms. Doc.}

NARANG, in Northern Afghanistan, a village situate on the right bank of the river Kooner, twenty-six miles north-west of the town of Bajour. Lat. 35° 20′, long. 71° 3′. _{E.I.C. Ms. Doc.}

NAREH, in Sinde, a village on the route from Sehwan to Larkhana, and fifty-three miles north of the former town. It is of considerable size, with houses built of burned brick. Its situation is in a level alluvial country, about a mile from the right bank of the Indus. Lat. 27° 7′, long. 68° 2′. _{E.I.C. Ms. Doc.}

NARI, a river of Beloochistan, has its origin on the eastern slope of the Hala mountains, about lat. 30°, long. 68°, and holding a course, generally in a southerly direction, for about fifty miles, it is joined near the village Eree, in lat. 29° 26′, long. 67° 58′, by the river Kauhee or Bolan. The united stream continues to flow southwards, and is finally lost in the arid plain of Cutch Gundava. When heavy rains fall it has a great body of water, and it is said that, when remarkably swollen, it sometimes even reaches the Indus. For many months in the year the stream disappears, and water can then be obtained only by digging in the bed, or from reservoirs made by excavation or draining. It is, however, of the utmost importance, being, in this sultry country, the only source from which water can be obtained for domestic purposes, or for irrigation. _{Pott. Belooch. 309; Masson, Kalat, 332; Bal. Afg. Panj. i. 341; Conolly, Jour. Eng. to India, ii. 225.}

NARRA[1] (Eastern), in Sinde, a large branch of the Indus, separating from the main stream on the eastern side, a few miles above Roree. Taking a southerly course, it passes by the ruins of Alore, where it is crossed by a bridge, and thence continues to flow in the same direction until its water, in the dry season, is absorbed or evaporated in the desert of Eastern Sinde. In the lower part of its course, about lat. 25° 50′, long. 69° 10′, it throws off during inundation a branch to the south-westward, bearing the name of Phuraun or Purani Deria, " the ancient river," and then turning to the south-east, flows by the fort of Omercote. Lower down it joins the united stream of the Purana and the Goonee or Fulailee, and falls into the sea by the Koree mouth, after a course of nearly four hundred miles. During the low _{[1] E.I.C. Ms. Doc. Burnes' Bokh. iii. 77, 267; Macmurdo on the Indus, in Jour. Roy. As. Soc.1834, p. 41.}

season of the Indus it ceases to be a stream, but when the inundation is at its height, it generally carries a very large body of water. In 1826 it overspread the desert to a great extent,[2] swept away part of the fortress of Omercote, though ninety miles from the main channel of the Indus, and forced its way to the sea by the *riunn* of Cutch, working for itself a passage through the Ullah-bund, a mound thrown up across its channel by the great earthquake of 1819.

[2] Leech, Rep. on the Sind. Army, 77.

NARRA (Western), in Sinde, a great and important branch of the Indus. It separates from the western side of the river about twenty-five miles below Sukkur, in lat. 27° 40′, long. 68° 34′, and takes a southerly course, in a direction in a great measure parallel to the main stream. At its extremity, in lat. 26° 30′, long. 67° 45′, it expands into lake Manchar. From the south-eastern part of this lake, the Arul, a navigable stream, flows, and discharges its water into the Indus. The direct distance from the place where the Narra divaricates from the Indus, to the expansion into lake Manchar, is about one hundred miles;* but measured along its very tortuous course, it will be found to be fully double that distance. The long, narrow island, insulated by the Indus, the Narra, lake Manchar, and the Arul, is one of the most fertile tracts in the world, very highly cultivated, and densely peopled. During the season of inundation, the Western Narra is preferred to the main channel of the Indus for the purposes of navigation, in consequence of the current being less violent. The word *Narra* signifies a snake in the vernacular language, and the name has, without doubt, been bestowed in consequence of the convolutions of the stream.

Burnes, iii. 268; Outram, 46, 47; Masson, i. 461; Kennedy, i. 176; Westmacott, in Jour. As. Soc. 1840, p. 1204.

NASSERABAD, in Beloochistan, a village on the route from Kedje to Gwetter, and twenty-five miles south-west of the former place. It is situate on the river Dustee, here called the Mooledanee. Lat. 26° 13′, long. 61° 57′.

E.I.C. Ms. Doc.; Pott. Belooch. Map.

NASUMON,[1] in the Northern Punjab, situate on the right or north bank of the Chenaub, and on the great route from India to Kashmir, through the Bainhal Pass. It is a small place, remarkable only for one of those bridges of rude ropes, called in the country *jhoolas*,[2] by which travellers pass the Chenaub, here about seventy or eighty yards wide. Nasumon is in lat. 33° 2′, long. 75° 11′.

[1] Forster, i. 346.

[2] Gerard, Koonawur, 33.

NATHO SALIMKE CHISTEE, in Bhawlpoor, a village

E.I.C. Ms. Doc.

* Westmacott erroneously states it at fifty miles (1204).

situate on the north-eastern frontier, near the left bank of the river Ghara. Lat. 30° 25′, long. 73° 39′.

NAUSHERA.—An extensive caravanserai on the route from Lahore to Kashmir, by the Pir Panjal pass. It is built of brick, faced at the gateways with stone, and was originally of such strength as to serve for a fortress as well as a caravanserai, but it is now in a ruinous state. It is situate on the river Tauhi[1] or Tihoi,[2] which, at eight or ten miles to the south-east, falls into the Chinab. An inscription on one of the gateways records that it was built by the Mogul emperor, Akbar. Naushera is in lat. 33° 6′, long. 74° 15′. [1] F. Von Hugel, Kaschmir, i. 179. [2] Moorcr. Punj. Bokh. ii. 300.

NAWA SUN.—See Chota.

NAWDREE, in Afghanistan, a collection of mud ruins, one mile and three-quarters south-east of Kandahar. This is a monument of the abortive attempt of Nadir Shah to found a city which should supersede Kandahar. Lat. 31° 36′, long. 65° 31′. E.I.C. Ms. Doc.; Atkinson, Exp. into Afg. 164.

NAWULA-JO-GOTE, in Sinde, a village on the route from Schwan to Larkhana, and sixteen miles north of the former town. It is inhabited by the cultivators of the adjacent fertile country. The road in this part of the route is straight and level, but not of easy transit for carriages, in consequence of neglect. Lat. 26° 35′, long. 67° 52′. E.I.C. Ms. Doc.

NECHARA, in Beloochistan, a village sixteen miles south-east of the town of Kelat. Lat. 28° 48′, long. 66° 40′. E.I.C. Ms. Doc.

NEEGAREE, in Beloochistan, a village of Cutch Gundava, on the route from Dadur to Gundava, and ten miles south of the former town. It is situate at the eastern base of the Hala mountains, a few miles south of the eastern mouth of the Bolan Pass. Lat. 29° 22′, long. 67° 41′. E.I.C. Ms. Doc.

NEELAUB.—See Nilab.

NEELOO, in the Punjab, a village twenty miles west of the town of Pind Dadun Khan. Lat. 32° 38′, long. 72° 34′. Walker's Map of N.W. Frontier.

NEEMBUJ, in Sinde, a village near the south-eastern frontier, and twenty miles north-east of Nuggur Packer. Lat. 24° 36′, long. 70° 50′. Ms. Map of Sinde.

NEEMLA, in Afghanistan, a small town with a fine garden, situate in the plain of Jelalabad, about three miles east of Gundamuk, and seventy in the same direction from Kabool. Here, in 1809, Shah Shoojah was defeated by Futteh Khan, and expelled from the kingdom of Kabool. Neemla is mentioned by E.I.C. Ms. Doc.; Burnes' Bokh. i. 125; Elph. Acc. of Caubul, 74; Hough, Narr. of Exp. into Afg. 301; Moorcr. Punj. Bokh. ii. 368.

Moorcroft under the name of Nimba. Lat. 34° 18′, long. 70° 8′.

E.I.C. Ms. Doc.
NEEMRA, in Sinde, a village on the route from Larkhana to Bagh, and forty-four miles north of the former place. It is situate in a barren country on the south-eastern border of the Run or arid desert of Shikarpoor. Lat. 27° 57′, long. 68° 8′.

E.I.C. Ms. Doc.
NELAEE, in Afghanistan, a halting-place on the route, by the Golairee Pass, from Ghuznee to Dera Ismael Khan, and fifty miles west of the latter place. The road to the west is very bad, and the place has no importance except from an abundant supply of water. Lat. 32° 3′, long. 69° 40′.

E.I.C. Ms. Doc.
NENKUR, in Sinde, a village on the route from Sehwan to Larkhana, and five miles north of the former town. It is situate two miles west of a large offset from the Indus, and four miles west of the main channel. The surrounding country is level, alluvial, and fertile, but little cultivated. The neglect of cultivation is more especially remarkable towards the Indus, in which direction the land is, for the most part, overrun with jungle. Lat. 26° 24′, long. 67° 54′.

Walker's Map of Afg.
NESH, in Afghanistan, a village on the northern route from Kilat-i-Ghiljee to Giriskh. Lat. 32° 10′, long. 65° 18′.

NEWAR BELOOCHWALA, in the Punjab, a village twenty-two miles east of the Indus. Lat. 31° 54′, long. 71° 30′.

Masson, Bal. Afg. Panj. i. 404.
NIAZPUR, in the Punjab, a village on the east bank of the Ravee. Here is a ferry over the river, which winds through a country of great fertility and beauty, densely peopled, and highly cultivated. Lat. 31° 27′, long. 73° 53′.

E.I.C. Ms. Doc.
NICETTA, in Afghanistan, a village situate on the right bank of the Kabool river, and near the confluence of the river Lundye therewith. It is about twelve miles north-east of Peshawur, in lat. 34° 6′, long. 71° 48′.

Walker's Map of N.W. Frontier.
NIHUNG, in the Punjab, a village situate eight miles from the left bank of the river Chenaub, in lat. 30° 54′, long. 72° 5′.

Elph. Acc. of Caubul, 90; Masson, Bal. Afg. Panj. iii. 222; Baber, Mem. 144.
NIJROW, in Afghanistan, a fertile valley in the Kohistan of Kabool, east of the valley of Punjschir. It is industriously cultivated, and has numerous orchards well stocked with pomegranate, walnut, and mulberry trees, besides abundance of vines. The overhanging mountains are covered with pines and hollies. The inhabitants are Tajiks, generally supposed

to be of Persian descent, with a few of a peculiar race called Pashai, who are said to speak a dialect similar to that of the natives of Kafiristan, and in some other respects to resemble that ancient and remarkable people. Though adjacent to the usual seat of the Afghan government, the inhabitants of Nijrow have, through their bravery, and the difficulty of their country, preserved their independence. Lat. 35° 10′, long. 69° 25′.

NILAB,[1] in the Punjab, a small town on the left or eastern bank of the Indus, a short distance below Attock, and close to the confluence of the Hurroo river. The name signifies "blue water," and has been assigned to it from the deep blue colour of the water of the Indus at this place. The great river here is narrow, rapid, and a hundred and twenty feet deep. There is a ferry at which, according to Wood, Timur crossed on his invasion of India; but Rennell[2] is of opinion that he crossed at or near Attock.* Lat. 33° 46′, long. 72° 17′.

[1] Wood, Oxus, 124.

[2] Memoir of a Map of Hindostan, 85; Elph. Acc. of Caubul, 111; Macartney, in Elph. 653.

NIL NAG, "blue lake."—In Kashmir, a great spring or piece of water, which gives rise to a stream falling into the Behut or Jailum, in the vicinity of Baramula, in lat. 33° 48′, long. 74° 32′. Like most other sources of rivers, it is regarded with superstitious veneration by the Hindoos. It is situate on the north-eastern declivity of the Pir Panjal, and twenty-five miles south of Serinagur.

Moorcroft, Punj. Bokh. ii. 383.

NINGANA, in Bhawlpoor, a village situate near the left bank of the Ghara river. Lat. 29° 38′, long. 72° 6′.

Walker's Map of N.W. Frontier.

NISHOWRA, in the Punjab, a large village situate on the route from Ramnugger to Lahore, and forty miles north-west of the latter town. The surrounding country is overgrown with thick grassy jungle, interspersed with patches of cultivation. Lat. 31° 59′, long. 73° 50′.

E.I.C. Ms. Doc.; Hough, Narr. Exp. in Afg. 356.

NOBRA, or NUBRA.—A division of Ladakh, or Middle Tibet. It is a singularly wild tract, of great elevation, on the south side of the Karakorum mountains, or eastern part of Hindoo Koosh, and is bounded on the north, the east, and the south sides by the Shy-Yok, or river of Nobra, which rising in

Moorcr. Punj. Bokh. i. 262, 315; Vigne, Kashmir, ii. 360, 364; Falconer, on Cataclysm of the Indus, in Jour. As. Soc. Beng. 1841, p. 617.

Pers. Narr. II.

* Burnes ascribes to Rennell a statement that Timur crossed the Indus not at Attock, but at Dingote, about seventy miles lower down. But he does not refer to the page, and the opinion of Rennell, as above quoted, is distinctly given in page 85:—"The Indus he (Timur) crossed, I take it for granted, at or very near the place where Attock now stands."

the Nobra Tsuh lake, or glacier, embosomed in the mountain, joins the Indus a few miles above and east of Iskardo. The lowest part of this tract is estimated by Vigne to be more than 11,000 feet above the sea, but though so elevated and very mountainous, it is described by him not only as picturesque, but as having a considerable degree both of culture and population. The fort and village of Nobra on the Shy-Yok is the principal place, and is in lat. 34° 38', long. 77° 10'.

E.I.C. Ms. Doc.
NOGRAMA, in Beloochistan, a village forty miles south of the town of Kelat, in lat. 28° 28', long. 66° 39'.

Jour. As. Soc. Beng. 1836, p. 468, Memoir on a Map of Peshawur, by M. A. Court.
NOHGIRA, in Northern Afghanistan, a village situate in the valley of Boonere, and fifteen miles from the right bank of the Indus. Lat. 34° 21', long. 72° 30.'

NOHUR.—See ISLAMGURH.

E.I.C. Ms. Doc.
NOOGONG, in the Punjab, a village on the route from Lahore to Ramnuggur, and fifteen miles south of the latter town, in lat. 32° 12', long. 73° 41'.

E.I.C. Ms. Doc.
NOONDROO, in Beloochistan, a village situate on the route from Kedge to Belah, and eighty miles west of the latter town. Lat. 26° 12', long. 65° 11'.

E.I.C. Ms. Doc.
NOON MIANEE, in the Punjab, a village situate on the left bank of the river Jelum, and five miles south of the town of Pind Dadun Khan. Lat. 32° 35', long. 72° 53'.

E.I.C. Ms. Doc.
NOORJA, in Sinde, a considerable village between Sehwan and Larkhana, and fourteen miles north of the former town. It is situate two miles west of the right bank of a large offset of the Indus, and three miles west of the main channel. The surrounding country is level, alluvial, and in many parts cultivated, but greatly broken up by numerous channels, cut for the purposes of irrigation. Noorja is itself supplied with water from wells. Lat. 26° 32', long. 67° 53'.

E.I.C. Ms. Doc.
NOOR JUMAL, in the Punjab, a village on the route from Ramnuggur to Jelum, and twenty miles south of the latter town. Lat. 32° 41', long. 73° 33'.

E.I.C. Ms. Doc.
NOORPOOR, in the Punjab, a village situate about twenty miles west of the Jailum river. Lat. 31° 49', long. 71° 41'.

E.I.C. Ms. Doc.
NOORZYE, in Afghanistan, a village on the route from Ghuznee to Shawl, and forty miles north of the latter place. It is situate in the fertile valley of Pisheen, in a well-watered country, exhibiting considerable cultivation. The road is good

in this part of the route, and supplies are abundant. Lat. 30° 38', long. 67° 2'.

NOOSHKY, in Beloochistan, a *toomun*, or fixed encampment, in the west of the province of Sarawan. It consists of about two hundred *ghedans*, or felt tents, ranged on the banks of the river Bale. The population are very barbarous, and depend for subsistence on their flocks and herds, the produce of which they barter for such grain and other articles as they require. It is governed by a sirdar, tributary to the Khan of Kelat. Lat. 29° 38', long. 65° 9'. <small>Pott. Belooch. 124.</small>

†NOSHARA,* in Bhawlpoor, a small town with a good bazaar, and surrounded by a wall. It is situate on an eminence at the western edge of a ravine, in a fertile country crowded with villages. Lat. 28° 26', long. 70° 16'. <small>Conolly, Jour. Eng. India, ii. 278; Mass. Bal. Afg. Panj. i. 386; Boileau, Rajwara, Map.</small>

NOSHURH.—See NOSHARA.

NOURAK.—See NOWRUT.

†NOUSHERA, in the Punjab, a village, with an adjoining fort, on the route from Attock to Kashmir, by Mazufurabad, from which last place it is distant about twenty miles south-west. It is situate at the western base of the mountains, inclosing Kashmir on the west. The surrounding country consists of parched, uncultivated plains, intersected at different distances by long, rocky, barren ridges. Noushera is in lat. 34° 7', long. 73° 7'. <small>Vigne, Kashmir, i. 117.</small>

†NOUSHERA, in Afghanistan, a town in the Peshawur territory, situate on the banks of the Kabool river, eighteen miles north-west of Attock. Here, in 1823, the Afghans were utterly routed by the Sikhs, commanded by Runjeet Singh. The Sikhs have a fort here, built for them under the direction of General Avitabile. It has four bastions and a double row of loopholes. Lat. 34° 3', long. 72° 2'. <small>Burnes' Bokh. i. 85; Hough, Narr. Exp. in Afg. 332; Masson, Bal. Afg. Panj. i. 125.</small>

†NOUSHERA, in the Punjab, a small town and fort on the route from Mazufferabad to Attock, and a few miles from the east bank of the Indus. Lat. 34° 6', long. 73° 10'. <small>F. Von Hugel, Kaschmir, iii. 54; Vigne, Kashmir, ii. 187.</small>

†NOUSHERA, in Sinde, a town in the division of Khyerpoor. Lat. 27° 48', long. 68° 39'. <small>Burnes, on Commerce of Shikarpoor, 24.</small>

NOUSHUHR.—See NOSHARA.

* This name, and the others in succession marked thus (†), appear to be different European modes of spelling نوشهرة "new towns," the singular for the plural, as in Kilat and similar instances.

E.I.C. Ms. Doc.	**NOWA DHERRA**, in Sinde, a village on the route from Larkhana to Sukkur, and twelve miles east of the former town. It contains about a hundred houses, and five wells. The road in this part of the route is a mere path through jungle. Forage and other supplies are abundant, and there is good ground for encampment on the north-west of the village. Lat. 27° 40′, long. 68° 22′.
Map of Sinde.	**NOWA GOTE**, in Sinde, a village situate on the right bank of the Indus. Lat. 27° 7′, long. 68° 3′.
	NOWAGYE.—See NAAGHI.
	NOWA MURGOH.—See KILLA-I-MURGHA.
E.I.C. Ms. Doc.	†**NOWCHARA**,* in Beloochistan, a village of Cutch Gundava, situate about twelve miles south of Dadur, on the road to Gundava, in lat. 29° 20′, long. 67° 39′.
E.I.C. Ms. Doc.	**NOWNEAS**, in Afghanistan, a village twelve miles south-west of Kabool. Lat. 34° 20′, long. 68° 59′.
E.I.C. Ms. Doc.	**NOWRUT**, in Afghanistan, a village situate on the right bank of the Turnak river, and twenty miles north-east of Kilat-i-Ghiljie. Lat. 32° 20′, long. 67°.
Hough, Narr. of Exp. in Afg. 27; Havelock, War in Afg. i. 157.	†**NOWSHARRA**, in Sinde, a considerable town on the western route from Roree to Hyderabad, and seventy miles south-east of the former town. It is a great mart for rice, and during the Talpoor dynasty was a principal depôt of the artillery of the Ameers. Lat. 26° 56′, long. 68° 8′.
E.I.C. Ms. Doc.	†**NOWSHARRA**, in the Punjab, a village situate on an offset of the Indus, and five miles from the left bank of the main stream. It is about six miles north of the town of Leia, on the route from Dera Ismael Khan to Mooltan. Lat. 31° 4′, long. 71°.
	NOWSHUR.—See NOWZER.
E.I.C. Ms. Doc.	†**NOWZER**, in Sinde, a village on the route from Shikarpoor to Larkhana, and seven miles and a half south-west of the former town. There are between two hundred and three hundred inhabitants. The place is supplied with water from two wells. Lat. 27° 50′, long. 68° 40′.
Map of Sinde.	**NUBEESUR**, in Sinde, a village situate on the route from Omercote to Dephlah, twenty-five miles south of the former town. Lat. 25°, long. 69° 42′.
E.I.C. Ms. Doc.	**NUFOOSK PASS**, in Afghanistan, lies over a ridge in the mountain range, rising between Sinde and the plain of Kahun.

* See note on preceding page.

Here, in August 1840, a British detachment, under the command of Major Clibborn, in advance to relieve the garrison of Kahun, defeated a greatly superior force of Belooches, but, in consequence of excessive heat and a total want of water, were compelled to make a disastrous retreat, in which all their guns, stores, carriages, and beasts of burthen, were lost. (See KAHUN.) The Nufoosk Pass is in lat. 29° 13', long. 69° 17'.

NULL, in Afghanistan, a village of Sewestan, twelve miles north of the town of Kahun. Lat. 29° 26', long. 69° 10'. E.I.C. Ms. Doc.

NULLUKH, in Western Afghanistan, a halting-place on the route from Kandahar to Herat, and one hundred and eighty-five miles north-west of the former place. It is situate on a small stream, called the Cheera, in a mountainous country, very thinly peopled, and scantily cultivated, but yielding forage from the spontaneous produce of the soil. The road winds through a succession of mountain valleys, and is rough and difficult. Lat. 32° 27', long. 63° 10'. E.I.C. Ms. Doc.

NUMMUL, in the Punjab, a thriving town twenty-four miles east of Kala Bagh, on the Indus. Here are indications of excellent coal. Lat. 32° 52', long. 72°. Wood, Rep. on Coal Mines of the Indus, 82.

NUNDANSUR.—See NANDAN SAR.

NUNDAWADAGAR, in the Punjab, a village situate sixteen miles east of the Chenaub river, in lat. 30° 55', long. 72° 20'.

NUNDEL, in the Punjab, a village on the route from Mooltan to Ferozpoor, and seventy-five miles east of the former town. It is situate on the right bank of the Ghara river, in lat. 29° 59', long. 72° 38'. E.I.C. Ms. Doc.

NUNDEWEEDAGUR, in the Punjab, a village situate near the left bank of the river Jailum, in lat. 31° 32', long. 72° 3'. E.I.C. Ms. Doc.

NUNGNEHAR, in Afghanistan, a name sometimes applied to the whole valley of Kabool, but in this place restricted to its more appropriate purpose, designating the hilly tract which extends along the northern base of Sufeid Koh, between the Khyber and the Kurkutcha ranges. The name Nungnehar vernacularly signifies nine rivers, and has been given with reference to the numerous streams which flow across this district from the Sufeid Koh to the Kabool river. The most direct road from the Khyber Pass to Kabool lies through it, but it is little frequented in consequence of the great number of defiles and the turbulent Wood, Khyber Pass, 2; Id. Oxus, 167; Baber, Mem. 141.

and predatory character of the people, who take pride in the name of *Yagistan*, or "Rebel Land," as the rough and inaccessible part of the region is called. The inhabitants, though habitually ferocious and inveterate robbers, are industrious cultivators, so that there is no spot neglected, where the labour of the husbandman can be beneficially employed. Where the plough cannot be used, its place is supplied by the spade, and every declivity, terrace, and earthy nook, is carefully and successfully tilled. Water is abundant, the soil being generally saturated with it, and where there are no rivulets wells are dug, which send forth perennial rills. This sequestered district exhibits a mixture of orchard, field, and garden, and abounds in mulberry, pomegranate, and other fruit-trees. The banks of the streams are fringed with rows of weeping willows, and during the greater part of the year enamelled with wild flowers and fragrant aromatic herbs. It lies between lat. 34° 20'—34° 35', long. 70°—71°.

E.I.C. Ms. Doc.

NUNGUL, in the Punjab, a village on the route from Amritsir to Vazeerabad, and forty-five miles south-east of the latter place. Lat. 31° 59', long. 74° 20'.

F. Von Hugel, Kashmir, i. 251; ii. 165.

NUNNENWARRE, a lofty mountain of Kashmir, in the range which bounds the valley on the north-east. Over it is the Bunderpoor pass, from Kashmir into Tibet. Von Hugel found the boiling water point on it to be at 186·8, which, according to the approximation usually adopted, would give about 11,000 feet for the height of the pass. North-west of this, the Nangaparvat attains a much greater elevation, the exact amount of which has not been ascertained. Lat. 34° 31', long. 74° 35'.

E.I.C. Ms. Doc.

NUNUKS DURRUMSALA, in Beloochistan, a halting-place, near the source of the river Aghor. Lat. 25° 35', long. 65° 35'.

E.I.C. Ms. Doc.

NUNWARRY, in Sinde, a village on the route from Sehwan to Larkhana, and thirty-nine miles north of the former town. It is situate near the north bank of a piece of stagnant water replenished during inundation by the Indus, the main channel of which is distant about a mile south. The inhabitants are engaged in the cultivation of the surrounding country. Lat. 26° 54', long. 67° 58'.

E.I.C. Ms. Doc.

NUR, in Bultistan or Little Tibet, a village situate on the right bank of the Indus, and twenty miles north-east of the town of Iskardoh. Lat. 35° 14', long. 75° 46'.

NURD, in Beloochistan, a village at the most southern flexure of the Moola pass, and equidistant from its extremities. It is situate in a small plain or valley, into which the pass expands in this part. Elevation above the sea, 2,850 feet. Lat. 27° 52′, long. 66° 54′. E.I.C. Ms. Doc.

NURPUR,[1] in the north-east of the Punjab, among the lower and southern mountains of the Himalaya range, a town of considerable importance, as being on the route from Hindostan to Kashmir. It contains a good and well-stocked bazaar, and has 6,000 or 8,000 inhabitants,* a large portion of whom are Kashmirians, employed in shawl weaving. There is a fort built of stones and mud on an eminence about two hundred feet high, at the base of which flows a small river, a feeder of the Ravee, which it joins about thirty miles lower down. It is commanded on every side by higher eminences. Nurpur is now held by the Sikh government, which has expelled the hereditary raja. Elevation above the sea, 1,924 feet.[2] It is in lat. 32° 12′, long. 75° 40′. [1] F. Von Hugel, Kaschmir, i. 114; Forster, Jour. Beng. and Eng. i. 267. [2] Journ. As. Soc. Beng. 1841, p. 111; Broome and Cunningham on Sources of Punjab Rivers. Walker's Map of N.W. Frontier.

NURRAH, in the Punjab, a village situate on the left bank of the Indus, in lat. 33° 12′, long. 71° 50′.

NURYOOB, in Afghanistan, a village thirty miles west of Kohat, on the route to Ghuznee. Lat. 33° 30′, long. 70° 57′. Walker's Map of Afg.

NUSSEERABAD, in Sinde, a village on the route from Sukkur to Shikarpoor, and four miles north-west of the former place. It is situate two miles from the right bank of the Indus, in a low, alluvial, fertile, and well-cultivated country. Lat. 27° 47′, long. 68° 52′. E.I.C. Ms. Doc.

NUSSEERPOOR, in Sinde, a town sixteen miles north-east of Hyderabad. It was formerly famous for its manufactures, especially of cotton; but these have been in a great measure superseded by those of Raneepoor and Gumbut. Lat. 25° 28′, long. 68° 39′. Burnes, on the Commerce of Hyderabad, 20.

NUTYAN, in the Punjab, a village situate near the left bank of the river Ravee, and on the route from Lahore to Mooltan. Lat. 31° 17′, long. 73° 42′. E.I.C. Ms. Doc.

NUZZERPOOR, in Sinde, a village situate on the right bank of the Goonee or Fulailee branch of the Indus, thirty miles south-east of Hyderabad. Lat. 25° 4′, long. 68° 37′. Ms. Map of Sinde.

* Vigne[1] states 15,000. According to Broome and Cunningham,[2] Nurpur, in 1839, was said to contain 7,000 Kashmerians.

[1] Kashmir, i. p. 144.
[2] Ut supra, 111.

NYAZ MUHUMUD, in Afghanistan, a village situate on the circuitous route from Herat to Siripool. Lat. 35° 39′, long. 64° 47′.

_{Walker's Map of Afg.}

O.

OBA—See OBEH.

OBEH, or OBA, in Afghanistan, a village in a fertile and well-watered district on the route from Kandahar to Ghuznee, and one hundred and seventy-two miles north-east of the former place. It is situate near the right bank of the Turnak; the road is good, and abundant supplies are obtainable. Lat. 33°, long. 67° 49′.

_{E.I.C. Ms. Doc.; Hough, Narr. of Exp. in Afg. 155.}

OIHMAN.—See OTMAN.

OIN, in the Punjab, a small town near the base of the mountains inclosing Kashmir on the south. It is situate on the river Jailum, the navigation of which here again becomes practicable after its interruption between Baramula and this place. Here rafts are made of deodar and other timber, the growth of the neighbouring mountains, and guided, by means of poles and paddles, to the towns lower down on the river. A practicable road runs down each side of the navigable course of the Jailum, as far as the town bearing the same name. Oin is in lat. 33° 40′, long. 73° 50′.

_{Moorcr. Punj. Bokh. ii. 306.}

OLEERA, in Sinde, a small town on the route from Shikarpoor to Khyerpoor, and six miles north of the latter place. It is situate amidst jungle and woods of stunted trees, in a low alluvial country, intersected by canals and watercourses from the Indus. Lat. 27° 34′, long. 68° 46′.

_{Conolly, Jour. from Eng. to India, ii. 254.}

OLIPORE,[1] in Afghanistan, a narrow valley in the north of the district of Lughman, and on the southern border of Kafiristan. Griffith considers that its natural characteristics strongly resemble those of the valleys of the Himalaya, especially in the abundance, large growth, and excellence of its timber trees. The bottom of the valley, which is about three thousand feet above the sea, produces very fine oaks, and thick forests of these extend up the sides of the inclosing mountains to the height of about four thousand five hundred feet above the same level. At

_{[1] Jour. As. Soc. Beng. 1841, pp. 707-801, Grif. Rep. on Subjects connected with Afg.}

that elevation commence the forests of *zaitoon*, or wild olive, which clothe the mountains for a farther height of two thousand feet. The *deodar* cedar grows in great abundance above this, to the elevation of ten thousand feet. The timber used at Kabool being of bad quality and high price, it would be very desirable for that place that favourable means should be found for transporting thither the produce of these fine forests. This, however, is impracticable, on account of the intervening difficulties; but the timber of Olipore could certainly be floated to the river of Kabool down the stream which flows through the valley, and is described by Griffith [2] as a large torrent. Once afloat on the Kabool river, there would be no insurmountable obstacle to its passage even as far as the ocean. Olipore is in lat. 34° 54', long. 70° 12'.

[2] Ut supra, 16.

OMARKOTE.—See OMERCOTE.

OMERCOTE,[1] in Sinde, a town and fort in the eastern desert. The fort is situate half a mile from the town, and is five hundred feet square, having a mud wall forty feet high, a strong round tower at each corner, and six square towers on each side. There is but one gate, which is on the eastern side, and is protected by an outwork. It was usually garrisoned by four hundred men. Though nearly a hundred miles from the Indus, a branch of that river finds its way hither in time of inundation, and, in 1826,[2] flowed with such violence as to sweep away the north-west tower. Water is to be had near the surface, and there is a pool twenty feet deep in the channel of this branch of the Indus west of the fort. Omercote was taken in 1813, by the Ameers of Sinde, from the Rajah of Joudpoor. It is celebrated as the birthplace of the renowned emperor Akbar, his father, Homayan, having in his exile taken refuge here.[3] Lat. 25° 19', long. 69° 47'.

[1] Leech, on Sind. Army, 77.

[2] Burnes, Bokh. iii. 315, 316.

[3] Price, Chronol. Retrospect, iii. 808.

OOBOWRAH, in Sinde, a village on the route from Subzulcote to Shikarpoor, and thirteen miles west of the former town. It is situate on the eastern bank of a *dund* or stagnant piece of water, in a low alluvial country, which is extensively flooded during the inundation of the Indus, but in the season of low water the road east and west of the village is level and practicable for carriages. Lat. 28° 10', long. 69° 30'.

E.I.C. Ms. Doc.; Hough, Narr. of Exp. in Afg. 424.

OOCH, in Bhawlpoor, a city situate four miles from the left bank of the Punjnud river, amidst beautiful groves. It is formed of three distinct towns, a few hundred yards apart, and each sur-

Masson, Bal. Afg. Punj. i. 22; Burnes' Bokh. iii. 90; Boileau, Rajwara, 63; Wood, Oxus, 74.

rounded by a ruinous brick wall. The streets are narrow and meanly built, but the bazaars are large, and well supplied with wares, and there is considerable general traffic. These towns are built on mounds, formed by the materials of great cities formerly existing here. In the immediate vicinity are prodigious quantities of ruins, still in such preservation that they could be easily rendered habitable. Ooch is regarded with veneration by Mahometans, in consequence of containing five shrines of deceased *pirs* or saints, *saiyids*, reputed descendants from Mahomet. Population, 20,000. Lat. 29° 13′, long. 71° 6′.

E.I.C. Ms. Doc.; Outram, Rough Notes, 149.

OOCHLAN, in Afghanistan, a village on the route from Ghuznee to Shawl, and fifty miles south of the former town. Lat. 32° 53′, long. 68° 10′.

E.I.C. Ms. Doc.

OODANA, in Beloochistan, a large village of Cutch Gundava, on the route from the town of Gundava to Shikarpoor, and twenty miles east of the former town. It is surrounded by a mud wall, outside of which are several wells, yielding a scanty supply of water. The road in this part of the route is good, lying over a level plain; but at fourteen miles west of the village it is crossed by a canal twenty yards broad and fifteen feet deep, with steep banks. There is some cultivation in the immediate neighbourhood of Oodana. Forage is abundant, but other supplies scarce. Seven miles to the east of the town are the ruins of old Oodana. The present town is in lat. 28° 30′, long. 67° 49′.

E.I.C. Ms. Doc.

OODAR, in Sinde, a halting-place on the route from Roree to Jessulmair, and fifty miles south-east of the former town. Here are two wells yielding good water, but no habitations nor supplies, except a little coarse grass as forage for camels. The fort which formerly stood here was, some years ago, swept away by a flood, and this event seems to indicate that the waters of the Indus sometimes find their way over this waste, though nearly fifty miles distant from the main channel. A mound with a few trees now marks this former site of the fort. Oodar is in lat. 27° 25′, long. 69° 30′.

Bokh. i. 58.

OODEENUGGUR, in the Punjab, a ruined city on the left or east bank of the Jailum, supposed by Burnes to be the remains of Niccea, built by Alexander on the field of his victory over Porus. Lat. 32° 49′, long. 73° 26′.

Elph. Acc. of Caubul, 26.

OODOO-DA-KOTE, in the Punjab, a village on the route

from Mooltan to Leia, and forty miles north-west of the former town. It is situate in a narrow tract of fertile ground, bounded on the east by the Desert and on the west by the Indus. The inhabitants are represented as peaceable, industrious, and skilful cultivators, drawing from their lands abundant crops of wheat, barley, cotton, and esculent vegetables. Lat. 30° 30', long. 71° 14'.

OOMEEPOOR, in the Punjab, a village situate twelve miles from the right bank of the Ghara river. Lat. 30° 9', long. 72° 40'. E.I.C. Ms. Doc.

OOMUR, in Beloochistan, a village fifteen miles north-west of Quetta. Lat. 30° 17', long. 66° 50'. E.I.C. Ms. Doc.

OONAPOOTLA, in Sinde, a village on the middle route from Bukkur to Hyderabad, and sixty miles north of the latter town. Lat. 26° 16', long. 68° 25'. E.I.C. Ms. Doc.

OONERPOOR, in Sinde, a large village on the route from Hyderabad to Sehwan, and twenty miles north of the former town. The right bank of the Indus, on which it is situate, is here considerably elevated above the water. Around is an alluvial country, rendered difficult for travelling in many parts during the inundation of the Indus, by marshes and watercourses. Half a mile to the north of the village is a good encamping ground. Lat. 25° 38', long. 68° 20'. E.I.C. Ms. Doc.

OONKAEE, in Afghanistan, a village four miles west of the route from Ghuznee to Kabool, and fifty miles south-west of the latter town. Lat. 33° 59', long. 68° 29'. E.I.C. Ms. Doc.

OONNA.—The most eastern of the six passes over the western extremity of the Hindoo Koosh, on the route from Kabool to Turkestan, by way of Bamian. It is about fifty-five miles west of Kabool, and is remarkable as forming the dividing ground between the waters which flow eastward into the Indus by the river of Kabool, and those of the river of Helmund, which flow south-westward to Seistan. Though having an elevation of 11,000 feet, according to the statement of Wood, "a mail-coach might be driven over it." Lat. 34° 21', long. 68° 12'. E.I.C. Ms. Map; Wood, Route of Kabool and Turkestan, 24; Jour. As. Soc. Beng. 1842, p. 68, Grif. Bar. and Ther. Mens. in Afg.; Burnes' Bokh. i. 175.

OOPLAUN, in Sinde, a village situate on the left bank of the Indus, at a point where a considerable canal passes off to the south-east. Lat. 24° 30', long. 68° 4'. E.I.C. Ms. Doc.

OORGHOON, in Afghanistan, a village of the Vizeree country, situate in lat. 33° 14', long. 69° 49'. Walker's Map of Afg.

Walker's Map of N.W. Frontier.	**OORMOOL**, in the Punjab, a village on the northern route from Amritsir to Ropur, and forty-five miles east of the former town. Lat. 31° 44′, long. 75° 34′.
Outram, Rough Notes, i. 181, 200, 261.	**OORNACH**, in Beloochistan, a village on the route from Bela to Nal, and fifty-five miles north-west of the former place. It is situate in the valley of Oornach, and south of the pass, near a stream bearing the same name as the village. Lat. 26° 56′, long. 65° 49′.
Id. 180; Masson, Bal. Afg. Panj. ii. 35.	**OORNACH**, in Beloochistan, a range of mountains, described by Outram as lofty, and by Masson as hills of some elevation. It is crossed by the Oornach pass on the route from Bela to Nal, and in lat. 26° 58′, long. 65° 48′. The road by this pass is good, and crosses the mountains by easy ascents.
Outram, Rough Notes, 181, 258; Masson, Bal. Afg. Panj. 35.	**OORNACH**, a river of Beloochistan, rises about lat. 27°, long. 66° 10′, first takes a course westerly for about twenty miles, then southerly for about ten, and, finally turning eastward, is lost in the wilds of Jhalawan. Where crossed by Masson, it was narrow, but had a good volume of water and a rapid course. Outram found it dry at the end of October.
E.I.C. Ms. Doc.	**OORUDANEE**, in Sinde, a village of the delta of the Indus, situate on the route proceeding by the right bank of the river from Tatta to Vikkur, and twenty-five miles south of the former town. Lat. 24° 28′, long. 67° 52′.
E.I.C. Ms. Doc.; Jour. As. Soc. Beng. 1839, p. 187, Carless, Acc. of a Jour. to Beylah.	**OOT**, in Beloochistan, two villages on the route from Lyaree to Bela, and five miles south of the latter town. They are situate on the gradual slope by which the plain of Lus is connected with the highlands of Kelat. Lat. 26° 2′, long. 66° 26′.
	OOTCH.—See OOCH.
E.I.C. Ms. Doc.	**OOTORAHGOTE**, in Sinde, a village on the route from Hyderabad to Sehwan, and forty-four miles north of the former place. It is situate a mile and a half from the right bank of a large offset of the Indus, and four miles from the main channel. The road in this part of the route is level, and suitable for the passage of carriages. Lat. 25° 53′, long. 68° 15′.
E.I.C. Ms. Doc.	**OOTPALANA**, in Afghanistan, the point at which the Sakhee Sarwar Pass penetrates the Suliman Mountains. The name signifies "camel's saddle," and is said to have been applied to it in consequence of the excessive steepness giving to the saddle a tendency to fall off in the ascent. Lat. 30° 2′, long. 70° 4′.

OOTUK, in Afghanistan, a village on the route from Ghuznee to Shawl, and a hundred and forty miles north of the latter town. Lat. 31° 43′, long. 67° 19′. E.I.C. Ms. Doc.

OOTUL, in Beloochistan, a small town of the province of Lus, situate on the route from Sonmeeanee to Bela, and twenty-five miles north of the former place. It is clean and well built, in a pleasant site, amidst groves and crops of grain and cotton. Provisions may be had in moderate quantities; honey is remarkably abundant and excellent. Good water is obtained from wells of a great depth. The population, about 2,000 persons, contribute annually four thousand rupees to the revenue of the Jam of Lus. Pottinger describes the people at the time of his visit as "very contented and happy. They have immense flocks of sheep and goats, besides herds of black cattle and camels." Ootul is in lat. 25° 44′, long. 66° 33′. E.I.C. Ms. Doc.; Pott. Belooch. 13; Masson, Bal. Afg. Panj. ii. 26, 165; Id. Kalat, 304.

OSANPOOR, in Bhawlpoor, a village situate on the left bank of the Indus, in lat. 28° 42′, long. 70° 12′. Walker's Map.

OSMAN, in the Punjab, between the Indus and Jailum, a small town situate at the base of the low range of hills which mark the rise from the plain to the Himalaya, in a fruitful and well-watered country. Lat. 33° 53′, long. 72° 52′. Burnes' Bokh. i. 70.

OTMAN, in Afghanistan, a halting-place on the route by the Goolairee pass, from Ghuznee to Dera Ismael Khan, and eighty-five miles south-west of Ghuznee. The road in this part of the route is bad, but there is a good supply of water from a stream, and hence the importance of the position in this arid region. Lat. 32° 33′, long. 68° 50′. E.I.C. Ms. Doc.

OUBAZEDEH, in Afghanistan, a village situate on the river Helmund, two miles south-east of Giriskh. Lat. 31° 42′, long. 64° 24′.

OUTCHE, in Northern Afghanistan, a village situate among the Laram mountains, in lat. 35° 6′, long. 72° 5′. Jour. As. Soc. Beng. 1830, p. 312, Court, Alexander's Exploits on the Western Bank of the Indus.

OUZBIN,[1] in Afghanistan, a village close to the Luttabund pass, and thirty-five miles east of Kabool. It is situate in a small elevated valley of the same name,[2] which in climate and aspect resembles the vicinity of Kabool. Lat. 34° 30′, long. 69° 40′. [1] E.I.C. Ms. Doc. [2] Elph. Acc. of Caubul, 99.

P.

PACENCE.—See PASSEENOE.

<small>Walker's Map of Afg.</small>
PACHLAWE, in Afghanistan, a village situate on the route from Kandahar to Khash, and seventy miles west of the former town. It is situate in the *doab*, or tract between the rivers Urgundab and Helmund, and close to their confluence. Lat. 31° 31′, long. 64° 17′.

PADEE ZHUR, on the coast of Beloochistan, an inlet of the Arabian Sea, on the west side of Ras Arubah. Lat. 25° 10′, long. 64° 21′.

<small>E.I.C. Ms. Doc.</small>
PADRA, in Sinde, a village on the middle route from Bukkur to Hyderabad, and a hundred miles north of the latter town. Lat. 26° 47′, long. 68° 13′.

<small>Walker's Map of N.W. Frontier.</small>
PADREE, in the Punjab, a village on the route from Julalpoor to Attock, and fifteen miles north of the former town. Lat. 32° 54′, long. 73° 13′.

<small>E.I.C. Ms. Doc.; Masson, Bal. Afg. Panj. ii. 116.</small>
PAEESHT KHANA, in Beloochistan, an expansion of the Moola pass, about forty miles south-west of its western termination. It is a fertile spot, inhabited by Brahuis, who live in dwellings made of mats, cultivate wheat, rice, and pulse, and keep numerous flocks of sheep and goats. The less fertile parts are overgrown with the *kuril*, or wild caper-tree; the *bar*, or Indian fig-tree, and *mimosas*. At this place the direct road, which proceeds nearly south from Kelat by Panduran, joins the Moola pass. The elevation of Paeesht Khana is 3,500 feet. Lat. 27° 59′, long. 66° 47′.

<small>E.I.C. Ms. Doc.; Elph. Acc. of Caubul, 27.</small>
PAHARPOOR, in the Punjab, a village on the route from Mooltan to Leia, and twenty miles south of the latter town. It is situate on the left bank of an offset of the Indus, in the low fertile tract stretching north and south between the main channel and the desert, and laid under water in the season of inundation. Lat. 30° 40′, long. 71°.

<small>[1] Burnes' Pol. Power of Sikhs, 5; Masson, Bal. Afg. Panj. 40.
[2] Acc. of Caubul, 34.</small>
PAHARPOOR,[1] in Afghanistan, a considerable town of the Derajat, situate where the route branches off westward to Tak, from the route northward through Dera Ismael Khan. Elphinstone[2] describes it as scarcely less than Dera Ismael Khan.

It was taken by Runjeet Singh, and held for a short time by a garrison of Sikhs, who were all massacred by the Esa Khail Afghans.[3] Lat. 32° 9′, long. 71° 2′.

[3] Burnes, Pers. Narr. 99.

PAIEN-I-DURAS, or PAIN DRAS, in Ladakh, a village on the route from Le to Kashmir, by the Bultul pass, from which it is distant twenty miles north-east. The land in the vicinity is in general employed for pasture, and produces the *prangos pabularia*, so highly esteemed by Moorcroft for winter fodder. Izzet Ullah,[1] who calls this place Panderras, observes that the road is good in this part of the route. Gholaum Hyder[2] styles the village Paeen-dur-rauz. Professor Wilson, the editor of Moorcroft,[3] considers that it should be called Pain-dras,[4] or "lower dras," but this does not seem justifiable, as the place lies higher up the course of the river and is more elevated than Dras. The elevation above the sea exceeds 9,000 feet.[5] Lat. 34° 20′, long. 75° 26′.

[1] Oriental Mag. 1825, March, 105.
[2] As. Jour. Sept. Dec. 1835, p. 189.
[3] Punj. Bokh. ii. 93.
[4] Note on Izzet Ullah, ut supra, 105.
[5] Vigne, Kashmir, ii. 393.

PAK PATTAN[1] (pure town *), in the Punjab, a town situate five miles west of the river Ravee, and eight miles from Mamoke Ghat, a much-frequented ferry over it. A perfectly level plain of four miles wide extends towards the river from the town, which, viewed at some distance, has the appearance of a citadel situate on the summit of a lofty eminence. It is built on the site of the ancient fort of Ajwadin, Ajodin, or Adjoodhun, and is celebrated as the place close to which Mahmud of Ghuznee, Tamerlane,[2] and several other invaders of Hindostan, crossed the river boundary of the Punjab on the east. The name of this town is considered to indicate its peculiar sanctity, in consequence of its having been for many years the residence of a celebrated Mahometan saint, Shekh Farid-u-Din, of whose miraculous powers many traditions are recounted by the natives. It is related, among his other wonderful deeds, that when hungry, he threw into his mouth handfuls of dust or pebbles, which immediately became sugar; and as he effected similar transmutations in innumerable instances for the benefit of other persons, he obtained the name of *Shakarganj*,† or "sugar store." The tomb or shrine is situate in a spot depressed below the rest of the mound on which the town is built, and which has an elevation of about forty feet above the plain. It is an unornamented and inconsiderable building, having

[1] Jour. As. Soc. Beng. 1837, p.191; Mackeson, Acc. of Wade's Voyage down the Sutlej.
[2] Ferishta, i. 488; Price, Mahommedan Hist. iii. 242; Rennell, 81.

* پاک پتن .   † شکرگنج .

but one small apartment, containing the remains of the saint in a grave, covered with faded drapery. There are in it two small doors, one to the north, the other to the east. The last is called the "door to Paradise," and is only opened on the fifth day of the first Mahometan month, called *Moharram*, and considered peculiarly holy, in reference to the belief that during the ten first days the Koran[3] was sent from heaven for revelation to men. This doorway is about two feet wide, but so low that it cannot be passed without stooping; and the chamber itself is of such contracted dimensions, that it can contain only about thirty persons. Those who rub their foreheads on the saint's grave are considered safe from perdition; the first who enters the chamber is believed to secure thereby a peculiarly high degree of felicity in a future state, and as the crowd of pilgrims, comprising Hindoos as well as Mussulmans, is immense, the crush is tremendous. The natives, however, assert that no accidents occur, in consequence of the tender care which the saint has for his votaries. Among other relics preserved here is a piece of wood in the shape of a cake, which, it is said, was used by the saint to solace himself when assailed by hunger during his long fasts. Pak Pattan is supposed by Masson[4] to have been the site of the colossal altars erected by Alexander to mark the eastern boundary of his conquests. Lat. 30° 20′, long. 73° 13′.

[3] D'Herbelot, ii. 684.

[4] Bal. Afg. Panj. i. 455.

PAKHA SIDHARO, in the Punjab, a village situate in lat. 30° 20′, long. 73° 3′.

Walker's Map of N.W. Frontier.

PAKRUN.—See DOOBAH RIVER.

PALALU.—See PULULU.

PALLIA, in Sinde, a small town on the route from Cutch to Hyderabad, and ninety miles south-east of the latter place. Lat. 24° 14′, long. 68° 51′.

Burnes, Rep. of Com. of Hydrabad, 17.

PAMBUR, in the north-east of the Punjab, a small town on the route from Kishtewar to Kashmir by the Muru Wurdwun pass. It is situate on the Muru Wurdwun river, forty miles above its confluence with the Chenaub. Lat. 33° 38′, long. 75° 40′.

Vigne, Kashmir, Map.

PAMGHAN, or PAMGHAAN.—See PUGHMAN.

PAMPUR, in Kashmir, a town about five miles west of the city of Kashmir, is situate on the north bank of the Jailum or Behut, in a level tract of great fertility, and presents most delightful views of the mountain ranges to the north. Here is a

Id. ii. 32; Moorcr. Punj. Bokhara, ii. 242; Ayeen Akbery, ii. 139.

bridge of several arches over the river. The town is surrounded by luxuriant orchards and gardens; it contains between three and four hundred houses,* a bazaar, and two Mahometan shrines. The neighbouring country is generally cultivated for the growth of saffron, and the produce is considered finer than that of any part of Hindostan. Lat. 34° 3′, long. 74° 46′.

PANALIA, in Sinde, a village on the route from Omercote to Nuggur Parkur, and twenty-five miles north of the latter place. Lat. 24° 40′, long. 70° 44′. Walker's Map of N.W. Frontier.

PANCH-GERAI, in the Punjab, a village situate on an offset of the Indus, about five miles from the right bank of the main stream. Lat. 31° 56′, long. 71° 14′. E.I.C. Ms. Doc.

PANDRENTON, in Kashmir, an antique temple of small dimensions, standing in a reservoir or tank about four miles south-east of Srinagur, the present capital of the valley. It is a striking specimen of the simple massive and chaste style which characterizes the architectural antiquities of Kashmir. The ground plan is a square of twenty feet, and the roof pyramidal. In each of the four sides is a doorway ornamented with pilasters right and left, and surmounted by a pediment. The whole is constructed of blocks of regularly hewn limestone. The interior is filled with water communicating with that without, which is about four feet deep; and as the building is completely insulated, it can be reached only by wading or swimming. The purpose of its construction is not known, but it is generally considered a Buddhist relic. It exhibits neither inscriptions nor sculptures, except the figure of a large lotus carved on the roof inside. Lat. 34° 2′, long. 74° 47′. Vigne, Kashmir, ii. 38; Moorcr. Punj. Bokh. ii. 246; F. Von Hugel, Kaschmir, i. 260.

PANDURAN, in Beloochistan, a village situate on the direct pass which, proceeding southwards from Kelat, joins the Moola pass at Pacesht Khana. It is built on the banks of a torrent, which commencing a little south-east of Kelat, flows southward, and joins the Moola river. The pass, which scarcely deviates in any place from the course of the stream, is much shorter than the upper part of the Moola pass, with which it is collateral, but is less available for military purposes in consequence of not being practicable for artillery. Panduran is in lat. 28° 36′, long. 66° 45′. E.I.C. Ms. Doc.

PANEEWAN, in Beloochistan, a village in the Moola or Gundava pass, on the route from Kelat to Gundava. It is situate E.I.C. Ms. Doc.

---

* Von Hügel describes it as a considerable town. Kaschmir, i. 262.

about 1,000 feet above the level of the sea, in a narrow part of the pass, which is here impeded with jungle and large rolling stones. Lat. 28° 6′, long. 67° 11′.

<small>Map of Sinde.</small>

PANJGADGERH, in Sinde, a village situate on the Khediwaree mouth of the Indus. Lat. 24° 14′, long. 67° 47′.

<small>Elph. Acc. of Caubul, 334; Jour. As. Soc. Beng. 1839, p. 306, Court, Exploits of Alexander on the Western Banks of the Indus.</small>

PANJKORA, a district north-east of Afghanistan, on the southern slope of Hindoo Koosh, and lying about the upper branches of the Lundye river. Hence its name, which signifies five rivers, that being the number of the principal streams. It has Chitral to the north; to the east are several small independent states, little known, but which extend north of the Indus to Bolor; to the south-east is Suwat; to the south, Afghanistan; to the west, Kafiristan. It has been overrun by the Yusuf Zais Afghans, who, having reduced the primitive inhabitants to a state of vassalage, maintain themselves in a turbulent independence. It is in general a maze of mountains densely wooded, except in the neighbourhood of the rivers, where cultivation is carefully attended to. The limits of Panjkora are ill defined, but the length cannot exceed eighty miles, and the breadth is about thirty. Panjkora, the principal place, is laid down in lat. 35° 25′, long. 72°.

<small>E.I.C. Ms. Doc.</small>

PANNOH-CA-PAR, in Sinde, a village situate in the eastern desert, and about forty-two miles north-east of Omercote. Lat. 25° 40′, long. 70° 21′.

<small>Vigne, Kashmir, ii. 38; Moorcr. Punj. Bokh. ii. 241.</small>

PANTUR CHUK, in Kashmir, a village five miles south of Sirinagur, on the road to Islamabad. It is situate on the right bank of the Behut or Jailum, which was here formerly crossed by a bridge, now totally ruined and impassable. Lat. 34° 1′, long. 74° 45′.

<small>E.I.C. Ms. Doc.</small>

PARAR, in the Punjab, a village on the route from Mooltan to Dera Ghazee Khan, and thirty miles west of the latter town. It is situate on an offset of the Indus, and two miles from the left bank of the main channel, in lat. 30° 5′, long. 70° 59′.

<small>Hough, Narr. Exp. in Afg. 352.</small>

PAREEWALLAH, in the Punjab, a small town ten miles from the right or west bank of the Chenaub. The surrounding country is regarded as peculiarly favourable to the constitution of the horse, and on this account the Sikh government has an extensive stud here. Lat. 32° 25′, long. 73° 36′.

<small>Outram, Rough Notes, 177, 256.</small>

PARKOO, in Beloochistan, a village of the province of Jhalawan, on the route from Kelat to Nal, and twelve miles north-west of the latter place. It is situate on a fine stream of water, amidst a few trees and traces of former cultivation, but is at present little better than a heap of ruins, having been destroyed by Mehrab Khan of Kelat. Lat. 27° 49′, long. 65° 54′.

PARKUTA, in Bulti, or Little Tibet, a small town with a fort, situate on the Indus, about twenty-five miles south-east of Iskardo, the capital. Before the late conquest of this country by the Sikhs, it was the residence of a raja, the brother of the sovereign of Bulti. It is a place of some trade, having a manufacture of saddles, which are much prized. Lat. 35° 3′, long. 75° 51′. Vigne, Kashmir, ii. 324.

PARNA, in Sinde, a village situate on the route from Omercote to Balmair, forty miles north-east of the former town. Lat. 25° 28′, long. 70° 21′. E.I.C. Ms. Doc.

PARTUR, in Afghanistan, a village among the mountains inclosing the valley of Kahun, and connecting the highlands of Hurrund and Dajel with the Hala range. It is situate on the Illiassee torrent, which, flowing from north-east to south-west, is lost in the arid plain of Cutch Gundava. Partur is in lat. 29° 9′, long. 69° 40′. E.I.C. Ms. Doc.

PARWAN.—See PURWAN.

PARWAN PASS.—See PURWAN.

PASSEENOE, or PACENCE, in Beloochistan, a village situate at the inner extremity of a deep bay of the Arabian Sea. A scanty supply of water and a few lean goats may be obtained here at a high price. Lat. 25° 17′, long. 63° 20′. Horsburgh, Ind. Dir. i. 495.

PASTAN, in Afghanistan, a village on the route from Herat to Andkhoo, and fifteen miles east of the former place. Lat. 34° 26′, long. 62° 25′. E.I.C. Ms. Doc.

PATAN,[1] in Kashmir, a village twenty-five miles north-west of the town of Sirinagur. It is situate close to a Kariwah, or table-land of fertile soil, once well cultivated, as is evident from the remains of canals constructed for the purpose of irrigation. At present it is a complete waste. [1] Moorer. Panj. Bokh. ii. 270.

This seems to have been an important locality during the predominance of Hindooism in Kashmir, as in the vicinity are the remains of two ancient buildings in a style similar to the celebrated temple at Matan.* Patan is still a place of pilgrimage for the superstitious Hindoos.[2] Lat. 34° 7′, long. 74° 21′. [2] F. Von Hugel, Kaschmir, ii. 384.

* Vigne, who took much interest in the architectural relics in Kashmir, gives the following description of the ruins at Patan:—"After Martund, the Kashmir, ii. 107.

PATAN KOT[1] (Afghan's Fort), in the north-east of the Punjab, and in the southern range of the Himalaya, fourteen miles north-west of Nurpur, and on the route to Kashmir. The fort has a fine appearance, is built substantially of brick, has a ditch and glacis, and being situate on level ground, is not commanded in any direction; it consequently admits of an obstinate defence. A lofty citadel in the interior rises above the ramparts. It was built by Shah Jehan, the Mogul emperor, during his attack on Nurpur. Notwithstanding its advantageous position and great strength, it seems to be allowed to fall to decay. Elevation above the sea, 1,205 feet.[2] Lat. 32° 18′, long. 75° 27′.

PATTEE, in Sinde, a village situate on the left bank of the Indus, ten miles north-east of Tattah. Lat. 24° 50′, long. 68° 9′.

PATTEN, in the Punjab, a village situate on the left bank of the Indus, about fifteen miles above Attock, in lat. 34° 1′, long. 72° 24′.

PAUK PETTAN.—See PAK PATTAN.

PAURIK, in Afghanistan, a village on the road from Ghuznee to Dera Ismael Khan. Lat. 33° 4′, long. 69° 2′.

PA YECH, in Kashmir, a very ancient ruin, situate at the northern base of the Kariwah, or table-land of No Nagur. It is of small dimensions, but in a tasteful and impressive style of architecture. It is thus described by Vigne, probably the only European by whom it has been surveyed. "The interior and exterior ornaments are particularly elegant. The building is dedicated, I believe, to Vishnu, as Surya or the sun-god, small sitting figures of whom are inserted in niches on the cornice outside. The ceiling of the interior is radiated so as to represent the sun, and at each corner of the square, the space intervening between the angle and the line of the circle is filled up with a gin, or attendant, who seems to be sporting at the edge of his rays." Pa Yech is in lat. 33° 50′, long. 74° 45′.

old ruin at Putun (Patan) is perhaps the best specimen of the square ruined temple to be found in the valley. The walls and colonnade of the peristyle are no longer in existence, and the interior of the remaining building, with its well-carved and graceful figures of Vishnu and Luchni, are well worth the inspection of the traveller, being scarcely inferior to those at Martund. At a little distance from it are the ruined walls of a smaller and separate building, and both and all are built of the mountain limestone occurring near Putun."

[1] F. Von Hugel, Kaschmir, 126.

[2] Jour. As. Soc. Beng. 1841, p. 111, Broome and Cunningham, Jour. to Sources of Punjab Rivers.

E.I.C. Ms. Doc.

E.I.C. Ms. Doc.

Walker's Map of Afg.

Vigne, Kashmir, ii. 40.

PEEDUR KUSSUR, in Beloochistan, a village situate on the route from Kedje to Bela, and a hundred miles west of the latter town. Lat. 26° 14′, long. 64° 52′. _{Walker's Map of Beloochistan.}

PEELINJABAD.—See FERINGABAD.

PEEPREE, in Sinde, a village situate on a feeder of the Garrah river in lat. 24° 49′, long. 67° 25′. _{E.I.C. Ms. Doc.}

PEEPUL, in the Punjab, a village situate on an offset of the Indus, and about five miles from the left bank of the main stream. Lat. 32° 15′, long. 71° 29′. _{E.I.C. Ms. Doc.}

PEEPULWARIE MUKAM, in Sinde, a village on the road from Kurrachee to Sehwan, and twenty-eight miles north-east of the former town. Lat. 25° 1′, long. 67° 21′. _{E.I.C. Ms. Doc.}

PEER ADAL, in Afghanistan, a town of the Derajat, on the road from Dera Ghazee Khan to Kandahar, by the Boree route. Population about 1,800. Lat. 30° 16′, long. 70° 41′. _{Leech, App. 40.}

PEER BUKSH, in Afghanistan, a village in the south of the Derajat. Lat. 29° 21′, long. 70° 35′. _{Walker's Map of Afg.}

PEER CHUTTA (the small saint), in Beloochistan, a shrine of a reputed Mahometan saint, situate at the north-eastern extremity of the Moola pass. Here a stream, falling into the Moola river, swarms with fish deemed sacred by the superstitious Belooches. Lat. 28° 20′, long. 67° 10′. _{E.I.C. Ms. Doc.}

PEERKA, in the Punjab, a village situate on the right bank of the river Ghara. Lat. 30° 40′, long. 74° 4′. _{Jour. As. Soc. Beng. 1837, p. 212, Mackeson, Jour.}

PEER LUKKEE, in Beloochistan, in the Moola pass, the abode of a fakir, or reputed Mahometan saint. It is situate in a part of the pass where the valley considerably expands. Elevation above the sea about 3,000 feet. Lat. 27° 56′, long. 67° 2′. _{of Wade's Voyage down the Sutlej. E.I.C. Ms. Doc.; Masson, Bal. Afg. Panj. ii. 117.}

PEER PUNJAH, in Sinde, a town on the route from Sehwan to Larkhana, and forty-eight miles north of the former place. It is situate three miles west of the right bank of the Indus, in a level alluvial country, having considerable cultivation, interspersed in some places with jungle. The road in this part of the route is tolerably good, and practicable for wheel-carriages. Lat. 27° 6′, long. 68°. _{E.I.C. Ms. Doc.}

PEER PUTTA (the young saint), in Sinde, a celebrated Mahometan shrine, and small town in the delta near Tatta. It is built on a low limestone hill, and, when seen from a distance, _{Wood, Oxus, 16; Kennedy, Sinde and Kabool, i. 75; Burnes' Pers. Narr. 10.}

its elevation and the brilliant white of its stuccoed walls render it a striking object. Lat. 24° 36′, long. 67° 55′.

Kennedy, Sinde and Kabool, i. 109.

PEER RADAN, in Sinde, a village near the right or western bank of the Indus. Here are three large *dunds*, or small lakes, filled by the Indus during inundation, and furnishing an ample supply of water for the irrigation of the adjacent country. Lat. 24° 50′, long. 68° 4′.

E.I.C. Ms. Doc.

PEER UKRA GOTE, in Sinde, a village on the route from Hyderabad to Sehwan, and fifteen miles north of the former town. It is situate about a mile from the right bank of the Indus, in a level alluvial country, reserved during the Talpoor sway as hunting-grounds for the Ameers of Hyderabad. Lat. 25° 34′, long. 68° 22′.

E.I.C. Ms. Doc.

PEESEE BHENT, in Beloochistan, a halting-place in the Moola pass. It is just below a very difficult part of the pass, where the cliffs, five hundred feet high on each side, approach within twenty or thirty yards of each other, so that those in possession of the heights above could effectually stop the progress of an army, by rolling down stones, there being, moreover, no possibility of turning the defile. Lat. 28° 10′, long. 66° 33′.

E.I.C. Ms. Doc.

PEHIE, in the Punjab, a village situate on the left bank of the Indus, close to the confluence of the Swan river. Lat. 33°, long. 71° 47′.

E.I.C. Ms. Doc.

PEIJHOUR, in Afghanistan, a village situate on the right bank of the Indus, thirty miles north-east of Attock. Lat. 34° 11′, long. 72° 34′.

PEMGHAN.—See PUGMAN.

Jour. As. Soc. 1836, p. 468, Court, Memoir on a Map of Peshawur.

PENJHUR, in Afghanistan, a village of Boonere, ten miles from the right bank of the Indus. Lat. 34° 15′, long. 72° 28′.

E.I.C. Ms. Doc.

PERE PYE, a village in Afghanistan, situate on the right bank of the Kabool river, fifteen miles north-east of Peshawer. Lat. 34° 3′, long. 71° 54′.

E.I.C. Ms. Doc.; Mil. Op. in Afg. 343.

PESH BOLAK, in Afghanistan, a village on the direct route from Peshawer to Kabool, and fifty miles north-west of the former town. It is situate at the eastern extremity of the desert of Butte Kote, in a district bearing also the name of Pesh Bolak. Lat. 34° 17′, long. 70° 55′.

Jour. As. Soc. Beng. 1836, p. 745.

PESHAWER, or PESHAWUR,[1] usually considered part

of Afghanistan, a very fertile and valuable territory, lying between the Indus above and below Attock and the Khyber mountains, through which is the great Khyber pass. It is bounded on the north by Suwat and the region lying between it and the Indus—on the east, by part of the last-mentioned territory, the Indus, and the territory of the independent Afghans holding the Salt or Kala range—on the south, by the possessions of the same Afghans, and on the west, by the Khyber mountains and the Afghan province of Jelalabad. It lies between lat. 33° 27' and 34° 22', and long. 71° 29' and 72° 12'. In the extent here assigned to this territory, it is sixty-five miles long, fifty miles broad, and about one thousand eight hundred square miles in extent. Its climate is very hot in summer, the thermometer frequently reaching 110° or 112° in the shade. The heat, however, is occasionally mitigated by the breezes from the neighbouring mountains, and as the country, naturally fertile, is well watered by the Indus, the Kabool river, the Bara, and some other streams of less importance, and is, moreover, well cultivated, it is amazingly productive. The water is applied to the purposes of cultivation by means of canals and innumerable small channels, from whence it is drawn up by means of a pole having a fulcrum in the middle and a bucket suspended at one end, which is raised by the hand pressing the other end; or where the depth is too great for this mode of operation, the water is obtained by the use of the Persian wheel, worked by camels or bullocks. Here, water is in general too near the surface to require the use of the draw-well. In consequence of this abundant supply, the country continues verdant during the whole year.[2] There are two regular and principal harvests in the year, and generally of crops completely distinct in their kind. The first,[3] called *rubbee*, sown in autumn and the beginning of winter, is cut in spring (about the end of April), and consists chiefly of wheat, barley, and pulse of various kinds, usually the staple crops of cooler climates. The second, or *khuseef*, is sown as soon as the other has been cleared away, and is reaped in autumn, the produce being rice,[4] maize, millet, and various other crops proper to hot climates. Peshawer produces the finest rice in the world. It is called Bara rice, because grown on ground irrigated by that river, and Runjeet Singh, ever watchful to secure to himself the best of every thing prized by man, exacted part of his tribute in this valued article. Esculent vegetables are cul-

Court, Memoir on a Map of Peshawur; Elph. Acc. of Caubul, 55; Masson, Bal. Afg. Panj. 131; Moorcr. Punj. Bokh. ii. 337; Burnes, Pol. Power of the Sikhs, 2; Id. Bokh. i. 86; ii. 319; Id. Pers. Narr. 112; Wood, Oxus, 154; Forster, Jour. Beng. Eng. ii. 56; Hough, Narr. Exp. in Afg. 321; Havelock, War in Afg. ii. 196-199; Atkinson, Exp. into Afg. 384; Baber, Memoir, 292-293.

[2] Burnes, ii. 326.

[3] Irvin, ix. 39.

[4] Elph. 300.

tivated with much success. Many of them are of the kinds known in England—carrots, turnips, radishes, cabbages, cauliflowers, onions; others are there of common occurrence in India. As a substitute for hay, corn and certain green crops are cut before ripe and dried for fodder. Barley, and sometimes wheat, are cut before they form ears and used for this purpose, and this treatment does not injure the crop. What is called here *paulaiz*, is a very important portion of the crop, and comprises musk-melons, water-melons, scented-melons, and various kinds of cucumbers, pumpkins, and gourds, produced in the greatest luxuriance, and consumed in the hot season in large quantities. The castor-oil-plant is cultivated, the oil, however, is not intended for culinary or medicinal purposes, but for any other in which a coarse oil may be required. Sesamum, mustard, and some other plants are reared for the sake of their oil. The sugar-cane is raised to be consumed as a sweetmeat; sugar itself being obtained from Hindostan. Ginger, turmeric, tobacco, and cotton, are also extensively cultivated. The ground is moved by the plough, the spade being little employed. Scythes are unknown, and crops of all kinds are cut with sickles. Oxen are used for ploughing, harrowing, and treading out the corn. Mulberry-trees abound, and silk is produced in moderate quantities. The principal fruits are plums, figs, peaches, pomegranates, mulberries, and quinces; but, though large, all except the last have an inferior flavour.[5] The quince of Peshawer is the only fruit that can lay claim to excellence, and it is said to surpass those of all other countries.

[5] Irvin. ix. 43.

Elphinstone, who entered the country in March from the great defile, through which the route from the south passes, describes the scene formed by the mountains, crowned with eternal snow, surrounding the luxuriant and picturesque plain, as at once grand and beautiful in the highest degree, and he found that a nearer survey increased his admiration. At the time of Elphinstone's visit, the population was so dense that thirty-two villages were counted within a circuit of four miles. It may be doubted whether the impressions of the European visitors on this occasion were not somewhat over sanguine, but it was their belief, "that never was a spot of ground better peopled." An estimate formed with reference to their views would give about half a million as the number of the inhabitants. Court[6] estimates the military force of the province at 40,000 cavalry and 1,000 infantry. Much

[6] 476.

of the happiness and prosperity then observed had passed away even when Moorcroft visited the country in 1834, and the events of the last few years have occasioned still greater desolation. In its decay, however, after the devastation caused by the Sikhs, Peshawer was estimated to yield a revenue of Rs. 1,000,000 per annum.

Through this fine province lies the great route from Khorasan and Kabool into India, by the passes of the Khyber mountains and across the Indus at Attock. It is, however, most perilously situated in being exposed to the incursions of the wild inhabitants of the mountains almost everywhere overhanging it, and the difficulty of crossing the Indus greatly embarrasses the communications with the Punjab, which has usually been the seat of more settled and civilized power. The Sikhs, who overrun the country by taking advantage of the dissensions of the Afghans, have regarded the population rather as present enemies than future fellow-subjects, and ruinously devastated both the capital city—Peshawer—and the whole country. The only act apparently at variance with their ordinary course of desolation was the construction of the fortress of Peshawer, and that of Futteghur, at Jamrood, at the eastern extremity of the Khyber pass, to command the passage into the plain. Besides the capital, there is no place of much importance, except the fortress of Hushtnuggur at the northern extremity. Acora, once an important place, is now in ruins.

PESHAWER, or PESHAWUR, the capital of the province of the same name, is situate about twelve miles east of the eastern extremity of the Khyber pass. In the early part of the present century, when visited by Elphinstone, it was a flourishing town, about five miles in circuit, and reported to contain 100,000 inhabitants. Twenty years later, Runjeet Singh, after defeating the Afghans in the decisive battle of Noushera, took Peshawer, demolished the Bala Hissar, at once the capital and state residence—destroyed the fine houses of the chief Afghans—desecrated the mosques, and cutting down the groves and orchards about the city, laid waste the surrounding country. The subsequent exactions and oppressions have effectually prevented its revival. The houses, built of mud or unburnt brick, have flat roofs, on which the inhabitants spend much of their time. The whole city has rather a melancholy appearance, presenting numerous ruins of great dimensions, the result, not so much of gradual decay, as of sudden and recent violence. The numerous mosques, many built in a splendid style of oriental architecture, have been intentionally polluted by the Sikhs, and are going to ruin. A vast and magnificent caravansera has been converted into the head-quarters of the Sikh governor. It is called Gorkhutru; it has quadrangular outlines, each side measuring two hundred and fifty yards, and contains extensive accommodation for all departments of government, as well as a spacious house for the governor. The fortress, recently erected by the Sikhs on the site of the Bala Hissar, is a square of about two hundred and twenty yards, and is strengthened by round towers at each angle, every curtain having in front of it a semicircular ravelin. There is a fausse braye all round of substantial towers and curtains, with a wet ditch. The height of the inner walls is sixty feet, of the fausse braye thirty, all constructed of mud. Within, are capacious and well-constructed magazines and storehouses. The only gateway is on the northern face, and it is protected by towers. Court, about ten years ago, estimated the population at 80,000; a mixed race of Afghans, Kashmirians, and Hindoos. It is believed to be now about 50,000. Peshawur was built by the Mogul emperor, Akbar, who affixed the name, signifying " advanced post," * in reference to its being the frontier town of Hindostan towards Afghanistan. Elevation above the sea 1,068 feet. Lat. 33° 59′, long. 71° 40′.

PETTEE.—See PUTTEE.

PEYHOUR.—See PEIJHOUR.

PHAGWARA.—See BAGHWARRAH.

PHALIAH, in the Punjab, a village situate about fifteen miles north-west of the town of Ramnugger, and five miles from the right bank of the Chenaub river. Lat. 32° 29′, long. 73° 26′.

PHELOKA, in the Punjab, a village situate on the left bank of the river Chenaub, six miles south-west of Oazeerabad. Lat. 32° 30′, long. 73° 58′.

PHOOGAN GARRA KOOND, in Sinde, a village situate on the road from Bukkur to Oomercote, on the left bank of the Narra river. Lat. 26° 10′, long. 69° 9′.

* Shakespear, in v. پیشاور

PHOOLERA, in Bhawlpoor, a town in the desert, close to the Bikaneer frontier. It has a good bazaar, but not much commerce. There is a fort with very high walls, surmounted by fine battlements and surrounded by a good trench, but all in great decay. The place has an antique but striking and pleasing appearance. On the north side of the town is an extensive piece of water. Lat. 29° 11′, long. 73° 4′. Masson, Bal. Afg. Panj. 24.

PHOR RIVER, in Beloochistan, a small stream rising in the hills east of Hinglaj, and, after a course of about twenty miles, falling into the Arabian Sea in lat. 25° 23′, long. 65° 51′. Its channel is fringed with a tamarisk jungle, and though the current intermits for a great part of the year, water may always be obtained by digging in its bed. E.I.C. Ms. Doc.; Jour.As.Soc.Beng. 1840, p. 51, Hart, Jour. from Kurrachee to Hinglaj.

PHULUDA, in Sinde, a village on the route from Subzulcote to Shikarpoor, and twenty miles east of the latter town. It is situate on the northern edge of an island in the Indus, at the ferry between Amil Got and Azeerpoor. Lat. 27° 52′, long. 69° 1′. E.I.C. Ms. Doc.

PHUMARA, in Sinde, a village situate on the route from Bukkur to Oomercote, near the right bank of the eastern Narra, in lat. 27° 5′, long. 69° 4′. E.I.C. Ms. Doc.

PHURAUN, a minor branch of the Indus.—See NARRA, EASTERN.

PHURRAH, in Beloochistan, a village in the province of Lus or Lussa. Lat. 25° 38′, long. 66° 11′. Walker's Map of Belooch.

PIND DADUN KHAN,[1] in the Punjab, a town lying near the right or western bank of the Jailum, from which it is separated by a narrow verdant plain. It consists of three small collections of houses, situate close to each other and about four miles from the river. The houses are built of mud, with a framework of deodar or cedar, the materials for which are floated down the river from the mountains to the north. Pind Dadun is a short distance south of the Salt range,*[2] which rising boldly from the right bank of the Jailum, stretches far into Afghanistan. Salt is raised in the vicinity for the supply of a great part of the Punjab. The formation of the rock containing the salt is sandstone, in strata vertical, or nearly so; the layers of salt, about eighteen inches in thickness,† conform to [1] Burnes' Bokh. i. 49. [2] Elph. 80.

* See Salt Range.

† According to Burnes,[1] "none of the layers exceed a foot and half in [1] Bokh. i. 55.

the arrangement of the rock, and consist of crystallized masses of a reddish tinge and of great brilliancy, which are separated from each other by thin layers of clay. The deposit is worked to great extent, the opening visited by Burnes being a gallery, a thousand feet long, leading into a chamber a hundred feet in height, excavated entirely in salt. The air was found to be very dry, and the temperature about twenty degrees higher than without. The salt is not very pure, and hence is unfit for curing meat. It is, moreover, considered unwholesome, in consequence, according to Burnes, of an admixture of magnesia. It sells at the mouth of the mine for nearly 5*l.* per ton, or about twenty times the price charged in England. The trade, as is usual in the East, is in the hands of the government, which realized a profit of above 1,000 per cent., and calculated, in the time of Burnes' visit, on obtaining from it an aggregate revenue of about 160,000*l.* per annum. The quantity raised annually is about 40,000 tons, but might be increased indefinitely, as the mines appear to be inexhaustible. The workings are conducted in the rudest manner, the salt being brought to the surface by unaided human labour, and in this way a man, his wife, and child may earn a rupee a day. The employment is both laborious and unhealthy in a very high degree. Pind Dadun Khan is the great mart for the produce of these mines, the salt being sent through it to be embarked on the Jailum. Population, 6,000. Lat. 32° 36′, long. 72° 52′.

E.I.C. Ms. Doc.   PINDEE BATTIANKA, in the Punjab, a village situate near the left bank of the river Chenaub. Lat. 31° 53′, long. 73° 8′.

PINDEE MULIK OULEA, or more properly PINDEE GAIBNE, in the Punjab, a village amidst the Salt range. It is
Pers. Narr. 115.   described by Burnes as a cheerful-looking place, though situate on an undulating upland moor, nearly destitute of vegetation. Lat. 33° 14′, long. 72° 7′.

PINIAREE RIVER.—See PINYAREE.

Map of Sinde.   PINJAREE DAREE, in Sinde, a village on the middle route from Roree to Hyderabad, and fifty miles south of the former town. Lat. 27° 2′, long. 68° 49′.

[2] Jour. As. Soc. Beng. 1843, p. 215, Jameson, Rep. of Geol. of Punjaub. [3] Voyage, v. 118.   thickness." Jamieson[2] speaks of the salt as being "very compact and imbedded in the marl, and from fifty to one hundred feet in thickness," &c. Jacquemont[3] states that cubical masses of ten or twelve feet cube could be obtained.

PINTEEANEE, in Sinde, one of the mouths of the Buggaur, formerly a great branch of the Indus, but latterly nearly deserted by the stream. In consequence, the Pinteeanee has become a salt-water creek. Its entrance is impeded and rendered dangerous by sandbanks; but in the channels there are fifteen feet of water at low tide, and boats of thirty tons can ascend for thirty miles. Lat. 24° 20', long. 67° 15'.

Carless, Official Survey of the Indus, 2; Burnes, Bokh. iii. 232.

PINYAREE, in Sinde, a great branch of the Indus, parting from the main stream on the eastern, or left side, at Bunna, in lat. 25° 4', long. 68° 18'. A little below this place, Burnes found the channel of the Pinyaree, during the low season, to be a mile broad, with a large sandbank in the middle. It is navigable downwards as far as Mughribee, where a bund, or dam, forty feet broad, was thrown across it by one of the Ameers in 1799. At Mughribee this great watercourse is called the Goongroo. Below this dam it is navigable southwards to the Seer mouth, at which it is two miles wide.

Burnes (James), Mission to Sinde, 40; Burnes (Alex.), Bokh. iii. 238; Pott. 358; Wood, Official Rep. in Carless, 17.

PIR JELALPOOR, in the Punjab, a town near the confluence of the Ghara and Trimab, or Chenaub. It contains a fine Mahometan shrine, covered with lacquered tiles, and adorned with minarets and cupola. There is a good bazaar; and the extensive ruins of brick-built structures in the vicinity indicate that it was formerly a place of importance. Lat. 29° 28', long. 71° 16'.

Masson, Bal. Afg. Panj. i. 395.

PIR PANJAL,[1] or the Saints' Mountain, a lofty range, forming part of the south-west boundary of Kashmir, and separating it from the Punjab. Its general direction is from north-west to south-east; its length from the Baramula Pass, at the former extremity, to the Pir Panjal Pass, or that of Nandan Sar, at the latter, is about forty miles. Its highest point is supposed to be about in lat. 33° 40', and is estimated to be 15,000 feet above the sea.[2] According to Vigne, the highest part is basaltic, consisting of amygdaloidal trap, which has upheaved; transition rocks appearing on its borders. Quartz, slate, and other primary formations are observable on the northern or Kashmir side. At the southwestern extremity is the pass, generally called the Pir Panjal Pass, or that of Nandan Sar, from a lake of that name near its northern extremity. It is about 12,000 feet high, and, though devoid of trees, is below the limit of perpetual congelation. The name of Pir Panjal, or the Pir's Mountain, has been given, from one

[1] Vigne, i. 264-5, 293.

[2] F. Von Hugel, i. 238; ii. 163; Bernier, ii. 289; Moorcr. ii. 295.

of its summits being the residence of a *Pir*,* or Mahometan saint, who gives benedictions to those who travel over the pass, and also supplies them with refreshments. This pass, though so elevated, must remain open to a late period in the year, as Von Hügel³ traversed it in the middle of November, with a numerous train of porters and other attendants from the plain.

³ I. 197.

PISHEEN,¹ in Southern Afghanistan, a table-land, or elevated valley, lying between the Toba and Khojeh Amran mountains and those of Tukatoo, and crossed by the great route from Sinde to Afghanistan, through the Bolan and Kojuck passes. Its elevation varies from 5,000 to 6,000 feet. It is about fifty miles in length from north-east to south-west, and about half as much in breadth. The elevation is very considerable, as the banks of the Lora river, or river of Pisheen, near Hydurzie, being the lowest part of the valley, are 5,000 feet above the level of the sea.² Being watered by the above-mentioned river, and possessing the advantages of a fertile soil and moderate climate, it is well suited for agriculture, which receives a large share of the attention of the inhabitants, though some of them are engaged in trade, and in the carrying business between Sinde and Afghanistan, for which their local knowledge and influence well adapt them. The chief products are wheat, artificial grasses, and various European fruits. The majority of the inhabitants are of the Tereen tribe, but there is a great number of Syuds, who claim descent from Mahomet, and bear a decent character for courage and morality, according to the scale of judgment prevailing in these parts. The successful resistance which these people gave to the British under General England, at Hykulzye, seems to justify an opinion creditable to their military spirit. They carry on a considerable trade in horses. Most of them are able to speak Hindostanee. The Tereens are much intermingled with the tribe of Caukers, or Khakas, and the Atchakzais, a clan of the Duranees; and the British force suffered much by their depredations in its passage through the valley. Pisheen lies between lat. 30° 20'—30° 50', long. 66° 30'—67° 20'.

¹ E.I.C. Ms. Doc.; Conolly (A.), Jour. to India, ii. 127; Masson, Bal. Afg. Panj. i. 321; Hough, Narr. Exp. in Afg. 63-78.

² Jour. As. Soc. Beng. 1842, p. 55, Grif. Bar. and Ther. Meas.

PITMUTEE, in Afghanistan, a village situate on the river Indus. Lat. 29° 26', long. 70° 42'.

Walker's Map of Afg.

PITTEE, in Sinde, the lower part of the Buggaur, formerly

Carless, Official Survey of the

* پیر literally, "an old man."

the great western branch of the Indus, but now nearly deserted by the stream, except during the inundation, and become, in consequence, merely a salt-water creek. It is five hundred yards wide at the mouth, is in the shallowest part there nine feet deep at low-water, and eighteen feet at high-water spring-tides, and is navigable for thirty miles for boats of twenty-five tons burthen. The Pittee mouth is in lat. 24° 41', long. 67° 8'. Indus, 2; Burnes, Bokh. iii. 233.

PIWAR, in Afghanistan, a village situate in lat. 33° 41', long. 70° 3'. Walker's Map of Afg.

PODSHEH, in Kashmir, a village situate in lat. 34° 22', long. 74° 28'. Map of Kaschmir.

POGHUARA, in the Punjab, a small town on the route from Filor to Amritsir, and sixteen miles north-west of the former place. It is situate in the *Doab* of Julinder, in a fertile country, having generally a soil of argillaceous loam. The principal inhabitants are Hindoos, engaged in commercial pursuits, or in the cultivation of the fine orchards and gardens which surround the town. Lat. 31° 15', long. 75° 41'. Jacquemont, Voyage, v. 53.

POKRUN, in Sinde, a halting-place on the route from Schwan to Kurrachee, and forty-eight miles south of the former town. It is situate on the river, or rather torrent, called, below the Dhurwal and still further downwards, Burran, but here, generally, the river of Pokrun. Though the current intermits for the greater part of the year, there are generally deep pools of good water in the bed. The road in this part of the route is very rocky and broken, and forage and other supplies are scanty. Lat. 25° 48', long. 67° 50'. E.I.C. Ms. Doc.

POOLAJEE, in Beloochistan, a small town of Cutch Gundava, at the southern base of the mountains inclosing the valley of Kahun, and connecting the highlands of Hurrund and Dajel with the Hala range. Here, in the beginning of May 1840, was the rendezvous of a British force marching to garrison Kahun, and thence subsequently, in the close of the following August, an expedition, under Major Clibborn, proceeded to relieve that post. After circumstances beyond human control had caused a disastrous result to the attempt of Major Clibborn, he fell back on Poolajee, with the loss of artillery, ammunition, stores of various kinds, all the beasts of burthen allotted to the expedition, and one hundred and seventy-nine men killed, ninety-two more being wounded. A month afterwards, the garrison of Kahun, having E.I.C. Ms. Doc.; Masson, Kalat, 332.

evacuated that fort, reached Poolajee in safety.—(See KARUN.) Water is obtained in wells at Poolajee, and the immediate vicinity yields supplies in moderate quantities. The heat in summer is probably as great as in any part of the world. Lat. 29° 3', long. 68° 30'.

POOLKEE, in Seistan, a great ruined town on the right bank of the Helmund, which here flows through a narrow tract of great fertility. The remains of this once extensive and flourishing city exhibit the ruins of ramparts, houses, and gardens, covering an extent of at least sixteen square miles. The river is here about two hundred yards broad, not fordable, and very picturesque. The beautiful and fertile country, formerly densely peopled and highly cultivated, is now occupied only by a few nomadic Belooches, who live in tents, never free from the terror of attacks from their fiercer and more predatory countrymen. Lat. 62° 30', long. 30° 30'.

E.I.C. Ms. Doc.

POOLSINGEE, in Afghanistan, a village six miles south of Kilat-i-Ghiljie, on the road to Kandahar. Lat. 32° 4', long. 66° 44'.

Pott. Belooch. 169.

POORA, in Beloochistan, a town on the route from Nooshky to Bunpoor, and two hundred and fifty miles south-west of the former town. It is neatly built, and is situate amidst groves of palm-trees, yielding fine dates, and forming the principal wealth of the inhabitants. This town, with its vicinity, originally held by the Mulikuh sept of Belooches, passed, by the event of war, to the Urbabis, whose chief, the Sirdar of Bunpoor, now holds it. Pottinger describes this people as the fairest tribe of Belooches which he met with, and adds, "there is a peculiar elevation in their countenances that pre-eminently distinguishes them amongst their countrymen. They are, without almost an exception, tall, handsome men, with great indications of activity. Their predatory character, on which they pride themselves, is sufficiently proved by their deeds." It seems, therefore, that the dignity of their physiognomical character is little in accordance with their habits of life. The population of Poora is about 2,000. Lat. 28° 17', long. 61° 57'.

Masson, Bal. Afg. Panj. ii. 31; Jour. As. Soc. Beng. 1839, p. 197, Carless, Mem. on Province of Lus.

POORALLY, a river of Beloochistan, rising in Jhalawan, flowing southward into Lus, and falling into the Indian Ocean in lat. 25° 23', long. 66° 30', a few miles west of Sonmeanee, after a course of a hundred miles. It is a shallow stream, running over a wide rocky or sandy bed; but when swelled by rains it becomes a furious torrent, sweeping along with it trees and stones. The trifling cultivation in the province of Lus is, for the most part, confined to its vicinity.

POORANAH, in the Punjab, a village situate in lat. 33° 24', long. 72° 29'. <small>Walker's Map of N.W. Frontier.</small>

POORANUH, in the Punjab, a village fourteen miles east of Julalpoor, and on the road from Jelam to Ramnuggur. Lat. 32', 46', long. 73° 30'. <small>E.I.C. Ms. Doc.</small>

POORUR, in Bhawlpoor, a village situate on an offset of the Indus, about five miles from the main stream. Lat. 28° 36', long. 70° 10'. <small>E.I.C. Ms. Doc.</small>

PORANADERA, in Sinde, a town on the route from Sehwan to Larkhana, and thirty-four miles north of the former town. It is situate a mile west of the right bank of the Indus, in a level fertile country, cultivated to a considerable extent. Lat. 26° 50', long. 67° 55'. <small>E.I.C. Ms. Doc.</small>

POREWALA, in the Punjab, a village situate in lat. 33° 41', long. 73° 5'.

POSHIANA, in the north of the Punjab, a small town near the highest part of the Pir Panjal Pass, or Nandan Sar Pass, into Kashmir. It is 9,500 feet above the sea, and the inhabitants, 600 or 800 in number, are supported by the intercourse on this route, the neighbouring country being too barren to yield them subsistence. Lat. 33° 33', long. 74° 23'. <small>Vigne, Kashmir, i. 269; Moorcr. Punj. Bokh. ii. 296.</small>

POTA, in Afghanistan, a village of the district of Jelalabad, is situate on the right bank of the Soorkh Rood, forty miles above its confluence with the Kabool river. Lat. 34° 14', long. 69° 58'. <small>E.I.C. Ms. Doc.</small>

POTEE, in Western Afghanistan, a village in the hilly country south of Lake Ab-i-stada, and on the route from Ghuznee to Shawl, ninety miles north of the latter place. It is situate near the left or southern bank of the Soorkh-Ab. It is inhabited by Barukzye Duranis, and exhibits cultivation sufficient to afford some scanty supplies. Lat. 31° 22', long. 67° 20'. <small>E.I.C. Ms. Doc.</small>

POULAUND, in Afghanistan, a village situate a little north of the road from Giriskh to Herat. Lat. 32° 20', long. 63° 52'. <small>E.I.C. Ms. Doc.</small>

POWAR GOTE, in Sinde, a village on the route from Hyderabad to Sehwan, and five miles north-west of the former town. The road in this part of the route is heavy with sand. Lat. 25° 25', long. 68° 18'. <small>E.I.C. Ms. Doc.</small>

POWAR GOTE, in Sinde, a village on the route from Sehwan to Larkhana, and seventeen miles north of the former town. It is situate on a considerable offset from the Indus, and a mile and a half from the main channel of the river. Lat. 26° 36′, long. 67° 55′.

E.I.C. Ms. Doc.

POWHUR, in Sinde, a village on the route from Hyderabad to Sehwan, and sixteen miles south-east of the former town. It is situate two miles west of the Indus, near the southern extremity of a *dund*, or small lake, replenished by that river during inundation. Lat. 26° 8′, long. 68° 2′.

E.I.C. Ms. Doc.

PUBB MOUNTAINS,[1] extending southward from the Hala range, and forming a natural boundary between the Beloochee province of Lus and Sinde. If we consider their northern limit to be in lat. 26°, where the Hala range becomes contracted to about thirty miles in breadth,[2] and their southern to be Cape Monze, their length will be found to be about ninety miles. In lat. 25° 3′, long. 66° 50′, they are crossed by the route from Kurrachee to Sonmeanee, at the pass of Guncloba, described by Hart[3] as " stony, of trifling ascent, and the descent equally gentle." The highest part appears to be about lat. 25° 30′, where native report represents the elevation as great, though it does not probably exceed that of the mountains of Western Sinde, considered to be about 2,000 feet.[4]

[1] E.I.C. Ms. Doc.; Masson, Kalat, 296; Jour. As. Soc. Beng. 1840, p. 135, Hart, Jour. from Kurrachee to Hinglaj.
[2] Pott. Belooch. 252.
[3] Ut supra, 135.
[4] Burnes, Bokh. iii. 265.

Boileau, Rajwara, Map.

PUBBERWALEE, in Bhawlpoor, a village between the town of Bhawlpoor and fort of Delawur, and eighteen miles south-west of the former place. It is situate on a canal, which conveys from the Indus a supply of water indispensable for irrigation, and even for the support of life in this arid region. Lat. 29° 11′, long. 71° 30′.

E.I.C. Ms. Doc.

PUCHKOOA, in the Punjab, a village situate on the left bank of the river Ravee, and in lat. 30° 30′, long. 72° 19′.

E.I.C. Ms. Doc.

PUDU DAVI, in the Punjab, a village thirty miles west of the town of Chumba, and situate in lat. 32° 26′, long. 75° 28′.

E.I.C. Ms. Doc.; Baber, Mem. 147; Wood's Oxus, 176; Moorcr. Punj. Bokh. ii. 384.

PUGHMAN, PEMGHAN, or PAMGHAN, a range of mountains in Afghanistan. It is a subordinate range to that of Hindoo Koosh, running along its southern base for about a hundred miles, in a direction in some degree parallel to the crest of that stupendous chain, and in general from north-east to south-west. Its northern face forms the southern boundary to the level and fertile valley of Ghorbund; its south-eastern brow overhangs the country near the town of Kabool and the delightful region of the Koh Daman, which is watered by numerous streams flowing from it. Though close to the location of British engineers for a considerable length of time, the elevation of its highest part has not been correctly ascertained, but it cannot be less than about 10,000 feet, and probably far exceeds that amount, as Baber, whose statements are usually very accurate, mentions that it is always covered with snow. By some it has been estimated as high as 13,000. These mountains are of primary formation. They are bleak, barren, and destitute of vegetation. From this destitution, and the uniformity of their appearance, they add little to the beauty of the scenery. Lat. 34° 40′, long. 68° 40′.

PUGMAN, or PEMGHAN,[1] in Afghanistan, a small town and fort in the Koh Daman, and thirteen miles west of Kabool. It is situate on a small feeder of the Kabool river, and at the eastern base of the snowy mountains of Pemghan. Baber,[2] in reference to Istalif and some other places in the vicinity, observes, that though not to be compared to them " in respect to grapes and fruits," it is beyond all comparison superior to them in point of climate. Lat. 34° 32′, long. 68° 51′.

[1] E.I.C. Ms. Doc.
[2] Memoirs, 147.

PUKATANGEE, in Afghanistan, a village situate on the river Kooner, fifteen miles north-east of Jelalabad. Lat. 34° 27′, long. 70° 40′.

E.I.C. Ms. Doc.

PUKLI,[1] in the north of the Punjab, a small tract east of the Indus. It is very fertile, and yields the Sikh government about a lac of rupees annually. Runjeet Singh obtained possession of it about twenty years ago, by expelling the Mahometan chief, Poyndu Khan, who took refuge in the island of Chuttoorbye, in the Indus, where he has maintained his independence. It is generally supposed to be the Peuceolatis[2] of Arrian, but erroneously, as that (Lib. iv. 22) was on the west side of the river, and Pukli,[3] is on the east. Lat. 34° 15′—34° 30′, long. 72° 50′—73° 15′.

[1] Burnes, Pol. Power of the Sikhs, 1; Wilson, Ariana Antiqua, 185; Ayeen Akbery, ii. 189.
[2] Rennell, 116.
[3] Jour. As. Soc. Beng. 1835, p. 393, 394, Court, Conjectures on the March of Alexander.

PULALUK, in Afghanistan,[1] a town on the route from Nooshky to Furrah, and a hundred and fifty miles north-west of the former place. It is situate on the left or southern bank of the Helmund, which, when seen at this place by Christie,[2] at the end of March, was " four hundred yards wide, very deep, and with uncommonly fine water." The current of the river here appears to have excavated a valley, which extends about half a mile from

[1] Jour. As. Soc. Beng. 1840, p. 724, Conolly (E.), Sketch of the Physical Geog. of Seistan, Map.
[2] App. to Pott. Belooch. 406.

each bank, and is bounded right and left by perpendicular cliffs, the brows of which, on both sides, are level with the desert. The narrow valley extending between those cliffs is fertile, and where cultivated and irrigated, by means of channels from the river, highly productive. When left in a state of nature, it becomes overrun with tamarisk jungle, and affords good grazing, in lat. 30° 30′, long. 62° 42′.

PUL-I-MALAN, in Western Afghanistan, a bridge near Herat, over the Herirood, which is itself sometimes called by the name of Pul-i-Malan. (See HERIROOD.)

E.I.C. Ms. Doc. PULLEEJA, in Sinde, a village situate on the left bank of the Indus, in lat. 27° 32′, long. 68° 25′.

E.I.C. Ms. Doc. PULLEEJA, in Sinde, a village on the road from Larkhana to Shikarpoor. Lat. 27° 48′, long. 68° 35′.

E.I.C. Ms. Doc. PULUNG, in Sinde, a village on the western route from Roree to Hyderabad, and fifteen miles west of the former town. Lat. 27° 40′, long. 68° 39′.

E.I.C. Ms. Doc. PUMJA GOTE, in Sinde, a village on the route from Hyderabad to Lucput, and seventy miles south of the former town. It is situate near the Goongroo offset of the Indus. Lat. 24° 25′, long. 68° 19′.

[1] Vigne, Kashmir, i. 248; F. Von Hugel, Kaschmir, i. 359; Moorcr. Punj. Bokh. ii. 293.

PUNCH,[1] in the Northern Punjab, a small town on the southern slope of the mountains bounding Kashmir on the south. It is situate at the foot of the Punch Pass, and on the banks of a river of the same name, discharging itself into the Chenaub. It was formerly the capital of a small independent *raj*, the raja of which was slain by Gulab Singh, the Sikh chief, who exposed his head, and that of his nephew, in an iron cage. At Punch, two much-frequented routes from the Punjab to Kashmir, that by Koteli and that by Rajawur, meet and proceed thence northward,

[2] Vigne, i. 249.
[3] Jacquemont, Voy. v. 166.

through the Baramula Pass. Elevation of the Punch Pass,[2] 8,500 feet; of the town, 3,280.[3] Punch is in lat. 33° 51′, long. 73° 53′.

PUNCH RIVER, in the Punjab, rises on the south-western declivity of the Pir Panjal Pass, about lat. 33° 33′, long. 74° 20′, and takes a direction generally north-westerly down the valley, dividing the Pir Panjal from the Ratan Panjal. After continuing in that direction for about fifty miles, it, close to the town of Punch, receives a feeder from the north, and below the confluence

[1] Punj. Bokh. ii. 297.

turns to the south-west. Here it is styled by Moorcroft[1] a rivulet, but Jacquemont, who mentions it under the name of

Tchaomok,[2] describes it as a torrent so rapid and powerful, that there is much danger in fording it, insomuch that a horse which loses its footing is swept down the stream, and irretrievably perishes. Holding a south-westerly course of about fifty miles, it, near Koteli, receives a considerable feeder, called the river of Rajour,[3] and is supposed ultimately to fall into the Chenaub. There is much obscurity, however, concerning the lower part of its course.

[2] Voyage, v. 165.
[3] Vigne, Kashmir, i. 251.

PUNCHSHIR,[1] or PUNJSHIR (five lions), in Afghanistan, an extensive valley furrowing the southern side of Hindoo Koosh. It extends for about sixty miles in a south-westerly direction, from the Khawak Pass, in lat. 35° 42′, long. 69° 53,′ to the *dasht* of Begram. The upper extremity has an elevation of 13,200 feet,[2] the lower of about 7,000. The general breadth is about a mile and a half, and it nowhere exceeds three miles. Numerous streams flow down from the inclosing ridges, and discharge themselves into the main river of Punchshir. The inhabitants are careful cultivators, and make the most of their sterile soil, which, scarcely producing a tree of spontaneous growth, is covered with orchards and groves of mulberry and other fruit trees, furnishing the principal means of subsistence to the population. The staple article of food is bread made of mulberries, dried and ground into flour.[3] Every spot capable of producing grain is carefully and successfully cultivated. According to the statement of Wood,[4] who traversed this valley, "though limited in range, the scenery of Punchshir is soft and beautiful. Its rugged red-tinged surface is dotted over with castellated dwellings, whose square-corner towers and solid walls, rising on every knoll, are relieved by the smiling foliage of fruit trees, and the lively green of the garden-like fields which surround them."

[1] E.I.C. Ms. Doc.; Baber, Mem. 145.
[2] Wood's Oxus, 416.
[3] Wood, ut supra, 419.
[4] 418; Elph. Acc. of Caubul, 313.

The people are Tajiks, considered to be of Persian descent, and their dispositions and habits are little in harmony with the fair scene described by Wood. Industry seems almost their only virtue. They are infamous for their rapacious and sanguinary crimes, and the valley is a scene of unceasing intestine wars. Notwithstanding this, the population is dense, and on an occasion calling forth public feeling, and suppressing for a time internal hostility, the valley could furnish ten thousand armed men. The inhabitants fight with firelocks and swords, and have the reputation of being good soldiers. Their most formidable enemies are the Siyah Posh Kafirs, who hold the mountains and valleys to the south-east of Punchshir, and make frequent inroads into it, never sparing the lives of those who fall into their hands. In night attacks, the cunning and agility of the Siyah Posh give them the advantage; but in day-time, the firelock of the Punchshir bestows on him the superiority over his more rudely armed enemy. The savage character of these conflicting parties completely stops the intercourse between Turkestan and Afghanistan by the Punchshir route,[5] across Hindoo Koosh, probably the easiest known. The same cause prevents the working of the silver[6] and lead mines, which lie in the upper part of the valley.

[5] Leech, Hind. Koosh, 34.
[6] Masson, Bal. Afg. Panj. iii. 168.

The Punchshiris are bigoted Mahometans of the *Sunni* persuasion. The name of Punjshir is supposed to have reference to a tradition concerning five sons of Pandu, an ancient monarch of fabulous renown.

PUNCHSHIR RIVER.—See PUNJSHIR.

PUNDEE, in the province of Sarawan, in Beloochistan, a village thirty-five miles north-west of the town of Kelat. Lat. 29° 20′, long. 66° 21′.

E.I.C. Ms. Doc.

PUNGRIA, in Sinde, a village on the route from Larkhana to Bagh, and twenty-four miles north of the former town. It is situate on a watercourse near the southern border of the *Rum*, *Pat*, or desert of Shikarpoor, yet the adjacent country, though much overrun with jungle, is in several places cultivated. Lat. 27° 50′, long. 68° 10′.

E.I.C. Ms. Doc.

PUNJ DEEN, or PUNJ DEH (five hamlets), in Khorasan, on the route from Herat to Merve, and a hundred and thirty miles north of the former town. It is a stationary camp of Turcomans, and consists of about three hundred tents of black felt, disposed in two squares. These are pitched amidst ruined vineyards and uncultivated fields, giving evidence of former industry and civilization, the fruits of which have been swept away by the devastating inroads of the nomadic tribes who now hold the soil. The tents are comfortable dwellings, being well provided with fine carpets and other furniture suitable for a migratory race. The Turcoman inmates are rather fair and handsome, though of Tartar physiognomy. They are described by Abbott as living in rude plenty, and, though in general lawless slave-dealers, to

Abbott, Heraut and Khiva, i. 20.

be scrupulous in observing the rules of conventional hospitality. Punj Deh is a frontier post of the kingdom of Khaurism, or the dominions of the Khan of Khiva. Lat. 36° 4', long. 62° 41'.

PUNJAB,[1] THE, an extensive territory on the north-west of India, so called from two Persian words,* signifying "five waters," the name having reference to five great rivers which flow through it. With respect to the propriety of the designation, it is, however, to be observed, that there are in fact six rivers, the Indus, the Jailum, the Chenaub, the Ravee, the Beas, and the Sutlej; but as the Beas has a much shorter course than the others, it seems to have been disregarded when the name of the country was bestowed. In semi-civilized states, and especially in those of Asia, the boundaries, at all times ill-defined, are subject to frequent changes; and this holds true in regard to the territory belonging to the independent Sikhs, a consequence of their incessant wars with their neighbours to the north and west. Any determination of boundary in these directions must therefore be in some degree arbitrary. In the present case the Punjab will be regarded as co-extensive with the empire of the independent Sikhs, with the exception of Peshawer and Damaun, or the Derajat, the two provinces of the Sikh empire, which are situated west of the Indus: these form the subject of separate articles, which appear under their respective names. If the Punjab be considered (as in this view it will) to include the recent conquests of the Sikhs over Iskardo,[2] Ladakh,[3] and some other hill states of less importance, it will be found to possess natural limits remarkably well defined. They are as follows:—on the north, the great mountain range, forming the extension of Hindoo Koosh to the east, and known variously by the names of Kouenlun, Mooz Taugh, and Karakorum;† on the north-west and west, the Indus; on the east and south-east, the river Sutlej and its continuation, the Ghara. The shape in outline approaches that of the sector of a circle, the centre of which is at the confluence of the Punjnud and the Indus, in lat. 28° 55', long. 70° 28'; the extreme radii, the Indus, holding in general a direction not greatly varying from north to south; the Sutlej and its continuation, the Ghara, holding a direction from north-east to south-west;

[1] Wilson, Ariana Antiqua, 195; Rennell, 80.

[2] Vigne, Kashmir, ii. 374.
[3] F. Von Hugel, Kaschmir, iv. 140.

* پنجاب from پنج "five," and آب "water."
† See Hindoo Koosh.

the arc in its highest latitude touching the 36th parallel. The most western point is the confluence of the Punjnud and Indus; the most eastern is about the 78th meridian. The length from north-east to south-west, from Nobra in Ladakh to the confluence of the Indus and Punjnud, is about six hundred miles; the breadth, measured at right angles to this from the Sutlej near Rampur, to the Indus at Derbend, about three hundred and fifty; the superficial extent, one hundred and twenty-five thousand square miles.* The outline of the extreme territory is almost completely formed by the course of the Indus and that of the Sutlej and its prolongation: the included region is watered or drained by those two great rivers or their feeders, and by the Beas, Ravee, Chenaub, Jailum, and a few others of less magnitude. The country thus marked out is bounded on the north by Bolor, or the unexplored mountain waste, lying between Yarkund and the Kouenlun range, and by Great Tibet; on the east, by Great Tibet and the hill provinces of British India; on the south-east and south, by British India and the state of Bhawlpoor; on the west, by Afghanistan; and on the extreme north-west, by the small territory of the independent Dards, by Yessen, Gilgit, and some other petty states.[4]

[4] Moorer, Punj. Bokh. ii. 264-271; Vigne, Kashmir, ii. 304-311; Jour. As. Soc. Beng. 1839, p.313, Court, Alexander's Exploits on the Western Bank of the Indus.

* If to this were added the dominions to the west of the Indus, comprising the Daman and Peshawer, containing about 10,000 square miles, the total area of the Sikh empire will be 135,000 square miles. A formal division of the Sikh realm might be thus stated:—

  Plain of the Punjab.
  Doab of Julunder.
  ——— Barie.
  ——— Rechna.
  ——— Jinhut.
  ——— Sindh Sagur.
 Mountain region:
  Country of Gukkers, and neighbouring tribes west of Kashmir.
  Kashmir.
  Rajpoot country east and south-east of Kashmir.
  Ladakh.
  Bulti.
 Territory west of the Indus:
  Derajat or Daman.
  Peshawer.

In addition to this great realm, the ruler of the Punjab holds on the left bank of the Sutlej, and under British protection and control, possessions as considerable as to yield an annual revenue equal to 75,000*l.* sterling.

Jacquemont, v. 46; Prinsep, Life of Runjeet Singh, 184.

No two regions can differ more in physical character than the northern and southern part of this territory. The former is throughout a maze of mountains, in general covered with perpetual snow, and in many places rising into summits not inferior in elevation to any of which there are ascertained measurements. Thus, the height of the mountains on the left bank of the Indus in Rupshu and in the north of Spiti is fixed by Gerard's[5] observation at 27,000 feet, and has been considered by Vigne[6] to be not less than 30,000. These vast masses may be classed into two groups; the southern constituting the western extremity of the Himalaya; the northern separated from the former by the great valley of the Indus, and known as the eastern part of the Hindoo Koosh, or by the names of Kouenlun, Mooz Taugh, and Karakorum. Of these, the southern or Himalayan group has, in consequence of the contact of European civilization, been the better explored, and more full and accurate particulars of its vast elevation have been registered. The statements made with regard to the greatest height of the northern group are vague and unsatisfactory. For instance, Vigne,[7] who reached the actual elevation of 16,000 feet in the mountains of Nubra, reports his having seen from thence that "the snowy sierra of the Muztak, extending from Hunzeh to Nubra, arose with conspicuous and most majestic grandeur."

[5] Koonawur, 6.
[6] Kashmir, ii. 340
[7] Id. 358.

The western Himalaya, or southern group, seen from the plain of the eastern Punjab, appears an unbroken chain of snow-clad summits, surpassing in majestic effect those rising farther east, between Undes and Hindostan.[8] Yet, on closer examination, these stupendous ranges are found to embosom many extensive and fertile valleys, forming the hill states of Kulu, Lahoul, and several others. In this range Hügel[9] mentions the following, occurring in the direction from east to west, as pre-eminent in height and grandeur:—the Mori, the Sansh range, the Buldawa, the Tricota, and the Ratan Panjal. The heights of none of these appear to be accurately determined, with the exception of that of the Ratan Punjal, which reaches 11,600 feet.[1] Westward still are the mountains in Kashmir, in few places exceeding 15,000 or 16,000 feet.* The mountains in general diminish in height as they stretch westward towards the valley, through which the Indus flows to the south; yet close to the

[8] P. Von Hugel, Kaschmir, ii. 157.
[9] Id. 157-163.
[1] F. Von Hugel, ii. 162.

* See Kashmir, table of heights.

bank of that river the summits of the Diarmul exhibit an elevation and grandeur scarcely inferior to any in the Himalaya. As seen by Vigne,[2] "mountain seemed piled upon mountain to sustain a most stupendous confusion of mist and glacier glistening with the dazzling and reciprocated brightness of snow and sunbeam, and whose outlines, pre-eminently bold, precipitous, and majestic, were rendered still more so by being discernible only for an instant."

[2] Kashmir, ii. 296.

The mountains inclosing the valley of the Indus are generally of primitive formation, granite,[3] felspar, quartz, gneiss, mica slate, roofing slate. The elevated table-land of Deotsun is of granite. In Rupshu, Spiti, and the adjacent part of Ladakh, mountain ranges of great extent and vast height have been ascertained to consist of secondary formations, in many places abounding with fossil remains.[4] In Kashmir and the adjacent regions, the prevailing rocks are those generally attributed to volcanic action, such as basalt,[5] trap, and gypsum, and these are overlaid in some parts with vast masses of limestone, containing numerous organic relics. Jacquemont[6] enumerates, as the prevailing rocks of this region, sienitic granite, quartz of various colours, grauwacke, limestone, schistose rocks of various forms, in general in transition from grauwacke to limestone, oolitic iron ore.

[3] Moorcr. i. 268; Vigne, ii. 261.

[4] As. Res. xviii. 264, Gerard, Obs. on the Spiti Valley.
[5] Vigne, i. 275; Moorcr. Punj. Bokh. ii. 199.
[6] Voyage, v. 315.

If a line be drawn in a north-westerly direction from the Sutlej, close to Ropur, and in lat. 31°, long. 76° 30', to Torbela, on the Indus, in lat. 34° 18', long. 72° 44', the section of the Sikh territory to the north-east of it, comprising about three-sevenths of the portion east of the Indus, will, with little exception, be found to be an Alpine region, with an elevation scarcely anywhere short of 5,000 feet, for the most part varying from 10,000 to 20,000, and in some instances approaching to 30,000. South-west of the supposed line, the surface slopes rapidly to the alluvial plain of the Punjab, which stretches in that direction several hundred miles, with scarcely any considerable eminences, except the salt range, connected with the southern base of the Himalaya by a maze of hills, forming a very rough, rocky, and difficult country.[7] Burnes,[8] who describes it as "a mountainous and rugged country, of great strength," says —"Our road lay in ravines. The chaos of rocks, their vertical strata terminating in needles from decomposition, the round pebbles that lay imbedded in the sandstone, and the wild scenery,

[7] Hough's Narr. Exp. in Afg. 338-345; Elph. Acc. of Caubul, 78.
[8] Burnes' Bokh. i. 63.

made this an interesting neighbourhood." About the town of Mundi, near the eastern frontier, and on the upper course of the Beas, in the most southern and lower ranges of the Himalaya, is an extensive tract of rocks and deposits, of recent formation,[9] of limestone, sandstone, gypsum, argillaceous slate, amidst which veins of quartz occasionally occur. This formation is important, in consequence of containing inexhaustible beds of fossil salt,* very compact and heavy, and of a reddish colour. On the west of the Punjab, and crossing the Doab, between the Jailum and the Indus, is the Salt range, which is cross-cut by the channel of the Indus, and which, to the north of the Daman, on the western side of that river, joins the Suliman and Khyber ranges. The Salt range,[1] sometimes (on the west of the Indus) called the Kalabagh range, holds a direction a little south of east, between lat. 32° 30'—33°, and terminates rather abruptly on the right bank of the river Jailum.[2] The elevation is not great, probably in few places exceeding 2,000[3] feet above the sea. The formations[4] composing it are grauwacke, limestone, sandstone, gypsum, and red tenacious clay, investing enormous deposits of common salt, or chloride of sodium. (See SALT RANGE and PIND DADUN KHAN.)

[9] Jacquemont, v. 318.

[1] Elph. Acc. of Caubul, 103; Wood, Oxus, 132; Burnes' Pers. Narr. 93.
[2] Jacquem. v. 109.
[3] Burnes' Bokh. i. 52.
[4] Jacquem. v. 109-116; Burnes, ib.

Altogether, the ascertained mineral wealth of the Punjab and its dependencies appears scanty in proportion to the great extent of its mountains. Gold is found in the sands of the streams of Bulti[5] and Ladakh,[6] also in those of the Chenaub,[7] the Huroo, and the Swan. Kashmir yields copper, lead, and iron.[8] Graphite or plumbago abounds in the Pir Panjal, bounding Kashmir on the south-west.[9] Iron is also raised in Mundi,[1] as well as common salt. The Salt range, besides the mineral from which it is named, produces antimony, alum, and sulphur. Nitre[2] is obtained in abundance from the alluvial plains. Coal[3] exists about the Salt range at Mukkud, on the left bank of the Indus, and in the localities of Joa, Meealee, and Nummul.[4]†

[5] Vigne, Kashmir, ii. 245, 287; Jour. As. Soc. Beng. 1835, p. 593, Wade, on Iskardoh.
[6] Moorcr. Punj. Bokh. i. 318; Id. in Jour. Royal As. Soc. 1824, p. 52.
[7] Burnes' Bokh. i. 80; ii. 401.
[8] F. Von Hugel, ii. 244, 245; Moorcr. ii. 162.
[9] F. Von Hugel, ii. 245.
[1] Moorcr. i. 175.
[2] Burnes' Bokh. ii. 402.
[3] Burnes, Rep. on Coal, 79.
[4] Wood, Rep. on Coal, 80.

* Moorcroft[1] states that the salt of this tract is found in grauwacke: the occurrence of this rock is not mentioned by Jacquemont.[2]

† Dr. Jameson,[1] an agent of the Anglo-Indian government, despatched to obtain information respecting the coal measures which Wood and Burnes reported they had examined in the Salt range, stated his opinion as follows:—" To the question, Is any good coal to be found in quantity in this

[1] Punj. Bokh. i. 159.
[2] Voyage, v. 318, 319.
[1] Jour. As. Soc. Beng. 1842, p. 2.

TABLE OF HEIGHTS.

		FEET
[1] Gerard, Alex., Koonawur, 6.	Summit on the left bank of the Indus, in Rupshu,[1] lat. 33° 20′, long. 78°	27,000
[2] As. Res. xviii. 255, Gerard, J. G., Obs. on Spiti.	Summit on frontier of Rupshu and Spiti,[2] about lat. 33°, long. 78° 30′	24,000
[3] Id. ut supra, 256.	Limit of perpetual snow in Northern Spiti,[3] lat. 33° 30′, long. 78° 40′	22,000
[4] Id. ut supra, 254.	Highest summit ascended by Gerard[4] on eastern frontier of Spiti, lat. 33° 5′, long. 78° 40′	20,400
[5] Id. ut supra, 359.	Mountain[5] rising north of Lake Chamoreril, lat. 33°, long. 78°	20,000
[6] Vigne, Kashmir, ii. 204.	Diarmul or Nanga Parbut mountain,[6] north of Kashmir, lat. 35° 10′, long. 74° 20′	19,000
[7] Jour. As. Soc. Beng. 1841, p. 2, Broome and Cunningham, Jour. to Sources of Punjab Rivers.	Summit of range[7] between the basins of the Beas and Sutlej, lat. 31° 40′, long. 77° 20′	18,000
[8] Gerard, quoted in note on Moorcr. Punj. Bokh. i. 215.	Lacha[8] range, between Lahoul and Rupshu, lat. 32° 40′, long. 77° 20′	17,000
[9] As. Jour. May—Aug. 1831, p. 90, Gerard, Jour. to Ladakh.	Bara Lacha, or Para Lassa Pass,[9] over Lacha range, about same lat. and long. as last	16,500
[1] Falconer, as quoted in Royle's Bot. of Himalaya, Introd. xxiv.	Skora,[1] a summit in Kouenlun or Mooz Taugh, north of Bultistan, about lat. 35° 30′, long. 76°	16,200
[2] Gerard, as quoted in note to Moorcr. i. 215.	Source of Surajbaga,[2] branch of the Chenaub, lat. 33° 12′, long. 77° 22′	16,200
[3] Vigne, Kashmir, ii. 358.	Pass in the mountains north of Le,[3] lat. 34° 15′, long. 77° 20′	16,000
[4] As. Res. xviii. 253, Gerard, Obs. on Spiti.	Table-land of Rupshu,[4] lat. 33°, long. 78°	16,000

district? we would at once answer, decidedly not." This *dictum* will probably seem precipitate and rash to those who know that the important coal fields of Flintshire, Denbighshire, and Gloucestershire are connected with the saliferous deposits of Cheshire and Worcestershire. It would be at once idle and illiberal to detract from the merits of the valuable information which Dr. Jameson has given respecting the Punjab,[2] but in such inquiries it is always well to remember Bacon's maxim,—" Prudens interrogatio dimidium scientiæ."

[2] Id. 1845, pp. 183, 226.

PUNJAB. 121

	FEET.	
Pass in Bultistan, between Iskardoh and Astor,[5] lat. 35° 14′, long. 75°	15,822	[5] Falconer, in Royle's Bot. Him. Introd. xxvi.
Kalee Debee Pass,[6] between Tandi and Chumba, lat. 32° 38′, long. 76° 24′	15,700	[6] Jour. As. Soc. Beng. 1841, p. 108, Cunningham, Jour. to Sources of Punjab Rivers.
Boorgee Pass,[7] about lat. 35°, long. 75°	15,600	[7] Falconer, in Royle's Introd. xxiv.
Thogjichenmo Lake,[8] in Rupshu, lat. 33° 18′, long. 77° 50′	15,500	[8] As. Res. xviii. 260, Gerard, on Spiti.
Chamoreril Lake,[9] in Rupshu, lat. 32° 45′, long. 78° 20′	15,000	[9] Gerard, ib.
Tzakala,[1] in Ladakh, lat. 33° 20′, long. 78° 45′	15,000	[1] Moorcr. i. 438.
Ritanka, or Rotung Pass,[2] lat. 32° 36′, long. 77° 11′	*13,300	[2] Moorcr. i. 191.
Source of the Beas,[3] lat. 32° 34′, long. 77° 10′	†13,200	[3] Moorcr. i. 187.
Deotsuh,[4] elevated desert between Kashmir and Iskardoh, lat. 34° 30′, long. 75°	13,100	[4] Falconer, in Royle, Introd. xxiv.
Chaol Ghaut,[5] in Kooloo, between the basins of the Beas and Sutlej, lat. 31° 50′, long. 77° 10′	10,170	[5] Broome and Cunningham, 2.
Koksur,[6] in Lahoul, lat. 32° 37′, long. 77° 10′	10,053	[6] Id. 5.
Le,[7] ‡ lat. 34° 11′, long. 77° 14′	10,000	[7] Vigne, Kashmir, ii. 341.
Tandi, in Lahoul,[8] lat. 32° 42′, long. 76° 57′	10,000	[8] As. Jour. May—Aug. 1831, p. 90, Gerard, Jour. to Ladakh.
Mount over Acho Hamlet,[9] and confluence of Hasora and Indus, lat. 35° 18′, long. 74° 25′	9,000	[9] Vigne, Kashmir, ii 302.
Chuarhoo,[10] in the north-east of the Punjab, lat. 32° 17′, long. 75° 46′	8,041	[10] Broome and Cunningham, 111.
Pass over the Ratan Panjal,[1] on the route from Lahore to Kashmir, lat. 33° 30′, long. 74° 16′	7,350	[1] Id. 113.
Gurys Valley,[2] north-east of Kashmir, lat. 34° 33′, long. 74° 36′	7,200	[2] Vigne, Kashmir, ii. 207.
Gau Ghautee,[3] in Kooloo, lat. 31° 35′, long. 77° 30′	7,093	[3] Broome and Cunningham, 1.
Burmawur,[4] in the north-east of the Punjab, lat. 32° 30′, long. 76° 30′	7,015	[4] Id. 108.
Hyderabad,[5] on the route from Punch to Baramula, lat. 34° 4′, long. 73° 54′	6,494	[5] Jacquem. v. 172.

* According to Broome, 13,000 feet.
† According to Broome, 12,941 feet.
‡ According to Moorcroft, more than 11,000 feet.

Jour. As. Soc. Beng. 1841, p. 4. i. 259.

122   PUNJAB.

		FEET
[6] Vigne, Kashmir, ii. 260.	Iskardoh,[6] capital of Bulti, lat. 35° 10, long. 75° 27'	6,300
[7] Vigne, i. 252.	Thana,[7] on the route from Lahore to Kashmir by the Pir Panjal Pass, lat. 33° 26', long. 75° 28'	5,000
[8] Id. i. 194.	Budrawar,[8] in the Northern Punjab, between the Chenaub and Ravee, lat. 32° 54', long. 75° 28'	5,000
[9] Jacquem. v. 149.	Town of Punch,[9] lat. 33° 52', long. 73° 52'	3,288
[1] Id. v. 146.	Height above Nekki,[1] about lat. 33° 18', long. 73° 30'	3,270
[2] Id. ib.	Village of Nekki,[2] lat. 33° 16', long. 73° 28'	3,436
[3] Gerard, Koonawur, Tables in Appendix.	Bed of Sutlej,[3] at Rampoor, lat. 32° 26', long. 77° 38'	3,260
[4] Broome and Cunningham, 110.	Chumba,[4] lat. 32° 22', long. 75° 56'	3,015
[5] Id. 113.	Rajawar,[5] lat. 33° 18', long. 74° 14'	2,800
[6] Jacquem. v. 122.	Highest summit of Salt range,[6] lat. about 32° 40', long. 72° 30'	2,150
[7] Broome and Cunningham, 111.	Nurpur,[7] lat. 32° 11', long. 75° 40'	1,924
[8] Jacquem. v. 121.	Village of Tobeur,[8] lat. 32° 26', long. 72° 40'	1,663
[9] Id. v. 143.	Nar,[9] lat. 33° 14', long. 73° 25'	1,624
[1] F. Von Hugel, iii. 140.	Jailum,[1] lat. 33° 2', long. 73° 36'	1,620
[2] Broome and Cunningham, 111.	Puthankot,[2] in the Northern Punjab, at the base of the lowest range of the Himalaya, lat. 32° 13', long. 75° 26'	1,205
	Bed of the Indus at Attok, lat. 33° 54', long. 72° 18'	*1,000
[3] Burnes, Bokh. iii.	Amritsir,[3] lat. 31° 42', long. 74° 47'	900
[4] Id. ib.	Lahore,[4] lat. 31° 36', long. 74° 14'	900
[5] Id. ib.	Confluence of the Indus and Punjnud,[5] lat. 28° 55', long. 70° 28'	220

From the bases of the Salt range and Himalaya, the plain of the Punjab slopes south-west with a regularity rarely broken by

[1] Hough, Narr. of Exp. in Afg. App. 74.

[2] Macartney, in Elph. Acc. of Caubul, 656; Wood, Oxus, 158.

* The height of Peshawer[1] above the sea is 1,068 feet. The stream which passes by Peshawer falls into the Kabool river about fourteen miles below the city, and, as its course lies through a plain, the fall to its confluence probably does not exceed two feet in a mile. From that confluence the course of the Kabool river to its junction with the Indus at Attok is about forty miles, and as it is navigable[2] for this distance, its fall cannot much exceed a foot per mile. This would make the elevation of the bed of the Indus at Attok about 1,000 feet.

PUNJAB.

any eminence of importance. The declivity of the surface from north-east to south-west is proved beyond question by the course of the rivers, which all descend in that direction. Jacquemont[6] considers that the courses of the Sarsouty and Gagra, which, flowing from the Himalaya, are lost in the desert of Bikanir, lie along an elevated tract dividing the basin of the Jumna from that of the Sutlej, and that barometric and other observations prove the plain of the Punjab to be below that of Eastern Hindostan. He thence concludes the bed of the Sutlej, in its course through the plain, to be lower than that of the Jumna; that of the Beas lower than that of the Sutlej, and so in succession westward with regard to the beds of the Ravee, the Chenaub, and the Jailum, to the Indus, flowing through the lowest part of this extensive basin.

[6] Voyage, v. 188.

No country of the same extent probably enjoys more largely than the Punjab the means of irrigation, and of inland navigation, by means of its six noble rivers. The most eastern, the Sutlej,* is generally believed to issue from the lake Rawan Radd,[6] in Undes, in lat. 30° 59′, long. 81°. Holding a south-westerly course of about five hundred miles,† it receives the Beas, below the confluence of which, taking place near Hurekee, and in lat. 31° 12′, long. 74° 55′, the united stream is called the Ghara for about three hundred miles to the confluence of the Trimab; thenceforward the aggregate body of water bears the name of the Punjnud for a further distance of about sixty miles to its confluence with the Indus. Next to the Sutlej, westward, is the Beas,‡ rising in lat. 32° 34′, long. 77° 12′,[7] and holding a sinuous course of about two hundred and twenty miles, in general to the south-west, to its confluence with the Sutlej. Farther to the west flows the Ravee,§ the least in the volume of its water, though not in the

[6] Gerard, Koonawur, 22; As. Res. xii. 469, Moorcr. Jour. to Lake Manasarovara; also, xv. 339, Herbert, Course and Levels of the River Sutlej.

[7] Moorcr. Punj. Bokh. i. 106.

[1] Ritter, Erdkunde Von Asien, iii. 666.

---

* Considered to be the Zadadrus,[1] Hesidrus, Hesudrus, of the classical writers; the Satadru, or Satahrada,[2] "the hundred channelled" of the Sanscrit.

† Gerard[3] considers its length of course to be five hundred and seventy miles, but this appears rather an over-estimate.

‡ Considered to be the Bibasis, Hyphasis, or Hypasis, of the classical writers;[4] the Bipasa, or Vipasa, of the Sanscrit.

§ Considered to be the Hydraotes,[5] or Hyarotes, of the classical writers; the Iravati of the Sanscrit. It is to this day called Iraotee[6] by the natives.

[2] As. Res. xv. 32, Wilson, Hist. of Kashmir; Id. Ariana Antiq.195, Rennell, 78, 82.
[3] Koonawur, 23.
[4] Arrian, vi.c.14; Ritter, Asien, v. 462; Wilson, Ariana Antiq. 195.
[5] Ritter, Erdkunde Von Asien, v. 457; Wilson, Ariana Antiq. 195.
[6] Burnes' Bokh. iii. 124, 397.

length of its course. Issuing from a lake[8] embosomed in the Himalaya, in lat. 32° 30′, long. 76° 36′, it holds a very tortuous course, but generally in a south-westerly direction, for about four hundred and fifty miles to its confluence with the Chenaub. This last-mentioned river,* usually regarded as the largest of the Punjab, flows in general west of that of the Ravee, though its source is more eastward as it sweeps in a wide flexure round the upper part of the smaller rivers. Rising in Lahoul, in lat. 32° 30′, long. 77° 40′,[9] the Chenaub pursues a circuitous course, but for the most part south-west, and at the distance of about five hundred and forty miles from its source, unites with the Jailum near Trimo Ferry.[1] The united stream, proceeding in the same direction for about fifty miles, receives the water of the Ravee;[2] below the confluence it loses the name of Chenaub, and is called the Trimab[3] † for a farther distance of a hundred and ten miles to the junction of the Ghara. From that point the river flows about sixty miles, as before mentioned, to its confluence with the Indus, being called the Punjnud,‡ a name derived from its conveying the accumulated water of the Beas, the Sutlej, the Ravee, the Chenaub, and the Jailum. This last river, the most westerly, except the Indus, rises in Kashmir,[4] the whole valley of which it drains. Soon after its issue therefrom, it receives a large tributary, the Kishenganga, or river of Mazufurabad, and after a course of about four hundred and fifty miles, generally in a south-westerly direction, it unites with the Chenaub near Trimo Ferry.§ The Indus forms the western boundary of the Punjab for about five hundred miles from Derbend, in the north, to the confluence of the Punjnud. These noble streams, besides their inestimable value for the purposes of irrigation, afford means of inland navigation scarcely equalled. Thus the Indus is navigable to Attok,[5] the Jailum to Oin,[6] the Chenaub[7] to Aknur, the Ravee[8] to Lahore, the Sutlej to Ropur.[9] There does not appear to be any direct and certain

---

* Considered to be the Acesines[1] of the classical writers.

† From تری "three," and آب "water."

‡ From پنج "five," and ند "a river."

§ The Jailum is considered to be the Hydaspes[2] of the classical writers; the Bitastha, or Vitastha, of the Sanscrit.

information as to the extent of navigation of the Beas, but as its volume of water is not inferior[1] to that of the Sutlej, it may with probability be concluded that vessels can ascend nearly to its efflux from the base of the Himalaya, or for a distance of about eighty miles. Thus the inland navigation of the Punjab may be stated as follows:—

[1] Macartney, in Elph. 662; Burnes' Bokh. i. 7.

	MILES.
Indus, from Attok to Mittun-kote	480
Punjnud	60
Trimab	110
Jailum, from confluence with the Chenaub to Oin	300
Jailum, in the valley of Kashmir	70
Chenaub, as far as Aknur	300
Ravee, as far as Lahore	180
Beas	80
Ghara	280
Sutlej	100
Total	1,960

In the plain of the Punjab, there are no considerable pieces of standing water. In the mountain region Kashmir contains three lakes—the city Dal,[2] or Lake; the Wulur,[3] and Manasa Bul.[4] In Ladakh are the two great salt lakes—that of Pangkung,[5] and that of Chamomeril;[6] and another, called Thogjichenmo,[7] of much smaller dimensions. There are many other pieces of water in the mountain region, but all of too inconsiderable dimensions to be designated as lakes.

The plain of the Punjab is divided by its rivers into five extensive natural sections, described by the native term *doab*,* signifying a great tongue of land lying in the bifurcation above the confluence* of two rivers. First, the doab of Julinder,[8] between the Sutlej and the Beas; second, the doab of Barie, between the Beas and Ghara on the east, and the Ravee and Trimab on the west; third, the doab of Rechna, between the Ravee and Trimab on the east, and the Chenaub on the west; fourth, the doab of Jinhut, between the Chenaub on the east, and the Jailum on the west; fifth, the doab of Sinde Sagur, between the Jailum,

[2] Moorcr. Punj. Bokh. ii. 111, 240; Vigne, Kashmir, ii. 62, 99; P. Von Hugel, i. 227.
[3] Moorcr. ii. 111; Vigne, ii. 158; F. Von Hugel, ii. 193.
[4] Moorcr. ii. 112; Vigne, ii. 147; F. Von Hugel, ii. 193.
[5] Moorcr. i. 434.
[6] Id. ii. 51; As. Res. xviii. 259, Gerard, Obs. on Spiti Valley; As. Jour. May, Aug. 1831, p. 91, Gerard, Tour in Ladakh.
[7] Moorcr. ii. 47; Gerard, As. Res. xviii. 299.
[8] P. Von Hugel, Kaschmir, i. 54; Ayeen Akbery, ii. 285, 287, 288, 290, 298.

* From دو "two," and آب "water."

Trimab, and Punjnud on the east, and the Indus on the west. Of these, that of Sinde Sagur is the most extensive, but that of Barie by far the most populous, as well as the most important, whether in a political, a commercial, or an agricultural point of view.

The regular and gradual slope of the great plain of the Punjab has been mentioned. Even the upper part is but of moderate elevation. Thus, Amritsir[9] and Lahore[1] are each 900 feet above the level of the sea, Jailum about 1,600, and the surface slopes regularly to the south-western extremity, where close to Mittunkote, the elevation is about 220 feet.[2] In consequence of the nearly unbroken flatness of the surface, the great rivers frequently change their courses in an extraordinary degree. "Bands of sand traverse the country in a north and south direction, which point out the old beds of rivers, and prove that all of them have been changed. The Sutlej, which formerly ran close to the town of Loodianah, is now seven miles to the northward; the Ravee, which twenty years ago washed the walls of the city of Lahore, runs in a channel three miles off to the northward; the Chenaub, which ten or twelve years ago ran close to the town of Ramnuggur, is now four miles distant, and the same applies to the Jailum."[3] So the Ghara, at no great distance of time, held, for above two hundred miles, a course considerably westward of the present and parallel to it.

Elphinstone[4] says, "The fertility of the Punjab appears to have been too much extolled by our geographers; except near rivers, no part will bear a comparison with the British provinces in Hindostan, and still less with Bengal, which it has been thought to resemble. In the part I passed through, the soil was generally sandy and by no means rich; the country nearer the hills was said to be better, and that further to the south worse; of the four divisions (*doabs*) east of the Hydaspes, the two nearest to that river are chiefly pastured on by herds of oxen and buffaloes, and that more to the east, towards the Hysudrus or Sutlej, though most sterile, is best cultivated. The two former are quite flat, the latter is wavy; there is not a hill to the east of the Hydaspes, and rarely a tree, except of the dwarf race of Baubool (*mimosa*). On the whole, not a third of the country we saw was cultivated." The most westerly doab, or that of Sinde Sagur, is probably the least productive, as the Salt range, and the rugged country be-

[9] Burnes' Bokh. iii. 298.
[1] F. Von Hugel, Kaschmir, iii. 142.
[2] Burnes' Bokh. iii. 209.
[3] Jour. As. Soc. Beng. 1843, p. 195, Jameson, Rep. on the Punjab; Jour. As. Soc. Beng. 1837, p. 191, Mackeson, Acc. of Wade's Voyage down the Sutlej.
[4] Acc. of Caubul, 81.

tween it and Attock, extend over it on the north, and the arid wilds, called by Elphinstone[5] the Little Desert, form nearly the whole of the southern part.[6] According to that eminent authority, the Little Desert extends from north to south upwards of two hundred and fifty miles, with a width, which was traversed by him in two marches, probably measuring together between thirty and forty miles. It occupies all that part of the country between the Jailum and the Indus which is not flooded by both those rivers, and extends northward from the thirtieth degree of latitude, where the inundated lands terminate, to the Salt range, seeming to be a part of the great desert of Rajpootana, cut off from the main body by the rivers and their rich banks. The outline being strongly marked and abrupt, the traveller, on leaving the fertile country, at once finds himself amongst sand-hills and the stunted shrubs and plants congenial to such tracts, and must be content with brackish water obtained from wells. The colour of the sand here is grey instead of the reddish-yellow of the Great Desert. The narrow tract, forming the southern part of the doab of Sinde-i-Sagur, is, however, rich and fertile through the entire breadth from one river to the other.[7] In the north also of this doab a tract of great fertility,[8] having a soil of black loam, extends for about thirty miles along the right bank of the Jailum, between the town of that name and Pind Dadun Khan. The small doab of Jinhut, between the Jailum and Chenaub, is barren and little cultivated. Jacquemont,[2] who from the Salt range viewed this doab in nearly its whole extent, describes it as a monotonous plain, broken by only one small hill which rises above the town of Lallee. It is thus noticed by Burnes :—" Nothing, however, can be more miserable than the country between the Acesines and Hydaspes; a sterile waste of underwood, the abode of shepherds, scantily supplied with water, which is sixty-five feet below the surface."[9] The doab of Reechna, though having in general a sandy soil, is a little more fertile and better cultivated than that just noticed. By means of wells, water can everywhere be obtained at a depth not exceeding twenty-five feet.[1] The soil and climate are suitable for the growth of the sugar-cane, and fruits and flowers are produced in great profusion, variety, and luxuriance.[2] Burnes[3] describes a garden visited by him, " as not a hundred yards square, but well stored with fruit-trees and flowers; most of the former," he adds, " were now in blossom, and an enumeration of them

[5] Acc. of Caubul, 25.
[6] Burnes' Bokh. iii. 301.

[7] Id. ib.
[8] Burnes, 56; Jour. As.Soc.Beng.1843, p. 195, Jameson, Rep. on the Punjab.

[8] Voyage, v. 124.

[9] Burnes, ut supra, i. 49.

[1] Id. i. 43.

[2] F. Von Hugel, Kashmir, iii. 155.
[3] Ut supra, i. 41.

would give a favourable idea of this climate: they consisted of the peach, apricot, greengage, fig, pomegranate, quince, orange (sweet and bitter), lime and lemon, guava, grape, mango, jamboo, bair, date, cardamom, almond, and the apple, with seven or eight other kinds, of which I can only give the native names,— the *gooler, sohaujna, goolcheen, umltass, bell, bussoora*. The walks of the garden were lined with beautiful cypresses and weeping willows; and in the flower-beds were the narcissus and rose-bushes of the *sidburg*, or an hundred leaves." "Most of the trees and flowers are indigenous, but many have been introduced." Still the cultivation is very limited in proportion to the qualities of the soil and the facilities for irrigation. From the elevation of the beds of the rivers, watercourses, and sources about the southern base of the mountains, and from the regular uninterrupted slope of the surface of the Punjab to the south, it is obvious that fertilizing streams might be conducted so as to spread abundance over most parts of that fine plain. The upper part of the doab between the Ravee and the Beas is at present sterile, from want of irrigation, as the canals made for this purpose during the Mogul dynasty have been allowed to fall to decay. In consequence of this neglect, the soil has become "a hard, indurated clay; sometimes gravelly, producing thorny shrubs and brambles, called by the natives *jund, kureel* (wild caper bush) and *baubool* (mimosa)."[4] Lower down, the soil of this doab appears, from Masson's[5] report, to be in general strong, and rather fertile, but little cultivated, and in consequence overrun with jungle and small woods. At the southern extremity, in the vicinity of Mooltan, the country is highly productive. According to the statement of Burnes,[6] "the soil amply repays the labour, for such is its strength, that a crop of wheat, before yielding its grain, is twice mowed down as fodder for cattle, and then ears," he continues, " and produces an abundant harvest. The indigo and sugar crops are rich, and one small strip of land, five miles long, which we passed, afforded a revenue of seventy-five thousand rupees." Tobacco, dates, and mangoes are produced in abundance and excellence. Jameson,[7] probably the latest authority on the subject, thus describes the actual state of the Punjab:—"At the present moment, the vast plain presents nothing but a waste, comparatively speaking, with here and there cultivation. Even in the neighbourhood of the very capital itself we meet with ex-

[4] Burnes, i. 10.
[5] Baf. Afg. Panj. i. 450—452.
[6] iii. 305.
[7] Jour. As. Soc. 1843, p. 104, Rep. on the Punjab.

tensive jungles, the luxuriance of their rank vegetation shewing what the country could be made." "We pass over vast uncultivated tracts, with here and there, in the centre of the bushy jungle, a small village, with some rich, cultivated fields around. Now and then, breaking up the monotony of the flat plain, we meet with the hillocks marking the sites of towns and villages which are now no more, but of which the streets and houses have left this memento of their former existence."

The climate of the mountainous regions, Ladakh, Kashmir, Bulti, Kulu, and Lahoul, is described in the respective notices on those places; that of the plain of the Punjab is in general characterized by dryness and warmth. Little rain falls, except in those parts extending along the southern base of the Himalaya, and where the south-west monsoon is partially felt, diminishing in its effect in proportion as it proceeds westward.[8] According to the statement of Elphinstone, the rain "in the north of the Punjab exceeds that of Delhi; but in the south of the Punjab, distant both from the sea and the hills, very little rain falls." Still the rains of the monsoon extend as far as Lahore,[9] and fall heavily there in midsummer. In the more southern part of the plain, the soil, where productive, is rendered so by irrigation. In addition to the facilities offered by the rivers and canals, the Persian wheel is employed to draw to the surface the water of numerous wells. The winters are cool even to the feelings of a European. Elphinstone[1] observes, in regard to his residence in Mooltan, at the end of December: "The weather was delightful during our stay; the thermometer, when at the lowest, was at 28° at sunrise; there were slight frosts in the night." During the march of the English army through this country in 1838, thin ice was formed on the water at the end of December,[2] whilst in the day the thermometer rose to 70°. At the end of December, Elphinstone,[3] marching through the doab between the Chenaub and the Indus, found a very cold wind; but it does not appear that snow falls in this part of the Punjab. Burnes[4] describes the weather in the beginning of February as cold and bleak, frequently rainy, and always cloudy. In January, 1839, the lowest state of the thermometer was found, on different nights of the month, to be respectively[5] 34°, 37°, 38°, 44°. In the day the thermometer, even in midwinter, is seldom below 70°, and in January generally reaches 80°, so that vegetation rapidly proceeds,

[8] Elph. Acc. of Caubul, i. 130; Jacquemont, Voy. v. 161; Vigne, Ghaznee, 16.

[9] Osborne, Court and Camp of Runjeet Singh, 200.

[1] 22.

[2] Hough, App. 58.

[3] 25.

[4] Bokhara, i. 44.

[5] Hough, App. 59, 70.

and the wheat harvest is gathered by the end of April.[6] Such, during winter, is the general temperature of the Punjab south of the Salt range. North of that, and even outside the limits of the mountains, the cold is greater, an effect attributable to a slight increase of elevation rather than to change of latitude. The British, in marching through that tract in December, 1839, found the cold severe, the thermometer during the night sinking to 2° below the freezing point.[7] The heat in summer is excessive; in the plains at Mooltan[8] it is so great as to be proverbial. At Lahore[9] it was found, in the beginning of June, to raise the thermometer to 112°, in a tent artificially cooled. A traveller who experienced the heat of this season describes it as "perfectly intolerable; we are unable," he adds, "to eat, drink, or sleep, and support existence by suction alone."[1] Bernier,[2] who had endured the heat of the most sultry part of Arabia, found that of the country between Lahore and Kashmir much more distressing, and each morning entertained a dread of being unable to survive till the evening. He describes his body as having become as it were a dry sponge, and he no sooner took a draught of water than it oozed from all parts of his skin, from which the cuticle had peeled, leaving the surface covered with pustules. Some of his companions died of heat even in the shade.

The indigenous vegetation of the plain of the Punjab closely resembles that of the drier tracts of Eastern Hindostan: trees are scarce, and there occur extensive tracts,[3] containing only a few bushes, principally babools of the mimosa species. Even the date-palm is, according to Burnes,[4] an exotic, introduced by the Mahometan invaders. The wild palm,[5] a species which produces no fruit, is in many places abundant; as are the *peloo* (Salvadora Persica), various species of willows, the *pepool* (ficus religiosa), divers species of acacias and tamarisk, the byr-apple or ju-jube (zizyphus ju-juba), and capparis, called here *kureel, juwassi*, or camel-thorn; the *talee*, a tree called *sissoo* in Eastern Hindostan, and sometimes of twelve feet girth, useful for boat-building; the *neem* (melia azadurachta), the *mudar* (tropœa), the *toolse* (ocymum sanctum), *kurmul*, or wild rue.[7] Fuel is scarce, in consequence of the general absence of trees, and cow-dung[8] is extensively used for the purpose. The towns and villages of the Punjab are, however, generally surrounded by groves, but these are usually of forced fruit-trees artificially cultivated,—date,[9] orange, pomegranate, mulberry, apple, fig, peach, apricot, plum, quince, almond, and a few others of less importance. The mango is cultivated, but does not attain high perfection except about Mooltan, and deteriorates in proportion to the advance northward.[1]

[9] Vigne, Ghuznee, 24; Masson, i. 19; Burnes, iii. 289.

[1] iv. 30.

The zoology of the Punjab is more rich and varied than its botany. No accounts[2] afford authority for concluding that elephants exist there in a state of nature, for though Arrian mentions the hunting of elephants on the banks of the Indus, the animals in question clearly appear to have been some turned loose by the natives in their hasty flight. Tigers lurk in the jungle and forests, and sometimes attain the enormous length of ten feet.[4] Lions are not uncommon.[5] The other beasts of prey are panthers, leopards, hyenas, lynxes, wolves,[6] bears, jackals, foxes, otters, martins, stoats, and divers other small *viverræ*; there are also nilgaus, wild hogs, porcupines, various animals of the deer, goat, and antelope species, monkeys and bats, including the large and hideous vampyre,[7] deemed sacred by the natives. Among the feathered tribes there are pea-fowl, parrots, jungle-fowl (the wild stock of our common domestic fowl), pheasants, various kinds of partridges, quails, water-fowl in great number and variety, herons, cranes, pelicans,[8] eagles, vultures, hawks, magpies, hoopoes, and doves of various kinds. The bulbul, or nightingale of Kashmir, is inferior in note to that of Europe, but very beautiful. A small species of alligator[9] swarms in the rivers, especially the Jailum. The porpoise ascends the Indus to a great distance. Among serpents, the more remarkable are the cobra di capello,[1] and a small snake, the bite of which is almost immediately fatal. The rivers abound with fish; the pulla, a delicious species of carp, swarming in the Indus,[2] forms an important article of subsistence. Of insects, the silk-worm thrives remarkably, and produces an article of admirable quality; bees also produce wax and honey in great abundance and of the finest kind, and this department of husbandry receives great attention, particularly in Kashmir. The more important domestic animals are the camel[3] (especially in the south) and the buffalo, of which great herds are kept in the neighbourhood of rivers, these animals being almost of an amphibious nature. Horses are bred extensively, especially in the plain country in the north-east, and receive great attention, the Sikhs being an equestrian people.

[2] Vigne, i. 117.

[4] Burnes, iii. 139; F. Von Hugel, i. 130.
[5] Vigne, Ghuznee, 14.
[6] Id. ii. 16; Burnes' Bokh. i. 10; Royle, Bot. of Himalaya, xxv.
[7] F. Von Hugel, i. 122.

[8] Id. ii. 293; Vigne, ii. 21.

[9] Burnes, i. 48; iii. 133.

[1] Vigne, i. 226; Osborne, 180.

[2] Burnes, iii. 253; Kennedy, i. 159.

[3] Masson, i. 20; Wood, Oxus, 51, 62.

The more important crops in the low, level, and fertile tracts, are indigo,[4] cotton, sugar, tobacco, opium, wheat, which is abundant and in quality excellent; buck-wheat, rice, barley, millet,[5] *juwaree* (holcus sorghum), *bajre* (holcus spicatus), *moong* (phaseolus mungo), maize, various sorts of vetches, oil-seeds, such as sesamum and mustard; peas and beans, carrots, turnips, onions, melons, cucumbers, and sundry kinds of cucurbitaceous plants. So plentiful is wheat, that it sells at Mooltan at from half a rupee to a rupee per maund. *Bang*, or hemp, is produced for the purpose of inducing intoxication; saffron, safflower for dyes, and a great number of less important products. Milk, butter, and wool are very important objects of rural economy, the former being almost the only * produce of the numerous herds of kine, as the slaughtering of these animals for food is not allowed by the Sikhs.

[4] Lord, Med. Memoirs, 66; Masson, i. 390; Burnes, iii. 303.
[5] Elph. 21; Vigne, Ghuznee, 24; Moorcr. i. 186; ii. 132.

The manufacturing industry of the Punjab is considerable. It is exercised principally in the silk and cotton productions of Amritsir, Lahore, Mooltan,[6] Shoojahbad, Leia, and some other places in the south; the fabrication of arms in Lahore; the shawl-weaving and manufacture of leather and of arms in Kashmir. Much of the commerce of the Punjab consists in the transit of the goods of Hindostan to the countries west of the Indus. The chief marts are Amritsir, Leia, and Mooltan, Lahore being in this respect of inferior importance. The imports from British India[7] are principally sugar, spices, and other groceries, dye-stuffs, cotton, woollen, and silk cloths; metals, and utensils of various kinds of metal; ivory, precious stones, glass, porcelain, and cutlery. From the west, the imports are gold, turquoises, silver, silk, madder, cochineal, assafœtida, safflower, fruits (fresh and dried), wool, horses, and a few of the more portable manufactures of Russia. The exports, whether in the way of transit or the produce of the country, are grain, ghee, or clarified butter, hides, wool, silk and cotton fabrics, carpets, shawls, silk, cotton, indigo, tobacco, gold, horses, and hawks, which last are so considerable an article of commerce as to bring Rs. 10,000 annually.

[6] Burnes, iii. 111; Masson, i. 294.
[7] Leech, Rep. on Commerce of Mooltan, 87.

The population consists of various races. The regions

* Leech (Report of the Commerce of Mooltan, p. 88) mentions hides as an article of commerce in the Punjab; they must be taken off kine which have died of disease or age.

north and north-west of Kashmir are generally inhabited by Tibetans belonging to the Mogol[8] variety of man. A small portion of the country included between the Kishengunga and the Indus, north of the Salt range, is held by the Eusufzye Afghans,[9] and Patans, the descendants of former Afghan conquerors, are scattered over the country in small numbers, as well as a few Moguls. The rest of the population is of Hindoo descent, though probably the majority have become converts to Mahometanism. This Hindoo stock may be classed as Kashmirians; Rajpoots holding the mountain tracts of Mundi, Jamu, Kishtewar, Rajawar,[1] and other small districts east of Kashmir; Gukers holding part of the country between the upper part of the Jailum and the Indus; and Punjabis, the greater part of whom are descendants from the Rajpoot tribe of Jats.* The only authority worth notice in regard to the amount of the population is Burnes, whose statement, however, is neither very explicit, nor invested with much pretension to accuracy. "It is with distrust," he says, "that I attempt an enumeration of the people subject to the Punjab, but I am informed that the Khalsa, or Sikh population, does not exceed 500,000 souls, and the remainder is composed of Sikhs, Mahometans, and Hindoo Juts, who may amount to 3,000,000." From various data, though far from satisfactory, an approximate computation may be made of the total population of the Sikh empire.

[8] Vigne, Kashmir, ii. 271; Jour. As. Soc. Beng. 1825, p. 597, Wade, Notes relative to Iskardoh; Moorcr. Punj. Bokh. i. 319; As. Res. xviii. 249, Gerard, Obs. on the Spiti Valley.
[9] Elph. Acc. of Caubul, 328.
[1] Burnes' Bokh. i. 60; Rennell, 86; Moorcr. ii. 306.

Punjabis	3,500,000
Ladakhis	160,000
Bultis	80,000
Kashmirians †	300,000
Other hill tribes	150,000
Afghans of the territory west of the Indus	500,000
Afghans of the Punjab	50,000
Total	4,740,000

The Sikhs are, for the most part, concentrated about their

* جاٹ.

† In the notice on Kashmir (i. 369) the amount of the population of the valley is estimated at 200,000, but great numbers of its native race are scattered through the neighbouring countries.

capitals, Amritsir and Lahore. The belief of this sect was originally, according to Malcolm,[2] a pure deism, but has so far degenerated that they now consider their founder entitled to divine honours, and regard him as a saviour and mediator with God. Their faith admits the doctrine of the transmigration of souls, either as a punishment, or a remedial process for moral deficiency, and of a future state of bliss for the good. To kill kine is considered by them a horrible impiety. Tobacco[3] is prohibited, but fermented liquors are allowed, and no kind of food is forbidden except beef. Malcolm[4] lays down the following as the great points by which they are separated from the strict Hindoos:—the renunciation of the distinctions of castes, the admission of proselytes, and the rendering the pursuit of arms not only allowable, but the religious duty of all. The sect, though it has but recently become powerful, was founded by Nanac, who was born in 1469 at Raypur,[5] sixty miles west of Lahore, and received the name of *Guru*,* or "spiritual pastor," from his votaries, who themselves assumed the appellation of *Sikhs*,† or "disciples." His followers were at first peaceable and humble, and remained so until the murder, by the Mahometans, of their fourth Guru in succession from Nanac, on which event his successor, Har Govind, in revenge, drew the sword which has never since been sheathed. Guru Govind, the fifth in succession from Har Govind, and the tenth from Nanac, is regarded as the founder of the temporal power of the Sikhs. His votaries were instructed by him always to bear arms, or at least steel in some form or other, about them, and to assume the name of Singh, or lion, previously affected only by the Rajpoots. By this name they are distinguished from the other Sikhs or followers of Baba Nanac. They ceased to have any spiritual leader ‡ after the death of Govind,[6] who was killed in 1708, and from that period until the power of Runjeet Singh became paramount, they constituted a turbulent and irregular republic, holding, in cases[7] of great emer-

[2] Sketch of the Sikhs, 171.

[3] Masson, i. 419.

[4] 189.

[5] Forster, Beng. Eng. i. 293.

[6] Forster, i. 303.

[7] Malcolm, i. 120

* گورو. † سکھ.

‡ So states Foster,[1] whose account is consistent, and probably accurate, and seems to be corroborated by that of Jacquemont,[2] in his notice of Amritsir—"Cette Rome du Pendjâb n'a point de pape." Burnes, however, makes mention of "the head of the Sikh church, the Bedee or Sahib Sing."

[1] v. 63.
[2] Bokh. ii. 286.

gency, a Guru-mata, or general diet, at Amritsir, but at other times engaged incessantly in petty warfare with each other. Runjeet viewed the congregated meetings at Amritsir with great jealousy, and built at that place the great fortress of Govindghur,[8] ostensibly to protect, but actually to overawe and control the excited followers of Govind, who resorted there. Those Sikhs who adhere to the original doctrines of Nanac are called Khalasa; they are less fanatical and warlike than the Singhs or followers of Guru Govind. Of these latter, a peculiar class is called Acalis,[9] or immortals, and sometimes Nihungs. Their fanaticism, Burnes observes, borders on insanity, and they seem to be at war with all mankind. They go about heavily armed, frequently bearing a drawn sword in each hand, two other swords in their belts, a matchlock on their back, and on their turbans[1] iron quoits six or eight inches in diameter, with their outer edges sharpened, and these, it is asserted, they throw with such force, as well as precision of aim, as to lop off the leg of a horse, or even of an elephant. Osborne,[2] however, who has frequently seen them try their skill, found them to be very bungling, and the missile in their hands to be very inefficient. They are a lawless and sanguinary class, and would have rendered the country desolate, had they not been vigorously coerced by Runjeet Singh.

[8] P. Von Hugel, iii. 398.
[9] Malcolm, 116; Burnes, i. 13.
[1] Masson, i. 437.
[2] Court and Camp of Runjeet Singh, 144.

The sacred books of the Sikhs are called *Granth* (scripture). The principal of them are the *Adi-Granth*, composed by Nanac, their first Guru, and the *Das Padshah ke Granth*, composed by Guru Govind, their last spiritual guide. They charge in battle to the war-cry, *Wai! Guruji ka Fath*, "O Victory to our master the Guru!" Their religious animosity is principally directed against the Mahometans, the slaughter of whom is enjoined in their *Granth*, while they are commanded merely to plunder and beat the Hindoos; yet great numbers of both are allowed to live under their sway, free, for the most part, from substantial injury, though treated with much contumely and exposed to many annoyances. The Mahometans especially are not allowed to pray in public, and they are subjected to a cruel death if detected in eating beef. The Sikhs carried their hatred of Islam so far as to devise and extensively to use a vocabulary[3] composed of terms which, while expressive of matters relating

[3] Leech, Grammar of Punjabee, 116.

to ordinary affairs, at the same time conveyed the most degrading and insulting allusion to Mahometanism.*

The Sikhs indulge in the grossest debauchery,[4] not excepting that species from which nature revolts; and among those addicted to this detestable vice, their late ruler, Runjeet Singh, attained an odious pre-eminence. As soldiers they appear in a more respectable light. Their repeated and signal successes against the formidable Afghans are conclusive evidence of their valour; they are patient of fatigue and privation, and, in case of reverse, readily rally. They are, however, as might be expected, prone to plunder,[5] retaining this propensity (a very common one with oriental troops) from the time when Sikh and robber were synonymous words; and, though easily disciplined so far as relates to the accurate performance of military evolutions, they are also easily moved to mutiny. Malcolm gives rather a favourable view of their character. "The Sikh soldier," he says, "is, generally speaking, brave, active, and cheerful, without polish, but neither destitute of sincerity nor attachment." But for the occurrence of some recent events, the present race of Sikhs might have claimed exemption from the charge of cruelty. Their celebrated Maharaja, Runjeet Singh, rarely shed the blood either of criminals or of his personal enemies, and he appears to have aspired to the praise of clemency. The countries which have fallen under the Sikh sway have indeed in general decayed in wealth and population, but this is to be attributed rather to their rapacity than to their innate cruelty.[6]

In person, the Sikhs bear a general resemblance to other people of Hindoo origin, but they are more robust, the result of a more varied and liberal diet: they especially excel others of the Hindoo race in having the lower extremities full, muscular, and symmetrical. Their women are esteemed beautiful, but they are frequently the victims of one of the most frightful of the enormities of Hindooism, which, banished from the British dominions in India, still lingers in unabated horror in a few

[4] Malcolm, 149; Jacquemont, v. 93, 100.

[5] Masson, Bal. Afg. Panj. i. 433.

[6] Id. 129; Masson, i. 433.

* A full account of the Sikh faith and "ecclesiastical polity" would be incompetent with the scope of this work. Ample information respecting them may be obtained from Wilson,[1] Forster,[2] Malcolm,[3] Masson,[4] and Ward.[5]

[1] As. Res. xvii. 291-239.
[2] Jour. Beng. Eng. 291-340.
[3] As. Res. xi. 197-292.
[4] Bal. Afg. Panj. i. 417-435.
[5] Religion of Hindoos, 270-289.

native states. Among the Sikhs, women often become *satis*,* or are burned with the dead bodies of their husbands. Nine[7] of the wives and female slaves of the Maharaja, Runjeet Singh, met this cruel fate on his death, in 1839.

The general dress of the male portion of the Sikh population consists of a jacket and trowsers reaching to the knee; of late, the chiefs have lengthened the trowsers to the ancles. They also wear shawls and scarfs, and wrap their heads in thin narrow cloths, so as to form a rude turban.[8] The favourite service of their soldiers is on horseback, using shields, swords, matchlocks, and spears, and some continue the use of the bow, for which they were formerly much celebrated. The irregular troops all serve on horseback, and are well suited for services in which such a force is required. The Sikhs are in general remarkably illiterate; Runjeet Singh[9] was unable to read or write, and most of his courtiers were alike destitute of these elementary attainments. This may, perhaps, be accounted for from the fact of most of the sect, including Runjeet himself,[1] tracing their origin to the Jets,[2] a Rajpoot tribe of very low order.

The language of the Punjab is called by Malcolm[3] a jargon compounded of various tongues. As spoken in large towns, it is a dialect of the Urdu[4] or Hindustani. In the villages, the dialect in use is Jathky, sprung from a cognate root, and originally the language of the country. On the southern frontier, Punjaubi contains a large admixture of Sindhi. There are two characters used, *Laude*, that of common translation, and *Gurmukhi*, or the character of the Granth. As before mentioned, there is also a dialect lately devised by the Sikhs, which enables them, while discoursing on the common business of life, to express their contempt for Mahometanism.

The present rule of the Sikhs extends over the whole of the Punjab, including Kashmir and the hill states of the north-east, comprehending Mundi, Kulu, and Kishtewar, in addition to Ladakh and Bulti. On the west of the Indus it comprises the provinces of Peshawer,[1] and the Derajat, or Daman, with its dependencies, as far south as the frontier of Sinde. The revenue

[7] Osborne, 223.

[8] Malcolm, 141; F. Von Hugel, iii. 244.

[9] Osborne, 93; Burnes, i. 44.

[1] Malcolm, 113.
[2] Malcolm, 136; Masson, i. 419.
[3] 24.

[4] Leech, Grammar of the Panjabi Lang. 116.

[1] Burnes' Pol. Power of the Sikhs, 1-6.

* ستی literally "chaste;" a virtuous wife according to Hindoo notions of virtue; a woman compelled to burn herself with her husband's body.

of the government is generally estimated, in round numbers, at something more than two and a half crores of rupees, or two millions and a half of sterling, which is allocated as follows:—

	RUPEES.
Kashmir[2]	*3,400,000
Peshawer[3]	1,000,000
Derajat and adjacent petty states[3]	1,500,000
Punjab	19,100,000
Possessions of Maharaja on left bank of Sutlej	750,000
	25,750,000

[2] F. Von Hugel, ii. 351.
[3] Burnes' Pol. Power of the Sikhs, 2.

or £2,575,000.

Runjeet Singh,[4] the late Maharaja of the Punjab, was believed to have accumulated ten millions sterling of treasure and moveable property.[5] This has been by native report exaggerated to thirty millions.

[4] Murray, App. to Prinsep, Life of Runjeet Singh, 185; Masson, i. 431.
[5] F. Von Hugel, iii. 309.
[6] Murray, in App. to Prinsep, 186.

The military[6] force was, in 1832, thus estimated:—

Regular and disciplined by Europeans	Cavalry	12,811
	Infantry	14,941
Undisciplined		26,950
Contingents of chiefs		27,312
Total		82,014
Artillery	Guns	376
	Swivels mounted on camels	370

[7] Kaschmir, iii. 244.

In 1836, Runjeet himself stated to Von Hügel[7] that his forces consisted of infantry, 27,000, of whom 15,000 were clad in armour; cavalry, 27,000; elephants, 100. Burnes states the army at 75,000, of whom 25,000[8] were regular infantry, 5,000 regular cavalry and artillery; and these being drilled in the European mode, were considered by this writer "fully equal to the troops of the Indian army." The artillery, according to the same authority, comprised a hundred and fifty guns. On occasion, however, of the interview which took place in 1838, at Ferozpoor, between the British Governor-General (Lord Auckland) and the Maharaja, it was remarked of the Sikh army,[9]

[8] Burnes, ii. 287.

Havelock, i. 86.

* An enormous and almost incredible amount for a population of 200,000; but the ill-fated district is fast sinking into utter destitution and depopulation.

"that the whole force, compared with the European standard, was indifferently equipped, the cavalry poorly mounted, and the artillery ill-harnessed."

There are few main and much-beaten routes in the Punjab, probably because the navigable rivers, and the level and open character of the country, admit of so many natural and unprepared lines of communication. The main route eastward from Kabool enters the Punjab at Attock, and takes a direction generally south-east to Rawit Pindee, where it divides, one route proceeding to the left by Jailum, the other to the right to Jelalpoor, and subsequently to Ramnuggur. The Jailum route subdivides at that town, the left-hand branch proceeding by Vazeerabad to Amritsir, and beyond that city to Filor, where it crosses the Sutlej into British India: the other takes a more southerly direction, through Ramnuggur to Lahore and Ferozpoor, into the same territory. The British army under Sir John Keane, and also that under General Pollock, returning from Afghanistan, pursued this route,[1] except that for a short distance they took a collateral road a little farther to the right, thus avoiding Lahore, to prevent collision with the Sikh forces, and to calm the alarm of the Maharaja. Another great route is that from Ferozpoor south-west to Mooltan, and thence into the Daman, west of the Indus. To the north-west of the route from Ferozpoor to Mooltan, and collateral and nearly parallel to it, a much-frequented route follows the course of the river Ravee. Three routes lead from Lahore, Amritsir, and the surrounding country, to Kashmir, one by Rihursi and the Banihal Pass, another by Bimber and the Pir Panjal Pass, a third by Punch and the Baramula Pass, by which pass there is also a frequented route from Attock. The route from the plain of the Punjab to Bultistan lies through Kashmir, leaving the valley by the Pass of Bundipur. The most frequented route to Ladakh lies also through Kashmir, which it leaves on the north-east by the Bultul Pass. There is another route to Ladakh by Lahoul and Rapstru.[2] Cross routes and roads of less importance are numerous, but appear in general to be little better than neglected paths or tracts.

[1] Hough, Narr. of Exp. into Afg. 357; Allen, March through Sinde and Afg. 366.

[2] Moorcr. i. 225.

The Sikh realm has many considerable towns; of these, the most worthy of notice are—Lahore, Amritsir, Kashmir, or Sirinagur; Mooltan, Peshawer, Dera Ghazee Khan, Dera Ismail Khan, Julinder, Vazeerabad, Leia, Nurpur, Le, Jelum, Jelalpoor, Shoojabad, and several others, especially noticed under their names in the alphabetical arrangement.

The Punjab was, in remote antiquity, the scene of some of Alexander's most arduous exploits. At the beginning of the tenth century of the Christian era, it was ravaged, widely and sweepingly, by Mahmood[3] of Ghiznee, "the Destroyer." Lahore, for about a century remained in possession of the successors of Mahmood, and was frequently the seat of their government, until 1186,[4] when the Ghaznevide dynasty was uprooted by Mahomed, Sultan of Ghore. Subsequently to this event, the Punjab became the prey of a succession of weak, licentious, and turbulent rulers, among whom the Afghans generally predominated, until, in 1526,[5] Baber gained the victory of Paniput, and, ascending the throne, established the sovereignty of the Timurian family. In 1748, Ahmed Shah Durani, finding the power of the Moguls broken by the invasion of Nadir Shah, overran the Punjab with an Afghan army, and made himself master of Lahore;[6] and in 1756 the Mogul emperor of India ceded to him these conquests. Soon after this, the power of the Sikhs began to assume a formidable aspect, and in 1768[7] they overran the country east of the Jailum, and, crossing that river, took the celebrated fortress, Rotas. In 1797[8] Shah Zeman Durani invaded the Punjab and took Lahore, but being immediately recalled by an insurrection at home, left the country in greater confusion than he found it. The expulsion of Shah Shooja in 1809, and consequent subversion of the Afghan monarchy, facilitated the rise of Runjeet Singh, a Sikh of the caste of Jats, one of the humblest but most numerous among the Rajpoots. In 1799, this adventurer had obtained from Zeman Shah Durani a grant of Lahore,[9] and in the same year[1] succeeded in expelling three rival Sikh chieftains, who had maintained themselves there. In 1809, having extended his power over the greater part of the Punjab, and some of the petty hill states, he carried his arms across the Sutlej, and attacked the Sikh chieftains under British protection. Negotiations ensued, and were brought to an amicable conclusion by a treaty providing "that the British government will have no concern with the territories and subjects of the Raja to the northward of the river Sutlej," and that Runjeet Singh would not commit or suffer any encroachment on the possessions or rights of the chiefs on the left bank of that river.[2] In 1818, Runjeet

[3] Ferishta, i. 47, 63; D'Herbelot, ii. 518; Price, Mahommedan Hist. ii. 281-294.
[4] Ferishta, i. 159.

[5] Id. i. 598; Baber, Mem. 367.

[6] Elph. Acc. of Caubul, 546.

[7] Elph. 556.

[8] Id. 570.

[9] Prinsep, Life of Runjeet Singh, 51.
[1] F. Von Hugel, Kaschmir, iv. 141.

[2] Prinsep, ut supra, 59.

Singh stormed Mooltan[3] and extended his power over the whole southern part of the Punjab, and in the same year marched a force across the Indus, and made himself master of Peshawer.[4] In 1819, the Maharaja of the Sikhs, as Runjeet styled himself, conquered the Derajat, on the west side of the Indus,[5] and Kashmir.[6] In 1831, at Rooper, on the Sutlej, an interview took place, amidst great pomp and display, between Runjeet Singh and Lord Auckland, the Governor-General of British India, and a paper was placed in the hands of the Sikh ruler promising him the perpetual amity of the British government. In 1835, Gulab Singh, a vassal of the Maharaja, reduced to subjection the extensive hill state of Ladakh, or Middle Tibet,[7] and five or six years later, the same chieftain subdued Bulti,[8] or Little Tibet. In 1838 Runjeet Singh became a party in the tripartite treaty with the British government and Shah Shooja, and succeeded in obtaining a stipulation securing to him the right to all the territories which he then possessed on both sides of the Indus.[9] Runjeet Singh died in July 1839, and was succeeded by his son Kuruck Singh. The latter died in 1840, and, as was generally believed, from the effects of poison. Before the funeral ceremonies for this prince were fully ended, his son and successor was killed by the falling of a beam—a catastrophe not accidental, though intended to have the appearance of being so. A competition for the vacant throne then ensued between the widow of Kuruck Singh and a reputed son of Runjeet Singh, named Sheer Singh, but who, though born in wedlock, had been subjected by his alleged father to the stigma of illegitimacy. Shere Singh finally succeeded, but his triumph was of short duration. Near the close of the year 1843 he was assassinated; and this was followed by a widely-spread, frantic, and sanguinary anarchy, which at this present time (1844) engages the anxious attention of the Anglo-Indian government.

[3] Id. 116.
[4] Id. 119.
[5] Id. 124.
[6] F. Von Hugel, Kaschmir, ii. 151.
[7] Id. iv. 140.
[8] Vigne, Kashmir, ii. 374.
[9] Tripartite Treaty, Corresp. on Sinde, 6.

PUNJAN GOOSHT, in Western Afghanistan, a range of mountains bounding the upper part of the valley of Furrah on the east. They are situate to the left of the route from Kandahar to Herat, and about two hundred and twenty miles northwest of the former town. They rise to a considerable height from the surrounding country, and as the latter is very elevated, their total altitude above the level of the sea is, probably, not less than 12,000 feet. Lat. 32° 30′, long. 63° 5′. E.I.C. Ms. Doc.

PUNJGOOR,[1] in Beloochistan, a town of Mekran, the [1] E.I.C. Ms. Doc.

principal place of a petty district, also called Punjgoor,[2] and containing ten small towns or villages. This little territory is a valley, and is one of the most productive places in Beloochistan, yielding in great abundance fine dates, grapes, grain, and esculent vegetables. Its fertility is owing to a never-failing supply of water from the river Boodoor or Dustee, which is replenished by a copious spring[3] issuing from its bed about three miles above the town. The population is in general agricultural, and greatly superior in character and habits to the other Brahooie tribes of the neighbourhood. The chief, a relative of the Khan of Kelat, was formerly his vassal, but has lately made himself independent. The annual income of this petty potentate is believed not to exceed an amount equal to 2,000*l.* sterling. Lat. 27° 20', long. 62° 42'.

PUNJNUD,* a great stream of the Punjab, discharges into the Indus the collected water of the Ghara and Trimab, and consequently of the Sutlej, Beas, Ravee, Chenaub, and Jailum. The great channel bearing the name of Punjnud commences at the confluence of the Ghara and Trimab, in lat. 29° 21', long. 71° 6', and, taking a south-westerly course of about sixty miles,[1] joins the Indus nearly opposite Mittunkote, and in lat. 28° 57', long. 70° 30'. Burnes[2] describes the commencement of the Punjnud, or confluence of the Trimab and Ghara, as "formed without violence, and the low banks of both rivers lead to constant alteration in the point of the union, which but a year ago was two miles higher up. This circumstance renders it difficult to decide on the relative size of these rivers at their junction; both are about five hundred yards wide, but the Chenaub (Trimab) is more rapid. Immediately below the confluence the united stream exceeds eight hundred yards; but in its course to the Indus, though it expands sometimes to a greater size, the Chenaub rarely widens to six hundred yards. In this part of its course it is likewise subject to change. The depth is greatest near its confluence with the Indus, exceeding twenty feet; but it decreases in ascending the river to about fifteen. The current is swifter than the Indus, running at the rate of three and a half miles an hour. The Chenaub (Punjnud) has some sand-banks, but they do not interrupt its navigation by the 'zohruks,' or flat-bottomed boats." Wade[3]

* From پنج "five," and ند "river."

found the Punjnud, abreast of Ooch, about nine hundred yards wide at the season of low water, and mentions that during the rains it is sometimes six miles across from that town to the opposite side. The Punjnud is by all accounts a very fine stream. It is navigated by large flat-bottomed boats without keels, but with perpendicular sides, which prevent them from making much leeway, even with the wind on the beam. The confluence of the Punjnud with the Indus takes place without noise or violence,[4] in consequence of the low, soft nature of the banks admitting of a considerable expansion of the channel there. An eddy sets to the opposite side, and depresses the surface of the water there below the general level, without, however, producing danger or serious impediment to navigation. Burnes[5] observes, that the name Punjnud appears to be a European refinement, and is unknown to the people living on its banks, and that this great stream is called Chenaub by the natives. The contrary, however, appears intimated by Boileau,[6] who states unambiguously that not one of the rivers of the Punjab retains its original name after falling in with another of nearly the same size, and adds explicitly, that after the junction of the Ghara with the Trimab, the united stream bears the name of Punjnud.

[4] Burnes, iii. 286.
[5] iii. 90, 286.
[6] Rajwara, 62.

PUNJOOK, in Beloochistan, a village of Cutch Gundava, on the route from Gundava to Larkhana, and ten miles south of the former town. Lat. 28° 20′, long. 67° 33′.

E.I.C. Ms. Doc.; Outram, Rough Notes, 59; Kennedy, Sinde and Kabool, i. 193.

PUNJSHIR, generally but corruptly called Panchshir, a river in Afghanistan, rises on the south-eastern declivity of the Khawak Pass, in lat. 35° 40′, long. 69° 50′, and at an elevation above the sea of 13,200 feet.[1] It holds its course in a south-westerly direction for about eighty miles, through the whole length of the valley of Punjshir, and, in lat. 35°, long. 69° 15′, receives the Ghorband river.[2] It then takes a south-easterly direction for about thirty-five miles, and receives the stream flowing westward from Koh Damun, and, proceeding from that confluence southwards for a farther distance of about twenty, falls into the Kabool river in lat. 34° 38′, long. 69° 47′.

[1] Wood's Oxus, 413, 416.
[2] Masson, Bal.Afg. Panj. iii. 130.

PUNNA, in Afghanistan, a village on the route by the Golairee Pass from Dera Ismael Khan to Ghuznee, and twenty-five miles south of the latter place. The road in this part of the route is good, and there is a supply of water from a subterraneous aqueduct. Lat. 33° 7′, long. 68° 10′.

E.I.C. Ms. Doc.

PUN—PUR.

<small>Elph. Acc. of Caubul, 35.</small>

PUNNAILAH, properly PUNIALLA, in Afghanistan, a village of the Daman, on the route from Dera Ismail Khan to Kala Bagh, and thirty-five miles north of the former town. Though situate at the southern entrance of the valley of Largee, a singularly barren and dreary tract, the immediate neighbourhood of the village is described by Elphinstone as "a cheerful and beautiful spot, such as one would figure a scene in Arabia Felix. It is a sandy valley, bounded by craggy hills, watered by a little stream, and interspersed with clumps of date-trees and with patches of green corn. The village itself stood in a deep grove of date-trees, on the side of a hill, from which many streams gushed through little caverns in the thickest part of the wood." The inhabitants are a mixed race of Belooche and Arab descent, and of notoriously predatory character. Lat. 32° 15′, long. 70° 58′.

PURANI DERIA, a minor branch of the Indus.—See NARRA, EASTERN.

<small>[1] E.I.C. Ms. Doc.</small>

PUREAN,[1] in Afghanistan, a village in the Punjshir valley, near the route from the Khawak Pass to Kabul, and about fifteen miles south-east of the crest of the pass. It is situate on a small feeder of the Punjshir river, and at a great elevation, as it lies on the mountain side above the fort of Khawak, which is 9,300[2] feet above the sea. Purean is in lat. 35° 32′, long. 70°.

<small>[2] Wood's Oxus, 416.</small>

<small>[1] E.I.C. Ms. Doc.; Leech, Memoir Hind. Koosh, 33-34; Wood's Oxus, 186-194; Lord, Koh-i-Damun, 49; Baber, Mem. 139.</small>

PURWAN,[1] in Afghanistan, a village in a valley of the same name, which furrows the southern side of Hindoo Koosh, in lat. 35° 10′, long. 69° 12′. The valley is very tortuous, and is in one part a narrow rocky defile; in another it is of softer character, the sides rising in terraces planted with mulberry-trees, the fruit of which, dried and ground, forms the staple subsistence of the inhabitants. A small river flows down the valley, and joins the Punchshir. Two passes proceed from this valley to Turkestan—that of Purwan Proper, and that of Sir-i-Ulung. The summits of both are probably very lofty, as a British party found them impassable from snow in the beginning of November; though those travellers, a few days later, succeeded in surmounting the pass of Hageguk,[2] the summit of which is 12,000 feet above the level of the sea. Purwan acquired some celebrity during the military operations in Afghanistan. Here, in November 1840, a British force attacked a party of Afghans, with the view of capturing Dost Mahomed Khan, but two squadrons of the

<small>[2] Jour. As. Soc. Beng. 1842, p. 69, Grif. Bar. and Ther. Meas. in Afg.</small>

2nd Bengal Native Cavalry, when ordered to charge, instead of responding to the command, fled in the most dastardly manner, deserting their officers; on this unhappy occasion, Dr. Lord,[3] the political agent, Lieut. Broadfoot, and Adjutant Crispin, were killed, and the remaining officers severely wounded.* Notwithstanding this event, Dost Mahomed immediately repaired to Kabool, and surrendered himself to the British envoy. Purwan is in lat. 35° 9′, long. 69° 16′.

[3] Indian News, i. 213; Atkinson, Exp. into Afg. 353; Burnes, Pers. Narr. 173.

PURWANA, in Khorasan, a village on the route from Herat to Merve, and eleven miles north of the former town. It is situate in a valley of considerable elevation, as the road from Herat ascends for the whole distance. Lat. 34° 34′, long. 62° 12′.

Abbott, Heraut and Khiva, i. 5, 7.

PUTTEE, in the Punjab, a town in the *doab* of Bari, and situate about twelve miles from the right or western bank of the Beas, in a country formerly fertilized by canals, and so well peopled and productive as to contain one thousand three hundred and sixty villages, and yield a revenue equal to 90,000*l.* per annum. The soil and climate are considered peculiarly favourable to the perfection of the breed of horses, and, in consequence, there is a great and well-selected stud belonging to the Sikh government. The town, which was founded in the reign of Akbar, is well built of bricks, and the streets are paved with the same material. Population about 5,000. Lat. 31° 17′, long. 74° 45′.

Burnes' Bokh. i. 11.

PUTTEHPOOR, in Sinde, a village on the route from Schwan to Larkhana, and thirty-two miles north of the former town. It is situate two miles from the right bank of the Indus, in an alluvial level country, much cut up by watercourses, which interfere with the practicability of the road. Lat. 26° 48′, long. 67° 54′.

E.I.C. Ms. Doc.

PUTTOOLA KILLA.—See FUTTOOLA KILLA.

PYRGHOWLA, in Afghanistan, a village among the Huzareh mountains. Lat. 35° 23′, long. 66°.

Walker's Map of Afg.

* Masson erroneously states that the conflict, marked by such disgraceful conduct, and producing such melancholy results, took place, not at Purwan, but at Tutam Dara, about five miles south-west of it. (See TUTAM DARA.)

Bal. Afg. Panj. iii. 129.

Q.

QUETTA, called also SHAWL, which see.

R.

Abbott, Heraut and Khiva, i. 8.

RABAHT, properly *ribat*,* "an inn," in Afghanistan, a halting-place on the route from Herat to Khooshk, and twenty miles north-west of the former town. It is situate on the Kytoo mountain, amidst a desolate tract, where neither tent nor fixed habitation could, at the time of Abbott's journey, be discerned for many miles, though the grass-covered hills appear well suited for the support of a pastoral population. Lat. 34° 41', long. 62° 2'.

E.I.C. Ms. Doc.

RABAT, in Northern Afghanistan, a village situate on the left bank of the Lundye river, in lat. 35° 12', long. 71° 59'.

E.I.C. Ms. Doc.

RADHWARREE, in Sinde, a village on the route from Kurrachee to Tattah, and twelve miles east of the former place. Lat. 24° 53', long. 67° 12'.

E.I.C. Ms. Doc.

RADO, in the Punjab, a village situate on an offset of the Indus, five miles from the left bank of the main stream. Lat. 30° 26', long. 71°.

Walker's Map of N.W. Frontier.

RAEPOOR, in the Punjab, a village situate on the left bank of the Jailum, ten miles south-east of Pind Dadun Khan. Lat. 32° 37', long. 73'.

E.I.C. Ms. Doc.

RAGEREE, in Sinde, a village on the route from Hyderabad to Sehwan, and twenty miles north of the former town. It is situate on the right bank of the Indus, in a shikargah or hunting-ground, formerly belonging to one of the Ameers of Hyderabad. Lat. 25° 49', long. 68° 19'.

E.I.C. Ms. Doc.

RAHIM DAD, in Northern Beloochistan, a village on the

* رباط.

route from Kelat to Shawl, and fifteen miles west of the last-mentioned town. Lat. 30° 6′, long. 66° 39′.

RAHMUK, in Afghanistan, a village fifteen miles east of Ghuznee. Lat. 33° 33′, long. 68° 30′. E.I.C. Ms. Doc.

RAJ, in Sinde, a village on the route from Hyderabad to Meerpoor, and eight miles south of the former town. It is situate on the left bank of the Indus, a little above the re-union of the Fulailee river. Lat. 25° 14′, long. 68° 20′. E.I.C. Ms. Doc.

RAJADARAH, in Sinde, a village on the route from Sehwan to Larkhana, and forty-five miles north of the former town. It is situate in a flat alluvial tract, on the right bank of the Indus. Lat. 26° 59′, long. 68°. Ms. Survey Map.

RAJA GOTE, in Sinde, a village about a mile to the east of the route from Sehwan to Larkhana, and forty-five miles north of the former town. It is situate on the right bank of the Indus, in a flat alluvial country, much cut up by watercourses. Lat. 26° 56′, long. 67° 58′. E.I.C. Ms. Doc.

RAJAK, in Afghanistan, a fort with a village in the Punchshir valley, and close to the left bank of the Punchshir river. Lat. 35° 21′, long. 69° 31′. Walker's Map of Afg.

RAJAPOOR, in Sinde, a village on the middle route from Roree to Hyderabad, and a hundred and twenty miles north of the former town. Lat. 27° 2′, long. 68° 22′. E.I.C. Ms. Doc.

RAJARIE, in Sinde, a village on the route from Roree to Jessulmair, and twenty-eight miles south-east of the former place. Though the neighbouring country is in general covered with low sand-hills, a few places have received the benefit of cultivation, and produce grain, principally wheat. The population consists for the most part of goatherds, who are supplied with water from four wells in the village. Lat. 27° 26′, long. 69° 17′. E.I.C. Ms. Doc.

RAJA SANSE, in the Punjab, a village six miles north of the town of Amritsir. Lat. 31° 46′, long. 74° 46′. Walker's Map of N.W. Frontier.

RAJAWUR,[1] in the north of the Punjab, a town situate on the banks of a stream, which rising in the Pir Panjal, or mountain bounding Kashmir on the south, falls into the Chenaub. The houses are generally built of mud, strengthened with frames of timber, but a few of those of the wealthier classes are of brick. Rajawur belongs to a petty rajah, who is dependent on the Sikhs. The chief crops of the small territory of Rajawur are rice and maize; the latter occupies the higher grounds, the former the level [1] Vigne, Kashmir, i. 232; F. Von Hugel, Kaschmir, i. 175; Moorcr. Punj. Bokh. ii. 300.

alluvial tract along the stream. The rice fields are kept constantly flooded, and hence the air is very unhealthy, and the population much subject to fever; goitre and leprosy are also very prevalent. The territory and revenue of the rajah have suffered so much from the encroachments of the Sikhs, that his annual income has decreased from a sum equal to 5,000*l.* to one-fifth of that amount. Elevation of Rajawur above the sea 2,800 feet.[2] Lat. 33° 19′, long. 74° 14′.

RAJH, in the Punjab, a village situate five miles west of Mooltan, and on the left bank of the river Chenaub. Lat. 30° 7′, long. 71° 23′.

RAJOORA, in the south-eastern desert of Sinde, a village situate fifty miles south-east of Omercote, on the road to Nuggur Parker. Lat. 24° 57′, long. 70° 31′.

RAJTULLA, in Sinde, a village situate on the Pinteeance mouth of the Indus. Lat. 24° 25′, long. 67° 16′.

RAJUNPOOR, in Afghanistan, a halting-place on the route from Dera Ghazee Khan to Kahun, and eighty miles south-west of the former town. Lat. 29° 21′, long. 70° 2′.

RAJUNPOOR, in Sinde, a village on the route from Subzulcote to Shikarpoor, and eighteen miles west of the former town. It is situate close to the east bank of an extensive *dund*, or piece of stagnant water, replenished by the inundation of the Indus. Lat. 28° 14′, long. 68° 54′.

RAJUR, in Sinde, a village situate on the road from Roree to Jessulmair, about thirty miles south-east of the former place. There is a swamp close to this village, and wells on the road about five miles to the left. Lat. 27° 25′, long. 69° 19′.

RAKNEE, in Afghanistan, a village situate where the Sangad pass intersects the Sakhee Sarwar Pass from Dera Ghazee Khan to Kandahar. It is distant forty miles west of the former town, and is a small place containing about forty mud huts; there is a good supply of water from a stream, which here divides into two branches, one going to Dajel, the other to Sang Ghar. There is a road practicable for wheel-carriages from Raknee to Kandahar. Lat. 30° 4′, long. 70°.

RAMNAGUR, in the Punjab, on the route from Chumba to Kashmir, by the Banihal Pass, is a considerable town with a large and stately castle, the residence of the deposed raja, and another the stronghold of the Sikh chief, his successor. It is one of the few places the condition of which has been ameliorated under Sikh dominion, having, since its acquisition by Suchet Singh, the present chieftain, been improved by the building of a large bazaar and several streets. Much encouragement is given to new settlers, and, in consequence, the population consists of various races—Sikh, Hindoo, Afghan, Kashmirian, and Persian. Lat. 32° 38′, long. 75° 13′.

RAMNEGHUR,[1] or RAMNUGGUR, in the Punjab, a walled town close to the left or east bank of the Chenaub, stands on a spacious plain, where, during the reign of Runjeet Singh, the Sikh troops frequently mustered for campaigns to the westward. There is a ferry here across the Chenaub, which, at its lowest season, was found to be three hundred yards wide, and for the most part nine feet deep, running at the rate of a mile and a half an hour. Two miles below the town there is, however, a ford, where the depth does not exceed three feet when the water is low. This place was called Rasulnuggur, or "prophet's town," until stormed in 1778 by Maha Singh, the father of Runjeet, when it received the present name,[2] signifying the "town of God." Lat. 32° 20′, long. 73° 38′. [1] Burnes' Bokh. i. 43; Hough, Narr. Exp. in Afg. 353. [2] F. Von Hugel, Kaschmir, iii. 343.

RAMTERETH, in the Punjab, a village situate on the route from Amritsir to Vazeerabad, ten miles north-west of the former town. Lat. 31° 44′, long. 74° 42′. E.I.C. Ms. Doc.

RANEEPOOR, in Sinde, a manufacturing town on the middle route from Roree to Hyderabad, and forty-five miles south-west of the latter place. It is irregularly built, but has a cleanly, healthy, and pleasant appearance, unusual in Sinde. The cotton manufactures here were formerly extensive and in high repute, but have latterly much decayed. Population 5,000. Lat. 27° 15′, long. 68° 30′. E.I.C. Ms. Doc.; Burnes, Com. of Hyderabad, 19; Leech, Rep. on Rampoor, 32.

RANJUNPOOR, in Afghanistan, a village of the Daman, situate on the right bank of the Indus. Lat. 32° 10′, long. 71° 13′. E.I.C. Ms. Doc.

RAS ARUBAH, or OREMARRAH, on the coast of Beloochistan, a remarkable headland projecting southward into the Arabian Sea, and forming deep bays on the eastern and western sides. Viewed from the east, it appears like an island, in consequence of the lowness of the land constituting the isthmus connecting it with the continent. The bay on the east side has safe ground, having regular depths of six or seven fathoms, decreasing Horsburgh, Ind. Dir. i. 494.

to three and four fathoms near the shore. A supply of water may be obtained from a rivulet called Jerkamutty, a little to the eastward. The bay on the west side has shoal water, and is destitute of shelter from south and west winds. Lat. 25° 8′, long. 64° 35′.

<small>Walker's Map of N.W. Frontier.</small> RASHUN BUSTEE, in the Punjab, a village situate on the left bank of the Ravee river. Lat. 30° 51′, long. 73° 9′.

RAS KOPPAH, in Beloochistan, a cape. Lat. 25° 14′, long. 62° 36′.

<small>Id. ib.</small> RAS MALAN, in Beloochistan, a headland projecting a short distance southward into the Arabian Sea. The shore in this part is bold and safe to approach, a bank extending southward for about four leagues, with a depth of twenty or twenty-five fathoms, and then deepening, so that soundings cannot be obtained. Lat. 25° 19′, long. 65° 9′.

<small>Id. i. 493.</small> RAS MOOARREE, at the north-western extremity of the coast of Sinde, a headland, also called Monze Cape (which see).

RAS NOO.—See GWADEL Cape.

RAS PASSEENOE.—See PASSEENOE.

<small>Id. i. 495.</small> RAS PISHK, in Beloochistan, a headland projecting a short distance south-east into the Arabian Sea. It forms the western side of the bay, of which Ras Noo or Gwadel Point forms the eastern. This bay, measuring about three leagues from east to west, and the same distance from north to south, has regular soundings of seven or eight fathoms at the entrance, and five or six inside, with a mud bottom, and is sheltered from all winds, except those blowing between east and south-south-west. Lat. 25° 7′, long. 61° 58′.

RAS SEEUNNEY, in Beloochistan, a small headland projecting into the Arabian Sea. Lat. 25° 15′, long. 64° 16′.

<small>Id. ib.</small> RAS SHEID, in Beloochistan, a headland projecting southwards into the Arabian Sea. It is a bluff point, appearing like an island when seen at a distance from the east. Lat. 25° 12′, long. 62° 50′.

RAS SHEMAUL BUNDER, in southern Beloochistan, a headland. Lat. 25° 13′, long. 62° 58′.

<small>[1] Jour. As. Soc. Beng. 1841, p. 100, Broome and Cunningham on Sources of Punjab Rivers.</small> RAVEE,[1] or RAVI, a river of the Punjab, rises in Kulu, on the declivity of a mountain called Bungall, and a short distance west of the Ritanka Pass. The source is situate about lat. 32° 30′, long. 76°. At the distance of about forty miles from the source, in a

south-westerly direction, the Ravee is joined by two feeders, the Nye and the Boodhill, the latter taking its rise in a lake called Munee Muhees, regarded as sacred by the superstitious Hindoos.* Where surveyed by Cunningham, four or five miles from Burmawur, at an elevation of about 7,000 feet, and in lat. 32° 30′, long. 76° 30′, it was found one hundred and sixteen feet wide. At Chumba, about sixty miles below and south-west of this place, or a hundred miles from its source, according to the statement of Vigne, the Ravee is crossed by a bridge. Forster[2] states that it is there "forty or fifty yards broad, and fordable at most seasons of the year." At Bisuli, to which the downward course is about twenty-five miles due west, Forster found it, early in April, about a hundred and twenty yards wide, very rapid, and unfordable. The statement of Vigne[3] is less explicit. "I have been twice ferried over the Ravi at Bisuli, once during the rainy season, when it was swelled to a roaring torrent, and once again in winter, when its stream was far more tranquil. On both occasions the natives made the passage upon buffalo hides. Its width is about eighty yards." From Bisuli, in lat. 32° 25′, long. 75° 28′, the Ravee takes a south-westerly direction, which it generally holds for the rest of its course. Macartney[4] found it, at Meanee ferry, on the route from Amritsir to Vazeerabad, and about two hundred and twenty miles from its source, to have, at the beginning of August and at the time of fullest water, a breadth of five hundred and thirteen yards, and a depth of twelve feet, where greatest. The deep channel was between thirty and forty feet in breadth, the rest of the waterway having a depth of from three to five feet. In the cold season, when lowest, the water is in no part more than four feet deep. Moorcroft[5] describes it at Lahore, about twenty-five miles lower down, as divided into three different streams or branches. These, he states, are "separated, in the dry weather, by intervals of half a mile, but in the rainy season the two most easterly branches †are

[2] Jour. Beng. Eng. i. 289.
[3] Kashmir, i. 171.
[4] In Elph. Acc. of Caubul, 661.
[5] Punj. Bokh. i. 108.

* Vigne considers the Boodhill river, flowing from the Munee Muhees, or Muni Mys, as the real Ravee, but the evidence of Cunningham, who approached nearer the locality, merits more credit. — Kashmir, i. 152.

† Moorcroft appears in error in stating the eastern branches of the Ravee to be the principal, as all other accounts represent the western as the main stream. There can be no doubt that he is in error in stating that Shahdehra, the burial-place of Jehanjir, is on the left bank of the Ravee, as Masson,[1] Burnes,[2] and Jacquemont,[3] agree that it is on the right or west bank.

[1] Bal. Afg. Panj. i. 415.
[2] Bokh. i. 30.
[3] Jacquemont, v. 102.

united, and form an expansive and rapid stream." "The two first branches are fordable, but the third, which is the principal one, has a ferry." He remarks, that the boats on the Ravee were the largest and best-built that he has seen in India. Burnes,[6] who navigated the Ravee from its confluence with the Chenaub to Lahore, says it " is very small, and resembles a canal, rarely exceeding a hundred and fifty yards in breadth in any part of its course. Its banks are precipitous, so that it deepens before it expands. Nothing can exceed the crookedness of its course, which is a great impediment to navigation, for we often found ourselves, after half a day's sail, within two miles of the spot from which we started. The water of the Ravee is redder than that of the Chenaub. It is fordable in most places for eight months in the year." From Lahore, its course south-west, measured according to the main direction of the stream, to its confluence with the Chenaub, is about two hundred miles, but along all the sinuosities, three hundred and eighty.[7] This point is in lat. 30° 33', long. 71° 46'. The Ravee joins the Chenaub by three mouths close to each other. Its total length, measured along the main direction of its course, is about four hundred and fifty miles.* It is considered to be the Hydraotes mentioned by Arrian,[8] and the Iravati of Sanscrit authorities: it is still known by the name of the Iraotee,[9] which might easily be corrupted by the Greeks into that which they appear to have given it.

RAWDON, in Sinde, a group of three or four villages on the route from Sehwan to Larkhana, and eleven miles north of the former town. It is situate close to a watercourse sent off from the Indus on the right side, and is two miles from the main channel. The road in this part of the route is level, and in general good, except that it is cut up in some places by channels formed for irrigation. The adjacent country is fertile and well cultivated. Lat. 26° 30', long. 67° 55'.

RAWIL PINDE, in the Punjab, between the Indus and the Jailum. It is a large, populous town, consisting of mud houses with flat roofs. It contains, what is called a palace, a wretched building of brick, constructed by Shah Soojah, on his expulsion from Kabool. There is a large bazaar, and a considerable business in the transit trade between Hindostan and Afghanistan.

* The estimate of Macartney is less, being only four hundred and fifteen miles, but he did not know the exact locality of its source.

The town is surrounded by a wall with bastions, and has an old fort, on which a few miserable cannon are mounted. Lat. 33° 40′, long. 73°.

REEPREE, in the Punjab, a village situate on the right bank of the Trimab, about twenty miles from its confluence with the Ghara. Lat. 29° 33′, long. 71° 6′. E.I.C. Ms. Doc.

REGAN, in Beloochistan, a village on the route from Nooshky to Bunpoor, and a hundred and eighty miles south-west of the former place. It is situate on the Badoor river, or torrent, the current of which intermits during great part of the year, and water can then only be obtained by digging in the bed. When visited by Pottinger, it was deserted, the inhabitants having emigrated in consequence of famine. Lat. 28° 20′, long. 62° 39′. Belooch. 135.

REG ROWAN,[1] * ("Flowing Sand,") in the Kohistan of Kabool, is a bed of loose sand on the slope of a hill. When put in motion by the wind or by the trampling of feet, undulations are caused, which produce a sound, described by Wood to be like that of a distant drum, mellowed by softer music. Close to it is a deep and unexplored cave, viewed with much awe by the Mahometans, who believe that their expected Imam Medi, the supposed precursor of the end of the world, has his retreat there until the appointed time of his appearance. [1] Jour. As. Soc. Beng. 1838, Burnes, on the Reg-Ruwan; Id. 1837, p. 403, Welsted, on the Djibbel Narkono, or Sounding Mountain of Sinai; Wood, Oxus, 181; Masson, Bal. Afg. Panj. iii. 167; Baber, Mem. 146; Lord, Koh-i-Damun, 56; Burnes' Pers. Narr. 158; Ayeen Akbery, ii. 183.

The bed of sand is a hundred yards wide, and it stretches up the face of the rock for two hundred and fifty yards with an acclivity of about 45°. The appearance of the sand is very curious, as if the hill on the side of which it lies had been cut in two, and that it had gushed out; but probably it has been accumulated by an eddy of the wind, which is here very powerful and constant.

The singular effects manifested at Reg Rowan did not escape the observant Baber, who thus alludes to them:—"They say that in the summer season the sound of drums and nagarets (Tartar drums) issue from this sand."† It is difficult to offer a satisfac-

* From ریگ "sand," and روان "flowing."

† Lieut. Newbold[1] describes a similar phenomenon at *Gebel Nakus*, on the eastern shore of the Red Sea, but he is unquestionably mistaken in his belief that such nowhere else occurs. Welsted,[2] who calls this place *Djibbel Narkono*, gives the following full and interesting account of his visit to it:—"The *Djibbel Narkono*, or sounding mountain, concerning which there has been so much doubt and discussion in Europe. I visited it on my way here—it is situated on the sea-shore, about eight miles from Tor. A solid slope of the finest drift sand extends on the sea face from the base to [1] Jour. Roy. As. Soc. May, 1842, p. 78. [2] Jour. As. Soc. Beng. 1837, p. 403.

tory explanation of that which is so unusual and has been so little considered. Prinsep[2] advances the opinion, that "the effect is produced merely by a reduplication of impulse setting air in vibration in a focus of echo." Reg Rowan is in lat. 35°, long. 69° 10'.

[2] Jour. Roy. As. Soc. Beng. 1845, p. 82.

E.I.C. Ms. Doc.

REJLA, in Sinde, a village situate on the right bank of the Indus, five miles west of the city of Hyderabad. Lat. 25° 23', long. 68° 18'.

E.I.C. Ms. Doc.

REMMUK, in Afghanistan, a village of the Daman, about five miles from the right bank of the Indus. Lat. 31° 21', long. 70° 50'.

E.I.C. Ms. Doc.

RETTA SOOLTAN, in the Punjab, a village eight miles east of the town of Ramnuggur, and on the road from thence to Vazeerabad. Lat. 32° 24', long. 73° 45'.

Carless, Official Rep. on the Indus, 2; Burnes, Bokh. iii. 234.

RICHEL, in Sinde, a mouth of the Buggaur, or great western branch of the Indus. Though now nearly filled up, it was at a former period one of the principal mouths of that river, and being frequented by shipping, was marked out by a *munorah*, or minaret, now fallen. In consequence of this distinction, the spot still bears the name Munorah. Lat. 24° 10', long. 67° 22'.

the summit, about six hundred feet, at an angle of about 40° with the horizon. This is encircled, or rather semicircled, if the term is allowable, by a ridge of sandstone rocks, rising up in the pointed pinnacle, and presenting little surface adapted for forming an echo. It is remarkable that there are several other slopes similar to this, but the sounding or rumbling, as it has been called, is confined to this alone. We dismounted from our camels, and remained at the base while a Bedouin scrambled up. We did not hear the sound until he had attained a considerable height. The sound then began rolling down, and it commenced in a strain resembling the first faint notes of an Æolian harp, or the fingers wetted and drawn over glass, increasing in loudness as the sand reached the base, when it was almost equal to thunder. It caused the rock on which we were seated to vibrate, and our frightened camels (animals, you know, not easily alarmed) to start off. I was perfectly astonished, as was the rest of the party. I had visited it before in the winter months, but the sound was then so faint as to be barely evident; but now the scorching heat of the sun had dried the sand, and permitted it to roll down in large quantities. I cannot now form the most remote conjecture as to the cause of it. We must not, I find, now refer it to the sand falling into a hollow; that might produce a sound, but could never cause the prolonged *vibrations*, as it were, of some huge harp-string. I shall not venture on any speculation, but having carefully noted the facts, I shall lay them, on my arrival in England, before some wiser head than my own, and see if he can make any thing out of them."

RIHURSI, in the Punjab, a town situate near the left or east Vigne, Kashmir, ii. 216. bank of the Chenaub, and on the southern slope of the most southern of the Himalaya ranges. Here is a fort considered by Vigne "one of the strongest, perhaps the strongest, and best constructed in the country." It is situated on a conical and rocky eminence south of the town, and is nearly square. The walls are built of stone: they are very lofty, and are rendered still more difficult to be scaled by their rising immediately from the precipitous sides of the hill, which are steeply scarped. There is a tower at each angle, and no pains have been spared to render these, as well as most of the buildings of the interior, bomb-proof. The garrison is supplied with water by means of two large tanks within the walls. The fort is separated, by a deep ravine, from an eminence of sandstone of the same height, about a mile distant. The town itself is an inconsiderable place, having about a thousand inhabitants. It belongs to Golab Singh, the Sikh chief of Jamu. Lat. 32° 51′, long. 74° 50′.

RILU, in the north-east of the Punjab, a small town situate Id. i. 142. among the mountains forming the lower ranges in the southern part of the Himalaya. It has a neat bazaar, and a fort with rampart, curtains, and bastions. Lat. 32° 5′, long. 76° 2′.

RIMBIARA RIVER, in Kashmir, rises on the north-eastern Id. i. 268; Moorcr. Punj. Bokh. ii. 110. declivity of the Pir Panjal, and holding a north-easterly course of about forty miles, falls into the Veshau Behut, or Jailum, in lat. 33° 48′, long. 74° 57′. It is frequently called the river of Shupeyon from flowing by the town of that name.

RINDAN, in Sinde, a village on the route from Sehwan to E.I.C. Ms. Doc. Larkhana, and fifteen miles north of the former town. It is situate in a fine grove close to the right bank of the Indus. Lat. 26° 33′, long. 67° 53′.

ROBAT, in Afghanistan, a halting-place on the route from E.I.C. Ms. Doc. Furrah to Giriskh, and twenty miles east of the former town. Lat. 32° 20′, long. 62° 26′.

RODA, in Sinde, a village situate on the right bank of the Ms. Survey Map. Indus. Lat. 28° 2,′ long. 69° 2′.

ROD BAHAR,[1] in Beloochistan, a valley through which the [1] E.I.C. Ms. Doc. route lies from Kelat to Beebee Nanee, in the Bolan Pass. Its name, signifying "river of spring,"* has probably been given in

* رود بهار

allusion to its fertility, pleasant aspect, and abundant irrigation. It extends for about eighteen miles in length, in a direction nearly from north-east to south-west, between lat. 29° 22'—29° 36', long. 66° 56'—67° 8'. Lying on the route between Beebee Nanee, having an elevation of 1,695 feet,[2] and Kelat, having an elevation of 6,000,[3] it can scarcely be less than 2,000 feet high, and is probably much more, as the inhabitants emigrate in winter with their flocks and herds to the low warm tract of Cutch Gundava. Rod Bahar is, throughout its whole length, supplied with water from the stream, which, flowing down the bottom of the valley, joins the Bolan river at Beebee Nanee. The soil is cultivated in patches with rice, wheat, millet, and esculent vegetables; orchards of mulberries, peaches, and apricots, yield abundance of fine fruit; and the inclosing mountains pasture numerous herds of goats and flocks of sheep. The annual migration of the inhabitants and their live stock takes place in November, and they previously bury their grain so artfully as to escape discovery until their return in the succeeding March. The ground produces two crops, of which wheat and millet are sown in August, and reaped in the beginning of April; rice is sown in the middle of May, and reaped in the middle of September. The route from Beebee Nanee to Kelat, passing through the valley, admits the passage of horses and beasts of burthen, but much labour and skill would be required to render it practicable for wheel-carriages.

RODBAR, near the south-eastern border of Seistan, a village situate on the left bank of the Helmund, which, though four hundred yards wide, rapid, and in general deep, is fordable near this place. It is held by the Towkee tribe of Belooches. Lat. 30° 30', long. 62° 33'.

ROGALIN, in Sinde, a village close to the north-west frontier, on the route from Shikarpoor to Gundava, and twenty-five miles north-west of the former town. Lat. 28° 14', long. 68° 26'.

ROGANI, in Beloochistan, a pass south of, and collateral with, the Kojuck Pass. It proceeds along the course of the Lora river, and through it lies the principal line of communication between the valley of Pisheen and Shorawuk, to the west of it. Lat. 30° 30', long. 66° 20'.

ROGHAN,[1] in Sinde, a village near the frontier of Cutch

Gundava, on the edge of the *Put*, or "arid desert," and on the great route from Shikarpoor to Afghanistan.[2] It is represented as a poor place, capable of furnishing some forage, but few or no supplies for human subsistence. There are several wells, but the water is stated to be of bad quality. Lat. 28° 13', long. 68° 26'.

[2] E.I.C. Ms. Doc.

ROH, in Afghanistan, a village on the route from Saugad to Raknee, and twelve miles north-west of the former place. Lat. 29° 46', long. 70° 32'.

E.I.C. Ms. Doc.

ROKREE, in the Punjab, a village situate on an offset of the Indus. Lat. 32° 41', long. 71° 32'.

Walker's Map of N.W. Frontier.

ROKUN, in Sinde, a village on the route from Sehwan to Larkhana, and thirty-three miles north of the former town. It is of considerable size, and is situate on the right bank of the Indus. Lat. 26° 48', long. 67° 53'.

E.I.C. Ms. Doc.

RONDU, or ROYAL, a small state or *raj*, dependent on Bulti, and situate on the right bank of the Indus, about forty miles north-west of Iskardoh. The communication along the right bank of the river, between Iskardoh and Rondu, is by means of a path not passable on horseback. The mountains abound in rock crystal and asphaltum. The raja, a vassal of the ruler of Bultistan, resides in a small fort. Lat. 35° 28', long. 74° 55'.

Vigne, Kashmir, ii. 305.

ROOD-I-ADRUSCUND.—See ADRUSCUND.

ROOD-I-GUZ, in western Afghanistan, a river, one of the feeders of the Adruscund, or river of Subzawur. It is a rapid stream, fifteen or twenty yards wide, crossing the route from Herat to Kandahar, fifty miles south of the latter place, in lat. 30° 36', long. 62° 14'.

E.I.C. Ms. Doc.; Conolly, Jour. to India, ii. 59.

ROODINJO,[1] in Beloochistan, a village on the route from Kelat to Belah, and twenty miles south of the former town. It is a poor place, having only about thirty houses, the inhabitants of which migrate in winter to the warm plain of Cutch Gundava. The vicinity of the village is barren and desolate, and the only circumstance rendering it of any importance is an abundant and excellent supply of fine water from a stream [2]* flowing close to it. Its elevation above the sea is about 5,800 feet, and the cold is very severe in winter. Connected with this circumstance is the tradition of a fact stated by Pottinger to have given rise to the name of the town. "Two merchants having accidentally

[1] E.I.C. Ms. Doc.; Masson, Bal. Afg. Panj. ii. 48; lii. 177; Id. Kalat, 320.

[2] E.I.C. Ms. Doc.

* Pottinger, however, with less probability, states, that "the people have no water except in wells, and that neither good nor plentiful."

Belooch. 38.

158 ROO—ROR.

met here on an extreme cold winter's night, the camels of one of them being laden with madder, and of the other with indigo—which two dyes are severally called in the Belooche language roden and jo—the merchant whose camels bore the latter exchanged some of that valuable article, to a great disadvantage, for a quantity of the former, with which he made a fire, and thereby preserved his life; while his more parsimonious fellow-sufferer would not apply the smallest particle of his remaining merchandize to the same purpose, and perished from cold." Roodinjo is in lat. 28° 40′, long. 66° 22′.

E.I.C. Ms. Doc.

ROOKENWALA, in the Punjab, a village on the route from Ferozpoor to Mooltan, and sixty miles south-west of the former town. Lat. 30° 37′, long. 73° 45′.

E.I.C. Ms. Doc.

ROOKUN, in Afghanistan, a village situate on the right bank of the Indus, in lat. 33° 4′, long. 71° 44′.

E.I.C. Ms. Doc.

ROOKUNPOOR, in Bhawlpoor, a village situate on the left bank of the Indus, in lat. 28° 59′, long. 70° 24′.

Pott. Belooch. 302.

ROOMRA RIVER, or rather torrent, in Beloochistan, has its source in some hills about thirty miles inland, and flowing in a southerly direction, falls into the Arabian Sea, in lat. 25° 20′, long. 63° 57′.

E.I.C. Ms. Doc.

ROREE, in Sinde, a village on the route from Sehwan to Kurrachee, and eleven miles and a half south-west of the former town. It is situate in a plain cultivated in several parts, and intersected by a watercourse, at all times yielding a good supply. Water is also to be obtained from three wells in the village. Lat. 26° 13′, long. 67° 50′.

[1] Westmacott, Jour. As. Soc. Beng. 1841, p. 393; Macmurdo, Jour. Roy. As. Soc. 1834, p. 236.
[2] Havelock, i. 118; Lord, Med. Rep. on Plain of the Indus, 59-64; Conolly, ii. 260; Burnes, iii. 73, 272; Kennedy, ii. 169; Wood, on the Indus, in App. to Burnes, 349; Id. Oxus, 51; Hough, 20; Leech, Rep. on Sindian Army, 79.

ROREE, or LOHUREE[1] (the ancient Lohurkot), in Sinde, a town situate on the eastern bank of the Indus, on a rocky eminence of limestone, interspersed with flint. This is one of those hills constituting a low range, of recent formation, stretching from Cutch Gundava[2] into Upper Sinde, and continued there by numerous knolls and peaks, sometimes nearly isolated, through part of which the Indus finds its way at Roree. The rocky site of Roree is terminated abruptly on the western side by a precipice of forty feet high, rising from the beach of the Indus, which, in inundation, attains a height of about sixteen feet above its lowest level. Westmacott is of opinion that it formerly must have risen to fifty feet, washing the brow of the eminence on which Roree stands, and that then the neighbouring rocky islets in the Indus were sunken rocks. According to the unanimous testimony of the natives, the level of the river during inundation continually decreases, and this is probably owing more to the wearing down of the rocky bed, than to any diminution of the supply of water in the upper part of the river's course.

Of the three islets in the Indus abreast of the town, the most important is that of Bukkur, a large oval rock of flint and limestone, rising twenty-five feet above the river, and crowned by the celebrated fortress of the same name. The road from the town to the ferry, communicating with Bukkur and the western bank, is for some distance excavated in the face of the rock. On the western side of the Indus, and opposite Roree, is the decayed, though once rich and populous, town of Sukkur. Of the two islets above Bukkur, the nearer is separated from it by a channel easily fordable when the river is low. One is covered with date-palms, the other with numerous tombs surmounted with spires of glazed porcelain. The bold and lofty banks, covered with groves and rich vegetation, the picturesque islets, the great fort of Bukkur, the antique towns of Roree and Sukkur, and the vast river, form a scene scarcely anywhere surpassed in grandeur and beauty.

Roree, when seen from without, has a striking and pleasing appearance, as the houses are four or five stories high, and of corresponding extent; but when surveyed more closely, they are found to be ruinous, in many instances rudely constructed with a slight timber-frame, filled up with wicker-work, and plastered with mud; and as whitewash, though very easily obtainable, is not used, they have a dingy and neglected appearance. The roofs are flat, and covered with straw, over which a layer of clay is placed, and they generally last twenty years or more, as they are exposed to little wet; but rain, when it does fall, causes great destruction amongst these frail buildings. The few more costly houses of burned brick were erected by wealthy merchants before the establishment of the dynasty of the late ameers, and are now generally unoccupied, oppression having either driven away the rich or reduced them to indigence. The flat roofs of the houses are surrounded by balustrades, and there the inhabitants spend much of their time in fine weather. The windows are not glazed, but those of the more wealthy inhabitants have shutters and lattices of wood. There are no chimneys; the apartments are in consequence stained with smoke, and indeed they are generally very dirty. The streets are so narrow that a camel in passing occupies the entire breadth from side to side. The air, in consequence, is very close and unwholesome, and this evil is increased by filth being allowed to accumulate, in great dunghills, in the open places of the town. Numbers of loathsome-looking, diseased, and famished dogs haunt the city, and are its only scavengers. There are forty mosques, in which prayers are still recited, and twice that number in a state of ruin and desertion. The great mosque stands on an elevated site in the north-east part of the town, and was built at the commencement of the seventeenth century by the lieutenant of the Emperor Acbar. It is a massive, gloomy pile of red brick, covered with three domes, and coated with glazed porcelain tiles. In an adjacent shrine is kept a hair in amber, in a gold case set with rubies and emeralds, and inclosed in another of wood enriched with silver. This the pious Mahometan undoubtingly believes to be a hair of the beard of his prophet, and a number of guardians of this precious relic are supported at the public expense.

Roree has a spacious and well-built serai, or lodging-place for travellers, but it has been allowed to fall into great decay. There are two bazaars, one for grain, the other for miscellaneous articles, and both are tolerably well supplied, but they are ill-built and ruinous. Manufactures are few and unimportant. They embrace the fabrication of paper of indifferent quality, leather, silks, and cottons, and the dyeing and printing of the last-named article. The population is mixed, consisting of Hindoos, indigenous Sindians, Belooches, Afghans, and Moguls, almost universally in a state of miserable poverty, and living in a very wretched manner. All trades and handicrafts, with the exception of works in gold, silver, and jewellery, are in the hands exclusively of Mahometans; the Hindoos devote themselves chiefly to banking, money-broking, and similar traffic. The population is estimated at about 8,000. Lat. 27° 44', long. 68° 53'.

ROTAS, in the Punjab, an extensive fort six miles west of the right or western bank of the river Jailum.[1] The interior is two miles and half long, and is of an oblong, narrow form, having its two sides and eastern end resting upon the edge of ravines, which divide it from a table-land of elevation equal to that of the hill on

[1] Moorcr. Punj. Bokh. ii. 309; Elph. Acc. of Caubul, 80; Ferishta, iii. 116.

which the fort stands. The western face of the plateau is washed by the small river Gham running at its base. Its works are of immense strength, consisting of massive walls of stone thirty feet thick, cemented with mortar, and strengthened with bastions, all crenated throughout, and provided with a double row of loopholes. Connected with the fortress is an immense well, lined with masonry, and having passages down to the water so numerous that from fifty to a hundred persons may draw water at once.[2]   [2] F. Von Hugel, Kaschmir, iii. 136.

The present fortress was built about the year 1540, by Sheher Shah,[3] the Patan Emperor of Dehly, who had driven Humaioon into exile, and he is said to have expended a million and a half sterling in its construction. When Humaioon returned, at the head of an army, to reclaim his empire, the fortress was given up to him without resistance. He demolished the palace raised within the fort by his rival and enemy, but found the massive defences too strong for the limited time and means which he could allow for their destruction. The fortress is at present in a ruinous state, and in one place a huge mass of the wall has tumbled down the precipice, and rendered the interior accessible. It is considered by military men indefensible against modern modes of attack.[4] Lat. 33° 2′, long. 73° 29′.   [3] Price, Mahomedan Hist. iii. 781; Burnes' Bokh. i. 62.   [4] Hough, 344.

ROW, in Sinde, a village situate on one of the mouths of the river Indus, in lat. 24° 35′, long. 67° 18′.   E.I.C. Ms. Doc.

ROZAN, in Sinde, a village situate on the route from Sukkur to Mittun Kote, and forty miles south-west of the latter town. Lat. 28° 39′, long. 69° 57′.   Ms. Survey Map.

ROZEH, in Afghanistan, a beautiful village, two miles north-east of Ghuznee, on the route to Kabool. It is celebrated as the burial-place of the renowned Mahmud of Ghuznee. (See GHUZNEE.) Its name, signifying "garden,"* has probably been bestowed with reference to its pleasant site.   E.I.C. Ms. Doc.

ROZEH-BAGH, in Western Afghanistan, a royal garden planted with fir-trees of great size and beauty. It lies on the route from Herat to Kandahar, and is seven miles south of the former town. Lat. 34° 18′, long. 62° 10′.   E.I.C. Ms. Doc.

ROZUR.—See ROZEH.

RUHUL, in the Punjab, a village situate fifteen miles from the right bank of the river Ghara. Lat. 30° 53′, long. 74° 5′.   E.I.C. Ms. Doc.

* روضه.

RUMZAN KHAN.—See KILLA-I-RAMAZAN-KHAN.

E.I.C. Ms. Doc. RUNGPOOR, in Afghanistan, a village situate on the right bank of the Indus, eighteen miles north of Dera Ismael Khan. Lat. 32° 3′, long. 71° 7′.

E.I.C. Ms. Doc. RUNNA, in Afghanistan, a village situate on the left bank of the Kabool river. Lat. 34° 18′, long. 71° 18′.

De La Hoste, Jour. As. Soc. Beng. 1840, p. 912. RUNNIE-KA-KOTE, in Sinde, a large fort near the town of Sunn, and about four miles west of the right or west bank of the Indus. It cost a sum exceeding 100,000*l.*, but it has never been occupied, as it has no regular supply of water, this all-important point having never, until after the completion of the structure, entered into the thoughts of the Ameers of Sinde, under whose orders the work was executed.* It is built of stone and lime-mortar, in the form of an irregular pentagon, and can contain two thousand men. A torrent from the Lukkee mountains, on the declivity of which it is situated, flows by it during heavy rains. Lat. 26°, long. 68° 10′.

Trebeck, in Moorcr. ii. 46; Gerard (J. G.), on Spiti Valley, As. Research. xviii. 244, 253. RUPSHU, in Ladakh, among the Western Himalayas, is a very elevated and barren plain, or extensive valley, bearing a scanty vegetation of grass and stunted furze; subjected, even in the height of summer, to frost and snow, and being swept over by the most impetuous whirlwinds. Its mean elevation is 16,000 feet. The climate is characterized by great aridity, and from this cause, and the intense cold, is peculiarly suited to the constitution of the yak and shawl-goat, which thrive here, notwithstanding the scantiness of pasture. Lat. 33° 20′, long. 77° 40′.

Burnes (James), Missions to Sinde, 36. RUREE, a town of Sinde on the route from Lucput, in Cutch, to Hyderabad, and on the edge of the desert. During the swell it is watered by a branch of the Indus, but suffers much from want of water at other times. There is here a magnificent mosque of great size and height. The town was formerly much more considerable than at present; its population is now scarcely 1,000. Near the town is a tank of good water. Lat. 24° 22′, long. 68° 30′.

E.I.C. Ms. Doc. RUSOOLPOOR, in the Punjab, a village situate about twelve miles from the left bank of the river Chenaub, in lat. 31° 58′, long. 73° 26′.

E.I.C. Ms. Doc. RUSTOM, in Afghanistan, a village thirty miles south of Lake Abistada. Lat. 32° 11′, long. 67° 57′.

* Yet Burnes (Bokhara, iii. 266) mentions "the copious supply of water within its walls."

S.

SAADAT,[1] in Western Afghanistan, a fort on the route from Kandahar to Herat, and ninety-five miles north-west of the former place. It was built by the celebrated but ill-fated Futteh Khan, as a residence for his mother, who maintained a petty court here, and was "renowned," says Conolly,[2] "for courage and goodness." The fort is strong and well constructed, being surrounded by a dry ditch, formidable from its section and the very hard granite in which it is excavated. The form of the fort is oblong; it is a hundred and eighty yards in length, forty in width; with round towers at the angles and sides. The entire space inclosed by the ditch is three hundred yards long and two hundred wide, the ground between the ditch and the walls being intended to protect cattle from an enemy. The supply of water is abundant, from subterraneous aqueducts, and in the vicinity is considerable cultivation. Lat. 32° 3′, long. 64° 19′.

[1] E.I.C. Ms. Doc.
[2] Jour. to India, ii. 83.

SADAN, in Sinde, a village near the right or western bank of the Indus. It is situate in a wooded country, at the eastern base of the extension of the Lukkee hills to the south. For a dozen miles south of the village the country is occupied by an extensive Sikargah or hunting preserve, formerly belonging to one of the Ameers of Hyderabad. Lat. 24° 56′, long. 68° 10′.

Kennedy, Sinde and Kabool, i. 111.

SADAUT.—See SAADAT.

SADI KHYLE, in Afghanistan, a village situate on the road from Peshawur to Kala Bagh through Kohat, from which latter town it is distant about fifteen miles. Lat. 33° 21′, long. 71° 32′.

E.I.C. Ms. Doc.

SAHEEWALL, in the Punjab, a village situate on the left bank of the Jailum river. Lat. 31° 47′, long. 72° 4′.

Walker's Map of N.W. Frontier.

SAHOO, in Bhawlpoor, a village situate on the left bank of the Ghara river, in lat. 29° 47′, long. 72° 12′.

Walker's Map of N.W. Frontier.

SAID KHAN, in Afghanistan, a village situate on the left bank of the river Turnak, twenty miles south of Kilat-i-Ghiljie. Lat. 31° 59′, long. 66° 34′.

E.I.C. Ms. Doc.

SAIDAN, in Afghanistan, a village situate on the route from Ghuznee to Kandahar, fifty miles south-west of the former town. Lat. 32° 56′, long. 67° 50′.

E.I.C. Ms. Doc.

SAIYADABAD,[1] in Afghanistan, a dilapidated fortress situate in the valley of Bamian, and close to the western side of the ruined city of Galgula. It is a huge, massive structure, originally of great strength, built of burnt bricks of extraordinary size. The entrance was formerly through a gateway of large dimensions on the western side, but this has been long built up, and admission to the interior is now gained by one much smaller on the south. The inmates live in rows of houses of two stories, each story being about twenty-five feet high. These rows are ranged along the inside of the ramparts, so that a small area is left in the middle of the inclosure. All the houses exhibit traces of having formerly been covered with domes of mud, but these have fallen in from the ravages of time, and the roofs are now flat, and supported on rafters. Water is at present obtained from a well, but there is a tradition that it formerly was supplied by subterraneous aqueducts, the situation of which being disclosed to a besieger by the daughter of a king who once held the place, its capture was the consequence. Hence it is called by the natives Killa Dokhtar, " daughter's castle."

Masson supposes that Saiyadabad formed part of the ill-fated city of Gulgula, and consequently fell with it before the arms of Zingis Khan.[2] In the early part of the present century the fort was repaired and rendered defensible, and its owner, confiding in its impregnability, acted as if independent of the ruler of Kabool. Being made prisoner, he was under the necessity of surrendering the place to the wily Haji Khan Khaka, so notorious for his tortuous and treacherous policy during the occupation of Kabool by the British. Connected with the fortress, and in the same architectural style, are the massive ruins of a mosque, from which circumstance Masson concludes that this stronghold was constructed by Mussulmans. Saiyadabad is in lat. 34° 50', long. 67° 50'.

SAIYADWALA, in the Punjab, a considerable walled town, situate near the right or western bank of the Ravi. A spacious and well-furnished bazaar extends quite across it. A few hundred yards to the west of the town is a mud fortress of considerable strength, surrounded by a trench. Lat. 31° 5', long. 73° 16'.

SAKHEE SAWAR PASS, in Afghanistan, on the route from Dera Ghazee Khan to Kandahar. It is a difficult pass, penetrating the Suliman mountains at Ootpalana in lat. 30° 2', long.

[1] Masson, Bal. Afg. Panj. ii. 425.

[2] As. Res. vi. 472, Wilford, on Mount Caucasus.

Masson, Bal. Afg. Panj. i. 403.

E.I.C. Ms. Doc.

70° 4', and, though greatly shortening the route, is little frequented, on account of the depredations of the mountaineers.

SAKHEE SURWAR, in Afghanistan, a large village in the Derajat, thirty-nine miles west of the Indus, and thirty-six west of Dera Ghazee Khan. It is often devoid of water, which has to be brought from a spring in the mountains five miles distant. It gives name to a celebrated pass on the route from Dera Ghazee Khan to Kandahar. The pass commences four miles west of the village, by a steep descent into a ravine, the bottom of which is covered with loose stones. The road is commanded by the steep heights on each side, and is little frequented on account of the depredations of the Marree freebooters holding the neighbouring hills. Sakhee Surwar is about twenty miles east of the great eastern acclivity of the Suliman mountains. Lat. 30° 2', long. 70° 26'. E.I.C. Ms. Doc.; Leech, App. 38.

SAKHIR, in Western Afghanistan, a village situate in lat. 32° 15', long. 62° 53'. Map of Afg.

SAKREE, in South-eastern Sinde, a village twenty miles north of Nuggur Parker, situate on the route from thence to Omercote, in lat. 24° 40', long. 70° 44'. Ms. Survey Map.

SAKUL, in Kashmir, a village situate at the eastern base of Pir Panjal, and eighteen miles west of the town of Sirinagur. Lat. 34° 4', long. 74° 28'. E.I.C. Ms. Doc.

SALAT, in the Punjab, a small town on the Dor river, within a few miles of the east bank of the Indus, and on the route from the Punjab to Kashmir through the Dub pass. Lat. 34° 5', long. 72° 56'. F. Von Hugel, Kaschmir, iii. 62; Vigne, Kashmir, ii. 187.

SALEHKEH, in Afghanistan, a fort situate on the route from Ghuznee, by the western shore of Lake Abistada, to Shawl, about ten miles north-west of the above-mentioned lake. Lat. 32° 40', long. 67° 45'. E.I.C. Ms. Doc.

SALIKI SERAI,[1] in the Punjab, a considerable town situate near the east bank of the Indus, on the great route to Kashmir by the Dub Pass. It has a large and well-supplied bazaar. Two miles from it is the fort of Krishen Ghur, which Vigne[2] declares the finest specimen of a "square, regular mud fort, which he had seen in the Punjab." Lat. 34° 5', long. 72° 55'. [1] P. Von Hugel, Kaschmir, iii. 65. [2] Kashmir, ii. 187.

SALLARAH, in Sinde, a village two miles from the left bank of the Indus, and twenty-two miles north of Hyderabad. Lat. 25° 41', long. 68° 27'. E.I.C. Ms. Doc.

SALULANG PASS (properly Sir Ulung, "meadow head"), E.I.C. Ms. Doc.; Leech, Passes of in Afghanistan, lies across the Hindoo Koosh mountain. The route by this pass proceeds northward up a gorge, which, at its southern extremity, opens into the Ghorbund valley, near the eastern entrance. The pass is practicable for horses during the summer months, but Wood found it impassable, from snow and excessive cold, as early as the beginning of November, and his Hindoo followers narrowly escaped perishing. The hamlet of Sir Ulung gives name to the pass, which is situate in lat. 35° 37′, long. 68° 55′.

<small>Hind. Koosh, 33; Lord, Koh-i-Damun, 48; Elph. Acc. of Caubul, 90; Wood, Oxus, 194.</small>

SALT RANGE.[1] — An extensive group of mountains stretching generally, in lat. 32° 30′—33° 30′, in a direction from west to east, from the eastern base of the Suliman mountains, in Afghanistan, to the river Jailum, in the Punjab. This range is, in different parts, known to the natives under various denominations, but is by Europeans comprehended under the general term Salt Range, in consequence of the great extent and thickness of the beds of common salt which it in many places contains. Though the southern part of this group terminates rather abruptly at the west bank of the Jailum,[2] the more northern part is, according to Jameson,[3] connected with the recent formation constituting the lowest and most southern range of the Himalaya, and runs " on by Bimber, Jummoo, Nurpoor, and down by the south of Belaspoor, crossing the Jumna at Fyzabad, and the Ganges at Hurdwar."[3] The general direction of the range is from north-west to south-east.

<small>[1] E.I.C. Ms. Doc.; Elph. Acc. of Caubul, 103.</small>

<small>[2] Jacquemont, v. 109.
[3] Jour. As. Soc. Beng. 1848, p. 195, on the Geol. and Zoology of the Punjab.</small>

<small>[3] Jameson, 195.</small>

This extensive range, of recent formation, may consequently be considered to contain not only the saliferous deposits of Kala Bagh and Pind Dadun Khan, but also those of Mundi, in the north-east of the Punjab. Its geological conformation has been examined on the west bank of the Jailum, at Pind Dadun Khan and Jelalpoor, and there found to comprise the following rocks ;[4]—1st, limestone compact, varying in colour from grey to black, and devoid of organic remains ; 2nd, sandstone ; 3rd, sandstone conglomerate ; 4th, red, yellow, and greenish clay ; 5th, sulphate of lime or gypsum ; 6th, conglomerate. All the strata are highly inclined (the angles varying from 30° to 60°), and they have no uniform direction. The conglomerate consists of a calcareous or silicious cement, containing boulders of granite, syenite, trap, quartz, and limestone, which last abounds in organic remains. The salt pervades all these formations, but is principally enveloped in clay, and occurs in enormous masses, one of those now worked being two hundred

<small>[4] Id. 196; Jacquemont, 114.</small>

feet thick.[5] In colour it varies from white to flesh-colour, or brick-red. It is granular, the concretions being very large and very compact, so that platters[6] and other utensils are made out of it, and take a high polish. Jameson[7] states it to be so pure as to require only grinding; Burnes, on the contrary, alleges it to have a considerable mixture of some substance, probably magnesia, which renders it unfit for curing meat.[8]

[5] Jameson, 199.
[6] Id. 201; Macartney, in Elph. 641.
[7] 201.
[8] Burnes, Bokh. i. 55.

The air of the salt-mines has deadly effects on the health of those employed in them, producing chronic and wasting catarrh, and distressing and fatal affections of the lungs. In consequence, the average length of life among the miners does not exceed thirty-five or forty years. Jameson[9] considers that considerable skill has been shewn in the working of these mines. They have been long known, being mentioned in the Ayeen Akbery.[1] At the time of the visit of Burnes,[2] in 1832, the total quantity of salt raised in a year, amounted to eighty million pounds, and it was sold at the mine at the rate of fifty pounds for a rupee. The present price is double, the advance having been made by Gulab Singh, who now holds the mines.

[9] 200.
[1] ii. 100.
[2] Bokh. i. 55.

The elevation of the Salt range is not considerable, and probably no summit attains the height of 2,500 feet above the sea.[3] Burnes[4] states that these mountains contain alum, antimony, and sulphur. Jacquemont,[5] Burnes,[6] and Wood,[7] obtained numerous specimens of coal from various parts of them. These are rejected by Jameson[8] as valueless, on the ground that they are "not true bituminous coal,"* a condemnation which, if just, must also apply to the vast and highly valuable deposits of anthracite and stone-coal in Wales, Ireland, and many other places.

[3] Id. i. 52; Jameson, 196; Jacquemont, v. 122.
[4] Bokh. i. 52.
[5] 113.
[6] Rep. on Coal, 78.
[7] Rep. on Coal, 86.
[8] 208.

* Dr. Jameson[1] elsewhere thus expresses himself:—"To the question, is any good coal likely to be found in quantity in this district? we would at once answer decidedly in the negative." But geology is a department of knowledge in which the field is so immense, and the data often so imperfect, that such sweeping conclusions can rarely be warranted. The opinion of a very weighty authority was widely different. Mr. James Prinsep, in reporting to government on the coal found on the western bank, stated that "four of the specimens were in fact of the very finest form of mineral coal, that in which all vegetable appearance is lost;" of one of the specimens, a kind of jet, he remarked "that, if found in sufficient quantities, it would not only answer well as a fuel, but be superior to all other coals for the particular object in getting up steam, from the large proportion of inflammable gas it disengaged under combustion."[2]

[1] Jour. As. Soc. Beng.
[2] Burnes, Pers. Nar. 113.

SALT RANGE.

The Salt range is remarkably barren. "Vegetation is scanty, and the bold and bare precipices, some of which rise at once from the plain, present a forbidding aspect of desolation."[9] About lat. 32° 50′, long. 71° 40′, the Indus traverses this range, making its way down a deep, narrow, rocky channel, on the sides of which the salt-beds come to light. Those parts of the range which lie on the west side of the river are denominated by Macartney[1] the salt-hills of Kala-Bagh or Karra-Bagh, from the name of the town where its geological structure is most fully exposed to view. Its appearance there is described by Elphinstone with his usual judgment and power of language. "Callabaugh, where we left the plain, well deserves a minute description. The Indus is here compressed by mountains into a deep channel only three hundred and fifty yards broad. The mountains on each side have an abrupt descent into the river, and a road is cut along their base for upwards of two miles. It had been widened for us, but was still so narrow, and the rock over it so steep, that no camel with a bulky load could pass. To obviate this inconvenience, twenty-eight boats had been prepared to convey our largest packages up the river. The first part of this pass is actually overhung by the town of Callabaugh, which is built in a singular manner upon the face of the hill, every street rising above its neighbour, and, I imagine, only accessible by means of the houses below it. As we passed beneath, we perceived windows and balconies at a great height, crowded with women and children. The road beyond was cut out of the solid salt at the foot of cliffs of that mineral, in some places more than one hundred feet high above the river. The salt is hard, clear, and almost pure. It would be like crystal were it not in some parts streaked and tinged with red. In some places salt-springs issue from the foot of the rocks, and leave the ground covered with a crust of the most brilliant whiteness. All the earth, particularly near the town, is almost blood-red, and this, with the strange and beautiful spectacle of the salt rocks, and the Indus flowing in a deep and clear stream through lofty mountains past this extraordinary town, presented such a scene of wonder as is seldom to be witnessed."[2]

The rocks in this part of the range are—first, magnesian limestone; second, new red sandstone; third, fossiliferous sandstone; fourth, red clay and sandstone, containing coal and mine-

---

[9] Burnes, i. 52; Elph. Acc. of Caubul, 80; Jameson, 203.

[1] In Elph. 640.

[2] Elph. Acc. of Caubul, 36, 37.

ral sulphur, rock-salt, gypsum, brown and red iron-ore, and alum-slate.[3] The lower beds contain no organic remains, but the upper abound in them. The iron-ore is a red or brown hematite, so rich that in many places the needle of the compass becomes quite useless, even at a considerable distance from the rocks, owing to their being highly magnetic, from the quantity of iron which they contain. The sandstone abounds with the exuviæ of enormous animals, either saurians or sauroid fishes. Most of the torrents of the Salt range carry down gold dust in their sands, which are washed, in search of the precious deposit, in numerous places,[4] throughout the greater part of the year. The hills at Kala Bagh contain great quantities of aluminous slate, from which alum is obtained at various manufactories at that town. The slate, well sprinkled with water, is laid in alternate strata with wood, until the pile reaches a height of from twenty-five to thirty feet; it is then lighted, and the combustion continued for about twelve hours, in which time the colour of the slate is converted from greyish black to dark red. This change of colour indicating that the process has been carried to a sufficient extent, the mass is thrown into a tank holding as much water as it is computed the alum is competent to saturate. After three days, the water, which becomes of a dark red colour, is drawn off, mixed with a due proportion of potash, and boiled down, the residuum on cooling becoming a solid mass of alum. It is sold at the rate of 1l. 19s.* (= 384 lbs.). Dr. Jameson expatiates[5] with the earnestness of sanguine excitement on the mineral wealth of the Salt range, concluding in these terms:—" Such is a rapid account of the riches of this district, and there are few, if any, districts in the world where iron, gold, sulphur, salt, gypsum, limestone, saltpetre, and *coal* † are met with in such quantity."

[3] Jour. As. Soc. Beng. 1843, p. 204, Jameson.

[4] Jameson, 212.

[5] Id. 213; Jour. As. Soc. Beng. 1842, p. 2.

SANDWALLE, in Afghanistan, a halting-place on the Boree or Mohavee route from Kandahar to Dera Ghazee Khan, and fifty miles west of the latter town. Lat. 30° 52', long. 69° 8'.

E.I.C. Ms. Doc.

SANGAD, or BUZDAR PASS, in Afghanistan, across the

E.I.C. Ms. Doc.; Leech, App. 39.

* This appears a very high price. Mohun Lal states it at only a fourth of a rupee per maund, which, on the other hand, is incredibly small.

Jour. As. Soc. Beng. 1838, p. 26, Acc. of Kala Bagh.

† It is, perhaps, needless to observe, that this statement respecting coal is at variance with the opinions expressed by Dr. Jameson in other places on the same subject.

Suliman mountains, in lat. 29° 50′, long. 70° 10′. It commences at the village of Sangad, on the route from Dera Ghazee Khan to Shikarpoor, and proceeds, in a north-westerly direction, to Raknee, on the Sakhee Surwar Pass, and thence north to the Mohavee pass. It is rather a good route, and practicable for wheel-carriages.

SANG GHAR, in Afghanistan, in the Derajat, on the west of the Indus, and between it and the Suliman mountains, is a dependency of Dera Ghazee Khan, and has a mud fort of considerable extent, but of little strength. The Sikhs have lately expelled its former chief, a Belooche, and seized the territory, which is fertile and productive. Lat. 30° 40′, long. 70° 45′.

Leech, App. 59; Masson, Bal. Afg. Panj. i. 36; Jour. As. Soc. Beng. 1839, p. 763, Irwin, Mem. on Afg.

SANGRAR, in Sinde, a town twelve miles south-east of Roree, on the route to Jessulmair. It has some trade with Marwar. Population about 1,000. Lat. 27° 36′, long. 69° 4′.

E.I.C. Ms. Doc.; Leech, on Sind. Army, 87.

SARAWAN, in Beloochistan, a province bounded on the north and west by Afghanistan, on the east by Afghanistan and Cutch Gundava, and on the south by Jhalawan, Kelat, and Mekran. It lies between lat. 27° 53′ and 30° 20′, and long. 64° and 67° 40′, is about two hundred and fifty miles in length from north-east to south-west, eighty miles in its greatest breadth, and has a surface of about fifteen thousand square miles. It is in general a very mountainous, rugged, and elevated tract, rising on its northern frontier into the lofty mountain Tukatoo,[1] supposed to have an elevation of between 11,000 and 12,000 feet, and on the east into the range which overhangs the Bolan Pass. On the west is the lofty range called the Sarawanee mountains. There are, however, some level and productive tracts.[2] The valley of Shawl, in the north, is fertile, well watered, well cultivated, and has a fine climate, though rather sharp in winter, the snow sometimes lying for two months together. It produces in abundance grain, pulse, madder, tobacco, and excellent fruits. At some distance south of this lies the valley or plain of Mustung, resembling that of Shawl in climate, soil, and productions, but superior to it in all these respects. Between them is the Dasht-i-Bedaulut, a plain of about twenty miles in diameter, barren and uninhabited, except in spring, when it is adequately supplied with water, and supports numerous flocks and herds. For the rest of the year water is very scarce, and then the plain becomes a cheerless waste, presenting only a scanty clothing of wild thyme, and similar plants, which thrive in arid and elevated tracts. Sarawan is in general re-

[1] Havelock, i. 249.

[2] Havelock, i. 251; Masson, Kalat, 311; Pott. 262; Hough, 57.

markably arid, having no considerable stream, except the Bolan, which flows through the Bolan Pass, into Cutch Gundava, where it is lost in the sands, and a few torrents rushing westward into the desert, where they all disappear from evaporation or absorption. Masson[3] estimates the population of this extensive province at 50,000 persons, an amount which seems incredibly small. The only places of any importance are Shawl, or Quetta, Sarawan, and Mustung. [3] Kalat, 327.

SARAWAN, in Beloochistan, in the province of the same name, a small town containing about five hundred houses, built of mud, and surrounded by a mud wall with bastions. It is situate in a barren district, and has nothing to recommend it but a perennial supply of fine water from the little rivulet Bale. The chieftain is exempt from tribute to the Khan of Kelat, but furnishes a contingent of two hundred men when required. Lat. 28° 47′, long. 64° 50′. Pott. Belooch. 128.

SARN, a small river in the Punjab, rises in the mountains west of Kashmir, and, joining the Dor, the united stream falls into the Indus above Torbela, in lat. 34° 12′, long. 72° 39′. F. Von Hugel, Kaschmir, iii. 47.

SARUNGKOL, in the Punjab, a village about thirty miles east of the Indus, in lat. 33° 2′, long. 72° 15′. E.I.C. Ms. Doc.

SATA, or SETTA,[1] in Sinde, the greatest eastern branch of the Indus, or rather the continuation of the main stream, which formerly sent off to the west a large arm called the Buggaur.[2] This last, however, is now almost completely closed during the season when the river is low, becoming then little else than a succession of *dunds*, or fresh-water pools.[3] The Sata below the divarication is generally about a thousand yards wide. It sends off, on the left or eastern side, two branches—the Mull and Moutnee, once great streams, but now, during the dry season, shallow rivulets. At the time that Carless wrote, in 1837, the Hujamree and Kedywaree mouths, which gave exit to two other branches sent off by the Sata on the right side, were navigable, but in 1839 the Hujamree[4] mouth was closed by a great alteration in the course of the stream. Having thrown off these branches on the right and left side, the Sata, still the main stream of the Indus, and known in the lower part of its course by the names Munnejah and Wanyanee, falls into the Indian Ocean by the Kookewaree mouth, in lat. 24° 2′, long. 67° 32′. [1] Carless, Official Survey of the Indus, 1. [2] Burnes, iii. 228. [3] Kennedy, i. 74. [4] Id. 230.

SATGHARRA, in the Punjab, a town on the left bank of Masson, Bal. Afg. Punj. i. 450.

the Ravee, having several small forts, whence its name, the "seven castles." It is situate in a country abounding in pasture, but in many places overrun with wood and jungle. Lat. 31°, long. 73° 20'.

Vigne, Kashmir, ii. 262.

SATPUR, in Bultistan, or Little Tibet, a defile by which the route from the elevated table-land of Deotsuh passes into the valley of Iskardoh on its south side. At the southern entrance of the pass is a lake nearly two miles long, and about a mile wide, and on the eastern side of this the path runs along the base of a steep mountain, so that an invading force would be exposed to certain destruction by rocks rolled down the declivity. The elevation of the pass is probably about 12,000 feet. Lat. 35°, long. 75° 24'.

E.I.C. Ms. Doc.

SAUGRA, in Kafiristan, a village situate in lat. 35° 41', long. 70° 51'.

Ms. Survey Map.

SAUL, in Sinde, a village situate on the right bank of the Indus, eighteen miles south-west of the city of Hyderabad. Lat. 25° 10', long. 68° 18'.

SCINDE.—See SINDE.

Walker's Map of Afg.

SEAH KHANA, in Afghanistan, a hamlet about sixty miles north-east of Subzawur. Lat. 33° 30', long. 63° 7'.

E.I.C. Ms. Doc.

SEALKEE, in the Punjab, a village situate on the right bank of the river Chenaub, fifteen miles south-west of the city of Mooltan. Lat. 30° 6', long. 71° 18'.

E.I.C. Ms. Doc.

SEAOUL, in Afghanistan, a village situate where the Shutul Pass over Hindoo Koosh opens into the valley of Punchshir. Lat. 35° '16, long. 69° 11'.

Elph. Acc. of Caubul, 136.

SEBEE, or SEWEE, in Afghanistan, a town situate near the southern frontier, and fifteen miles east of the town of Dadur. During the war in Afghanistan, Sebee was occupied by a British garrison, which was withdrawn on the final evacuation of the country in 1842. The intense heat of the climate is noted by a native proverb—" O God! when you had Sewee, why need you have made hell?" Lat. 29° 30', long. 67° 59'.

Carless, Official Survey of the Indus, 2; Burnes' Bokh. iii. 238.

SEER, in Sinde, the mouth of the Goongroo or Pinyaree branch of the Indus, which, in its lower part, is, in consequence of the dam thrown across it at Maghribee, deserted by the stream, except during the highest state of the inundation. This estuary is navigable for boats of forty tons. The Seer mouth is in lat. 23° 36', long. 68° 13'.

SEERANNEE, in Sinde, a village on the route from Hydera- E.I.C. Ms. Doc.
bad to Lucput, and sixty-five miles south-east of the former
place. Lat. 24° 27′, long. 68° 45′.

SEETAREE, in the Punjab, a village situate on the left Walker's Map of
bank of the Indus, in lat. 29° 31′, long. 70° 55′. N.W. Frontier.

SEHAMA, in Kashmir, a village six miles east of the town of Ms. Survey Map.
Baramula, and in lat. 34° 10′, long. 74° 18′.

SEHKOH, in North-western Afghanistan, a village situate Walker's Map of
in lat. 35° 12′, long. 65° 30′. Afg.

SEHRA, in the Punjab, a village on the route from Koteli to E.I.C. Ms. Doc.
Punch, and twelve miles north of the former town. Lat. 33° 39′,
long. 73° 50′.

SEHWAN,[1] in Sinde, a town situate on an eminence at [1] Burnes, Bokh.
the verge of a swamp on the right or south-west bank of the iii. 55, 265; Pers.
Arul, which flows from the Lake Manchur into the Indus, and nedy, i. 171;
which abreast of the town is about a hundred yards wide, and of Khyrpoor, in
when lowest twelve feet deep. The Indus, a few years ago, Jour. As. Soc.
flowed close to the town, but is now two miles distant from it. 1209; Macmurdo
Ruined houses, mosques, and sepulchres cover here a wide space, Roy. As. Soc.
and bear evidence of the greatness of this city before it was 1834, p. 295.
ruined by the Kalora princes of Sinde. The houses of the present
town are of mud, often several stories high, and arched. They
are superior to those usually to be seen in the towns of Sinde;
but the bazaar, long, crooked, narrow, and covered with
mats to exclude the scorching beams of the sun, is ill supplied
with goods, and has little trade. The manufactures are inconsiderable, consisting of caps, shoes, and petty silken fabrics.
The inhabitants are chiefly fishermen or beggars, which last class
are supported by the pilgrims who flock to the shrine of Lal
Shah Baz, whose memory stands high for sanctity, not only with
Mussulmans, but also with Hindoos. The remains of this reputed saint, who was originally from Khorasan, lie in a tomb
inclosed in a quadrangular edifice, covered with a dome and lantern, ornamented with smaller domes and spires, and with glazed
porcelain tiles, bearing numerous inscriptions in Arabic characters. The gate is of hammered silver, as is the balustrade round
the tomb, which is covered with rich cloths. The sepulchre is
reputed to contain a considerable treasure, and its keepers are
endowed with the gardens of Sehwan and several villages. Great
numbers of pilgrims flock to this spot from all parts of Sinde and

the neighbouring countries, and, according to the popular belief, even the fish pay the same homage to the saint's memory. But neither the possession of so sacred a deposit, nor the example of so much devotion, has any beneficial effect on the morals of the population, who are remarkable for idleness and profligacy. North-west of the town, and separated from it by a deep channel, is an eminence about eighty feet high, having its sides cased with a brick wall. The summit is oval, and is twelve hundred feet long and seven hundred and fifty wide.[2] It is covered with ruins and fragments of pottery; the remains of towers are visible along the circuit of the wall, and two fine arched gateways are in tolerable preservation. The population of Sehwan is estimated by Burnes* at about 2,000. Lat. 26° 21′, long. 67° 55′.

[2] De La Hoste, in Jour. As. Soc. Beng. 1840, p. 913.

SEISAN, in Sinde, a village situate on the west side of Lake Manchur. Lat. 26° 28′, long. 67° 40′.

Ms. Survey Map.

SEISTAN,[1] on the western frontier of Afghanistan, a district of late years sometimes under Persian, at others under Afghan sway, according as the power of either nation acquired the ascendancy. It was formerly called also Segestan, and sometimes Nimroz,[2] † or "the country of mid-day or the south." Its boundaries are set out by D'Herbelot to have been at the remote period of which he treats—on the west, Khorasan; east, Mekran; south, desert of Fars; north, India. In its present extent,[3] Seistan measures about a hundred miles in length from north to south, sixty miles in breadth from east to west, has a nearly oval outline, and an area of about five thousand square miles.‡ It lies between lat. 30° 30′—32°, long. 61°—62° 30′, and is bounded on the north by Khorasan; on the east by Afghanistan; on the south by the great desert dividing the last-mentioned country from Beloochistan; on the west by Persia. Conolly, to whom is due the credit of any accurate information

[1] Elph. Acc. of Caubul, 492.

[2] D'Herbelot, iv. 288.

[3] Jour. As. Soc. Beng. 1840, p. 710, Conolly (E.), Phys. Geog. of Seistan.

* Personal Narrative, 41. Elsewhere (Bokhara, iii. 55, 227) at 10,000.

† Nimroz, نيمروز mid-day, or half a day. Kinneir relates an idle tradition that this country was called Nimrose, because being "once entirely under water, but having been drained in the short space of half a day, by the genii, it hence received the name of Nimrose."

Geog. of Persia, 189.

‡ Christie states the area at only five hundred square miles, or a tenth of the amount set forth in the text. Conolly, however, was enabled to afford the subject a much more careful notice, and the outline laid down in his map gives the larger amount.

In App. to Pott. Belooch. 407.

which we possess respecting the physical geography of this country, gives the following description of the arrangement of its surface:—" The southern limit of the lower ranges of that portion of the great Caucasian chain of mountains, which lies between the 62nd and 65th meridians of east longitude, is well defined by the lower or Delaram road from Girishke to Furrah. From this line a vast desolate tract extends, part of that great desert named, rather loosely, by Malcolm the salt desert. Sloping gradually to the south-west, it descends, like the plains of Tartary, in steppes, till its progress is arrested, on the south, by a high sandy desert, and on the west by a broad and lofty chain of hills, which stretches, in a south-west direction, from probably near Ghorian to the Surhud, and thus, perhaps, connects the Parapomisan mountains (Huzarah mountains) with the southern Kohistan (highlands of Mekran). The south-west corner of this thus interrupted plain, the last and lowest steppes,* are Seistan."[4] It is, in fact, a basin or plain, having on every side higher grounds, and receiving in its most depressed part the waters of a system of drainage extending over above a hundred thousand square miles. From the east it receives the great river Helmund, the Khash Rood, the Ibrahim Joi, and some others of less note; from the north, the Furrah Rood, the Adruscund or river of Subzawur, and some smaller streams. The only one of its streams which flows from the west is the Bundau river, thus described by Conolly:[5]—" During the wet season, a mountain torrent rather than a river flows south-east into the lake (Hamoon) from Bundau, by the name of which place it is known. The Bundau has a course of fifty miles, and only deserves notice as being, as far as our knowledge extends, the solitary stream which enters Seistan on the west." The salt and sultry desert of the south of course supplies no streams. All the above, even the Helmund, partake of the nature of mountain torrents—at one time of the year rushing down with great rapidity and violence, and with a large volume of muddy water; at other times a shallow stream of clear water rolls along the bottom of their beds, which in the smaller rivers are often dry, or become a succession of pools. The Helmund, however, at all times retains a considerable body of water. Christie found it, at the end of March, four

[4] Conolly, 710.

[5] 713.

* Conolly here mistakes the German *steppe*, meaning " heath," for the English " step " of stairs, or similar ascent.

hundred yards wide, very deep, and with uncommonly fine water. The contents of these streams stagnate in the more depressed parts of the country, forming shallow lakes or morasses, the number, extent, and shape of which occasionally change as their basins are filled up with matter deposited by the currents, or as unusual quantity of water lodges on any particular spot. Of these swamps the principal are the Great Hamoon,* about seventy miles long and fifteen or twenty wide; the Duk-i-Teer, about a third of its size, and communicating with it on the eastern side; the swamp of Aishkineik, and a few others. The Hamoon of Zirreh, so denominated from a ruined town of that name on its border, at one time extended over a considerable space south of the Great Hamoon, but is now nearly dried up, in consequence of the Helmund, which formerly replenished it, having some years since deserted that part of the country. So variable are the limits of these Hamoons, or swamps, that they have different shapes in every different month of the year. The whole of Seistan is completely level, except one small hill, the Kohizor, or Koh-i-Khwajah, rising over the Great Hamoon, near its eastern border, and not a stone is to be found, except a few rounded pebbles in the beds of the rivers. The soil is either a light and friable earth, similar to that of the neighbouring desert, or a rich alluvial loam; but, notwithstanding its fertility, forest trees are unknown, though dense jungles of tamarisk in many places overspread the surface.

The country on the banks of the Helmund, at the eastern frontier, is described by Christie[6] in favourable terms:—"There the banks of the river are well cultivated and fruitful, having a fine rich soil, irrigated by the stream; but the utmost breadth of this fertile strip does not exceed two miles, whence the desert rises in lofty cliffs, and extends over an uninterrupted tract without water or vegetation to the great road from Herat to Kandahar on the one side, and on the other down towards the route pursued by Lieutenant Pottinger from Nooshky to Dizuk and Bunpoor. The country, though now only inhabited by Afghans and Beloochees in felt tents, still bears the marks of former civilization and opulence, and there are ruins of villages, forts, and windmills along the whole route from Rodbar to Dooshak." The elevation

[6] Pott. 407.

* See HAMOON in the alphabetical arrangement.

of Seistan* does not appear to have been ascertained, but an approximation to its determination may be attempted. Kandahar is supplied with water by canals from the Urghundab, and consequently the bed of that river, at the place of their divergence, five or six miles to the west, cannot lie below the town, ascertained to have an elevation of 3,484 feet.[7] The course of the continuous streams, Urghundab and Helmund, from the vicinity of Kandahar to the Great Hamoon, is, in round numbers, two hundred miles; and if we allow to each mile a fall of five feet, which would render the current an unnavigable and very rapid torrent, the elevation of the most depressed part of Seistan would reach about 2,500 feet. This elevation is not incompatible with the very high temperature of Seistan, as Kandahar, in the same latitude, and having a greater elevation by a thousand feet, has a very hot climate.† The heat in Seistan, however, exceeds that of Kandahar, and is so great as to preclude the comfortable enjoyment of life, except during the three winter months.[8] The Gurmseh,[9]‡ especially on the banks of the Helmund, in the east of Seistan, is noted for the great heat of the climate.

[7] Jour. As. Soc. Beng. 1842, p. 57, Grif. Bor. and Ther. Obs. in Afg.; Hough, Narr. Exp. in Afg. App. 74.

[8] Conolly, ut supra, 718, 725.
[9] Elph. Acc. of Caubul, 137.

The air throughout Seistan is unhealthy, producing various kinds of fevers, especially intermittents. The country is remarkably subject to wind, a strong steady gale blowing, during the warm six months, from the Huzareh mountains on the north, to supply the rarified air which ascends from the sultry desert lying southwards.[1] This wind sweeps clouds of saline dust over the country, and is so distressing to the eyes that one man in every five suffers from diseases of those organs. Sometimes the wind is so loaded with sand as completely to overwhelm towns.[2]

[1] Conolly, ut supra, 718.

[2] D'Herbelot, iv. 188; Elph. 492.

As is frequently the case with bodies of water having no outlet, the various Hamoons are impregnated with salt to a greater or less

* Humboldt, in the hypsometrical map annexed to his *Asie Centrale*, states the elevation half-way between Yezd and Lake Zirreh (the Great Hamoon) at 350 toises (= 2,205 feet), but giving neither the authority nor grounds for this position, it of course is of doubtful weight.

† Baber[1] states that the heat in Hindostan is not to be compared with that of Kandahar, not being above half so warm as it. Atkinson,[2] on the 30th of July, found "the weather intensely hot. The paper," he says, "on which I am writing curls up, and is as crisp as if it was before a blazing fire."

[1] Memoirs, 334.
[2] Exp. in Afg. 181.

‡ گرم "warm," and سال "a place."

degree, so as in some instances not to be drinkable. The soil of the southern desert is for the most part sandy; that, on the contrary, of the north-western is a hard, compact, light-coloured clay, generally devoid of vegetation, but in some places producing a growth of tamarisks and other stunted shrubs, or of harsh dry grass. D'Herbelot mentions that Seistan, according to common report, so abounded in gold, that it used to spring from the earth as if by a vegetative process. Conolly does not appear to mention gold as found in Seistan. It may, probably, be gathered from the sands of the numerous rivers.

The beasts of prey are leopards, wolves, otters, jackals, hyænas, foxes. There are also porcupines, hedgehogs, kangaroos, and rats. Wild asses and deer are very numerous. Wild hogs lurk in the marshes in great numbers, whence they issue to devastate the crops, of which it is computed that they destroy one half. They are hunted with dogs and destroyed with spear and matchlock; but the Mahometan prejudices of the Seistanis preclude them from eating the flesh of this animal; it is, therefore, abandoned to the dogs. Cows grow very fat on the reeds and sedge of the Hamoons, but are frequently subject to great mortality: horses cannot be kept in Seistan, being either destroyed by a species of venomous fly, which swarms there in surprising quantities, or by a bloody discharge from the bowels, to which the animal is liable in this country. Camels and sheep are subject to a less degree of mortality, but do not thrive very well. Water-fowl are very numerous; those of most common occurrence are pelicans, geese, and ducks.

Travellers in Seistan observe numerous traces of its former populousness and industrious cultivation. Thus, according to Conolly,[3] "the violent action of the swollen streams was in a great measure moderated, by large bodies of water being drawn off in canals, which were conducted in some places as far as forty miles through dry and sandy tracts. Massive embankments had also been constructed by rich and enlightened governments, which prevented the water from flowing without control, and confined it within certain bounds for the purposes of cultivation." To the same purport is the statement of Elphinstone,[4] that "the numerous ruins which it still contains, testify Seistan to have been a fertile country, full of cities, which in extent and magnificence are scarcely surpassed by any in Asia." Though the fertility of

[3] Ut supra, 711.

[4] Acc. of Caubul, 492.

Seistan is in many places very great, the country is for the most part a desert, except a few spots under cultivation, producing wheat, rice, millet, cotton, tobacco, grapes, and melons; there are scarcely any trees, the largest being stunted pomegranate trees and tamarisks. The scantiness of produce appears to result from the want of industry and skill in the inhabitants to make use of their natural advantages.

The majority of the people are Tajiks, considered to be of Persian descent; with these are intermixed Belooches and Afghans. The morasses are inhabited by a very barbarous race, distinguished from the rest of the population by their tall athletic frames, dark complexions, ugly features, long faces, and large black eyes.[5] Besides their occupation as herdsmen, they fish and fowl on rafts, amidst the reeds and rushes of the swamps. The Tajiks are Shia Mahometans; the Belooches and Afghans, Sunnis.[6] There are also a few Hindoos. The total population, probably, does not exceed fifty or sixty thousand persons. The language is broken Persian according to Leech, who, in a hundred and fifty words, found about thirty of that language. Pushtoo is also spoken by many. The country is divided amongst a number of petty chiefs, who, according to the latest accounts, acknowledge the supremacy of the ruler of Herat.[7] The only places worth notice are Ilumdar, Dooshak, or Jelalabad, Laush, Kash, and Furrah, and even the three last of these are not strictly within the limits assigned by Conolly to Seistan. Yet this wretched country, as observed by Elphinstone, Christie, and Conolly, contains numerous ruins of vast magnitude, indicating the high prosperity which it formerly enjoyed. Thus at Dooshak, or Jelalabad, the ruins of the ancient city cover as much ground as Isfahan. At Poolkee they extend over sixteen square miles. At Peshawuroon they are described by Christie[8] as of immense extent, insomuch that he rode five miles across them.

Seistan is classic land to the Persians. In the words of Elphinstone,[9] "There is no country to which an admirer of Persian poetry and romance will turn with more interest than to Seistan, and there is none where his expectations will meet with so melancholy a disappointment." It is especially celebrated as the ordinary residence of Rustum,[1] of romantic celebrity among the Persians, and, at a later period, of the valiant Jacob Ben Laith. The prosperity of Seistan was terminated in the latter

[5] Elph. 493.
[6] Leech, Descrip. of Seistan, 156.
[7] Jour. As. Soc. Beng. 1841, p. 310, Jour. of a Visit to Seistan, by Conolly (E.).
[8] In App. to Pott. 409.
[9] 402.
[1] D'Herbelot, iii. 288.

part of the fourteenth century, being, after a brave resistance, conquered in 1383, by Tamerlane,[2] who exterminated the population, and reduced the town to heaps of ruins.

<small>[2] Price, Mahomedan Hist. iii. 46; Malcolm, Hist. of Persia, i. 459.</small>

SENEE, in Afghanistan, a village situate about twelve miles west of the Indus, in lat. 33° 30′, long. 71° 54′.

<small>E.I.C. Ms. Doc.; Conolly, Jour. to India, ii. 57.</small>

SERAI-I-SHAH BEG, in Western Afghanistan, a halting-place on the route from Herat to Kandahar, and thirty miles south of the former place. It is situate on the river Adruscund, near its source, and nearly opposite to the point where it receives the Rood-i-Guz. The contiguous country affords forage, but no other supplies. The elevation above the sea is 6,500 feet. Lat. 33° 58′, long. 62° 10′.

<small>E.I.C. Ms. Doc.</small>

SERI GOBINDPOOR, in the Punjab, a halting-place and caravanserai situate on the right bank of the Beas river, forty miles east of Amritsir. Lat. 31° 43′, long. 75° 24′.

<small>Walker's Map of Kashmir.</small>

SERMIH, in Bultistan, a village situate on the left bank of the river Indus, here called Sinh-kha-bab, in lat. 35° 6′, long. 75° 48′.

<small>E.I.C. Ms. Doc.; Boileau, Rajwára, Map.</small>

SESSARAH, in Bhawlpoor, a village on the route from the town of Bhawlpoor to Bekanir, and seventy miles south-east of the former. It is situate in the great eastern desert of Bhawlpoor, and, though the ordinary halting-place, is devoid of water. Lat. 28° 45′, long. 72° 83′.

SEWESTAN, in Afghanistan, an extensive tract, but little known, our scanty information concerning it being confined, in a great degree, to what the diligence and sagacity of Elphinstone[1] enabled him to glean from native report. Its limits on the north appear to be undefined; on the east it is bounded by the Suliman mountains; on the south by the mountains inclosing Kahun, and by Cutch Gundava; on the west by the Toba and Hala ranges. With reference to the most trustworthy information that exists, it may be stated to be between lat. 29° 30′—30° 30′, long. 69° 30′. According to Elphinstone's description, "it is a flat dry plain of hardened clay; its natural defects being in some places corrected by streams from the hills, and round the town of Sewee at least it is highly cultivated." It is inhabited principally by the Punnee division of the great Cauker or Khaka tribe. The mountains about Kahun are, however, held by Belooches, in general engaged in hostilities with their Afghan neighbours. Sewestan is crossed throughout its whole extent, from east to

<small>[1] Acc. of Caubul, 450.</small>

west, by the route from Dera Ghazee Khan to Kandahar, by the Sakhee Surwar Pass.[2] Baber,[3] in 1505, took this route in his march from the Indus to Lake Ab-istada, and mentions the privations endured from want of supplies for his troops in their progress. The climate is excessively hot, Sewee or Sebee, one of its few towns, being proverbially compared, on this account, to the infernal regions.[4]

[2] E.I.C. Ms. Doc.; Leech, App. to Passes over Hindoo Koosh, 38.
[3] Memoirs, 164.

[4] Elphin. 136.

SEZKOH, a village situate to the north of Bultistan, at the northern entrance of the valley of Shighur, in lat. 35° 40′, long. 75° 19′.

Vigne's Map of Kashmir, by Walker.

SHADABAD, in the north of the Punjab, and on the route from Lahore to Kashmir, by Rajawur, a spacious and magnificent caravanserai, built by one of the Mogul emperors. It is a rectangular structure, uncovered in the middle. The walls are nearly twenty feet thick, and contain cavities close to each other, and at regular intervals. These cavities, or deep niches, as they may be termed, open into the uncovered space in the middle, and are the apartments for the accommodation of travellers. Lat. 33° 2′, long. 74° 19′.

Vigne, Kashmir, i. 250.

SHADADPOOR,[1] in Sinde, a town on the route from Larkhana to Gundava, and twenty-five miles north-west of the former place. It is situate in a barren tract, nearly destitute of population, and described by Kennedy as "more like the bed of a salt lagoon, in an interval of spring tides, than an inland district." To the north-west stretches the dreary tract called the *Pat*, or desert, of Shikarpoor, noticed by the same writer as "a boundless level plain of indurated clay of a dull earthen colour, and shewing signs of being sometimes under water. At first a few bushes were apparent here and there, growing gradually more and more distant, until at last not a sign of vegetable life was to be recognized."[2] Lat. 27° 46′, long. 68°.

[1] E.I.C. Ms. Doc.; Kennedy, Sinde and Kabool; Leech, on Sind. Army, 86.
[2] Kennedy, i. 190.

SHADAYWARA, in the Punjab, a village situate on the left bank of the river Ravee, about twenty miles south-west of Lahore. Lat. 31° 27′, long. 74° 6′.

E.I.C. Ms. Doc.

SHADEEZYE.—See SHAHDAZYE.

SHADEHUR, in Beloochistan, a village of Cutch Gundava, situate on the route from Gundava to Larkhana, and forty miles south of the former town. It is situate at the eastern base of the Hala mountains, here excessively rugged, with a surface devoid of vegetation. Lat. 27° 59′, long. 67° 41′.

E.I.C. Ms. Doc.; Kennedy, Sinde and Kabool, i. 192.

SHA.

E.I.C. Ms. Doc.

SHAEEWAN, in Afghanistan, a village and usual halting-place on the route from Kandahar to Herat, and two hundred and forty miles north-west of the former place. It is situate on the Furrah Rood, or river of Furrah, in a remarkably fertile country, having considerable population and cultivation. Lat. 32° 37', long. 62° 21'.

E.I.C. Ms. Doc.

SHAGURH, in Sinde, a village situate on the Great Desert, about a mile and a half from the eastern frontier, and forty-two miles west of the town of Jessulmair. Lat. 26° 56', long. 70° 22'.

Vigne's Map, by Walker.

SHAH AHUN, in Kashmir, a village situate fourteen miles east of Sirinagur. Lat. 34° 2', long. 74° 58'.

Ms. Survey Map.

SHAH ALUM, in Sinde, a village about three miles west of the Poorana offset of the Indus, in lat. 24° 44', long. 69° 1'.

Vigne, Kashmir, i. 323; Moorcr. Punj. Bokh. ii. 249; F. Von Hugel, Kaschmir, i. 251.

SHAHBAD, in Kashmir, a town formerly a favourite residence of the Mogul emperors, but now ruinous and neglected. It is situate in a long, narrow valley, bounded on the south-west by the Panjal of Banihal, and on the north-east by a ridge of green hills several miles in length, dividing it from the valley of Bureng or Breng. The valley in some places has a width not exceeding a thousand yards. It is watered by a stream flowing from the celebrated spring of Vernag, and which lower down, where increased by several small feeders, is called the river Sandaren. Accounts received by Vigne represented the valley to be very rich in mines of iron and copper, which were worked in the time when the Afghans held it, but are now neglected, in consequence of the ignorant rapacity of the Sikhs, who would compel the natives to labour without remuneration; to avoid which hardship, those oppressed people conceal both their knowledge of the situation of the veins and of the mode of working.

The neighbourhood of Shahbad is celebrated for its fruits, especially apples, and for its wheat, considered the finest in Kashmir. The town, when visited by Moorcroft, had a bazaar and a few shops, at which provisions, coarse cloth, and very fine honey, were sold. It was formerly the residence of the most powerful of the seven hereditary Maleks, or wardens appointed by the emperor Akbar to watch over the passes of Kashmir. The Malek of Shahbad had charge of the pass of Banihal, and enjoyed a considerable income from lands held in jaghire, which have been seized by the Afghans, so that the Kashmirian who has succeeded to the dignity receives no emolument from it. Shahbad has an elevation of 5,600 feet above the sea. Lat. 33° 30′, long. 75° 10′.

SHAH BILLAWAL, in Beloochistan, a hamlet of Lus, regarded with veneration by the Mahometans in consequence of its containing the tomb of a reputed saint. It is situate in a narrow valley embosomed in the Hubb mountains, and watered by a small stream flowing from a fine spring which never fails. The soil may be considered fertile as compared with the adjacent barren hills: it produces vines, mango, orange, and tamarind trees, besides a number of large and fine *babool* trees (mimosas). Here is a mosque, with a cemetery attached to it, and the Beloches believe that peculiar blessings attend the souls of those buried there. Lat. 25° 49′, long. 67° 5′. E.I.C. Ms. Doc.

SHAH BUNDER, in Sinde, in the delta of the Indus, a small place on the east bank of the channel, which discharges its water into the sea by the Mull mouth. Hither the English factory was removed from Aurungabunder or Dehrajamka, in consequence of this latter place being deserted by the water of the Indus. Previously to the dissolution of the factory here in 1775, its establishment for navigating the Indus consisted of fourteen small vessels, each of about forty tons burthen. Subsequently, this place also was deserted by the stream, and, on the reestablishment of the factory in 1799, Lahorebunder, thirty-five miles north-west, on the Buggaur, or western branch of the Indus, was selected as its site. Shah Bunder is in lat. 24° 10′, long. 67° 46′. Burnes, Rep. on the Ports of the Indus, 2.

SHAHDAZYE,[1] in Afghanistan, a *khail* station or village in the Pisheen valley.[2] It is situate on a stream, or, as it is vernacularly termed, a *lora*, which rises at Sir-i-Aub, ten miles south of Quetta, or Shawl, and flows northwards about forty miles to Kyderzye Khail, thence westward twelve miles to Shahdazye, and four miles below that place joins the Pisheen *lora*. The united streams flow on past Shorawuck, a hundred and twenty miles, into an *abistada*, or lake, about eight miles in circumference, which nearly disappears in the dry season.

[1] E.I.C. Ms. Doc. [2] Conolly, Jour. to Ind. ii. 128.

Shahdazye is inhabited by *Saiyads*, or Mahometans, claiming to be descended from the prophet. The Shahdazye Saiyads are one of the three great septs of these claimants of sanctity, who inhabit the valley of Pisheen, the other two being the Hyderzye and the Kerbolahe Saiyads. All three, according to tradition, are sprung from a wandering descendant of the prophet, who visited the valley and settled there many centuries ago. The Shahdazye Saiyads are considered superior to the others, and are in high repute for miraculous powers among the ignorant and superstitious population. They had formerly extensive estates, but these were seized by the *Sirdars*, or rulers of Kandahar, and the Saiyads are now compelled to maintain themselves by commerce and pastoral pursuits.

The khail of Shahdazye consists of about a hundred and fifty families, whose houses occupy two villages close to each other, and situate two hundred yards from the crumbling bank of the stream. A few of the best habitations are built with thick mud walls, and have roofs supported on beams, but the greater number are mere hovels. None of the inhabitants, however, are in a state of extreme indigence, and they are represented as living in concord and the exercise of mutual good-will—a happy contrast to the state of society prevailing through a large part of Afghanistan. Shahdazye is in lat. 30° 30', long. 66° 43'.

Walker's Map of Sinde.

SHAHKOOGUD, in Sinde, a village situate on the right bank of the Indus, in lat. 27° 58', long. 69°.

E.I.C. Ms. Doc.

SHAH KOT.—A village in the Punjab, situate on the road from Mooltan to Bhawlpoor, ten miles south of the former city. Lat. 30°, long. 71° 30'.

[1] Masson, Bal. Afg. Panj. i, 415; F. Von Hugel, Kaschmir, iii. 258; Moorcr. Punj. Bokh. i. 92; Burnes' Bokh. iii. 160.

SHAHLIMAR.[1]—A splendid pleasure-ground, about three miles east of Lahore, made by order of the Mogul emperor Shah Jehan, but now in the possession of the ruler of the Sikhs. Here were numbers of pavilions and other buildings for ornament and pleasure, but many of them were demolished or defaced by Runjeet Singh, to obtain the marble materials for the embellishment of his residence in Lahore, and the construction of his religious capital of Amritsir, and of the neighbouring fortress of Govindghar. Still there is much to cause admiration, especially the numerous beautiful fountains, abundantly supplied with water brought in an aqueduct a hundred and twenty miles in length, from Shah Jehanpoor, in the Himalaya.

[2] Court and Camp of Runjeet Singh, 140.

According to Osborne,[2] the scene is not unworthy the magnificence of the Mogul dynasty. The following account is given by that author: "These gardens are very beautiful, and are said to have cost 300,000*l*., but for many years have been totally neglected; and Faqueer Uzeezoodeen tells me, that within his recollection, they were so overgrown with jungle as to have become the haunts of tigers and other wild beasts. They are now, however, kept in tolerable order, and, under the superintendence of any person of taste, might be made very picturesque and pretty; and even now, when the fountains are all playing and the orange-trees in blossom, their appearance is very eastern and handsome. They consist of three large terraces, inclosed within a wall of about from three to four miles in circumference. There is a small tower over every gateway, of which there are four, and a low minaret at each corner of the wall. They are filled with beautiful orange, pomegranate, and mango trees, and vines, with paved stone walks, and a canal running through the centre, with a large square tank in the middle of the gardens, from which some hundred fountains are constantly throwing water, and adding considerably to the coolness of the atmosphere." The splendid baths built by the Mogul emperor have been destroyed, and fragments of the marble sculptures and beautiful mosaic employed in their construction now encumber the walks. The gateways, encased in enamelled porcelain, are still in tolerable repair. Lat. 31° 36′, long. 74° 21′.

SHAH MAHOMED, in the Punjab, a village situate near the right bank of the river Chenaub. Lat. 30° 50′, long. 71° 56′. E.I.C. Ms. Doc.

SHAH MUKSOOD, in Afghanistan, a village situate about three miles south of the Urghundab river. Lat. 31° 22′, long. 65° 10′. E.I.C. Ms. Doc.

SHAH MUSHUD, in Afghanistan, a village situate on the right bank of the river Moorghab. Lat. 34° 57′, long. 63° 55′. Walker's Map of Afg.

SHAHPOOR, in Beloochistan, a small town of Cutch Gundava, on the route from Shikarpoor to Kahun. It has good water in wells dug in the bed of a torrent, the surface of which is dry during the greater part of the year. The neighbouring country, now nearly desolate, has traces of former cultivation to a considerable extent. Lat. 28° 43′, long. 68° 43′. E.I.C. Ms. Doc.

SHAHPOOR, in the Punjab, a village situate on the left bank of the Jailum river, in lat. 32° 8′, long. 72° 15′. Walker's Map of N.W. Frontier.

SHAIK KA RAJ, in Southern Beloochistan, a village situate about ten miles north of the town of Sonmeanee, on the route to Pott. Belooch. 13; Masson, Bal. Afg. Panj. ii. 165.

Belah. It is the first inhabited spot on the road northwards from Sonmeanee, the intervening country being one continued salt marsh. There are about sixty houses, amongst which are a few shops kept by Hindoos. Lat. 25° 33′, long. 66° 33′.

<small>Burnes (James), Mission to Sinde, 38; Pott. (Wm.), on the Indus, in Jour. Royal As. Soc. Beng. 1834, p. 204.</small>

SHAKAPORE, in Sinde, a town on the great route from Cutch to Hyderabad. About a mile north-east of the town are the ruins of a large city, built of excellent burnt brick, and still in such a state of preservation that the walls and bastions are plainly discernible. To the north-east of these ruins is the large bed of a great branch of the Indus, now completely devoid of water. Shakapore has, at this time, no pretensions to importance either in point of wealth or population. Lat. 24° 34′, long. 68° 26′.

<small>Walker's Map of N.W. Frontier.</small>

SHAKHUR, or SHENKHUR, in the Punjab, a village on the route from Baramula to Mazufurabad, and ten miles west of the former town. It is situate on the right bank of the Jailum, where it holds a rapid course down the southern slope of the Pir Panjal. Lat. 34° 10′, long. 74° 1′.

<small>E.I.C. Ms. Doc.; Lord, Koh-i-Damun, 45; Wood, Oxus, 177; Masson, Bal. Afg. Panj. iii. 115; Burnes' Pers. Narr. 146.</small>

SHAKR DARA, in Afghanistan, a handsome village and collection of delightful gardens in a valley on the east side of the Pughman range of mountains, and distant twelve miles north-west of the city of Kabool. Lat. 34° 40′, long. 68° 45′.

<small>E.I.C. Ms. Doc.</small>

SHALKOT, in the Punjab, a fort and village on the route from Lahore to Rihursi, and sixty miles north-east of the former town. Lat. 32° 23′, long. 74° 33′.

<small>E.I.C. Ms. Doc.</small>

SHARGULLEE, in Afghanistan, a village and halting-place on the route from Ghuznee to Shawl, and sixty miles north of the latter place. The surrounding country is rough, barren, and nearly impracticable for a military force or other large body of persons, from the difficulty of the routes and the scantiness of supplies. Lat. 30° 49′, long. 67° 19′.

<small>[1] E.I.C. Ms. Doc. [2] Wood, Oxus, 112, 127.</small>

SHARKEE,[1] in Afghanistan, a village on the right bank of the Indus, thirty miles above Kala Bagh. It is situate at the southern base of the rocky range, which, rising south of Attock, is traversed by the Indus in a deep and narrow channel. Below Sharkee the channel expands, the declivity decreases, and the stream becomes smoother and less violent. Above, during the season of inundation, the upward navigation of the Indus is utterly impracticable. Lat. 33° 13′, long. 71° 46′.

SHARUK.—See SHEHERUK.

SHAWL.

SHAWL,[1] in Beloochistan, a small town with a fort, the principal place in the valley of the same name. Though generally mentioned by British writers under this name, it is better known to the natives under that of Quetta.* It is meanly built of mud, and surrounded by a crenated wall of the same material, twelve hundred[2] yards in circumference, and containing four gates. Amidst these houses, and overlooking them, is a small castle on a mound of earth, seventy or eighty feet high. Hough[3] describes it as a most miserable mud town, with a small castle on a mound, on which there was a small gun on a ricketty carriage." The description given by Allen[4] is much more favourable:—"This was certainly the prettiest spot I had seen in these lands. The fertile and well-watered valley of Shaul is surrounded by hills of the boldest form, and several thousand feet in height. In the middle of the valley is the little town surrounded by a mud wall, in the centre of which rises the citadel upon a mound seventy or eighty feet high, whether artificial or natural no one could inform me." As the elevation above the sea is great, exceeding 5,000 feet, the cold in winter is severe, and the seasons as late as in England. Thus the British force which marched into it on the 20th of April found the spring then opening, and as the immediate vicinity of the town is fertile, well watered, and graced by numerous orchards, the scene as described by Kennedy[5] was very pleasing:—"We rested on a noble orchard. Fine standards of the size of forest trees, apple, pear, peach, apricot, and plum, were surmounted and overhung with gigantic vines, which, wreathing round the trunks, and extending to the remotest branches, festooned from tree to tree, in a wild luxuriance of growth, such as I had never dreamed of seeing in fruit-trees and the vine. It was the first month in spring, and they were covered with blossoms which perfumed the air, and presented a picture of horticultural beauty surpassing description." There is an abundant supply of fine water from numerous kareezes, or subterraneous aqueducts. During our military operations in Afghanistan, this was an important post in the line of communication between Sinde and Kandahar. It was occupied in April, 1839, by the army of the

[1] E.I.C. Ms. Doc.
[2] Havelock, War in Afg. i. 246; Masson, Bal. Afg. Panj. i. 328.
[3] Narr. Exp. in Afg. 61.
[4] Diary, 118.
[5] Sinde and Kabool, i. 227.

* Probably for کوتاه Persian plural, from کوت "a fort." According to Masson, Quetta is a word used by the Afghans as an equivalent for fort. Kalat, 312.

Indus in the advance on Kandahar, and retained by a garrison of two [6] Bengal native regiments under General Nott. In the close of the same year, the Bengal detachment, returning from Kabool, marched through it; and on the arrival of the force there, General Willshire marched to storm Kelat.[7] After General Nott removed to the command of Kandahar, possession of Shawl was retained by a regiment of native infantry cantoned in an entrenched camp near the town.[8] In the beginning of March 1842, General England, marching from Dadur to reinforce the garrison of Kandahar, made Shawl his head-quarters, and fell back on it when repulsed at Hykulzye, in the close of the month, in his advance towards the Kojuk Pass.[9] A month after this reverse, General England marched from Shawl, and with little difficulty forced his way to Kandahar: in the close of the following August he returned to it, having succeeded without loss in withdrawing over the Kojuk Pass thirteen pieces of artillery, and an enormous amount of baggage, conveyed by between nine and ten thousand beasts of burthen.[1] On the 1st of October,[2] 1842, the British force totally and finally evacuated Quetta, and marched through the Bolan Pass to Sinde. Shawl has been ascertained, by barometrical measurement, to be 5,563 feet[3] above the sea. The population is probably about 2,000. Lat. 30° 8′, long. 66° 56′.

[6] Kennedy, ii. 149.

[7] Outram, Rough Notes, 158.

[8] Allen, 118.

[9] Mil. Op. in Afg. 220.

[1] Id. 373.
[2] Id. 418.

[3] Jour. As. Soc. Beng. 1842, p. 55, Grif. Bar. and Ther. Obs. in Afg.

SHAWL,[1] in Beloochistan, an elevated valley or table-land, bounded on the east by the Kurklekkee mountains overhanging the Bolan Pass, and on the west by the heights connected with Chehel Tan; on the north it has the Tukatoo mountains; on the south it ascends, with a very gentle acclivity, towards Mustoong and Kelat. Limits substantially the same with these are assigned to it by Masson:[2]—" To the north, Shawl extends to the Khaka district of Toba; to the south it joins the district of Mastung and the plain called Dasht Bedowlat; to the east it has the Khaka district of Hanna; to the west, Peshing and Sherrud, belonging to Afghan tribes." According to this writer, the valley of Shawl is twelve miles in length, with an average breadth of three or four miles. It lies between lat. 30° 2′—30° 14′, long. 66° 55′—67°. The drainage of the few scanty streams which water it is effected through an opening in the heights bounding it on the west. As the elevation everywhere exceeds 5,000 feet[3] above the sea, the climate is cold in winter and

[1] E.I.C. Ms. Doc.; Elph. Acc. of Caubul, 451.

[2] Kalat, 312.

[3] Jour. As. Soc. Beng. 1842, p. 55, Grif. Bar. and Ther. Obs. in Afg.

moderate in summer. Snow lies for two months in winter, and then such of the inhabitants as have the means emigrate to Cutch Gundava.[4] The soil is generally fertile, being a rich black loam, yielding wheat, barley, rice, lucerne, and similar vegetation suited for fodder, besides madder, tobacco, and esculent vegetables. The wildest parts of the inclosing mountains are the haunts of wild sheep and goats; the more accessible tracts yield ample pasture to the herds and flocks of the mountaineers. The lambs are proverbially excellent. Orchards are numerous, and produce in great perfection and abundance apples, pears, plums, peaches, apricots, grapes, mulberries, pomegranates, quinces, and figs. The whole number of fixed population is supposed to be about 4,000 or 5,000, and consists of Afghans and Belooches, probably in nearly equal proportions. Besides Shawl or Quetta, the chief place, the valley contains Ispunglee, and a few other insignificant villages.

[4] Masson, Bal. Afg. Panj. i, 329.

SHAWPOOR, in Afghanistan, a village situate in the south of the Derajat. Lat. 29° 12′, long. 70° 27′.

E.I.C. Ms. Doc.

SHEAUL, in Sinde, a village on the middle route from Roree to Hyderabad, and sixty-five miles south-east of the former town. Lat. 26° 53′, long. 68° 17′.

Ms. Survey Doc.

SHEER.—A village in Afghanistan, forty miles south-west of Ghuznee. Lat. 33° 8′, long. 67° 52′.

E.I.C. Ms. Doc.

SHEERKAIL, in Afghanistan, a village about two miles from the left bank of the Turnak river. Lat. 31° 49′, long. 66° 12′.

E.I.C. Ms. Doc.

SHEHERUK, in Western Afghanistan, on the route from Kandahar to Herat, and one hundred and forty-five miles south of the latter place. It lies in a hard level plain, bounded on the south by a very lofty range of mountains. There is an abundant supply of water, and considerable cultivation in the neighbourhood. Lat. 32° 34′, long. 62° 37′.

E.I.C. Ms. Doc.

SHEK, in Beloochistan, on the south-eastern frontier, a village situate on the right bank of the Hubb river. Lat. 25° 12′, long. 67° 1′.

E.I.C. Ms. Doc.

SHEKABAD, in Afghanistan, a village and large fort on the route from Ghuznee to Kabool, and fifty miles south of the latter place. It is situate on the right or south bank of the river of Logurh, in a fertile and well-cultivated valley, containing numerous forts and villages. Elevation above the sea, 7,473 feet. Lat. 34° 6′, long. 68° 30′.

E.I.C. Ms. Doc.; Hough, Narr. Exp. in Afg. 242; Jour. As. Soc. Beng. 1842, p. 65, Grif. Bar. and Ther. Meas. in Afg.

SHEKWAN, in Western Afghanistan, a village thirty miles north-west of Herat. Lat. 34° 33′, long. 61° 46′.

SHELGHUR, in Afghanistan, on the route from Ghuznee to Dera Ismael Khan, and fifteen miles south-east of the former place. It consists of a fort surrounded by a considerable village, inhabited by Lohanis, a commercial tribe of Afghans. The number of inhabitants in the village and adjacent district, which bears the same name, is about 3,000. There is a good supply of water from a subterraneous aqueduct. Lat. 33° 23′, long. 68° 22′.

SHELLY SOLA, in Afghanistan, a village twenty-four miles south of Ghuznee. Lat. 33° 11′, long. 68° 14′.

SHERANOW, in Beloochistan, a village on the western route from Shawl to Kelat, and twenty-five miles south of the former town. Lat. 29° 49′, long. 66° 40′.

SHER DUNDAN, in Afghanistan, on the route from Ghuznee to Kabul, and eight miles north of the former place, is a defile through an elevated tract, from two to three hundred yards wide, running between low hills; capable, however, of being defended against a greatly superior force. It is sometimes called the Ghuznee Pass. The elevation above the sea is estimated at 9,000 feet. Lat. 33° 40′, long. 68° 26′.

SHERI, in Northern Bultistan, a village situate in the valley of Shighur, and in lat. 35° 40′, long. 75° 16′.

SHER-MAHOMED-KILLA, in Afghanistan, a fort on the route from Ghuznee to Kabool, and thirty miles south-west of the latter place. It is situate on the bank of a feeder of the river of Kabool, near the southern entrance of the fine valley of Maidan. Lat. 34° 16′, long. 68° 45′.

SHER-I-SAFA, in Afghanistan, a ruin on the route from Kandahar to Ghuznee, and forty miles north-east of the former place. It consists of a mound about fifty feet high, all that remains of a city reduced to desolation in the eleventh century, by Mahmood of Ghuznee, "the destroyer."* This remarkable object stands a mile from the right or west bank of the river Turnak, in a well-cultivated country. Elevation above the sea, 4,618 feet. Lat. 31° 51′, long. 66° 10′.

SHEROO, in Afghanistan, a village of the Derajat, situate

* Havelock states that it is mentioned by Forster as a remarkable hill of a conical shape. But no such passage can be discovered in that traveller.

near the right bank of the Indus, in lat. 29° 42′, long. 70° 51′.

SHESHA NAG.—A lake in the Punjab, among the mountains inclosing Kashmir on the north. Its water is discharged into the Lidur, one of the principal feeders of the Jailum or Behut, and by some considered the genuine head of that river. It lies in a limestone formation, and is 13,000 feet above the sea. Lat. 34° 7′, long. 75° 34′. Vigne, i. 376.

SHIGHUR, in Bultistan, or Little Tibet, a fort on a spur of rock running from one of the ranges connected with the southern part of the great mountain of Mooztaugh. It is naturally accessible on the side next the mountain, and in another part has been made so by means of stairs cut in the rock. The valley, twenty-four miles long and four or five wide, is very wild, and marked by features of great sublimity, being inclosed by vast rocky mountains with summits always covered with snow. At its upper extremity is a copious spring, having a temperature of 109°. A considerable river, rising in the Mooztaugh, holds a southerly course along the bottom of the valley, and falls into the Indus at Nynsuk, opposite to the rock of Iskardo. Lat. 35° 21′, long. 75° 40′. Vigne, ii. 250, 269, 283.

SHIKARPOOR,[1] in Sinde, a town the most important in the country in a commercial point of view, and probably the most populous, though not possessing the distinction of being regarded as the capital. It is situate fifteen miles due west of the Indus, in a country so low and level that, by means of canals from that river, it is, during the inundation, extensively flooded, and so completely is the soil saturated with moisture, that, by digging to the depth of twelve or fifteen feet, water may at any time be obtained in quantity almost without limit. The Sinde canal, dug from the Indus, passes within a mile of the town, and proceeds south-west to Larkhana. It is navigable for large boats during four months of the year. Though the inundation[2] leaves extensive tracts covered with stagnant water, and the heat is excessive, the climate is not considered insalubrious, except towards the end of September, when agues prevail. The soil is alluvial, being the deposit of the waters of the canals and channels. It is so rich as to require no manure, producing very great crops in return of culture and irrigation. The town is surrounded by flourishing groves and orchards, yielding in abundance dates, mangoes, oranges, mulberries,

[1] Burnes, iii. 227, 277; Wood, Oxus, 54; Burnes' Pers. Narr. 57; Id. Rep. of Commerce of Shikarpoor, 22, 32; Leech, Rep. of Trade between Shikarpoor and Marwar, 68, 70.

[2] Postans, Memorand. on Shikarpore, Jour. As. Soc. Beng. 1841, p. 20; Havelock, i. 109; Kennedy, ii. 167; Hough, 25; Conolly, ii. 241.

and other fruits the usual produce of this country. Sugar-cane is cultivated more with a view to its consumption as a sweetmeat than for producing sugar.

The wall by which Shikarpoor was once fortified is now in ruins, but eight gates may still be traced. The circuit of the wall is 3,831 yards. The approaches to the town are bad, and when reached it exhibits nothing attractive. Much waste ground is interspersed among the houses in the inhabited part; the streets are narrow and very filthy, and the houses in general wretched. The mansions of the opulent Hindoo merchants are large, massy, gloomy piles, inclosed and secluded by high brick walls. Shikarpoor contains no public edifice worthy of notice. The character of the place is thoroughly commercial, almost every house having a shop attached to it. The bazaar extends for about eight hundred yards through the centre of the city, and is covered with rafters thatched with palm leaves. This arrangement is intended to afford protection against the rays of the sun, but it renders the air stagnant, oppressive, and injurious to health. Trade, however, appears to thrive. Conolly[3] observes that "the shops seemed to be well filled with the necessaries of life and various merchandize, and the people had that busy air which characterizes men engaged in active trade." Burnes states the number of the shops in the bazaar in 1837 at 884. Postans in 1841, represents the number of Hindoo shops as 923. The laborious trades and handicrafts are followed exclusively by Mahometans. Burnes states the total annual value of the manufactures of Shikarpoor at 5,000*l.*, but this is beyond question preposterously too small, and there does not appear to be any means of making a safe estimate of the amount. The transit trade is important, as the town is situate on one of the great routes from Sinde to Khorasan and Afghanistan, through the Bolan Pass, and also on that which leads northward to the Derajat, by the western side of the Indus. There is likewise a route to Kurrachee by way of Sehwan, and one to Hindostan and the eastern side of the Indus by the ferry at Roree and Sukkur, besides others of less importance. "The direct trade of the town of Shikarpoor itself," Burnes[4] observes, "is not extensive; its port is Kurrachee, from which it receives goods to the amount of 21,000*l.* annually." By this he seems to mean goods intended for the consumption of the town itself. The trade with Khorasan

[3] ii. 242.

[4] Rep. on the Commerce of Shikarpoor, 25.

SHIKARPOOR.

and Kandahar is considerable, but there is scarcely any with Northern Afghanistan, that being conducted through the Punjab and Bhawlpoor. The transit[5] trade is principally that from Marwar and the adjacent parts of Hindostan to Khorasan and Persia; but banking and other branches of monetary traffic constitute the more important departments of the commercial operations of Shikarpoor. There are several Hindoos possessing large capitals, which appear to have been accumulated under the supremacy of the Afghans.[6] The improvidence of the latter left the management of money matters to these acute financiers, who, by farming the revenue, and exacting exorbitant interest on loans, public and private, have amassed immense wealth. These capitalists are represented as enterprising, vigilant, and ravenous for gain;[7] living impersonations of heartless avarice, but at the same time, specious, civil, and intelligent to an extraordinary degree. Their lingual acquirements are extensive, as they usually understand Persian, Belooche, Pushtoo, Hindostanee, and Sindee. Their credit stands so high that their bills can be negotiated in every part of India and Central and Western Asia, from Astracan[8] to Calcutta. In every important town throughout this vast extent they have agents, whose families remaining at Shikarpoor are a sort of hostages for their fidelity. The commerce and general prosperity of the town have rapidly declined since it has fallen under the power of Sindian rulers, but may be expected * to revive under the lately established supremacy of the British. So much disorganized had society become when Masson visited the place a few years ago, that to pass the walls was almost to incur the certainty of being robbed.

The annual revenue in Shikarpoor in 1840,[9] according to Postans, amounted to 7,100*l.*, divided between the Hyderabad and the Khyrpore Ameers, the former receiving 4,000*l.*, the latter the residue. Masson[1] states that 2,500*l.* could only be obtained by extortion, loudly complained of. The population is estimated at 30,000.[2]† Of these 20,000 are Hindoos, characterized by great laxity in respect to their peculiar tenets, flagrant licentiousness, and

[5] Leech, Rep. on the Trade between Shikarpoor and Marwar, 68; Postans, on Shikarpoor, Jour. As. Soc. Beng. 1841, pp. 12, 26.

[6] Masson, i. 354.

[7] Conolly, ii. 243.

[8] Burnes, on the Commerce of Shikarpoor, 24.

[9] Postans, 23.

[1] i. 358.

[2] Postans, 19; Burnes on the Commerce of Shikarpoor, 24.

* Burnes (25) states that there is no mint at which gold or bullion can be coined. Masson (i. 359) makes a statement apparently at variance with this.

† Kennedy (ii. 168) states the amount at 50,000. It is probable that all the estimates are very far removed from correctness.

general disregard of principle, morality, and decency. The remaining 10,000 are Mahometans, of whom 1,000 are Afghans. These share in the general bad character of the population, being considered ignorant,³ crafty, contentious, and cowardly. It may be hoped that the prevalence of evil is but the result of the long course of oppression, extortion, and cruelty to which the people have been subjected by their rulers,⁴ and that under better auspices the tone of morals will be raised, while increased security will be afforded to life and property.

³ Masson, i. 357.

⁴ Kennedy, ii. 167.

Shikarpoor was founded in 1617,⁵ and has risen on the ruin of Lukkee. Lat. 27° 55′, long. 68° 45′.

⁵ Burnes, ut supra, 23.

SHIKARPUR.—See SHIKARPOOR.

SHING, a village situate on the right bank of the Indus, ten miles north of its confluence with the river of Gilghit. Lat. 35° 37′, long. 74° 30′.

E.I.C. Ms. Doc.

SHINKEE, in Afghanistan, a village situate on the right bank of the Indus. Lat. 32° 22′, long. 71° 23′.

Walker's Map of Afg.

SHINIZA, in Afghanistan, a village on the road from Ghuznee to Dera Ismael Khan. Lat. 32° 54′, long. 68° 33′.

E.I.C. Ms. Doc.

SHOOJUABAD.—See SHUJABAD.

SHOOKRABAD, in the Punjab, a halting-place on the route from Punch to Baramula, and fifteen miles north of the former town. It is on the southern slope of the ridge, the crest of which forms the Punch Pass. The name, signifying literally "thanks-town," seems to have been intended to remind the traveller of the gratitude* due to those who erected a caravanserai, situate here for the accommodation of those toiling up the painful steep. The caravanserai, however, is now ruinous and comfortless. Lat. 34°, long. 73° 55′.

Vigne, Kashmir, i. 248.

SHORAB,¹ in Afghanistan, a halting-place on the route from Giriskh to Furrah, and thirty miles north-west of the former town. The name signifies "salt-water,"† yet as Forster² remarks, the water at Shorab is fresh. Lat. 32° 3′, long. 63° 55′.

¹ E.I.C. Ms. Doc.

² Jour. Beng. Eng. ii. 123.

SHORABAK, in Afghanistan, a village on the road from

E.I.C. Ms. Doc.

* From شکر "gratitude," and آباد "town." This seems a curious coincidence with the famous resting-place, called "Rest and be thankful," on Marshal Wade's road in the Highlands.

† From شور "salt," and آب "water."

Furrah to Giriskh, ten miles west of the latter place. Lat. 31° 50', long. 64° 11'.

SHORAEE KHOJAKE, in the Punjab, a village situate about twenty miles north of Lahore. Lat. 31° 49', long. 74° 12'. E.I.C. Ms. Doc.

SHORANDAN, in Afghanistan, a village on the route from Kandahar to Ghuznee, and five miles east of the former place. It is supplied with water by a small stream, but affords scarcely any provision or forage, the surrounding country, though level, being almost entirely devoid of vegetation. Lat. 31° 37', long. 65° 31'. Atkinson, Exp. into Afg. 181.

SHORAWUCK.—A barren tract south of Kandahar, on the borders of the Great Desert of Beloochistan. The waters of the Lora, flowing from the valley of Pisheen, are lost in a swamp in the south-western part. On the banks of this stream there is considerable fertility, and fine crops of wheat, barley, and maize, are produced; but the rest of the country is a bare plain of hard clay, quite flat and very arid. It is inhabited by the Afghan tribe of Baraich. Lat. 30° 30', long. 65° 30'. Elph. Acc. of Caubul, 426; Masson, Bal. Afg. Panj. i. 307; Conolly, Jour. to India, ii. 128.

SHORKACH, in Afghanistan, a village on the eastern route from Kabool to Shawl, and ninety miles south of the former town. Lat. 33° 23', long. 68° 42'. E.I.C. Ms. Doc.

SHORKOT,[1] in the Punjab, a small town situate on the route from Jung to Tolumba, and twenty-six miles north of the latter town. Here are some ruins, which Burnes[2] states to be similar to those of Sehwan, but more extensive. The most remarkable object is a mound of earth, surrounded by a brick wall, and so high as to be seen for a circuit of six or eight miles. Native tradition represents it to have been the capital of a rajah of the name of Shor, who was conquered by a king from the west, considered by Burnes to have been Alexander the Great. In the Ayeen Akbery,[3] mention is made of Syalkote and of Shoore, two towns in this part of the Punjab, and Shorkot may, perhaps, be the ruins of one of these. Lat. 30° 50', long. 72° 19'. [1] E.I.C. Ms. Doc. [2] Bokh. iii. 131. [3] ii. 289.

SHORUN, in Beloochistan, a village of Cutch Gundava, situate on the road from Gundava to Dadur, and twenty-two miles north of the former town. Lat. 28° 46', long. 67° 30'. E.I.C. Ms. Doc.; Kennedy, Sinde and Kabool, i. 200.

SHUDAPOOR.—See SHADADPOOR.

SHUFTUL, in Afghanistan, a halting-place on the route from Kandahar to Ghuznee, and one hundred and seventeen miles north-west of the former town. The road to the southward, in E.I.C. Ms. Doc.; Hough, Narr. Exp. in Afg. 152.

this part of the route, is hilly, rugged, much cut up by watercourses, and with difficulty practicable for guns. There are considerable supplies of forage, and abundance of water from the river Turnak, near the west bank of which it is situate. Elevation above the sea, 6,514 feet. Lat. 32° 28′, long. 67° 12′.

SHUHR ROGHAN, in Beloochistan, in the province of Lus, a very remarkable relic of some troglodyte people who formerly held this country, at present so desolate and neglected. It is a town of caves, resembling, though on a small scale, the celebrated excavations at Bamian. As no abridgement could convey the effect of the description given by Carless[1] of this place, his account will be quoted in his own words:—"About nine miles to the northward of Beylah, a range of low hills sweeps in a semicircle from one side of the valley to the other, and forms its head. The Poorally river issues from a deep ravine on the western side, and is about two hundred yards broad. It is bounded on one side by very steep cliffs forty or fifty feet high, on the summit of which there is an ancient burying-ground, and the water runs bubbling along it in two or three small rivulets, among heaps of stones and patches of tamarisk jungle. Having crossed the stream, we pursued our way up its bed amongst the bushes, until we gained the narrow ravine through which it flows, and then, turning into one of the lateral branches, entered Shuhr Roghan. The scene was singular. On either side of a wild, broken ravine, the rocks rise perpendicularly to the height of four or five hundred feet, and are excavated, as far as can be seen in some places, where there is footing to ascend, up to the summit: these excavations are most numerous along the lower parts of the hills, and form distinct houses, which are uninjured by time. They consist in general of a room fifteen feet square, forming a kind of open verandah, with an interior chamber of the same dimensions, to which you gain admittance by a door; there are niches for lamps in many, and a place built up and covered in, apparently intended to hold grain. Most of them had been plastered over with clay, and in a few, when the form of the rock allowed of its being done, the interior of the apartment is lighted by small windows. The houses at the summit of the cliffs are now inaccessible, from the narrow, precipitous paths by which they were approached having been worn away, and those at the base appear to have been occupied by the poorer class of inhabitants, for many of them are

[1] Jour. As. Soc. Beng.1839, p. 191, Acc. of a Jour. to Beylah.

merely irregular-shaped holes with a rudely-constructed door." These excavations, like those at Bamian,[2] are made in a conglomerate of no great consistency or hardness. After recounting the native legend of a beauteous princess (Buddul Tumaul), harassed, like the bride of Tobit, by demons, who slew her seven lovers (the seven friends) in succession, and who was at length rescued by Syful Mullik, the son of the king of Egypt, the description proceeds:—" A short distance above the entrance of the city, the broken, precipitous ravine in which it is situated decreases in width to ten or twelve yards, and forms a deep natural channel in the rock. For about half a mile the cliffs are excavated on both sides to a considerable height, and, taking the remains of the houses into account, I think there cannot be less altogether than fifteen hundred. In one place a row of seven was pointed out by the guides as the residence of 'the seven friends,' and further on we came to the grandest of all, the palace of Buddul Tumaul. At this part, the hill, by the abrupt turning of the ravine, juts out in a narrow point, and towards the extremity forms a natural wall of rock, about three hundred feet high and twenty thick; half-way up it had been cut through, and a chamber constructed about twenty feet square, with the two opposite sides open; it is entered by a passage leading through a mass of rock partly overhanging, and on the other side of the apartment two doors give admittance to two spacious rooms. The whole had once been plastered over, and, from its situation, must have formed a safe and commodious retreat. At the summit of the hill, near it, there is another building, which my attendants said was the mosque where the princess was rescued by Syful Mullik, when the demons attempted to carry her off." Exclusive of the fanciful tradition already alluded to, all record is silent respecting the origin of these singular relics. Shuhr Roghan is in lat. 26° 18', long. 66° 19'.

[2] Jour. As. Soc. Beng. 1833, p. 7, Gerard, Route from Peshawar to Bokh.; Burnes' Bokh. i. 183.

SHUHROVA, in the Punjab, a village situate on the left bank of the river Ravee, ten miles from its confluence with the Chenaub. Lat. 30° 34', long. 71° 55'.

E.I.C. Ms. Doc.

SHUJABAD, in the Punjab, a town about four miles from the east bank of the Chenaub, and thirty miles south of Mooltan. Its size is considerable, and at a distance, with its lofty and irregularly-built fortifications, it has a striking and picturesque appearance. The walls are mounted with a few guns, and defended by

Masson, Bal. Afg. Panj. i. 394.

a small garrison. There is a good and well-supplied bazaar. Its principal manufactures are cottons and wood-turnery; the excellence of the latter is much celebrated. The gardens belonging to the town are extensive and luxuriant, and the surrounding country is fertile as well as highly cultivated, yielding great crops of sugar-cane, cotton, grain, and indigo. It belongs to the Sikhs. Lat. 29° 47′, long. 71° 18′.

[1] F. Von Hugel, Iii. 76.

SHUJANPOOR,[1] in the Punjab, a small town about eight miles east of Attock, remarkable for a splendid Serai, or place of accommodation for travellers, built near it by one the Mogul emperors. This place seems to be noticed by Hough[2] as situated north-east of Shumsabad, and having about three hundred houses. Lat. 33° 53′, long. 72° 25′.

[2] Narr. Exp. in Afg. 337.

Wood, Oxus, 131.

SHUKUR DARAH, in Eastern Afghanistan, an important pass a little north of Kala Bagh, on the western bank of the Indus. By it, proceeds the great route from the Derajat to Peshawer, through the Salt range. Lat. 33° 5′, long. 70° 35′.

Walker's Map.

SHULY WUKYL, in Afghanistan, a village situate on the right bank of the river Helmund. Lat. 34° 20′, long. 67° 38′.

E.I.C. Ms. Doc.

SHUMKOOL, in Afghanistan, a village on the route from Ghuznee to Dera Ismael Khan, and thirty miles west of the latter place. The road is good in this part of the route, and there is a supply of water from a subterraneous aqueduct. Lat. 31° 50′, long. 70° 25′.

Hough, 337.

SHUMSABAD, in the Punjab, a small town near the left bank of the Indus, and a few miles east of Attock. It is situate in a fertile and well-cultivated plain, and is built on an artificial mound. Population about 1,000. Lat. 33° 56′, long. 72° 28′.

E.I.C. Ms. Doc.

SHUND, in Western Afghanistan, a village thirty miles south-west of Khash. Lat. 31° 17′, long. 62° 53′.

F. Von Hugel, Kaschmir, i. 102; Vigne, Kashmir, i. 255; Moorer. Punj. Bokh. ii. 290.

SHUPEYON, in Kashmir, a small town at the base of a hill, close to the Huripoor, or Dumdum river, and on the route from the Pir Panjal Pass to Sirinagur. Close to it was fought, in 1819, the decisive battle, by which the Sikhs won Kashmir from the Afghans. The summit of the hill is 7,480 feet; the town 6,550 feet above the sea. Lat. 33° 42′, long. 74° 45′.

Vigne, i. 297.

SHURJI-MURGA.—A small river of Kashmir, rising in the Futi Panjal, one of the mountains bounding that valley on the south. It has a north-westerly direction of about twenty miles, and falls into the Veshau, or Jailum, a little above the beautiful cataract of Arabul, in lat. 33° 32′, long. 74° 39′.

SHUTUL.—A pass over the Hindoo Koosh from Afghanistan to Turkestan. It is entered from the Kohistan of Kabool, by proceeding up the Punjshir river for a few miles, and then turning to the left northwards, in which direction the general course of the route lies for about thirty miles to the summit of the pass, a short distance beyond which point, at Rhinjan, in Kunduz, it joins the road by the Koushan Pass. The elevation is, probably, very considerable, as the Khawak Pass, forty-five miles to the east, is 13,200 feet high, and the Koushan Pass, fifteen miles to the west, 15,000. The summit is in lat. 35° 33′, long. 69° 8′. E.I.C. Ms. Doc.; Leech, Acc. of Koushan Pass, 35; Wood, Oxus, 416; Lord, Koh-i-Damun, 48.

SHYRKHOWI, in Afghanistan, a village situate on the river Hury, or Herirood. Lat. 34° 22′, long. 64° 6′. Walker's Map of Afg.

SIAH KOH, or the Black Mountain of Afghanistan, is so called as contradistinguished from the Sufeid Koh, or White Mountain, farther south, and parallel to it. The Siah Koh bounds the plain of Jelalabad on the north, and extends between long. 69° 45′ and 70° 20′, in lat. 34° 25′. It is of moderate height, probably nowhere more than 3,000 feet above the plain of Jelalabad. Wood, Khyber Pass, 6; Jour. As. Soc. Beng. 1842, p. 119, MacGregor, Geog. Notice on the Valley of Jullalabad.

SIB, in the Punjab, a village situate on the route from Mooltan to Ferozpoor, and about forty miles north-east of the former town. Lat. 30° 1′, long. 72° 1′. E.I.C. Ms. Doc.

SICKEELALE, in the Punjab, a village situate on the road from Vazeerabad to Julalpoor. Lat. 32° 36′, long. 73° 41′. E.I.C. Ms. Doc.

SIDA, in the Punjab, a village situate on the right bank close to the junction of the Jailum and Chenaub rivers. Lat. 31° 5′, long. 72° 5′. E.I.C. Ms. Doc.

SIKUNKA, in Bhawlpoor, a village situate on the left bank of the river Ghara. Lat. 30° 9′, long. 73° 3′. Walker's Map of N.W. Frontier.

SIMMASUTTEE, in Bhawlpoor, a village situate on the river Ghara, about twelve miles west of the town of Bhawlpoor. Lat. 29° 33′, long. 71° 30′. E.I.C. Ms. Doc.

SINAOW, in Sinde, a village situate on the road from Jessulmair to Halla. Lat. 26° 30′, long. 70° 3′. Ms. Survey Map.

SINDE, an extensive and important country of Western India, so called, probably,[1] from the river Sinde * or Indus. Others 1 79; McMurdo, on the Indus, Jour. of Roy. As. Soc. of Beng. 1834, p. 22.

* From *Sindh* or *Sindhu*, Sanscrit for sea or "collection of water," سندُ Shakespear in v. There are numerous similar instances in various

consider that the name, both of the river and the country, is derived from the word Sindhi,[2]* synonymous with Hindi, as the inhabitants from the first dawn of recorded knowledge have principally been of the great Hindoo family. It is bounded on the north by Beloochistan, Afghanistan, and Bhawlpoor, on the east by Jessulmair and Marwar, on the south by Cutch and the Indian Ocean, on the west by Beloochistan, and is situated between lat. 23° 32'—28° 50', and long. 66° 37'—71° 16'. It is three hundred and eighty miles long from north to south, three hundred miles in its greatest breadth from east to west, and contains a surface of about sixty thousand square miles.† Its sea-coast, washed by the Indian Ocean, extends a distance of one hundred and fifty miles, in a north-west direction, from the Koree or greatest mouth of the Indus (long deserted by the stream), situate in lat. 23° 30', long. 68° 25', to Cape Monze,[3] or Ras Mooarree, in lat. 24° 48', long. 66° 38'. This whole extent of coast, except the part intervening between Kurrachee and Cape Monze, which are distant from each other about fifteen miles, is very low, being merely a series of mud banks deposited by the Indus, or, in a few place, low sand-hills,[4] blown in from the sea-beach. With the exception of those few sand-hills, "the shore," observes Carless, "is low and flat throughout, and at high water partially overflowed to a considerable distance inland. With the exception of a few spots covered with jungle, it is entirely destitute of trees or shrubs, and nothing is seen for many miles but a dreary swamp. Whenever this occurs, the land is scarcely discernible two miles from the shore." Wood[5] also observes—"The coast line is submerged at spring tides, when the delta of the Indus resembles a low champagne tract of verdure, with tufts of mangrove dotted along its seaward edge." Burnes, too, states that the coast of Sinde is not distinguishable a league

[2] Notice of Wathen's Sindhi Grammar, in Jour. As. Soc. Beng. 1837, p. 347.

[3] Horsburgh, Ind. Dir. i. 493; Pott. Belooch. 251.

[4] Carless, Official Rep. on the Indus, 3; Wood, Oxus, 11.

[5] Oxus, 10.

parts of the world of great tracts denominated from rivers, as many states of North America, departments of France, and circles of Germany.

* According to the native Sindian history, in the usual style of national vanity—"Sindh is so called from Sindh, the brother of Hindh, the son of Noah, whose descendants for many generations ruled that country."—Postans, Extracts from Tóhfat ul Kiram and the Chach Nameh. (Transacts. of As. Soc. of Bengal, 1838, 298; and 1841, 184.)

† This estimate is given from careful measurement on Walker's excellent map of the north-west frontier. The estimate given by Burnes (iii. p. 213) of 100,000 square miles is unquestionably exaggerated.

from the shore. Westward of the Garrah estuary, and between it and Kurrachee, the southern extremity of the Hala[6] or Pubb mountains approaches the shore, the point of Munoora, which forms the southern shelter of the harbour of Kurrachee, being rocky;[7] but with the exception of this point, the coast itself is like that eastward, low[8] and alluvial, and so continues westward to Cape Monze or Ras Mooarree, which rises from the sea to a moderate height. The sea of the coast is very shallow, so that, according to Wood,[9] a vessel of 1,000 tons could scarcely come in sight of the Sindian coast;[1] the soundings, however, in general decrease so gradually and regularly, that in the fine season there is no danger in approaching it. The shallowness of the sea appears to be mainly owing to the enormous quantity of mud deposited by the water of the Indus. A bank[2] extends all along the coast from Kurrachee to Cutch, reaching from two or three miles to five or six from land, and being in most places dry at low water. The only shoal which projects to any considerable distance is the Great Munnejah Bank, which has a hard, smooth bottom, and which should be approached with much care by large vessels. The tides[3] are extremely irregular, both in direction and height, rising in the south-eastern part of the coast about four feet, and among some of the great channels as much as twelve feet.[4] The flow and ebb are exceedingly violent and rapid, sweeping over the low lands, and retiring with a velocity and force not easily conceived by those who have not witnessed them. The influence of the tide is perceptible for seventy-five miles from the ocean, or about twenty-five miles above Tatta. The[5] south-west monsoon reaches the coast of Sinde, and though it does not bring much rain, blows with extreme violence, rendering navigation perilous after the beginning of March. Of the eleven mouths of the Indus, only two, the Hujamree* and Kookewarree, are navigable in sea-going vessels from the sea to the main channel of the river; and as on the bar of the former there are only thirteen[6] feet of water at full tide, on the latter only ten[7] feet, while the sea breaks violently on them during the stormy season, it is inevitable destruction for a ship then to attempt to

[6] Burnes, iii. 10.

[7] Pott. 343; Leech, Rep. on Sind. Army, 78.

[8] Horsburgh, i. 493.

[9] App. to Burnes' Pers. Narr. 310.

[1] Carless, 3.

[2] Id. ibid.

[3] Id. ibid.

[4] Burnes, iii. 241.

[5] Id. ib.; Wood, in Official Rep. by Carless, 23; Elph. Acc. of Caubul, 181.

[6] Carless, 4.

[7] Id. 8.

* According to the account of Kennedy, however, the Hujamree mouth was closed in 1839 by one of those violent changes frequent in the shifting shoals and channels of the Indus, "and has now no river communication with Tatta, or junction with the main stream."

Sind and Kaubool, ii. 220.

enter them. In the winter months the weather is very mild; the fleet,[8] which in 1838 conveyed the British armament to the mouth of the Indus, remained for nearly the whole month of November at anchor in the open roadstead, at the mouth of the Hujamree, and during that time experienced no inconvenience. The capability of the coast of Sinde for the purposes of navigation is thus summed up by Wood[9]:—"It is plain to all who are conversant with nautical affairs that Kurrachee is the only safe seaport for the valley of the Indus. When the season is favourable, the merchant may indeed send his goods direct to the mouth of the Indus; but every thing here is subject to such constant change—the weather, the depth of water, the channels, and the very embouchure itself—that this voyage, even in February, is not without hazards." He then observes, that as the danger of entering the river is greater than of leaving it, exports may be sent from the mouths in November, December, and January, but that all imports should be brought by Kurrachee. It should be observed, however, that though sea-going ships of 400 or 500 tons can at no time safely enter the river,[1] yet smaller vessels, if their draught do not exceed six or seven feet, may do so. An inland navigation, or even a ship canal, could probably be easily made from Kurrachee to the deepest and most navigable part of the Indus below Hyderabad, as the Garrah, a small stream [2] communicating with the Indus, falls into the sea* at that port, and is navigable from it for boats as far as Garrah Kot, a distance of forty miles.

Kurrachee, the only port in Sinde for sea-going ships of burthen amounting to four or five hundred tons, has, at high water, a depth of two fathoms and a half,[3] and at spring tides of three fathoms; but, during the south-west monsoon, the swell is so great on the bar, that it is highly dangerous to cross.[4] The Kookewarree,[5] called the Gora by Burnes,[6] the principal mouth

* Carless (Official Report on the State and Navigation of the Indus, p. 6) uses these words:—"The Garrah, a small stream that conducts them (large boats) *to the harbour of Corachee;*" and Masson [1] states, that "the salt water creek of Garrah has a communication with Karachi;" but in the MS. map of Sinde of the Quartermaster-general, No. 1, the mouth of the Garrah is laid down on the eastern side of Kurrachee Bay, and ten miles east of the entrance into the harbour. The intervening country is, however, represented by Pottinger [2] and Horsburgh [3] as perfectly level, and consequently a canal could easily be dug through it.

of the Indus, is one thousand one hundred yards wide; the Hujamree, until lately next in importance, five hundred; the Pittee,[7] five hundred at low water—at other times between eight and nine hundred yards. The Koree mouth is the most eastern, forming the boundary of Sinde towards Cutch. It has long been deserted by the stream, except in very great inundations, when sometimes the Poorana[8] and Fulailee branches pour their waters into it. Burnes states its breadth at Cotasir, twenty miles from the sea, to be seven miles, and that it increases, proceeding downward, until neither shore can be seen. He however adds, very justly, that it is nothing more than an arm of the sea.*

[7] Id. iii. 232.

[8] Id. iii. 238.

The base or seaward line of the delta of the Indus measures, from the Garrah mouth, in lat. 24° 43′, long. 67° 9′, to the Sir mouth, in lat. 23° 35′, long. 68° 15′, about one hundred and twenty-five miles.[9] If it be regarded as having the shape of a triangle, to which it in some degree approximates, the perpendicular measured from the sea-shore to the vertex, near Tatta, where the great branches of the Indus—the Sata, or eastern, the Buggaur, or western—divaricate, is about fifty miles, and its surface is about three thousand square miles; but as the river has in

[9] Id. iii. 230-31.

* This statement is probably referred to by Zimmerman (Geographische Analyse der Karte von Inner-Asien), s. 115, where he states the breadth of "eine Indus-Mündung" at twelve miles, and quotes Arrian, Burnes, and Carless, without giving any exact reference, an inconvenient practice, and which on this occasion tends to implicate the last-mentioned authority, generally highly accurate and judicious, in what cannot be regarded otherwise than as a gross exaggeration. Pottinger[1] states, the western branch, or Buggaur, falling into the sea at lat. 24° 8′, and consequently at the point corresponding with the actual position of the Khedjwarree mouth, to have a breadth of nine miles at Darajee and of twelve miles at its mouth, and this error has been copied into a vast number of elaborate and expensive maps from that prefixed to his account of Beloochistan. As if this were not sufficient, Kennedy[2] states that Pottinger informed him that the breadth was upwards of *twenty* miles! When the British army forded this branch in 1838, during the low season, it was fifty yards wide and two feet and a half deep; and Burnes,[3] in 1830, found it two hundred yards wide near Meerpoor. Pottinger, indeed, furnishes an apology for the more extravagant dimensions, in declaring that they were "from the best native information I could procure." It has been suggested that a great change has taken place in the dimensions of that part of the river since Pottinger wrote, but in various charts of the coast given by Dalrymple, there are no such vast openings as those in question.

[1] 360.

[2] i. 71.

[3] iii. 34.

some degree deserted a considerable portion of the south-eastern part, the present delta proper does not probably contain more than two thousand five hundred square miles. Unlike the densely wooded delta of the Ganges, it is nearly destitute of timber, resembling in this respect that of the Nile. It is almost level, of alluvial soil, apparently brought down by the Indus, and consisting of vegetable mould, clay, and sand, which becomes hard soon after being deposited,[1] even in the channels of the river. There are, however, even within the limits of the delta proper, and eastward of the Buggaur or western branch of the Indus, some rocky hills,[2] known by the name of the MUKALI HILLS (which see). Near the Pittee,[3] or western mouth of the river, is a dangerous rock, the only point in the delta south of the range just described which is not alluvial.

Along the sea-coast, and for several miles inland, the delta is one of the most miserable countries in the world. The tide overflows the ground, and, on receding, leaves a dreary swamp, covered, wherever the water is brackish, with stunted mangrove trees, yet affording pasture for numerous herds of buffaloes, but in most places destitute of fresh water, which must be brought from a distance.[4] The inundation here, during the summer months, is very extensive,[5] and, in consequence of the shifting nature of the channel, vessels are frequently left aground. Burnes[6] estimates that one-eighth of the delta is occupied by streams or canals. Where water cannot be obtained at such a level as to admit of being conducted through the fields by means of channels, it is raised by the Persian wheel. The soil, where not well watered, becomes a clay nearly as hard as if it were baked, producing tamarisks,[7] *mimosa, euphorbia*, furze, cactuses, and various saline plants. In the dry time of the year, this clay is raised in clouds of dust,[8] so dense as to threaten suffocation. Under the influence of water, however, the soil is very productive, especially of a gigantic grass, attaining the height of twelve or eighteen feet, and so thick that it is difficult to force a passage through it. Where the alluvial soil of the delta has been long deposited, it produces lofty acacias, attaining a girth of seven or eight feet. On the fall of the waters of the Indus, numerous *dunds*, or extensive pieces of water, are left, and swarm with the finest fish, which, with those

---

[1] Carless, 6.

[2] Wood, Oxus, 10; Outram, 16; Kennedy, i. 76, 96; Burnes' Pers. Narr. 10, 21.
[3] Burnes, iii. 16; Wood, Oxus, 12.

[4] Burnes, iii. 250.
[5] Lord, Mem. of the Plain of the Indus, 66.
[6] Rep. on the Navig. of the Indus, 3.

[7] Carless, 11; Outram, 14; Burnes, iii. 250.
[8] Kennedy, i. 75.

drawn from the sea and river, form a very considerable proportion of the subsistence of the inhabitants.

In some degree similar to the delta, but superior to it in scenery, soil, cultivation, and climate, is the alluvial tract, extending on each side of the Indus for a distance varying from two to ten or twelve miles. But extensive portions of this country have been depopulated[9] by the Ameers of Sinde, to form *Shikargahs* or hunting-preserves, now consisting of dense thickets of tamarisks, saline plants, shrubs, and brambles. One of the finest parts is a long, narrow island, extending from north to south, a distance of about one hundred miles, with an average breadth of about eight; inclosed by the Indus on the east, and on the west by the Narra. The greatest extent of this alluvial land in the upper part of Sinde appears to be about Khyerpoor, Shikarpoor, and Larkhana,[1] where canals and watercourses, communicating with the Indus, during inundation cover the surface to a wide range with water, which both irrigates the ground and deposits on it a fertilizing slime. According to Postans,[2] the soil is so rich that no manure of any kind is used, though it regularly produces two crops every year, and sometimes three; and Macmurdo[3] states, that "the fertility of this province in those parts which are exposed to the floods of the Indus is exceeded by that of no tract of country on the earth." Throughout the alluvial tracts of Sinde, the soil contains saltpetre in great abundance, and it is largely extracted both for home consumption and for exportation.

An extensive alluvial region stretches eastward of the fertile tract along the Indus, but being now generally deserted by the water of the river, it has become a desert,[4] yielding a scanty pasture to camels or horned cattle, and in the less frequented parts occupied only by the fleet *goorkhur*,[5] or wild-ass. Through it flows the Eastern Narra during the height of the inundations of the Indus. The great doab contained between this branch and the Indus is on an average about seventy or eighty miles wide; the soil consisting generally of a hard sun-baked clay,[6] like the rest of the alluvial soil of Sinde where devoid of water. In this doab are two low ranges of recent limestone; the more southern, that of Hyderabad, about one hundred feet high, and on one part of which that city is situate; the more northern running north-westward from the vicinity of Jes-

[9] Burnes, iii. 257; Wood, 34.

[1] Postans, 21.

[2] Memorandum on Shikarpoor, Jour. As. Soc. Beng. 1840, p. 17.

[3] Jour. Roy. As. Soc. 1834, p. 228.

[4] Macmurdo, on the Indus, Jour. Roy. As. Soc. 1834, p. 41.

[5] Elph. 7; Burnes, iii. 321.

[6] Lord, Mod. Mem. on the Plain of the Indus, 58, 59.

sulmair, and towards the Indus attaining an elevation of a hundred and fifty feet, and abounding in flint, which forms, almost exclusively, the rocks on which Roree and Bukkur stand. These ranges are not, however, completely continuous, being cut by valleys, through one of which the Narra already mentioned holds its course; through another, the Fulailee branch, insulating Hyderabad.

The stiff nature of the deposit of the river is, probably, owing to its course in the upper part generally lying through a very mountainous region, principally of primitive formation. In the more southern part of Sinde, the soil has a very large admixture of sand, and is sometimes so impregnated with common salt that, as Lord observes, " it is not uncommon to see the same soil, which during the season of irrigation had yielded crops of grain, transferred afterwards to the Salt-pan, and furnishing, by the simple process of pouring water over it, which is subsequently evaporated, an abundant supply of salt." The moisture, so indispensable to the productiveness of the soil, is altogether supplied by the water of the Indus,[6] rain in Sinde being very scanty and uncertain. In consequence, the country, where destitute of the means of irrigation, becomes a desert. Of this nature, on the north-east, is the *Pat*,[7] or desert of Shikarpoor, lying between that town and the Bolan Pass, and apparently consisting of the clay deposited by the Bolan, the Nari, and other torrents which flow down from the Hala mountains, and which are all lost in this dreary tract. It is about ninety miles across, and, according to Kennedy, in some places resembles " the dry bed of a salt lagoon in an interval between spring tides;" in others, it is a level plain of indurated clay of a dull earthy colour, and having the appearance of being occasionally under water, but during the dry season exhibiting, at long intervals, a few wretched, parched, and stunted shrubs, but without a single blade of grass or other herbage. In the eastern part, and in general reaching to within twenty miles or even a less distance of the river, is a region called the *Thur*, or desert, having considerable resemblance to that just described, except that it is much more sandy; extensive tracts being covered with sand-hills,[8] varying and shifting under the influence of the tempests of the wilderness. Yet,[9] in many places there is a considerable growth of low shrubs, coarse herbage, and prickly, saline, or aromatic plants, affording pas-

[6] Lord, 61.

[7] Masson, 350; Outram, 57; Kennedy, i. 189; Havelock, i. 184; Hough, 47.

[8] Elph. 8, 9.
[9] Macmurdo, on Sinde, in Jour. Roy. As. Soc. 1834, p. 231; Masson, i. 19.

turage for camels, buffaloes, kine, sheep, and goats, all in continual motion in search of water, or its concomitant, vegetation. Numerous beds of rivers long dried up intersect this arid tract, appearing to indicate that the waters of the Indus, or of some of the Punjab rivers, once found their way throught it. Vestiges of ancient towns also may be observed, in great quantities of fragments of bricks and pottery in some places strewed over the surface. That the Indus, which now finds its way through the limestone rocks at Roree, might at one time have poured its waters in many branches over this waste, at present parched, is by no means improbable, as there are unequivocal indications, that it formerly flowed fifty feet[1] above its present level, in the channel between Sukkur and Roree, and that the country on both sides of the river along the base of the limestone range was at that time under water. The old course of the river[2] may also be traced along the northern base of that rocky range, which stretching nearly one hundred miles to the south-eastward, must have sent the water of the Indus over the surface of the country now become the Eastern Desert since it has been deserted by the stream. This limestone range, commencing in Cutch Gundava, proceeds, as already mentioned, south-east towards Jessulmair, being cut by the channel of the Indus between Roree and Sukkur, where way may have originally been made for the stream by one of those earthquakes the traces of which are observable elsewhere in that region. The passage here, however formed originally, it is certain has, in a long course of ages, been deepened greatly by the force of the current, and thus an adequate efflux afforded for the water, which may formerly have been poured over the *Thur*, and found its way to the sea by the eastern mouths and the *Run*, or great salt-marsh of Cutch. With the exception of this range of hills stretching from Roree towards Jessulmair, and the Gunjah hills[3] east of the Indus, on which Hyderabad is built, in Lower Sinde, the eastern part of this country is quite level. On the west[4] of the Indus, the Hala, or Brahooic mountains, under various denominations, stretch, with diminished height, to the bank of the river at Sehwan, and southward, to the sea at Cape Monze. Of these, the Pubb range is the most western, its ridge forming the boundary on the side of Beloochistan. Among its valleys and ravines runs the Hubb, the only permanent river of the country, except the Indus. It

[1] Westmacott, Acc. of Roree, Jour. As. Soc. Beng. 1841, p. 303.
[2] Kennedy, ii. 169; Lord, Med. Mem. 59.
[3] Pott. 361.
[4] De La Hoste, Rep. on the Country between Kurrachee and Sehwan, Jour. As. Soc. Beng. 1840, p. 911.

rises near the north-east corner of the province of Lus, and runs southward, discharging itself into the sea immediately west of Cape Monze. The whole of that part of Sinde between Kurrachee and Sehwan is a maze of hills, known by various denominations, Jutteel, Keertar, and Lukkee. The Lukkee are considered the highest, having an elevation, where greatest, variously estimated at 1,500[5] and 2,000 feet.[6] They terminate abruptly on the west bank of the Indus.[7]

[5] Kennedy, i. 163.
[6] Burnes, Bokh. iii.
[7] Outram, 40.

The climate of Sinde is remarkably sultry and dry. As Lord[8] observes:—"Situated on the verge of two monsoons, it is unrefreshed by the waters of either. The south-west monsoon," he proceeds, "terminates at Lucput Bunder (on the western coast of Cutch), as accurately as though it covenanted not to violate the Sindh frontier." The north-west monsoon, which deluges the country to the west, comes no farther than Kurrachee, and even there the annual fall of rain does not exceed six or eight inches. At Hyderabad, the rain of an entire twelve-month amounted only to 2·55* inches; and farther north, at Larkhana. Three years had elapsed continuously without rain, at the time of Hamilton's visit in 1699; the consequence was a pestilence, which cut off one-half of the population.† But Burnes, in travelling through the delta on the 10th of April, experienced very heavy showers, and a severe fall of hail; and in June, 1809, during the visit of the British mission, the rain[2] fell so heavily there that the streets frequently resembled rivulets, and none could stir abroad. In the following August the rains were again excessively heavy during the stay of the mission at Hyderabad. The N.W. monsoon commences in February, and continues about four months,‡ rendering the navigation[3] along the coast at that

[8] Med. Mem. of the Plain of the Indus, 58.

[1] Lord, Med. Mem. 61.

[2] Pott. 354, 385.

[3] Carless, Official Survey of the Indus, 9; Lord, 61.

* Lord quotes Wood's Meteorological Tables, but those given by Wood in the Official Survey of Carless contain some astounding statements; e.g. in p. 39 it is stated that fifty-two inches of rain fell on the 13th of July, a quantity which probably never fell in any one day in any country in the world since the deluge. An error, therefore (probably the omission of the decimal point), is to be suspected. The total quantity during the month he states at fifty-eight inches.

† Such is strictly the substance of the statement made by Hamilton (New Account of the East Indies, 8vo. Edin. 1727, vol. i. p. 122). Burnes, referring to it, says: "I observe in Hamilton's India that there is frequently dearth of it (rain) here for three years at a time," which is not correct.

‡ Postans (Observations on Commerce of the Indus, 8) states, that the

time dangerous, and nearly impracticable. Notwithstanding the discrepancy in our information on the subject, there can be little doubt that, throughout Sinde, the climate is generally too dry for the purposes of agriculture, except in the parts irrigated by means of the river. On this subject the Ameer of Khyerpoor remarked to Burnes,[4] that rain always brought disease, and that they were better without it. The temperature is very high in summer. Lord[5] states the mean maximum of the temperature of the atmosphere at Hyderabad, during the six hottest months, to be 98·5° in the shade, and considers it the greatest* hitherto registered in an authenticated form. The water of the Indus at that time attains the temperature of 92° or 93° when highest, and consequently very nearly blood-heat. There appears reason for concluding that the temperature is still higher in Northern Sinde, where the cooling influence of the ocean cannot extend. Burnes[6] states it at 96° at Khyerpoor in the beginning of April. In Northern Sinde, however, frost is not unknown, and ice has been observed in February.[7] In January the difference of the temperature at night and during the day has been found as much as 40°, the thermometer ranging to 84° and upwards. So high, however, in general is the temperature in Lower Sinde, that there is, in fact, no winter.[8] The great heat in summer, the innumerable stagnant pools left by the inundation, and the decaying vegetable matter deposited on the surface or mixed with the soil, produce in many places pestilential exhalations[9] very fatal to health, especially in strangers, and in the dry season the winds sweep from the surface vast clouds of dust impregnated with common salt and nitre, highly injurious to the lungs, and still more to the eyes. The unwholesome nature of the water obtained from the wells increases the evils of the climate, and produces fatal complaints of the bowels, liver, and urinary organs. Violent catarrh or influenza is at some periods of the year general. Fever[1] and ague prove very fatal in moist situations, and Kennedy informs us that the British force stationed at Tatta[2] "suffered a sickness and mortality beyond all he had ever known among native troops in India." The most unwholesome[3] communication is closed, during the monsoon, for the months of May, June, July, and a portion of August.

[4] Pers. Narr. 37.
[5] 64.
[6] Pers. Narr. 57.
[7] Hough, 60.
[8] Macmurdo, on the Country of Sinde, Jour. of Roy. As. Soc. 1834, p. 227.
[9] Id. 226.
[1] Pott. 368.
[2] ii. 217.
[3] De La Hoste, on the Country between Kurrachee and Sehwan, in Jour. of As. Soc. Beng. 1840, p. 914.

* Lord quotes Wood, but his tables, as given in Carless, do not shew so high a temperature.

season is autumn, and during that of 1840, the whole of the 26th regiment, stationed in Lower Sinde, was, with the exception of three persons, attacked with fever, and nearly one hundred died. The climate and air of Kurrachee are by far the most salubrious in Sinde. In consequence of the unwholesomeness of the climate in Lower Sinde,[4] the infirmities of age are in general premature in their approach, and life is of short duration.

[4] Burnes' Bokh. iii. 254.

The natural history of Sinde has not received the attention due to so important a subject. The shores of the delta and its numerous inlets are overgrown in most places with mangrove trees (*Cocoloba uvifera?*), where the brackish water reaches.[5] It is a low tree, but frequently has a girth of twelve feet. The ground everywhere in the delta, where deserted by the water, becomes a jungle of tamarisk, springing up so closely as to present, when a few inches high, the appearance of a verdant field, and affording, in the tender shoots, an excellent food for cattle. It furnishes the common fuel of the country, and also the wood principally employed for carpentry and boat-building.[6] Its twigs are used for mats, baskets, and similar purposes. It is called *lye* by the natives, but appears to be the *Tamarix orientalis* or *articulata* of our botanists. The other trees are *babool*, or *mimosa*, of which several kinds, yielding good fuel, abound in the arid wastes; *jal*, or *pelloo* (*Salvadora Persica*), is found chiefly where the irrigated tract and desert join. Besides these may be mentioned the *neem* (*Melia azadarachta*), the *pepul* (*Ficus religiosa*), the *bir* (*Zizyphus jujuba*), the elegantly-formed *Parkinsonia aculeata*, the Jerusalem thorn of the West Indians; the *juwassi*, a prickly shrub, a favourite food of the camel; the *tallee*, the most valuable of the timber trees of this country; the *kurreel*, or caper, a stunted tree, with crooked wood, well suited for boat-building; the *kundie*, resembling the last in size, and in being suited for the same purposes. A few others of no importance, besides various sorts of wild and fruitless palms, might be added to the list. The date-palm,[7] according to tradition, was introduced by the conquering armies of the Khalifs. Wild rue, and other odoriferous plants, occasionally enliven the arid deserts, accompanied often by various species of *salsola*, or saltwort, turned to advantage by the natives, who burn them, and extract soda from the ashes; the *toolse*, or *Ocymum sanctum*, abounds, but is supposed to have been introduced from Central Hindostan: the egg-

[5] Wood, Oxus, 10; On the Indus, in App. to Burnes' Pers. Narr. 335; Kennedy, i. 74.

[6] Lord, Med. Rep. 60; Burnes' Bokh. iii. 274.

[7] Burnes, iii. 120.

plant (*Solanum melongena*) is abundant, and much esteemed as an esculent.* A gigantic[8] grass, called *cana*, and in some places *moonj*, is very abundant in moist situations, where it grows to the height of from twelve to twenty feet, and is so thick, strong, and crowded together, as to form a sort of thicket, through which it is very difficult to force a way. It is very useful for making mats, baskets, thatch, ropes, and for other similar purposes.

A large collection illustrative of the zoology of the country was made during the exploratory expedition of Burnes[9] in 1837, but the results do not appear to have been given to the public.† The *goorkhur*, or wild ass, a species of the genus *equus*, and in shape resembling the *quagga* of Southern Africa, roams in large herds over the *Thur*, or Eastern Desert, which is also frequented by various species of antelopes.[1] Tigers[2] abound in the jungle by the river side; also hyænas, wolves, jackals, foxes, otters, badgers, wild hogs, deer, hog-deer (*Axis porcinus*), porcupines, hares. Porpoises, or some similar *cetacea*, called by the natives *bolun*,[3] abound in the Indus. The *guryal*,[4] or slender-snouted alligator, is also common in the river and creeks, and is considered harmless. The common alligator[5] swarms in the hot pools formed by the thermal springs near Kurrachee. Two hundred large ones are said to have been found in one piece of water one hundred and twenty yards in circumference. Snakes, scorpions, and centipedes are to be met with. Leeches are numerous in many places, and much used for surgical purposes. There are birds in great number and variety, especially water-fowl. The flamingo,[6] or phœnicopter, frequents the shores of the delta, as does the pelican, which attains a great size, being inferior in this respect only to the ostrich; one taken by Burnes[7] stood four feet high, and measured nine feet eight inches from tip to tip of its wings. Water-fowl are so plentiful that in some places a wild goose[8] may be bought for less than a halfpenny, and two or three ducks for the same sum. Bustards, partridges, quails, jungle-fowl (the wild stock of our com-

[8] Wood, Oxus, 15; Westmacott, Acc. of Khyrpoor, Jour. As. Soc. Beng. 1840, p. 1188.

[9] Pers. Narr. 41.

[1] Elph. 7; Burnes, Bokh. iii. 274.
[2] Wood, Oxus, 61.

[3] Westmacott, 1192; Wood, 25.
[4] Burnes' Pers. Narr. 8.

[5] De La Hoste, Rep. on Western Sinde, in Jour. As. Soc. Beng. 914; Kennedy, ii. 212.

[6] Id. i. 56.

[7] Pers. Narr. 7.

[8] Masson, i. 21.

---

* Lord[1] states that both the *pepul*, or *Ficus religiosa*, and the *banyan*, or *Ficus Indica*, grow in Sinde. Burnes[2] states that the banyan is not to be found there.

† Burnes states, that the drawing and information obtained in his mission of 1837, concerning the zoology of Sinde, comprised, of genera and species, twenty *mammalia*, one hundred and ninety-one birds, thirty-six fishes, eleven reptiles, besides two hundred in other departments of natural history.

[1] 60.
[2] iii. 274.
Id. 41.

mon domestic fowl), various kinds of parrots and perroquets, *merops*, or bee-eaters, crows, and several sorts of small birds, are of common occurrence. The birds of prey are the vulture, and various kinds of falcon. Burnes [6] enumerates five varieties of them. Fish is peculiarly abundant, and forms the principal animal food of the lower orders,[7] who are often reproached with this circumstance by neighbouring nations, and supposed to be rendered stupid by the nature of their diet. The fishermen and their families form a considerable portion of the population, living on the river in boats during the inundation, and in temporary huts of boughs and reeds when the river is low. Burnes [8] estimated that a thousand boats are employed on Lake Manchar alone.

[6] Pers. Narr. 51.
[7] Burnes, iii. 87.
[8] Pers. Narr. 42.

An extravagant addiction to field-sports characterized the Ameers of Sinde, who sacrificed to it the welfare and even the existence of their subjects, laying waste and inclosing extensive cultivated tracts to form their *shikargahs*, or hunting-jungles. One of the Ameers, some years ago, depopulated, near the capital, an extensive tract of fertile ground, and converted it into a shikargah, though this foolish and monstrous act of tyranny caused a loss of revenue equal to 20,000*l.* or 30,000*l.* a year.[9] Another razed a village to the ground, because the noise of the population and domestic animals was considered to disturb the game of a neighbouring preserve.

[9] Burnes (James), Mission to Sinde, 79.

There are generally two harvests [1] in Sinde; the *rubbee*, or spring harvest, reaped from seed sown in autumn, and the *kureef*, or autumn harvest, which is sown in spring. The rubbee crops in general consist of wheat, barley, oil-seeds, millet (*Holcus sorghum*), the *durra* of the Arabians, and called here *bajree*, opium, hemp, tobacco; the kureef crop consists of those productions which require considerable heat to bring them to maturity, such as rice, sugar-cane, cotton, indigo, maize. Pulse and pumpkins, cucumbers, melons, and esculent vegetables, are sown for both crops, and some products are sown indifferently for either. Rice appears to be the staple crop, and, with maize and wheat, forms the principal article of diet, besides being exported in great quantities. The fruits are dates, mangoes, plantains, *Musa paradisiaca*, pomegranates, limes, citrons, figs, apricots, apples, plums, tamarinds, mulberries, pistachio and some other kinds of nuts, and melons. They, in general, are of inferior quality; the grapes especially are small and sour. The plantations of date-palms are very

[1] Jour. As. Soc. Beng. 1840, p. 1102, Westmacott, Acc. of Khyrpoor.

general and extensive, and the fruit is used largely for food and for distillation, by which process a strong spirit is drawn from it. As food, it is found to be of a very heating nature.

Camels[2] are bred in great numbers in the salt-marshes of the Indus, and, though such tracts might seem very uncongenial to the nature of that animal, those reared there are considered very hardy, strong, and enduring, especially of thirst, in consequence of the scanty supply of fresh water in their original soil. The value of the camel is not confined to its virtues as a beast of burden: its milk is a favourite article of diet (though it spoils if not used very fresh), and its hair is woven into coarse cloths. Buffaloes are kept in great numbers in the swampy tracts, where they may be seen wallowing in the mud with their heads[3] only above water. Their flesh is excellent, and their milk is preferred to that of cows, yielding better butter, which, when clarified, forms, under the name of *ghee*, a great article of commerce. A considerable trade is also driven in the hides of these animals. Sheep and goats abound in Upper Sinde, especially on the borders of the *Pat* of Shikarpoor, and of the *Thur*, or Eastern Desert. The former district, called Boordgah, produces the best wool in Sinde, both of goats and sheep, and both animals are kept throughout Upper Sinde,[4] as well for their fleeces as for their milk and flesh. The wool is taken from the carcase of the animal only when slain for food, as the heat would cause its death after losing its fleece. The coarser wool is manufactured into bags, ropes, and strong cloths. The finer might be obtained in such quantities as to be an important branch of commerce, for which, however, there has been hitherto but little encouragement. The horses of Sinde are small and of mean appearance, but hardy,[5] active, and enduring. They are mostly used for the saddle, the beasts of burden being the camel, the mule, and the ass. The camel is the dromedary or one-humped variety, and the finer descriptions are used for the saddle, carrying generally the rider and his attendant.[6] The breed of asses is small, but they are neatly made, strong, active, capable of enduring great fatigue, and of living and thriving on the coarsest fare. The mules are large, strong, handsome, and quick in pace.

As the import trade of Sinde is inconsiderable, the demand of its people for manufactured goods must be, in a great measure, supplied from their own skill and labour; but that demand is

[2] Burnes, iii. 253.

[3] Wood, Oxus, 61; Westmacott, 1191.

[4] Burnes' Rep. on the Commerce of Shikarpoor, 29; Mohun Lal, on the Commerce of Khyrpoor, 37.

[5] Westmacott, 1191; Havelock, i. 125.

[6] Macmurdo, on Sinde, in Jour. Roy. As. Soc. 1834, p. 230.

small, as they are for the most part very poor, and their habits very simple. The state of manufacturing industry is generally rude, and few articles are produced suited for exportation. The peasantry of the delta manufacture a few coarse cloths and felts from the hair and wool of their flocks and herds, and mats[7] of reeds, sedge, straw, and grass, for constructing their moveable houses. At Hyderabad, the fabrication of swords,[8] spears, fire-arms, and other arms, offensive and defensive, has been greatly encouraged by the Ameers, and in consequence is carried to a degree of perfection surprising among a people in general so unskilled. Weaving and embroidery are also skilfully conducted there. Paper[9] is manufactured to some extent, and of good quality, at Roree, Shikarpoor, Larkhana, and some other towns. Tanning[1] is successfully carried on, especially at Larkhana, where excellent shoes, sword-belts, and leather water-bags are made. The bark used is generally that of the acacia. Potteries are universally diffused, and the ware produced, though not in general distinguished by elegance, is sound and strong, the clay being of excellent quality. The pottery[2] of Halla forms an exception to the usual style, being remarkable for tasteful shape and colouring. The Belooches of Sinde, instead of turbans, wear caps, like high-crowned hats without a brim, and these are manufactured in great quantities, and in a handsome style, of cotton, silk, and wool. The manufacture of woollens[3] is both trifling and unskilful, though the Sindians have wool in abundance, and much admire British woollen cloths, which, however, they are in general too poor to purchase. Gunpowder is manufactured in most towns. Silk goods are fabricated at Tatta,[4] Roree, Khyerpoor, and Shikarpoor, the raw material being principally obtained from Persia and Central Asia. Tatta also manufactures loongees, or rich narrow cloths of silk and cotton, sometimes intermixed with golden thread, and embroidered. Loongees of a coarser description are made at Raneepoor, and some other towns in the vicinity of Khyerpoor. Coarse cottons are produced at Tatta, Khyerpoor, and the neighbouring towns, Muttaree, Larkhana, Shikarpoor,[5] and, indeed, at most towns; but this branch of manufacture has been impaired by the importation of cheaper and handsomer fabrics from Hindostan and Britain. Dyeing is an extensive branch of manufacture, the principal dyes being indigo, madder, and *sakur*, which last some describe as a knot[6]

---

[7] De La Hoste, Rep. of Country between Kurrachee and Sehwan, 908; Burnes, iii. 251.
[8] Pott. 370, 372; Leech, on Sind. Army, 67.

[9] Westmacott, 1190.
[1] Id. 405.

[2] Wood, Oxus, 37.

[3] Burnes, on the Commerce of Hydrabad, 20.

[4] Burnes, Commerce of Tatta, 11; Westmacott, 1189.

[5] Postans, Sikarpore, 19.

[6] Mohun Lal, on the Trade of Khyrpoor, 37.

or excrescence on the tamarisk; others,[7] as its blossom, dried and pulverized. *Kirmiz*, extensively used for giving a crimson colour, is the product of the *coccus querci*, and is frequently confounded with cochineal, though a different article.

[7] Westmacott, 1189.

The transit trade between the British possessions in India and the countries west of the Indus has hitherto been principally conducted through Bhawlpoor and the Punjab. Now that the navigation of the Indus is kept open and protected by the British Government, and that many improvements, by means of steam and otherwise, will probably be introduced in the mode of conducting it, the greater portion of the trade may be expected to take its course either through Kurrachee, Sehwan, Larkhana, and Shikarpoor, by the Bolan Pass, or else up the Indus, through the Derajat, by the middle and northern passes. The principal transit trade at present passes by three courses—first, by Hyderabad to Larkhana, or Shikarpoor, and subsequently by the Gundava or Bolan passes; secondly, from Marwar[8] and Central India, across Khyerpoor and by Shikarpoor, to the Bolan Pass; thirdly, from Kurrachee, by Sehwan, Larkhana, and the Bolan Pass. The principal imports, either for transit or home consumption, are silk,[9] cotton, and woollen goods, raw silk, opium, and other drugs; madder and various other dyes; groceries, hardware, metals, turquoises, and other precious stones; glass, chinaware, shields of leather, timber, cordage, bamboos, and dried fruits. Sinde at present has few exports; the more important are rice, and other grain; ghee, or clarified butter, and hides (all sent principally by sea); from the Delta, fish, wool, salt, saltpetre, oil, and oil-seeds; *pabbadee*,[1] or nuts of the *Nymphæa Nelumbo*, bark for tanning, vegetable alkalis, firewood, and gum; a few coarse drugs, and dye-stuffs, sulphur, camels, and horses. To these, under proper management, might be added cotton, silk, tobacco, and opium. The sugar of Sinde is considered of inferior quality. In 1837, when Burnes[2] wrote, the custom-dues of Kurrachee were farmed for 7,000*l.*; those of Darajee for 700*l.*; those of Vikkur for 4,000*l.*; those of Maghribee for 3,200*l.*, and those of Hyderabad for 12,500*l.*; a total of 27,400*l.** for Lower Sinde. The estimated amount of the duties of Khyerpoor, or

[8] Leech, Trade between Shikarpore and Marwar, 68-70.

[9] Pott. 344; Burnes, on the Commerce of Hydrabad, 15-22; Postans, Trade of Shikarpore, Jour. As. Soc. Beng. 1841, p. 12-16.

[1] Leech, on Commerce of Mandavie, 52.

[2] Rep. on Commerce of Hydrabad, 15-22.

* Such would be the amount, taking the rupee at two shillings; but as the standard of this coin is lower in Sinde, the actual amount is something less.

Upper Sinde, at the same time, was 10,000*l.* annually.[3] The vessels belonging to the port of Kurrachee were about one hundred dingees,[4] or small sea-going vessels, drawing from nine to twelve feet of water, and of burthen from fifty to two hundred tons, ill-constructed and put together, unable to weather severe storms, and hence lying idle during the violence of the monsoons.[5] From four hundred to five hundred sea-going boats sailed out of the port of Vikkur in 1836, but this channel, according to the statement of Kennedy,[6] was closed up in 1839. Burnes[7] estimates the whole of the imports of Lower Sinde at four lacs of rupees, or 40,000*l.*; and if 30,000*l.* be allowed for Upper Sinde, the whole will amount to 70,000*l.* annually for a population probably not less than 1,000,000.

The Sindians of the present day are a mixed race, consisting partly of the Juts, probably aboriginal Sindians,[8] of Hindoo extraction (many of whom have been converted to Mahometanism), and the Belooches, who have settled here in recent times. Those Hindoos who have adhered to their original religion and manners are divided into *Bhattias*[9] and *Lohannas*, with their respective *gurus*, or pastors, and the *Pokarna* and *Sarsat Brahmans*. They deviate much in their mode of life from the Hindoos of Hindostan Proper, and this laxity is more particularly observable in the Lohannas, who are the most numerous. These last decline no means of subsistence, and readily entered into the service of the Ameers, in which case they were obliged to wear their beards[1] like the Mahometans. Compulsory conversions to Mahometanism were not unfrequent; the helpless Hindoo being forcibly subjected to circumcision on slight or misconstrued profession, or the false testimony of abandoned Mahometans.[2] It is still more remarkable, that this forcible conversion was sometimes inflicted as a punishment, and in all instances operated as an irreparable loss of caste. The Mahometan population sprung from the converted Hindoos are a peaceable race, generally engaged in agriculture, and are despised by the Belooches, who affect a bold and martial character. In this, the latter have been encouraged by the Ameers of the same descent as themselves. Besides these distinctive races, there is a large part of the population the offspring of their intermarriages. The Hindoos, however, in many places, form a very large proportion of the population; at Shikarpoor,[3] for instance, they are estimated at two-thirds. There are likewise

---

[3] Burnes, Commerce of Shikarpoor, 30.
[4] Id. on the Commerce of Hydrabad, 16.
[5] Burnes, Practical Notes on the Trade to the Indus, 6.
[6] ii. 220.
[7] Commerce of Hydrabad, 19.
[8] Pott. 375.
[9] Macmurdo, on Sinde, in Jour. Roy. As. Soc. 1834, p. 247.
[1] Postans, Memorandum on Shikarpore, Jour. As. Soc. Beng. 1841, p. 20.
[2] Macmurdo, 252; Burnes, Pers. Narr. 15.
[3] Postans, 18.

a few Afghans, especially in the north-western part of the country. The Sindians,[4] collectively, are described as handsome, though of dark complexions; well limbed, but inclined to corpulency, and above the middle size. The beauty of their women is proverbial, and Pottinger[5] remarks, that among the numerous sets of dancing girls whom he saw, there was not one who did not display loveliness of face or symmetry of figure. The Belooches, and the mixed race between them and the Hindoos, are considered the finest part of the population. They have "an oval contour of face,[6] aquiline nose, arched eye-brows, and high forehead, with expressive eyes." The character of no people, perhaps, has been visited with greater obloquy than that of the Sindians. Pottinger[7] represents them as "avaricious, full of deceit, cruel, ungrateful, strangers to veracity;" and adds, that among bordering nations, the term "Sindian dog" is synonymous with "treacherous liar." Macmurdo[8] observes, that "with most, if not all, the vices common to Asiatics, the Sindians appear to possess few, or none, of their virtues," and declares them "the most bigoted, the most self-sufficient, and the most ignorant people on record." Burnes, on the contrary, gives a favourable estimate of their character; having found those with whom he had transactions kindly,[9] grateful, faithful, and of unimpeachable honesty; as the traveller and his company lost nothing in their progress through the country, though all they possessed was at the mercy of the rude individuals casually drawn to serve as guards or servants; and when the British army, in 1839, marched through Sinde to Afghanistan, the people acted with great honesty, and it was observed, that a similar camp[1] "would have suffered more from robberies in one night in Guzerat, than we [the British] had done for the three months we had been in Sinde." The charge of cruelty, also, is discountenanced by reference to the various occasions on which British envoys and agents visited and explored Sinde, with views dreaded and detested by its rulers, but without becoming the victims of any Sindian cruel or treacherous actions. They are charged with adulation, but their expressions and manners in this respect appear to amount to little more than awkward and overstrained attempts at politeness. The natural results, indeed, of their semi-barbarous state and long-continued misgovernment are apparent. The people are grossly ignorant and bigoted, and inclined to be tricky in matters of business.[2] The Hindoos engaged

[4] Pott. 377; Macmurdo, 243.
[5] 377.
[6] Macmurdo, 243.
[7] 376.
[8] 244.
[9] Burnes' Bokh. iii. 86, 225.
[1] Kennedy, i. 167.
[2] Conolly, ii. 243.

in mercantile concerns are especially avaricious and overreaching. Their warriors are swaggering and boastful; individually brave, but deeming it no disgrace to take to flight if their first onset fail.[3] This class consists almost exclusively either of men of Beloochee descent,[4] or of Belooches by birth, who have been driven by want to leave their native mountains, and whose warlike and predatory character became well known to our troops during the late military operations. So frequently have this class recourse to arms, that it is rare to see one of them without several sword wounds.[5]

The country, though remarkable for fertility, being, from social and political causes, so ill cultivated, that it with difficulty maintains its very limited population, swarms with a vagrant and " idle [6] race of men, alternately soldiers, beggars, and thieves." These, in great numbers, seek service with foreign powers, and, in Western India, hold the next place to the Arabs as mercenary troops. The Mussulmans are generally *Sunnis*,[7] or of the more numerous class of Mahometans, who recognize the succession of the three first Khalifs; but the Ameers, and others of the great, were *Shias*, or votaries of Ali. There is a great number of *Saiyids*, or those who claim descent from Mahomet, and who, upon the strength of their claims, have succeeded in obtaining considerable grants of lands from successive rulers, and are among the most prosperous[8] persons in the country. The country is also overrun with a prodigious number of Fakeers,[9]— lazy, worthless mendicants, who, under the guise of religion, subsist on arms or contributions extorted by importunity or threats. The Beloochian Sindians differ from other Mahometans in wearing the hair of the head long, as well as that of the beard. The dress of the men consists of a loose shirt, a pair of trowsers gathered at the ancles, a kummerbund or scarf round the waist, and a quilted woollen or cotton cap, shaped like a hat without a brim,[1] and often ornamented with embroidery of silk or gold round the bottom. The great wear turbans of enormous size, Pottinger[2] having seen some two feet or two feet and a half in diameter, and containing seventy or eighty yards of gauze from eight to twelve inches in breadth. The women dress like the men, except that they do not wear the cap, and that, when out of doors, they wrap themselves in a long, loose cloth, having one end fastened on the crown of the head, so that it can be drawn

[3] Macmurdo, 245.
[4] Leech, on the Sind. Army, 68.

[5] Pott. 377.

[6] Macmurdo, 245.

[7] Pott. 377; Macmurdo, 252.

[8] Burnes, Bokh. iii. 63.
[9] Wood, Oxus, 50; Pott. 364.

[1] Id. 378.

[2] 368; Macmurdo, 246.

over the face on the approach of a stranger. The filth of the Sindians cannot be denied or extenuated; it is proverbial, and may, perhaps, be attributed to their poverty.[3] Sinde is supposed by Sir William Jones to have been the original country of the gypsies,[4]* who, according to Adelung,[5] fled from India to escape the massacres of the ruthless Tamerlane. The Sindian language is a branch of the Sanscrit or Indo-Germanic stock, merely a little differing in spelling and inflexion from the pure Hindi[6] of Upper India, and is by some considered the elder of the two, being more elaborate and regular in the inflexions of its nouns and verbs. Macmurdo[7] states, on the authority of native scholars, that "it has fewer modern innovations, and a greater number of Sanscrit words, than the Gujarati, which is a pure Hindoo dialect." It has a character peculiar to itself, which is written from left to right. Belochee,[8] another of the Indo-Germanic tongues, is of course largely spoken, especially in the hilly country; and Persian may be regarded as the language of the court[9] and of the higher order of the people.

[3] Burnes, Bokh. iii. 87; Macmurdo, 247.
[4] As. Res. iii. 7.
[5] Mithridates, i. 198; iv. 488.
[6] Notice of Wathen's Grammar of the Sindhi Language, in Jour. As. Soc. Beng. 1837, pp. 348, 349.
[7] In Jour. Roy. As. Soc. 1834, p. 248.
[8] Leech, Grammar of Belochee, 101.
[9] Havelock, I. 151.

From the period when Sinde was visited by the Greeks under Alexander, its history is in a great degree a blank. Native annalists appear to be magniloquent in regard to the grandeur, power, and resources of some of its princes; and, on the event of a revolution, brought about through the criminal passion of a queen for a young Brahmin, who was enabled by her favour to ascend, first to the office of chief minister, and subsequently to the throne, the historian who records the facts indulges in the following burst of mingled grief and admiration:[1]—" Such was the close of the race of Rajah Sazee, which had governed the kingdom of Sinde for upwards of two thousand years; whose princes, at one period, received tribute from eleven dependent kingdoms, and who had set the threats of the greatest monarchs of the world at defiance." According to Pottinger,[2] the dominions of the Rajah Sazee (including his tributaries) are described by native authorities as extending, "on the north, to the present provinces of Kashmir and Kabool; southward, to Surat and the island now called Dieu; westward, along the sea-coast to Meck-

[1] Pott. 387.
[2] 386.

* Besides the older work of Grellman on this subject, see "Harriot on the Oriental Origin of the Gypsies," in Transact. of Royal As. Soc., vol. ii. 518—558; also Richardson on the Bazeegurs, vol. vii. 457, of As. Researches; and Klaproth (Asia Polyglotha) on the branches of Sanscrit.

ran; and eastward, to the provinces of Marwar, Beckaneer, &c." In the sixth century of the Christian era the country was invaded by the Persians, and to this invasion probably refers the allusion of the enthusiastic chronicler above quoted to the defiance offered by the royal house of Sinde to "the greatest monarchs of the world." The result, however, was disastrous to the reigning prince, though unproductive of any permanent change in the relation of the two countries. The Persians defeated the Rajah in a pitched battle, in which the prince fell. But the object of the invaders appears to have been not so much conquest as plunder, and, having secured as much booty as they had the means of carrying away, they departed. Among the spoils which they bore from Sinde were some thousands of its most beautiful women.

At an early period of the Khalifate, the reputed wealth of Sinde seems to have excited the cupidity of the representatives of the prophet, but their attempts, for a time, were unsuccessful. A subsequent invasion was attended by a different result. The Khalifs were in the habit of importing slave-girls from Sinde, and a party of the followers of the Khalif Abool Mulik, in charge of a selection of Hindoo beauties, destined for the harem of their master, were attacked by the Rajah's troops, some of them killed, and the remainder made prisoners. This occurrence provoked a hostile visit from a Mahometan army. The Rajah was permitted to remain quiet in his capital while the enemy were ravaging his dominions with fire and sword, and when, at last, he left the city with his army, it was but to encounter disaster, defeat, and death. The events of the battle transferred the kingdom to Mahometan rule.*

* The victory gained by the Mahometans was followed by a remarkable instance of oriental revenge. Among the captives were two daughters of the Rajah, esteemed, it is said, the most beautiful women in Asia, and who, in conformity with Eastern custom, were reserved to grace the harem of the Khalif. The princesses meditated vengeance on the general, whose success deprived their father of his throne and life, and reduced them to captivity in a foreign land; and, on their arrival at Bagdad, effected their object, by accusing him of conduct which involved a breach of duty to his master, as well as an outrage on the feelings of his illustrious prisoners. The Khalif, enraged at the alleged insult, ordered the supposed offender to be sewn up in the raw hide of a cow, and in this manner brought into his presence. The sentence was inflicted, and the unfortunate general, thus ungratefully recompensed for

Some centuries later, Sinde became a tributary to the empire of Ghuznee. On the dissolution of that empire, the Sindian chiefs asserted their independence against the Ghoorun during many years, and with various success. Ultimately they were compelled to yield, and Sinde became a constituent part of the Imperial dominions. In the time of Baber, it was invaded and conquered by the prince dispossessed by that emperor at Kandahar. The invader was subsequently compelled to yield the larger portion of his conquest. He soon made an effort to regain what his father had lost, but found new enemies, to whom he was compelled to make large sacrifices. Sinde then, for a time, maintained a claim to independence, but was the scene of great disorders, two successive princes being afflicted with insanity in its most outrageous form. Late in the sixteenth century it yielded to the emperor Akbar, and for about a hundred and fifty years it remained in the usual condition of oriental dependencies; its chiefs usually professing unqualified submission to the emperor; paying tribute when they could no longer postpone it, but scrupulously evading that acknowledgment of supremacy whenever their fears were not sufficiently active to prompt to a different course. In 1739, Sinde fell to the Persian conqueror, Nadir Shah. On his death, and the consequent dismemberment of his empire, it seems to have reverted to its nominal subjection to the imperial throne of Delhi. In 1756, Sinde was included in certain territories forming part of a dowry bestowed by the reigning emperor upon Tymur, son of Ahmed Shah Durani. It is thenceforward to be regarded as an appendage of Kabool, the new relation being maintained precisely in the same mode as that previously existing with the sovereign of Delhi. In 1779, a rebellion was raised by the Talpoor tribe of Belooches against the reigning Nawaub of the Kuloora tribe, who was defeated and forced to fly. He was reinstated in his dominions by the aid of the ruler of Kabool, and the in-

---

his success, died on the third day after being subjected to the punishment. The tale was subsequently discovered to have been fabricated, and the vengeance of the Khalif, then directed towards the beautiful, but vindictive princesses, was manifested in a mode not less characteristic of Eastern cruelty, than was the punishment inflicted on their victim. He ordered them, after being totally divested of clothing, to be tied by the hair of their heads to the tails of horses, and in this manner dragged through the streets of Bagdad till they were dead. The horrible sentence was executed, and the mangled remains of the sufferers then ignominiously cast into the river. Pott. 380, note.

surgents retired. They soon, however, returned, deposed the Kuloora prince once more, and took possession of his throne and power. The ruler of Kabool again advanced to maintain the rights of his dependent, but the usurpers had collected an army superior to that of the Afghans, which they totally defeated. This was in 1786. Fortune being against the Afghan prince, it only remained for him to make the best terms he could. The battle was followed by negotiation; in virtue of which, the Talpoor chief engaged to discharge all arrears of tribute, and to meet the accruing payments in future with punctuality. Within little more than three years, presuming on the inability of the nominal emperor to coerce them, the rulers of Sinde signified their indisposition to paying tribute at all, and the weakness of the Duranie government insured to them for a time impunity. Zeman Shah approached their frontier in 1794, to enforce the demand of his house, but was prevailed on to return with a small portion only of the arrears due. A similar result attended the advance of Shoojah-ool-Moolk in 1809. He received a sum equal to something more than one-third of the amount which had accumulated, and returned, perhaps not altogether indisposed to congratulate himself on his good fortune in obtaining any thing. The disturbances which subsequently prevailed in Afghanistan were admirably calculated to gratify the dislike of the Ameers to dispensing any part of their treasures in the shape of tribute.

[1] i. 140.

The government of Sinde, under the Talpoor dynasty, has been quaintly described by Kennedy,[1] as "a tailor-like personification of royalty, requiring precisely nine Ameers or princes to make up one sovereign." In 1786, when Meer Futteh Ali, the Belooche chief of the Talpoor tribe, succeeded in expelling the Calora dynasty, and was recognized by the Durani monarch,[2] he assigned large tracts of country to those of his relatives who had aided his enterprise to Sohrab Khyrpoor and Northern Sinde, to Thara Meerpoor in the south-east, with the adjoining country, at the same time investing them with independent powers. He reserved Hyderabad and the greater part of the country for himself and his three brothers, residing with them in the same palace, and publicly administering the government with them in the same common *durbar* (hall of audience). Thus the country became divided into the three states—Hyderabad, Khyrpoor, and Meerpoor—each having their little knot of Ameers, or

[2] Pott. 400; Burnes (James), Outram, 20.

SINDE.

rulers. In 1839 there were four Ameers of Hyderabad, the sons of the first who enjoyed the dignity. There were, at the same time, three Ameers at Khyrpoor, and one, or according to Kennedy[2] two, at Meerpoor. The revenue of the three states has been estimated by Pottinger[3]* at sixty-one lacs of rupees, or 610,000*l*.; by Macmurdo,[4] about twenty years later, at half a crore, or 500,000*l*.; by Burnes,[5] about the same time, at thirty lacs, or 300,000*l*.; of which he assigns 150,000*l*. to Hyderabad, 100,000*l*. to Khyrpoor, and 50,000*l*. to Meerpoor. So necessarily uncertain and liable to error must statements of this nature be respecting such barbarous and ill-governed states. Burnes, in the same page, states, " the treasure, it is said, amounts to about twenty millions sterling, thirteen of which are in money, and the remainder in jewels." He does not, however, explain how this enormous sum could have been saved in less than fifty years, out of an annual income not exceeding 300,000*l*. sterling. The revenue was derived in part from customs, dues, and other imposts, but principally from a proportion of the produce of such lands as have not been granted in *jaghir*, or feudal tenure, to individuals. In some cases the revenue was collected in kind, in others in money. The amount, exacted in proportion to the gross produce,[6] was regulated by the greater or less fertility, or facilities for irrigation, and being in some instances a third, in some a fourth, and in some as low as a fifth. These rent-payments are in general as moderate as those required on similar accounts in India, and more so than those usually exacted in Britain.

The government under the Talpoor Ameers appears to have been a military despotism, unchecked, except by a regard to the dogmas of Islam. The Ameers[7] held courts of justice every Friday, and reserved to themselves the right of deciding in cases of life and death. Those potentates,[8] in time of peace, had no more standing army than was sufficient to guard their persons and treasury, to collect the revenue, and retain the forts. Their avarice made them keep the regular military force so low in point of number, that it probably did not exceed one thousand five hundred men. For great and important occasions of national warfare, the army consisted of a feudal soldiery,[9] maintained by the respective chieftains, to whom had been allotted jaghires or

---

* Who wrote between 1813, which year he mentions (p. 401), and 1816, when his work was published.

[2] i. 140.
[3] 401.
[4] In Jour. Roy. As. Soc. 1834, p. 241.
[5] Bokhara, iii. 213.
[6] Macmurdo, 240, 241.
[7] Id. 243.
[8] Leech, on Sind. Army, 67.
[9] Westmacott, Acc. of Khyrpoor, in Jour. As. Soc. Beng. 1840, p. 1195; Leech, ut supra, 67.

grants, on condition of bringing into the field a proportionate number of men, for whom they were responsible, incurring forfeitures in cases of serious misconduct. These retainers usually belonged to the tribe of their chiefs, and worked in their lands and households when not on military service. When called out, these troops received in addition a scanty pay from the Ameers. These men were either Belooches, or of the mixed race descended from them and the Hindoos, and were overloaded with arms, carrying shield, sword, matchlock, and knife. They generally move to the field of battle mounted on camels, horses, mules, or ponies, and there dismount, and, after a few shots from their matchlocks, throw them away; and, being excited with large doses of opium, rush sword in hand, and with loud shouts, on their enemy. They are represented as ignorant of manœuvring, and, if not immediately successful, as ready to break and take to flight; yet, in their late conflicts with our troops, they displayed steady and enduring bravery. Leech[1] estimates the total number of irregular troops enrolled for the service of the Ameers, and available for emergencies, at one hundred and two thousand men; but adds, that sixty thousand by the Hyderabad and Meerpoor Ameers, and thirty thousand by those of Khyrpoor, are as many as could be brought into the field. Even this number is unquestionably too large an estimate, and the true amount probably did not exceed half of it. The artillery was wretchedly inefficient, consisting of a few guns of various and irregular sizes, ill-constructed originally, and for the most part nearly useless from decay, mounted on rude and crazy carriages, and ill-served. The gunpowder also was of inferior quality, though saltpetre may be had in great abundance, and sulphur is obtained from the hills on the western frontier. The forts, Omercote, Hyderabad, Islamcote, Deejy, Munorah, and Bukkur, are described under those respective names.

The population of the towns of Sinde has been very variously estimated; and the following table, though it has received much care, can be regarded only as a tolerable approximation to the truth:—

[1] 76.

SINDE.   225

Hyderabad, the residence of the principal Ameers						20,000[1]	[1] Burnes, iii. 227.
Shikarpoor	...	...	...	...	...	30,000[2]	[2] Postans, 19.
Khyerpoor	...	...	...	...	...	15,000[3]	[3] Burnes, iii. 227.
Kurrachee	...	...	...	...	...	15,000[4]	[4] Id. ib.; Pott. 344, 13,000.
Tatta	...	...	...	...	...	12,000[5]	[5] Outram, 18.
Meerpoor	...	...	...	...	...	10,000[6]	[6] Burnes, iii. 227.
Halla	...	...	...	...	...	*10,000[7]	[7] Burnes, iii. 227.
Larkhana	...	...	...	...	...	10,000[8]	[8] Id. ib.
Roree	...	...	...	...	...	8,000[9]	[9] Id. iii. 272.
Alla yar ka tanda	...	...	...	...	5,000[1]	[1] Id. iii. 227.
Subzulcote	...	...	...	...	...	5,000[2]	[2] Id. ib.
Sukkur	...	...	...	...	...	4,000[3]	[3] Id. iii. 272.
Muttaree	...	...	...	...	...	5,000[4]	[4] Id. iii. 227.
Beyan†	...	...	...	...	...	2,000[5]	[5] Id. iii. 264.
Majinda	...	...	...	...	...	2,000[6]	[6] Id. ib.
Sehwan	...	...	...	...	...	2,000[7]	[7] Burnes, Pers. Narr. 41.
Sunn	...	...	...	...	...	2,000[8]	[8] Burnes, Bokh. iii. 264.

The population is in general most dense at a distance of two or more miles from the banks of the Indus, as the lands may there have the advantage of irrigation without the dangers incurred by nearer proximity to the stream. The immediate banks[9] are in general overrun with jungle, and deserted, except during the fishing season, when they are frequented by busy crowds. The total population of Sinde is stated by Burnes at 1,000,000, or something more than sixteen to the square mile: an estimate which, when the great extent of arid desert and the general imperfect cultivation are considered, seems too high.

[9] Wood. Oxus, 45; Burnes' Bokh. iii. 264; Macmurdo, 242.

The relations of the British government with Sinde were at no time very close or very friendly. It was always characterized by coldness and suspicion on the part of the Sindian authorities, and sometimes by stronger marks of dislike. The agents of the East-India Company resorted thither for the purposes of trade, but early in the present century the commercial resident of the Company was violently expelled, and a large amount of property in his custody seized. According to Pottinger,[1] an attempt was made to murder the resident. That author deems it matter for regret that on that occasion the Ameers were not "made to feel

[1] Belooch. 492.

---

* Yet Burnes (iii. 264) states the population at 2,000!

† Probably the Beeah in the alphabetical arrangement of the present work.

the force of our arms within their dominions; had that been the case," he continues, "their conduct would doubtless have been of a very different nature towards the late missions to their court." Those missions were treated in various instances with great indecorum, and attempts were made to cast indignity on them in matters of *etiquette* and ceremony. In 1809, however, a treaty was concluded,[1] the most important article of which was the following: "The government of Sinde will not allow the establishment of the tribe of the French in Sinde;" it being then an important point to exclude from the vicinity of our Indian possessions an enemy who had long been desirous of attacking them. In 1820, another treaty was concluded, the chief object of which seems to have been the exclusion of European and American adventurers from the dominions of the Ameers. A new treaty was formed in 1832, the most important provisions of which are those relating to the opening of the roads and the river of Sinde to the merchants of India. This privilege is stipulated for by the third article, and by the fifth, fixed and moderate duties are to be levied; but the concession was shackled by three conditions: First, that no military stores should pass; second, that no armed vessel or boat should come by the river; and third, that no English merchant should settle in Sinde, but should come as occasion might require, transact their business, and return to India. The third restriction was a step in retrogression, it having been stipulated in the treaty of 1820, that " if any of the subjects of either of the two states (the British and the Sindian) should establish their residence in the dominions of the other, and should conduct themselves in an orderly and peaceable manner in the territory to which they may emigrate, they will be allowed to remain in that situation." The change sufficiently marks the jealous feeling of the Ameers towards the British Government; while the first and second of the restrictions operated materially to diminish the value of the opening of the Indus. A commercial treaty was concluded in the same year, and thus rested the relations of the Anglo-Indian Government and Sinde till 1836, when Runjeet Singh prepared to carry into effect a design which he had long meditated, of reducing Sinde to subjection to himself. By the interposition of the Government, however, he was prevailed upon to suspend his progress, and the opportunity being thought favourable for establishing a closer connection with Sinde, Colonel

[1] Corresp. relating to Sinde.

Pottinger was despatched to negotiate for the purpose. After a measure of delay, proportioned to the practice of Eastern courts, a treaty was concluded in April, 1838, which possessed at least the merit of brevity. It contained only five articles; by the first of which the British Government engaged its good offices to adjust the differences between the Ameers and Runjeet Singh; by the second, it was stipulated that an accredited British minister should reside at the court of Hyderabad, and that the Ameers should be at liberty to depute a vakeel to reside at the court of the British Government.

The British Government was now engaged in a series of measures designed to erect a barrier to the Anglo-Indian empire, by settling Afghanistan under a prince believed to be friendly to British interests, and an invasion of that country was meditated for the purpose of restoring Shoojah-ool-Moolk to the possession of the dominions then held by Dost Mahomed Khan and his relations. With a view to this, a tripartite treaty was concluded in July, 1838, the parties thereto being the British Government of India, the exiled Shah Shoojah-ool-Moolk, and the Sikh chieftain Runjeet Singh. Preparatory to carrying out its object, it became necessary to establish some more satisfactory relation with Sinde, and measures were taken accordingly, on which the treaty above mentioned was signed; a copy of it with other papers, illustrative of the existing policy of the British Government, was transmitted to Colonel Pottinger,[2] who was instructed to the following effect:—He was to apprize the Ameers of the conviction of the Governor-General, that a crisis had arrived at which it was essentially requisite to the security of British India that the real friends of that power should unequivocally manifest their attachment: he was to inform them of the intentions of the British Government with regard to the westward, and to point out articles in the tripartite treaty, by which that government engaged to arbitrate on the claim of Shoojah-ool-Moolk, as sovereign of Afghanistan, upon the Ameers of Sinde, and proposed to bring also to a final settlement the claims of Runjeet Singh, as connected with the Shah and with the territories along the course of the Indus, formerly included within the dominions of the Afghan kingdom. Colonel Pottinger was also to intimate the approach of Shah Shoojah, supported by a British force, to express a hope, on the part of the Governor-General, in the friendly dispositions of the

[2] Corresp. I. 40, 42.

Ameers, and to warn them that the disappointment of that hope would render necessary the temporary occupation of Shikarpoor and of as much of the adjacent country as might be required to afford a secure basis to the contemplated military operations, while, by neglecting to avail themselves of the proffered mediation in regard to the claim of Shoojah, they would become exposed to the full effect of any measures which he might deem proper for the enforcement of his claim, which, under such a supposition, the Governor-General could not interfere to control. The instructions advert to some other points, but the above are the chief.

Colonel Pottinger, in the discharge of his duty, had to encounter a full share of the impediments usual in Oriental diplomacy, and the general conduct of the Ameers of Hyderabad was such as to lead to an unqualified suspicion of their hostile feelings; the British army, however, passed without molestation, and the members of the British mission were compelled to take their departure. Alexander Burnes's was somewhat less difficult, though here a great obstacle to the conclusion of terms existed in the demand of the British Government for the surrender of the fortress of Bukkur. The Ameers at length gave way, and signed a general treaty of alliance, together with the most unpalatable article conveying to his ally the right of occupying the strongest hold in his dominions. The Hyderabad Ameers also finally gave way, and after various unsuccessful attempts at agreement, ratified a treaty originally consisting of twenty-one articles, but which had been cut down by the Governor-General, Lord Auckland, to fourteen. Among the articles expunged were several prescribing the manner in which intercourse should be carried on with the port of Kurrachee. Hostile possession of that place had previously been taken by a British force, and the Governor-General regarded this fact as placing in the hands of the captors the power of dictating the terms on which intercourse with the fort should be carried on. The general effect of the treaty was to place the territory of the Ameers of Hyderabad in a state of subsidiary dependency on the British Government. A treaty, nearly corresponding with that entered into with the Hyderabad chiefs, was subsequently concluded with Mere Shere Mohamed Khan, Ameer of Meerpoor.

These arrangements did not prevent the recurrence of disputes.

The disasters encountered by the English in Afghanistan were calculated to call forth the latent particles of enmity to that power wherever they might lurk, and some of the Ameers at last were confidently believed to have passed beyond hostile wishes, and to have committed themselves to acts inconsistent with their relations of perfect amity and alliance with the British Government. These circumstances were thought to call for some considerable changes in the existing treaties, and Sir Charles Napier was intrusted to negotiate new treaties,* his diplomatic functions being sustained

* The terms proposed to the Ameers will be found in the following extract from a letter addressed by the Governor-General, Lord Ellenborough, to Sir Charles Napier, 4th November, 1842:—

"Having stated to you, in my letter of yesterday's date, the position in which it appears to me that the British Government stands with respect to certain of the Ameers of Upper and Lower Sinde, I will now communicate to you my views as to the course which should be pursued.

"2. The free navigation of the Indus through the dominions of the Ameers of Lower Sinde, and the free introduction of all articles of consumption into the British cantonments, are already provided for by the treaty of 1839; and the strict observance of these provisions must be enforced.

"3. They appear to be sufficient for the purpose without any alteration in words.

"4. The engagement of Meer Roostum Khan in the treaty of 1838, that he would acquiesce in the arrangements made by other powers for the free navigation of the Indus, must be construed as binding him to the performance of the engagements subsequently entered into by the Ameers of Lower Sinde for that object; but it will be necessary to proceed one step further, and to require that all articles of consumption shall be freely introduced into the British cantonments.

"5. I have always considered that the obligation on the part of the native State to pay tribute to our Government is one which places us in a false position. No character can be more offensive than that of an exacting creditor, with which this obligation invests us. It gives rise to constant discussion of an unfriendly nature between our Government and that of the native States, and it makes us appear to be the cause of all the exactions which the native State inflicts upon its subjects. I desire, therefore, to base the new arrangements to be made with the Ameers of Lower Sinde upon the abolition of all tribute now payable by them to the British Government.

"6. In exchange for the tribute given up by us, we should exact the cession of territory. In the first instance, the surrender of territory would be as painful to the Ameers as the exaction of tribute; but the latter is a grievance constantly recurring, brought continually to the recollection by incessant applications for payment, which the debtor State continually invents excuses

by a considerable military force to act against the Ameers in case of necessity. The Ameers hesitated, but ultimately the treaty to evade or defer. The cession of territory is a grievance which, once submitted to, is in time almost forgotten; and in this case a large portion of the territory to be demanded is of recent conquest, not a part of any ancient possession.

"7. Another provision which it appears to me to be expedient to introduce into a revised treaty with the Ameers, is one for the establishment of uniformity of currency in their dominions.

"8. The inconveniences and evils which arise from the intermixture of currencies of various and changing values are constantly forcing themselves upon my attention. I desire ultimately to establish one uniform currency throughout India. This is a convenient opportunity for introducing a provision to that effect with respect to Sinde. I am aware that native States attach much importance to the right of coinage. I shall endeavour, as far as any feelings of pride are concerned, to save those feelings, by an engagement to coin for the native States rupees, bearing on one side whatever inscription or device they may prefer, but, on the other side, the head of the Sovereign of England; such rupees to be of the same intrinsic value as those which are called 'Company's rupees,' and the whole charge of the coinage to be borne by the British Government.

"9. The exaction of a provision to this effect is but a lenient penalty for the offences which the Ameers have committed, and to this I propose to add another, strongly recommended by you,—a provision securing to us the right to cut wood upon both banks of the Indus for the use of the steamers.

"10. At the same time I know that, on the part of the Ameers, there will be more repugnance to this provision than to any other we could require; and I cannot but doubt whether it would not be found more economical to make use of coal imported from England, than of wood to be cut upon the banks of the Indus. However, for our own security, we must have this provision. It would be expedient to make it as little painful to the Ameers as possible, and to resort to the enforcement of the right to be conceded only in the event of their not furnishing, at the price and at the places to be fixed from time to time, the quantity of wood demanded by the officers of our Government.

"11. The lands we might demand as an equivalent for the tribute we are prepared to abandon, and those of which we may require the cession by Meer Roostum Khan and Meer Nusseer Khan of Khyrpore, as the just penalties for their designed hostility, are in value beyond what are wanted for our own purposes; for it would be highly inexpedient for us to possess upon the Indus any larger extent of territory than may be sufficient to afford full security to the trade upon that river, and to give us the entire military command of it. It is to me a subject of great satisfaction that this circumstance will afford the means of conferring a great reward upon our most faithful ally and friend the Nawab of Bhawulpore.

was signed by those of Lower Sinde, amidst the clamours of a host of infuriated Belooches, who openly insulted the officers of

"12. I consider it to be a measure of true policy to shew to all the States of India, that while we punish the infraction of engagements, we reward fidelity; and it will be in our power, by compelling the cession to the Nawab, by Meer Roostum Khan and Meer Nusseer Mahomed Khan, of the pergunnas of Bhoong Bara and Subzulcote, which were wrested from Bhawulpore thirty-three years ago, to confer a favour the most gratifying to the Nawab and his people.

"13. It appears that the late Meer Moobaruck Khan possessed a very large portion of the fertile territory between Subzulcote and Roree; and it might be desirable that this territory also should be ceded by Meer Nusseer Khan of Khyrpore, his son, if he should now be in possession of it, to the Nawab of Bhawulpore, so that the dominion of the Nawab might extend to Roree, and we might have one continued line of friendly territory on the left bank of the Sutlej and Indus from Ferozepore to Roree. I am not, however, acquainted with the value of these pergunnas formerly belonging to Meer Moobaruck Khan, nor with their exact position; and it is possible that some of them, or all, may have been allotted to his other sons, and not to Meer Nusseer Khan, who alone, as far as I am informed, has placed himself in the position of an enemy by his conduct.

"14. If these pergunnas should belong to the late Meer Moobaruck Khan's other sons, the surplus tribute to be surrendered by us (in excess of the annual value of the lands to be demanded) may be made the means of compensation to the present possessors, the tribute being in all cases exchanged for land; for it is undesirable that there should be any payments of money to be made amongst the Ameers themselves. They are the constant source of dissension: and I have no wish to afflict them by the introduction of this perpetual element of quarrels into their family.

"15. I have already stated that I am desirous of confining the acquisitions of territory to be made by us to such as are necessary for the full protection of the trade upon the Indus and the military command of the river.

"16. These objects will be accomplished by the possession of Kurachee, Tatta, Sukkur, Bukkur, and Roree, together with such arondissement as may be necessary for the secure and convenient occupation of the places, and to give ample room for the extension of the towns and cantonments.

"17. I have no information with respect to Tatta. At an early period of the Afghan war, it was considered desirable to have possession of it as the place of embarkation upon the Indus. It would, I conclude, be very valuable as a possession; and in any case it would be advisable to insert in any revised treaty, provisions not only securing to us the free use of that place of embarkation, but likewise the free use of the navigable creek between Kurachee, Tatta, and of the road from that creek to Tatta.

"18. I have not introduced into the Draft of Treaty, which I annex to this letter, any provisions for the entire freedom of the internal trade of Sinde, principally because I doubt the power of the Ameers, even if well disposed,

the British residency, and their servants. On the following day the residency was attacked, and its inmates were obliged to seek safety elsewhere.* Sir Charles Napier immediately advanced,

to effect that object beyond the Indus; and further, because, even on the left bank of the Indus, it would be difficult for us to detect all the practical infractions of such a provision, and to enforce the observance of it.

"19. You may, however, bear in mind, that my ultimate object is the entire freedom of internal trade throughout the whole territory between Hindoo Koosh, the Indus, and the sea, and that I only await the favourable occasion for effecting this purpose, and for introducing uniformity of currency within the same limits.

"20. To these great benefits, to be enjoyed equally by 140 millions of people, I desire ultimately to add the abolition of all tributes payable by one State to another, and the substitution for such tributes of cessions of territory, so made, by means of mutual exchanges, as to bring together into masses the dominions of the several sovereigns and chiefs. These various measures, which would impart to the people of India the most considerable of the advantages derived from union under the same empire, it may require much time to effect; but it is desirable that they should always be held in view as the ultimate object of our policy, not inconsistent with the real independence of any State, and conducive to the happiness of the subjects of all."

* The following is the account of this transaction given by the resident, Major Outram, to Sir Charles Napier:—

"My despatches of the last few days will have led you to expect that my earnest endeavours to effect an amicable arrangement with the Ameers of Sinde would fail; and it is with much regret I have now to report that their highnesses have commenced hostilities by attacking my residence this morning, which, after four hours' most gallant defence by my honorary escort, the light company of her Majesty's 22nd regiment, commanded by Captain Conway, I was compelled to evacuate, in consequence of our ammunition running short.

"At 9 A.M. this morning, a dense body of cavalry and infantry took post on three sides of the agency compound (the fourth being defended by the *Planet* steamer, about 500 yards distant), in the gardens and houses which immediately command the inclosure, and which it was impossible to hold with our limited numbers. A hot fire was opened by the enemy, and continued incessantly for four hours; but all their attempts to enter the agency inclosure, although merely surrounded by a wall varying from four to five feet high, were frustrated by Captain Conway's able distribution of his small band and the admirable conduct of every individual soldier composing it, under the gallant example of their commanding officer and his subalterns, Lieutenant Harding and Ensign Pennefather, her Majesty's 22nd regiment, also Captains Green, of the 21st regiment of Native Infantry, and Wells, of the 15th regiment, who volunteered their services, to each of whom was assigned the charge of a separate quarter; also to your aide-de-camp Captain Brown, Bengal Engineers, who carried my orders to the steamer, and assisted in work-

gave battle to the enemy, and though the Belooches fought bravely, succeeded in achieving a signal victory—a result greatly aided by the superiority of the arms of the British forces over those of their

ing her guns and directing her flanking fire. Our ammunition being limited to forty rounds per man, the officers directed their whole attention to reserving their fire, and keeping their men close under cover, never shewing themselves or returning a shot, except when the enemy attempted to rush, or shewed themselves in great numbers, consequently great execution was done with trifling expenditure of ammunition and with little loss. Our hope of receiving a reinforcement and a supply of ammunition by the *Satellite* steamer (hourly expected) being disappointed, on the arrival of that vessel without either shortly after the commencement of the attack, it was decided at 12 A.M., after being three hours under fire, to retire to the steamer while still we had sufficient ammunition to fight the vessel up the river; accordingly I requested Captain Conway to keep the enemy at bay for one hour, while the property was removed, for which that time was ample, could the camp followers be induced to exert themselves. After delivering their first loads on board, however, they were so terrified at the enemy's cross-fire on the clear space between the compound and the vessel, that none could be persuaded to return, except a few of the officers' servants, with whose assistance but little could be removed during the limited time we could afford; consequently much had to be abandoned, and I am sorry to find that the loss chiefly fell upon the officers and men, who were too much occupied in keeping off the enemy to be able to attend to their own interests. Accordingly, after the expiration of another hour (during which the enemy, despairing of otherwise effecting their object, had brought up six guns to bear upon us), we took measures to evacuate the Agency. Captain Conway called in his posts, and all being united, retired in a body, covered by a few skirmishers, as deliberately as on parade (carrying off our slain and wounded), which, and the fire from the steam-boats, deterred the enemy from pressing on us as they might have done. All being embarked, I then directed Mr. Acting Commander Miller, commanding the *Satellite* steamer, to proceed with his vessel to the wood station, three miles up the river, on the opposite bank, to secure a sufficiency of fuel for our purposes ere it should be destroyed by the enemy, while I remained with the *Planet* to take off the barge that was moored to the shore. This being a work of some time, during which a hot fire was opened on the vessel from three guns which the enemy brought to bear on her, besides small arms, and requiring much personal exposure of the crew (especially of Mr. Cole, the commander of the vessel), I deem it my duty to bring to your favourable notice their zealous exertions on the occasion, and also to express my obligations to Messrs. Miller and Cole for the flanking fire they maintained on the enemy during their attack on the Agency, and for their support during the retirement and embarkation of the troops. The *Satellite* was also exposed to three guns in her progress up to the wood station, one of which she dismounted by her fire. The vessels were followed by large bodies for about three miles, occasionally opening their guns upon us to no purpose; since then we have pursued our voyage up the Indus, about fifteen

234   SINDE.

opponents.* Triumph continued to attend the career of the victorious general. He was again successful in defeating the army of

miles, without molestation, and purpose to-morrow morning anchoring off Muttaree, where I expect to find your camp. Our casualties amount to two men of her Majesty's 22nd regiment and one camp follower killed; and Mr. Conductor Kiely, Mr. Carlisle, agency clerk, two of the steamer's crew, four of her Majesty's 22nd regiment, two camp followers wounded, and four camp followers missing : total, three killed, ten wounded, and four missing."

* Subjoined is the official report of the battle by Sir Charles Napier:—
" The forces under my command have gained a decisive victory over the army of the Ameers of Upper and Lower Sinde. A detailed account of the various circumstances which led to this action does not belong to the limited space of a hasty despatch, I therefore begin with the transactions belonging to the battle. On the 14th instant, the whole body of the Ameers, assembled in full durbar, formally affixed their seals to the draft treaty. On leaving the durbar, Major Outram and his companions were in great peril: a plot had been laid to murder them all. They were saved by the guards of the Ameers; but the next day (the 15th) the residence of Major Outram was attacked by eight thousand of the Ameer's troops, headed by one or more of the Ameers. The report of this nefarious transaction I have the honour to inclose. I heard of it at Hala, at which place the fearless and distinguished Major Outram joined me, with his brave companions in the stern and extraordinary defence of his residence against so overwhelming a force, accompanied by six pieces of cannon. On the 16th I marched to Muttaree. Having there ascertained that the Ameers were in position at Meeanee (ten miles' distance), to the number of twenty-two thousand men, and well knowing that a delay for reinforcements would both strengthen their confidence and add to their numbers, already seven times that which I commanded, I resolved to attack them, and we marched at 4 A.M., on the morning of the 17th. At 8 o'clock the advanced guard discovered their camp ; at 9 we formed in order of battle, about two thousand eight hundred men of all arms, and twelve pieces of artillery. We were now within range of the enemy's guns, and fifteen pieces of artillery opened upon us and were answered by our cannon. The enemy were very strongly posted; woods were on their flanks which I did not think could be turned. These two woods were joined by the dry bed of the river Fulailee, which had a high bank. The bed of the river was nearly straight, and about 1,200 yards in length. Behind this and in both woods were the enemy posted. In front of their extreme right, and on the edge of the wood, was a village. Having made the best examination of their position, which so short a time permitted, the artillery was posted on the right of the line, and some skirmishers of infantry, with the Sinde irregular horse, were sent in front, to try and make the enemy shew his force more distinctly ; we then advanced from the right in echelon of battalions, refusing the left, to save it from the fire of the village. The 9th Bengal light cavalry formed the reserve in rear of the left wing, and the Poona horse, together with four companies of infantry, guarded the baggage. In this order of battle we advanced, as at a review, across a fine plain, swept by the cannon of the enemy. The artillery, and

the Ameer of Meerpoor,* and the result was the complete subjugation of Sinde, and its annexation, with the exception of the

her Majesty's 22nd regiment in line, formed the leading echelon, the 25th native infantry the second, the 12th native infantry the third, and the 1st grenadier native infantry the fourth.

"The enemy was a thousand yards from our line, which soon traversed the intervening space. Our fire of musketry opened at about a hundred yards from the bank, in reply to that of the enemy, and in a few minutes the engagement became general along the bank of the river, on which the combatants fought, for about three hours or more, with great fury, man to man. Then, my lord, was seen the superiority of the musket and bayonet over the sword and shield and matchlock. The brave Beloochees, first discharging their matchlocks and pistols, dashed over the bank with desperate resolution, but down went these bold and skilful swordsmen under the superior power of the musket and bayonet. At one time, my lord, the courage and numbers of the enemy against the 22nd, the 25th, and the 12th regiments, bore heavily in that part of the battle. There was no time to be lost, and I sent orders to the cavalry to force the right of the enemy's line. This order was very gallantly executed by the 9th Bengal cavalry and the Sinde horse, the details of which shall be afterwards stated to your lordship, for the struggle on our right and centre was, at that moment, so fierce, that I could not go to the left. In this charge the 9th light cavalry took a standard and several pieces of artillery, and the Sinde horse took the enemy's camp, from which a vast body of their cavalry slowly retired fighting. Lieutenant Fitzgerald gallantly pursued them for two miles, and, I understand, slew three of the enemy in single combat. The brilliant conduct of these two cavalry regiments decided, in my opinion, the crisis of the action, for, from the moment the cavalry were seen in the rear of their right flank, the resistance of our opponents slackened; the 22nd regiment forced the bank, the 25th and 12th did the same, the latter regiment capturing several guns, and the victory was decided. The artillery made great havoc among the dense masses of the enemy, and dismounted several of their guns. The whole of the enemy's artillery, ammunition, standards, and camp, with considerable stores and some treasure, were taken."

* The following is an extract from Sir C. Napier's report of the battle: —"The forces under my command marched from Hyderabad this morning at daybreak. About half-past 8 o'clock we discovered and attacked the army under the personal command of the Meer Shere Mahomed, consisting of 20,000 men of all arms, strongly posted behind one of those large nullahs by which this country is intersected in all directions. After a combat of about three hours, the enemy was wholly defeated with considerable slaughter, and the loss of all his standards and cannon.

"His position was nearly a straight line; the nullah was formed by two deep parallel ditches, one 20 feet wide and 8 feet deep, the other 42 feet wide and 17 deep, which had been for a long distance freshly scarped, and a banquette made behind the bank expressly for the occasion.

"To ascertain the extent of his line was extremely difficult, as his left did

236 SIN.

territory added to Bhawlpoor, to the British dominions. Such is the substance of the latest intelligence that has been received (March, 1844).

SINH-KHA-BAB.—See INDUS.

E.I.C. Ms. Doc. SINZAVEE, in Afghanistan, a village on the gun-road not appear to be satisfactorily defined, but he began moving to his right when he perceived that the British force outflanked him in that direction. Believing that this movement had drawn him from that part of the nullah which had been prepared for defence, I hoped to attack his right with less difficulty, and Major Leslie's troop of horse artillery was ordered to move forward and endeavour to rake the nullah; the 9th light cavalry and Poona horse advancing in line, on the left of the artillery, which was supported on the right by her Majesty's 22nd regiment, the latter being, however, at first considerably retired to admit of the oblique fire of Leslie's troop. The whole of the artillery now opened upon the enemy's position, and the British line advanced in echelons from the left, her Majesty's 22nd regiment leading the attack.

" The enemy was now perceived to move from his centre in considerable bodies to his left, apparently retreating, unable to sustain the cross-fire of the British artillery; on seeing which, Major Stack, at the head of the 3rd cavalry, under command of Captain Delamain, and the Sinde horse, under command of Captain Jacob, made a brilliant charge upon the enemy's left flank, crossing the nullah, and cutting down the retreating enemy for several miles. While this was passing on the right, her Majesty's 22nd regiment, gallantly led by Major Poole, who commanded the brigade, and Captain George, who commanded the corps, attacked the nullah on the left with great gallantry, and, I regret to add, with considerable loss. This brave battalion marched up to the nullah under a heavy fire of matchlocks, without returning a shot till within forty paces of the entrenchment, and then stormed it like British soldiers. The intrepid Lieutenant Coote first mounted the rampart, seized one of the enemy's standards, and was severely wounded while waving it and cheering on his men. Meanwhile the Poona horse, under Captain Tait, and the 9th cavalry, under Major Story, turned the enemy's right flank, pursuing and cutting down the fugitives for several miles. Her Majesty's 22nd regiment was well supported by the batteries commanded by Captains Willoughby and Hutt, which crossed their fire with that of Major Leslie. Then came the 2nd brigade, under command of Major Woodburn, bearing down into action with excellent coolness. It consisted of the 25th, 21st, and 12th regiments, under the command of Captains Jackson, Stevens, and Fisher, respectively; these regiments were strongly sustained by the fire of Captain Whitlie's battery, on the right of which were the 8th and 1st regiments, under Majors Brown and Clibborn: these two corps advanced with the regularity of a review, up to the intrenchments, their commanders, with considerable exertion, stopping their fire, on seeing that a portion of the Sinde horse and 3rd cavalry, in charging the enemy, had got in front of the brigade. The battle was decided by the troop of horse artillery and her Majesty's 22nd regiment."

from Dera Ghazee Khan to Kandahar, and one hundred and fifty miles west of the former place. It has a population of about 1,500, living in wretched huts, and is only important for its supply of water from a spring. Lat. 30° 19′, long. 68° 30′.

SIR MOUTH, an estuary of the Indus (which see). Lat. 23° 38′, long. 68° 12′.

SIRA, in the Punjab, a village situate on the route from La- E.I.C. Ms. Doc. hore to Mooltan, along the left bank of the Ravee. Lat.31° 7′, long. 73° 28′.

SIRA DURGA, in Afghanistan, a village on the road from E.I.C. Ms. Doc. Babur-ka-killa to Dera Ismael Khan. Lat. 31° 48′ long. 68° 48′.

SIRAHUH, in the Punjab, a village situate on a small feeder E.I.C. Ms. Doc. of the Hirroo river, and thirty miles south-east of Attock. Lat. 33° 43′, long. 72° 45′.

SIR CHUSMAH, properly SIR CHUSHMAH, "Fountain- [1] E.I.C. Ms. Doc.; head,"* in Afghanistan, the source, according to some, of the Outram, Rough Notes, 138; Kabool river, through a stream rising ten miles farther west,[1] and Wood, Oxus, 197. [2] Moorcr. Punj. higher on the mountain receives the water from this spring. Here Bokh. ii. 382. are two natural ponds replenished from springs, "so full of trout [3] Burnes, Bokh. i. 174; Sale, Dis- as to baffle description or credibility."[2] These fish are treated as asters in Afg. 417. sacred by the superstitious Afghans.[3] There is a small town here, [4] Jour. As. Soc. Beng. 1842, p. 68, defended by a fort. Elevation above the sea, 8,836 feet.[4]† Lat. Grif., Bar. and Ther. Obs. in Afg. 34° 20′, long. 68° 15′.

SIRDARCOTE, or WALOUR, a village near the south-eastern frontier of Bhawlpoor, and situate on the route from the town of Bhawlpoor to Bhutnea. Lat. 29° 16′, long. 73° 16′.

SIRDAR GHUR.—See GOTTARAO.

SIREE, a village in Afghanistan, on the road from Tull to E.I.C. Ms. Doc. Dera Ghazee Khan. Lat. 30° 3′, long. 70° 12′.

SIRGAE, in the Punjab, a village situate on the right E.I.C. Ms. Doc. bank of the Ravee, about eight miles from its confluence with the Chenaub. Lat. 30° 35′, long. 71° 53′.

SIR-I-AB, in Beloochistan, a copious spring in the Dusht-i- E.I.C. Ms. Doc.[1] Hough, Narr. Exp. Bedowlut, or table-land north-west of the Bolan Pass, is im- in Afg. 57; portant as lying on the great military and commercial route from Jour. As. Soc. Beng. 1842, p. 55, Sinde and Lower India to Afghanistan. Its name, *the head of* Grif. Bar. and *the river*, is derived from its being the source of the Shah de Tell Ther. Obs. in Afg.

* From سر "head," and چشمه "fountain."
† In Wood's MS. Survey, 8,400.

Lora river. Elevation above the sea, 5,793 feet. Lat. 30° 3', long. 66° 53'.

SIR-I-ASP, in Afghanistan, a halting-place on the route from Kandahar to Ghuznee, and ninty-four miles north-west from the former place. It is a monument raised over a horse, on the right or west bank of the river Turnak, and hence the name, signifying "horse's head." The road here is good, and country fertile and well cultivated. Elevation above the sea, 5,973 feet. Lat. 32° 14', long. 66° 54'.

SIRINAGUR,* " the town of Surya or the Sun," the capital of Kashmir, and at present more generally known by the same name as that of the valley at large.† The town extends about four miles along both banks of the Jailum, or Behut, which here, deep and sluggish, winds in a very picturesque manner through the town, and adds much to the prospect, by the enlivening effect of the numerous and variously constructed vessels by which it is navigated. The north-west part of the town is the principal, and is situate on the right bank of the river; on the south-east and south is the suburb of Sher-Gerh, which has fortifications of no great strength, and contains the usual residence of the governor. This seat of government has two stories overtopping the ramparts and a principal entrance communicating with the river by broad wooden stairs.[2] On the north of the city rises a hill, called the Kohi Maran, Hari Parbat, or Hirney Parvat, of trap formation, and having an elevation of about two hundred and fifty feet above the Jailum; on the summit is an ill-constructed fort of slight strength, though, according to Hügel,[3] it might easily be made impregnable. On the edge of the cliff, which rises perpendicularly over the town, two or three large guns are mounted and command the city; the fortress itself has no cannon, being roofed over and having no embrasures. According to the statement of Vigne, the Mogul emperor, Akbar, caused a wall to be built round the base of the hill, a circuit of about four thousand paces. Of the five gates in this wall, one bears an inscription, stating that the tower Naginagur, thus inclosed, was built A.H. 1006, cost eleven millions of rupees,[4]

* From سور "the sun," and گر "a town."

† According to Hügel, the Hindoos call it Sirinagur; the Mahometans, Kashmir.

and that two hundred master-builders were employed on it. Of this great undertaking nothing remains but a handsome mosque, the rest has been reduced to a vast extent of shapeless ruins, at present totally uninhabited. Moorcroft[5] draws a very repulsive picture of the city of Sirinagur. "The general character of the city of Kashmir is that of a confused mass of ill-favoured buildings, forming a complicated labyrinth of narrow and dirty lanes, scarcely broad enough for a single cart to pass, badly paved, and having a small gutter in the centre, full of filth, banked upon each side by a border of mire. The houses are in general two or three stories high; they are built of unburnt bricks and timber, the former serving for little else than to fill up the interstices of the latter. They are not plastered, are badly constructed, and are mostly in a neglected and ruinous condition, with broken doors or no doors at all, with shattered lattices, windows stopped up with boards, paper, or rags, walls out of the perpendicular, and pitched roofs threatening to fall. The roofs are formed of layers of birch-bark covered by a coating of earth, in which seeds, dropped by birds or wafted by the wind, have vegetated, and they are constantly overrun with grass, flowers, and seeds. The houses of the better class are commonly detached and surrounded by a wall and gardens, the latter of which often communicate with a canal. The condition of the gardens is no better than that of the building, and the whole presents a striking picture of wretchedness and decay."

[5] ii. 118.

The public buildings of this city are not in much better style than the private dwellings. The oldest structure is the tomb of the mother of a Kashmirian king, who reigned in the middle of the fifteenth century. It is built, in an octagonal form, of brick, the walls being seven or eight feet thick, and surmounted by a dome constructed with great strength and solidity, but altogether devoid of architectural beauty. The Jama Musjid, or "great mosque," is the most celebrated building of the city, and native estimate, which is probably exaggerated, represents it capable of containing sixty thousand persons. The foundation and lower part of the walls are built of stone, the upper of brick. The whole is surmounted by a dome and spire rudely constructed of timber, and partly supported on pillars of the same materials, and of these there are three hundred and eighty-four.[6]* Every pillar is a

[6] Moorcr. ii. 129.

* There is a most extraordinary and unaccountable variance between this

pile of square deodar logs, each about a foot thick, and laid one over another as beams are usually stored in a timber-yard, so that each face presents a succession of butts and sides. These pillars are about ten feet high, and seem to have been devised with a precautionary view against earthquakes, which are here of frequent occurrence, and have damaged the rest of the structure without shaking them, or causing them to deviate from the perpendicular. The deodar is a timber so durable that though these pillars have stood nearly two centuries, they exhibit no symptoms of decay. The ground-plan of this spacious building is a square of about four hundred feet.[6] The mosque of Shah Hamedan is built of deodar in a singular style of architecture, resembling the Chinese, but less fantastic and meretricious. The Jailum is crossed by seven bridges. The piers of these are formed of deodar logs, arranged as in the pillars of the great mosque, the road being formed by beams of the same timber stretching from one pier to another. There are no parapets nor side-rails of any kind, and as the beams are in most places some distance asunder, the passage of these singular bridges is not altogether free from danger. So durable is the material, so gentle the current of the Jailum, and so exempt the climate of Kashmir from storms, that some of these apparently frail structures have lasted for several centuries. Houses are built on some of them, and in many places trees have spontaneously grown up. Close to the east of Sirinagur is the city Dal, or Lake, described by Vigne[7] as five miles in length from north to south, and two and a half miles in breadth from east to west. The water is very clear and not deep, in few places exceeding eight or ten feet. The lake is divided into two nearly equal parts by an artificial causeway made across it in the direction from south-west to north-east. This is covered with rushes, and has the appearance of a green line traversing the water. A single opening, bridged over, admits the passage of

[6] F. Von Hugel, i. 249.

[7] ii. 62.

account and that of Vigne.[1] "The foundations are of stone, but the roof of the surrounding cloister, or interior, is supported by two rows of pillars, three hundred and ninety-two in all, on plain stone bases, *each pillar being formed of a single deodar-tree, about thirty feet in height.*" In attempting to decide between such discordant statements, it should be borne in mind that Vigne was an eye-witness, and that the work styled Moorcroft's Travels is a compilation from materials which the learned *rédacteur* was "compelled to compress unmercifully."[2]

[1] ii. 81.

[2] Wilson in Pref. to Moorcr. liii.

boats from one part of the lake to the other.[8] Various tongues of land divide the Dal into inlets or basins, which have distinctive names. It is supplied with water by a stream called the Tybul, but which descends from the mountains bounding the valley on the north-east. This beautiful lake communicates with the Jailum by a canal having floodgates, which remain open when the current sets from the lake towards the river. During inundations of the Jailum, the floodgates are closed by the first rush of water towards the lake, which is thus prevented from overflowing the lower part of the city. That part of the city situate between the Jailum and lake is in several places intersected by canals, which, with proper care, would serve important commercial purposes and contribute to salubrity and cleanliness, but in their present neglected state they must rather be classed amongst the deformities and disadvantages of this fallen city.

[8] F. Von Hugel, i. 231.

The Mar canal is described by Vigne[9] as a singular monument of the ancient prosperity of the city. "Boats pass along as at Venice. Its narrowness, for it does not exceed thirty feet in width; its walls of massive stone; its heavy single-arch bridges and landing-places of the same material; the gloomy passages leading down upon it, betoken the greatest antiquity, whilst the lofty and many-storied houses that rise directly from the water, supported only by thin trunks of deodar, seem ready to fall down upon the boats with every gust of wind. It could not but remind me of one of the old canals in Venice, and, although far inferior in architectural beauty, is perhaps not without pretensions to equal singularity." The verdant and level margin of this beautiful piece of water was the favourite resort of the Mogul emperors and their courtiers, and is still in many places overspread with the relics of their pleasure-grounds and palaces. Of these, the most celebrated is the Shahlimar, where Moore's imagination has pictured the closing scene of Lalla Rookh. This pleasure-ground, laid down by the emperor Jehan Gir, is shaded by noble *chunars*, or plane-trees, now, from age, verging to decay. It is, according to Vigne,[1] seven or eight hundred yards in length by two hundred and eighty in breadth.* The principal building is placed at the upper end of this inclosure, and is thus described by Vigne in rather singular terms:—"It is of

[9] ii. 89.

[1] ii. 100.

* According to Hügel, three hundred and seventy-six paces long, and two hundred and twenty broad.   i. 232.

polished black marble, and consisting of two rooms on either side of a passage, which runs through the centre of the building. On the east and west sides of it there is a corridor, six and a half yards wide, formed by a range of six polygonal pillars, about thirteen feet in height, and of the same material. They are said to have been taken from the ruins of a Hindoo temple, but the capitals and bases appear to have been the work of a Mahomedan architect, and the latter in particular are most beautifully scalloped and polished. The building itself is twenty-four yards square, the north and south sides being ornamented with Saracenic reliefs. It stands in the centre of a square reservoir, which is also lined with black marble, whose sides are about fifty-four yards long, and in its whole circumference, contains one hundred and forty-seven fountains, which are made to play on holidays, the reservoir being filled by the stream, which enters it in the shape of a cascade. The height from the stone floor to the roof is about twenty feet. The latter may originally have been pointed like the Tuscan roof, but as it is now covered with thatch, its original shape cannot be determined. The stream thence descends from the reservoir by a shallow canal cut through the centre of the gardens, and lined with marble, and it falls over an artificial cascade at each of the three lodges through which it passes in its way to the lake. A broad causeway, or walk, runs on each side of it, overshadowed by large chunar-trees, and here and there, a few turfed walks branch off at right angles into the shrubberies, in which are little else than wild plum-trees, planted for the sake of their white blossoms. At the end of one of these is a decayed bath, built of brick, and the walls around are covered with ivy." The view of the lake from the vicinity of the city is very beautiful, the entrance lying between two striking eminences—Huri Parbut on the west, and on the east the Tukhti Suliman, of greater elevation and more imposing aspect. Between these, a magnificent crescent of mountains rises on the north, the east, and south-east, and on the north-west the huge summit of Haramuk towers in the distance with great grandeur. The foreground is formed by the expanse of the clear water of the lake, in many places mantling with the rich green leaves and brilliant blossoms of the water-lily (*Nelumbium speciosum*), and studded with green islets, in many instances tufted with trees. The beauty of this delightful scene is heightened by the appearance of the shore, teeming with the richest verdure, and ornamented with groves of noble plane-trees and poplars. The floating gardens, formed of matted reeds, weeds, and sedge, overlaid with earth, and bearing abundant crops of melons and cucumbers, though on account of their singularity attracting the notice of the traveller, form no feature in the landscape, being at a short distance nearly undistinguishable from the contiguous bank. The scene is, however, enlivened by the numerous boats employed in taking the fish with which the lake abounds. Formerly many persons lived by taking the countless water-fowl which frequent the lake, but these are now unmolested, in consequence of the strictly enforced orders of the Sikh rulers. The appearance of the antique city falling piecemeal into ruin, when viewed at some distance, is no unpleasing feature in the prospect. "The aspect of the city itself is curious, but not particularly striking.[2] It presents an innumerable assemblage of gable-ended houses, interspersed with the pointed and metallic tops of musjis or mosques, melon-grounds, sedgy inlets from the lake, and narrow canals, fringed with rows of willows and poplars. The surface of the lake itself is perfectly tranquil, and the very vivid reflections which cover its surface are only disturbed by the dabbling of wild-fowl, or the rippling that follows the track of the distant boat." In the more prosperous ages of Kashmir, this lake was the scene of the frequent pleasure-parties of the volatile and voluptuous Kashmirians. According to Forster,[3] "when a Kashmirian, even of the lowest order, finds himself in the possession of a few shillings, he loses no time in assembling his party, and, launching into the lake, solaces himself until the last farthing is spent." This fondness for festive pleasures is especially displayed at the "Feast of Roses," which flowers are produced in Kashmir of unrivalled beauty and fragrance. "The season when the rose first opens into blossom is celebrated with much festivity by the Kashmirians, who resort in crowds to the adjacent gardens, and enter into scenes of gaiety and pleasure rarely known among other Asiatic nations."[4] As oppression and consequent misery have "frozen the genial current of the soul," in the Kashmirians, that romantic festival has degenerated into the feast of *Singaras* or water-nuts, celebrated on the first of May by ascending to the summit of the Tukhti Suliman and feasting there, "eating more particularly of singaras."[5] Sirinagur was formerly much celebrated for its manufacture of

[2] Vigne, ii. 61.

[3] Jour. Beng. Eng. ii. 26.

Forster, ii. 18.

[5] Vigne, ii. 93.

shawls, paper, leather, firearms, and attar of rose,* but these have nearly disappeared under the cruel oppression which has long crushed the energies of a people naturally ingenious, industrious, and persevering. Notwithstanding the notorious pusillanimity of the Kashmirians, the Sikhs, conscious of the hatred with which they are regarded, maintain a garrison of about fourteen hundred men, to coerce the miserable population of Sirinagur, computed by some not to exceed forty thousand persons.[6] Moorcroft,[7] who visited the city in 1823, estimated the population at two hundred and forty thousand; the judicious and cautious Elphinstone,[8] in the early part of the present century, at " from a hundred and fifty to two hundred thousand." This appalling reduction of the population in so brief a period has been the combined effect of oppression, pestilence, and famine.† Sirinagur is generally considered to have been founded by Pravarasena, who reigned in Kashmir from A.D. 128 to 176.[9] It is supposed to have succeeded to a more ancient city of the same name, the ruins of which are conjectured by some to be observable at Wentipur,[1]‡ by others at Matan.[2] The elevation of Sirinagur above the sea has been the subject of much controversy, though stated by several intelligent Europeans who have resided at the city for a considerable time, and made this point the specific object of their notice. There can be little doubt that it exceeds 5,000 feet, and falls below 6,000, and 5,500§ may be taken as the mean and probable amount. Lat. 34° 5′, long. 74° 41′.

SIRINGNAGHUR.—See SIRINAGUR.

SIRI POOL,‖ or "Bridge End," in Afghanistan, a town close to the northern frontier, where the Huzareh mountains slope towards the lowlands of Kunduz. It is held by an Uzbeg chieftain, who can muster about a thousand horsemen, and con-

[6] F. Von Hugel, ii. 258.
[7] Punj. Bokh. ii. 123.
[8] Acc. of Caubul, 507.
[9] As. Res. xv. 40, Wilson, Hist. of Cashmir.
[1] Vigne, ii. 25.
[2] F. Von Hugel, i. 288.

Burnes, on Herat and surrounding Countries, 43.

---

* See the notice on Kashmir, i. 362.

† Vigne,[1] as well as Cunningham,[2] estimates the population at 80,000, Jacquemont[3] at 250,000, and there seems too much reason to conclude that the lowest estimate is nearest the truth.

‡ Wilson,[4] from Sanscrit authorities, attributes the founding of Wentipur, Ventipur, or Avantipur, to Avanti Verma, who reigned in Kashmir A.D. 876. It consequently could not be identical with the ancient Sirinagur.

§ See the notice on Kashmir, i. 352, note, for the various authorities on this point. Cunningham states the elevation at 5,046 feet.

‖ From سر "head," and پل "bridge."

[1] ii. 118.
[2] Jour. As. Soc. Beng. 1841, p. 114, on the Sources of the Punjab Rivers.
[3] Voyage, v. 291.
[4] As. Res. xv. 61.

Jour. As. Soc. Beng. 1841, on the Sources of the Punjab Rivers.

trives to maintain a precarious independence. Lat. 36° 11′, long. 65° 44′.

SIR-I-SUNGA, in Afghanistan, a fort on the route from Ghuznee to Kabool, and twenty-two miles south-west of the latter place. It is built of stone on a hill in the fertile valley of Maidan, and completely commands the road. Lat. 34° 20′, long. 68° 46′. — E.I.C. Ms. Doc.

SIRKANY, in the Punjab, a village situate on the left bank of the Indus, on the route from Mooltan to Dera Ismael Khan, and fifteen miles north of the town of Leia. Lat. 31° 10′, long. 70° 59′. — E.I.C. Ms. Doc.

SIRNAWAREE, in Sinde, a village situate on the right bank of the Eastern Narra, on the route from Bukkur to Omercote, and forty miles north-west of the latter place. Lat. 25° 44′, long. 69° 26′. — E.I.C. Ms. Doc.

SIRRA KILLA.—A village in Afghanistan, situate in the Pisheen valley, three miles north of Hykulzie. Lat. 30° 35′, long. 66° 53′. — E.I.C. Ms. Doc.

SIR-ULUNG, in Afghanistan, a pass over Hindoo Koosh, from the Kohistan of Kabool to Turkestan. It is entered from Afghanistan, by following up the course of the Ghorbund river for a few miles, and then turning to the right northwards. Its course lies in general north for about thirty miles, to the summit near which it debouches into the route by the Koushan Pass. The elevation of the summit must be very considerable, as in the beginning of November it was found impassable from snow by Lord and Wood, though a few days after they succeeded in making their way over the Hageguk Pass, 12,000 feet above the level of the sea. The pass of Sir-Ulung is very difficult, being open only from June to November, and even during that interval passable only for ponies. Lat. 35° 36′, long. 68° 55′. — E.I.C. Ms. Doc.; Acc. of Koushan Pass, 33; Lord, Koh-i-Damun, 48; Wood, Oxus, 191; Burnes, Pers. Nar. 173.

SMALAN.—A village in Afghanistan, in the road from Nooraye to Dera Ghazee Khan. Lat. 30° 26′, long. 68° 14′. — E.I.C. Ms. Doc.

SOBARAH.—A halting-place on the route from Roree to Jessulmair, and seventy miles south-west of the former town. The road in this part of the route is difficult, being over sand-hills covered with brushwood and dry grass. Lat. 27° 21′, long. 70°. — E.I.C. Ms. Doc.

SODR WAD.—A village in Daman, Afghanistan, forty miles south-west of Dera Ghazee Khan. Lat. 29° 47′, long. 70° 22′. — E.I.C. Ms. Doc.

SOE.—See DHERIA GOTE.

SOFAHUN, in Kashmir, a small town at the south-eastern extremity of the valley. Here are the only iron-mines in Kashmir. The works here have greatly fallen away, and employ only two hundred men, or about half their former number; the diminution resulting from the exactions and short-sighted oppression of the Sikhs. The iron is considered inferior to that obtained from Bajour and Chinese Tartary. Sofahun is in lat. 33° 32′, long. 75° 12′.

Vigne, Kashmir, i. 338.

SOHRAB, in Beloochistan, on the route from Kelat to Khozdar, and forty miles south-west of the former town. Here is a collection of villages, situate in a fertile and well-watered valley, displaying in summer luxuriant verdure, but in winter dreary from cold, resulting from the elevation, which is between five and six thousand feet. Lat. 28° 33′, long. 66° 9′.

E.I.C. Ms. Doc.; Masson, Bal. Afg. Panj. ii. 47, 112, 177.

SOLEIMAN MOUNTAINS.—See SULIMAN.

SOLTANPOOR.—A village in Bhawlpoor, situate on the route from Bhawlpoor to Subzulcote, about fifty-five miles north-east of the latter town. Lat. 28° 30′, long. 70° 29′.

E.I.C. Ms. Doc.

SONAWARUN, in the Punjab, a lofty peak among the mountains bounding Kashmir on the north-east. Lat. 34° 6′, long. 75° 26′.

Vigne, i. 279.

SONDANWARAN.—A village situate on a small river to the east of Kashmir. Lat. 34° 8′, long. 75° 25′.

Walker's Map of N.W. Frontier.

SONEAUT.—A village in Southern Sinde, ten miles from the border of the Great Western River. Lat. 24° 24′, long. 70° 23′.

E.I.C. Ms. Doc.

SONMEANEE,[1] properly SOUMEANEE,* in Beloochistan, a small town on the shore of the Arabian Sea. It is situate at the northern extremity of an inlet, called the Bay of Sonmeanee, and described, probably in too favourable terms, by Pottinger,[2] as " a very noble sheet of water, said to be free from rocks or shoals, and is capable of affording anchorage to the largest fleet." This bay is formed by the projection of Cape Monze on the east. According to the competent authority of Carless,[3] "the harbour, which has been formed by the Poorally river, is a large irregular inlet, spreading out, like that of Kurrachee, in extensive swamps, and choked with shoals. The channel leading into it is extremely narrow, and has a depth of sixteen or seventeen feet at high water in the shallowest part, but it shifts its position every year,

[1] *Horsburgh, Ind. Dir. i. 493.*

[2] *Belooch. 9.*

[3] *Jour. As. Soc. Beng. 1839, p. 201, Mem. on Province of Lus.*

* According to Hart, from سُو *su*, "neat," and *meanee*, signifying, in Sindhi, " a fishing station."

Jour. As. Soc. Beng. 1840, p. 138, Acc. of a Jour. from Kurrachee to Hinglaj.

and vessels of any size could not navigate it without great difficulty until it has been buoyed off inside. There are six or seven, or even ten, fathoms in some places, but towards the town the channels become shallow, and the trading boats cannot approach it nearer than a mile. At the spot where they anchor, they are always aground at low water. During the south-west monsoon the harbour cannot be entered, for the bar at the entrance is exposed to the whole force of the swell, and the breakers on it are heavy." This bar, according to Horsburgh, has two fathoms of water when the tide is out, but the depth is every year diminishing, and will probably be soon too little to admit vessels; at the same time the sea is encroaching on the land, and threatens soon to sweep away the present site of the town.[4] Sea-going vessels, in general, anchor outside the bar, at the distance of about two miles from the town, and are much exposed to the sea and the weather. The cargoes are discharged into small boats, and so landed. Horses for exportation are made to swim to the vessels. The town is mean and dirty, and has about five hundred houses, built of mud, and each surmounted by a *badgeer*, or small turret or flue, open on one side to the sea-breeze, which it sends downwards in the interior of the building, for the purpose of mitigating the excessive heat. It was formerly surrounded by a mud wall, which is now so decayed that scarcely a vestige of it remains. Water can be obtained only by digging in the sand a little above high-water mark, and is so brackish as to be scarcely drinkable, insomuch that the British vessels, when stationed here, were supplied from Kurrachee. The inhabitants live principally by fishing, and are extremely poor, except a few Hindoos, who have the whole trade in their hands. The imports from Bombay are silk, cloths, iron, tin, steel, copper, pepper, sugar, and spices; from the Persian Gulf, dates and slaves; from Sinde, coarse cotton cloths. The exports are horses, butter, wool, hides, oil, grain, dried fruits, and gum. In 1808 this place was burned by Arabian pirates, and the trade has much decayed since that time. Its traffic is at present much injured by the predatory Belooches, who interrupt the communication with the interior. The population is estimated by Carless at about two thousand. Lat. 24° 25', long. 66° 35'.

[4] Masson, Kalat, 306.

SOOKAD.—A village in Northern Afghanistan, situate on the left bank of the Alingar river. Lat. 35° 21', long. 70° 41'.

E.I.C. Ms. Doc.

E.I.C. Ms. Doc.	SOOLTAN-KA-KOTE, in the Punjab, a village situate near the left bank of the Indus, on an offset of that river, and on the route from Mooltan to Dera Ismael Khan. Lat. 30° 46′, long. 71°.
E.I.C. Ms. Doc.	SOOLTANKHEL.—A village in Afghanistan, twenty-six miles north-east from Ghuznee, on the road to Kabool. Lat. 33° 54′, long. 68° 29′.
E.I.C. Ms. Doc.	SOOLTANPOOR, in the Punjab, a village situate about twelve miles from the right bank of the Sutluj, on a small feeder of that river. Lat. 31° 12′, long. 75° 9′.
Burnes (James), Mission to Sinde, 38.	SOOMERJEE WUSSEE, in Sinde, is a town on the left or eastern bank of the Indus, and on the route from Cutch to Hyderabad. Lat. 25°, long. 68° 30′.
Ms. Map.	SOONA CHANDA-KE-BINDEE.—A village in Sinde, situate near the river Indus. Lat. 27° 2′, long. 68° 3′.
E.I.C. Ms. Doc.	SOOPUR, in Sinde, a village situate on the left bank of the Narra river, on the road from Sehwan to Larkhana, about five miles north of Lake Manchur. Lat. 26° 33′, long. 67° 48′.
Ms. Map.	SOORBAN, in the Punjab, a village situate near the right bank of the river Chenaub, twelve miles south of its confluence with the Jailum river. Lat. 31°, long. 72° 1′.
E.I.C. Ms. Doc.	SOORGOORGYE.—A village in Afghanistan, on the road from Ghuznee to Dera Ismael Khan, by the Gomul Pass. Lat. 32° 36′, long. 68° 42′.
	SOORK DEWAR.—See ALI BOGHAN.
E.I.C. Ms. Doc.	SOORKH-AB (Red River), in Afghanistan, takes its rise in the hilly country between the Toba mountains on the south, and Lake Ab-istada on the north, in lat. 31° 35′, long. 67° 23′. The route from Ghuznee to Shawl proceeds up its course nearly to its source. After a course of about twenty miles in a north-westerly direction, it falls into a river flowing south-westerly, by Maroof, and which appears to be lost in the unexplored country between the Toba mountains and Kandahar.
	SOORKH-AB is a name sometimes given to the Soorkh Rood (which see).
E.I.C. Ms. Doc.; Kennedy, Sind. and Kabool, ii. 135.	SOORKHOW, in Afghanistan, a halting-place on the route from Ghuznee to Shawl, and fifty miles north of the latter place. It is situate on the southern declivity of the Toba range, in a very barren and dreary country, through which winds a road

scarcely passable for cannon, and in general little else than the bed of some mountain torrent. Lat. 30° 50', long. 67° 20'.

SOORKHPOOR.—A village in the Punjab, situate in lat. 30° 34', long. 73° 24'. ^{Walker's Map of N.W. Frontier.}

SOORKH ROOD,[1] or SOORKHAB* (Red River), in Afghanistan, a tributary of the Kabool river, falling into it from the south at Darunta, about ten miles west of Jelalabad, and in lat. 34° 28', long. 70° 22'. The Soorkh Rood rises on the northern slope of the Sufeid Koh, or White Mountains, and receives numerous streams, so that, though neither deep nor broad, it is a very rapid river, with a violent current. It was forded by a British party at Hissatuck in June, 1838. The water at that place was then stirrup-high, and the stream about two yards wide. It is crossed, in lat. 34° 19', long. 69° 56', by the route from Kabool to Jelalabad, by means of "a bridge, built by Ali Mardan Khan in the reign of Shah Jehan, A.D. 1606, but recently repaired by Akram Khan. The bridge was one hundred and seventy yards long and eighteen broad, with a single arch. It was flat at top, with a low parapet on each side. The river, which comes from the south-west, about twenty miles off, was flowing in a rocky bed with much rapidity."[2] During the Talpoor dynasty, it belonged to the Ameer of Khyerpoor, but in 1843 was, with the surrounding district, transferred[3] by the British Government to Mahomed Bouhawul, Khan of Bhawlpoor. It derives its name from its water being tinged by the red earth suspended in it.

[1] E.I.C. Ms. Doc.; Wood, Oxus, 169; Baber, Mem. 142; Masson, Bal. Afg. Panj. i. 181; Moorcr. Punj. Bokh. ii. 362; Jour. As. Soc. Beng. 1842, p. 119, Macgregor, Geog. Notice of the Valley of Jullalabad; Hough, Narr. Exp. in Afg. 301.

[2] Moorcr. ii. 371.

[3] Corresp. on Sinde, 502, 507.

SOORKOON.—See SOORKHOW.

SOORMADANE, in Bhawlpoor, a village situate on the left bank of the Ghara river. Lat. 29° 45', long. 72° 20'. ^{Walker's Map of N.W. Frontier.}

SOORMASING.—A village in the province of Jhalawan, Beloochistan, and situate on the road from Kelat to Southern Beloochistan, about thirty miles south-west of the above-mentioned town. Lat. 28° 34', long. 66° 13'. ^{Ms. Survey Map.}

* سرخ Surkh "red," and رود rud "river," آب ab "water." According to MacGregor,[1] "it is called the Red River from the colour of its water;" and of similar import is the statement of Burnes:[2] "We continued our march to Jugduluk, and passed the Soorkh Rood, or Red River, by a bridge, with a variety of smaller streams, which pour the melted snow of the Sufued Koh into that rivulet. The waters of all of them were reddish; hence the name." Havelock,[3] on the contrary, makes mention of its "crystal waters."

[1] 119.
[2] Bokh. i. 126.
[3] War in Afg. ii. 179.

E.I.C. Ms. Doc.

SOOUK DEEVAL, in Afghanistan, on the route from Dera Ghazee Khan to Ghuznee, and thirty-five miles west of the former place. The road is good here, and there is a supply of water from a subterraneous aqueduct. Lat. 31° 55′, long. 70° 13′.

Vigne, Kashmir, ii. 157; F. Von Hugel, Kaschmir, i. 153; Moorer. Punj. Bokh. ii. 279.

SOPUR, in Kashmir, a small town at the point where the Jailum, here two hundred yards wide, flows from the Wulur lake, and commences that rapid course which it holds downwards until it enters the plain of the Punjab, above the town of Jailum. It is protected by a small fort. Lat. 34° 15′, long. 74° 20′.

E.I.C. Ms. Doc.

SORAH, in Sinde, a village situate on the route from Bukkur to Omercote, about two miles from the right bank of the Narra river. Lat. 26° 57′, long. 69° 1′.

E.I.C. Ms. Doc.

SORAH, in Northern Afghanistan, a village situate in the valley of Bamian, four miles east of the city of the same name, and on the route to Kabool. Lat. 34° 49′, long. 67° 54′.

E.I.C. Ms. Doc.

SORAHANEE.—A village of Sinde, situate on the left bank of the Mulleeree river. Lat. 24° 52′, long. 67° 14′.

E.I.C. Ms. Doc.

SORETNEE, in the Punjab, a village situate on the circuitous route from Mooltan to Ferozpoor, and six miles from the right bank of the Ghara river. Lat. 29° 53′, long. 72° 20′.

Walker's Map.

SOUN LEAD MINE, in North-eastern Afghanistan, situate near the right bank of the Lundye river. Lat. 35° 25′, long. 72° 15′.

E.I.C. Ms. Doc.

SPEENCHA, in Afghanistan, a village on the road from Ghuznee to Dera Ismael Khan, by the Gomul Pass. Lat. 32° 14′, long. 68° 35′.

Elph. Acc. of Caubul, 100; Jour. As. Soc. Beng. 1841, p. 802, Grif. Rep. on Subjects connected with Afg.; Id. 1842, p. 12), Macgregor, Geog. Notice of the Valley of Jullalabad. E.I.C. Ms. Doc.

SPEENGHUR.—The Pushtoo name of the high mountains in Eastern Afghanistan, more generally known by the Persian name, Sufeid Koh, or White Mountains. (See SUFEID KOH.)

SPINAWAREE, in Afghanistan, a halting-place on the route from Ghuznee to Shawl, and one hundred and twenty miles north of the latter place. It is remarkable for an artificial mound, and is situate in a valley well supplied with water. Near this place the route from Dera Ismael Khan to Kandahar intersects that from Ghuznee to Shawl. Lat. 31° 43′, long. 67° 22′.

E.I.C. Ms. Doc.

SPUNDOW, in Western Afghanistan, a very lofty mountain on the route from Kandahar to Herat, and one hundred and seventy miles north-west of the former place. Lat. 29° 28′, long. 63° 10′.

E.I.C. Ms. Doc.; Conolly (A.),

SUBZAWUR, in Western Afghanistan, a decayed though once

considerable town on the banks of the Adruscund, sometimes called the river of Subzawur. It is situate in a fertile valley, containing a great number of walled villages, and is itself protected or commanded by a mud fort, about two hundred and fifty yards square. There are seven rounded bastions on each face, one gate on the southern face, and a slight ditch. All these defences are in a state of dilapidation, so that it is a place of no strength, and might easily be taken by a *coup-de-main*. It is nominally governed by a son of Shah Kamran, of Herat. The residence of this powerless governor is in a small citadel in the centre of the fortress. He possesses scarcely any sway over the surrounding country, which is in a state of great anarchy, and fast verging to ruin. Subzawur is situate about eight miles west of the route from Herat to Kandahar, and distant seventy miles south of the former place. Lat. 33° 20′, long. 62° 10′. *Jour. to India, ii. 61; Jour. As. Soc. Beng. 1840, p. 713, Conolly (E.), Physical Geog. of Seistan; Id. 1841, 319, Jour. of Travel in Seistan; Fraser, Jour. Khorasan, App. 29.*

SUBZJOO, in Afghanistan, a village ten miles south-east from Furrah, a little south of the road from that town to Giriskh. Lat. 32° 20′, long. 62° 15′. *E.I.C. Ms. Doc.*

SUBZULCOTE.—The northern frontier town of Sinde, towards Bhawlpoor. It is surrounded by a wall mounting three decayed cannon, and has a bazaar well supplied with various wares. Without the town are many wells of good water. There is some trade, but not so much as formerly. Outside the walls is a small fort manned by an insignificant garrison. Population, 5,000. Lat. 28° 13′, long. 69° 42′. *Masson, i. 376; Burnes, iii. 278; Hough, 13; E.I.C. Ms. Doc.*

SUDER GHUR.—See GOTTARAO.

SUDOJA, in Sinde, a village situate on the left bank of the river Indus. Lat. 28° 4′, long. 69° 4′.

SUDOO SHAW, in the Punjab, a village situate on the left bank of the Indus. Lat. 33° 21′, long. 71° 59′. *Walker's Map of N.W. Frontier.*

SUDUK RIVER.—A small river in Beloochistan, which rises in lat. 26°, long. 63° 12′, and after a southerly course of about eighty miles falls into the sea in lat. 25° 26′, long. 68° 29′. Its banks are covered with a stunted growth of trees in the lower part of its course, and as the channel is navigable for ten or twelve miles from the sea, traders ascend in boats for that distance to cut wood. *Pott. Belooch. 302.*

SUDUR GHUR.—A village in the north-eastern desert of Sinde, situate on the road from Roree to Jessulmair, in lat. 27° 12′, long. 70° 13′. *E.I.C. Ms. Doc.*

SUFEID KOH,* or "the White Mountain," is a lofty range, bounding the valley of the Kabool river on the south, as the Hindoo Koosh does on the north. These two ranges are about seventy miles apart, and this distance may be considered as the extreme breadth of the valley of the Kabool river. The Sufeid Koh range runs nearly east and west along the parallel of lat. 33° 50′, commencing eastward near Attock in long. 72° 16′, and terminating westward in long. 69° 36′. Its western extremity sinks into a maze of hills, stretching like net-work to the Kohistan of Kabool. The Sufeid Koh is generally of primary formation, consisting of granite, quartz, gneiss, mica, slate, and primary limestone. There are three ranges running nearly parallel, and rising in height as they recede from the river; the two lower are covered with pine forests; the highest and most distant has a very irregular outline, is steep and very rocky, yet furrowed by many beautiful and fertile vales. The highest part is between the meridians of 69° 40′ and 70° 30′, and attains the elevation of 14,100 feet, being covered with perpetual snow. The Soorkh Rood, the Kara Su, and many other shallow but impetuous streams, rush down its northern face, and are discharged into the river of Kabool, which conveys their water to the Indus. The Khyber mountains connect the eastern extremity with the Himalaya, as the Kurkutcha do the western, and between them lies the plain of Jelalabad.

[margin: E.I.C. Ms. Doc.; Wood, Khyber Pass, 4; Id. Oxus, 166; Baber, Mem. 142; Moorcr. Punj. Bokh. ii. 371; Jour. As. Soc. Beng. 1842, p. 121, Macgregor, Geog. Notice of Valley of Jullalabad; also, 1841, p. 802, Grif. Rep. on Subjects connected with Afg.; Masson, Bal. Afg. Punj. i. 177; Burnes, Bokh. i. 123; Id. Pers. Narr. 183; Hough, Narr. of Exp. in Afg. 209; Havelock, War in Afg. ii. 180; Elph. Acc. of Caubul, 100.]

SUFFIN JO VHAN, in Sinde, a village situate on the left bank of the river Indus, near the road from Bukkur to Hyderabad, viâ Nowsharra. Lat. 26° 31′, long. 68°.

[margin: Ms. Survey Map.]

SUHOYUM,[1] or "Burning Ground," in the Punjab, in Kashmir, at the north-western extremity of the valley, at an elevation of 6,000 feet above the sea. Here are well-marked indications of volcanic action still at work, as from time to time the heat is so great as to fuse the soil and send forth volumes of smoke. Phenomena of this kind occurred about forty years ago, and Abul Fazl,[2] in the sixteenth century, described them in the following words:—"The soil of this place is so intensely hot that it destroys the trees, and if a kettle be set on the ground it will boil." Lat. 34° 16′, long. 74°.

[margin: [1] Vigne, Kashmir, i. 280. [2] Ayeen Akbery, ii. 148.]

SUKKERUNDA, in Sinde, a village situate on the road from

[margin: E.I.C. Ms. Doc.]

* سفید "white," and کوه "mountain."

Bukkur (viâ Nowsharra) to Hyderabad. Lat. 26° 2′, long. 68° 18′.

SUKKUR,[1] in Sinde, a decayed town on the west or right bank of the Indus, and opposite Roree, on the eastern bank, the island fortress of Bukkur lying between them. It is situate where a low limestone range slopes down to the river's bank, clothed in the neighbourhood of the town with luxuriant groves of date-palms. These groves, combined with the ruined but picturesque town of Sukkur, the river, the huge fortress of Bukkur, and the town of Roree, situated on the bold precipice opposite, form a very noble landscape. In 1839, a British cantonment was made at Sukkur, which, for a time, became converted from a scene of desolation and wretchedness to one of activity and prosperity. Sukkur has still a few towers, mosques, and minarets standing. One minaret is in a state of considerable preservation, and, according to Kennedy,[2] is a hundred feet high, and may be ascended by a winding stone staircase, affording access to the summit, whence is a noble prospect. It is a heavy, ill-proportioned column,[3] without ornament. The population of Sukkur is stated by Hough[4] to be about 500. Burnes[5] states it to be half of that of Roree, and estimates this last at 8,000. There can be no reasonable doubt that the actual number considerably exceeds the estimate by Hough. Lat. 27° 44′, long. 68° 52′.

[1] Leech, Rep. on Sind. Army, 79; Masson, i. 362; Burnes, on the Commerce of Shikarpoor, 30; Id. Bokh. iii. 73, 272; Wood, Oxus, 51; Kennedy, ii. 168, 202; Burnes, Pers. Narr. 53; Macmurdo, in Jour. Roy. As. Soc. 1834, p. 235; Havelock, i. 119; Hough, 22.

[2] ii. 175.

[3] Westmacott, in Jour. As. Soc. Beng. 1840, p. 1095.
[4] 22.
[5] Bokh. iii. 272.

SUKYT,[1] in the Punjab, a small town nearly midway between the Beas and Sutluj, and on the route from Bilaspur to Mundi. It is situate in the valley of Sukyt-Mundi, eight or ten miles long, three or four broad, fertile, well watered, and highly cultivated, down the middle of which the river of Sukyt flows northward, and falls into the Beas. Vigne[2] observes that "perhaps no country of equal extent could boast of so many strongholds." Lat. 31° 32′, long. 76° 52′.

[1] Moorcr. Punj. Bokh. i. 43.

[2] Kashmir, i. 79.

SULDERA, in the Punjab, a small town on the route from Ferozpoor to Mooltan, and in the Doab of Barie. Lat. 29° 49′, long. 72° 5′.

Vigne, Ghuznee, 13.

SULIMAN MOUNTAINS, an extensive and lofty range in Eastern Afghanistan, are, in their northern extremity, a continuation of Sufeid Koh, or the "Snowy Mountain," which bounds the valley of Kabool to the south. They may be considered to commence in lat. 33° 40′, and from that quarter, stretch due south in nearly the seventieth meridian of longitude to the moun-

Id. 102; Elph. Acc. of Caubul, 100; Wood, Oxus, 80; Masson, Bal. Afg. Panj. i. 47; Jour. As. Soc. Beng. 1841, p. 802, Grif. Rep. on Subjects connected with Afg.

tains about Hurrund and Kahun, and to lat. 29°, attaining their greatest height in lat. 31° 35', where the Takht-i-Suliman, or "Suliman's Seat," called also Khaisa Ghar,* is 11,000 feet above the sea. This summit does not enter within the limit of perpetual congelation, being devoid of snow during the height of summer. Of its geological structure scarcely any thing is known. Vigne, almost the only European who has visited this range, only states that "it consists of recent formations, principally sandstone and secondary limestone, abounding in ammonites and other marine exuviæ, the strata being much shattered and contorted, and often overlaid by shingle." The eastern declivity dips rather steeply to the valley of the Indus, giving rise to numerous watercourses, which fertilize the Derajat, and are expended by absorption or irrigation. The western declivity is much more gradual to the desert table-land of Sewestan. It is remarkable that no stream rising in this range is known to reach the sea in any direction, or by any channel, except the Kurum, which discharges a scanty volume of water into the Indus, above Kala Bagh. The greatest dimension of the range is from north to south, and is a little more than three hundred miles. The Suliman range is generally considered the peculiar seat of the aboriginal Afghans. Nowhere is vegetation more vigorous and varied. The sides of the mountain nearly to the summit are clothed with dense and lofty forests, and the valleys overgrown with a great variety of indigenous trees, shrubs, and flowers.

Hough, Narr. Exp. in Afg. 36.

SULLEEANEE, in the Punjab, a small town of the Doab of Barie, on the route from Surrukpore to Ferozpoor, and about half-way between the Ravee and Ghara. Lat. 31° 10', long. 74° 8'.

Moorcr. Punj. Bokh. i. 171; Vigne, Kashmir, i. 99.

SULTANPOOR, or KULU, in the north-east of the Punjab, and on the southern slope of the Himalaya, is the capital of the *raj*, or small state, of Kulu. It is situate on a triangular tongue of land between the river Beas and a feeder flowing into it on the right side. The southern, or lower part, which is next the river, contains

App. to Elph. 640.

* Macartney states the greatest elevation of the range in the same part, as ascertained by trigonometrical measurement, at 12,831 feet above the sea. Walker, in his elaborate and valuable map of " the countries between the Satluj and Oxus," notes the elevation as 12,000 ; probably thinking it least objectionable to state a mean between two authorities, each so eminent, yet in this instance so widely differing.

the residence of the rajah; and north of this, and separated from it by a small bazaar, is the upper part of the town, consisting of the houses of traders, shopkeepers, and artificers. The principal imports are chintzes, coarse cottons, and woollens, and the returns are made in opium and musk, the traffic being conducted by wandering mendicants, of whom great numbers arrive here on their route to various places of pilgrimage in the mountains. The place is, as Moorcroft observes, "of no great population or extent." Lat. 32° 7', long. 77° 2'.

Jour. As. Soc. Beng. 1842, p. 78, Grif. Bar. and Ther. Meas. in Afg.; Id. 1842, p. 122, Macgregor, Geog. Notice of the Valley of Jullalabad; Hough, Narr. Exp. in Afg. 302; Masson, Bal. Afg. Panj. i. 181.

SULTANPOOR, in Afghanistan, a small town west of Jelalabad on the route to Kabool, is celebrated for its fine springs, gardens, and orchards. Elevation above the sea 2,286 feet. Lat. 34° 24', long. 70° 19'.

SULTAREE, in the Punjab, a village situate on a road on the left bank of the Chenaub, in lat. 31° 47', long. 73° 3'. E.I.C. Ms. Doc.

SUMABOO, in Bhawlpoor, a village about six miles south-west of the town of Khanpoor on the route to Subzulcote. Lat. 28° 36', long. 70° 35'. E.I.C. Ms. Doc.

SUMARAKOTE, or SOMANAKOTE, in Sinde, a small town in the Delta, about twenty miles north of Vikkur, is situate near the right bank of the Hujamree branch of the Indus, and on a slight eminence amidst a grove of well-grown acacias. Lat. 24° 30', long. 67° 45'. Kennedy, Sinde and Kabool, i. 71; Outram, Rough Notes, 14.

SUMBI.—A village in Afghanistan, situate on the right bank of the Kabool river, twenty-six miles east of Kabool. Lat. 34° 32', long. 69° 32'. E.I.C. Ms. Doc.

SUMBUL, SIMBUL, or, according to Moorcroft, SUMBHELPUR.—A village of Kashmir, on the left bank of the Jailum, a short distance above the point where it communicates with the Manasa Bul Lake. A little lower down a canal proceeds from the left side of the Jailum to the west, in which direction it extends about ten miles to Sopur, thus avoiding the navigation of Lake Wulur during inundations or tempestuous weather. Sumbul is distinguishable at a great distance by its lofty grove of trees. The Jailum opposite the village is about a hundred yards wide, and six or eight feet deep, and is crossed by a large bridge built of *deodars* in the usual Kashmirian style. Sumbul is in lat. 34° 11', long. 74° 30'. Moorcr. Punj. Bokh. ii. 276; Vigne, Kashmir, i. 146.

SUMMA KA BUSTEE, in Sinde, a village situate on the Ms. Survey Maps route from Hyderabad to Omercote, nine miles west of the latter place. Lat. 25° 22', long. 69° 40'.

Ms. Survey Map.   SUMMANI, in the Punjab, a village situate on the route from Vazeerabad to the town of Punch. Lat. 33°, long. 74° 5'.

E.I.C. Ms. Doc.   SUMMEE, in Sinde, a village on the western route from Roree to Hyderabad, and fifty miles south-west of the former town. Lat. 27° 17', long. 68° 19'.

E.I.C. Ms. Doc.   SUNDUM.—A village situate to the north-east of Afghanistan, in lat. 34° 32', long. 72° 14'.

E.I.C. Ms. Doc.; Hough, Narr. Exp. in Afg. 77.   SUNGAW RIVER, in Afghanistan, in the valley of Pisheen, rises at the southern base of the Toba mountains, and, taking a westerly course, falls into the Lora. Eight miles north of Hydurzie, it crosses the route from Shawl to Kandahar. This point, distant twenty-six miles north of Shawl, is in lat. 30° 29', long. 66° 52'. The river here has rather high banks, with a stream about eight yards wide, and twenty inches deep. The elevation above the level of the sea is about 5,000 feet.

E.I.C. Ms. Doc.   SUNGLAKHL, in Afghanistan, a village at the southern base of the Pughman mountains. It is situate between Kabool and Bamian, on a feeder of the river of Kabool. Lat. 34° 25', long. 68° 28'.

E.I.C. Ms. Doc.   SUNGRAR, in Sinde, a village situate on the road from Roree to Jessulmair; this route crosses the Narra river a little to the right of this place. It is in lat. 27° 37', long. 69° 4', about twelve miles south-east of Roree.

E.I.C. Ms. Doc.   SUNGSA, in Afghanistan, a halting-place on the route from Poolajee to Hurrund, and forty miles east of the former place. It is situate at the southern base of the mountain inclosing the valley of Kahun. Sungsa is in lat. 29° 1', long. 69° 12'.

SUNGUR.—A village of North-western Afghanistan. Lat. 36°, long. 64° 30'.

E.I.C. Ms. Doc.   SUNGUR, in Sinde, a village on the road from Larkhana to Bagh, in Cutch Gundava. Lat. 28° 56', long. 68° 8'.

E.I.C. Ms. Doc.   SUNJEREE, in Western Afghanistan, on the route from Kandahar to Herat, and twelve miles south-west of the former place. It is situate about a mile from the right or north-western bank of the Urghundab, here generally fordable, being about forty yards wide and from two to three feet deep. As the current is very rapid, the ford cannot safely be attempted when the depth exceeds three feet. The surrounding country is very fertile, being irrigated by numerous watercourses from the river. Lat. 31° 35', long. 65° 18'.

SUNN, in Sinde, is a small town of about one hundred houses,* situate on the right or west bank of the Indus, at the mouth of a torrent running during rains from the Lukkee mountains. Near it, to the west, is Runnie-ka-kote, a vast fortress built by the Ameers of Sinde, but unoccupied. Lat. 26°, long. 68° 16'. — De La Hoste, Journ. As. Soc. Beng. 1840, p. 912.

SUNNABAKE BOONGA, in Bhawlpoor, a village situate on the left bank of the river Ghara. Lat. 30° 1', long. 72° 57'. — Walker's Map.

SUNNEE.—A village of Cutch Gundava, situate on the route from Gundava to Dadur. Lat. 29° 2', long. 67° 36'. — Ms. Survey Map.

SUNNEWEH, in the Punjab, a village situate on an offset near the left bank of the Indus, and thirty-five miles north-west of Mooltan. Lat. 30° 20', long. 71°. — E.I.C. Ms. Doc.

SUNTPOOR, in the Punjab, a village situate about thirty miles north-west of Lahore. Lat. 31° 53', long. 74°. — E.I.C. Ms. Doc.

SURANOTERANO, in the Punjab, a village situate on the right bank of the Ravee river, in lat. 30° 48', long. 72° 54'. — Walker's Map of N.W. Frontier.

SURDHEE.—A village in the Punjab, situate in lat. 32° 43', long. 72° 30'. — Walker's Map.

SURGE, in Afghanistan, a village on the route from Ghuznee to Dera Ismael Khan, and sixty miles south-east of the former place. The road here is through the mountains forming part of the Suliman range. There is a stream of good water. Lat. 32° 46', long. 68° 37'. — E.I.C. Ms. Doc.

SURNA-KOT-KILLA, in the Punjab, a village situate about twenty-five miles south-east of the town of Punch. Lat. 33° 41', long. 74° 6'. — E.I.C. Ms. Doc.

SURRUKPOOR, in the Punjab, on the west bank of the Ravee, which was here, at its lowest season, found to be two hundred and fifty yards wide, and crossed by a ferry. There is a good ford close to this, passable in the season when the river is lowest. Lat. 31° 28', long. 73° 53'. — Hough. 348.

SURTAF, in Afghanistan, a steep ridge in the group of mountains inclosing the valley of Kahun, and connecting the Hala with the Suliman range. It is crossed by the route from — E.I.C. Ms. Doc.

* Burnes (Bokhara, iii. 264) assigns to it, under the name of Sen, a population of 2,000.

Poolajee to Kahun, and admits the passage of guns, as in August, 1840, the British force which marched over it to attempt the relief of Kahun was provided with three pieces of artillery. The summit of the ridge is dreary, rocky, and devoid both of vegetation and water. Surtaf is in lat. 29° 11′, long. 69° 5′.

Ms. Survey Map.

SURWOD.—A village situate on the northern frontier of Cutch Gundava, on the circuitous route from Bagh to Kahun. Lat. 29° 21′, long. 68° 30′.

SUTLEDGE.—See SUTLUJ.

SUTLUJ.—The most easterly of the rivers of the Punjab. It does not appear that its source has been visited by any European, in consequence of their vigilant exclusion by the Chinese, within whose territory it lies. Moorcroft, in his journey to Manas Sarovara,[1] seems to have approached nearest to the source, having, about lat. 31°, long. 80° 40′, come upon the Sutoodra or Sutluj. Lloyd[2] and Gerard, who with Moorcroft have done more for the geography of this region than any others, give the following account: "The most remote source of the Sutluj is said by my informants to be at a place named Chomik Tongdol,[3] where a small stream gushes out of the ground and runs into Goongeoo Lake. This place must be very much elevated, for, allowing a moderate fall for the river, it will come out 19,000 or 20,000 feet more than Lake Man Sarowur, which I think I have pretty good data for estimating at 17,000 above the sea." This spot is, in the map of the authors just quoted, placed in lat. 31° 5′, long. 81° 6′, and appears to be on the south side of the Kailas, or "Peaked Mountain," on the north of which the Indus is thought to have its source.[4] From this point it takes its course to Rawan Hrad,[5] or Goongeoo Lake, situate close to that of Manas Sarovara, and supposed by some to receive its waters. It subsequently issues from the north-western extremity of this lake, being there in the dry season thirty feet broad,[6] and takes a north-westerly course of about one hundred and fifty miles, through a country of awful and even terrific sublimity, as far as Nako, in lat. 31° 50′, long. 78° 36′. Close to this it receives the river of Spiti from the north-west.[7] Above the confluence, the Sutluj is seventy-five feet wide; its bed 8,600 feet above the level of the sea. Gerard observes, "It is not easy to form an estimate of the water contained in the Sutluj, for although the breadth can be determined, yet within the mountains there is scarcely a possibility of

[1] As. Res. xii. 473, 476.
[2] Tour in the Himalaya, ii. 184.
[3] Gerard, Koonawur, 139.
[4] Moorcr. Punj. Bokh. i. 262.
[5] As. Res. xv. 309; Herbert, Levels of Setlej.
[6] Gerard, Koonawur, 27.
[7] Jour. As. Soc. Beng. 1839, Hutton, Trip through Kunawur, 947. Lloyd and Gerard, ii. 161.

sounding it, on account of its great rapidity."[8] The depth at this [8 Koonawur, 26.] spot must be very great, as the volume of water is considerable even eighty miles further up, where, at Ling, the river is too broad to admit of a rope-bridge, and is crossed by one of iron chains: the breadth thereabouts being one hundred and twenty yards; the depth, at the lowest season, one foot and a half; the rapidity seven or eight miles an hour; the impetus of the stream such as that it can be forded only by yaks or Tartarian kine if the depth exceed two feet. The bed[9] of the river, a short distance below this, in lat. [9 Lloyd and Gerard, Map.] 32° 38', long. 79° 4', is 10,792 feet above the sea. Here the river is by the natives called Langzhing-Khampa, or the river of Langzhing; lower down, Muksung; then, Sanpoo; lower still, Zeung-tee; lower down, Sumeedrung; in Busehar, Sutoodra, or "hundred-channeled," whence the names Zadadrus[1] and Hesu- [1 Rennell, 83.] drus of the classical writers; lower down, it is generally called the Sutluj, by which name it is also known up to its source. Though the river[2] is in the upper part of its course a raging torrent, fall- [2 Gerard, Koonawur, 12.] ing in several places a hundred or a hundred and fifty feet per mile, with a clamorous noise, and displaying heaps of white foam, yet so severe is the climate that for two hundred miles it is completely frozen for two months every winter. Where not fordable, it is crossed either by a *sango*, or wooden bridge; by a *jhoola*, or rope-bridge, which the traveller passes on a seat suspended by a loop made to slide along the rope, by means of a long string, pulled by men stationed on the further bank; or by means of a *szum*, or foot-bridge, formed of cables, stretched parallel to each other. These frail suspension-bridges frequently give way, and the passengers are dashed to pieces.[3] There are also a few chain [3 Gerard, Koonawur, 34-5.] bridges. At the confluence of the Spiti and Sutluj, the bed of the river is 8,494 feet above the sea. The scene is described as awfully sublime; according to Lloyd and Gerard,[4] "the charac- [4 ii. 14.] ter of the gulf at the confluence is certainly one of the wonders of the world." The Lee, or river of Spiti, issues forth from a rocky channel, so narrow and deep as almost to seem subterranean, with a calm blue deep current. The Sutluj is muddy and breaks violently on the rocks with a tremendous roaring. The Spiti has probably a larger body of water than the Sutluj.[5] The [5 Gerard, Koonawur, 26, 30.] former river averages from two hundred and fifty to three hundred feet in breadth; the latter, a short distance above the confluence, is seventy-five feet broad. Below the confluence, the stream is so deep and rapid that no bottom could be found with a ten-pound sounding lead. From this remarkable point its general course is south-west, with a very rapid declivity.[4] At Namptoo (lat. 32° 45′, long. 78° 36′), the height of its bed is 8,220 feet, its breadth 106; at Wangtoo (lat. 32° 32′, long. 78° 1′) the height of its bed is 5,200 feet, the breadth is 92; at Rampoor (lat. 32° 26′, long. 77° 38′), the height of the bed is 3,360, the width 211. These measurements were made at the narrowest places, where bridges have been constructed, but in other places it is 150 yards wide. From Rampoor to Bilaspoor, in lat. 31° 21′, long. 76° 41′, its course is generally west-south-west.[5] Forster, who crossed it here, describes it as a very rapid stream, about one hundred yards broad. Hence it holds a very tortuous course, but in general west-south-west to Ropoor, lat. 30° 58′, long. 76° 29′, where it makes[6] its way through the low sandstone range of Jhejwan, and enters the plain of the Punjab. It is here thirty feet deep and more than five hundred yards wide in its season of greatest fulness,[7] and is crossed either in boats or on floats of inflated buffalo-hides.[8] As is the case with all the rivers descending from the Himalaya, it is far fullest in June, July, and August. At the ferry of Filor, or Faloor, in lat. 31°, long. 75° 51′, it was found, in the season when lowest, to be two hundred and fifty yards wide,[9] seven feet deep, and moderately rapid. Burnes, who crossed it here in August, when fullest, found it seven hundred yards wide, with a depth, where greatest, of eighteen feet, but on an average of only twelve. Up to this point it is navigable at all seasons for vessels of ten or twelve tons burthen.[1] Its confluence with the Beas is a little above Hurekee, and in lat. 31° 11′, long. 74° 54′. According to Macartney,[2] the Beas has the larger body of water. Gerard appears to over-estimate, by seventy or eighty miles, the distance which it runs from the source to the confluence with the Beas. According to his statement,[3] "the whole length of the Sutlej thus far is five hundred and seventy miles, four hundred and forty of which lie within the mountains." Below this confluence, as far as the confluence of the Chenaub, the united stream bears the name of Ghara. From about thirty miles above Rampoor to the frontier of Bhawlpoor, a distance of about three hundred and fifty miles, the continuous streams, Ghara and Sutluj, form the north-west

---

[4] Lloyd and Gerard, Map.

[5] i. 239.

[6] Gerard, Koonawur, 23.

[7] Vigne, Kashmir, i. 53.
[8] F. Von Hugel, i. 50; Moorcr. i. 40.

[9] Gerard, Koonawur, 26.

[1] Journ. As. Soc. Beng. 1837, p. 169, Mackeson, Acc. Wade's Voy. down the Sutlej.
[2] Elphinstone, 662.

[3] Koonawur, 23.

[4] Ritter, Erdkunde von As. v. 464.

boundary of the British territories. As before mentioned,[5] the Sutluj is considered to be the Zaradrus, Zadadrus, or Hesudrus of the ancients, and the Hypanis mentioned by Strabo.

[5] Rennell, 51; Wilson, Ariana Antiqua, 195—231.

SUTTA WALLA.—A village in that part of Afghanistan called Daman, situated on the banks of the Indus. Lat. 32° 42′, long. 71° 26′.

Walker's Map of Afg.

SUWAT,[1] on the north-eastern frontier of Afghanistan, a secluded territory very little explored, extending west of the upper part of the Indus to the Lundye, or river of Panjkora. It is said to be a very fine country, fertile, well watered, and, notwithstanding its elevated position on the southern slope of Hindoo Koosh, possessing a good climate. The inhabitants, a semi-civilized race, are fanatical Mahometans, though not very well acquainted with the tenets of the religion they profess. They are partly Eusufzai Afghans, who are the ruling race, and partly indigenous Swatis, reduced by the former to a state of helotism. Dhyr, the residence of the chief, is said to have a population of about 3,000. It is watered by the river Suwat, which, rising in the Hindoo Koosh, takes a south-westerly course, and falls into the Lundye, or river of Panjkora, in lat. 34° 42′, long. 71° 48′. In the reign of Akbar, Suwat formed part of the Mogul empire, being a *sircar*, or subdivision of the *subah*, or government of Kashmir.[2]

[1] Elph. Acc. of Caubul, 332; Burnes, Pol. Power of the Sikhs; Jour. As. Soc. Beng. 1839, p. 307, Court, Exploits of Alexand.

[2] Ayeen Akbery, ii. 170.

SUYUD BUKAS, in Sinde, a village situate on the left bank of the Narra river, on the route from Bukkur to Omercote. Lat. 25° 50′, long. 69° 20′.

E.I.C. Ms. Doc.

SWAN, a river of the Punjab, rises in a subordinate range of the Himalaya, west of Kashmir, and in lat. 33° 55′, long. 73° 10′. It holds a south-westerly course of a hundred and twenty miles, and falls into the Indus[1] on the left side, about ten miles below Mukkud, and in lat. 33°, long. 71° 46′. Elphinstone,[2] who crossed it in lat. 33° 37′, long. 73° 3′, and about thirty miles from its source, describes it to be, where forded, " a large rivulet, which, though only up to our horses' girths, was so rapid as to be scarcely fordable. Several of our camels were swept down by the stream." Hough,[3] who crossed the Swan when the water was low, describes it as having " a stony bed, not broad, and one foot of water." Burnes,[4] who crossed this stream in lat. 33° 6′, long. 72° 12′, found it there " rapid, red, and swollen," and stirrup-deep.

[1] Wood, Oxus, 108.
[2] Acc. of Caubul, 77.
[3] Narr. Exp. in Afg. 340.
[4] Pers. Narr. 115.

E.I.C. Ms. Doc.; Hough, Narr. Exp. in Afg. 242.	SYADABAD, in Afghanistan, on the route from Ghuznee to Kabool, and fifty-four miles south of the latter town. It is a large fort, situate on the right or eastern bank of a considerable feeder of the Logurh river, and in a well-cultivated tract gradually sloping towards the north. Lat. 34° 1′, long. 68° 40′.
Ms. Survey Map.	SYAGARD.—A village of Afghanistan, situate in the valley of Ghorbund. Lat. 34° 56′, long. 68° 46′.
E.I.C. Ms. Doc.	SYEDAD, in Beloochistan, a village of Cutch Gundava, situate on the route from Bagh to Larkhana, and thirty miles east of Gundava. Lat. 28° 30′, long. 67° 57′.
Walker's Map of Afg.	SYNABAD.—A village in South-western Afghanistan, situate on the banks of the Helmund river. Lat. 30° 34′, long. 62° 28′.
	SYNDABAD.—See SYADABAD.
E.I.C. Ms. Doc.	SYNDABAD, in Sinde, a village situate about three miles from the left bank of the river Indus, thirty-five miles north of Hyderabad, on the road to Bukkur. Lat. 68° 24′, long. 25° 50′.
E.I.C. Ms. Doc.	SYNDAN, in Afghanistan, a village eighteen miles west of Bamian. Lat. 34° 49′, long. 67° 28′.
Ms. Survey Map.	SYUDGAUM, in Sinde, a village situate about four miles from the left bank of the Indus, on the road from Hyderabad to Bukkur, thirty miles north-east of the former. Lat. 25° 46′, long. 68° 31′.
Walker's Map.	SYUDGOTE, in the Punjab, a village situate on the right bank of the river Ravee. Lat. 30° 40′, long. 72° 45′.
E.I.C. Ms. Doc.	SYUD KA GOTE, in Sinde, a village situated near the Richel mouth. Lat. 24° 19′, long. 67° 41.
E.I.C. Ms. Doc.	SYUDS GOTE.—A village in Afghanistan, on the road from Kandahar to Quetta, sixteen miles north from Quetta. Lat. 30° 20′, long. 66° 53′.

T.

E.I.C. Ms. Doc.	TAB, in the Punjab, a village situate on the left bank of the Chenaub, and seventy miles north of Lahore, on the route from that town to Kashmir by the Banihal Pass. Lat. 32° 32′, long. 74° 43′.

TAGOA, a river of Afghanistan, has its rise in the Hindoo Koosh near Farajghan, and runs southward about eighty miles, through the valley of Tagoa, emptying itself into the Kabool river sixty miles east of the city of Kabool, in lat. 35° 24′, long. 69° 45′. The valley of Tagoa is inhabited by Taujiks and Saufees, an Afghan tribe, nearly independent of the government of Kabool. It is fertile and populous, being studded with numerous castles, the strongholds of the turbulent natives. Elph. Acc. of Caubul, 99; Masson, Bal. Afg. Panj. iii. 178.

TAHIRBEGY.—A village in North-western Afghanistan, about twenty miles north-west of the town of Mymunuh. Lat. 35° 54′, long. 64° 23′. Walker's Map of Afg.

TAK, in Afghanistan, a thriving town of the Derajat, is situate north of Dera Ismael Khan, and twenty-six miles west of the Indus. It is surrounded by a strong and high mud wall, surmounted by towers; within is a citadel of burnt brick, having a high tower at each of the four corners, and mounted with twelve pieces of cannon. It has some transit trade, being situate on a route from east to west, which crosses the Suliman range to the north of the Goolairee Pass. The surrounding country is fertile and populous, being crowded with good villages, but it is not healthy, the heat in summer being intense, and the water bad. The Afghan khan or chief has a revenue of about 150,000 rupees per annum, on which he lives in petty state, though obliged to pay the Sikhs a tribute of 60,000 rupees annually. Tak is celebrated for fine fruits, grapes, oranges, pomegranates, apples, and especially mulberries. Lat. 32° 14′, long. 70° 50′. Burnes, Pol. Pow. of Sikhs, 4; Masson, Bal. Afg. Panj. i. 49, 147.

TAKAREE, in Beloochistan, a pass from Cutch Gundava to Sarawan, across the eastern brow of the Hala range, in this part called the Takaree. The road by it is intricate and narrow, having room only for the passage of one camel or horse at a time. It extends in a direction generally from east to west, south of the Bolan, and north of the Moola, and consequently lies somewhere between lat. 28° 20′—29° 30′, and in long. 67° 30′. Such is the scanty amount of information concerning it deducible from native report, as it does not appear to have been explored by Europeans. Masson, Kalat, 319; Bal. Afg. Panj. i. 338; Leech, Rep. on Sindh. Army, 87.

TAKEAH, in Bhawlpoor, a village situate on the left bank of the Ghara river, in lat. 29° 43′, long. 72° 13′. Walker's Map of N.W. Frontier.

TAKEE.—A village in Afghanistan, on the road from Ghuznee E.I.C. Ms. Doc.

to Kabool, thirty miles north-east of the former town. Lat. 33° 55′, long. 68° 33′.

E.I.C. Ms. Doc.

TAKHT, in Beloochistan, a village situate in an elevated plain or valley, on the route from the town of Kelat to Beebee Nanee, in the Bolan Pass. There is here no fixed population, this sterile tract being frequented only in summer by a few wandering shepherds. Even water is not to be had except during rains, and for a short time after. Lat. 29° 20′, long. 66° 55′.

E.I.C. Ms. Doc.;
Vigne, Kashmir, ii. 160.

TAKIPUR, in Kashmir, a village on the route from Sopur to Lolab, and twenty miles north of the former place. Close to it is a warm chalybeate spring. Lat. 34° 24′, long. 74° 20′.

Masson, Bal. Afg. Panj. i. 147.

TAKKAL, in Afghanistan, a village in the district of Peshawer, about six miles west of the city of Peshawer, and on the route through the Khyber Pass. Lat. 33° 58′, long. 71° 34′.

Jour. As. Soc. Beng. 1839, p. 312, Exploits of Alexander on the Indus, by Court.

TAL.—A river in Northern Afghanistan, which rises in the Laspissor mountains, in lat. 36° 14′, long. 73° 6′, and flows in a south-westerly direction for about a hundred and twenty miles, to its confluence with the Panjkora, in lat. 35° 28′, long. 72°.

Walker's Map of Afg.

TAL.—A village of Northern Afghanistan, situate on the left bank of the river of the same name, in lat. 35° 40′, long. 72° 10′.

Jour. As. Soc. Beng. 1839, p. 307, Court, Exp. of Alexander on Western Banks of the Indus.

TALACHE, in Afghanistan, a ruined town in the bifurcation between the rivers of Suwat and Panjkora. All the information existing respecting this place is due to Court, who ascertained from native report that amidst its massive and immense ruins exists an enormous cupola of elaborate architecture, embellished around its base with a number of *basso relievos*. Lat. 34° 56′, long. 71° 58′.

Walker's Map of N.W. Frontier.

TALAFRU.—A village in the Punjab, situate on the route from Doda to Chumba, in lat. 32° 42′, long. 75° 7′.

Ms. Map.

TALEE.—A village of Sewestan, in Afghanistan, on the road from Dadur to Tull. Lat. 29° 42′, long. 68° 13′.

TAMEEHAK, in the Punjab, a small town on the route from Attock to Rotas. It has a small fort. The surrounding country is singularly rugged and difficult. Hough observes, "When you got on the table-land, you looked back on the most frightful ravines ever seen," and considers the country worse than the most dreaded passes of Afghanistan. Lat. 33° 17′, long. 73° 19′.

Narr. Exp. in Afg. 343.

Map of Sinde.

TAMULSIR.—A village near the eastern frontier of Sinde. Lat. 25° 45′, long. 70° 31′.

TANDDA, in the Punjab, a village situate about twelve miles west of the river Jailum. Lat. 31° 8', long. 71° 54'. _{E.I.C. Ms. Doc.}

TANDI, in the Punjab, a village of the district of Lahoul, is situate at the point where a considerable feeder of the Chenaub falls into that river, which immediately below the confluence is two hundred feet wide,[1] with a steady current. Here are a store and office belonging to the ruler of Kulu, and appointed for the receipt of the revenue, which he derives in grain from Lahoul. The vicinity is wooded, producing pines, yews, and willows. Buck-wheat is the principal crop, though barley and wheat are cultivated, but the great elevation, probably exceeding 8,000 feet, and consequent lowness of temperature, frequently render the crops of these two last sorts of grain abortive.[2] Lat. 30° 41', long. 74° 56'.

[1] Moorcr. Punj. Bokh. i. 193.

[2] Jour. As. Soc. Beng. 1841, p. 5, Broome and Cunningham on Sources of Punjab Rivers.

TANGEE TURKAI, in Afghanistan, a very difficult pass, east of and close to Khurd Kabool, on the southern route, through the Kurkutcha range of mountains, between Kabool and Jelalabad. Here, on the disastrous attempt made by the British to retreat from Kabool in 1842, they were nearly all massacred, so that the remnant was disabled from making any further resistance. This pass is about eighteen miles south-east of Kabool. Lat. 34° 51', long. 69° 20'.

E.I.C. Ms. Doc.; Eyre, Mil. Op. at Kabool, 228.

TARA.—A village of Sinde, on the road from Tattah to Meerpoor, twelve miles south-west of the former place. Lat. 24° 41', long. 67° 50'. _{E.I.C. Ms. Doc.}

TARIANA.—A village situate in the south-eastern desert of Sinde, sixty miles south-east of Omercote, on the route to Nuggur Parker. Lat. 24° 50', long. 70° 33'. _{Ms. Map of Sinde.}

TATARA PASS, in Afghanistan, through the Khyber mountains, between Jelalabad, is north of the Khyber Pass. It leaves the route through the Khyber Pass a little east of Jamrood, takes a circuit to the north, and rejoins it at Duka, its western termination. It is very difficult, being scarcely practicable for cavalry, yet of great importance, as, if left undefended, it affords a means of turning the Khyber Pass. In the commencement of 1842, when the Khyber Pass was closed, communication was frequently effected by the Tatara Pass, between Peshawer and Jelalabad. The Tatara Pass is in lat. 34° 10', long. 71° 20'.

Leech, Khyber Pass, 11; Mil. Op. in Afg. 63.

TATTA, in Sinde, a town formerly very famous, but now much

TATTA.

[1] Carless, Official Rep. on the Indus, 11; Kennedy, i. 81, 83; Burnes, iii. 34; Burnes (James), Mission to Sinde, 128; Masson, i. 468; Pott. 347.

decayed,[1] is situated about three miles west of the right or western bank of the Indus, and four miles above the point where the Buggaur or western, and the Sata or eastern, branches of the river separate. Its site is consequently close to the vertex of the delta of the Indus, the channel of which is here about a mile and a quarter wide, with a muddy stream, in the low season occupying only a third of this space. The present city is built on a slight eminence, composed of the rubbish of former buildings, in an alluvial valley at the foot of the Mukali hills. It is in consequence exceedingly unhealthy. The British troops stationed here in 1839 suffered dreadful loss from diseases,[2] resulting from the pestilential air and bad water, which last is not only unwholesome, but fetid and offensive to the senses.[3] The town appears to have been formerly insulated by the water of the Indus,[4] and is still nearly so during the season of inundation; when this passes away it leaves numerous stagnant pools which infect the air. Dr. Burnes[5] states that it was once thirty miles in circuit, judging no doubt from the vast space in the vicinity overspread by tombs and ruins; but these are with much probability considered by Wood[6] to be the relics of successive cities, built on various but contiguous sites, to avoid the ravages, or take advantage of the navigation, of the shifting currents of the Indus. These extensive ruins are scattered from Peer Puttah, about ten miles south of Tatta, to Sami-Nuggur, three miles north-west of it. The ruins of the great fortress of Kulancote shew it to have been constructed with much labour and skill, in a massive style of building. "The vast cemetery of six square miles," observes Kennedy,[7] "may not contain less than a million of tombs—a rude guess—but the area would admit of four millions." In these ruins the masonry and carving, both in brick and stone, display great taste, skill, and industry. The bricks especially are of the finest sort, nearly equalling porcelain. Kennedy observes,[8] "The finest-chiselled stone could not surpass the sharpness of edge and angle, and accuracy of form." Tatta, viewed at some distance from the outside, presents a very striking and picturesque appearance, as its lofty houses rise over the numerous acacias and other trees, everywhere interspersed, and which, says Kennedy,[9] "formed altogether as fine a picture of city scenery as I remember to have seen in India." But the illusion is dissipated on entering the town, where the houses are everywhere falling into

[2] Kennedy, ii. 217.

[3] Burnes, Pers. Narr. 12; Wood, in App. to Carless, 30.

[4] Pott. 347; Macmurdo, in Jour. of As. Soc. Beng. 1834, p. 234.

[5] Mission to Sinde, 128, 129.

[6] Oxus, 20.

[7] i. 87.

[8] i. 85.

[9] i. 80.

ruin, to which they are prone, being constructed for the most part of a timber frame-work,[1] on the outside of which are nailed laths, which are plastered over with mud of a grey colour, so as when new to have the appearance of a solid wall of masonry. These structures are sometimes three or four stories high, and covered with flat roofs of earth. From the fragility of the materials they can last but a short time, and this work of ruin is continually in progress in the town. All the houses are surmounted by *bad-geers*,[2]* a sort of ventilator, built somewhat in the shape of a windsail, and conveying, even in the most sultry weather, a current of cool and refreshing air. The appearance of the town is mournful. The streets are deserted, the bazaars in ruins, and every thing indicates depression and poverty; the inhabitants are dirty, squalid, and of unhealthy appearance.[3] The only building worth notice is the brick-built mosque of Shah Jehan, itself crumbling into ruins. Of the decayed manufactures of Tatta, the principal is that of *loongees*, a thick, rich, and variegated fabric, having a warp of silk and a woof of cotton,[4] with (in the more costly kinds) much gold thread interwoven. The silk is imported from Persia, Kabool, and Turkestan; the cotton from Eastern India. The number of persons employed in this manufacture at present is not more than one hundred. Coarse cotton fabrics, both plain and coloured, were formerly manufactured in considerable quantity, but have lately been superseded by those of England. British woollens are greatly prized, but the poverty of the people prevents an extensive sale of them. The total value of the silk and cotton manufactures in 1837 was 41,400*l*., of British goods imported 3,000*l*. The number of tradesmen and artificers in the same year was ascertained by Wood to be 982. It is said that in 1742,[5] when Nadir Shah entered this city at the head of his army, there were 40,000 weavers, 20,000 other artisans, and 60,000 dealers in various departments. Alexander Hamilton, who visited Tatta in 1699, calls it a very large and rich city, about three miles long, and one and a half broad, and states that 80,000 persons had, within a short time previously, died of the plague, and that one-half of the city was uninhabited.†
This would lead us to the conclusion, that previously to that

[1] Pott. 353.

[2] Id. 354; Wood, App. to Carless, 30.

[3] Wood, Oxus, 18; Outram, 18; Pott. 353; Kennedy, i. 81.

[4] Burnes, Rep. on Commerce of Tatta, 10.

[5] Pott. 350.

* "Wind-taker," from باد *bad*, "wind," and گیر *gir*, "seizer," or "taker."

† New Account of the East Indies. Edin. 1727, 8vo. London, 1744, 8vo.

calamity the population was above 150,000.* The present population is variously estimated—at below 2,000,[1] at less than 10,000,[2] at 12,000,[3] 15,000,[4] 18,000,[5] 20,000,[6] and 40,000.[7] The number of artisans and traders ascertained (as mentioned above) by Wood affords grounds for estimating the population at about 10,000. Tatta has been supposed to be the Pattala of the ancients.[8] Pottinger states that the earliest mention he has found of it is in the ninety-second year of the Hegira,[9] but he does not give any reference to the place of such mention. Burnes says, "the antiquity of Tatta is unquestioned."[1] Outram[2] assigns its foundation to 1445, but does not cite his authority. Macmurdo states,[3] from native authorities, that it was founded 900 of the Hegira, or A.D. 1522. In 1555[4] it was pillaged and burned by some Portuguese mercenaries. In A.H. 1000, it was, according to this last authority,[5] again destroyed in the Mogul invasion by Akbar, and never completely recovered. In 1758 a British factory was established there, and withdrawn in 1775. In 1799 an abortive attempt was made to re-establish it. The house belonging to the factory is yet in good repair. In the beginning of 1839 it was occupied by a British garrison. Tatta is in lat. 24° 44′, long. 68°.

[Margin notes: ¹ Kennedy, i. 81. ² Burnes, Rep. on Commerce of Tatta, 8. ³ Outram, 18. ⁴ Burnes, Bokh. iii. 30, 227. ⁵ Macmurdo, Jour. Roy. As. Soc. 1834, p. 234. ⁶ Pott. 352. ⁷ Burnes (James), Sinde. ⁸ Burnes, Bokh. iii. 31. ⁹ 351. ¹ Bokh. iii. 31. ² 18. ³ Jour. Roy. As. Soc. 1834, p. 30, 233. ⁴ Postans, in Jour. As. Soc. Beng. 1841, p. 279; Burnes, Rep. on Nav. of the Indus, 3. ⁵ 234.]

TAWISK.—A village in Afghanistan, twelve miles south of Furrah, and near the left bank of the river of the same name, in lat. 32° 16′, long. 62° 2′. [Margin: E.I.C. Ms. Doc.]

TAZEEN.—A village at the eastern foot of the pass of the Huft Kotul, and in a valley of the Kurkutcha mountains, twenty-six miles from Kabool, on the route to Jelalabad. It was one of the scenes of the prolonged and exterminating massacre of the British troops, in their attempted retreat from Kabool, in January 1842. Here, subsequently, in September of the same year, the British, under General Pollock, entirely defeated a greatly superior force of Afghans. Elevation of the pass above the sea, 8,173 feet; of the valley, 6,488. Lat. 34° 21′, long. 69° 28′. [Margin: E.I.C. Ms. Doc.; Wood, Khyber Pass, 3; Mil. Op. in Afg. 395; Hough, Narr. Exp. in Afg. 296; Moorcr. Punj. Bokh. ii. 279; Jour. As. Soc. Beng. 1842, p. 74, Grif. Bar. and Ther. Meas. in Afg.; Allen, Diary of March through Sinde and Afg. 330. E.I.C. Ms. Doc.]

TEBHEE.—A village in the Punjab, situate near the right bank of the river Ghara, and on the route from Mooltan to Ferozpoor. Lat. 30° 7′, long. 72° 51′.

* Pottinger[1] mentions, that Hamilton states that the citadel of Tatta could contain 50,000 men and horses. This is indeed the number, as given in the London reprint of his work (1774),[2] but in the original Edinburgh edition (1727),[3] the number is stated with more probability at 5,000.

[Margin: ¹ 352. ² i. 116. ³ i. 115.]

TEE—TER.   269

TEENDO.—A village in Sinde, situate on the right bank of the Indus, on the route from Larkhana to Sukkur. Lat. 27° 46′, long. 68° 40′. _{Ms. Survey Map.}

TEER ANDAZ,* in Afghanistan, on the route from Kandahar to Ghuznee, and fifty-one miles north-east of the former place. Here is a pillar of brick, between thirty and forty feet high, said to have been built to mark the spot where fell an arrow shot from a neighbouring hill by Ahmed Shah, the founder of the Durani empire, and hence the name, which signifies the circumstance. The distance, however, proves the falsehood of the story. Lat. 31° 55′, long. 66° 18′. _{E.I.C. Ms. Doc.; Jour. As. Soc. Beng. 1842, p. 58, Grif. Bar. and Ther. Meas. in Afg.; Hough, Narr. of Exp. in Afg. 146; Havelock, War in Afg. ii. 44.}

TEEREE, or TEERA, in Afghanistan, a small town and district, situated in the Salt range, south of Peshawer, and west of the Indus. The mountains here are of secondary formation, and contain iron, coal, and salt. Teeree is the southern of the two chiefships of the Khuttuks, Acora being the northern. The town, or rather village, of Teeree is a very insignificant place. Lat. 33° 18′, long. 71° 22′. _{Burnes, Pol. Pow. of the Sikhs, 3; Masson, Bal. Afg. Panj. i. 115; Moorcr. Punj. Bokh. ii. 341.}

TEEREE.—A village in Afghanistan, five miles from the left bank of the Helmund river. Lat. 32° 32′, long. 65° 41′. _{Walker's Map of Afg.}

TEEREE,[1] in Northern Beloochistan, a town in the province of Sarawan, is situate on the route from Shawl to Kelat, and seventy miles north of the former place. The road to the north of this town is good; to the south, and in the direction of Moostung, it passes through a deep ravine, and is broken up by watercourses. Teeree is surrounded by a wall having two gates, and the immediate vicinity abounds in productive orchards and gardens.[2] The elevation is considerable, as the road ascends from Shawl, which is 5,563 feet above the sea.[3] Teeree is in lat. 29° 51′, long. 66° 57′. _{[1] E.I.C. Ms. Doc. [2] Masson, Bal. Afg. Panj. ii. 70; Kelat, 311, 318. [3] Jour. As. Soc. Beng. 1842, p. 55, Grif. Bar. and Ther. Meas. in Afg.}

TEHER, in the Punjab, a village situate on the route from Ferozpoor to Mooltan, about twelve miles from the right bank of the Ghara river. Lat. 30° 30′, long. 73° 35′. _{E.I.C. Ms. Doc.}

TENGHI.—A village in Afghanistan, situate on the left bank of the Lundye river, thirty miles north of the town of Peshawer. Lat. 34° 24′, long. 71° 41′. _{E.I.C. Ms. Doc.}

TERIE, in Sinde, a village on the eastern route from Roree to Hyderabad, and twelve miles south-west of the former town. Lat. 27° 36′, long. 68° 47′. _{Map of Sinde.}

* From تیر tir, "arrow," and انداز andaz, "cast," or "throw."

270   TEY—TIB.

E.I.C. Ms. Doc.

TEYAGA.—A village of Cutch Gundava, in Beloochistan, situate on the road from the town of Bagh into Sewestan. Lat. 29° 4′, long. 68° 46′.

TEZEEN.—See TAZEEN.

Hough, Narr. Exp. in Afg. 356.

THABOOL, in the Punjab, a small town on the route from Ramnegurh to Lahore, and twenty-two miles south-east of the former town. Lat. 32° 6′, long. 73° 30′.

Vigne, Kashmir, i. 252; Jour. As. Soc. Beng. 1840, p. 113, Cunningham, Sources of Punjab Rivers.

THANA, in the Northern Punjab, a small town on the route from Lahore to Kashmir, through the Pir Panjal Pass. Here is a large serai, or public lodging for strangers, built of red brick by the emperor Akbar. The town contains three or four hundred inhabitants, most of them Kashmirian shawl-weavers. It is embosomed in groves of walnut and mulberry trees, and prettily situate on the summit of a bank, rising precipitously from the Rajawur river, and has small streams flowing through every pathway. Its height above the sea is 5,000 feet. Lat. 33° 26′, long. 74° 16′.

Moorcr. ii. 50; Gerard (J. G.), on the Spiti Valley, in As. Res. xviii. 260.

THOG-JI-CHENMO, in Ladakh, a lake on the elevated plain of Rupshu. Its extent is considerable, as Trebeck travelled for nearly a day along it. Innumerable wild-fowl frequent it, though the water is very bitter and brackish. The elevation is 15,500 feet. Lat. 33° 5′, long. 78° 4′.

Burnes (James), Mission to Sinde, 38.

THOORA, in Sinde, a small town on the route from Cutch to Hyderabad, and fifty-five miles south of the latter place. Lat. 24° 30′, long. 68° 28′.

E.I.C. Ms. Doc.

THULLADA, in the Punjab, a village situate on the route from Mooltan to Ferozpoor, in lat. 29° 52′, long. 72° 5′.

E.I.C. Ms. Doc.; Burnes, Pers. Narr. 116.

THUTHA, in the Punjab, a village on the route from Pind Dadun Khan to Attock, and twenty-five miles south of the latter place. Lat 33° 35′, long. 72° 21′.

E.I.C. Ms. Doc.

THYREH, in Afghanistan, a village situate on the river Bahreh, twenty-five miles south-west of the town of Peshawer. Lat. 33° 47′, long. 71° 21′.

Vigne, Ghuznee, 13.

TIBA, in the Punjab, a village in the Doab of Barie, between the Ghara and the Chenaub, and on the route from Ferozpoor to Mooltan. Lat. 30° 8′, long. 71° 56′.

E.I.C. Ms. Doc.

TIBBEE, in Afghanistan, a village of the Daman, situate near the right bank of the Indus. Lat. 31°, long. 70° 48′.

E.I.C. Ms. Doc.

TIBBY, in the Punjab, a village on the route from Leia to Kaheree ferry over the Indus, and twenty-five miles north of Leia.

It is situate on an offset of the Indus, and about four miles east of the main channel. Lat. 31° 18', long. 71°.

TIBEE, in the Punjab, a small town about five miles from the western bank of the Ghara. Lat. 30° 6', long. 72° 47'. Vigne, Ghuznee, 13.

TIGADEE.—See TURGHURREE.

TIRA, or SHAH JEHANPUR, a town and stronghold in the north-east part of the Punjab, is situate on a rock of sandstone, several miles in circumference and flat at top. The Beas flows along its base on one side, and on every other it is surrounded by precipices eighty or a hundred feet high. It contains about twelve or fifteen hundred houses, and five thousand inhabitants. It was formerly the residence of Sansar Chand, the independent rajah of Kotoch, who at one time had a revenue of 350,000l., and was so powerful as to rival Runjeet Singh. After the death of Sansar Chand, his descendants were dispossessed by Runjeet Singh, who took possession of Tira, which is still held by the Sikhs. Lat. 31° 36', long. 76° 26'. Moorcr. Punj. Bokh. i. 125; Vigne, Kashmir, 111; Masson, Bal. Afg. Panj. i. 429.

TISSA.—A village situate in the Shighur valley, in Northern Baltistan. Lat. 35° 33', long. 75° 20'. Vigne, Map of Kashmir.

TOBA,[1] in Afghanistan, an irregular range of rocky mountains, extending northwards from the north side of the valley of Pisheen. They are about a hundred and fifty miles in length, and a hundred in breadth, and lie between lat. 30° 40'—32° 40', long. 66° 40'—68° 20'. They are estimated to have an elevation of about nine thousand feet above the sea,[2] or between three and four thousand above the valley of Pisheen. The country overspread by these mountains, though in general rugged, has many fertile and pleasant spots. According to native report received by Conolly,[3] " between the long and severe winters which the inhabitants of these hills experience, they enjoy a very delicious climate. The tops of the hills are table-lands, which are greatly cultivated by means of springs everywhere in abundance. One enthusiastic resident of this part of the country, in describing it, said that even if there was not water there, the very air would raise the crops." "The water was like running diamonds, the plentiful fresh verdure as a carpet of emeralds, and the air like the odour of musk." This tract is principally inhabited by the tribe of Caukers, or Khakas, so infamous for their rapacious, treacherous, and sanguinary dispositions. A native gave Conolly a lively ac- [1] E I.C. Ms. Doc.; Elph. Acc. of Caubul, 165.
[2] Kennedy, Sinde and Kabool, i. 326.
[3] Jour. to India, ii. 71, 120.

count of the zest with which, in spring, those savages enjoy the pleasures of their pastoral state. " The shepherds of Toba, he said, would, at this blithe season, pitch their camps together, and entertain each other for joy of the increase which the new year brought to them; feasting on lamb and fresh curds, and all the varieties which their wives made with milk; hunting with hawks and greyhounds during the day, or, perhaps, following a wolf or a hyena to his lair and tying him there; while at night, they would sit out late in social parties, conversing and telling stories, or dancing the *attun*."

TOE.—A stream of Afghanistan, rises in the mountains inclosing Kohat, about lat. 33° 30′, long. 71° 10′, and after a course of about forty miles, generally in a south-westerly direction, falls into the Indus on the right side, opposite the Soheili rocks[1], a dangerous group in its channel. Elphinstone[2] styles it a brook not deserving the name of river; yet where he crossed it, about twenty miles above its mouth, he found it at the end of February, a deep, clear, and rapid stream.[3] It is made extensively useful, nearly the whole of its stream being dispersed in numerous channels for the purposes of irrigation.[4]

[1] Wood, Oxus, 126.
[2] Acc. of Caubul, 114.
[3] Id. 39.
[4] Wood, Oxus, 136.
E.I.C. Ms. Doc.

TOGA.—A village in Afghanistan, fifteen miles east of the town of Kohat. Lat. 33° 32′, long. 73° 39′.

[1] Vigne, Kashmir, i. 192; F. Von Hugel, Kaschmir, ii. 161.

TOHI.—A river of the Punjab, rising in the southern or lowest range of the Himalaya, near the left bank of the Chenaub, and about lat. 32° 55′, long. 75° 10′. It holds a south-westerly course of about eighty miles, flowing by Chinini and Jamoo, about fifteen miles below which last town it falls into the Chenaub, lat. 32° 32′, long. 74° 41′. Where crossed by Broome and Cunningham[2] in the beginning of September, it was found to be a great river, running deep and red, and full of quicksands, which rendered the passage dangerous as well as tedious.

[2] Trans. As. Soc. Beng. 1841, p. 112; Forster, Jour. Beng. Eng. 244.

E.I.C. Ms. Doc.

TOKURUK.—A village in Afghanistan, on the route from Ghuznee to Shawl, and eighty miles north of the latter town. It is situate in a valley, on the banks of a fine stream. The road northward, in the direction of Ghuznee, is for several miles very bad, in some places a path not being traceable; on the south it becomes more practicable. Lat. 31° 10′, long. 67° 23′.

Vigne, Kashmir, ii. 325; Gerard, Koonawur, 34.

TOLTI, in Bultistan, a large village, situate on the left bank of the Indus, which is here deep and rapid, and is crossed by a *suzum*, or rude suspension-bridge of twisted twigs. A castle stands here on the edge of the lofty cliff rising over the river. Lat. 34° 55′, long. 76°.

TOONEA.—A village of Cutch Gundava, in Beloochistan, and situate on the route from Gundava to Larkhana, thirty miles south of the former town. Lat. 28° 5′, long. 67° 27′. E.I.C. Ms. Doc.

TOONEE, in Sinde, a village on the route from Larkhana to Gundava, and twenty miles north-west of the former town. It is situate on a watercourse along which the Moola river, in time of inundation, finds its way to the Indus. Lat. 27° 41′, long. 68° 2′. E.I.C. Ms. Doc.

TOORKUBAR, in Beloochistan, a halting-place on the route from Bela to Khozdar, and sixty miles north of the former town. According to Pottinger, "this spot is said to owe its name to a celebrated deeve or demi-god, called Toor, whose grave is marked by a neighbouring eminence, and of whose exploits the most fabulous accounts are related." Lat. 27° 1′, long. 66° 25′. E.I.C. Ms. Doc.; Pottinger, Belooch, 33.

TOOT-I-GUSSURMAN, in Afghanistan, on the route from Kandahar to Herat, and half-way between them, or one hundred and eighty-five miles from each. It is near the summit of a pass about 1,200 feet above the general level of the country. To the north, the mountains in the Tymunee country about Ghore rise to a very great height, probably not less than from 13,000 to 14,000 feet. Lat. 32° 32′, long. 63° 10′. E.I.C. Ms. Doc.

TORBELA.—A small town in the north of the Punjab, and on the left or eastern bank of the Indus, a little below where it issues from the mountains and flows over the plain in a broad and shallow, yet still very rapid current.[1] Below Torbela, and between it and Attock, are the five fords of the Indus. These are dangerous at all times, from the icy coldness and extraordinary rapidity of the stream; and in summer they are, in consequence of the swell of the stream, totally impracticable. The river[2] is here smooth, rapid, and about two hundred yards wide. Lat. 34° 12′, long. 72° 44′. [1] Leech, Fords of the Indus, 19; Burnes, Pers. Nar. 119.
[2] Vigne, Kashmir, ii. 188.

TORGAD, in Bhawlpoor, a town where the Khan of Bhawlpoor defeated the Ameers of Sinde. Lat. 28° 23′, long. 69° 46′. Leech, Rep. on Sind. Army.

TORGO.—A village in Bultistan, ten miles east of the capital town, Iskardo. Lat. 35° 10′, long. 75° 36′. Ms. Map of Kashmir.

TOUDA CHEENA, in Afghanistan, a village on the route from Ghuznee to Dera Ismael Khan, a hundred and twenty miles E.I.C. Ms. Doc.

west of the latter place. It is situate in the pass of Gomul, and near the river of that name. Lat. 32° 11', long. 69° 7'.

TRAHAL, in Kashmir, a valley, furrowing the south-western slope of the great Bultul mountain. It is about six miles in length and of varying width. Vigne describes it "to be as little worth seeing as any part of Kashmir, it being a comparatively barren and stony tract." It is the principal residence of that race called Kashmirian Sikhs, or those whose ancestors came into the valley of Kashmir in the service of Raja Suk Juwan, a Hindoo of Shikarpoor, who about seventy years ago was appointed governor by Timur Shah. The village of Trahal is in lat. 33° 54', long. 75°.

Kashmir, ii. 29.

TRANEE.—A village in Sinde, situate on the south side of Lake Manchar, in lat. 26° 22', long. 67° 44'.

E.I.C. Ms. Doc.

TRANKAR, or **DANKAR**, in Ladakh, is a hill-fort of the valley of Spiti, nearly inaccessible, as it can be reached only by a path a foot wide, and which could be rendered impassable by rolling down stones from above. It is rudely constructed of stone intermixed with unburned brick. Its elevation is 13,014 feet. Lat. 32° 6', long. 78° 12'.

Gerard (J. G.), on Spiti Valley, in As. Res. xviii. 267; Trebeck, in Moorc. ii. 58; Gerard (A.), Map of Koonawur.

TREMOU, in Sinde, a village, on the route from Khyerpoor to Jessulmair, and eight miles east of the former place, from which the road lies through a level, and in general well-cultivated country, though occasionally overspread with jungle. There are several shops in the village, and abundant supplies can be obtained there. Lat. 27° 32', long. 68° 53'.

E.I.C. Ms. Doc.

TRICCUL, in Sinde, a small town where an offset from the river Fulailee rejoins the main channel of the Indus. Lat. 25° 7', long. 68° 21'.

Wood, in Official Rep. by Carless, 17; Burnes (J.), Mission to Sinde, 38. F. Von Hugel, Kaschmir, i. 155.

TRICOTA, a lofty mountain in the north of the Punjab, and on the south of the valley of Kashmir, has such an elevation as to be covered with snow the greater part of the year. North of it is a remarkable spring, from which the water gushes at very short and regular intervals, as if expelled by pulsations, and is received into a spacious reservoir. During December, January, and the beginning of February, the water is too warm for the hand to bear immersion in it, but at other times cold. According to Von Hügel, this is caused by the water produced by the melting of snow on the heights cooling that yielded by the fountain, which being heated by subterranean fire, has this naturally high temperature during the winter months when the snows and ice-bound streams withhold their cold admixture. This natural wonder causes the place to be considered holy by the Hindoos, and consequently to be visited as a place of pilgrimage. Lat. 32° 58', long. 74° 37'.

TRILOKNATH (TEMPLE OF), in Lahoul, a celebrated Hindoo fane dedicated to Siva, or Triloknath, the lord of three worlds —heaven, earth, and hell. It is a square building surmounted by the trident of Siva, which deity is represented here by an image of white marble with six arms. The village of Toonda, in which the temple is situated, was, in 1838, overwhelmed by an avalanche, which destroyed most of the inhabitants. It is subject to the Rajah of Chumba. Lat. 32° 50', long. 76° 41'. *Jour. As. Soc. Beng. 1841, p. 105, Cunningham, on Sources of Punjab Rivers.*

TROOHAWALA, in Bhawlpoor, a halting-place on the route from the city of Bhawlpoor to Ghosghur, and sixty miles south-east of the former town. It is situate in the *Thur*, or Great Desert, overspreading the eastern part of Marwar. Lat. 28° 47', long. 72° 4'. *E.I.C. Ms. Doc.; Boileau, Rajwara, 77.*

TRUG, in Afghanistan, a village situate on the route from Kala Bagh to Dera Ismael Khan, and twenty miles south-west of the former town. Lat. 32° 47', long. 71° 24'. *E.I.C. Ms. Doc.*

TRUGGAR, in the Punjab, a village situate twenty miles south of the town of Mooltan, on the road to Bhawlpoor. Lat. 29° 51', long. 71° 31'. *E.I.C. Ms. Doc.*

TSOK.—A village in Bultistan, situate twenty miles north-west of the capital town, Iskardo, in lat. 35° 15', long. 75° 15'. *Walker's Map of Kashmir.*

TUBUKSIR.—A village in Western Afghanistan, situate on the left bank of the river of Khash. Lat. 31° 54', long. 62° 55'. *Jour. As. Soc. Beng. 1840, p. 724. Conolly (E.), Physical Geog. of Seistan, Map.*

TUGAO PEAK, in Northern Afghanistan, situate about eight miles to the east of the river Tagao, in lat. 35° 5', long. 69° 55'.

TUKANEE.—A village in Afghanistan, situate on the Kabool river, in lat. 34° 20', long. 68° 24'. *E.I.C. Ms. Doc.*

TUKATOO, on the borders of Afghanistan and Beloochistan, a range of mountains bounding the valley of Shawl to the north. The forked summit of the range is estimated by Havelock to be 6,000 feet above Shawl, and as this is 5,600 feet above the sea, the elevation of Tukatoo must be nearly 12,000 feet. Lat. 30° 20', long. 66° 55'. *Havelock, War in Afg. i. 249; Conolly, Jour. to India, ii. 197; Elph. Acc. of Caubul, 106.*

TUKHTAPOOL, in Afghanistan, a village and halting- *E.I.C. Ms. Doc.; Hough, Narr. Exp.*

place on the route from Shawl to Kandahar, and twenty-six miles south-west of the latter city. It is situate on the river Doree, here about three feet deep, with brackish water, yet not so much so but that it may be drunk. The road in this part of the route is good, and the country cultivated. The elevation above the sea is 3,630 feet. Lat. 31° 18′, long. 65° 42′.

<small>in Afg. 92; Masson, Bal. Afg. Panj. ii. 185.</small>

<small>E.I.C. Ms. Doc.</small>

TUKHT-I-SIKUNDUR, in the Punjab, a village situate near the left bank of the Jailum, eight miles south of the town of Jailum, on the road from thence to Ferozpoor. Lat. 32° 50′, long. 74° 33′.

<small>Forster, Jour. Beng. Eng. ii. 12; Moorcr. Punj. Bokh. ii. 115; Vigne, Kashmir, ii. 59.</small>

TUKHT-I-SULIMAN, or "Solomon's Seat," in Kashmir, a lofty hill* close to the city of Sirinagur or Kashmir, on the eastern side. The view from it is very noble, extending over the city, the contiguous lake or dal, and the whole of the valley of Kashmir, bounded on every side by mountains in most places crowned with perpetual snow. It is three-quarters of a mile long, rocky, bare of trees, but covered with grass where there are any patches of earth. Its rocks are of trap. On the summit is a massively-built Buddhist temple, having every mark of extreme antiquity. It is now converted into a mosque, and dedicated to Solomon, who, according to popular belief, drained the valley, by making at Baramula a miraculous exit for the water, which formerly rendered it a lake. Elevation above the sea, 6,950 feet. Lat. 34° 4′, long. 74° 43′.†

<small>Ms. Map of Sinde.</small>

TUKROW.—A village in Sinde, situate about five miles from the right bank of the Eastern Narra river. Lat. 26° 3′, long. 69° 4′.

<small>E.I.C. Ms. Doc.; Jour. As. Soc. Beng. 1840, p. 724, Conolly (E.), Physical Geog. of Seistan, Map; Leech, App. 39. E.I.C. Ms. Doc.</small>

TULKAB.—A village in Afghanistan, sixteen miles east of Khash, on the road to Giriskh. Lat. 31° 39′, long. 62° 59′.

TULL, in Afghanistan, a small town in the desert of Sewestan, and on the route from Dera Ghazee Khan to Dadur, through the Lakhee Surwar Pass, which is scarcely passable for cavalry. Tull is in lat. 30° 5′, long. 69° 7′.

---

* Vigne (ii. 42) states its height at 450 feet; Von Hügel (i. 238) states it at 1,200 above the surface of the lake.

† Vigne (ii. 47) states, that between this and the next mountain is a gully, whence "is constantly blowing a breeze that must tend to prevent the stagnation of its (the lake's) waters." Von Hügel, on the contrary (ii. 235), states that there is so complete a calm in the valley, that you can never see a wave on the lake.

TULLAR.—A village in the Punjab, situate on the road from Leia to Kote, on the Chenaub river. Lat. 30° 34′, long. 71° 27′. E.I.C. Ms. Doc.

TULL-I-KUMAN.—A village in Afghanistan. Lat. 32° 29′, long. 63° 28′. E.I.C. Ms. Doc.

TULUMBA, or TOOLUMBA.[1]—A town of the Punjab, on the left bank of the Ravee river. It is large, populous, and surrounded by a high mud wall. Close are the ruins of an ancient mud fortress of great height and strength, and probably that laid in ruins by Tamerlane in 1398.[2] It is supposed by Masson to be the capital of the Malli mentioned by Arrian. Lat. 30° 28′, long. 72° 9′. [1] Masson, i. 456.
[2] Price, Mahomedan Hist. iii. 239.

TULWANDEE.—A village in the Punjab, about twenty miles south of the town of Vazeerabad, on the route from thence to Amritsir, in lat. 32° 20′, long. 74° 4′. E.I.C. Ms. Doc.

TUMBOO.—A village of Cutch Gundava, in Beloochistan, and situate on the road from Bagh to Larkhana. Lat. 28° 16′, long. 68° 1′. E.I.C. Ms. Doc.

TUNDEH, in the Punjab, a village situate on the road from Attock to Jailum, and twenty-five miles north-west of the latter town. Lat. 33° 15′, long. 73° 20′. E.I.C. Ms. Doc.

TUPPEE.—A village in Afghanistan, thirty miles north of the town of Kala-Bagh. Lat. 33° 16′, long. 71° 30′. E.I.C. Ms. Doc.

TUPPERAH.—A village in Afghanistan, about five miles south-east of the town of Kohat. Lat. 33° 30′, long. 71° 32′. E.I.C. Ms. Doc.

TURAHNU, in the Punjab, a village situate on the left bank of the Ravee. Lat. 30° 46′, long. 72° 55′. Walker's Map of N.W. Frontier.

TURGHURREE, in Afghanistan, a walled village in the province of Lughman. Here, in 1842, the British prisoners spared from the massacre in the attempted retreat from Kabool, received refuge for a short time. Near it is a tomb, called by the Afghans Kubber-i-Lamech, being supposed by them to be that of Lamech, the father of the patriarch Noah, and much visited by pilgrims. Lat. 34° 51′, long. 70° 9′. Sale, Disasters in Afg. 283; Eyre, Mil. Op. at Cabul, 267; Masson, Bal. Afg. Panj. iii. 197; Baber, Mem. 142.

TURNAK RIVER, in Afghanistan, rises on the southern declivity of the high lands of Ghuznee, or those connecting the Huzareh mountains with the Suliman range. The remotest source is about five miles north of Oba, and in lat. 33° 5′, long. 67° 48′, and at an altitude of 7,500 feet; thirty-five miles farther down it receives from the west a large feeder, which is generally considered the main stream, though having a much shorter E.I.C. Ms. Doc.; Jour. As. Soc. Beng. 1842, p. 60, Grif. Bar. and Ther. Meas. in Afg.; Elphin. Acc. of Caubul, 116, 121; Masson, Bal. Afg. Panj. i. 269; Hough, Narr. Exp. in

course of about ten miles. This feeder rises in numerous copious springs at Sir-i-Chushma (Springs-head), at the base of a mountain having an elevation of 2,000 feet above the general level of the country. After this, the united stream is about eight yards wide and two and a half feet deep, with a clear rapid current. It receives few accessions of any importance in the lower part of its course, and loses much water, drawn off right and left to irrigate the fertile valley down which it flows in a south-westerly direction. It is almost everywhere fordable, and is, in fact, crossed by a ford eight miles above Julduk, on one of the routes from Kandahar to Ghuznee, though the most frequented proceeds along the right bank of the river nearly to its source. In the lower part of its course, in consequence of the draughts from it for the purpose of irrigation, the Turnak, in summer, becomes completely dry, as it was found to be eight miles east of Kandahar in the end of April, when the bed was crossed by the British army. Some miles lower than this place it was crossed by Conolly at the end of October, and found to be a narrow stream. Continuing a south-westerly course a few miles farther, it, at such times as the current is continuous, joins its scanty water with that of the Urgundab, in lat. 31° 23', long. 65° 8', having, about fifteen miles above this point, received from the east the stream of the Doree.

Afg. 156; Conolly, Jour. to India, ii. 93; Atkinson, Exp. into Afg. 195; Havelock, War in Afg. i. 331, ii. 51; Kennedy, Sinde and Kabool, ii. 5; Outram, Rough Notes, 103

E.I.C. Ms. Doc.

TURTEE, in Sinde, a village situate on the right bank of the Western Narra. Lat. 27° 11', long. 68° 1'.

E.I.C. Ms. Doc.

TUSHAT, in Kashmir, a village situate on the east shore of the lake or *Dal* of Sirinagur, in lat. 34° 8', long. 74° 44'.

E.I.C. Ms. Doc.

TUTAM DARA, in Afghanistan, a village on the Ghorbund river, and at the eastern entrance of the valley of that name. Here, at the end of September, 1840, Ali Khan, a refractory Afghan chieftain, was attacked by a British force, under Sir Robert Sale, and, after a brief and ill-sustained attempt at resistance, put to flight. Though the position was strong, being defended by several forts, the casualties of the British on this occasion were very trifling in a numerical point of view. Six sepoys were wounded, but Captain Edward Conolly, an officer of high professional and intellectual character, was killed. The country in the vicinity is fertile, being principally laid down in gardens and orchards. Artificial irrigation is extensively and skilfully practised, by means of three fine canals diverging from the Ghorbund river, and each extending for about ten miles in a southerly direction.* Tutam Dara is in lat. 35° 6', long. 69° 6'.

TUTHEE, in the Punjab, a village situate about eight miles from the right bank of the Swan, in lat. 33° 20', long. 72° 28'. _{Masson, Bal. Afg. Panj. iii. 129.}

TUTT, in Sinde, a village situate on the left bank of the Indus, in lat. 26° 53', long. 68° 3'. _{E.I.C. Ms. Doc.}

TUTWANU.—A village in the Punjab, situate on the right bank of the Ravee. Lat. 30° 39', long. 72° 39'. _{Map of Sinde.}

TYVERA.—A village in Afghanistan, situate on the northern route from Subzawur to Giriskh. Lat. 32° 40', long. 63° 39'. _{Walker's Map of N.W. Frontier.}

U.

UDDOOREE.—A village in Sinde, situate near the Poorana or Phurraun river, in lat. 24° 46', long. 69'. _{E.I.C. Ms. Doc.}

UDHURANA, in the Punjab, a small town on the route from Attock to Rotas, is situated in a very difficult country and on the bank of the Kasee river. Lat. 33° 2', long. 73° 21'. _{Hough, Nar. Exp. in Afg. 344.}

UDRANA.—See UDHURANA.

UKRIE, in Sinde, a village situate on the road from Sehwan to Kurrachee, eight miles from the former place. Lat. 26° 16', long. 67° 50'. _{E.I.C. Ms. Doc.}

ULEEL KOOND, in Southern Beloochistan, and situate at the source of the Hingol river, in lat. 25° 40', long. 65° 36'. _{E.I.C. Ms. Doc.}

ULLABAD.—See ALLAHABAD.

ULLABAD.—See ALLA-YAR-KA-TANDA.

ULLAH BUND,[1] on the southern frontier of Sinde, a ridge of earth of slight elevation, thrown up by the earthquake of 1819, across the Phurraun or Poorana branch of the Indus. The name signifies "the mound of God," and was given to it by the natives, in allusion to the fact of its not having been made by human

_{[1] Burnes, Bokh. iii. 314.}

---

* Masson, though in general remarkable for accuracy, is mistaken in assigning Tutam Dara as the scene of the action at Purwan, in which Dr. Lord, Lieutenant Broadfoot, and Adjutant Crispin were killed, in consequence of the dastardly backwardness of two squadrons of the 2nd Bengal native cavalry. (See the notice on Purwan.)

efforts. It is thus described by Burnes:[2] "The Ullah Bund, which I now examined with attention, was, however, the most singular consequence of this great earthquake. To the eye it did not appear more elevated in one place than another, and could be traced both east and west as far as it could reach. The natives assigned it a total length of fifty miles. It must not, however, be supposed to be a narrow strip, like an artificial dam, as it extends inland to Ramoaka-bazaar, perhaps to about a breadth of sixteen miles, and appeared to be a great upheaving of nature. Its surface was covered with saline soil, and I have already stated that it consisted of shells, clay, and sand." In 1826, a great inundation of the Indus poured such a stream over the desert that it cut through the Ullah Bund, forming a channel thirty-five yards wide and about thirty feet deep, and immediately below that bank expanded into a lake, covering a surface of two thousand square miles. This watery expanse[3] received from Burnes the name of the Lake of Sidree, being that of a small fort which it overwhelmed. The place where the Ullah Bund was intersected by the Phurraun is in lat. 24° 5′, long. 69° 4′.

UMDANEE, in Afghanistan, a village of the Daman, eight miles west of the Indus. Lat. 30° 30′, long. 70° 48′.

UMRITZIR.—See AMRITSIR.

UREUHAL, in Kashmir, a village situate about six miles north-west of the town of Islamabad, on the road to Sirinagur. Lat. 33° 44′, long. 75′.

URGHANDEE BALA, or UPPER URGHANDEE, to distinguish it from another in the vicinity, is a commanding position on the road from Ghuznee to Kabool, and about ten miles west from this last place. Here on the 4th of August, 1839, Dost Mahomed Khan had posted his army with twenty-eight cannon, to give battle to the advancing British, but being deserted by his troops, took to flight, abandoning his guns, which were in consequence captured. Elevation above the sea 7,628 feet. Lat. 34° 28′, long. 68° 33′.

URGUNDAB.—A river of Western Afghanistan, which rises in the unexplored Huzareh country, south-west of Koh-i-Baba, and ninety or a hundred miles north-east of Kandahar, about lat. 33°, long. 67°, and holds a south-western course, passing by Kandahar, and, twenty-five miles below that city, receiving the water of the Turnak, flowing from the north-east. It then takes a westerly direction for about seventy miles, and falls into the river Helmund, after a course of two hundred and fifty miles, in lat. 31° 30′, long. 64° 10′. The banks of the river between Hourz-i-Muddud and Kandahar (about twenty-six miles) are thickly studded with gardens and villages. Where crossed by the route from Kandahar to Herat, about twelve miles south-west of the former place, the Urgundab is, in its ordinary state, about forty yards wide, and from two to three feet deep, and fordable. In inundations it becomes much increased in volume, and travellers are then prevented from crossing it, though for no great length of time. It is a very valuable stream, the greater part of its water being drawn off to fertilize the country about Kandahar.

URGUNDAB.—A village in Afghanistan, situate on the right bank of the river of the same name, and about twenty-five miles west of Kelat-i-Ghiljie. Lat. 32° 11′, long. 66° 25′. E.I.C. Ms. Doc.

URNEEYARAH.—A village in Sinde, situate in the Little Desert. Lat. 24° 33′, long. 70° 12′. E.I.C. Ms. Doc.

URS BEHGEE.—See ARS BEGHEE.

URUMBEE, in Afghanistan, on the route from Shawl to Kandahar, and ninety-seven miles south-west of the former place. It is situate in the valley of Pisheen, near a feeder of the Lora river, and in a country having some cultivation. Lat. 30° 40′, long. 66° 40′. E.I.C. Ms. Doc.; Hough, Narr. Exp. in Afg. 78.

USTAD.—A village of Cutch Gundava, on the great route from Sinde to Kandahar and Ghuznee. There is here a small lake of fresh water. Lat. 28° 47′, long. 67° 53′. Id. 40.

UTCH.—A village in Sinde, situate in the Delta, near the Joa mouth of the Indus. Lat. 24° 19′, long. 67° 23′. E.I.C. Ms. Doc.

UWUR, in the Punjab, a village situate on the left bank of the river Chenaub. Lat. 33° 10′, long. 75° 41′. Walker's Map of N.W. Frontier.

UZEERPOOR.—See AZEEZPOOR.

V.

VAZEERABAD, or VAZIRABAD, a town in the Punjab, is situate about three miles from the left or eastern bank of the Chenaub, here half a mile broad. The country imme- F. Von Hugel, Kaschmir, iii. 149; Vigne, Kashmir, i. 236.

diately about it is exceedingly fertile, and the view of the Himalaya probably the most extensive and magnificent anywhere. It is one of the handsomest towns in India; General Avitabile, an Italian officer in the service of Runjeet Singh, having caused it to be rebuilt in the European style, with wide streets, and a handsome and commodious bazaar. Runjeet Singh made here a pleasure-ground, and palace of singular construction, and covered outside with rude full-length figures of the ten *Gurus,* or spiritual leaders of the Sikhs, painted in fresco. Lat. 32° 30′, long. 74°.

E.I.C. Ms. Doc.

VEHRAB JAGOTE.—A village situate on the Pubb mountains, in Southern Beloochistan, in lat. 25° 36′, long. 67° 7′.

VENTIPUR, or WANTIPUR, in Kashmir, a village containing ruins, considered by some to be those of the original capital of the valley. It is situate near the right bank of the Jailum, on the route from Sirinagur to Islamabad, and twenty miles south-east of the former town. According to the chronicles of Kashmir, it was founded about A.D. 876, by Avanti Verma, king of the valley, who, after his own name, called it Avantipur.[1]* Here are the ruins of two great buildings, resembling in plan and character those described in the notice on Matan.[2] The greater ruin is called Vencadati Devi, the less Ventimadati. They are in a state of extreme dilapidation, yet, according to the detailed account of Moorcroft,[3] are still striking monuments of early architecture. "About half a mile further on we came to an interesting ruin on our right. Like others of the same kind, it is called by the peasants a building of the Pandus, the heroic princes of Hindoo epic verse, but believed here to have been giants. The edifice must have been a square temple, with four doors, approached by broad and spacious porches, and inclosed by a wall with four gates opposite to the doors of the central structure. A part of one of these was still standing, but of the walls the foundation alone remains, and the temple itself is a confused mass of ruins. The most remarkable feature of these remains was their magnitude. All the blocks were of immense size, and many of them could not have weighed less than ten tons. At the adjacent village of Wantipur we found similar remains, and here also one of the gateways was nearly entire. This was much richer than

[1] As. Res. xv. 61, Wilson, Hist. of Kashmir.

[2] Vigne, Kashmir, ii. 25.

[3] Punj. Bokh. ii. 243.

Kaschmir, ii. 266. * According to native tradition, as related by Hügel, Ventipur was built by Ven, the last Hindoo sovereign of Kashmir.

in the first edifice, and was covered with ornaments, scrolls, and figures. Two masses of stone on each side of the entrance, and each supported by a single pillar, were of an extraordinary size. The shape of the temple was undefined, and the principal part of its fragments seemed to be carved cornices, or portions of the roof. The stone of which these buildings were constructed is a limestone, which is susceptible of a high polish, and might be termed grey marble." The natives attribute the destruction of those solid edifices either to the zeal of the first Mahometan converts,[4] or the reckless cupidity of individuals, not scrupling to level those great structures for the sake of their materials. Moorcroft,[5] however, considers such agents to have been inadequate to produce their destruction. "It is scarcely possible, however, to imagine that the state of ruin to which they have been reduced has been the work of time, or even of man, as their solidity is fully equal to that of the most massive monuments of Egypt. Earthquakes must have been the chief agents in their overthrow." The slope of the mountain rising north of Ventipur was, during the ages of Kashmirian prosperity, formed, with wonderful industry, into a succession of terraces, the faces of which were supported by massive walls, and the horizontal surfaces overlaid with earth, for the purposes of cultivation.[6] The vicinity of Ventipur, dreary and desolate enough in the present depression and depopulation of Kashmir, was far otherwise sixty years ago, when visited by Forster,[7] who describes it with his usual simple felicity of expression: "The evening was serene, and the variegated view of populous villages, interspersed through a plain which was waving with a rich harvest, and enlivened by the notes of a thousand birds, filled the mind with harmony and delight." Ventipur is in lat. 33° 54′, long. 74° 55′.

[4] Jacquemont, v. 271.
[5] ii. 245.
[6] F. Von Hugel, Kaschmir, i. 265.
[7] Jour. Beng. Eng. ii. 9.

VERAWOW, in Sinde, a village near the south-east frontier. It is situate on the route from Omercote to Nuggur Parker, and fifteen miles north of the latter place. Lat. 24° 33′, long. 70° 46′.

E.I.C. Ms. Doc.

VERE, in Sinde, a small village or station, having a scanty supply of brackish water, on the route from Cutch to Hyderabad. Lat. 24° 8′, long. 68° 40′.

Burnes (J.), Mission to Sinde, 38.

VERNAG,[1] in Kashmir, in the south-eastern extremity of the valley, is celebrated for a magnificent spring, which rises with a great volume of water, in a basin about a hundred and twenty yards in circumference, built by the order of the Mogul emperor

[1] Vigne, Kashmir, i. 333; Moorc. Punj. Bokh. ii. 250.

Jehan Gir, the ruins of whose palace here are still to be seen. The water, which is very clear, swarms with trout, and flows off in such quantity as to form a considerable stream,[2] one of the principal feeders of the Jailum. Lat. 33° 26′, long. 75° 10′.

VESHAU, a river of Kashmir, rises in the Kosha Nag Lake, in the Futi Panjal, one of the mountain ranges which bound Kashmir on the south. After a very sinuous course of about fifty miles, and generally in a northerly direction, it joins the Haripoor or Dumdum river, and soon after the united stream falls into the Behut or Jailum river, of which it is by many considered the principal head. Lat. 33° 48′, long. 74° 58′.

VEYRE.—See VERE.

VEYUT.—See JAILUM.

VHEMDARA KA.—A village in Sinde, situate on the left bank of the Western Narra, on the road from Sehwan to Larkhana, in lat. 27°, long. 67° 48′.

VIGIPARA.—See BIJBAHAR.

VIKKUR,[1] or GHORABAREE, in Sinde, a small and wretched town, situate twenty miles from the sea, on the right or western side of the Hujamree branch of the Indus, which in its ordinary state is, opposite this place, a hundred and seventy yards wide and four or five fathoms deep close to the bank. In consequence of this advantage, it for some time was the port for the greater part of the commerce of the delta. About a mile below the town is a bar across the river, having only seven and a half feet of water at high tides. Near the town is the hull of a Dutch-built brig of war, of two hundred tons, and pierced for fourteen guns, imbedded in the earth so completely that tamarisk-trees grow on the deck. Her draught of water does not exceed six feet.[2] The town contains about a hundred and twenty houses, built of reeds and grass, and, with the adjoining villages, has a population of 1,200 persons. Its trade is not considerable; the exports averaging about 7,000*l.* per annum, and the imports about 5,000*l.* In December, 1836, there were eighty-four boats of all sizes lying at the landing-place. Here, at the close of 1838, the British troops from Bombay, marching for Afghanistan, were landed. According to Kennedy,[3] its navigation from the sea has become impracticable, in consequence of the Hujamree mouth having, in the course of 1838, been closed by a great change in the bed of that estuary of the Indus. Lat. 24° 14′, long. 67° 36′.

VINDOOR RIVER.—A small river, or rather torrent, in South-eastern Beloochistan, which, after a course of about twenty miles, falls into the Bay of Sonmeanee, in lat. 25° 15′, long. 66° 40′. It is of trifling width, and has a sandy bed, except in rainy weather, after the ceasing of which in a few hours it becomes dry. E.I.C. Ms. Doc.; Jour. As. Soc. Beng. 1840, p. 136, Hart, Jour. from Kurrachee to Hinglaj.

VIZEERABAD.—See VAZEERABAD.

VIZEEREE.—A village in Afghanistan, situate to the north of the Derajat, and twenty miles east of the Suliman mountains. Lat. 32° 46′, long. 70° 27′. E.I.C. Ms. Doc.

VUDDIA.—See GOORBAN RIVER.

YUNG, in the Punjab, a village on the route from Julalpoor to Rawul Pindee, ten miles north of the former town. Lat. 32° 48′, long. 73° 15′. E.I.C. Ms. Doc.

YUSAVA.—A village in the Punjab, situate about ten miles west of the river Chenaub, in lat. 31° 6′, long. 72°. Walker's Map of Afg.

W.

WADOLE.—A village in Sinde, situate on the route from Bukkur to Omercote, thirty-three miles north-west of the latter town. Lat. 25° 42′, long. 69° 30′. Ms. Map. of Sinde.

WADOR, or WADER, in Afghanistan, a town in the Derajat, twenty miles west of the Indus, and seventeen west of Dera Ghazee Khan. When other sources of water fail, it is supplied from a well a hundred and twelve feet deep. It is situate on the great route from Dera Ghazee Khan to Kandahar by the Sakhee Sarwar Pass. Population about 2,000. Lat. 30° 2′, long. 70° 40′. E.I.C. Ms. Doc.

WAH, in the Punjab, close to Hussun Abdul, a ruined palace and pleasure-ground, laid down according to the order of the emperor Akbar, who was so delighted when he saw it finished that he exclaimed, "Wah!" signifying admiration, and hence the name. The situation is very beautiful, and the ruins indicate that refined luxury was combined with elegance of taste in the design. Lat. 33° 54′, long. 72° 42′. (See HUSSUN ABDUL.) Moore, Punj. Bokh. ii. 317; F. Von Hugel, Kasch. iii. 97; Elph. Acc. of Caubul, 78; Vigne, Kashmir, ii. 188; Burnes, Bokh. i. 73; Hough, Nar. Exp. in Afg. 338.

WANGA BAZAAR.—See WUNGA.

WANJUMAL.—A village in Afghanistan, eleven miles north E.I.C. Ms. Doc.

of Kandahar, situate on the left bank of the Urgundab river, in lat. 31° 47', long. 65° 31'.

WANTIPUR, in Kashmir, also called Ventipura (which see).

Burnes, Bokh. iii. 236; Carless, Official Rep. on Indus, 9.

WANYANEE, in Sinde, is the lower part of the Sata, or great eastern branch of the Indus, and also bears the name of the Munejah. Its mouth, the Kookewaree, is the principal channel for the discharge of the waters of the Indus. Lat. 24° 2', long. 67° 32'.

Walker's Map of N.W. Frontier.

WARA.—A village in the Punjab, situate on the left bank of the Chenaub river, in lat. 31° 28', long. 72° 36'.

[1] E.I.C. Ms. Doc.

WAREEARA.—A village in the province of Lus, in Beloochistan, about twenty miles south of Belah, on the eastern route from that town to Sonmeanee. It is situate in a flat, sandy, barren country, having a scanty supply of brackish water. Pottinger[2] describes it as a miserable place, having about a dozen houses, or rather sheds. Lat. 25° 55', long. 66° 33'.

[2] Belooch. 14.

E.I.C. Ms. Doc.; Conolly, Jour. to India, ii.

WASHEER.—A village in Afghanistan, on the road from Kandahar to Herat, and a hundred and forty miles north-west of the former town. It is situate amidst hills, where the mountains of the Huzareh country slope downwards to Seistan. Lat. 32° 15', long. 63° 44'.

E.I.C. Ms. Doc.

WAUNEH.—A village in Afghanistan. Lat. 32° 16', long. 69° 40'.

E.I.C. Ms. Doc.

WEESHANA, in Afghanistan, a village thirty-five miles south of Kabool. Lat. 34° 4', long. 18° 57'.

E.I.C. Ms. Doc.

WESSERPOOR.—A village in the Punjab, situate on the route from Ferozpoor to Mooltan, and ten miles from the right bank of the Ghara river. Lat. 30° 34', long. 73° 40'.

Survey Map of Sinde.

WHAND.—A village in Sinde, situate on the route from Omercote to Bailmair, thirty miles north-east of the former town. Lat. 25° 27', long. 69° 17'.

E.I.C. Ms. Doc.

WINGEE.—A village situate in the south of Sinde, on the road from Ballyaree to Nuggur Parker, and five miles from the boundary of the Great Western river. Lat. 24° 16', long. 70° 3'.

E.I.C. Ms. Doc.

WOGUNI, in the Punjab, a village situate on a small branch of the Chenaub river, and on the route from Lahore to Kashmir, by the Banihal Pass. Lat. 33° 7', long. 75° 6'.

E.I.C. Ms. Doc.

WOWAPOORA.—A village in the Little Desert of Sinde, thirty miles south-east of Omercote. Lat. 25° 7', long. 70° 10'.

WOWREE, in Sinde, a village in the Desert, is situate forty-five miles south-east of Omercote. Lat. 24° 50′, long. 70° 9′. ^{E.I.C. Ms. Doc.}

WOWRIE.—A village in Sinde, situate in the Little Desert, fifty miles south-east of Omercote, on the road to Nuggur Parker. Lat. 25° 2′, long. 70° 30′. ^{E.I.C. Ms. Doc.}

WUDD,[1] in Beloochistan, a plain of the province of Jhalawan. It is about six miles in extent from north to south, and still greater from east to west, in which last direction the country, viewed from the town of Wudd, is open as far as the eye can reach.[2] The eastern part is the most fertile, producing abundance of wheat and millet. The town or village of Wudd is described by Pottinger[3] as very small and ill-built, and Masson does not draw a much more favourable picture. According to him, " Wudd is a small town comprising two parcels of mud houses, distant about one hundred yards from each other. The western portion contains about forty houses, principally inhabited by Hindoo traders; the eastern portion contains some twenty-five or thirty houses, tenanted by Mahometans. Among these are the residences of the sirdars or chiefs of the great Minghal tribe, Isa Khan and Wali Mahomed Khan, for the town, such as it is, is the capital of one of the most numerous tribes of Beloochistan. The house of Isa Khan is distinguished from the others by a single tree within the walls, and none of the houses have a second story." Wali Mahomed Khan, the sirdar above mentioned, fell fighting in the defence of Kelat when it was stormed by the British,[4] 1839. Wudd is in lat. 37° 19′, long. 66° 31′.

[1] E.I.C. Ms. Doc.
[2] Masson, Bal. Afg. Panj. ii. 38; Kalat, 328.
[3] Belooch. 36.
[4] Outram, Rough Notes, 168.

WULLEEJEE, in Sinde, a village of the Delta, on the route from Kurrachee to Tatta, and thirty-five miles east of the latter town. It is situate on the Ghara river, falling into the Arabian Sea. Wulleejee is in lat. 24° 48′, long. 67° 30′. ^{E.I.C. Ms. Doc.}

WULLOOKHAN.—A village in Afghanistan, situate on the route from Ghuznee to Kandahar, and on the left bank of the Turnak river. Lat. 32° 37′, long. 67° 23′. ^{E.I.C. Ms. Doc.}

WULUR, in Kashmir, is the largest lake in the valley, and may be regarded as a dilatation of the river Jailum. It is, according to Hügel, twenty-one miles long from west to east, and nine wide from north to south, abounds with fish and water-fowl, and produces the *singara*, or water-nut, in such abundance that it supports a considerable portion of the population. So important is this nut as an article of food, that Forster

Vigne, Kashmir, ii. 153; P. Von Hugel, Kaschmir, i. 343; Moore, Punj. Bokh. ii. 111; Forster, ii. 41; Jacquemont, Corres. ii. 156.

mentions that in his time, government derived an income of 12,000*l.* for granting the privilege of selling it. These nuts are the roots of the plant (*trapa bispinosa*), and are obtained by dredging the bottom between two boats, in a manner similar to that by which the deeper-lying shell-fish are taken upon our coasts. In the lake is a small island, which contains the extensive ruins of a Buddhist temple of great antiquity, destroyed by the fanatic Mahometans. The lake is subject to very violent squalls, which cause the loss of such craft as may be exposed to their fury. Lat. 34° 17′, long. 74° 22′.

E.I.C. Ms. Doc.

WUNG, in Afghanistan, a village on the route from Mittunkote to Kahun, and five miles north of the former town. Lat. 28° 59′, long. 70° 29′.

Burnes, iii. 316.

WUNGA, in Sinde, a small town, is situated on the Purana, or Phurraun, a branch of the Indus, generally deserted by water. In 1826, however, in consequence of a violent inundation, this channel was made navigable to the Koree mouth of the Indus, and continued so some years. Wunga is in lat. 24° 30′, long. 69° 9′.

Vigne, Kashmir, i. 211; Ayeen Akbery, ii. 140.

WURDWUN.—A village on the eastern frontier of Kashmir. It is situate at the eastern base of the Nabog Nyh Pass and at the head of the Muru Wurdwun valley. The village is merely a collection of a few log-houses on the banks of a feeder of the Chenaub. Lat. 33° 50′, long. 75° 30′.

Map of Sinde.

WURR.—A village situate at the south-eastern extremity of Sinde, on the borders of the Great Western river. Lat. 24° 21′, long. 70° 5′.

E.I.C. Ms. Doc.

WURZEH, in Afghanistan, is a village in the district of Jelalabad. It is situate in a valley of the Sufeid Koh mountains, in a well-watered, fertile, and well-cultivated spot. Lat. 34° 18′, long. 70° 18′.

Pott. Belooch. 298.

WUSHUTEE MOUNTAINS, in Beloochistan, a range in Mekran, extending from east to west, about lat. 28°, and between long. 62°—64°. It also bears the name of "Much" (date), as that fruit is produced in excellence in its valleys. This range separates the sandy desert on the north from the more elevated and fertile region stretching southwards through Mekran.

E.I.C. Ms. Doc.

WUZEERKHAN, in Afghanistan, a small fort on the route from Kabool to Bamian, and fifty miles west of the former place. Lat. 34° 20′, long. 68° 14′.

Y.

YAGEE BUND, in Afghanistan, a village on the route from Kabool to Peshawer, and forty miles south-west of the former town. Elevation above the sea about 8,000 feet. Lat. 34° 17', long. 69° 45'. <small>E.I.C. Ms. Doc.</small>

YERGHUTTOO, in Afghanistan, a village with a fort, on the route from Kandahar to Ghuznee, and eighteen miles south-west of the latter town. It is situate at the eastern extremity of a plain about fifteen miles across, fertile and well cultivated. Lat. 33° 20', long. 68° 9'. <small>E.I.C. Ms. Doc.</small>

YOEE.—A village of Beloochistan, on the route from Nooshky to Bunpoor, and two hundred and fifty miles south-west of the former place. It is situate a little south of the southern limit of the desert of Afghanistan, in a hilly country, of considerable irrigation, fertility, and cultivation. Lat. 28° 20', long. 61° 56'. <small>Pott. Belooch.149. E.I.C. Ms. Doc.</small>

Z.

ZALEE.—A village in Afghanistan, situate about eight miles from the right bank of the Helmund river. Lat. 33° 20', long. 66° 38'. <small>Walker's Map of Afg.</small>

ZANSKAR,[1] in Ladakh, or Middle Tibet, an elevated region lying between the Indus on the north, and the Chenaub on the south. It is about eighty miles long from south-east to north-west, sixty wide from south-west to north-east, and lies between lat. 33°—34° 30', long. 76°—77° 20'. This region not having been explored by any European, little is known concerning it, except that it is drained by a large stream called the river of Zanskar, which rising near Labrang, on the southern frontier, and holding a northerly course of nearly a hundred miles, receives several tributaries and joins the Indus on the left side, about twenty-five miles below Le, and in lat. 34° 13', long. 77° 2'. <small>[1] Moore. Punj. Bokh. i. 263-417.</small>

Its confluence with the Indus, here called the river of Le, and higher up the Sinh-kha-bab, is thus described by Moorcroft:[2] "The river of Le, flowing from east by south, was a clear and placid stream; that of Zanskar, from west by south, came rushing with great rapidity, and dashed its turbid waters into the Sinh-kha-bab with so much vehemence as to cause a reflux current for several yards. The height at which the union of the two rivers takes place is nearly 12,000 feet." All parts of the basin of the Zanskar river must of course have a very great elevation, exceeding that of the confluence.

ZARRAH, or ZIRRAH.—See HAMOON.

ZARSHOE, in Afghanistan, a village of the Kohistan or Highlands of Kabool, is situate on a feeder of the Pinyshreen river. Lat. 35° 7', long. 69° 42'.

ZARUS.—A village in Western Afghanistan, situate on the left bank of the Helmund river. Lat. 30° 21', long. 64° 2'.

ZEERUK, in Western Afghanistan, a halting-place on the route from Kandahar to Herat, and ninety-six miles north-west of the former place. It is situate in a plain, and has a good supply of water from subterraneous aqueducts. The road in this part of the route is good over an undulating country, but supplies for an army are very scanty, in consequence of want of cultivation. Lat. 32° 8', long. 64° 14'.

ZEHREE, in Beloochistan, a town of Jhalawan, is the residence of the *sirdar*, or chief of that province. It is described by Pottinger as having from two to three thousand houses, surrounded by a mud wall; but this number is doubtless greatly exaggerated, as it would give to this obscure place a population of between 10,000 and 15,000 persons. The surrounding country, also called Zehree, is of less elevation, and consequently warmer, than Kelat, and other tracts lying northward. The soil is comparatively fertile, and, being watered by numerous rivulets, is productive of grain, pulse, and esculent vegetables. Lat. 28° 22', long. 66° 34'.

ZEINPORE, in Kashmir, a hamlet situate on a *kariwa*, or elevated table-land, fifteen miles north-west of the town of Islamabad, in lat. 33° 44', long. 74° 51'.

ZHOBE, in Afghanistan, a river of Sewestan, rises near the north-eastern base of the Toba mountains, whence it pursues a north-easterly course, about one hundred and seventy miles, and joins the Gomul at Sirmaughan. Lat. 32° 2', long. 69° 40'.

ZIAN.—A village situate to the north of Kashmir, on the route to Astor, by the Husareh valley, and near the right bank of the Kishengunga river. Lat. 34° 35', long. 74° 42'. E.I.C. Ms. Doc.

ZINNAH, in the Punjab, a village situate on an offset of the Indus, and six miles east of the main stream. Lat. 31° 31', long. 71° 5'. E.I.C. Ms. Doc.

ZIRCHABY.—A village in North-western Afghanistan. Lat. 35° 51', long. 64° 56'. Walker's Map of Afg.

ZOHAK'S FORT, in Afghanistan, is a spacious ruin in the valley of Bamian (which see).

ZOORGONSHAH, in Afghanistan, a village thirty miles south of Kabool. Lat. 34° 7', long. 69° 1'. E.I.C. Ms. Doc. Jour. As. Soc. Beng. 1834, p.

ZOORGOONSHUR, thirty miles north-east of Lake Ab-istada, in Afghanistan, a halting-place on the route by the Gomul Pass from Dera Ghazee Khan to Ghuznee, and fifty miles south of the last-mentioned town. Lat. 32° 55', long. 68° 24.' 178, Honigberger, Route through the Veziri country.

ZOOTAN DARRA.—A village in Northern Afghanistan, situate on a feeder of the Punjshir river, about eight miles north-east of the town of Charikar. Lat. 35° 6', long. 69° 6'. E.I.C. Ms. Doc.

ZUKIR.—A village on the left bank of the Turnak, eight miles south-east of Kandahar. Lat. 31° 31', long. 65° 35'. E.I.C. Ms. Doc.

ZUMMAWALEE, in the Punjab, a village ten miles east of the Indus, in lat. 32° 53', long. 71° 51'. Walker's Map of N.W. Frontier.

ZURNAC, in Afghanistan, a fort on the route from Ghuznee to Kabool, and forty-four miles south-west of the latter place. It is situate about two miles from the right bank of the river of Logurh. Lat. 34° 6', long. 68° 38'. E.I.C. Ms. Doc.

ZUR SUNG, in Afghanistan, a village in the Huzareh country, situate on a feeder of the Herirood or Huro. Lat. 35° 26', long. 65° 19'.

ZURUD, in Beloochistan, a village on the route from Shawl to Kelat, and fifty miles north of the former town. It is a *ziarat*, or place of pilgrimage, in consequence of containing the tomb of some deceased person of reputed sanctity. There are about twenty houses, the inhabitants of which are supplied with water from a good stream. Lat. 29° 33', long. 66° 30'. E.I.C. Ms. Doc.

APPENDIX.

The following Routes are submitted as being some of the more useful through the [country] to which the "Gazetteer" relates. The particulars recorded are the results of [observ]ation made for official purposes, by parties actually traversing the routes to which [they] respectively relate.

ROUTE from KANDAHAR to HERAT, performed in 1839.

Distances			REMARKS		
	British				
Miles	Furlongs	Yards	Water and Ground for Encampment.	Forage and Supplies.	Nature of Road, Rivers, Hills, and general Observations.
					Left Kandahar at seven o'clock on the evening of the 21st of June from camp near the Herat gate.
7	—	—	The river Arghand at within 500 yards of the high road, an irrigation channel furnishing also an abundant supply of water. Ground for the encampment of a considerable force might be taken up here in a strong position.	The jowassa plant and grass abundant; bhoosa (chopped straw) and lucern also procurable, but in no great quantity, the greater portion having been carried into Kandahar for sale to the British army now encamped there.	The first three miles of road pass through the surrounding inclosed gardens and suburbs of the city, and the road crosses the several canals drawn from the Arghandab for irrigating the valley of Kandahar. Arrangements should be made previous to the march of any large force in this direction, for widening the

narrow portions of the road, and sloping down the banks of the watercourses, or what would be better, bridging them. There are two roads, if not more, by which troops and baggage may pass through the suburbs in this direction.

5	—	—	Water procured from an irrigation canal drawn from the Arghandab, the river one mile distant S.E. of the encamping ground. Ample room for the encampment of the largest force near this village.	Sufficient forage for the camels and horses of a large force at the present season. Bhoosa and lucern also procurable.	The road stony in some places, but generally good. An abrupt descent into the bed of the river, which would give a morning's work to forty pioneers to render easy for heavy guns; the ford across the Arghandab easy. The river at this time does not exceed two and a quarter feet in depth,

having fallen about six inches since the latter end of May. A ford about three-quarters of a mile lower down the river is generally pointed out as the best for guns to cross at, and the eighteen-pounders passed the river

294 APPENDIX.

Names of Halting Places.	Distances. British			REMARKS.		
	Miles.	Furlongs.	Yards.	Water and Ground for Encampment.	Forage and Supplies.	Nature of Road, Rivers, Hills, and general Observations.
Houz-i-Muddud Khan	14	—	—	at this point in May, 1839; but this ford is to be preferred, as crossing the river above the point where several irrigation channels are led from it, which render it troublesome to convey large guns across the low plain on the right bank of the Arghandab. In times of flood, and whenever the depth of the water in this stream exceeds three feet, it must, on account of its great velocity, prove a serious obstruction to travellers. It is, however, stated that the river never remains at this height for more than a day or two at a time. It is fordable generally almost everywhere. The stream is at this season about forty yards wide. Beyond the Arghandab one or two artificial water-courses have to be crossed, and the labour of a few pioneers would be required to facilitate the passage of heavy guns. N.B. The two marches above noticed might, without much difficulty, be made in one by a small force, where time was an object; but, under ordinary circumstances, it would be desirable to allow a day for the artillery and heavy baggage accompanying an army to cross the river, particularly if the river were in flood.		
				The same canal that supplies water at Sunjeree runs nearly parallel to the road the whole of this march, and affords an abundant supply about half a mile south of the reservoir now dry. Ground for the encampment of a large force, level and ample.	Jowassa for camels in abundance; grass in the immediate vicinity of the camp rather scarce, but plentiful a few miles to the southward, in the direction of the river, distant about five miles. Several villages, and (for Khorasan) much cultivation in the vicinity; some large flocks of sheep and goats observed.	The road lies across a hard level plain, across which a brigade might move in line. Water is found close to the road, a short distance beyond the village of Budwan, two and a half miles from Sunjeree; and a force halting at the former instead of the latter village would divide the stages more equally, shortening the last march, which is not, however, distressing, on account of the excellence of the road.
Kooshk-i-Nakhood	15	6	135	N.B. The foregoing distances not measured for want of a perambulator; they are taken on estimate, aided by the Sketch of a Route to Girishk, surveyed by Captain Patton, of the Quartermaster-General's department.		
				Water supplied from two khareezes (artificial water-courses) good and abundant. No water found on the road, though the beds of several small water-courses, quite dry, except after heavy rain for a short time, are crossed on the march. Ample ground for a large camp.	Jowassa plentiful, grass scarce; but little cultivation near the encamping-ground. A village of some note, called Maimund, lies about ten miles to the N. of the encamping-ground; in which direction, also, a valley opens at some distance, said to be well cultivated.	A hard, level, gravelly road, without obstacle or difficulty. At the distance of ten miles from Houz-i-Muddut Khan the road closely approaches a range of hills of trifling elevation, beyond which a higher range runs in a N.E. and S.W. direction.
Khak-i-Chapan	9	5	178	Water procurable from khareezes in sufficient quantity for a considerable force; but	Forage for camels less abundant than at the other halting-places on this route already	The road generally good and level; sand lies rather deeply on it for a short distance, and some slight un-

APPENDIX.

	Distances.			REMARKS.	
	British				
Names of halting places.	Miles.	Furlongs.	Yards.	Water and Ground for Encampment.	Forage and Supplies.	Nature of Road, Rivers, Hills, and general Observations.
				it is not so plentiful as to preclude the necessity of posting guards to prevent waste or pollution. The ground for encamping is somewhat irregular, but no difficulty would be found in arranging the disposition of a large camp.	passed, and grass scarce. Cultivation, and villages with gardens lie two or three miles to the south of the encamping-ground, and several large flocks of sheep observed on the march.	dulations in the ground met with towards the end of the march.
Bank Hel-d R.	22	3	58	Water abundant, as well from irrigation-channels as from the river. Ground for the largest force to encamp available, either on the low meadow land near the river, or on the dry plain above.	An ample supply of forage for camels and horses. Very little cultivation on this side the river, and but few dwellings; and, excepting the village of ferrymen, no inhabitants observed.	Road generally good and hard, the first part slightly undulating, and one or two sandy patches. About half-way is a well, with a scanty supply of water, sufficient for a few travellers, but not to be mentioned in calculating on the movements of even a small force. Further on are the remains of a garden and artificial water-course, neglected and suffered to fall to decay within the last few years. It would not, it is said, be a work of much labour to re-open the water-course, which would allow of this long march being divided. A line of 100 laden camels made this march in nine hours.
nk. R. Hel-nd ...	1	4	—	Water from irrigation-channels abundant; the river a mile distant to the S.E. Ground for an encampment sufficient, somewhat broken by water-courses and damp spots.	Forage, both for camels and horses, excellent and most abundant. Many small villages and much arable land, but comparatively little cultivation; nevertheless, the produce of the valley of the Helmund is said to be considerable; but the supplies for 500 of Shah Shoojah's infantry, now encamped here, are procured from Kandahar. It cannot, however, be doubted that considerable supplies of grain could be procured in this vicinity in ordinary	Crossed the Helmund river at a point nearly a mile above the usual ferry. The stream is barely fordable for infantry, taking off their arms and accoutrements; and with a strong wind, and ripple on the water, could not be deemed fordable at the point where the detachment crossed it. There are, however, easier fords within a short distance higher up the stream. Laden camels crossed the river with ease. Its depth was about three feet nine inches, width of the widest branch seventy yards, there being two or three others shallower and

296   APPENDIX.

Names of Halting Places.	Distances. British			REMARKS.		
	Miles.	Furlongs.	Yards.	Water and Ground for Encampment.	Forage and Supplies.	Nature of Road, Rivers, Hills, and general Observations.
				seasons, if necessity compelled a resort to vigorous measures. feet; at that time the stream was crossed by rafts made of rum kegs, which were rowed across by sappers; but in the event of it being again necessary to cross a force at the time the river is in flood, it is suggested that a suspension-bridge of ropes supported on trestles should be thrown across, the conformation of the banks immediately above the ferry presenting a favourable locality for constructing a bridge of this description; four 5-inch or 5½-inch ropes, with treble blocks, and a few stout spars (with the lighterlines and gear for the platform, most of which would be procurable at Kandahar), would be a sufficient provision for the purpose. The fort of Girishk is an insignificant place; the defences might be taken off by nine-pounders, were this preliminary found necessary, and the place carried by escalade; or a favourable spot where there is no ditch selected for mining, and the wall breached without difficulty; the gateways, also, are weak, and the gates of wretched construction. At a short distance from the river cultivation ceases, and a high gravelly bank, with an almost desert plain above it, extends	narrower. Velocity of current three miles per hour. Since 21st May, this river had fallen upwards of four	for several miles to the northward.
Zeeruk ..	20	7	85	Water procurable from several khareezees. Water good and abundant. An open plain for encampment.	Forage for horses and camels plentiful. Some cultivation in the vicinity, but not to so great an extent as to promise supplies for a single regiment. Fuel here, as at the former halting-places on this route, is scarce; the dried bushes found on the plain being almost the only fuel procurable. At most of the stages, however, there are mulberry-trees, which would only be used in the event of a greater deficiency of firewood than need be apprehended.	The first six miles of the road on this stage stony and undulating, the beds of several torrents, which drain the desert plain, crossing the line. After thus much of the road is passed, it becomes level and easy, till the fort of Saadaat, eighteen miles from Girishk, is reached. Beyond Saadaat, the road again passes over undulating ground within two steep slopes, till Zeeruk is close at hand. We passed the fort of Saadaat about midnight, and by the imperfect light it was difficult to examine the place so closely as was desirable. It appears, however, to be a strongly-planned little ghurree, surrounded by a dry ditch, formidable from its section, and the very hard gravel in which it is excavated. The fort was abandoned, and the gates removed, but otherwise seemed in good repair. The form of the fort was oblong, with round towers at the angles, and on the sides, about 180 by 140 yards; the ditch inclosed a space of nearly 300 by 200 yards, the space between it and the walls of the fort being intended to protect cattle and horses from a hostile force. The accompanying marginal section is submitted as an approximation to the truth. There is an abundant supply of water at Saadaat, and a large force might halt there in preference to proceeding three miles farther to Zeeruk.
Dooshakh .	12	7	76	Water from khareezes, good; abundant ground for the encampment of a large force available. Passed khareezes with water	Jowassa and grass plentiful. One or two villages, and some cultivation in the vicinity, but the villages were deserted, and no sup-	The road hard and level the whole way. At the village of Sur, six miles from Zeeruk, water and forage are procurable; and if Saadaat were made a

Distances.			REMARKS.		
	British				
Miles.	Furlongs.	Yards.	Water and Ground for Encampment.	Forage and Supplies.	Nature of Road, Rivers, Hills, and general Observations.
			flowing from the town of Sur.	plies could be expected.	halting-place, Sur would form another, at a distance of five miles from it.
21	7	195	Water abundant from two or three khareezes. Ground for encamping rather irregular close to the village, but ample; village available a short distance to the west.	Good forage for the camels. Grass for the horses. More cultivation than we have seen since leaving Girishk, there being several villages in the vicinity. It is possible that some small supplies might be collected here if compulsion were resorted to.	The first part of the road good and level; excellent water found at a distance of three miles from our encamping-ground, and to a force halting at Saadaat and Sur this would form a third good halting-ground at a distance of ten miles and a half from the place last named. At a distance of eight miles and a half, en-

tered a range of hills, the path leading over which shortly afterwards became contracted in several places so much that a laden camel could barely pass. The ascent gradual; no steep slopes; the road broken and stony; the character of the hills on either side smooth, gravelly, and not abrupt, except occasionally, when the naked rock projects above the surface. This is mentioned as affording a tolerably sure indication that difficult places in the beaten track might be turned by previous inquiry being made. The apparent summit of the pass, judged to be about 900 feet above the level of Dooshakh, was reached at a distance of three miles from the base, and from this point to the end of the march, the road wound among declivities, and followed the beds of water-courses, passing over much difficult ground. The march proved a very distressing one to the camels, and occupied thirteen hours and a half; but by daylight it is probable easier paths might have been selected. Vegetation in the beds of the water-courses was very luxuriant, indicating either the recent presence of water in the bed, or its nearness to the surface. Tall reeds and tamarisk bushes abounded in the hollow places, and the hills were dotted over with a great many khunjuk trees. We were informed that another route lay to the westward of the path we pursued, stated to be shorter, easier, and better supplied with water. The route, as thus pointed out, is entered in the map, and is as follows:—From Dooshakh to Kurra Khan, six miles, where there is water; from Kurra Khan to Ujrum, four miles, water; from Ujrum to a shéla, or pool of water, called Guswâp, four miles; from Guswâp to a point half-way between Khoosh-i-Sufeid and Washere, eight miles, water; from the above point to Washere, five miles; total, twenty-seven miles. By the road we followed, the distance is thirty-five miles. In its present state, the hill path we came over is not practicable for artillery, but it might be rendered so without great labour. The other road is said to be free from obstacles, but the information obtained on this head is not quite satisfactory.

9	5	215	Abundance of water from khareezes. Ground for encampment irregular, but not otherwise objectionable.	Jowassa and grass plentiful. Many villages in the vicinity of Washere, and several gardens. Supplies for small parties of travellers are, it is understood, procurable here, and, with	The road runs down a valley, with several small villages and inclosed gardens in it, watered by khareezes laid in an oblique direction down the sides of the slopes, the water-course at the bottom being quite dry. The road is hard and good,

298   APPENDIX.

Names of Halting Places.	Distances. British			REMARKS.		
	Miles.	Furlongs.	Yards.	Water and Ground for Encampment.	Forage and Supplies.	Nature of Road, Rivers, Hills, and general Observations.
Left Bank of Khash Rood	12	2	97	Excellent water from the river. Ground for a large camp, not good, much broken, stony, and irregular; but no real difficulty would exist in making a sufficiently convenient disposition.	previous arrangement and preparation, a few kharwaas of grain might be collected at Washere. Forage for camels abundant on the banks of the river. The grass met with not plentiful, and did not appear of good quality. No villages in sight, and the country on either side the river dry, stony, and almost a desert.	with a gentle descent the whole way, till within a mile or two of Washere, when it is undulating and stony; in some places there is, however, no obstacle of importance. The road stony and uneven ; at the distance of a mile came on the source of a small stream called Ausiaub, and followed its course for nearly six miles down a narrow valley lying between low hills. The last four miles of the march, the road winds down a dry water-course; the road not good, but practicable for artillery; the descent into the bed of the Khash Rood steep and bad.
Ibrahim Jooce	16	7	188	Water abundant. Ground for a large encampment, not good, the banks of this small stream being high, irregular, and stony.	Jowassa not very plentiful, but sufficient for a small force. Grass and reeds procurable in the bed of the stream. Bhoosa obtained from villages a few miles distant. Fuel, as elsewhere, scarce; but, if thought requisite, a stock might, in two or three days, be procured from the neighbouring hills.	Forded the Khash Rood, a river formidable during floods, and detaining caravans several days on such occasions. At this season it is thirty-seven yards wide, eighteen inches deep, and has a current of one mile and a quarter per hour. Its banks, however, bear all the marks of having at times to sustain the rush of an impetuous torrent; beyond the river the road pursued a tortuous course

Looking up the valley of this river, a succession of ranges of mountains, the most distant of which are very lofty, are visible to a distance of at least fifty miles. The bearing of the highest peaks about thirty E. of N.; the general direction of the chain apparently E. and S.

among hills of conglomerate for about three miles, at which distance a small spring is found, a few hundred yards to the north of the road; beyond this point it leads across a hard level plain for about nine miles, without any obstacle beyond the dry beds of two considerable torrents; then, at the termination of the plain, entered a range of hills, of moderate elevation, the path being in some places narrow and difficult, and crossed in many places by the dry beds of mountain torrents. The march proved a very fatiguing one for the cattle, their labour being much increased by a strong north-west wind, which from this date invariably got up an hour or two after noon, and continued to blow from the above quarter till morning, during the remainder of the march. The Kohi Doozdan, a large insulated mountain, which has been visible during the last three marches, was passed to-day; we left it to the south of the road, and the present encampment is immediately below a

APPENDIX. 299

	Distances. British		REMARKS.		
	Furlongs.	Yards.	Water and Ground for Encampment.	Forage and Supplies.	Nature of Road, Rivers, Hills, and general Observations.
	13	4	10	Water from a running stream good and abundant. Ground for a large encampment sufficient.	Forage for camels and horses plentiful. Very little cultivation near the encampment, though some passed on the march.	The encampment is on the bank of a small stream called the Cherra. The road, after leaving our last encampment, lay among hills for a mile, then debouched on a plain skirting a range

of precipitous and lofty hills for three miles and a half; road good: again turned into another mountain gorge, and ascended the valley for five miles to a spot called Guncemurgh, where there was a plentiful supply of water from a khareez, and lights from khails or villages were seen. The road continued to thread a succession of mountain valleys without any abrupt slopes, either ascent or descent, over rather difficult and broken ground, till the end of the march, which was accomplished by laden camels in seven hours.

| | 6 | 5 | 95 | Good water from a khareez. Sufficient ground for encamping a large force. Passed water on the road at a village called Cherra, where there is also a small fort, and others (all contemptible) seen to the west of the road. | Forage for both camels and horses abundant. Fuel procured from the numerous dry shrubs near the encamping-ground. There was some cultivation in the Cherra valley, but none nearer our camp; the country could not afford supplies. | Road among hills the whole way, but not difficult; very high mountains towering before us, the road ascending gradually as we advance towards them. |
| | 15 | — | 59 | Water from the khareez good and abundant. Ground for a large encampment, irregular, but sufficient. | Plenty of jowassa for the camels; grass rather scarce. There are several villages near the camp, but the inhabitants seem all to have fled. In detached patches there is some cultivation near our present ground. | A difficult road; after leaving Toot-i-Kusurman the road pursues a northerly direction for about two miles, then turns to the westward, and follows the course of a mountain valley from three-quarters of a mile to two miles wide, bounded by lofty and rugged peaks on either side. At |

a half from Toot-i-Kusurman, the summit of the pass, which is supposed to be full 1,200 feet above the last encamping-ground, is gained. The path then descends, and towards the foot of the slope water is found in the bed of a stream, completely overgrown by long grass, bushes, and rushes; here the valley widens out to three or four miles, and the road continues tolerably level till Suroward Khareez is reached. The road over the pass much broken, crossed by numerous beds of torrents, and in some places very stony. Laden camels would find crossing this pass by night very inconvenient; by daylight little difficulty is experienced, the march having been accomplished by them in seven hours; but for artillery, the road in its present state is not practicable, but there is no obstacle on the road which the labour of a company of pioneers might not remove or remedy in two days. If it were necessary to bring guns by this route, they should not be carried up this hill-pass till the road had been improved and reported on; and even then, it is probable a strong

300   APPENDIX.

Names of Halting Places.	Distances. British			REMARKS.		
	Miles.	Furlongs.	Yards.	Water and Ground for Encampment.	Forage and Supplies.	Nature of Road, Rivers, Hills, and general Observations.
				working party would be required to drag them across the more difficult places. These hills are thickly sprinkled with khunjuk trees, and many bushes fringe the water-courses; very lofty hills, their height above the level of the sea being estimated at 10,000 feet, rise to the right and left of the road in crossing the pass.		
Sheheruck	15	5	115	Abundance of good water for an encampment. Level plain for the encampment of a large force.	Jowassa and grass plentiful; villages and cultivation near, but the inhabitants not willing to sell supplies on any terms.	The road commonly adopted by Caplaghs going by this line to Herat is to the northward of that adopted by our party on this march; it passes by Cheetran, crosses the Furrah
				Rood, at Dowlutabad, and falls again into our line of march at or near the spring of water called Chah-i-Jehan. The first four miles of road passing over undulating ground, then entered a low but very rugged range of hills, through which the road wound for about two miles; a second range of low hills, met with eleven miles from Largehur Khareez, is crossed without difficulty, and at the twelfth mile the road enters upon the hard level plain which extends for twenty-seven miles to the banks of the Furrah Rood. The chain of hills, on the end of which we came at Toot-i-Kusurman, runs parallel to our line of march; the remarkable peaks called Punj Angoosht are included in the range, and are seen several miles to the left; a break in the range occurs a few miles to the west of the Punj Angoosht, the hills receding to the southward forming a valley, said to be highly cultivated, in the gorge of which is situated the village of Sour; two others were also seen under the range, but my closing in prevented their position being ascertained.		
Sehwan ..	15	12	175	Numerous canals for irrigation. Ground for encampment broken by watercourses and inclosures near the village, but at a small distance from them ample room.	Abundant forage. The banks of the Furrah Rood, on which we are encamped, thickly dotted with villages, and much cultivation at this point. We are informed the valley is equally fertile and	For ten miles, the road passed over a hard level plain; then slightly undulating ground was met with, as we came on the alluvial soil of the river; and from this point to its banks watercourses and cultivation were frequently met with.
				productive as far down the stream. Supplies of grain for our party were procured here without difficulty. Fruit was cheap and very plentiful. It cannot be doubted that if depôts were, previously to march of an army, established at convenient spots on the banks of this stream, partial supplies for an army might be collected. At Sheheruk a field of wheat had just been reaped; at Sehwan the harvest had been completely gathered for some days.	as Furrah, forty miles	A high range of hills, with a very remarkable projecting peak, at a point between this village and Sheheruk, lies to the south of our march. A valley called Durra-i-Khoon Khar, the produce of which is said to be considerable, is pointed out as lying beyond the point alluded to.
R. Bank of the Furrah Rood	1	3	45	Water of great purity from the river. Ground for the encampment of a large force procurable on the high bank above river.	Forage for a large force would not be plentiful on this side the river. The low watered ground is on the left bank at this part of its course, and there it is abundant, the grass being more luxuriant than any seen since leaving Gi-	Forded the Furrah Rood, a river which must, in times of flood, be a most difficult one for an army to pass. The bed is very irregular, forming alternate rapids and deep pools, and when in flood, the current is said to be extremely rapid;

APPENDIX. 301

Names of Halting Places	Distances. British.			REMARKS.		
	Miles.	Furlongs.	Yards.	Water and Ground for Encampment.	Forage and Supplies.	Nature of Road, Rivers, Hills, and general Observations.
				rishk; but, except in times of flood, cattle could ford the river with ease, and find pasture immediately on the other side. Fuel scarce.		caravans being detained on its banks occasionally for weeks. Its breadth at this season, at the point where the detachment crossed it, did not exceed thirty-five yards, the greatest depth being two feet and a quarter; the velocity of the current one mile and a half per hour. The bed of shingle. The water of the greatest clearness and purity.
Lookhoor-nah	21	3	50	Water from a spring, not very good, but wholesome. The spring amply sufficed for our small party; but for a force precautions would be necessary to prevent the soft bed of the water-course being trodden by animals or the water wasted. Ground very irregular.	Forage for camels sufficient. The encampment placed on a small meadow of turf, which, if reserved for the purpose, would afford a supply of grass. No villages or cultivation near the encamping-ground.	For fourteen miles the road traverses a hard stony level plain. Traces of former irrigation and cultivation for six miles from the river-bank; then entered low hills, and traced for some miles the bed of a mountain stream full of reeds, in which at fifteen miles and a half distance from the Furrah Rood, was a pool of water. Hills round us the rest of the march; road gradually ascending.
Sub-i-Jehan ..	17	2	17	Water tolerably good from springs, and ample for a small force; but with a large one, or, indeed, in any case where water is procured from springing in soft ground, guards are requisite to prevent from stirring up the mud and polluting the water; and at its place the supply, with every care, would not more than suffice for the wants of an army. Here (also at Ab-i-Koormah) the supply might be increased by digging wells previously in the bed of the watercourse. Ground for encampment good.	Forage both for camels and horses abundant; vegetation in the bed of water-course very luxuriant; no villages or cultivation near. animals going to drink	The road somewhat rough and stony at 10½ miles from Ab-i-Koormah. There are two roads leading to the halting-ground; that to the left, leading up the face of a hill, a short but steep ascent, was followed by the horsemen, laden yaboos; the one to the right was taken by the laden camels. Both routes were examined; that to the left is shorter and better than the other, excepting only the steep slope, which would be difficult for laden camels; with a little improvement it might be rendered quite practicable for light artillery. The difference in distance is about a mile and a half; that entered shews the longer route, on which, though generally not so smooth as the other, there is no obstruction worth noticing.
Urzabad..	20	1	135	Abundance of water from several kharee-zes. Ground for encampment ample; the plain is at this time rather marshy, from	Forage for camels and horses good and abundant; fuel scarce. The plain on which we are encamped is amply supplied with	The road generally good and level; at part of it winds through hills of no great elevation, but which, in places, approach close to the road, and would, from

Names of Halting Places.	Distances. British.			REMARKS.		
	Miles.	Furlongs.	Yards.	Water and Ground for Encampment.	Forage and Supplies.	Nature of Road, Rivers, Hills, and general Observations.
				water of the numerous khareezes formerly employed in cultivation having been suffered to run to waste.	water, and is apparently susceptible of high cultivation. Villages, consisting of a few houses surrounded by a wall, with round gardens attached, are numerous, and the whole	their position, afford a strong post to a force wishing to defend the pass against an army approaching from Herat.
L. Bank of the Adruscund	22	2	25	Water from the river of excellent quality. As already mentioned, water was found in abundance at a khareez, three miles and a half north of our encampment at Hyzabad on the march. Water was also found at a stream fifteen miles in advance of Hyzabad sufficient for a force. A spring at the top of the pass, eighteen miles on the road, and water again at eighteen miles and a half. Sufficient ground for an encampment, but rather irregular.	Forage and fuel abundant, the bed of the river being fringed by willows and bushes, among which much dry wood may be collected. No signs of cultivation or inhabitants near the river, nor indeed are any villages seen between the valley of Subzawur and that of Herat.	A fatiguing and difficult march; no force should attempt it. From Hyzabad, if it encamped there, a force might change ground to the verge of the cultivation and irrigated land of the Subzawur plain to the northward, which would shorten the march about four miles. It might then halt at the stream called, it is believed, Khojih Omeih, where there is abundance of forage, making a march eleven miles. The water was said to be brackish, but the spahies, and some of the officers, drank of the stream, and found it not unpalatable. This arrangement would leave seven and a quarter miles to the river,

plain as far as Subzawur, distant about eight miles, has been thickly populated and cultivated to a much greater extent than is now the case. Still the province of Subzawur is reported one of the richest, if not eminently the richest, district of the present kingdom of Herat, and as such is governed by a man of the first influence in the country, the eldest son of the prime minister. The southern route to Herat falls into that we pursued at Subzawar, and a depôt for supplies established at this place, or in its vicinity, would enable an army advancing on Herat from Kandahar to halt and recruit the cattle for a few days, before encountering the toilsome marches in advance of this plain. Our halting-ground was chosen at the first khareez met with on the plain. Advancing from the southward, the most northerly stream we passed on the plain is three miles and a half in advance of our present encampment. It has not been noticed in the proper place, that between Chah-i-Jehan and Hyzabad. Pools of water are found in the bed of a water-course called Gundutsan, at four miles, and again at seven miles and a half from the former place.

on which portion of the march a difficult hill pass has to be surmounted; after leaving the irrigated land, much of which was marshy, from the overflowing of the khareezes, came in a hard stony plain, with a gentle ascent, over which we travelled for six miles; then entered hills, and continued ascending five miles and a half by a winding road, when we reached a table-land, or rather basin, surrounded by low eminences thickly spread with reeds and bushes, and bearing the appearance of being occasionally under water. High peaks rose to the eastward, the summits of which are judged to exceed 10,000 feet in height above the level of the sea. The table-land two miles and a half

APPENDIX. 303

Names of halting places	Distances			REMARKS		
		British.		Water and Ground for Encampment.	Forage and Supplies.	Nature of Road, Rivers, Hills, and general Observations.
	Miles.	Furlongs.	Yards.			
				across, when there is a further slight ascent, the elevation reached being considered 1,500 feet above the level of Subzawur. The descent into the valley of the Adruscund is steep, rocky, and tortuous, and would require the labour of a company of pioneers for a day to make it practicable, and for three or four to make it moderately easy for heavy guns.		
Serai-i-Shah Bed	22	3	195	Water from a stream in front of the Rui Serai. Ground for encampment sufficient; it is rather irregular, and commanded by a hill to the eastward; indeed all the encamping-grounds among hills are commanded on this route.	Forage for camels and horses good and abundant. No supplies of any description procurable.	For nineteen miles from the Adruscund the road is one continued ascent among hills, the elevation attained supposed to be full 1,500 feet higher than the spot where we crossed the Adruscund, or 6,500 feet above the sea. Forage was observed plentiful throughout the march, and water was found at convenient distances the whole way. The
				road stony, and in some places difficult, but quite practicable for artillery. The Rood-i-Guz, which falls into the Adruscund immediately opposite our last encampment, runs for nearly six miles parallel to the first part of this march.		
Rozeh Bagh	21	—	210	Numerous artificial channels of excellent water. Abundance of room outside the garden, with access to water for a large force. Passed a spring of water four miles and a half from our last halting-ground. Also a khareez near the Howz-i-Meer Daood, six miles from the Rozeh Bagh.	Jowassa for camels plentiful, grass very scarce; bhoosa procurable from numerous villages. We are now in the valley of Herat, and not more than seven miles and a half from the city.	On leaving the Serai of Shah Bed the road ascended for about three miles, attaining an elevation of about 700 feet above our last encamping-ground; it then commenced a gradual, but regular and continued descent to the end of the march, falling, it is conjectured, 2,000 feet. We passed a caravanserai, called the Serai-i-Meer Daood, about eleven miles from the Serai-i-Shah Bed, but the khareez which formerly supplied it
				with water is dried up. From this point the eye ranges over great part of the valley of Herat, but the city itself, concealed by an intervening range of hills, called the Koh-i-Dooshakh; the distant mountains of the Huzareh country are seen, far overtopping a range of hills of considerable elevation on the other side of the valley. These mountains appear from the distance to be twelve or fourteen thousand feet high; but as the Serai-i-Meer Daood is considerably elevated above the plain, this appearance may be deceptive. The road is good the whole way from the foot of the hill. The Rozeh Bagh is a royal garden, planted with Scotch firs, now of great size and beauty.		
Bank of Heri Rood	4	2	70	Water good. Ground for encampment ample. Channels for irrigation leading from the river would be convenient in furnishing water for a large camp.	Forage plentiful. A meadow of considerable size on the river-bank would supply grass. The quantity of jowassa would depend materially on the ab-	Forded the Heri Rood, a wide shingly bed, over which the river runs in several separate channels. The largest may be forty yards wide and eighteen inches deep, the current having a

Names of Halting Places.	Distances. British.			REMARKS.		
	Miles.	Furlongs.	Yards.	Water and Ground for Encampment.	Forage and Supplies.	Nature of Road, Rivers, Hills, and general Observations.
					sence or otherwise of cultivation. At present a great deal of land has been suffered to run to waste, which has been, and probably will again be, under cultivation. This spot is but three miles from the bazaars of the city.	velocity of one mile and a quarter per hour. A great portion of the water is drawn off at this season for the purpose of irrigation. In the season of flood, the river is deep, and exceedingly difficult to cross. The body of water in it, however, appears greatly inferior to that of the Helmund. An old irregular bridge of numerous arches, unequal in size, formerly spanned the river. Three of the arches have altogether failed, and the whole structure is in a state of great dilapidation. The river, also, has partially deserted the bed in which it formerly flowed, a branch flowing round either end of the bridge.
Herat, the Kandahar Gate.....	3	—	180	The city is supplied with water from the river by aqueducts, with wood troughs running across the ditch. It is stored in large reservoirs of masonry, of solid construction, arched over. In time of siege, an ample supply is obtainable from wells dug from twelve to fourteen fathoms below the surface.	The valley round Herat is fertile and productive, when cultivated; supplies, even in ordinary years, used always to be most plentiful and cheap; now the city is little better than a ruin, the country round laid waste and desolate, the valley having been swept of inhabitants by the Persians, few of whom have returned. Forage for camels and horses is abundant; grain, &c. very scarce.	From our encampment on the meadow land, near the river to the city, the road passes through a succession of villages, all or most of the houses in which are now roofless and deserted; and inclosed gardens, the walls of which have been partially thrown down, and the trees generally felled or destroyed. The road is also crossed by numerous water-courses, over some of which narrow and awkward or dangerous bridges are thrown. The road has been paved, is quite worn out, and is very bad, but practicable.

ROUTE from HERAT to JELALABAD, performed in 1838.

Names of Stations, &c.	Distance in Miles.	Direction.	REMARKS.
Herat			On leaving the town, the road to Kandahar leads due south, through a succession of gardens and fields, intersected by numerous water-courses. About three miles from the town, the Herirood or Pul-i-Malaum river is crossed. Formerly, a fine bridge of burnt brick spanned the stream at this point, but the river has formed for itself a new channel, and now flows round one end of the bridge. The breadth of the river at the place where I crossed was about 150 yards; the stream was exceedingly rapid, and the water reached to our saddle-flaps. Several fatal accidents had lately occurred to persons who had attempted to ford the stream, when it had been swollen by a fall of rain in the adjacent mountains. To the south of the river is a fine tract of pasture-land, thickly studded with villages and gardens.
Houz (reservoir of water)	14	S.	Situated in an opening of the range of hills, to the south of the town.
Meer Daoud	4	S.	Caravanserai in good repair, with a fine stream of clear water from a khareez, or succession of wells, connected by an underground passage, which conducts the stream from its source.
Shah Beg	12	S.	Ruined caravanserai. Abundance of water.
Meer Allah	12	S.	Ruined caravanserai. Five and a half miles beyond Shah-Beg, a spring of sweet water on the left of the road. The caravanserai of Meer Allah, surrounded by cultivation, and a fine stream of water runs under the walls.
Rood-i-Guz	6	S.	A rapid stream, fifteen or twenty yards broad.
Rood-i-Adruscund	5	S.	Stream, one mile beyond Rood-i-Adruscund, a rocky pass, with springs of fresh water.
Khajeh Ourieh	6	S.	A ziaret-gâh, or place of pilgrimage, a ruin perched on the summit of a rocky hill, at the foot of which runs a stream slightly brackish.
	4	S.	Road turns off to Subzawur, leaving that which leads direct to Kandahar on the left.
Houz	7	S.W.	Reservoir of water, ruined.
Subzawur	10	S.S.W.	A small mud fort, 200 or 250 yards square, with seven circular bastions on each face, one gate on the southern face, scarcely any ditch, the walls in a state of dilapidation; a small ark or citadel, the residence of the prince governor, in the centre of the place. Subzawur is a place of no strength, and might be taken with little loss by a *coup-de-main*. It is situated in the midst of a richly cultivated tract of country, studded with innumerable villages, which are inhabited by Noorzais. Each village is about sixty yards square, surrounded by a mud wall, with towers at the

Names of Stations, &c.	Distance in Miles.	Direction.	REMARKS.
			angles. A range of hills, of inconsiderable elevation, to the south of the town, distant about two miles. The road between Herat and Subzawur is good and level, and passable for wheel-carriages of every description. Abundance of fresh water in every part of this route; but provisions are not procurable at any point between Herat and Subzawur. Shahzadeh Iskunder, a son of Shah Kamran, was nominally the governor of this district when I passed through it; he possessed, however, little weight or influence anywhere, and none beyond the walls of his fort; he seemed to be a half-witted and imbecile person. He had made no attempt to succour his father, or even to divert the attention of the Persians. The surrounding country was in a state of utter disorder. Bands of plunderers were roving about in every direction, and these men were described as acknowledging neither God nor king.
——	13	E.	At this point the road from Subzawur joins the main road, between Herat and Kandahar. The range of hills to the south of Subzawur terminates four miles from the town in a long spur, upon which the remains of an extensive fort are visible. This is called the "Kulla-i-Dookhter," or maiden's castle; and at a short distance from it, on a mound in the plain, are the ruins of another castle, called "Kulla-i-Pisr," or the youth's fort. The plain is thickly studded with villages and khails (encampment) of Noorzais; abundance of water; road perfectly level.
Kharuck	30	S.E.	A grove of khunjuck trees, with a fine stream of water, situated under a range of hills, running W.S.W. and E.N.E. Wells or springs at every six or eight miles, but no provisions procurable. For the last four or five miles the road hilly, and difficult for wheel-carriages, but a road, which is described as being good and level, strikes off to the right, three miles before Kharuck, and after turning the Kharuck range, crosses the plain to Dowlutabad, where it again joins the road which I followed. Encampments of Noorzais are occasionally formed in the vicinity of Kharuck, but these cannot be depended on for furnishing supplies even to a small force.
Summit of Pass	3	S.	Road, or rather pathway, impassable for wheel-carriages.
Dowlutabad	15	S.E.	A ruined fort on the right bank of the Furrah-rood; several large encampments in the vicinity. The valley of the Furrah-rood runs from N.E. to S.W., and is said to be richly cultivated. In the vicinity of the town of Furrah, about forty miles below Dowlutabad, supplies to almost any extent, and of every description, might be drawn from the district of Furrah. A son of Kamran, with the title of Saadut-ool-Moolk, resides at Furrah, and is the governor of the district; he, like the Subzawur prince, has not attempted to aid his father.

APPENDIX. 307

Names of Stations, &c.	Distance in Miles.	Direction.	REMARKS.
Checkaub	22	S.E. by E.	On the 29th of May, the river was fordable at a point where it was divided into five streams, about three hundred yards above a large solitary tree, which stands on the water's edge, and is remarkable as being the only tree near Dowlutabad. Checkaub is the name given to a fine spring of water, near which was an encampment of Noorzais. The road from Dowlutabad passable for wheel-carriages. No water between the Furrah-rood and Checkaub, except a few brackish streams. Abundance of water, and a good deal of cultivation, wheat and barley, in the immediate vicinity of Checkaub.
Largebur Khareez	9	E.	Gardens, half a mile to the right of the road, with abundance of water. Some encampments of Atchikzais in the vicinity.
Carwan Cazee	4	S.E.	Water.
Tooti Gusserman	10	E.	Several encampments near some mulberry-trees, which are said to mark the half-way distance between Herat and Kandahar. Abundance of water and cultivation. Road from Largebur Khareez hilly and stony; difficult for wheel-carriages.
—	8	S.	
Gunneemurgh	6	E.	Gardens and encampments of Atchikzais, near a fine stream; country hilly, but road good.
Ibrahim-jooee River	7	S.S.E.	We turned off the main road at this point, and ascended the right bank of the stream.
Tull-i-Kuman	7	N.E.	Mud fort belonging to Mem Khan, a chief of Noorzais, on the left bank of the stream. There are about thirty other forts higher up the stream, inhabited by the Badirzai branch of the Noorzais. There are two branches of the Noorzais—the Chulakzye and the Badirzai. The head of the former is Mahomed Haleem Khan (at present in the Persian camp before Herat; he was with Sheer Mahomed Khan when Ghorian was given up to Mahomed Shah), and Hassan Khan, at present in Herat, is the head of the latter. It is said that the two branches of this tribe muster from six to seven hundred families. There is no such fort as Kila Sufeid, as mentioned by Lieutenant Conolly, and inserted in Arrowsmith's map; but I was told the Tull-i-Kuman was built upon the site of what had once been the Kila Sufeid, which, like all other Kila Sufeids, is assigned to the days of Rustam and the white demon. The Tull-i-Kuman is surrounded by encampments, and is used as a "keep" for the flocks and herds of the chief and his people. In times of danger, these people retire to caves and hiding-places in the adjacent hills. The Tull-i-Kuman and its dependent forts are nominally under the authority of the Tyfool Moolk (a son of Shah Kamran, who resides at Ghore, said to be about thirty-five miles north of Toot-i-Gusserman, but he has not been able, for a long time past, to extract

Names of Stations, &c.	Distance in Miles.	Direction.	REMARKS.
			any thing from them in the shape of revenue or taxes, and they enjoy their fields and their flocks without paying any regard to the constituted authority, which is too weak to enforce its demands.
——	9	S.E. & S.	Came again upon the high road; abundance of water on the road between the Tull-i-Kuman and this point; passed several gardens and encampments.
Khaush-rood River..	6	E.S.E.	A fine stream twenty or thirty yards broad, running from the north; fordable. This is the boundary between Kamran's territory and that of the Kandahar sirdars.
Washeer............	14	E. by S.	Four forts, situated on a fine stream, and surrounded by rich cultivation and gardens.
Byabanck..........	24	E.	Village, with a stream from a khareez. The road in some places rugged, but passable for wheel-carriages. No fresh water during the first ten or twelve miles. This road is to the south of that followed by Conolly, which leads through the villages of Poosand and Numzand.
Dooshaukh.........	5	E.	Village, surrounded by a mud wall and towers.
Lur	3½	E.	Deserted fort, with a stream from a khareez; no encampments in the vicinity.
——	7	E.S.E.	Stream near a deserted fort, and some encampments of Baurikzais. Road perfectly level.
Sadant..	4	E.S.E.	Fort small, but strong; in good repair. This fort was built by Futteh Khan Baurikzai for his mother, who is said to have held a petty court here. Abundance of water.
Girishk...........	21	S.E.	The fort of Girishk is built upon a mound, about two miles from the right bank of the Helmund. Girishk is a place of considerable strength, and, if properly garrisoned, would require a force of three or four thousand men, with a small train of artillery (four iron guns and two or three mortars would be sufficient), to insure its capture. There are four or five old guns in the fort, but they appeared to be in an unserviceable state.
			Between the river and the fort is a fine chummun (pasture land) intersected by water-courses, and dotted with gardens, and groves, and villages. The country round the fort might be easily flooded, and the approach to it thus rendered exceedingly difficult to a besieging force. Mahomed Siddik Khan, a clever, intelligent young man, one of the sons of Sirdar Kohundil Khan (the eldest of the Kandahar brothers), rules at Girishk, and is the governor of the frontier district. He is attempting to form a corps of infantry, to be drilled and disciplined after the European manner. I saw about a hundred of his recruits, armed with sticks in lieu of muskets, being drilled by a fellow who looked very much like a runaway sepoy, dressed in a gay English uniform. When I passed through Girishk, Mahomed Omar Khan, and Mahomed Osman Khan, two sons of Kohundil Khan, were encamped

Names of Stations, &c.	Distance in Miles.	Direction.	REMARKS.
Rood-i-Helmund River	2	E.	in the vicinity, with about two hundred followers, on the way to join the Persian army before Herat. The measure was most unpopular, and it was given out that, after a sufficient force had been collected, the young chiefs would in the first instance undertake a plundering expedition against Furrah and Subzawur. The Etymander of the ancients. Broad and exceedingly rapid river, not fordable at this season. The distance between the banks is about a thousand yards, but in spring it is said to spread itself over the low ground on its right bank, and sometimes to approach within a few hundred yards of the walls of Girishk. The Helmund takes its rise on the mountains to the west of Cabul, and after a course of six hundred miles, during which it is joined by several considerable streams, the principal of which are the Turnak, the Urghundab, the Shahbund, and the Khaush-rood, it falls into the Lake of Tumah. There is usually a small boat at this place, by which travellers cross the river when the stream is not fordable, but this had been destroyed a short time before our arrival, and we crossed the river on an elephant, the water being in some places about seven feet deep, 3rd June.
Chak-i-Chapan	24	E.S.E.	A grove of mulberry-trees, with a small stream. There is no water between the Helmund and this place.
Kooshk-i-Nakhood, or Khoosh Nakhood	7	E. by S.	A great deal of rich cultivation, and several fine groves and gardens in the vicinity. Abundance of water. The ruins of an ancient fort, called the Kulla-i-Nadir, which must have been a place of considerable strength in its day, about two miles to the west of Khoosh Nakhood.
Houz-i-MuddudKhan	14	E.	A large tank on the right of the road.
Kandahar	26	E.	The Urghundab, a fine stream, about half a mile to the right of the road. The banks of the river thickly studded with gardens and villages. The Urghundab, after passing Kandahar, takes a westerly course as far as the Houz-i-Muddud Khan, and then turns to the south, not as it is laid down in Arrowsmith's map. The road from the Houz to Kandahar passes through a succession of fields, and gardens, and villages, which cover this fertile and delightful valley, the breadth of which varies from three to nine miles. Nearly the whole of the water of the Urghundab is taken off by canals for the purpose of irrigation. The route by which I travelled from Herat to Kandahar, was nearly the same as that followed in 1828 by Lieut. Conolly, to the accuracy of whose statements and descriptions I can bear ample testimony. I calculated the distance to be $380\frac{1}{2}$ miles by the average rate of a fast-walking horse, which I found to be four miles an hour on level ground. The journey is performed by horsemen in ten, and

Names of Stations, &c.	Distance in Miles.	Direction.	REMARKS.
			sometimes in nine days, but caravans of laden mules are usually from sixteen to eighteen days between Herat and Kandahar. The country is occupied by pastoral tribes, chiefly of the Noorzai, Atchikzai, and Baurikzai branches of the Doorance Afghans. They are possessed of numerous flocks and herds, and in the vicinity of their *khails*, or encampments, they raise a sufficiency of grain for their own consumption. These khails, which generally consist of from fifteen to fifty tents, are scattered over the face of the country, and as they are usually at some distance from the road, it is impossible for a mere traveller even to make a rough guess at the extent of population, or the amount of the resources of the country. To the south of the route above described is another, which passes through Bakwa, and which was followed by Forster in 1783, since which time I believe no European has travelled it. This southern or Dilaram road, as it is usually called, is described as being perfectly level, and not more than forty or fifty miles longer than the northern or more direct one; but there is a scarcity of water on it, some of the halting-places being upwards of thirty miles apart. It is, however, travelled by caravans and horsemen, and for an army it would have the advantage of passing within a short distance of Furrah and Subzawur, from which places supplies almost to any extent are procurable.
Kulla-i-Khalek dad Khan..........	13	E. & E.N.E.	A half-ruined village. Road, for the first two or three miles, led through gardens and cultivation, after which we travelled over an open, uncultivated plain. Good level road, free from stones. Water only amongst the gardens and cultivation.
Kulla-i-Azim Khan..	3	E. by N.	A small fort, in tolerable repair, with a stream of clear water.
	8	E. by N.	Opening in a low range of hills.
Khail-i-Akhoond, or "Dominies Khail"	7	E.N.E. & N.E. by E.	Road good, but stony. A few houses built round the tomb of a sainted schoolmaster, situated on the right bank of the river Turnak; the course of the Turnak (N.E. and S.W.) is marked by a green line of tamarisk-trees. A good deal of cultivation round the village.
Bivouac on the right bank of the Turnak	20	N.E.	Road excellent, cultivation the whole way, but no villages or khails to be seen, the people having retired from the vicinity of the highway to avoid the extortions of the great men who frequent the road.
Teer Andaz	4	N.E.	A minaret, about forty feet high, on the right of the road, said to mark the spot where an arrow of Ahmed Shah's fell, when that monarch was shooting from an eminence which is pointed out on the left of the road.
Khawer Taneh......	16	N.E.	No habitation to be seen. Bivouacked on the right bank of the Turnak, in the district of Khawer Taneh. Two or three miles beyond the minar, at a place called "Jalloogeer," or the bridle-pull, the road

APPENDIX. 311

Names of Stations, &c.	Distance in Miles.	Direction.	REMARKS.
			bad and stony for a short distance; with this exception, the road perfectly level and good, following the right bank of the Turnak. The valley of the Turnak is now (12th of June) a sheet of waving corn ripe for the sickle.
Jelduk	4	N.E.	A village, surrounded by gardens, about a mile to the left of the road.
Jud	8	N.E.	Crossed the Turnak near a mill, which marks the boundary between the country of the Dooranees and that of the Ghiljies. Here we diverged from the direct road, which leads along the right bank of the Turnak, and passes Kelat-i-Ghiljie, but which is now seldom taken by travellers, in consequence of its being infested by robbers or lawless Ghiljie chiefs, who either send their followers to attack caravans, or levy contribution themselves, under various pretences. The principal of these are the sons of one Shaabaden Khan, and are considered as the chiefs of this part of the country. They are upwards of twenty in number, and are seldom mentioned by their own names, being generally called "Buchahee Shaabaden," the sons of Shaabaden. They reside at Kelat-i-Ghiljie, and in the forts of this district, between the territories of the Ameer and the Sirdars, and are uncontrolled by either, although nominally their country is under the rule of the latter.
Kulla-i-Ramazan Khan	8	E. by N. E.N.E.	A small fort. Our route from the river lay amongst low hills; road stony, but passable for wheel-carriages. Black-mail was levied upon us at this place by Shaabaden's men, who had heard of our being in the vicinity.
Koorrum	22	N.E.	Small garden, and khareez, in the district of Koorrum. Passed several forts and khails, with slips of cultivation. At the fourteenth mile, Deewalik, a ruined fort, which is said to have been once a considerable place. As far as Deewalik, the country is inhabited by the Hotukee branch of the tribe of Ghiljie. The district of Koorrum is inhabited by Tokhees; the river Turnak, two or three miles distant, behind some low hills to the westward.
Kulla-i-Jaafferee	30	N.E.	Several forts. The road from Koorrum over undulating ground, passable for wheel-carriages. Khails and forts on either hand, but at some distance from the road. At the eighth mile, Glondee, said to be a large village (we passed it in the dark), the residence of one of the sons of Shaabaden. At the Kulla-i-Jaafferee we again entered the valley of the Turnak. Forts and khails are seen in every direction. Rich fertile tract of country on the banks of the stream.
Ford	11	N.E. W.N.E.	Crossed the Turnak, water reaching to horses' knees.
Gudh or Ghar	1		The first fort of the district of Mookur, which forms part of the government of Cabul.

y 2

Names of Stations, &c.	Distance in Miles.	Direction.	REMARKS.
Source of the Turnak	16	N.N.E.	Several fine springs under a range of hills. Road for the last ten miles lay through fields of waving corn (wheat and barley), clover, and madder. Forts thickly spread over the country, and abundance of water at every step: these forts form the district of Mookur. Road level, and free from stones.
Khareez in the district of Obeh or Oba	14	N.N.E.	Road sandy. Obeh is a pastoral district, the whole plain covered with flocks of sheep and goats, and droves of camels, but few forts are to be seen. Some khails under the hills, on either side of the road, at the distance of six or eight miles.
Chardeh	16	N.N.E.	One of the thousand forts of the fertile district of Kala-Bagh, which is chiefly peopled by Huzarehs. The whole country, as far as the eye can reach, one large field of wheat. The harvest is gathered in early in July.
Kareiz*	6	N.E.	Good level road.
Kareiz*	2	N.E.	Road execrable: sand and large round stones.
Water-mills	16		In the district of Nânee, between this district and Kala-Bagh, is that of Moorakee, which is said to be very populous, and to contain many forts; but I saw nothing of it, as I passed it in the dark.
Chehl Buchegân	8	N.E.	Fine grove. A place of pilgrimage. Road good. Numerous villages, chiefly on the right, inhabited by the Underee division of the Ghiljies. The whole plain covered with green wheat and fine clumps of trees. Abundance of water.
Ghuznee	4	N.N.E.	The present town of Ghuznee is a small place, not more than four hundred yards square; said to have been the citadel of a former town. It was built by the Jagatars four hundred years ago, and is situate on the southern slope of a hill to the S.W. of two minars, which are said to mark the spot upon which, or near which, stood the bazaar of Sultan Mahmood's city. The walls of modern Ghuznee are lofty, and stand upon a khareez, or fausse braye, of considerable elevation; but the ditch is narrow, and of no depth; and the whole of the works are commanded by some hills to the N.E. and N. of the place. At the northern and upper end of the town is a hill, upon which has been constructed a small citadel, forming the palace of the governor, Gholam Hyder Khan, a son of Ameer Dost Mahomed Khan. I saw one large, unmanageable gun, and four smaller ones, as I passed from the gate of the town to the citadel; I had no opportunity, however, of examining their state. The approach to Ghuznee from the south is highly picturesque; and the citadel, from its great height, looks formidable. The river of Ghuznee flows from the north, under the western face of the town, and supplies the place and the surrounding country with an abundance of water. Ghuznee may contain nine hundred or a thousand families—Tanjiks, Dooranees, and Hindoo shopkeep-

* This undoubtedly means the same as "Khareez," so often used, but approaches nearer the proper spelling, "Kariz." The "K" should not be aspirated.

Names of Stations, &c.	Distance in Miles.	Direction.	REMARKS.
			ers and merchants. As Ghuznee commands the high road between Kandahar and Cabul, it would be necessary that a force advancing from the former upon the latter place should take possession of it; but this would be easily accomplished, as the works are of no strength, and are commanded as above mentioned.
Tomb of Sultan Mahomed	2	N.E.	This celebrated place of pilgrimage is situated in the midst of a large village, surrounded by fine gardens, with several running streams.
	6	N.E.	Narrow defile, called the "Tung-i-sheer," a very strong position, but, I believe, it may be turned.
	1½	N.E.	End of pass.
Shusgao	2½	N.E.	Village; water and cultivation.
Sydabad	23	W.	Village. The country between Shusgao and Sydabad highly cultivated, a fine valley between low hills, villages at every step, abundance of water, road good, but stony in some places.
Logur River	4		Bridge called the Pull-i-Shaikhabad. The Logur river runs here from N.W. to S.E., crossing the valley, and entering some hills to the eastward.
Top	6	N.	Village.
River of Cabul	12	N.	Ford; rapid stream, about twenty yards broad; water at this season (June) stirrup-deep. The Cabul river comes from a break in the hills, to the N.W. of this point, and runs in a S.E. direction through a similar break, called the Tung-i-Lullunder, in the eastern range.
Mydān	½	N.	A collection of villages to the left of the road; rich cultivation, abundance of water. The country between Ghuznee and Mydān is chiefly inhabited by Wurdeks, who claim descent from the Emaum Teilabadeen; they number about twelve thousand families, and pay Rs. 90,000 to government; they are divided into three banches:—1. Malyar (chief, Koorumkhan); 2. Noosai (Tein Khan); 3. Meer Khail (Jan Mahomed Khan).
Arghunder	9¼	E.N.E.	Several fine villages, forming the district of Urghundee, about a mile to the north of the high road.
Cabul	14	E.	Half-way from Urghundee, the village of Kulla-i-Hajee. From this place to the city the road passes through a succession of gardens and fields, the whole country intersected by water-courses, brought from the river of Cabul; road excellent; villages and gardens as far as the eye can reach. The approach to Cabul from the west is through a narrow defile, which forms as it were the western gate of the city, and through this defile runs the river of Cabul, which afterwards flows through the centre of the city. The hills on both sides have been fortified with lines of wall, flanked at regular intervals by massive towers; but the works, which have fallen to decay, are too extensive to be properly defended, and the height may be easily turned. The citadel, or Bala Hissar, situated at the eastern

314   APPENDIX.

Names of Stations, &c.	Distance in Miles.	Direction.	REMARKS.
			extremity of the city, is a place of no strength, being commanded by heights in the vicinity.
There are about forty guns in Cabul, most of which are in a serviceable state.
The route between Kandahar and Cabul, above described, is generally blocked up by snow during four months of winter, but at the other season is good, and passable for all descriptions of wheel-carriages. Water is abundant, and supplies are procurable at any season for an army of twenty or thirty thousand men. A caravan travels between Kandahar and Cabul in fifteen days, but horsemen perform the journey in eight days, and couriers in six.
I estimated the distance at 317 miles, but the direct route, viâ Kelat-i-Ghiljie, is shorter by about ten or fifteen miles.
Cabul Bool	12	E. by N.	Village; road good, through gardens and fields.
Khak Teezee	25	S.E. & E.	Ditto, situated on the skirt of a range of lofty hills; at the fourth mile entered a defile called Tung-i-Khood Cabul, about three miles in length, ascended a small stream, which is crossed by the road every fifty yards; after passing the defile, the road enters an open country, the villages of Khood Cabul two miles to the right.
Twelve miles beyond, Bootchak, another defile; road hilly and stony, in some places impassable for guns.
Between the second defile and Teezee the road passes over the "Huft Kothul," or seven passes. Khooda Buskh Khan is the chief of this district.
Hissaruk (Pissaruk of Arrowsmith's Map)	17	E. by S.	Cluster of villages on the Soor-khrood stream, after leaving Teezee, steep ascent for about five miles, mountains covered with pine and hollyoak, magnificent scenery, road impassable for guns, abrupt descent for about two miles. The road or pathway in the bed of a mountain-stream.
The Soorkhrood flows from a break in the mountains to the east of Hissaruk. The skirt of these mountains covered with gardens and villages.
Ishpan	4	E.S.E.	Village on the left of the road. Between Cabul and this place the country is inhabited by Ghiljies; but we here enter the districts peopled by Khogianees. Forded the Soorkhrood, a clear rapid stream, near Hissaruk. Water at this season (June), stirrup-deep, and about twenty yards broad.
The Soorkhrood, after being fed by numberless mountain-streams, which come down from the ranges called Sufeid Koh, joins the Cabul river near Jellalabad.
Mookoor Khail	12	E. by S.	Large village. Abundance of water, fine cultivation, road stony, but passable for wheel-carriages. Crossed several mountain-streams running from south to north.
Wurzeh	14	E. & E.S.E.	Village, in a valley running down from the Sufeid Koh. Abundance of water, gardens and cultivation.

Names of Stations, &c.	Distance in Miles.	Direction.	REMARKS.
			After leaving Nookur Khail, the road descends into a valley, with a mountain-stream flowing through it. Road stony and bad. Villages and gardens on the southern side of the valley. At the sixth mile, passed the celebrated garden of Neemla, about a mile to the left; at the tenth mile, villages and gardens, on the skirts of the Sufeid Koh range.
Agaum............	7	E.S.E. & S.E.	Village, situated in a valley similar to that of Wurzeh. Fine stream, gardens, and rich cultivation. Villages as far as the eye can reach.
			Road stony, but passable for guns. Sirdar Mahomed Akber Khan, a son of Ameer Dost Mahomed Khan, was encamped with his troops in the valley of Agaum. This young man, although not the eldest, is said to be possessed of more power and influence than any of the other sons. He has acquired a high character for courage, and he certainly displayed this quality in the affair of Jumrood. The government of Jelalabad has been intrusted to him; and, if he is not greatly respected by the people, he is certainly the least unpopular of the family. His immediate dependents are said to be devoted to him. His troops were scattered in the different villages near Agaum, when I passed through that place; but I believe he has twelve guns, chiefly six-pounders, in a serviceable condition; a corps of 1,500 Jazarjurchees—a fine body of men, armed with long, heavy guns, which are fired from a rest, and will carry a ball 400 yards with precision—and two or three thousand good horses.
Jelalabad	24	N.N.E.	Village. The road, or rather pathway, for the first six miles, led through gardens and rice-fields. The whole country flooded.

ROUTE from KANDAHAR to CABUL.

STAGES.	Distances.		REMARKS.
	Miles.	Furlongs.	
Kandahar..............			From Cabul gate.
Shorandan	5		A village about two furlongs on the right of where the army encamped. A small river; has a stream of water and some coarse grass about its bed; yet forage for camels and horses is but scanty here, and no firewood except the wild thyme.
Killa-i-Azim Khan	9		A fort and village nearly in ruins; there are some few inhabitants in the fort, and several huts of cultivators in the fields, and an open village about three miles N.E. from the fort. There is considerable cultivation about this place, plenty of water from khareez (the artificial water-courses, as distinguished from natural streams or rivers). The road is good and open, crossing Junnoo Khareez at 4½ miles, which is muddy in some places. Good camel-forage; for horses, plenty of wheat-straw to purchase at present (the time of harvest); firewood the wild thyme, which is the general, and in most places the only, fuel throughout this route.
Kheil-i-Akhund	15	2½	A small village and mausoleum, from which the village is named, situated on the right bank of the river Turnak; there is also a large village on the opposite side of the river, about two miles from the other. There is a good deal of cultivation along the Turnak river here, the valley of which is entered by this route, about one mile before reaching the village. Forage and grazing good. The road is good and open the first seven miles, when it enters between a range of hills, continuing to wind among them until the last mile, with many ascents and descents, all of which are stony, and some a little steep. Half a mile after entering the hills an old fort is passed; and Manjore, a large place about one mile beyond it, situated in a narrow valley. Jookun is on the other side, but not in sight.
A highway was pointed out going round the hills to the right, which is reported a good gun-road, but of course must be two or three miles longer, joining this again where it meets the Turnak river.			
The Turnak river continues a fine stream, from five to eight yards wide, and twenty inches deep, running rapidly.			
Shahr-i-Safa	10	4	Ruins of an ancient city destroyed by Sultan Mahomed of Ghuznee, nearly one mile from the Turnak river; encamped beyond the ruins along the river. There is considerable cultivation, and several temporary encampments along the level of the valley, which varies in breadth from half a mile to three miles, to the rising grounds on the left, amongst which the permanent villages are built; the lower or level valley of the river being covered with snow to a great depth during the three winter months, and on the melting of which
Two villages, about one mile on the left, and two on the right, about three miles, a considerable distance from the road, about five miles from Kheil-i-Akhund, are called Poutee, by which passes the winter route to Cabul.			

APPENDIX. 317

STAGES.	Miles.	Furlongs.	REMARKS.
			it is overflowed with water; this is the reason assigned for there being no villages or forts in the plain here, and some of the stages in front. There is good grazing for camels, and forage for horses. About Shahr-i-Safa the road, the first three miles, is confined between a large water-course and the rising ground on the left, with several stony ascents and descents; afterwards it is good.
Terandaz	11	7	A pillar built to mark the flight of one of Ahmed Shah's arrows to the point of the hill on the left. There are six villages from one to three miles among the rising ground on the left. The Turnak river is about a quarter of a mile on the right. Camel-grazing good; horse-forage, the short green grass about the river, and some wheat-straw for purchase. The road is good, with the exception of being swampy at the five water-courses near the river, between the third and fourth mile, and the Khorzana Kotil, or pass, at 5¼ miles. About two furlongs of ascent and descent, slightly stony, and not very steep.
Jelloogheer	2		A narrow pass near the river, the name implying bridle-pull; it is also the name of the district. There are several villages among the rising ground at a distance on the left. There is much cultivation along the river here. There are several water-courses and broken ground in the first mile, besides the pass above mentioned.
Hulmee "Chukee"	6	7	Road to Hulmee good.
Camp Thoor .... from Terandaz, 10m. 5fr.	1	6	Thoor, the name of the spot the army encamped at; but no village. Some temporary huts in the fields, encamped along the Turnak river. Camel-forage moderate; for horses, the green grass of the river, and wheat-straw for purchase.
Aband of Jadak	5	5	Some small villages on the left, and considerable cultivation from thence towards the Turnak. A dry river and deep nullah, both from the left, are crossed here. The road is also confined, but good between the river and the rising ground, one mile before reaching this place. Some ruined gardens here, and buildings two miles further on, were pointed out, and stated to have been a place of importance in the times of the kings; and this is the usual stage.
Azeeree Chukee	4	3	A corn-mill, and considerable cultivation. Forage as above. Encamped along the Turnak river, two miles before reaching the chukee.
Kelat-i-Ghiljie, 84m. 2½fr. The ruins are high and extensive, the top "Balance" is seen a great way off; it has several fine springs on the top, which run down on two sides of the hill.	12		The ruins of an ancient fort and city. Encamped one mile beyond, between Amo Khans killas and the Turnak river. There are two forts here, an open village, and encampments of felt, with much cultivation; and supplies were furnished in limited quantity. It is stated that the family of Amo Khan was lately

318   APPENDIX.

STAGES.	Miles.	Furlongs.	REMARKS.
			driven from this place, and that it is now in possession of one of the Shaboodeen chiefs. The road is confined at Azeeree Chukee between the river, the water-course, and the rising ground on the left, for a short distance. Baggage and cavalry are recommended to go round it, by crossing the river. A road runs off to the right from Azeeree Chukee by a small stone bridge, which is the boundary between the Ghiljies and Dooranees. The protected road through Shahboodeen's country runs this way, along on the other side of the river, where the tolls are collected. The road on this side is reported as only passable to a large force, on account of the marauding practices of the people; the country opens out on the right from Azeeree Chukee, and several important forts appear.
Sar-i-Asp	10		A small round tower, being a monument over a horse; no village near, but considerable cultivation all along, and temporary huts. Turnak river near. The road is crossed by a large water-course in the first mile, muddy and inconvenient, and confined by it again in the second mile, to the hill or rising ground on the left; keeping still along the road, it crosses it again at six miles and a half, in four separate streams, some of them muddy and inconvenient; recrossing the road again at eight miles, in one large stream, three yards wide; some slight ascents and descents, generally stony, combine to render this stage fatiguing: some supplies were brought in for sale; forage as above.
Nauruk .... Name of the spot the army encamped at.	9	1	The road, the first mile and a half, is confined by the water-course that runs along the base of the rising grounds on the left, with several ascents and descents; the whole of the road after is a continuation of slightly stony ascents and descents. No village near: Nauruk is the name of this part of the valley. Considerable cultivation commences on the N.E.; camel-grazing good; forage, the green grass of the river, and wheat-straw for purchase; a few supplies were brought in here.
Tazee Chukee		3	A water-mill here; no village, but there are several killas in sight on the other side of the river, which is a quarter of a mile on the right. Much cultivation appears on the other side. Camel-grazing good; horse-forage, some short green grass, and wheat-straw for purchase. Road, the first three miles, is confined between the water-course and the base of the low hills on the left; afterwards good and open.
	8		
Shuftul	6	1	No village here: encampment near the Turnak river. Forage as above. The road crosses five deep dry nullahs, which are avoided in a considerable degree by keeping to the left.
Chasma-i-Sadee, or Chasma-i-Sar	9	4½	Several fine springs of water; much cultivation. Turnak river about one mile on the right. No village near

STAGES.	Distances.		REMARKS.
	Miles.	Furlongs.	
			here, but several killas of Takhae independent Ghiljies on the left, towards the hills, and on the opposite side of the river there are many small forts. From two to four miles off, the road is good and open, crossing a deep nullah with water in it at three miles and a half. Camel-forage good; for horses, green grass about the springs and river, and straw for purchase.
Chasma Panguk	5	5	Several fine springs, and Turnak river about two miles on the right; no village near, but several forts of Tinkhae Ghiljies on the left, towards the hills: there is much cultivation along the plain here. Forage as above. The road is good, excepting where it crosses a water-course in a deep wide nullah at two miles.
Ghojan................	12		Four forts, about two miles on the left of the road, and one khareez, a good stream of water, which runs across from the forts on the left to the extensive plain on the right. Camel-forage indifferent near the camp. A considerable quantity of lucern, green grass, and wheat. Straw was brought into camp, and supplies of flour, barley, &c. in abundance: road good.
Mukur, or Sir-i-Chusma .	12	1	The source of the principal feeder of the Turnak river, which issues from the base of the hill here on the left in many fine streams. This is a very extensive plain on the right, containing many forts and cultivation, and is midway between Kandahar and Cabul. Forage and supplies abundant; the road is good, with the exception of some uneven ground, and a deep dry ditch at five miles and a half; the best road is round the head of the springs at Mukur, close to the hill, as immediately below it is deep and swampy: the district of Mukur is in the province of Cabul.
Oba...................	14	2	A fine spring of water, the stream from which turns several mills. No village here, but several small forts at a distance on the right and left, and much cultivation along the plain. Two small streams cross the road at the tenth and eleventh mile. Forage, wheat, straw, and some short grass; camel-forage good: road good, over an open country the whole way.
Camp Futtehpore, near Moordan	11	4½	There are many forts in the plain here, some good streams, and much cultivation; a fine spring is passed at nine miles. Forage and supplies abundant here; the road is good and open, but crosses twelve dry nullahs.
Karabagh-i-char Deh Huzareh	3	4	This is a large killa, on the right of the road; three others near it, and the ruins of the Chuperkana, or stage of the mounted dawk of the kings, on the left of the road. Karabagh is the name of the district between Oba and Mooshakee, more particularly on the road, and to the right, as the plain on the left to the hills is very extensive, containing many forts and villages, both Afghans and Huzarehs. The country

STAGES.	Distances.		REMARKS.
	Miles.	Furlongs.	
			around appears populous and well cultivated. Road good : cross two streams.
Mooshakee	5	2½	Mooshakee is a small district on the right, of about eight killas, and considerable cultivation; the camp was formed south of a fakeer's place and peer on the high road, where there is good khareez of water, and a cultivated plain ; the road crossing eight streams of water in the cultivated plain, some of which are swampy and inconvenient for baggage: the last two miles ascents and descents, stony, along the base of some rising ground. Forage good : lucern in considerable quantity.
Yerghuttoo Camp Urghesan	8	7	Yerghuttoo is a small fort and village, about two miles on the left, entering, between the low hills, the plain on the right; is very extensive and cultivated, several killas appearing across the plain, which extends in that direction upwards of fifteen miles. Water, a good stream from the hills, on the left ; camel-forage good; for horses, grass was brought in for sale, as also supplies. The road is good the first two miles and a half, when it crosses, and runs along some very sandy nullahs ; a slight ascent then commences, which, for upwards of a mile, is a very stony, dry river-bed, which most of the baggage avoided to the right and left; the rest of the road is gravelly ; slight ascents and descents.
Nanee	6	6	A large place, a mile and a half on the right of the road. Camp at the ruins of the Chuparkana, or stage of the mounted dawk of the kings, which is on the left of the road here. There is a very extensive plain on the right, called the Shulgurh district. The ruins of the city of Shulgurh, and a high mound of earth, its citadel, or Balasir, is pointed out. About ten miles on the right there is much cultivation, and several large villages near Karabaghee, a large place about three miles N.E., with many gardens. The road is generally good ; a slight descent ; is stony at one mile; a river is crossed near the camp, which has a good stream of two or three yards here, and a wide stony bed. Supplies and forage abundant; lucern, green and dry.
Ghuznee	13	2	A fortified town, about one mile in circumference; appears to be very populous. The general height of the walls or rampart is forty feet, and in some places much more, independent of the depth of the wet ditch, which goes nearly round it. Its bazaar appears extensive, and is stated to be an entrepôt for merchandize, and many articles of supply between the Punjab, the Indus, and this country, and to be one of the principal sources of supply to Cabul. A fine river runs close past on its west and southern sides, over which are two bridges to the town. Much cultivation, and many

STAGES.	Distances.		REMARKS.
	Miles.	Furlongs.	
			killas and villages within a few miles on each side. The road from Nanee is moderately good in the first six miles, crossing one or two dry nullahs and five running streams. At six miles, some sandy, light, gravelly, deep road, and a broad sandy river-bed is crossed; at 7¼ miles, a fine clump of trees on right, and peer, with a remarkable tomb of forty children, called Chilbucha-Ghaum, on the left hand. A deep, narrow water-course is passed here, from whence the road is good to Ghuznee, passing many killas, gardens, and cultivated country.
Chasgon	14	4	Six killas on left. Khareez water a good stream; and considerable cultivation. Camel-forage moderate; for horses, lucern and straw for purchase. The road is good the first two miles and a half, until after it passes through the town of Roza, or suburb of Ghuznee, and burial-place of Shah Mahomed, which is large, with many gardens; the road then commences to ascend along the side of the hill, crossing six dry nullahs, and considerable ascent and descent for three miles, when it crosses a plain about three miles more to the entrance of Ghuznee pass (or Leana-i-Sher) from a ruined killa at the bottom, to the chokee at the top of the pass; it is two miles three furlongs; the ascent considerable, but easy, and in general of good breadth, and slightly stony in some parts. It is infested by notorious thieves, to guard against whom the chokees have been built. The road descends a little from this, and is good and open to Chasgon.
Huft Asya	9	1	Huft Asya is the name of the district in this part of the valley, where there are from ten to twelve walled villages in the last two miles and a half on the left. Khareez water, and considerable cultivation. Encamped near Sheenraz. Camel-forage good; for horses, a considerable quantity of short grass, straw, and lucern for purchase. The road is good, excepting some ascents and descents; slightly stony after the third mile, when the road runs along the base of the rising ground and small hills on the right. The walled villages near the road and district of Lora, or Lehda, on the left, is passed here. Several streams of water cross the road from the hills on the right at four miles; afterwards the road is again good.
Hyderkhail	11		A fort on the right, and another one mile on the left, with much cultivation. Forage for horses and camels good, and supplies water in khareez. A good stream crosses the road here at a peer, and small river a mile and a quarter on the left. These killas belong to, or are called, Khoja Russool Syuds, and lie between the districts of Tuckia and Saidabad. The road running between the base of the hilly ground on the right, and

STAGES.	Distances.		REMARKS.
	Miles.	Furlongs.	
			the cultivation on the left, is confined from the sixth to the ninth mile, especially near Tukea Killa, crossing three streams with stony ascents and descents from the right, which are muddy and inconvenient. Some water of the same description is crossed at a tower chokee. At the third mile the road has a general descent. Many killas are passed on the left in the first three miles. The district is called Sheeneez, and for the last five miles in the Tukea district. It was here that Futteh Khan, the vizier and elder brother of Dost Mahomed, was murdered.
Shekabad Camp .... Two miles beyond the large killa.	9	5½	Shekabad is a large killa on the left, with six other walled villages near, in a fine, cultivated valley, through which the river runs to the right; the same which, passing through the Loghur district, runs past the right of Cabul city. Encamped on the north of the river towards Zurnae Killa, which is on the left, two miles north of Shekabad. Forage and supplies plentiful. The road, after crossing the river at two miles, has Naib Gool Mahomed on the left, and the large killa of Shaidabad on the right, and is confined in several places by the water-courses and rising grounds on the left, from which the water runs through cultivated fields to the river on the right. The cultivation and killas of Shaidabad continue until the fifth mile, four killas on the left and six on the right, when two deep stony nullahs are crossed; the road is then good, though slightly stony, to the river, at Shekabad, which is about twenty yards broad, and eighteen inches deep, and has a narrow wooden bridge over it; there are several water-courses in this valley from the river, which are muddy and inconvenient for an army; the road in general descends gradually.
Bheenee Badam Camp....	10	7	Six killas, two, one mile, and four from two to two and a half miles on the left, and two or three killas on the right, two miles from the road. This is an extensive plain, with much cultivation; water one khareez at Bheenee Badam. The road is in general good, but confined a little about Tope, at three miles, by some nullahs and cultivation-banks. Tope is an ancient artificial mound, about one mile on the left, from which this district is named, and consists of six killas, terminated by Tope Chokee on the right; at the fifth mile the hills then retire further from the road, and it continues an extensive open plain to beyond Bheenee Badam.
Maidan Camp, about two and a half miles after entering the valley of Maidan............	7	4	An extensive cultivated valley, with many killas, inclosures, gardens, and a fine river; the same which runs through the city of Cabul: forage for horses and camels, good and plentiful, as also supplies. The road from Bheenee Badam crosses four large nullahs in the first three miles from the hills on the left, which are then

STAGES.	Distances.		REMARKS.
	Miles.	Furlongs.	
Urghandee Lower Camp Killa Kass-im, one mile beyond Urghandee Chokee .... Upper Urghandee is eight killas (from one to three miles) to left to the chokee.	12	2	near, and the road over them is in some parts stony, and, for some distance, runs along sandy nullahs. The road descends slightly to where it turns off to Maidan, passing Sher Mahomed Killa at three miles and a half, and, turning to the left at four miles and three-quarters, over a stony ascent and descent of about two furlongs, enters the valley of Maidan; the road is then good to the river, which is crossed at six miles. The road, after crossing the valley, is confined, muddy, and slippery; between the cultivation, a watercourse, and the base of the hill on which Sirisunga, a stone fort, is situated, which completely overlooks the road here, which then runs along the base of the hills,—on the right, a slight ascent, and stony in parts. Upper and Lower Urghandee is a district containing about fifteen killas on the left of the road here, a small river, with a good stream, and much cultivation. Killa Kass-im is an old or deserted killa on the bank of the river. Forage for camels indifferent, for horses good and plentiful, for purchase, as also supplies. The road from Maidan continues along the base of the hills on the right, and is confined and stony where it turns round the corner of the hills, leaving the valley at two miles and a half, and a little after a short ascent and descent, and after crossing a plain of two miles, some uneven ground, and a slight ascent, crossing four nullahs to a chokee, at seven miles, called Kotulac Fught; the road is then good, with a slight descent, to Urghandee Chokee, where the river is crossed; it is broad and stony. A large dry nullah continues on the right from near Kotulac Fught, and one is crossed before reaching Upper Urghandee, at nine miles and three-quarters behind which, the Cabul guns, abandoned by Dost Mahomed, were drawn up when the army passed.
Cabul City	13	4	To the west gate, through Mozung village. The road from Urghandee moderately good, passing Killa Kazee at five miles three furlongs; six forts on the right of the road: Sher Mahomed Killa at seven miles six furlongs and a half; Top-chee Bashee at eight miles three furlongs; Deh-i-Booree Pool at nine miles seven furlongs and a half; Mazung village, at eleven miles three furlongs, and the chokee at the bridge across the river to the right, where the works, or walls, run down the hills on either side, confining the road on each side of the river to a narrow passage: this road goes on this side of the river by Assamaee Chokee, and, crossing the river to the city gate, by Pool-i-Shai Dooshum Sherra, thirteen miles four furlongs. From Killa Kazee, the country on each side of the road is occupied by forts, villages, inclosures, gardens, and cultivation, to the city gate.

ROUTE from GHUZNEE to DERA ISMAEL KHAN.

Stages.	Koss.	REMARKS.
Ghuznee.		
Sheloghur	6	A village. Road good. Water from a khareez.
Wusta Joga	5	A small village. Good road. Water from a khareez.
Punna	5	Do. Water from a khareez. Road good.
Kakajan	5	Do. Good road. Water from a khareez.
Dund	4	Do. Water from river. Road good.
Zogun Shuhr	6	Do. Road indifferent. Water from a khareez.
Hundgaee	5	No village. Road as last stage. Water from a mountain-stream.
Surgo	4	A small village. Water from a mountain-stream. Road through hills.
Kalagur	5	Do. Water from river. Road indifferent.
Otman	4	No village. Road bad. Water from river.
Serae Mama Chular	4	Do. Road as before. Water from river.
Shedan	4	Do. Road indifferent. Water from river.
Khair Dongur	3	Do. Do. Do.
Ahmed Shah Kateh	4	Do. Road and water as before.
Turpurneea	4	Do. Do.
Parsuk	3	Do. Do.
Ispan Paee Kat	3	Do. Do.
Lemlakut	4	Do. Do.
Kota Raee	3	Do. Road very bad. Water from a mountain-stream.
Postcut	3	Do. Road as before. Water from do.
Shardan	3	Do. Road and water as before.
Dangubraee	3	Do. Road very bad. Water from do.
Rumoo	3	Do. Do. Water in abundance.
Nelace	4	Do. Road and water as before.
Jeraee	3	Do. Do.
Cheirjagarain	3	Do. Do.
Maj-gurra	4	A village. Road good. Water from a khareez.
Soouk Deeval	4	Do. Do. Do.
Shumkool	3	Do. Do. Do.
Geraee Reman	4	Do. Do. Do.
Darabund	4	A large town. Water from a khareez. Road good.
Goondee Azim Khan	4	Do. Do. Do.
Metaee	3	Do. Water and road good.
Dera Ismael Khan	7	A large town on the Indus.
Total	136	

At least one month's supplies required to be carried along with an army. Forage for horses and camels is abundant throughout. The road is represented to be easy for troops and carriage. The road at Kota Raee, and from Dangubraee to the foot of the ghaut at Maj-gurra, will be found difficult for artillery.

ROUTE from DERA GHAZEE KHAN to KANDAHAR, through the Sakhee Sarwar Pass and Buzdar Pass.

No. I.

Dera Ghazee Khan.

Charatta—Nine miles, two hundred houses, two wells, six miles and a half from Dera Ghazee Khan; the Sharya canal crosses the road. It is thrown off by the river, nine miles above, at Gurmanee, and waters the country to five miles below, at Paga; at a mile further, the Manika canal crosses the road. It is thrown off by the river, at a place called Chainsalla, twenty-seven miles above, and extends twenty-five miles to the south, to a place called Hawan.

Wador, through brushwood..} Nine miles; four hundred houses; one well, one hundred and twelve feet deep.

Sakhee Sarwar, a stony road } 18 miles { a large village and a mausoleum. } { Water brought from a spring in the mountains, five miles distant. }

Siree.—Fourteen miles, through an uninhabited road; a desolate fort; a fine stream. The pass commences four miles out of Sakhee Sarwar, by a steep descent; it then runs through a ravine, whose bed is covered with large stones. It is commanded by the steep faces of the hill. The mountains have been deserted on account of the frequent attacks of the Marus. Runjeet Singh has in his employ two influential men of these mountains, viz. Jata Omalonee and Bidda Amadanee; both, however, under the command of Jalal Khan Lagharee.

Ascent of the Suliman range (Kalee-roh) at a place called Ootpalana, or camel-saddle: some say from the shape of the hill, some say from the steepness, which causes even a saddle to fall off in the ascent.

This is a zig-zag road for horses and camels; the face of the mountain covered with loose stones, that each shower brings down. There is an easier road to the south, that goes to Raknee, but not for a moment to be reckoned a gun-road.

A table of 5 miles, and a descent of the same, to a place called Raknee	10 miles.	40 reed huts of Languee Kathryans, under Meer Hajee Khan, of Darazoo Kot.	A rivulet.

The gun-road from the Derajat to Racknee enters the mountains from Sangad, and is as follows:—

Sangad, commencement of the pass, fort of Roh	16 miles.	50 houses of Jaths.	A stream and valley.
Sude wad	14 miles.	Scattered huts of Buzdars of the Backaree clan, under Pandee.	The above stream.
Ambar	13 miles.	A granary of the Buzdars and Sadhwanees, in caves.	Ditto ditto.
Manjawal	14 miles.	Uncertain habitations of Buzdar shepherds.	Ditto ditto.
Raknee	12 miles.	A good gun-road.	

From Sangad to Kandahar is a gun-road. There are quantities of grain, wheat, rice, and barley in Ambar, Darazoo, in Barakam, Chotyaly, Tal, Dukkeede, in fact, on the whole road; water is plentiful, as well as firewood, except at Baghas and Samalan. There are sheep to be procured along the whole road. Camels are procurable at Tal, Barakam, Kholoo, and Pishing. The inhabitants are quiet. There is a road from Racknee to Chotyaly, as follows:—

APPENDIX.

Raknee.

Darazoo-ka-Kot, the residence of Hajee Khan and 400 Kathryans.	20 miles.	A large village, 600 houses.	A stream from Kholoo, called Han, as well as rain-water.
Kooh, the head of the Han stream.	5 miles.	No habitation, except in the neighbourhood, which is inhabited by Kathryans.	
A difficult, steep, narrow ascent and descent, Nika Pannee	12 miles.	No habitations.	Sufficient water for drinking.
Fort of Dhost Mahomed Khan, a level road from the former stage.	5 miles.	200 houses of Zarkan Pathans.	Rain-water in wells.
Fort of Fazulkhan	1 mile.	100 houses ditto ditto.	ditto ditto.
Ditto ditto Alykhan	1 mile.	100 houses.	ditto ditto.
Chotyaly, over hills passable for camels and horses	36 miles.		

There is no water to be met with on the road, except in most inconsiderable quantities and uncertain places, which, however, when found, is too salt to drink.

The remaining gun-road from Racknee to Kandahar is as follows:—

Racknee.

Chobara	4 miles.	200 houses, Ishyanee Kathryans, under Mahar, and Dakoo Malaks.	A rivulet, as well as water in tanks.
Darazoo Kot	16 miles.	Before described.	
Kooh, the head of the Han stream.	5 miles.	Before described.	
For Chapper, or Black Hill: not to be passed	10 miles.	No habitations: a rivulet.	The road level: a slight ascent; soap-stone met with.
Baba Dakai, a hill which is turned; the road leading through the bed of the stream	8 miles.	No fixed habitations; shepherds sometimes come here for a few months.	
Swang, or ford; knee-deep. The stream called Hanokee	6 miles.	No habitations.	
Palyanee	14 miles.	Twenty habitations: Zarkan Pathans, under Sabab Khan, who is under Fazal Khan, of Kholoo.	
Chotyaly	12 miles.	400 houses of Tareens, under Biland Khan.	Water from Baree.
Sobha Khan's fort	1½ miles.	200 houses of Usturijanees.	The former rivulet.
Tal, famous for wheat, which is produced to a great extent	12½ miles.	700 houses of Tareens, under Sobha Khan, Faizulla Khan, Huzur Khan, Abdulla Khan, and Baboo Khan.	Ditto, ditto, and tanks.
Durkkee, or Rah	14 miles.	400 houses of Tareens, under Gul Rag.	Water from Baghao; plentiful cultivation.
Baghaw	10 miles.	600 houses. Dhumad Kukads, under Hufam Khan and Peraz Khan.	A stream rises here.
Sinzaoee	7 miles.	300 houses of Dhumads.	A spring of water.
Chinjan	11 miles.	Uninhabited. In the neighbourhood are Zikhpel Dhumads.	A stream, from which a few acres are cultivated.

APPENDIX. 327

Chadee	11 miles.	{ A few houses of Sanatya Kakads.	{ A stream, in the bed of which the road runs.
Karez	8 miles.	{ 300 houses of Sanatya Kakads.	} Springs of water.
Ingland	9 miles.	{ 60 houses of Sanatya Kakads.	} Sets of springs.
Bazaar in the valley of Pishing ..	13 miles.	{ 30 houses of Battezai Tareens, under Painda Khan.	} The river of Surkhab.

Gulisthan Karez, sixteen miles, before described; this road is a gun-road. Hajee Khan Kakad brought two guns with him from Kandahar, and engaged the Tareens of Tal-Hajee Khan. Could secure protection and aid to an army passing by this road.

No. II.

The road of ROD BAHAR, from BEEBEE NANEE, in the Bolan Pass, to KELAT.

Beebee Nanee.

Jam, and Baradee, twelve miles: 100 houses of Prij Belooches. They do not pay tribute to Mihrab Khan, and are generally employed in guarding caravans through the pass of Bolan. The water is in mountain-springs. Rice, wheat, barley, and juwarree are cultivated here, and there are gardens of mulberries, apricots, peaches, and grapes. Indeed, the fertility of this road may be inferred from its name—Rod-bahar, signifying the valley of spring. From Beebee Nanee, the first six miles is in a plain; the road then enters the pass, which is 150 yards wide, in which a half-hid stream runs. The two villages of Jam and Baradee are off the road, on an elevated plateau. The next stage is Zer-i-Kotal, "foot of pass," a distance of twenty miles. There are no habitations here, nor on the road. The stream at the stage is plentiful. After leaving Jam Baradee, the valley opens out to the breadth of three miles, in which the tamarisk-tree forms a jungle, and in which plain the water is lost. The pass is then formed again, and the water again appears; at four miles distant from the foot of the pass, the stage is level. On the top of the pass, three-quarters of a mile from the bottom, are the ruins of an old town, the streets of which are still to be traced, and several sunken spots denote the site of wells or reservoirs. The natives have searched in vain for old coins. The city is said to have belonged to Giours (Greeks).

The road from the old town then descends a little—again ascends—and finally, has a considerable descent, and takes a level nature and a third descent, to Sar-i-Deh. A collection of wild fig-trees, and water in stagnant pools, a distance of eighteen miles. This stage goes by the name of Rod Bahar; it is supplied throughout its length with water, and is cultivated in patches of wheat, rice, and juwarree; peaches, apricots, mulberries, &c. also abound in small gardens. In this stage there are about four hundred houses of Prij Mughandooee and Kulooe Brahiris, who are cultivators. Firewood is plentiful. The next stage is Irarmookh, four miles, inhabited in the summer by Brahui shepherds, viz. Ladees, Janooees, and Kulooees, to the amount of 150 tents. The water is in three wells, and the cultivation depends on the rain. This stage is out of the pass. Narmookh is on a plain, which is divided from the plain of Takht by a projecting range of hills. From Narmookh, the next stage is Takht, fourteen miles, inhabited only in the summer months by wandering shepherds. If rain falls, water will be found at Takht. The next stage is Johan, fifteen miles, a fort containing thirty houses of Johanees, under Kadar Dad, the son of Sahab Khan Johanee. The water here is in a running stream.

Rice and wheat are cultivated to some extent, and there are a few gardens. The next stage is Kishan, twelve miles, containing ten houses, under Jangee Kishanee.

z 2

The water is in a running stream. Rice and wheat are cultivated to some extent, and there are a few gardens. The next stage is Kishan, twelve miles, containing ten houses, under Jangee Kishanee. The water is in a running stream. There is some cultivation. Kelat is thence fifteen miles.

This road is passable to cavalry and camels, but by no means to guns. Snow does not fall in the pass, its boundary being Narmookh (Narmool of maps). The inhabitants begin to emigrate to Cutchee (Cutch Gundava) by the middle of September, some on account of the cold, others on account of the scarcity of grass for their flocks, and the remaining cannot stay behind, as they would be too weak to withstand the plundering attacks of the Dhumad Kakuds. The heaviest falls of snow in Kelat do not cover the ground knee-deep, and it never remains on the ground for more than seven days. Snow begins to fall in the beginning of December, and lasts to the end of February.

When the inhabitants of Rod Bahar emigrate to Cutchee, they first bury their grain, and cover it very artfully, so as to escape observation. The inhabitants return to Rod Bahar by the end of March. Wheat is sown in the end of August, and reaped in the beginning of April. Rice, or the rabbee crop, is sown in the middle of May, and reaped in the middle of September.

There is grazing-ground on the mountains, for flocks, during March, April, and May, and forage for horses might be procured during May. The wheat-stalks could be given to horses as long as they lasted.

No. III.

Road from MANZILJAH, at the entrance of the Bolan Pass, to KELAT.

Manziljah, in the Dasht Khurd, or small plain called Bedoulat. There are no habitations here, neither is there water. It is said, however, to have been brought by Meer Nusser Khan, Brahui chief of Kelat, from Zadakhoo, a spring ten miles to the north, by means of a small duct, to furnish the army of Ahmed Shah Duranee. From Manziljah to Marow is ten miles, over a level road, having only one slight hill. This village contains five hundred houses of Koodds, under Sardar Ala Dinna. There is plenty of good spring-water. Wheat and juwarree are plentifully cultivated. From Marrow to Isplinjee is ten miles, over a level road. The water is in springs. The village contains five hundred houses, of Bangulzais Brahuis, under Noor Mahommed Wadera (Patel). From Isplinjee to Koohak is sixteen miles, over a level road. The water is in wells. The village is only inhabited in the summer, as are the other villages on the road, to the extent of six hundred houses, of Bangulzais Badoozais, who pay taxes to the Mahommud Shahees, the owners of the soil.

From Koohak to Gazah, a set of worked springs in the district of Mangochar, twenty-four miles; a level road, having no water or habitations on the way. Mangochar is three miles distant to the right. It contains two thousand houses of Sangaws. It is under Kelat. From Gazah to kareez (spring) of Girance is ten miles. There is a spring called Shireenah, four miles from Gazah. The road is level. Karez-i-Girance contains, in the winter, thirty habitations, and in summer two hundred, of mixed Brahui tribes. The water here is remarkably good compared with that of Kelat. From Karez-i-Girance to Kelat is eight miles, the last three miles being through fields and gardens.

No. IV.

Road from KOT (Kwettah of maps) to KELAT, from my journal.

Left Kot, the road passing between two hills, and reached Saryab, a distance of seven miles. There are no habitations here. The water is in worked springs, in which are a quantity of fish. This is an extremely cold place in winter. A report prevails that two caravans, one of indigo and one of madder, proceeding from Hindostan, were caught in a fall of snow; the madder-merchant offered to burn his madder if the other would share the cost. The indigo-merchant refused, encamped at a distance, and perished in the night from the cold.

Passing a hill at four miles from Saryab, entered a plain, and keeping along the skirt of the hills to the left, to avoid the deep rugged nullahs that cut up the lower plain, reached Pilingabad, a further distance of eight miles. The town of Teeree is in the neighbourhood. Pilingabad contains about three hundred houses of Afghans, and is surrounded by fine gardens of apricots, almonds, mulberries, and grapes. The former grow to the height of English elm-trees, and the vines are trained up them.

Marched four miles and a half to Mastung, a walled town, situated in a wilderness of gardens. It contains about 3,500 houses; and a naib, or governor, on the part of Mehrab Khan, generally resides here. Mastung is famous for its melons. The inhabitants in the neighbourhood are Mashwanees and Sangaos, and a sprinkling of the different other tribes of Sarawan Brahuis. The seasons in Mastung are twenty days in advance of those of Kelat.

The direct road from Mastung to Kelat is then, *viâ* Mangochar, as follows:—

Mastung Cha (well) of Guroo: situated in the Kad (vale) of Mastung } 12 miles. No habitations. { The road is perfectly level.

Mangocha .. .. 16 miles. Before described.

This road is only chosen when express is required, on account of the distances between the watering-places.

The other road, the same by which I travelled, is as follows:—

Left Mastung and marched by the roundabout road to Kelat. Halted at Shirenab; no habitations. The water is in worked springs and salt to the taste. The distance is twelve miles. The neighbourhood abounds in hares.

Marched seven miles to khareez (worked springs) of Dost Mahomed, the road running through a valley. Thirty habitations. Cultivation.

Marched nine miles to the Zyarat (mausoleum) of Zard. Twenty houses inhabited, and the like number in ruin. At half a mile in front is a garden, the fruit of which was this year destroyed by a blight.

Marched eight miles to Sar-i-Khareez. No habitations, except twelve in ruins. A small stream. Mangochar was visible to the left.

Marched sixteen miles to Zyrat, a village containing two hundred houses. Mehrab Khan's stud is stationed here.

Marched four miles to Kelat. This road is a gun-road throughout.

ROUTE from GHUZNEE to QUETTA.

STAGES.	Distances.		REMARKS.
	Miles.	Furlongs.	
Ghuznee to Mooshakee	26		*Vide* Route from Kandahar to Cabul.
Killa-i-Bukshee	10	2	Road over an extensive plain, bounded by a high range of hills to the north, and a lesser range to the south; road excellent the whole way, with the exception of some water-courses to cross, of no great difficulty. Several villages passed both on and near to the road, besides encampments of felt tents belonging to Loohanees, who come here during summer for pasturage for their camels. Killa-i-Bukshee is a collection of several walled villages. The inhabitants about here are Turkhee and Andharee Ghiljies. Supplies abundant and cheap.
Atuk	10		Road good over undulating ground, with a low range of hills to the right. Passed a good many water-courses, besides several dry nullahs. Supplies not very abundant. Atuk, and the hamlets belonging to it, are inhabited by Populzee Dooranees. The district is called Jamrad.
Islam Killa	13	3	Road excellent, with a slight descent, passing, at seven miles and a half, a peer's tomb, on the left, situated on an eminence. Supplies and forage abundant. Islam Killa is in the Mookur district; and this part is called Seer-i-Mookur (the head of it).
Camp about two miles N. of Jaz	12	2	Road good, over a dusty plain, crossing a deep ravine soon after leaving our camp, which was to the north of Islam Killa. Passed two walled villages on our route; the first called Kurdee Killa, the second Ars Behgee, after its owner, now a prisoner at Cabul. The Mookur district terminates here. Supplies were not brought in any quantity to camp; but the district is a very rich one.
Munsoor Khareez	12	5	Road good over undulating ground, crossing two large, dry ravines. Munsoor Khareez is a collection of three or four hamlets, situated on the bank of the Abistada lake. Supplies were scarce, and very little cultivation was seen. Our camp was on the border of a small stream of fine water running into the lake. This is the first stage in the country of the independent Ghiljies, under the sons of Shaboodeen Khan, whose principal fort of Nowa is about twenty miles to the west, and south of the range of hills that bound the valley of the Turnak on the left bank. The Abistada lake is about forty miles in circumference; the water is brackish, and its banks are deeply incrusted with salt: its great feeder is the Ghuznee river, and

STAGES.	Distances.		REMARKS.
	Miles.	Furlongs.	
			is formed from the water not being able to find a passage out at the S.W. corner; the brackish taste to it is given by the quantity of salt in the soil. There are only two or three wretched villages situated on its banks, and its silent water, with the surrounding mountains and barren country, presented a melancholy appearance.
Bara Kail............	13	2½	The road followed the western bank of the lake for five miles and a half, when it crossed a range of hills, but passable for guns, then over a plain to our encampment. Bara Kail is the name of several large open villages near to each other. Supplies were abundant. This district is inhabited by Khan Turkee Ghiljies, the chief of whom resides in his fort, about ten miles south of this place.
Jumeeat	11	7½	The road, this march, took a more easterly direction, in consequence of our having altered the line of route from hence to Quetta. The road was good, with the exception of some dry water-courses. Several villages were visible to the right and left of the road; but Jumeeat itself is a small place.
Kishanee............	8		Road good, nearing a range of hills running from east to west, under which we encamped. Kishanee is the name of several villages, or rather hamlets; that close to our camp is called Mapan. The Ghiljies here belong to the Astuk tribe.
Ghondan	11	0½	The road, this march, was very bad; and the guns were with difficulty taken over it; the first seven miles was a succession of ascents and descents, across the range of hills noticed in the last march; the last descent into the opposite valley was good. This is called Julloo Kotul. Passed, at 8½ miles, a small hamlet and a saint's tomb; and encamped on the bank of a dry, deep ravine, with a good stream of water in a small canal close to it. Ghondan is a lofty hill close to the left of our camp, and gives name to this district. The Ghiljies in this valley are called Tokhees; their chief, Kullul Khan, has a fort about two miles N.E. of our camp.
Busoor Kail	10	0¼	The road ascended gradually for about two miles, then a descent to the dry bed of a large nullah, after which, at about four miles, crossed a range of hills by the Sheree Kotul. The road was not good, but our light guns met with no obstruction. Busoor Kail is a small village, with two or three similar ones near it. We have ascended considerably since leaving Jumeeat.
Spinawaree	11	5½	The first five miles of the road winds amongst the hills, but with a considerable descent. At five miles passed the hamlet of Moosa Astuk. Spinawaree is the name of a small mound in the valley, and by which

STAGES	Miles	Furlongs	REMARKS
			the district is called. A large ravine, with a good deal of water, runs to the rear of our camp. A road from Dera Ismael Khan to Kandahar, used by the Kaffillas,* crosses here.
Soorkab	10	2	The road, for the first seven miles, winds amongst the hills, with several ascents and descents; it then joins the Soorkab river, and follows its windings, with a considerable ascent, to where we encamped; near a few huts called Nadir Deh, a little forage was found in pits, secreted by the inhabitants, but no supplies obtained. The river is confined between ranges of high hills, and the road along the bed of the river was over loose stones, making it very laborious for the horses dragging the guns.
Sir-i-Soorkab	10	0½	The road follows the windings of the river the whole distance, ascending considerably, and was of the same description as the last part of the preceding march; a few huts were passed, but all deserted; we encamped near the source of this branch of the river.
Khardoo Chummum	13	3½	Passed several wells on the road, called Babur-kacha, said to have been dug by the Emperor Babur, and encamped near a small stream of running water coming from the hills to the east. The road followed the Soorkab river for the first mile, it then ascended considerably, crossing a range of hills, it then descended gradually for some miles, again crossing a smaller range near to our encampment. No village of habitation seen during the march, but a few villagers came into camp and shewed where forage was to be had. The road to-day was very fatiguing for both horses and camels.
Kudunee	7	6	The road followed the bed of the stream near our last camp, ascending to its source, passing at one mile and a quarter the small village of Patee, inhabited by Baurikzai Dooranees; it then crossed a range of hills and descended to a few huts on the branch of the Kudunee river, having a good supply of water, near which we encamped. Some forage for our horses was procured.
Tokuruk	11	0½	The road to-day was very bad, having to cross a range of hills, where at times even a foot-path was not to be seen. We encamped in a hollow, on the bank of a fine stream of water, near a few huts inhabited by Sudozai Dooranees. Tohuruk is the name of the district.
Cutch Toba	12	3	The road this march was better than the last three, generally following the bed of a river, having to cross some low hills before reaching our encampment. No village near, but in the hills are several hamlets inhabited by the Kawkers, whose country extends to the valley of Pisheen, and who are under Hajee Khan,

* The proper spelling is "Kafilah."

STAGES.	Distances.		REMARKS.
	Miles.	Furlongs.	
Hajee Khan's Fort of Toba	7	3	the noted chief that has played so conspicuous a part in the politics of Afghanistan. We encamped about two miles west of the fort, the road following a small stream for about five miles, when it passed over a small range of hills, and we halted close under another range on the opposite side of the valley. Hajee Khan's fort was deserted, and no supplies to be had.
Shargullee	12	6	The road for the first two miles ascended the bed of a nullah; it then descended down a deep ravine, confined by very high ranges of hills, to where we encamped, passing a small village called Soorkhow, about one mile from the place we halted at. This is the last range of hills to be crossed, as the water here runs to the Lora river, in Pisheen. The road was very bad to-day, lying in the bed of a mountain stream, covered with loose stones. The inhabitants had not deserted the village, and some few supplies were procured.
Hassin Khan's Village, in Badshara	8	2	We descended the same valley as yesterday, leaving the river to our left for the first four miles; the road was better than for several marches, and the valley much broader; several villages were passed, and many of the inhabitants had remained; whereas, from Busoor Kail we found the country generally deserted. Supplies of grain and flour were procured, but very dear.
Camp between Toresha and Pacen Killa	16	2	The road followed the bed of the river for about seven miles, with a range of hills on each side, when it entered the valley of Pisheen, the river running north of the route. From this the road was excellent, passing the villages of Noorzai, Moleeka, and Toresha to our camp, which was on the bank of a fine stream, called the Soorkab. Supplies abundant.
Hydurzye	14	2	Road excellent, joining the Kandahar route two miles before arriving at Hydurzye.
Quetta	21	2½	*Vide* Route to Kandahar.

ROUTE from SHAWL to KELAT.

STAGES.	Miles.	Furlongs.	REMARKS.
Quetta to Ispunglee	5	4	Road good, excepting having to cross a deep nullah about half-way. There is a more direct road to Kelat from Quetta, but not practicable for guns.
Burg	9	6½	Road excellent, leading up a valley about eight miles wide; a small running stream, and four or five villages, on the right, some distance towards the hills.
Kunuk	12	6	Road as yesterday, leading up the same valley, and equally good. A stream of water on the right of the camp, and the village of Kunuk visible about two miles south-west.
Mustoong	15	2	Road good as far as Teree, a large village; about eleven miles on the road from thence had a deep ravine, and several water-courses between it and Mustoong. From Teree there is a direct road to Kelat, leaving Mustoong to the left; but it was necessary that we should have gone there, on account of supplies that had been laid in for the troops. Mustoong is a place with a good many gardens near, but the town seems to be going to decay. The district was under the Khan of Kelat, who had a Naib here, but, since Merab Khan's demise, is to be given over to Shah Shoojah. The inhabitants are Belooches and Hindoos.
Shireen-ab	11	6	After marching due west for about eight miles, the road sweeps to the south, and enters a valley, the same as from Ispunglee to Kunuk, and is equally good. There was no village near our camp, but the name of a small river to the right, where we halted, with plenty of water in it.
Khareez Dost Mahomed	9	3¼	A small village, with a spring of water from the hills, besides the Shireen-ab river. Road excellent, with a slight ascent. The village was almost deserted, both on account of the troops, and it being the custom of the inhabitants to emigrate to Cutch Gundava on the approach of winter.
Zurd	12	2	Two or three small villages, but deserted; a good stream of water, and the road excellent, still continuing up the same valley as before.
Bureen Chinar	9	4½	An aqueduct, and much cultivated ground, but the village was deserted. This is near the head of the valley. Mungoocha was visible to the left, by which the direct road comes from Kelat, but is not convenient for troops, on account of a scarcity of water.
Girance	17	7	Encamped on a fine stream of water; several villages near, and the road good.

STAGES.	Distances.		REMARKS.
	Miles.	Furlongs.	
Kelat	8	2	A strong walled town, besides a lofty inner citadel. The suburbs are also very extensive, and a good many gardens to the east. This is the residence of the Khan of Beloochistan. The road from the last ground was very good, with hills on both sides, until within a mile of Kelat. A river runs to the east of the suburbs of the town.

ROUTE from KELAT to KOTREE.

STAGES.	Miles.	Furlongs.	REMARKS.
Kelat to Rodenjo	14	7	A village of about fifty houses, but deserted since the fall of Kelat. A fine stream of water runs past the village, which comes from the hills on the east. The first two miles of the road was up the bed of a dry river, with an ascent; the rest of the road is very good, over a plain, with a slight descent. No appearance of cultivation until we reached Rodenjo.
Soorma Sing	12		Name of a river about one mile west of the encamping-ground, in which there is plenty of water. Road excellent, over a plain of the same description as the latter part of the first march.
Sohrab	16	3	A collection of several villages, generally deserted since the approach of the troops; but in times of peace had a large population, with sixty or more Hindoo shops. Water in streams, from the hills to the east. Road very good, and over a plain.
Angeera	14	1	Three or four houses lately deserted, formerly inhabited by Zehree Belooches, under Sirdar Rusheed Khan, whose tribe extends from this through the Moola Pass as far as Kotree. We encamped about half a mile north of the village, close to a small running stream, that comes from the west. The first part of the road went close to the hills on the right; there descended, and entered the dry bed of a nullah, which is the source of the river that runs through the pass. The road to Soomeana Bunder branches off to the right.
Bapow	11	6¾	A good-sized village, about a mile to the north of the road, surrounded by fruit-trees; deserted on the approach of the troops. Water from the hills, in a running stream above the village. There was a considerable descent in this march. The road, soon after leaving camp, entered the bed of the river, dry for the first three miles, after that a running stream a few inches deep, having to cross it several times. This march may be said to be in the pass. Very high mountains visible in every direction.
Pesee Bent	12	5	No village. Bent means an opening in the valley, and Pesee is the name of a fruit which grows wild in the pass. This march lay entirely in the bed of the river, dry for about ten miles, where a stream gushes out of the rocks to the right, and we had water for the rest of the way, but not deep. There was a considerable but gradual descent during this stage, and at about ten miles and a half the hills on each side sud-

APPENDIX.

STAGES.	Distances.		REMARKS.
	Miles.	Furlongs.	
Putkee	11	7	denly closed, and approached to within twenty or thirty feet, and at least five hundred feet high, almost perpendicular. An enemy might here make a stand, and effectually prevent any troops from passing, merely by rolling a few blocks of loose stone down into the pass, which would close it, and there is no possible way of turning the defile. Passed at seven miles the deserted village of Mordana: considerable signs of cultivation. Here the road leaves the river for about a couple of miles, which goes to the right, and joins it again before arriving at the place we encamped at. The river was crossed several times, but the water was not deep. A good deal of tamarisk jungle this march. The valley was about three hundred yards wide at our halting-ground.
Paeesht Khana	10	4	The first five miles of the march was very tedious, having to cross the water several times, and the bed of the river very stony: from thence the hills opened into a large plain, with a much better road, the river taking a sweep to the north-east, to meet another stream which comes from Panduran. The ruins of a village were at Paeesht Khana, which is the name of this open plain. A direct road from Kelat joins here, which comes by Joorgee and Panduran. It is not practicable for guns.
Nurd	11	6	At three miles passed Peer Luttoo, a fakeer's abode, close to the left of the road; at eight miles Dodandan, two peaks on a high range of hills to the right. The first half of the march had to cross the river several times; the river then turns to the right and joins another stream, following which is a road to Kozdar, by Guz Gooroo and Zeedee. A few huts near our camp, and some supplies were obtained. The hills were close on each side for about six miles; the valley there opened a good deal.
Jang-i-Kooshta	12	2	From Bapow to Nurd, our direction had been about south-east, but from the commencement of this day's march it took a sudden turn to the north, and continued so for about six miles; then for half a mile nearly south; then again north. At six miles and a half, passed the tomb of Lakka—the mausoleum of the saint of that name, the adopted son of Lal Shah Bbaz, whose shrine is at Sehwan. Road, as usual, generally followed the course of the stream, with a considerable descent.
Bent-i-Jah	10	4	Passed the village of Hootachee, at seven miles. First part of the road very good, having the river to the right. A village here, and some supplies.
Camp, one mile a half short of Kohow	11	2½	First part of the march left the river to the right, passing Pancewun to the left; after that, a jungle to go through, and the last two miles crossed the water

STAGES.	Distances.		REMARKS.
	Miles.	Furlongs.	
Kullar	10	0¼	several times. The road abounding in large stones; the valley very confined where we encamped. The first mile of the road very bad, having the water to cross; it then left the river, and ascended an elevated plain to the right, when at six miles it descended again, and enters the pass of Nowlung, having to pass the river several times with the hills close on each side. Kullar, the name of a ruined village, and is the end of the pass.
Kotra	13	2¾	Left the river, which goes to the east, and marched over a plain to Peer Chutta, a place where there are sacred fish; the road then for a short distance entered the bed of a river, very stony; then ascends, and is excellent to Kotra, passing half-way from Peer Chutta, the tomb (a handsome building) of Mahomed Eltozai. Kotra is a large place with a good bazaar, principally inhabited by Hindoos from Shikarpoor.

ROUTE from DADUR to KANDAHAR.

STAGES.	Distances.		REMARKS.
	Miles.	Furlongs.	
Dadur to Kondilan and Kundye	10	5	The names of places where kafilas usually halt, situated on either bank of a fine running stream. About five miles after leaving Dadur, the pass is entered, and the road occasionally crosses a stream of water from a few inches to about two feet deep; the breadth of the valley generally about half a mile wide, and the hills running to five or six hundred feet high. There is a slight ascent the whole way, and the road, although stony, offers no obstruction to guns. Camel forage scarce, and only some coarse grass to be had for horses.
Garmal, near Kirta	10	3	The road in this march still ascends, crossing the same stream as yesterday seventeen times, and, altogether, a more difficult march than the first. Camel and horse forage the same as the first stage.
Beebee Nanee	9	3	A good road over a plain, with a slight ascent passing about half-way through a small pass, called Jellowghur. Our encampment still on the same stream, but which takes a sweep some more miles to the right. Forage of all kinds scarce, and which is indeed the case until you reach Seri-ab-Beebee Nanee: lies on an elevation of 1,400 feet.
Ab-i-goom	9	6½	A more perceptible ascent to-day, Ab-i-goom being 2,200 feet above the sea, and the march fatiguing to the men, from the road lying in the dry bed of a river (the same we had during the march from Dadur), the water of which loses itself here, and does not appear again until near Beebee Nanee.
Sir-i-Boolan	8	5	This is the head of the spring, there being no water from this to Sir-i-ab; it is a fine stream, gushing out of a rock on the left of the road: ascended during this march 1,800 feet.
Sir-i-ab	27	6½	From Sir-i-Boolan to the top of the pass is ten miles; from thence the road to Sir-i-ab is over a desert plain, called Dost-i-Beh-Dowlut. Not a drop of water, and nothing seen but wild thyme. The top of the pass is 5,100 feet high. Sir-i-ab is the head of a fine spring, and has several small villages near. Camel forage good, and lucerne to be bought.
Quetta	8	1	Road good. A large town, sometimes called Kote, and at other times goes by the name of Shawl, of which district it is the chief place.
Abdool Rahim Khan	2	7	A small village, with a running stream, and some cultivation.

STAGES.	Distances.		REMARKS.
	Miles.	Furlongs.	
Ascent commences	3	1	The road to this crosses three running streams and two river-beds; they are shallow, but one of them is muddy, and has a small stream of water. The other streams are swampy in some places.
Top of the ascent	2	1½	The ascent is very gradual but stony, crossing five stony nullahs from the high hills on right.
Descent to the level plain, and cross two streams.	1	4	The descent for one furlong is rather steep; the guns came down with the drag-chain, without unyoking the horses. Afterwards, along the bottom of the defile, gradual, but rough and stony, like the dry bed of a river. The heights require to be guarded from the attacks of plunderers. Two large streams come out from the base of the hills on right here, which are crossed to the level plain, in which Kuchlack lies.
Some report of a better road to the left was current among the Shawl people; the plain appears to run on from both sides, in that direction quite open; it may be a little longer.			
Kuchlack	1	2½	Kuchlack is a small village on the bank of the brook, with a small fort three furlongs beyond it. There are several other forts and villages near, in this extensive plain, and much green cultivation. This village is between two and three miles from the base of the Tukatoo mountain, the double point of which is the highest in the range; it was wreathed with snow a great way down, and stated to be upwards of eight thousand feet above the level of the sea. The inhabitants retired to the mountains on the approach of the army: they were induced to return by the Bombay division when they passed, and brought some few supplies for sale.
Camp, 11 5½ General direction, N.		5½	
Cross Lora River ...... (Eighty yards wide)	2		A good stream, five or six yards water, eighteen inches deep, between thirty and forty feet beneath the level of the plain; banks perpendicular in some places.
Cross a deep Nullah	3	2	The road now winding a little among low sandy hills or rising ground, but good; dusty, but not deep.
Cross another deep Nullah	1	3	
Cross Lora River	1	2	A good stream, twenty inches deep, three or four yards broad, thirty feet below banks muddy.
Ditto ditto again		6	Do. do.
Hydurzye..............		5	A small village, with considerable cultivation. There is another village, about one mile to the left, on the opposite bank of the river, inhabited by Syuds. The village was deserted on the approach of the army: a few of the men remained during the time. Care should be taken to guard the baggage from the Kowkur Beloochees who infest the higher range on left. The Syuds, though not plunderers themselves, through fear connive at the thievery of the Kowkurs.
Camp, 9 6 N.18 E.		4	
Cross a large Nullah	3	4	Over a fine open plain.
Cross a dry River, 10ft.deep N. 10 E.		3	Another road runs along the side of the hills on left, said to be more direct; the open plain continues on right, with short green grass.
Cross a dry Nullah, 6ft.deep N. 15 E.	3	3	Road good. The low hills continue on left, and approach on right at intervals on an open plain.

STAGES.	Distances.		REMARKS.
	Miles.	Furlongs.	
Cross the Sungaw River.. N. 45 W.	1	4	The low hills close on the road, about a mile before reaching the river, turning N. 45 W.; a stream three yards broad and twenty inches deep, banks moderate. The road winds along the base of some low sandy hills for a mile further, where the baggage requires to be well guarded against plunderers.
Hykulzie and Khedazie .. 10 7 A canal runs close to the south of the village. N. 55 W.	2	1	A large village with walls: Khedazie is open. This is a very extensive plain, with much cultivation, and several other villages near. The river runs past, three furlongs to the south of Hykulzie, which is principally inhabited by the Syuds, most of whom speak Hindoostanee: were civil, and brought in many supplies from the surrounding villages.
Cross Lora River to Camp 7 1	7	1	There is no village here. The road runs, after the first two miles, along a deep nullah, which is crossed at four miles and three-quarters twice; it is fifteen feet deep, rough and difficult; a road for the carriages was made over it. The road after runs along between deep and dangerous nullahs of the same description; the ground along river for a great way is of the same uncertain description, with intervals of good level ground. The river has seven or eight yards of water, two feet deep, between forty and fifty feet beneath the level of the plain, with double banks on each side; the guns were brought over by fatigue-parties for about four hundred yards. Forage is scarce on the plain here, but there is a good deal of thin grass in the higher bed of the river.
Tookanee, on left.........	1	5½	A small village.
Koolazy	3	7	A large village on left; Mazye, a large village further to the left beyond it about one mile. None of these villages were entirely deserted when the leading division passed, and much cultivation appeared all round.
Urumbe .... 7 5½ N. 50 W.	2	1	The plain or district here about is called Urumbee. The camp was formed a mile and a half beyond Koolazy, one mile on right of a fort and village, at a good stream or canal of running water. Forage and some supplies were brought into camp. The road was good, and the country covered with lye-bushes to near Koolazy, apparently nearly all withering away from drought.
Camp, two miles and a half north of Killa Abdulla 6 1	6	1	Camp on the left bank of the river, which is broad and shallow, and has a small stream running here, which disappears a little further down. Considerable green grass was found between the low hills on right, and green corn and grass were brought from about Killa Abdulla. Supplies came in in great quantities. Abdulla is in possession of a battalion of infantry, belonging to the Shah.

STAGES.	Miles.	Furlongs.	REMARKS.
Kojuk Pass .... N. 45 W.			The distance is a very gradual ascent, which, though a good road, fatigued and knocked-up the cattle.
To the foot of the Pass	6	6	
Top of the first ascent....	1		The road now narrows to from twenty to twelve feet broad, and the ascent increases considerably until the last two furlongs, which is steep, and the forty yards near the top much more. A spring of water crosses the road half-way up the steep ascent, which is cut for the guns, along the side of the hill.
First descent		1½	The descent is nearly as steep as the ascent. A good stream of water here crosses the road, and another road comes in on left, by which part of the baggage came.
Top of second ascent		2½	This ascent is fully as steep as the first, especially at a narrow turn near the top; the best camel road is turning to the left from the gun road about half-way up this ascent for about half a mile, when a good road for camels will be found leading down a small watercourse, with a gradual descent, but only sufficient for one camel at a time. Care must be taken to avoid following a path which runs to the right of this, which runs over a small ridge, by which some came down, but many fell in attempting to do so in the ravine on left, which is the road. Guards should be placed at all paths leading from the high road, to prevent any one entering them, and the heights must be well protected as the baggage passes, the hills being, as usual, full of plunderers.
Bottom of second steep descent, on the gun road to a small stream		3½	This is longer and steeper than any of the other ascents, turning sharp round a point near the top, on the brink of a precipice. The carriages were dragged up and lowered down at these places by strong parties of European infantry.
Chumun .... 11 4 N. 55 W.	2	6½	A few springs in a hollow on right, with some short grass. A better road than either of the above is reported to run off to the right from the stream of water after passing the first ascent and descent, joining the gun road again about two miles and a half beyond the bottom of the last steep descent by a more gradual one. Forage for horses was scarce at Chumun, but some more springs and green grass were discovered more to the right of the usual halting-place. Camel forage pretty good. Foraging parties from this should be alert and well guarded.
Dund-i Gollai .... N. 40 W.	15	6	This is a reservoir of water, supported by a canal from the hills from a great distance on right. There are other pools of standing water, but not sufficient for more than a small party. The canal was turned off on the second day when the leading division passed, on a pretext of not receiving remuneration. The

STAGES.	Distances.		REMARKS.
	Miles.	Furlongs.	
			descent continues but gradual for three or four miles after leaving Chumun over a dry plain, crossing seven or eight shallow nullahs with green bushes about them, but no water. A small pool was passed at twelve miles and a quarter. The dry bed of a large nullah or river is then crossed, and ascend a number of low sand ridges, which continue for about a mile and a half. Forage was scarce, and no village near.
Puttoola Killa .... Camp one mile and a quarter south of the fort. N. 45 W.	9	2	This fort and village was deserted on the approach of the army, and the canals cut off from the same place as those belonging to Dund-i-Gollai; both coming from the same hills, reported about fifteen miles to the right; encamped about four miles and a quarter south of the fort; the standing corn was brought in as forage, which must otherwise be scarce for a force; about four or five miles to the left are several good wells, and in a more direct line to the camp of Mele, by the plain, avoiding the hilly ground north of Puttoola Killa; part of the baggage came round these hills, and reported the road good.
Mele, or Melamanda .... Deduct 1½ mile from this, as the distance beyond camp to head-quarters. N. 55 W.	11	3	There are the remains of several small villages, but lately deserted, a small stream in the bed of the river, and some wells; there are several wells and springs in the road that comes through the hilly pass from Puttoola in the last mile, which the generality of the army followed, encamped on the bank of the river to the right; there were several other wells and pools of water found north of the camp one mile and a half; forage from the river and nullah-beds, and the standing corn. The road ascends very gradually until about four miles north of the fort, when a succession of rough ascents and descents over nullahs between the two hills, which approach here to a narrow pass, occur, descending then gradually all the way to the river. In the event of Puttoola remaining drained of water, the route to the left over the plain would have every advantage over the other.
Mele, or Melamanda, to Doree River .... Or Tuktapool, N. 9 W.	14	4	No village near, but a good deal of cultivation along the river. The road is over undulating, dry, stony ground for ten miles and a half, covered with katara and wild-thyme bushes, passing at a narrow part between the hills at six miles on the north-west out of the valley of Melamanda, where the road is confined a short way and more stony; crossing afterwards three or four large nullahs; at twelve miles several cucha wells were passed, two only had water; they are deep. There is some grass about the river, a good deal of lye-bushes and other camel forage. The river had four or five yards of water, eighteen inches deep.
Deh-i-Hajee .... N.W.	7	4	A large place, with a good deal of green cultivation around, two other inclosed villages, one on the right

STAGES.	Distances.		REMARKS.
	Miles.	Furlongs.	
			and one on the left, at from one and a half to two miles; this is a very extensive place, and some other villages appear near. A considerable quantity of supplies came in here, forage, some short grass, lucerne, and green corn; water from the aqueduct. The road from the Dorce river is good, crossing eight nullahs, all small, running to a large nullah, with high banks, and ruined buildings on left.
Koosh-aub, 9 7½, Camp at the Aqueduct, 2 2½ N. 35 W.	12	2	Koosh-aub is a general name given to the villages in this part of the plain; there are six or seven large villages all within two or three miles of this camp, and much green cultivation. The village passed at ten miles on the right side of the road is large and populous, and well supplied with water, forage, a good deal of green grass, and lucerne.
Zankur Village 2 2½			A large village, with many inclosures and gardens, besides very extensive cultivation along on the left, over a very extensive plain.
Kurazee 2 6			A large village, many supplies exposed for sale here on the approach of the army; gardens and inclosures as above, with much cultivation.
Populzie, on right .. 0 3			Inclosures, gardens, and habitations, called also Koolcha Bagh.
Nawdree, on left .. 0 2			Buildings and ruins of the city of Shah Nadir.
Kandahar City 1 6	7	4½	Shikarpoor gate, Kandahar city is nearly a rectangular figure, one mile in length, nearly north and south, and three-quarters of a mile in breadth; the country outside is open on the south and west, but a few inclosures on the north end, and extensive cemeteries, durgahs, and peers; the west side is more inclosed, especially at the south-west, where gardens, inclosures, and villages at intervals confine the country, for between two and three miles.

ROUTE from DADUR to KANDAHAR.

From Dadur to the Shikarpoor gate of Kandahar, the Perambulator ran 225 miles and 5 furlongs, divided as follows :—

	M.	F.
Distance—Dadur to Shawl or Quetta	84	7
Kandahar	140	6
Total	225	5

Road.—The road itself from Dadur to Kandahar cannot be said to be a bad one, as all our wheeled carriages, including some heavy pieces of ordnance, traversed it, and the famous Bolan Pass, which was expected to offer many difficulties, was easily surmounted. The Kojuk Pass, however, over the Amran range, is very bad, and the descent on the northern face so abrupt, that all the guns had to be handed down by working parties of European infantry.

Ascents and Descents.—From Dadur, which is itself six hundred feet above the level of the sea, there was a very perceptible rise to the top of the Bolan Pass, until we reached an elevation of 5,100 feet, giving a rise of 4,500 feet in about fifty-seven miles; consequently we experienced a considerable improvement in climate as we advanced. From the top of the pass to a descent of about five hundred feet, between Shawl and Koochalk, the first march from it, the road was over a level country; the same may be said of the road between Koochalk and Killa Abdoola Khan, near the foot of the Kojuk Pass. After crossing this pass, the road gradually descends to Kandahar, passing two or three low ranges of hills.

Rivers, Water.—From Dadur to Sir-i-Boolan, we encamped daily near a fine stream of water, which rises at the latter place. Between this and Sir-i-ab, for thirty miles, not a drop of water is to be found, consequently both our people and cattle were much distressed. When the country is under our rule, and our influence firmly established, one of the first acts of the local Government should be to dig an aqueduct from Sir-i-ab to the top of the pass, and bring down one of the many mountain-springs in which this country so happily abounds, the soil easily admitting of its being dug. From Sir-i-ab to the foot of the Kojuk Pass, water is abundant at every stage, and is also plentiful from springs on the northern side of the hills. From this place, however, we had to make a forced march of twenty-four miles before water could be found, with the exception of a dirty pool at Dund-i-Goolaee; and when we reached Killa Footoola, the water there had been turned from its usual channel, so that the army was much distressed. From this latter place to Kandahar we found water at every stage.

Mountains.—I have before stated that from Dadur to the top of the Bolan Pass we ascended 4,500 feet, and our route was bounded by mountain ranges many hundreds of feet higher, being shoots from the main chain on which we found ourselves on arriving at the top of the pass. From thence there was little perceptible descent until we went down the pass between Quetta and the first march to

Kandahar, but very lofty hills were on each side of our route a few miles distant, and with snow on them. The next range we came to were the Amran hills, which intersected our line of route at the Kojuk Pass; these are about 1,200 feet above the surrounding plain. From this no other elevated range occurred near our line of route, although hills of some magnitude are visible in all directions.

Boundaries.—Dadur, in times of peace, and when the rule of the kings was in force, paid tribute to them; but I believe the district bearing the same name does not extend beyond the entrance of the pass itself, which may be considered debateable land under no authority, but chupased by several marauding tribes of Beloochees, who collect black mail from any traveller they fall in with, and unable to resist their demands, and in most cases their exactions are coupled with murder.

From the top of the pass, as far as Koochalk, the district of Shawl extends, which belongs to Merab Khan, of Kelat, and here commences the territory of Kandahar.

Inhabitants.—The Bolan Pass is infested by many tribes of Beloochees, who subsist principally by plunder and chupasing different districts. Their habitations are some distance from the high road, and I believe they generally reside in caverns. They have large flocks of sheep, and cultivate small patches of ground. Either their antipathy to us must have carried them to commit acts of violence beyond their usual custom, or their natural character must be cruel and ferocious. The latter, I fear, is the case; and even this is not coupled, as it often is, with courage, for their excesses were always committed upon our unarmed followers, or when they knew it was not possible to attack them.

From Dadur, the whole way to Kandahar, whenever any hilly country occurred, we always found it infested by the same class of persons, either Beloochees or Affghans, of equally bad character. The few villages we passed in the plains were generally deserted; but, from signs of considerable cultivation, the inhabitants most probably were of a more peaceable character.

The villages in the vale of Pisheen are generally inhabited by Syuds, who keep up a considerable traffic with Bombay, principally in horses; they remained in their villages; most of them spoke Hindoostanee, and very willing to furnish what supplies they had to part with.

Produce.—The first cultivation we met with was in the Shawl district. Wheat was the general produce, besides artificial grasses. There are many orchards, in which, for the first time, we saw several European fruits.

The Pisheen valley is also well cultivated; the same kind of produce as before mentioned from this to Kandahar; cultivation was very limited until we approached this city.

Climate.—Dadur was very hot when we left it. In April it rose to 105°, but the nights were cool, the glass falling to 52°; the first two marches in the pass it was still higher, but from that an improvement took place daily until we passed Quetta. Dadur is said to be insupportable during the months of May, June, July, and August, and very unhealthy; the Bolan Pass still worse, no one but kossids venturing through it in these months. We have since heard that detachments of our army with convoys have marched through it, but the sickness they suffered is sufficient proof that only in great necessity should it be attempted. The climate of Shawl is very good, but the winter severe; the first detachment of British troops that ascended the pass had a fall of snow in the beginning of April.

By all accounts, the whole country we passed through, from Shawl to Kandahar, is considered very healthy, although the heat in the summer months at times is very oppressive. The following was the range of the thermometer from our departure from Dadur to the day we left Kandahar, kept in a tent:—

	1st to 15th April.	To 30th April.	May.	June.
Maximum	105°	90°	103°	110°
Minimum	52	45	53	56
Mean maximum	94	90	100	102
Mean minimum	62	58	59	61
Medium	77	75	79	82

Very little rain falls; we had not one shower during the whole of this period. Snow falls more or less during this line, the melting of which is principally depended on for watering the fields.

Manners and Customs.—During the whole march we saw but few of the inhabitants of the country, excepting the wild tribes of the hills that infested our line of route for plunder, and a more lawless set of rascals it is not easy to imagine. Blood with them is cheap as water; even the cultivators go armed; and the constant feuds between different tribes, coupled with their plundering habits, renders this necessary. Every person seemed well dressed; and, but for the insecurity of life and property, might be happy and contented, the country yielding every thing necessary for their support, with the advantage of a fine climate.

ROUTE from DADUR to SUKKUR.

STAGES.	Distances.		REMARKS.
	Miles.	Furlongs.	
Dadour to Nowsherra....	7	4	
Myhysir	15	3	At nine miles cross a deep nullah from Nowsherra, with little water in it, but muddy. Road good. Water in a nullah south-west of the village. Myhysir contains about two hundred houses and ten shops. Plenty of forage for camels, and kirby for horses. Encampment on the north-east of the village.
Bhag	14	6	In this march cross six nullahs, one of which has water in it. Road good, and cultivation of juwarree in the vicinity of this place. Water bad, and from a tank filled in by the fall of rain. Bhag is a large place, with plenty of supplies; it contains about two thousand houses and one hundred shops. Forage for camels in the vicinity of this town, and kirby for horses. Juwarree fields all the way from last stage; encamping-ground on the east of the village.
Kassim-ka-joke	20	6	Cross five nullahs in this march, one of which runs on the left of the road, with pools of water in it. Road good, with cultivation of juwarree on both sides at some places. This village is small, with seventy-five houses and eight shops; supplies limited; plenty of forage for camels at one mile from the village, and kirby for horses; encamping-ground south-west of the village.
Kunda	15	7	In this march cross five nullahs, with one running on the left of the road, as before. Road, a foot-path, and bad; cultivated fields of juwarree on both sides of the road. Kunda is a small, but good village, with about two hundred houses and thirty shops; water in a nullah, on the left of the village, till the end of February, when it could be had by digging in the bed of the nullah; plenty of forage for camels and kirby for horses; encamping-ground south-west of the village.
Rojan	35	3	At five miles three furlongs, pass the village of Roree, where the guns were halted, and from whence desert of twenty-six miles is crossed. Road good, on a plain all the way. Rojan is a poor village, with few huts; water bad, and in three wells, built of burnt brick. No supplies; forage for camels and kirby for horses; encamping-ground south-east of the village.
Janeederrah	11	2	Road good from the last march. Janeederrah is a small ghurry, in which commissariat supplies are stored, and guarded by a party of infantry from Shikarpoor: this village is deserted. Water in five wells, two of

STAGES.	Distances.		REMARKS.
	Miles.	Furlongs.	
			which are now dry. Sufficient forage for camels, and kirby for horses. Supplies very limited; encamping-ground on the east of the village.
Jagghan	11	5	In this march pass four dry nullahs; road good. Jagghan is a small village, with sixty houses and few shops. Water from five kutcha wells. Forage for camels in abundance, and kirby for horses; supplies very limited. Encamping-ground on the south-east of the valley.
Shikarpoor	12	2	Road good, through thick jungle, having no nullahs to cross in this march. Shikarpoor is a large town, with considerable supplies and population. Encamping-ground on the south-east of the town, where there are several wells.
Kheahyee	14	7	In this march cross eight dry nullahs; road good, through jungle. Kheahyee is a small village, with about one hundred houses and eight shops; supplies few; water from two pucka and ten kutcha wells; plenty of forage for camels and kirby for horses. Encamping-ground on the south-east of the village.
Sukkur	13	3	Cross seventeen nullahs in this march; road good, but through thin jungle; at seven miles on the left of it the river Indus is met; and on the right bank of which Sukkur is situated; is the head-quarters of the brigade in Upper Sinde.

ROUTE from ROREE to JEYSULMEER.

STAGES.	Distances.		REMARKS.
	Miles.	Furlongs.	
Roree			Roree is built on the eastern bank of the Indus. It is a good place; the houses are built in the same manner as those of Hyderabad, being a framework of wood, with mud plaster. The bazaars are good. Outside the town there are the ruins of several large mosques and tombs, which shew that it must have been a place of considerable importance. The banks of the Indus, about Roree, are thickly lined with date-trees. There are also many Persian wheels used to water sugar-cane and wheat-fields.
Khyerpoor	16	6	A good road, with many villages, and cultivation; water is to be procured from wells at every place. Khyerpoor is a large town, the capital of Meer Roostum Khan. Supplies of all kinds plentiful.
Tremon	8	5	Road over a level country, with low jungle. There is a good deal of cultivation round the villages, which are numerous. Supplies abundant. Cross a small canal, which, during the inundation, brings water from the Indus; there is a narrow stone bridge of three arches over it. The village contains twenty-five shops.
Ghurree	15	3¾	Two miles from last ground, pass some rather handsome tombs; two miles further, cross a low range of stony hills, which extend from Roree to the south eighty miles. The country after this is level, with jungle and small hamlets, till you come to the banks of a branch of the Indus, called the Narra, which is filled during the inundation; it is about fifty yards broad and twenty feet deep; there was a little water in it, flowing to the south. This branch is supplied by three feeders from the river, and passes near Omerkote and Luckput. Bunder Ghurree is a pretty good village, with ten shops; supplies moderate. There are two more villages within a few miles. A shorter road from Tremon passes by Saleka Budra, but the Narra is difficult to cross, on account of mud.
Rajarie	16	5	N.B. The direct road from Roree joins in here. It passes by Sungrar, a large village, distance twenty or twenty-four miles; road through dense jungle of tamarisk, with low sand-hills; at three miles, pass a large sheet of good water, which remains throughout the year from the inundation; there are some wheat-fields along the road, and occasionally a few miserable huts. Rajarie is inhabited by goatherds. There is one good well, and three small ones; but water can

STAGES.	Distances.		REMARKS.
	Miles.	Furlongs.	
			always be obtained at a few feet below the surface. Coarse grass abundant, but no supplies.
Oodur	16	5½	Road through low jungle, with sand-hills on each side. Pass two small hamlets of goatherds: the first, Muttee, ten miles, five huts and one good well, water three feet deep; the second, Banahon, two miles and a half further, has one good well two furlongs off the road. There are two good wells at Oodur, and one filled up; also a little coarse grass, but no inhabitants. The fort was destroyed by a flood nine years ago; a small mound, with trees, is all that remains of it.
Metrao	15	6	Sandy road, with low jungle; about half-way, pass the hamlet of Karora, where there are three good wells. Metrao is a small mud fort, with a party of five or six matchlock-men to prevent robberies. There are five good wells, and one shop, but scarcely any supplies.
Sobarah	18	3	Road very heavy over sand-hills, covered with low brushwood and tufts of grass.
Surdar Ghur, or Gottarao	37		There are three small ponds of rain-water along the road: one at five miles six furlongs; the second, called Buniah Wallee, at eight miles six furlongs; and the third, half-way to Surdar Ghur, called Sobarah, eighteen miles three furlongs. They are sufficient for small parties, not exceeding a wing of a regiment of infantry, but could be easily deepened. The water does not remain during the hot season. Coarse grass very abundant. Surdar Ghur is a brick fort with round bastions, about two hundred yards square; the gate is on the south face. The outer wall may be ten feet without the parapet, the inner one twenty or twenty-five feet, and the keep about ten more. It appears in good order, and mounts two guns. The Ameer of Khyerpoor maintains one hundred matchlock-men in it. There are five wells, 150 feet deep—two within the fort, and three outside, close to the walls. In the village there are two shops, but supplies are very scarce.
Mourdalie	24	4	Eleven miles, road the same as last march when you pass the boundary of the Khyerpoor and Jeysulmeer states. The sand-hills here end, and the road is pretty hard, at twenty-four miles four furlongs; and about half a mile off the road is the village of Mourdahie, consisting of a number of shepherds' huts, and a few small muddy ponds. About a mile further on there are twelve small wells, amongst sand-hills; they contain a little good water, but could be easily concealed. Neither the ponds nor wells are to be depended on, except after the rains. There is coarse grass at Mourdalie.

STAGES.	Distances.		REMARKS.
	Miles.	Furlongs.	
Koorah	33		Koorah is a small stone fort and village, with six wells and three shops. Supplies very scarce.
Kuchrie	9	3	Good road. There are thirteen stone wells and a small pond with good water, and coarse grass, but no village.
If from Mourdalie	18	3	
Chutrail	15	6	Over a good road, with a tank of rain-water at twelve miles three furlongs and a half. There are five good wells here, and coarse grass, but no village.
Jeysulmeer	14	7	Stony road at four miles, and off the road is the village of Soudra; three shops, and wells. Two miles from Jeysulmeer pass the village of Oumer Sagur: twenty shops, and a fine tank. Water is found in tanks, and one nullah, all along this march. Jeysulmeer supplies most abundant. Long-cloth and coarse blankets are manufactured here.

ROUTE from TATTA to KOTREE.

STAGES.	Miles.	Furlongs.	REMARKS.
Tattah to Chuttai-ka-Gote, on the left	4	5½	Kullaree river, dry; pass Goolam Hussain, Seir-ka-Gote; both are small villages, and water not procurable.
Chilkya, on right	2	4½	Water not procurable; an inclosed shikargah runs one mile on right from Chuttai.
Shaik Radaw Peer	1	7	A white tomb on a hill to the right; there are two large tanks, around which there is plenty of grass. Forage is plentiful in an inclosed shikargah; on right, the ground in the vicinity is hilly and stony.
Kunjur Dund, or Lake, seven furlongs on left of the road	5	2	The water is brackish, but not bad; plenty of grass at the north end, and in the shikargahs near the Ameer's bungalow, on the right of the road.
Heleya-ka-gote, on right of the road	1	6	A pond of good water, but small, half a mile beyond the village, among some thick bushes on left of the road.
Soonda	6	3	Two miles from the bank of the river, an open plain, south of the village, to the north; it is hilly—no grass in the vicinity, but plenty in the shikargah, on right. Pass Jutta-ga-Gote at one mile on right, Tarunja at two on left, and pass Somraka at two miles and three-quarters on right, and Kurramka at four miles and a half on right.
Jirkh, or Jerrick	9	5	On the bank of the river, boats come close to the bank here; road along the foot of a range of hills, but not stony.
Raja-ka-gote	4		A large village on an open plain, close to the bank of the river; encamping-ground north of the village. Grass can be procured from the banks of a tank, about two miles and a half in front, on the road to Mozawur.
Mozawur, or Shaik Peer	5	2	Situated among the tall trees, conspicuous at a distance. There are two or three wells, but the water is not good.
Sorunjee Wassee	5	3	Three-quarters of a mile from the bank of the river, which is shelving and soft; the jungle round the village is thick, with no grass; encamping-ground sufficient between the river and village; tolerably open.
Kotree Hyderabad is about four miles across the river from Kotree.	8	4	Kotree is situated in a large clump of trees, on the bank of the river; ground in the neighbourhood open and level. Boats can come close to the bank at Kotree. The river is 844 yards wide here, but there is a bank of sand opposite the town, which extends some distance below it. The road, for three miles from Wassee, winds among sand-hillocks.

ROUTE from KOTREE and GUNDAVA to SUKKUR.

STAGES.	Distances.		REMARKS.
	Miles.	Packings.	
Kotree.			
Gundava	7		
Oodauna	14	7	A walled village, with considerable cultivation around. Water from cutcha wells outside; at this time scarce, and insufficient for a small force. The road good, over a level desert plain, crossing a large canal at six miles, twenty yards broad and fifteen feet deep, with steep banks. Cultivation commences at one mile from Oodauna. Forage abundant, supplies few.
Kunda	10	4½	A large walled town; water in canals, but indifferent. Much cultivation, and several other villages around at a distance of from one to three miles. Road over a level country, but more bushy passing one village on the right at three miles, and the ruins of old Oodauna with some cutcha wells, and two or three large villages on left at seven miles. Supplies plentiful at Kunda.
Burshooree	9	2	Two walled villages, with considerable cultivation around, on the edge of the Runn desert. Water from small cutcha wells. Road good all the way, and for the first two miles and a half through cultivation; then a desert plain, until within one mile and a quarter of Burshooree. Forage abundant, but few supplies.
Rojan	26		Two walled villages on the eastern side of the Runn or desert, with a little cultivation and one good pukka well. The road over the Runn is very good. Parties with laden cattle should march just so late in the evening as to arrive across it by daylight. Forage abundant; few supplies.
Janeedera	11	2	A large square fort and a village; the village at present in ruins, having been destroyed some time ago by a plundering band of Beloochees. There is considerable cultivation around, and some of the population scattered in huts in the fields. There are four good pukka wells, one of which is inside the fort. Khangaum, a large and populous place, is about four miles to the northward; at present an outpost from Shikarpoor. Road good, except at the ninth mile, where it is deep in sand. Forage plentiful, and some supplies.
Jaghan	11	4½	A fort and village, with some lofty square fortified buildings outside. Considerable cultivation, and some good pukka wells. The road is over a level but more woody country, passing two or three villages on the

STAGES.	Distances.		REMARKS.
	Miles.	Furlongs.	
			right and left. Jaghan has a small but good bazaar, with considerable supplies, and forage plentiful.
Shikarpoor	13	4	A large town or city, the capital of Upper Scinde, with extensive bazaars and abundant supplies. A large fort on the east side of the town. The buildings are in general lofty; the country around an extensive level, bushy plain, with much cultivation. Water plentiful from wells. Road good, over a level but very bushy or jungly country.
Kahee	14	¼	A large village, and also much cultivation. The road winds a good deal over a level but a very bushy or jungly country, with many fine clumps of trees, and several villages at a distance from the road.
Sukkur	12	6	To the bank of the Indus river, near the flying bridge, to Bukkur Killa. The road from Kahee is in general good, but crosses about ten water-courses, or nullahs, all at present dry. Pass Thoomance at 1½ miles on right; Rubail on left at 2¼; Durraha at 5¼, and Soomar at 6½, both on right; Jaffrabad 7¼ on right; Nusseerabad at 7¾ on left; and Abad at 9½: all small villages, with many trees and considerable cultivation about them.

ROUTE from KOTREE to SEHWAN.

STAGES.	Miles.	Furlongs.	REMARKS.
Kotree (north end of) to Cawnpoor on left	1	5½	Road good after first half-mile on the river bank.
Ismael Puttan	1	6	A fine tope of trees on right, between the road and river; some buildings, and a garden of the Ameers.
Powar-gote on right	1	6¼	River about seven furlongs on right.
Lalloo-meerjut on left		2½	Cross a nullah between, and another at Lalloo. Sand very heavy.
Rajurrah-gote come on		3½	Road broken. Sand-banks—in parts deep, and confined by four-feet bushes.
River bank again	2	1½	This distance over a low, level plain of rice-fields.
Boda	1	1½	A large village. Road good along river bank; fine open space before reaching it for encamping.
9 2¾			
Sikarpoor, a Syud's gote	1	2½	
A ditch and some broken ground		4½	Open, level country.
Some broken ground		6	The last two furlongs deep sand.
Rising ground		7½	This distance over an elevated, stony plain; the stones are smooth pebbles, generally small.
Meer Soobedar's Shikargah on right, 1½ coss.		1	Road good, over hard, sandy plain.
Shikargah, 4 frls. on right		5	Barren plain all round; road good.
Ditto, edge of	1	1¼	The last distance a succession of ascents and descents among some low hills, stony, but road tolerably passable for carriages.
Peer Ukra-gote	1	6½	A few scattered huts, and peers' places and graves. Road gravelly, but good. The shikargah terminates here, and, after a short interval, where the river one mile off, Meer Mahomed's shikargah commences; road runs along its fence some short distance.
Manjae-gote on right, four furlongs, Peer Ukra Nullah dry	1	5½	River two furlongs beyond it.
Musjid and Peer on a hill on left	1		Road winds along the bottom of these.
Nullah		½	Hills, and to Oonderpoor crosses a low marshy plain, now hard, and confined by stunted bushes. Oonderpoor is a large village on the bank of the river, which has high banks; here a horse can only go down at Dadoo Mogul.
Ditch, deep and narrow		4	
Oonderpoor		6½	
11 2¾			
Cross a ditch	1	4½	Half a mile south, or at the village half a mile north of Oonderpoor, fine encamping. Forage seems scarce.
Shora Boodnapoor	1	1¼	Small village, about twenty huts; a nullah is crossed at it, and another a little beyond. The road, which to this is excellent, now becomes sandy, and winding between the cultivation and shikargah on right.

STAGES.	Distances.		REMARKS.
	Miles.	Furlongs.	
Koraejae-na-gote	3	5	This is a large place, and the river close by. The road this last distance winding among the trees of the Shikargah, very deep; light dust in most places.
Beah		4½	This is also a large place; fine trees, and much cultivated ground; some rough cultivation-banks; a deep ditch between the two villages. The road runs through its bazaar, and a furlong further comes on the river-bank.
Kanotch-go-gote	1		This is also a large village, with much cultivation.
Gangreh-gote		4¼	A small village. A ditch and some rough road, afterwards good.
Cross a deep ditch		1	
Cross two large ditches, a hundred yards apart	1	3	
Large ditch, fifteen yards wide	1	2½	This is very rugged. The ground, about ten yards in front, low marsh, now hard and rugged.
Kassye Gopang		3½	This is a large village on the bank of the river.
11 5½			
Gopang		3½	A smaller village, but much cultivation.
Rajree on right		7½	A small village in the Shikargah, and some cultivation.
Old Rajree, deserted	1	6	
Two or three Nullahs, within a hundred yards of each other	3	7½	
Pareez Moot on left		6	A small village. The Shikargah continues on right all the way from Rajree to this.
Halan Syuds on right		6½	
Majinda		6½	This is a large place, with an extensive bazaar. Good water. The plain is entirely without vegetation, slightly uneven, and very dusty near the road and river here. The road is a good gun-road all the way.
9 3½			
Ootorah-gote and Peer ...	1	3½	Ootorah is a small village: cross a ditch in the first half-mile.
Kachee	1	0½	This is a pretty large place, part belonging to Meer Nusseer and part to Meer Soobedar, whose territory then continues all the way to Sun.
Lakaw-gote	1	2½	A large village on left. There are some sandy hillocks before reaching it, about two hundred yards, and bushes, otherwise the road is very good, and continues so to Lalloo.
Lalloo-gote	1	1½	A small village.
Fakeer Mahomed's-gote .	1	1	A small fakeer's place, as is a little north-east of it, where there is a wet nullah, dammed up at the road. The country, as far as Lakaw, on the left side, is a barren waste to the hills, but on the right it is a continuation of green cultivation and low green lye bushes.
Noorpoor	1	0½	Noorpoor is a middling village, with many fine trees, and a pucka well and wet nullah. The fort is old, and not inhabited, but entire.

STAGES.	Distances.		REMARKS.
	Miles.	Furlongs.	
Syud Bakul Shaw	2	1½	A middling-sized village, with extensive cultivation, which continues in the bed and east bank of the standing river all the way to Sun.
Chota, or Nawa Sun		5	This is a small village.
Sun, or Sen	1	6	This is a large place, about half the size of Majinda, but appears to be poorer, and its bazaar much inferior. From the tree in the front or east of the town, up to the bed of the dry river, is heavy sand.
11 5			
Hashim-chicher, small village	2	4½	This territory belongs to Meer Noor Mahomed; after crossing the dry river, which comes from the hills, the road becomes good shortly after leaving the river-bed.
Meershawudda on right		7	
Burobera on right		5	These are pretty large villages, with much green cultivation.
Gancha on left		4½	A small village on left.
Dehru Khan Gancha	1	2½	Large village, with much green cultivation.
Mahir-chir	1	7	Small ditto ditto.
Burra-chicher	1	2⅓	This is a good-looking or apparently thriving place, with a large white Mujeed peer, and tombs in its front, with much cultivated ground. Good encamping-ground, and a good bank in front for watering; the road is very good until beyond this village, where some sand-hillocks occur a short distance, and for about a mile the sand is rather deep, but pretty level and open.
Amree	3		Amree is small, and appears to be rather a poor village, yet there is a great quantity of green cultivation near it. There is a small hill, about fifty feet high, on its north side, from whence an immense quantity of green cultivation is seen in the dry bed of the river, at a bend beyond it, running a great way to the north-west from the river.
12 1			
Lonara on right	3	2	Four or five huts of cultivators. The road runs along the standing river. The main river is said to have run this way some time ago, and does now in the monsoons. The road is good. The Pukka or high road runs off to the left a little half-mile.
Tittee on left	1	6	On an eminence a mosque, and large square building; but few houses besides.
Powhur on left	2	3	A large collection of thatched houses, but a permanent village.
Abad		5½	A scattered village of the same description as Powhur.
Bajoorah	1	1½	The road, winding along the bank of the standing water and fields, requiring a little opening. There is a good deal of grass about this water, where the Ameers, Sepoys, and Jemadar stop.
Inclosure on right	1	2	
Lukka		4½	The Hakeem of the town is a Syud, and is distinct or independent of the Jemadar. The camp is pretty clear, and clean ground at Lukka, across from the
11 0½			

APPENDIX. 359

STAGES.	Distances.		REMARKS.
	Miles.	Furlongs.	
			inclosure to the town, and southward from the water along the high road.
Tchewan	1	0½	A small and poor-looking village. The high road turns off a little beyond, and going by it would avoid some bad road at Batchaw.
Batchaw	1	2	Such another village as the above. A ditch is crossed to it, which runs along its right, and is very uneven. Road good.
Kottanga	2	0½	A small, poor village; crossing over the fields to the main road from Batchaw, to avoid some uneven ground which appears in front. This is an encampment for people going over the pass to Sehwan. Road good.
Old Chokee on left	1		A little beyond this, at the turn, the hill stands nearly perpendicular over the road, which is confined by the little hill on its right.
Pass commences	1	2	It narrows to the river-bank for upwards of two hundred yards, before the ascent commences, to seven feet in some places, composed on either side of blocks of stone, nearly two feet square some of them; and in two places, for a short distance, ledges of rock lie on the inner side, so as to raise it above the other nearly two feet.
To the top About eighty or ninety feet high perpendicular.		3	The two sharp turns at the bottom would require widening; some more parts slope sideways from the direction of shelving rock; and one brow of solid rock, ten paces, would render it dangerous for horses, unless assisted by a strong party with drag-ropes. The ascents altogether, including some easy parts, make a total of about three hundred paces, as shewn in a bird's-eye view on the other side. The laden camels come up easily.
Descent to the plain	2	0½	The descent is rough in some places, but slopes along the side of the hill more gradually, and is comparatively easy.
Kottai	1	3	This is the only place where a good camp can be found all the way to the city. The road, after descending, runs in the bed of a dry river a short distance, which is heavy sand; the road is sandy all the way to the town; in a few places heavy.
Sehwan	2	5	
From Lukkah 13 1			

ROUTE from SUKKUR to LARKHANA.

STAGES.	Miles.	Furlongs.	REMARKS.
Camp Sukkur to Bangudjee	10		In this march, pass four dry nullahs. Road, a foot-path, but good, through thin jungle; ten houses and one shop: water from the Indus, and encamping-ground on the bank of it. Plenty of forage for the camels, and kirby for horses.
Shaleanee	8	2	Pass eight dry nullahs in this march. Road, a foot-path, through thin jungle, and leading through the bank of the river; twenty houses and four shops. River-water and encamping-ground on the bank of the Indus; plenty of forage for camels, and kirby for horses.
Maddehjee	9	5	Pass seven dry nullahs in this march. Road, a foot-path through thin jungle, leaving the river at about three miles from the last stage; about a hundred and fifty houses and twenty shops. Water from six pucka wells; supplies plentiful; encamping-ground on the south-west of the village. Lots of forage for camels, and kirby for horses.
Nowadehra	9	4	In this march pass seven dry nullahs. Road, a foot-path through jungle; about a hundred houses, eight or ten shops; water from four or five pucka wells. The river is left about three miles from this place. Supplies plentiful; encamping-ground on the north-west of the village; forage for camels and kirby for horses.
Larkhana	12	3	Cross nine dry nullahs in this march; road good, through thick jungle. Larkhana is a large town; abundance of supplies.

ROUTE from SEHWAN to LARKHANA.

STAGES.	Distances.		REMARKS.
	Miles.	Furlongs.	
Sehwan to cross Arrub River		0¼	The road runs through Kurmpoor, and is good, with the exception of deep sand in parts, and in particular for three furlongs, runs along the bed of a broad ditch, heavy in sand.
Kurmpoor	2	4	
Cross a wet ditch	1	2½	This is narrow (two feet), but runs into a large wet ditch on the left, from the standing river, which runs along on the left, about two furlongs off, from three furlongs beyond Kurmpoor, the last distance, over a low grassy plain, not much above the level of the water; road good; many stumps of cut bushes occur here, from one to two feet high, near the road, amongst the high grass.
A road to Turitee, to the left along the Standing River		3½	This appears to be more direct, but for a little way, which was examined, not so open, following it two furlongs; the water appears all along to the front, and the country beyond, for two miles, with several villages on or near its banks.
Halipootra		7½	A village on the right, amongst high trees: the country appears level, but very bushy beyond it towards the river.
Nenkur and Meanee		5	A small village. Meanee is a village of fishermen near the water.
Turritee, or Turrotee, one half-mile on left		1½	A large village; much cultivation appears from Halipootra and on to the left, for a great distance beyond Turitee.
Bullalpoor, on right	2	1	A large village; from thirty to forty shops: the last distance over a level open plain, damp in some places from the late rain. Encampment in front of Turitee, or at Bullalpoor, good and open.
North corner of Town		1	
8 2¼			
Bullalpoor			
Rawdan on left, 4 fs.	2	4½	Three or four villages on the left; road good, excepting at the ditches; much green cultivation.
Bubria on left		7½	A small village; several villages on the right and left; cultivators, and much cultivation; two ditches; require labour for carriages.
Hiddaw-gote, left		7½	A small village; road over some rough irrigation-banks and cultivated ground; dusty in parts.
Syud Talib	1		A small village of cultivators; Ameenana and Noorja on the left (to which a road turns off before this village), which appear to be large places, and the main or high road to Dadoo runs beyond them; but said to have no water: these places have pucka wells.
Rindan on right	1	4	A large scattered village; some fine trees.

APPENDIX.

STAGES.	Miles.	Furlongs.	REMARKS.
Nawula-jo-gote	1		Small: a village of cultivators. The road comes straight on from Rindar, but perhaps the line outside over the fields would save labour for carriages.
Powar-gote		3½	A small village; much cultivation and irrigation from this nullah, though apparently small.
Jullaw-gote		5¾	A middling village; Chotta Churnaut on its left, and Bumbeya in front, both close on the apparent monsoon bank of the main river, which is now distant a mile and a quarter.
9 0¼			
Jullow-gote			
Koorania	4	1	Good camp, and water from standing nullah. The river is one mile and a half off on the right. The road is across a large ditch, with easy slope, and some rough ground before reaching Koorania.
Through a bushy plain, but open, to the open plain, one mile east of Dadoo	2	3	This is very good road, over a short turfy grass, with patches of cultivation.
Seal-jo-gote	2	1½	Along the hedge which divides the green from the dry cultivation ground.
Moondra	2	6½	Moondra is a large place. The water in the nullah and the wells of the town with care would be sufficient. The camp is good.
11 4			
Moondra			Some report the river two coss and some one-half. Cultivators and considerable cultivated open ground.
Sheerdas on left	1	7	
Davouch on right		6	Lassaree and Chandid are pointed out to the left, and the high road beyond or near them; but water is there scarce.
Tawraw on right		5	
Puttehpoor on left	1	0½	Some rough ground over cultivation-banks and at the ditches.
Chotta Lassaree		3½	
Poranadera on right	1	3½	A large village, and much green cultivation towards the river, which now appears, i. e. its opposite high bank all along on the right, a fine open plain, behind Poranadera.
Kokun		3	A large place on the bank of the river, which is here from fifteen to twenty feet high, but low opposite the wand, before reaching Rokun, where there is considerable green cultivation.
6 4½			
Boating or landing-place		6½	
Bappa	1	3½	Small cultivating village: the road is close along the bank; bushy, but good.
Chandia		5⅙	
Nunwarry	1	4⅓	Cultivators and some cultivation.
Tewnan	2		
Shikaree and Powar	1	6	Much green cultivation commences, irrigated from the standing river by a ditch to this.
Chotta Gulloo	1	5	This appears to be the best place for a camp, as the country appears more bushy beyond Gulloo. Chotta Gulloo is on the bank of the water. The ground is good, but a good many kurree bushes on it also. The road the last half-mile is rather uneven from irrigation ditches.

APPENDIX. 363

STAGES.	Miles.	Furlongs.	REMARKS.
Gulloo-gote		5	A middling village, and Raja-gote on its right.
10 4 17 0½			
Gulloo-gote			From the camp at Chotta Galloo the road is made all the way to near Meraub Lukie.
Chotta Seeta on left	1	3	A small village on the bank of the river.
Seeta on right	1	7½	A large place, pucka-built.
Nareh on left	4	5½	A large place, pucka-built.
Daderah on right	1	2½	A large village.
Wujut Churanan on left		7½	The road to Peer Punjah runs off to the left here. The new road is cut through a thicket, and runs across the cultivated fields, avoiding the village in a direct line.
Peer Punjah on left	1	1	A large good-looking town three furlongs on left.
Agra on right	2	0¼	A small village.
Meraub Lukia	1	4¾	The road is made to within a mile of Meraub Lukia, when a nullah occurs, and afterwards the cultivation-banks near the camp.
To the bank of the Standing River 15 6		6¼	
A point on the river, seven furlongs east of Meraub Lakyca.			
Mahomed Ali	2	1	The made road commences here.
Dheria-gote, or Sooee	3	1 }	The road turns off from the river here. Chunna on a branch of the river.
Chunna		5 }	
6 2			
Vear	1	6	A large village. The present road from Vear is very narrow, and confined by the cultivation hedges along the bank of a nullah the first five furlongs.
Kulporah		6	A large village. Road confined here a little way. High hedges.
Sowar Gadde	1	4	A large village, completely surrounded by green cultivation.
Chukra		6	A middling village, with good watering and open ground for encamping.
4 3			
Vear			A pucka-built village.
Chukra on right	3	1	A middling ditto.
Futtipoor on right	1	5	A large ditto.
Dublee on right		3	The road is cleared to three furlongs beyond this.
Shaik on right	1	7	The road is narrow and confined for guns in some places.
Through the jungle to cultivated fields	4		Road through the jungle is in general good. Some rough ground after leaving it, in the clayey tracked ground of the nullah and for one hundred yards between the fields, a track on the middle of the road being deep and narrow.
Hussainwah, north end	1	3	A moderate village on the bank of a standing river. Very little clear ground for encamping.
12 3			
Hussainwah to Darragote.	1	2	The first six furlongs of road confined in parts, and slightly uneven.
Bagae-gote		5½ }	These are small villages, of from five or six to ten or twelve huts. The road through the jungle is very good and open.
Bagae Dunwullee	2	1½ }	
Areejaw	1	6	A large village after coming through the jungle.

STAGES.	Distances.		REMARKS.
	Miles.	Furlongs.	
Buckranee	2	4	A middling village. The road from Areejaw is over cultivated fields, now vacant.
To the Ferry		2	
8 5			
Camp Buckranee			From the point at the ferry and a large tree two furlongs from the village.
To the Ford opposite Toonia Hashem	1	4	The ford starting from the tree on the south side two furlongs beyond Toonia to within one furlong back again to Toonia.
Toonia Hashem		6	
To where the two roads separate		5	The usual route was followed; it was reported good and shorter than the other.
Mahomed Amroo	1	3½	A small village. The road is good, over a level waste field, some vacant cultivation, and along the bed of a ditch. The banks of the ditches would be an obstacle to carriages only.
Booguie		6	A small village.
Bukapoor	1	2½	A large village and deserted fort. The road is good at these villages.
Larkhana Fort	1	7½	The ground along the left of the fort good encamping-ground, and has many wells on each side.
To the encamping ground north of the City	1		Crossing a large canal about forty yards broad, now dry, excepting a pool near the eastern extremity of the town. It is reported unfit for cattle to drink, on account of the quantity of dye from coloured clothes washed there.
9 2½			

ROUTE from SEHWAN to LARKHANA, *viâ* ARRUL RIVER.

STAGES.	Miles.	Furlongs.	REMARKS.
From Sehwan to *Changur	12		A cluster of villages: on their right flows a branch of Arrul river; direct unto, from Sehwan, is *viâ* "Buza," but a heavy fall of rain had stopped that road. Supplies and forage good and plentiful: road very good. Direction, west by north.
*Shahuson	11	6	A large town on banks of Arrul: a risala of the Meer's horse stationed there, under a jemadar. Supplies and forage good and plentiful: road very good. Direction, north-west.
*Chinee	6	4	Large village; branch of Arrul river. Supplies and forage good and plentiful: this is a thievish village: road good. Direction north about.
*Choll	12		A cluster of villages; branch of Narra river. A jemadar's party of Meer's sepoys stationed here; large cultivations around. Supplies and forage good and abundant: road very good. Direction, north by east.
*Darigz	6		A cluster of villages; Loree Nuddee branch of Narra river. Supplies and forage good and abundant: road very good. Direction, north-east.
*Poligee	4		Cluster of villages; the same river supplies, and forage good and abundant.
*Thurree	3		Cluster of villages; same river supplies, and forage abundant; good road; direction, north by east.
*Toree	10		Cluster of villages; same river supplies moderate; forage plentiful; many villages along the road, all supplied by the Loree river, branch of Narree; road good; direction, north-east by east.
*Maduh	8		Cluster of villages; branch of Narra river; supplies and forage moderate; road good; direction, north-east by east.
Yojaha	12		A small village; branch of Narra river; supplies moderate; road good; direction, north by east.
*Tarodakhura	10		Small village; Cheela river, branch of Narra; supplies scarce; road good; direction, north-east.
*Dera	12		A small village; branch of Cheela river; supplies moderate; road good; direction, north-east.
*Gwrilla	6		Large village; Cheela river; supplies moderate; road good.
Kulorah	2		Village; Cheela river; supplies moderate; and road good.
*Larkhana	7		

Villages thus marked * are halting-places.

The road throughout is very good, but the country, as you approach Larkhana, is cut up with deep though narrow water-courses, and branch streams; some are bridged, and all are fordable. From the Arrul and Narra rivers these water-courses are only filled during the hot months, and become dry as the waters of the inundation are drawn off; the villagers then resort to their wells, of which there are generally one or two in each village. There are numerous villages along the road, but, on account of the inundation, they are built on the rising ground, and generally about two miles from the bed of the rivers. Supplies and forage are good and abundant, till within forty miles of Larkhana, when provisions become rather scarce. Though I saw a vast tract of land under cultivation, the grain, I was told, is carried off to Larkhana or Sehwan. Fresh guides should be procured from the villages along the route, in preference to one from Sehwan for the whole way: the former have a better knowledge of the country, and are more to be relied on.

ROUTE from LARKHANA to KYRA-KA-GURRA.

STAGES.	Miles.	Furlongs.	REMARKS.
Larkhana to Futtypoor	6		Good road through a jungly country. Futtypoor, a small village, with only one well giving water. Moderate quantity of supplies.
Daamrah	3		Small village, with two wells. Supplies scarce.
Kyree Dehroo	6		Tolerably good, through thin jungle. A large village, with four wells and small stagnant pools of water. Supplies abundant. Encamping-ground close to village.
Tullhoo	1		Small village; two wells.
Shera Sookra	2	4	Country about these two villages open and cultivated.
Meeanee		4	Seven wells in the villages and their immediate vicinity. Road, in places, intersected by dry watercourses.
Chundia	3		Good road, over an open country. In Chundia, plenty of supplies, and four wells.
Uosu Boota	3		Country cultivated near village; two wells.
Pungria		4	Small village, near dry bed of a canal.
Bund	1		Small village, with one well.
Sujawul		4	Large place. Supplies very abundant. Eight wells in the village and its neighbourhood. A great deal of cultivation carried on by irrigation. Good encamping-ground near the village. Forage in large quantities everywhere on this day's march.
Sooar Buth	1		Good road, through sandy country. Large village, with three wells.
Goolab Seah	5		Waste country, with low bushes growing on it. Goolab Seah, a small village, with brackish water.
Tay-lugaru	5		Road over a parched desert tract of country. At the village, two large wells, and a moderate quantity of supplies.
Sunjur	2		Large village; two wells. There are said to be several in the neighbourhood, but the people studiously concealed them from us.
Neemra	4		Village, a little distance from the road; barren country.
Kyree Gurra	4		Walled town, on the edge of the desert. Two good wells; twelve Bunyans' shops. Road on this march good.

ROUTE from SHIKARPOOR to LARKHANA.

STAGES.	Miles.	Furlongs.	REMARKS.
Shikarpoor to Samun Kote	4	2½	A small village; about ten houses and two shops. Water from two wells.
Nowser	3	2½	Ditto; thirty houses and six shops; supplies limited; water from two cutcha wells.
Kumboowa	1	5	This village contains about twenty houses; one shop: water of wells.
Khairr		6½	This is a good village of about fifty houses; seven shops: water of wells in the village.
Gahay-ja	4	3½	A good village, containing about one hundred houses; twelve shops: water of wells.
Bungool Dehra	2	6½	Ditto, ditto, forty houses, seven shops, and one well.
Bambut Poora	6	3	Ditto, ditto, forty ditto, three ditto, ditto.
Rahooja	1	1½	A deserted village.
Nowadehra	2	7	A large town; abundant supplies. This village has about one hundred houses, ten or twelve shops. Forage for camels, and kirby for horses, abundant.
Larkhana	12	3	

ROUTE from SEHWAN to KURRACHEE.

STAGES.	Distances.		REMARKS.
	Miles.	Furlongs.	
Sehwan to Roree	11	4½	From the gardens south of the town near the river. Two small choppered villages, with some cultivation. Three wells. A nullah was found, with a good supply of water, about one mile on the south-west of the village. A small stream runs through Arer Peer, about a mile and a quarter to the westward, and a good supply of water always to be found one mile further in the same direction in the bed of the river. The road is very good, over a level plain.
Tairae, a middling village, is passed at four miles and a quarter, and Cuchee, Bajar, and Jangur, three large villages, from two to three miles distant, on the right bank, about nine miles from Sehwan. Forage was got by the grass-cutters about Arer Peer, also kirby to purchase.			
Warkee River, near its junction with Chorla River	14	6	The Warkee river is small, and joins the Chorla river about half a mile on the right, near which there is a pool of water, at the foot of a rock, which terminates Loond Hill, and which lasts all the year. Warkee camp appears to be the usual halting-place, and had more grass about it than where the dragoons encamped. There are two roads, which separate at the place where Dheeng river is crossed, about four miles from Roree, one running on each side of Loond Hill, and meeting again one mile in front of Warkee. The road running to the right of Loond Hill, along the Chorla river, is longer, but reported better. The halting-place by it is called Chorla Mukam, near some ancient tombs, where there were also fine pools of water in the river. The other road is more stony, as it crosses the Dheeng river two or three times.
Forage was scarce, but furnished by the grass-cutters from the banks of the river.			
Camp at Mulleeree River .	10		Some good pools of water, stated to last all the year. Forage scarce, but procurable by grass-cutters about the river and the hills on the right. The ranges of hills on each side approach much closer, and at four miles the road enters the defile of the Joorung river, and continues along its bed and banks for about three miles very rough and stony, and some rocky nullahs afterwards are crossed before reaching camp.
Pokrun Camp, on Pokrun River	12	3½	Extensive pieces of deep water, and a small stream running. There is no village seen since leaving Roree, though some of the shepherds of the country brought in some goats here. There is a good deal of thinly-scattered jungle, amongst which the shepherds' huts are located. The road continues to ascend slightly, until the fifth mile, crossing four or five rocky nullahs, running into Mulleeree river. The road is then better, with a slight descent, and crosses some nullahs, running southward into the Pokrun river. Forage more plentiful, but procured in the same manner by the grass-cutters about the river-banks.

STAGES.	Distances.		REMARKS.
	Miles.	Furlongs.	
Kajoor Camp	9	4½	Good pools of water. This is the same river with the Pokrun, but the forage not so plentiful. The road is pretty good in general, crossing the river at the sixth mile. At the eighth mile it is confined between the hills and river for a short distance, where it is rocky, and crosses the river again to camp. Roads run off here and about midway to Moohun Kote, a fort of the Ameers, beyond the hills on the left.
Doobah Camp, on the Doobah River	8	2	Good pools of water on the same river, here called the Doorbah. Forage as above. The road is pretty good all the way, through thin jungle, crossing ten or eleven nullahs, some of which are stony.
Murraie Makam, on the Murraie River	9	3½	Water in the sandy bed of a broad river. Ahmedkhan's Tana, a large village, with good supply, is about two miles south-west, further up the river; it is the residence of the soobedar of the district. Two other small villages lie between it and the road, called Mahomedkhan and Janser; but neither have any supplies. There are two roads here, one running on each side of a low range of hills; that to the left is the usual route, and the halting-place at Meerkhan Tana, a village with two or three shops, and is also on the bank of the Murraie river, with water from pits in its sandy bed. The guides brought the detachment by the other road, as having more water, and on account of its being nearer the large village of Ahmedkhan. The road pretty good.
Dumajee	9	6½	A small village of about twenty choppered huts, and a few banian supplies. Water from two wells, and a pool of rain-water in the bed of the river, all of which were exhausted, and found insufficient for the detachment, and part of the camels were not watered. Forage more plentiful, but some distance on the plain to the front, and rear of the stage by the road. The road pretty good.
Irak Mukam, at Irak River 9 3½			The Irak river is crossed at nine miles and a quarter, and water is found in its bed at all seasons, about two miles on the left, at the base of the hills through which it passes to the southward. The distance is not increased by going to this point, though so far off the beaten camel-road, as paths go direct to and from it before reaching the river. Forage abundant, and the road good through jungle; and some cultivation at the fourth mile.
Bhool Camp 2 7½ The roads to Jerakh and Hyderabad cross here.	12	3	A place at the Huttul Ke-bhoot hills, where a nullah contains a good supply of water from the late rains, with plenty of forage. Country covered with thin jungle and grass; but Irak should be the halting-place, making Kuttajee the next stage.
Kuttajee Mukum, at Kuttajee River 12 3			The river about six furlongs on the right has good pools of water, which never fail, especially at the base of

STAGES.	Distances.		REMARKS.
	Miles.	Furlongs.	
Goorban Camp, at Goorban River ...... 6 1 {This long march was made from an expectation that, from not having gone off the road to Irak, a distance of from three to four miles had been saved, which was not the case, as it proved.}	18	4	the hills here, where it passes through the range to the south-west. Forage as above. The road is in general good, excepting where it crosses some nullahs, and is a little confined between the river and some low hills on the left, at the eighth and ninth miles, where it is stony; then good through jungle-bushes to Kuttajee.
Dumba Camp	10	2	The confluence of the Goorban and Kuttajee rivers, both having small running streams and large pieces of standing water. Forage not so plentiful. The road at two miles from Kuttajee has a slight but stony ascent, at the top of which the Gohar Talloo occurs, at present filled with rain-water. At three miles and a half, a rocky ghaut or defile commences, and continues an easy descent passable for guns; but being most of it bare rock, is rough, and crosses two stony nullahs at the bottom. At four miles some more rising ground is passed from the nullah, when the road is good again, along the Kuttajee river to camp, crossing the river at the junction.
Camp Kurrachee, to the lines of the Grenadier Regiment, by the high road	17	1½	Camp Dumba is on the Dumba river, which has good pools, and a small stream of water running. Forage is procurable by the grass-cutters in considerable quantities about Dumba, but more plentifully a few miles before reaching it. The road is in general good, and passes Peepulwaree river and Mukum at six miles and a quarter, which has water in some small wells, at present dug in its bed, and a good deal of short grass and thin jungle.
Kurrachee Town	2		This road is that generally travelled, and is longer than that by Dozan about one mile, but stated to be much better, the first thirteen miles being over an extensive level plain, in most parts thin jungle; but good well-beaten tract at ninth mile. Reekee Koree and two huts are passed on left; but the well is small. Amree Nullah, at present containing pools of water, from the late rain, is passed at ten miles. At thirteen miles the road runs through some rocky ridges, and uneven hard ground, passing a pool of salt-water at thirteen miles and a half on the left, and is then good to camp.

ROUTE from KURRACHEE to KAJA JAMOTE.

Names of Places.	Bearing.	Distances. Miles.	Distances. Furlongs.	Supplies.	Water.	REMARKS.
From the town to Muggeh Peer	N. 10 E.	9	1	none	hot springs	This is the Muggeh tank described by Lieut. Carless. There are pools of warm water, a few date and coco-nut trees, and some mud huts, in which a few fakeers reside.
Chukkora Nullah	N.	11	3	none	in pools	This is a halting-place. Water brackish. No village.
Hubb River	N.	5	6½	none	plenty	A fine stream of excellent water, eighteen inches deep at the place crossed; in many parts there are pools of a depth of twenty and forty feet, abounding with fish and alligators, or rather crocodiles. No village. The inhabitants of this part of Sinde wander about with their numerous herds of cattle, as the country affords pasturage. The Hubb river is said to rise in the mountain-range called Pubb, near Zeedee; it enters the sea twenty miles west of Kurrachee. Second guide, one Sing, has surveyed the route from hence to the point.
Loharie Nullah	N. 10 E.	1	3½	none	scarce	Here the good footpath ends.
Baboora River	N. 4 W.	13	4	none	scarce	Water salt. Road rocky; bad.
Vehrab River	N.	3	3	none	scarce	Road between hills; very bad.
In bed of river	N.W.	2	4			
Vehrab-ja-gote	N. 10 E.	2	2	two shops	abundant	Forty huts. Water from pools in the bed of the river. Plenty of sheep, goats, and buffaloes. Supplies for fifty or sixty men. Inhabitants, Loomires and Guddrals.
Cross Vehrab River	..	2	5½			
Junction of Vehrab and Amrie Rivers	..	8	4½	none	scarce	From holes in bed of river.
Amrie river ends	N. 5 E.	8	..	..	..	Road very bad, hardly passable by camels.
Shaw Billawl, to turning of road N. 10 W., after	W.	3	2	..	..	It will be seen by the protracted route, that the position of this place is singular, being a narrow valley (in which 1,500 men might encamp), producing fruit-trees of various kinds—mango, orange, tamarind—vines, and flowers. A fine spring flows out of the rock and fertilizes the valley, the only inhabitant of which is an ancient

APPENDIX. 373

Names of Places.	Bearing.	Distances. Miles.	Distances. Furlongs.	Supplies.	Water.	REMARKS.
						fakeer (eighty years old), who has resided here upwards of forty years. There is a pukka musjid, and tomb of Awlea Shaw Billaest. It is said the present resident never eats food, but lives on some heavenly substance supplied to him by the genii—an extraordinary assertion, but credited by the people in the vicinity. The spot is sacred, and those who can afford to be buried there esteem themselves fortunate.
On right bank Shah River		4	..	..	..	
Cross river	..	2	..	none	scarce	The bed of river is full of very large babool trees and stones.
Ruins of a village	N.E.	8	2	none	none	
Junction of Shah and Samot River	..	1	..	none	none	
Cross the Samot River	..	6	1	none	none	Very bad road, full of large stones.
River, deserted village, lately occupied by Sahib Khan	N. 10 E.	..	7	none	plenty	Nullahy and stony country.
A spring of fresh water in a nullah	..	6	2	none	plenty	
Foot of small pass (Lesk)	W.	..	..	..	..	The small pass is as if it were paved with common flat stones.
Ascent ditto	..	..	6	..	..	
Descent ditto	..	..	5	..	..	The large one nearly perpendicular. The camel could scarcely go up it, and even then would not have succeeded unless assisted by the ropes.
Commence ascent of the large pass	..	..	5	..	..	
Descent	..	..	4½	..	..	
Vindher River	..	2	½	none	good by digging	Bed full of tamarisk and stones.
Juma Jamote	W. 40 S.	..	1	none	river	Deserted, except in the rains.
Kunaraj River cross	..	14	1	none	plenty	Running stream, three feet deep.
Cross again	..	3	2	none	plenty	
Deep nullah and spring	..	..	1	none	plenty	
Another ditto	..	..	7	none	plenty	
Hoja Jamote-ka-gote	N. 25 W.	2	2	four shops	plenty	Forty huts; 160 inhabitants; can bring into the field 100 matchlocks. This is similar to other villages of the description given—mat huts, and merely temporary. It is probably by this time abandoned, as the people say they merely were there in the rains and hot weather, when the heat on the Hubb river is insupportable. Hoja is the name of the chief. Jamote is the name of the tribe: they are Moosulmen.

VOL. II.   2 C

ROUTE from SUBZUL to SHIKARPOOR.

Surwelee, the last stage in Bhawal Khan's country, is a small village, bearing the tomb of Nawab Moosa Khan; direction, north-east, 80°; distance, eight miles from Subzulkote, and the road leads through slight jungle; a nullah about half-way, with a wooden bridge, and a village: the frontiers of Sinde.

Subzulcote is a pretty large village, having a good bazaar, and many wells, out of the town, of good water. To the north is the dund or lake, which is fast drying up. The spot chosen for encamping-place is among some broken ground by the plough, south-east of the town, in the neighbourhood of wells, and a small jungle which can soon be cleared.

Oobowrah is about thirteen miles distant from Subzul, due west. The encamping-ground lies north-east by south-east, the same spot where the Shah encamped on his way to Shikarpoor. There are three good wells about the vicinity; guidance, a date-tree near the lake, and one of them undergoing repairs: on the other side, in a grove of large tamarisk-trees, another well; and in a plantation, marked by a few plum-trees (Ber), one well, independent of the wells in the village, and the nullahs, over which the pucka bridge is built, which is going to decay, containing water all the year round, and teeming with fish. The road to be traversed is inundated ground when the overflow of the River Indus takes place; at present dry, and considered a good road, with the exception of a slight jungle. Oobowrah, distance from Subzul, is about thirteen miles.

From Oobowrah, next stage is Bagoodra. The road, on the first onset, is over bogs of mud and water, and over a nullah with a wooden bridge. The jungle runs from here about a mile distant, after which a good road until about half a mile near the village of Mammadpoor; before reaching this, you pass a lake and the village of Rajunpoor, and Sooee to the left, distance about three-quarters of a mile from the road, and Zig, one mile; also a garden and well. Leaving Mammadpoor, you meet the small village of Koraeen and the Muswaee drain, running on to Meerpoor; and on reaching Bagoodra, a nullah is crossed: distance from Oobowrah, thirteen miles. The encamping-ground is on the south of the village, having the command of five good wells of water, and where the Shah once encamped.

Surhad is about nine miles' distance from Bagoodra, and, after leaving a jungle, runs for about one mile until it reaches Tutta Malna; after which a slight jungle until reaching the drain, when a pretty thick one commences to near the village. A well, and a few habitations of shepherds, with the village of Janpoor, is seen to the right. A good encamping-ground, with more than nine wells in the neighbourhood. Shah Shooja encamped here.

Gotkee from Surbad is about nine miles; a pretty good road almost all the way. About the midway is a canal thirty feet broad, but rendering no obstacle, and perfectly dry. There are also two small drains to be passed before reaching Gotkee.

From Gotkee to the next stage is Dadoola; distance about thirteen miles; direction south-west 70°, passing three villages—Bammoowala, Bhishtee, and Malloodee; all the way a slight jungle, which can soon be cleared with a little trouble. The encamping-ground is on the north side of the village, having the use of three wells on the lands. This part of the country is well peopled, and cultivation is getting on prosperously.

Thence, Choonga, after passing Bhelar and a drain, which should be avoided by treading on the east side; the road is free from jungle: direction, south-west 64°. This village is situated on the dund and deep water which runs on to Azeezpoor and Hoosein Belee. The encamping-ground had better be on the bank of the dund, which is about ten, twelve, and fourteen feet high; the road leads on the bank and over jungle, and in one place over a cotton field, on to Azeezpoor, which is also near the river; but the ferry, commonly known by the name of Azeezpoor-ka Pattan, is at the village of Hoosein Belee. Azeezpoor, from Choonga, is about four miles distant.

The next halting-place is Hoosein Belee; at the ferry, after crossing a deserted dund, completely dry at the road, and some small jungle. There are two streams at the present ferry, one the dund, about 150 feet broad, with two, three, and four feet water; the best is an extensive one. Two boats ply here, one on each stream, and people land on the Bet, having to go about a mile and a half, when they again embark, and land on the other side. The two ferries made here is a matter of choice of the boatmen, to save themselves the trouble of plying to a long distance, for there is a good ferry higher up, where the army should cross.

The Indus, on the western bank, contains water twelve, sixteen, and eighteen feet, and at the centre stream, more than thirty and forty feet deep, with a strong running current, near the Bet (an island), ten, twelve, and eighteen feet water; and, on the east bank, four, six, and eight feet water. There are two villages situated on the northern bank of the river, named Syud Ameer Mohamed and Phoolooda-got. Crossing the ferry, the place of encampment pitched on is at the village of Got Amil, about a mile from the river, and in a fine plain; the river water is used here, and there is but one small temporary well.

From Got-Amil, taking a direction north-west 80°, about a mile on the road, is the small village of Motar-mar, and then, about half a mile further, is a good drain, over which is a temporary bridge, all shattered; horsemen are obliged to keep to the left, and pass the drain, taking the same direction, and leaving Rubbun and Enjmut to the left, the latter a comfortable village. You pass a small jungle on to Kaee, where is the encamping-ground of the army on the south of the village. The difficulty here to be experienced is from the well-water, which is not good.

Leaving Kaee, the direction varies to north-west 60°. Distance from Got-Amil to this place is little more than twelve miles. Shikarpoor is the next stage, before coming to which you pass through a good path-road, on both sides free from jungle, and, after reaching Lubauna, you pass the Scinde canal. Lubauna is a village under Meer Ali Moorad, and to appearance, the inhabitants are in a comfortable way; patches of cultivation mark the road on to Shikarpoor. Distance from Kaee nearly twelve miles.

ROUTE through SINDE, BELOOCHISTAN, KHORASSAN, to KANDAHAR.

STAGES.	Miles.	Furlongs.	REMARKS.
Bamnigote	—	—	A small village near Vikkur and Gora-baree.
Jullalkote	9	1	Ditto, crossed the river on pontoons.
Shuamroo	7	7	A moderate village.
Golamshaw	18	4	A large village on the bank of the river.
Tuttah	11	4	Encampment on the south-west side of the city.
Shaik Radan Peer	9	2	No village, water from two large tanks.
Soonda	13	3	A large village.
Jirrikh	9	5	Ditto, on the bank of the river.
Mozauwur	9	2	Encampment ditto ditto.
Kotree, near Hyderabad	13	6	A large village, four miles from the city.
Bada	9	2½	A village on the bank of the river.
Oonderpoor	11	3½	A large village ditto.
Kassye and Gopang	11	1	Two villages on the bank of the river.
Majunda	10	0	A large town on a creek.
Sun, or Sen	12	1	A large place.
Amree	10	7½	A small village on the bank of the river.
Lukkee	11	1	A large village, and a fine piece of water.
Sehwan	13	1	A large town, Arrul and branch of Indus crossing Lukkee Ghaut half-way.
Turratee and Bullalpoor	8	1	One mile asunder, both large villages.
Jullan and Baumbeya	9	4	A moderate village, one mile and a half from the river.
Moondra	11	3	A large town, wells and standing water.
Rokun	6	7	A large village on the bank of the river.
Gulloo	10	2	A moderate village, and fine piece of water.
Nowaderra	15	6½	Encampment one mile and a half on left of Nowaderra.
Chunna	6	2	A moderate village on a branch of the river.
Futtepoor	7	0	A large village, and fine piece of water.
Buckrance	15	6	A moderate village, near Narra river.
Larkhana	9	7	A large town, and Larkhana canal, now dry.
Kumber	15	1½	Ditto, with good wells.
Dustalee	9	7½	A moderate village, where kafilahs assemble going northwards.
Shudautpoor	15	4	A moderate village, near the runn lately deserted.
Kechee	30	0	A village near the hills, crossing the runn or desert.
Jhull	19	1	A large town, and fine streams of water, the principal one of the Moongsee Beloochee.
Punjoke	13	5½	A large village, and fine streams of water.
Gundawa	11	3½	A large town, ditto ditto.
Gajen	5	3½	A large village, ditto ditto.
Shorun	14	3	A moderate village at present, but the principal one of the Rind Belooches.
Sunnee	23	3½	A small village.
Nowshara	18	1	A large village, with good bazaar.

STAGES.	Miles.	Furlongs.	REMARKS.
Dadur	7	4	A large town, the principal of the district.
Kondeelauna	10	5	No village, the first stage in the Bolan defile, forage scarce.
Kirts	10	3	A small village lately deserted, the second stage in the Bolan Pass.
Beebeenaunee	9	3	No village, the third stage in the Bolan defile, forage scarce.
Abigoom	9	6½	Ditto, fourth ditto ditto.
Siri-Bolan	8	5½	Ditto, fifth ditto ditto.
Busht-beh Dhowlut	12	7½	Encampment in the desert beyond the head of the pass, no water.
Siriab	14	7	Encampment, and some good water, villages deserted.
Shawl	8	1½	The principal town in the district.
Kuchlak	11	5½	A small village, at present deserted; water good.
Hydurzye	9	6	Ditto, and river near.
Hykulzye	10	7	A large village, running and river water.
Lora River	7	1	Very steep and deep banks, few yards of water.
Urumbee	7	5½	
Killa Abdulla	5	1	A village near the Kojuck Pass.
Chummum	12	6	Some wells in a hollow, after crossing the hills of the Kojuck Pass; no village near.
Dund-i-Goolai	13	6	Some tanks, dependent on the canals from the hills, which were turned off by the natives on some disagreement about a remuneration with the advance.
Futtoolah	9	2	A small village, its water cut off as at Dund-i-Coolai.
Mhela, or Mhelamaunda	12	2	Encampment near a small stream in a river bed.
Tuktapool	14	4	A fine stream, no village near.
Deh-i-Hajee	7	4	An extensive place, aqueduct water.
Kocshaub Abdull Karez	10	1½	
Kandahar	8	4½	

INDEX.

TO VOLUME I.

Aasnee	Page 1	Aknur	Page 48
Abad	1	Akora	49
Abad	1	Ak Serai	49
Abasabad	1	Alee Boolghan	49
Abdalla-i-Boorj	1	Alem Khan	49
Abdool	1	Alghoee	49
Abdooruhman	1	Aliabad	49
Abdulla Azeer	1	Aliar-Ka-Tanda	49
Abdul Rahim Khan	1	Ali Bagh	49
Ab-i-Goom	2	Ali Boghan	49
Ab-i-Koormeh	2	Ali Bunder	49
Ab-Istada Lake	2	Ali Musjid	50
Ab-i-Tulk	3	Alingar	51
Abkhana	3	Aliphur	51
Abkhor-i-Roostum	3	Alipoor	51
Abookhan	3	Alipoor	51
Acesines River	3	Alishang	51
Acora	3	Alizye	52
Adam-Khan-Ka-Maree	3	Allahabad	52
Adampoora	4	Alla-Yar-Ka-Tanda	52
Adawaon	4	Alli Jah's Killa	52
Adeean	4	Alma-di-Got	52
Adhee Bahr	4	Altumgot	52
Adrek	4	Altumoor	52
Adruscund, or Rood-i-Adruscund	4	Am	52
		Amawanee	52
Afghanistan	4	Amb	52
Agaun	46	Ambar	53
Aghor, or Hingol River	46	Amdabad	53
Agra	46	Ameenana	53
Ahmedabad	46	Ameen-la-ka-jo-gote	53
Ahmed Khan	46	Ameer Altalta	53
Ahmed Khan Ka Magha	46	Amerkote	53
Ahmed Khan's Tanda	47	Amil Got	53
Ahmedpoor	47	Amoo Mahomed	53
Ahmedpoor	47	Amrajee Kote	53
Ahmedpoor Chuta	48	Amran Mountains	53
Airul	48	Amree	54
Aisabad	48	Amree Nullah	54
Akaligurh	48	Amrie	54
Akkehu	48	Amritsir	54
Akmuk	48	Amurgurh	56

Amurnath	56	Baghwarrah	64
Anardurra	56	Bagoo	64
Andavre	56	Bagoodra	64
Andkhoo	56	Baguramee	64
Angeera	57	Bagwana	65
Anghorian	57	Bahawulpoor	65
Anian	57	Bahram	65
Anjeera	57	Bahreh River	65
Anjyruk	57	Bahur	65
Antre Roustam	57	Baida	65
Aowbuh	57	Baidyanathpur	65
Arabul	57	Bairan	65
Arak	58	Bajar	65
Aredo	58	Bajoorah	65
Areejaw	58	Bajour	65
Arghasan, or Urghessann	58	Bakasir	66
Ars Beghee	58	Bakerala	66
Arul, or Airul	58	Bakkar	66
Asloo	59	Bala Bagh	66
Astor, or Husara	59	Baladeh	67
Astola	59	Bale River	67
Atgah	59	Balla Atta Khan	67
Atlah	59	Balloo Jirda Ree Ka Koobeh	67
Attauree	59	Ballyaree	67
Attock (اتک) Atak, "obstacle")	59	Balti, or Baltistan	67
		Bamboora	67
		Bambut Poora	67
Atuk	61	Bameekutair	68
Atuk	61	Bamian	68
Augoo	61	Baminacote	73
Augoomanoo	61	Bamnoo Chakur	73
Auk Tuppa	61	Banahou	74
Awan	61	Banaul	74
Awchiri River	61	Bandee	74
Azeezpoor	61	Bander Vikkar	74
Azeree Chukee	62	Bangudjee	74
Azim Khan	62	Banihal	74
		Banoo, or Bunnoa	74
		Bapaw	74
Bab	62	Bappoo	75
Baba Hadjee	62	Bara	75
Baba Kara	62	Baradree	75
Baba Moorghab	62	Barak	76
Baber-Ka-Cha	62	Barakail	76
Babla	63	Barakhail	76
Baboora River	63	Barakzye	76
Baboos	63	Baral	76
Baboo Saboo	63	Baramgula	76
Babur-ka-Killa	63	Baramula	76
Babutu	63	Barata	77
Badabeer	63	Barra Ahmedpoor	77
Baddra	63	Barshoree	77
Badoo River	63	Barsnow	77
Badoor	63	Baruk	77
Bagae Gote	63	Baramgula	77
Bagh	64	Barus Ke Got	77
Baghaw	64	Bashkala	77
Bagh-i-Alum	64	Bashoree	77
Baghwan, Bagwana, or Bunkar	64	Bassowal	77

Baster Bunder	77	Bhoong Bara	107
Batchaw, or Butcha	77	Bhoor	107
Bau Sooltan	78	Bhooraiwala	107
Bayla	78	Bhoorka-Mu	107
Bazaar-Ahmed-Khan	78	Bhugwur River	107
Bazaruk	78	Bhullee-de-Chak	107
Beah River	78	Bhusool	107
Beas	78	Bhyrawul	107
Bed Tilla	79	Bhyrowalah	107
Beeah	79	Bijbahar, or Vigipara	108
Beebee Nanee	79	Bijore	108
Beebeenaunee	79	Billundee	108
Beeboo Triggur	79	Bimber (بيمبر Bhimber)	108
Beelalpoor	80		
Beelun	80	Bindeh	108
Beraloo	80	Binoa	108
Beetun	80	Biralee	109
Beghram	80	Birozabad	109
Behut	81	Bisuli	109
Bela	81	Bitngee	109
Beloat	82	Boda, or Baida	109
Beloochistan	82	Bokharee	109
Belur	99	Bolan Pass	109
Bemanjoporo	99	Bolan	112
Benee Badam	99	Bonakot	113
Beneer	99	Bonyr	113
Bent-i-Jah	99	Boodooke	113
Berawul	99	Boodoor River	113
Bereng	99	Booloo	113
Bermul	99	Boom	113
Berravol	99	Boombulpoora	113
Berravol	100	Booneere	113
Berravol	100	Boonga	114
Beta	100	Boonga	114
Betsul	100	Boonj	114
Bezaise	100	Booquie	114
Bhag or Bagh (باغ Bagh, "a garden")	100	Boorhan	114
		Boorkhoe	114
Bhagah-ki-Tanda	101	Boothauk (بت خاک But-khak, "idol-dust")	114
Bhahall	101		
Bhat	101	Bootia	115
Bhauda	101	Bootla	115
Bhawlpoor (Buhawulpur)	101	Boree	115
Bhawlpoor	105	Bowynuh	115
Bheem-ka-Kubba	106	Breng	115
Bheenee Badam	106	Brijky	115
Bhekee	106	Brygy	115
Bhelar	106	Bubuk	115
Bhera	106	Buchoo	116
Bheranah	106	Buckranee	116
Bhetlee	106	Buddeeabad	116
Bhimbur	106	Budeena	116
Bhira	106	Budrawar	116
Bhirhtee	106	Budwan	116
Bholan Pass	106	Buggaur	116
Bhoodluh	106	Bugut	117
Bhool	106	Bukapoor	117
Bhooldra	107	Bukerala	117

Bukkur (بهكر Bhukur)	117	Byabanck	130
		Bye Dera	130
Bukkur	118	Bye Deru	130
Bukrala	118		
Bukwa	118		
Bukwa-a-Karaiz	119	Cabool, or Cabul	130
Bulameen	119	Cabulpoor	130
Bulbut	119	Caferistan	130
Buleas	119	Candahar	130
Bulloo	119	Caroppa, or Kadapa, Pass	130
Bulria	119	Carwan Cazee	130
Bulti, or Bultistan	119	Cashmere, or Cashmir	131
Bul-Tul, or Kantal	123	Catarh	131
Bumbeya	123	Caubool, or Caubul	131
Bumbra	124	Chacher	131
Bumbutpoora	124	Chachera	131
Bund	124	Chadooh	131
Bunda	124	Chagai	131
Bundee Boree	124	Chuga Serai	131
Bunder Gurree	124	Cha Gooroo	131
Bund-i-Burbur	124	Chah-i-Jehan	131
Bundipur, or Bundurpur	124	Chah-i-Meerza	131
Bungala	125	Chah-i-Moosuk	131
Bungool Dehra	125	Chaikal	131
Bungush	125	Chain	132
Buniah Wallee	125	Chamoreril	132
Bunka	125	Chandee	132
Bunkar	125	Chandee-Ja-Gote	132
Bunna	125	Chandia	132
Bunnoo	125	Chandia	132
Bunpoor	126	Chandkhote	152
Bura	126	Chandkoh	133
Burakhail	126	Chandoo, or Chandra	133
Buranghur	126	Chandookee	133
Bureen Chenon	127	Chandra	133
Bureen Chinar	127	Chandra	133
Bureng, Bereng, or Breng	127	Chandrabhaga	133
Bureng River	127	Chang	133
Burg	127	Channi-Khan-Digot	133
Burguna	127	Chaogaonwa	133
Burmawur	128	Chappar	133
Burobera	128	Charan	134
Burra Chicher	128	Charatta	134
Burran	128	Charbagh	134
Burrindoo, or Bonyr	128	Chah Boorjuk	134
Burrukullan	128	Chardar Pass	134
Burshoree	128	Chardeh	134
Burt	129	Chardeh	134
Burukhanu	129	Chardeh	134
Busseen	129	Charee Chuckoo	134
Busseerah	129	Charikar	134
Bussoor Khail	129	Charna	135
Bussoul	129	Charratta	135
Butcha	129	Charsia	135
Butcheal Lugaree	129	Chasgo, or Shushgao	135
Butchral	129	Chatchur	136
Butora	129	Checheneh	136
Butte Kote	129	Chechoke	136
Buzdar Pass	130	Checkau, or Checkaub	136

Cheeaput	136	Chotta Lassaree	144
Cheehawutnee	136	Chotta Seeta	144
Cheela	136	Chotyaali	144
Cheendee	136	Chouchuck	145
Chegha	136	Choukooli	145
Chehar Bagh	136	Choutra	145
Chehel Tan	137	Chuch	145
Chehl Bucha Gum	137	Chuck	145
Chehl Dochtur	137	Chuckerala	145
Cheirjagarain	138	Chuckrealee	145
		Chuckree	145
Chenaub (چناب Chinab)	138	Chuckwundee	145
Chepkedar	140	Chuhkowal	146
Cheran, Cherat, or Shah Nurud		Chukkora-Nulla	146
Dyn	140	Chukra	146
Cherra	140	Chulluk	146
Cherra	140	Chumba	146
Chesgow	140	Chumba	146
Cheychun	140	Chummun	146
Cheylar	140	Chumorereel	146
Cheylee	140	Chuman Chokee	146
Chiaguz	140	Chund	146
Chiarbag	140	Chunderwon	147
Chiarbag	140	Chundha	147
Chibree	140	Chundia	147
Chichundee	140	Chundia	147
Chiganuk	141	Chundranee	147
Chikon	141	Chundun	147
Chiliya	141	Chungal	147
Chilney, or Churna	141	Chungond	147
Chinab	141	Chungur	147
Chinee	141	Chunna	147
Chinini	141	Chupper Mount	148
Chinjan	141	Churcha	148
Chioukiatan	141	Churna	148
Chir	141	Churra Fort	148
Chirnat	141	Chusma I Jadee	148
Chitral	142	Chusma Punguk	148
Chitral	142	Chuta Ahmedpoor	148
Chittrooree	142	Chutka	148
Choakee	142	Chuttai Ka Gote	148
Choatilloh	142	Chutterbai	148
Chobara	142	Chuwari	149
Choho	142	Cohan	149
Chokundee	142	Cohast Gurnode	149
Cholalaj Pass	143	Coleew	149
Choll	143	Col-Narawa	149
Chooashahgunee	143	Colul	149
Choonee	143	Coondor	149
Choonga	143	Coruchie	149
Choonka	143	Cuchee	149
Chore	143	Cuchee	149
Chorla	143	Culdan	149
Chorla Mukam	144	Cudjerab, or Kuteherie	150
Chota, or Nawa Sun	144	Cundye	150
Chotta Churnaut (signifying		Cutch Gundava	150
"small," strictly چھوٹا		Cutch Toba	152
chota)	144	Daamrah	152
Chotta Gulloo	144	Dabhu	152

Dadarah	153	Dera Deen Punah	162
Dadoola	153	Dera Deen Punah	162
Dadun Khan Pind	153	Dera Fati Khan	162
Dadur	153	Dera Ghazee Khan	162
Daebraz	154	Dera Ismael Khan	163
Daho	154	Derajat	164
Dajel	154	Derbend	164
Daka	154	Deristan	165
Dalana	154	Derra Guz	165
Damajee	155	Derwazeh	165
Dama-Ka-Kot	155	Dewalan	165
Daman, or The Border	155	Dewalik	165
Damunkoh	155	Deyhifaiz	165
Dan	155	Deyplah	165
Daneh Chekow	156	Deyrah	165
Dar	156	Dhak	165
Dara	156	Dheeng	166
Darah	156	Dheengee	166
Darajee	156	Dher	166
Darapoor	156	Dheria Gote, Soe, or Sovee	166
Darazoo-Ka-Kot	156	Dheyrialee	166
Darbarra	157	Dhoda	166
Darragote	157	Dho Dace	166
Darunta	157	Dhowler	166
Dasht-i-Bedaulat	157	Dhanneeal	166
Davouch	158	Dhurwal	166
Dawun	158	Dhyr	166
Debalpoor	158	Diarmul, or Nanga Purbut	167
Deedled	158	Die	167
Deedwal	158	Dilaram	167
Deejy	158	Dilawur	167
Deela	159	Dilazak	167
Deembra	159	Diliar	167
Deenarh	159	Dincana, or Deengana	167
Deengah	159	Dingana	168
Deengana	159	Dingee	168
Deengurh	159	Dirawul, or Dilawur	168
Deerah Jallah	159	Dobre	168
Deeshoo	159	Dobundee	168
Deewalik	159	Doda	168
Deh Hindoo	159	Do Dundan	169
Deh-i-Hajee	159	Dola	169
Deh-i-Kepuk	160	Doobah	169
Deh-i-Nou	160	Doobah	169
Deh-i-Subz	160	Doob Gau	169
Deh Koondee	160	Dooboorjie	169
Deh Lahour	160	Doodee Ghat	169
Dehr	160	Doo Kooee	170
Dehra	160	Doonah	170
Dehra-Jam-Ka, or Aurunga Bunder	160	Doondey	170
		Doora	170
Dehra Khan Gancha	160	Dooshak	170
Dehree Kote, or Dera Ghabi	160	Dooshank	170
Deh Zirgaran	161	Dor	170
Deo Chundaisur Mahadeo	161	Doraha	170
Deogonda	161	Doree River	170
Deotsuh	161	Doshak	171
Depaulpoor	161	Dost Mahomed's Fort	171
Dera	162	Doulutpoor	171
Derabund	162	Dour	171

INDEX TO VOL. I.

Dowd Khail	171
Dowlatabad	171
Dowlutdyar	171
Dowlutpoor	171
Dowulutpoor	171
Dozan	171
Drabogam	172
Drabund, or Derabund	172
Dras	172
Drey	172
Dribbar	172
Droubund	172
Drubbee	172
Drumtoor	173
Dub	173
Dubar	173
Dublee	173
Duchin	173
Dufehr	173
Duka, or Daka	173
Dukkee	174
Dulhuk	174
Dullah	174
Dumajee	174
Dumba	174
Dumdum	175
Dumtaur, or Dharum Tawur	175
Dumtaur	175
Dund	175
Dundal	176
Dundee	176
Dundi Goolai	176
Dundya	176
Dunwullee	176
Durajee	176
Duras, or Dras	176
Durasind	176
Durawat	177
Duraz	177
Durban	177
Duree	177
Duria Khan	177
Durkkee	177
Durmagee	177
Durnameh	177
Durraha	177
Durruk River	177
Durwaza Pass	178
Durya	178
Dusht-i-Bedowlut	178
Dustalee	178
Dustee	178
Duturna	178
Eebibul	178
Eejmut	179
Eekung-Choo, or River of Ghertope	179
Eesa Khan	179
Eleegill	179
Emaum Ghur (امام گڑھ)	
Imam Garh, "Priest-fort"	179
Emenabad	180
Endreesa	180
Erak	180
Eree	181
Esott	181
Essun de Wustee	181
Eyzulat Khan	181
Fakir Mahomed Ka Kote	181
Falour	181
Fapree	181
Farajghan	181
Fatta Dur	182
Fazilpoor	182
Ferai Kholm	182
Feringabad	182
Ferzah	182
Ferengal	183
Fezan Khyle	183
Filor, or Falour	183
Footakea	183
For Chapper	184
Frinjal Pass	184
Fulailee	184
Fuqueerka Kooh	184
Fureedabad	184
Furrah	184
Furrah Rood, or River of Furrah	185
Furza River	185
Futeh Jung	185
Futehpoor	185
Futighur	185
Futi Panjal	186
Futteghur	186
Futtegurh	186
Futtehabad	186
Futtehpoor	186
Futtehpoor, Fatipoor, Futtipoor فتحپور "town of victory"	186
Futtehpoor	187
Futtehpore	187
Futteynli Jullailee	187
Futtihpoor	187
Futtipoor	187
Futtoolah Killa, or Puttoola Killa	187
Futty Khan	187
Fyzabad	188

Gad, or Ghar	188	Gomul	204
Gahayja	188	Gomul	204
Gahrah	188	Gomul Pass	204
Gajen	188	Gonne, or Goonee River	204
Gajin	188	Goobla	204
Gancha	188	Goodake	205
Ganga	188	Goodeoobushd	205
Gangreh Gote	188	Googoo	205
Gansyh Bul	189	Googroe Bheerun Luk	205
Gardou	189	Goojah	205
Garrah	189	Goojeranwala	205
Garrah	189	Goojerat	205
Gartope, Gardokh, or Garo	189	Goolab Seah	205
Gazah	190	Goolairee	205
Gazin	190	Goolam Ali	206
Geedur Gullee	190	Goolam Hooseingola	206
Gerace Reman	190	Goolam Hussain Seir Ka Gote	206
Geramnee	191	Goolam Ja Gote	206
Ghah Kirbeh	191	Goolaub Shee	206
Ghain i-Bala	191	Goolistan	206
Ghar	191	Gooljatooe	206
Ghara	191	Goolkoo	206
Ghazee-abad	191	Goolkuts	207
Ghizni	191	Gool Mahon	207
Ghojan	192	Goomeran	207
Gholam-Shah-Ka-Kote	192	Goondee Azim Khan	207
Gholam Shah	192	Goonee River	207
Ghondan	192	Goongree	207
Ghondee Jooma	192	Goongroo River	207
Ghoorka	192	Goorab Sing	207
Ghorabaree	192	Goorban	207
Ghora Trup	192	Goorban	207
Ghorbund	193	Goordoo Bagh	208
Ghore	193	Goorjeanuh	208
Ghoro Trop	194	Gooroo	208
Ghosgurh, or Rookhunpoor	194	Gooroo Killa	208
Ghospoor	194	Gooruh	208
Ghulghuleh	194	Goorzywan	208
Ghunymut Huzaruh	194	Goostang	208
Ghurruk	194	Gootie	208
Ghurry	194	Goozarat	208
Ghuzamuridee	194	Goozur-i-Khashi	208
Ghuznee (غزني Ghizni)	195	Goozuristan	208
		Gopang	208
Ghuznee	201	Gopang	208
Gidrawala	202	Gorazan	209
Giduri Ke Patun	202	Goree	209
Gilghit	202	Goreewala	209
Girdee	202	Gorian	209
Girishk	202	Gotkee	209
Gironee	203	Gottarao	209
Gisry	203	Gourjeanuh	210
Goberunce	203	Guddra	210
Goda	204	Guddra	210
Gohar Tulao	204	Gugah	210
Goindwal	204	Guggeira	210
Gol	204	Guggur	210
Golakee	204	Gujerat	210
Goma Ghondu	204	Gujuru-Walla	210

Gulamurg	211
Gulbahar	211
Gulgula	211
Gulistan Karez	212
Gullah	212
Gullah	212
Gullean Ka Gote	212
Gumbut	212
Gumba	213
Gunaidio	213
Gundamuk	213
Gundava Pass	213
Gundava	213
Gunderra	214
Gundutsan	214
Guneemurah	214
Gunga Bal	214
Gungatee	214
Gunguni	214
Gunjatee	214
Gunneemurgh	214
Gunysh Bul	215
Guranee	215
Gurdaiz	215
Gurdan Dewar	215
Guribai Pass	215
Gurilla	215
Gurmab	215
Gurmab	216
Gurmab	216
Gurmsehl (گرمسیر Gurmseer, "warm region," or گرمسهل Gurmsahl, "warm plain")	216
Gurnagh	217
Gurnee	217
Gurree	217
Gurseah	217
Guruk Teelah	217
Gurunee	217
Gurys	217
Guswap	217
Guz	217
Gwadel	217
Gwadel Cape, or Ras Noo	218
Gwalian Pass	218
Gwazgar Pass	218
Gwetter	219
Gydur Khyle	219
Hagah	219
Hageguk	219
Haidaree	220
Hajamaree	220
Hajeechurm	220
Hajeeka	220
Hajeekajoke	220
Hajee Kurreemdad	220
Hajeepoor	220
Hajeguk	220
Hakrit Sar	220
Halachee	220
Hala Mountains	220
Halan Syuds	223
Halipootra	223
Halla	223
Hamoon	223
Hangu, or Hangoo	226
Haramuk	226
Harapa	227
Harawug	227
Haripoor	227
Haripoor (هریپور "Town of Hari," or Vishnoo)	227
Haripoor	228
Harnavee	228
Haroot	228
Haru	228
Hashim Chicher	228
Hassan Khan	228
Hattyaree	228
Havalee	228
Hazarjooft	229
Heddeealee	229
Helai	229
Helmund	229
Herat	230
Heri Rood, or Hury River	234
Hidda	235
Hiddawgote	236
Hiliya	236
Hiliya	236
Hillaya	236
Himtut	236
Hindan	236
Hindoo Koosh	236
Hinglaj	249
Hingol	249
Hirroo River	249
Hisaruk	249
Hissaruck	249
Hissaruck	249
Hoblal	249
Hoja Jamote Ka Gote	250
Honshaira	250
Hoormara	250
Hoormuk	250
Hoosenee	250
Hooshiarpoor	250
Hoossein Bela	251
Hoshyarpur	251
Houzi Ahmed Khan	251
Houzi-Meer Daoud	251
Houz-i-Muddud Khan	251
Hubb	251

Hubb 252
Hudeah Khad 252
Huft Asya, or Huftasaya 252
Huft Kotul 253
Hujamree 253
Huleejee 253
Humboowa 254
Hungoo 254
Hunjunby 254
Hurdeh 254
Hureekee (ہری کی پتن)
  Huri ke patan, Town of
  Huri, Hari, or Vishnoo) 254
Huripur Fort 254
Hurjpur 254
Hurreah 254
Hurroo 255
Hurrund, or Hurroond ... 255
Hurvoob 255
Hury River 255
Huryh 255
Husara 255
Hushtmy 255
Hushtnuggur 255
Husseinwah 255
Hussee 255
Hussun Abdul 255
Hutial 256
Huwelee 256
Huzara, or Huzroo 256
Huzareh Country 256
Huzrelwala 260
Huzroo 260
Hydaspes River 260
Hyderabad 260
Hyderkhail, or Hyderkhel 262
Hyder Khan 262
Hydrabad 262
Hydurzie, or Hydurzye ... 262
Hykulzye 262
Hyphasis 263

Ibrahim Bannas 263
Ibrahim Joee River 263
Illiassee 263
Indus 264
Inlkawn 283
Irak Mukam 283
Irak River 283
Ishikaghasy 283
Ishpan 283
Ishpee 283
Iskardoh 283
Islamabad 286
Islamcote 286
Islamgurh, or Nohur ... 286
Islam Killa 287

Islamkote 287
Ismail Puttan 287
Isphawk 287
Ispinglee 287
Ispunglee 287
Istalif 287
Isturgateh, or Isturgeteh 288

Jackree 288
Jadak 288
Jaffrabad 289
Jafur 289
Jagan 289
Jaghan, or Jaghun 289
Jailpoor 289
Jailum, or Jelum 289
Jailum, Jelum, Jilum, Veshau,
  Veyut, or Behut (جہام
  Jhilum) 290
Jainpoor 292
Jairula 292
Jaitanu 292
Jalendher 292
Jalk 292
Jallinder 292
Jam 292
Jamhallaka Tanda 292
Jamote Hoja 292
Jampoor 293
Jampoor 293
Jamrood 293
Jamu 293
Jamut Thura 293
Jana 294
Janee Ka Sung 294
Janehdurra 294
Jangur 294
Jannoo Kareez 294
Janpoor 294
Janser 294
Jareja 294
Jaya 294
Jehangroo 294
Jeja, or Jeya 294
Jelalabad 294
Jelalabad 296
Jelalabad 296
Jelalpoor 296
Jelloogheer 297
Jelum 297
Jemel Khans Kooa 297
Jendialeh 297
Jendoul 297
Jesool 297
Jesrod, or Jesroute ... 298
Jewa, or Jewah 298
Jewala Muki 298
Jeykeir 299

Jhalawan	299	Jurroop	306
Jhow	300	Jurruk	306
Jhubbher	300	Jussa	306
Jhung	300	Jutta Ka Gote	306
Jilum	300	Jutteel Mountains	306
Jimpoor	300	Juttoo	307
Jindala	300	Jym Kila	307
Jindialeh	300		
Joa	300		
Joa	300	Kabool	307
Joageh Walla	300	Kabool River, or Jui Shir	316
Joali	301	Kachee	318
Jodhake	301	Kadirpoor	318
Joga Syn	301	Kadurra	318
Johan	301	Kaee	318
Jok	301	Kaffir Ka Bund	318
Joke	301	Kafiristan	318
Jokhay	301	Kafir Kila	327
Jokhe	301	Kafir Kote	327
Jolunee	301	Kafir Tunjee	327
Jooa	301	Kafr Kot, or the Infidel's Fort	327
Jooee Cirear	301	Kaggalwalla	327
Joogewallah	301	Kahag	327
Joorg	302	Kahee	327
Joorgee	302	Kaheer	327
Joreend	302	Kaheree	328
Josa	302	Kahun	328
Jourey	302	Kailleeawala	329
Jubbra	302	Kaimpoor	329
Jugbarah	302	Kajoor	329
Jugdee Khaee	302	Kajoor	329
Jugduluk	302	Kaka	329
Jujja	303	Kakajan	329
Julalpoor	303	Kakapore	330
Jalalpoor	303	Kakur	330
Julduk	303	Kala Bagh	330
		Kalagur	330
Julinder (جالند)	303	Kalaichi	331
Jull	303	Kala Kullai	331
Jullai Kaet	304	Kalee, Cave of	331
Jullalkote	304	Kaleesa Rabat	331
Jullal Khan	304	Kale Sura	331
Jullaree	304	Kalloo	331
Jullawgote	304	Kallora	331
Julloo Kotul	304	Kaloo	331
Julraiz	304	Kama River	331
Juma	304	Kamalia	332
Juma Jamote	304	Kambar	332
Jumburum	304	Kamjee	332
Jumedarah	305	Kandahar	332
Jumeeat	305	Kandairoh	336
Jumlaira	305	Kanegorum	336
Jumrajee Wussee	305	Kanghur	336
Jundra	305	Kanhi	336
Jung	305	Kanoteh-ka-Gote	336
Jungalee	305	Kantal	336
Junnoo Kareez	305	Kantasir	337
Junruck	305	Kapoortheila	337
Jupp	305	Kapourdigueri	337

Kara Bagh	337	Khangur	378
Karachi	337	Khangur	378
Karaila	337	Khangurh	378
Kara-Su, or Black River	337	Khanjee	379
Kara Tuppa Fort	337	Khankail	379
Karatupuh	338	Khanpoor	379
Kardo	338	Khanpoor	379
Kareez Dost Mohamed	338	Khanpoor	379
Karmel	338	Kharan	379
Karora	338	Kharan	380
Karuk	338	Khardoo Chummum	380
Kasbah	338	Kharuck	380
Kasee	338	Khash	380
Kashgar	339	Khash Roduk	380
Kashmir	339	Khash Rood, or River of Khash	380
Kasien	372	Khatian	381
Kasimpoor	372	Khawak	381
Kason	372	Khedaree	381
Kassye Gopang	372	Khediwaree Mouth	381
Kasunka	372	Kheewa, or Keewa	381
Katachee	372	Kheil-i-akhund	382
Kataike	372	Khelat-i-Ghiljie	382
Katakchund, or Kartakshee	372	Khengunpoor	382
Katawas	373	Khenj	382
Kateychee-ke-Ghurree	373	Kheorah	382
Katia	373	Kher	382
Kator	373	Khewa	382
Kauhee	373	Khimpoor	382
Kedje, or Kedge	373	Khirpoor	382
Kedywaree	374	Khirpoor	382
Keechree	374	Khoar	382
Keehal	374	Khodabad	383
Keehal	374	Khodad Khan	383
Keer	374	Khoja Amran	383
Keertar	374	Khoja Khidree Julgha	383
Keertee	374	Khonck	383
Keewa	374	Kholoo Choytyally	383
Kehchee	374	Khood Zye	383
Kelal	374	Khoosh-ab	383
Kelat	374	Khooshk-i-Sufaid	383
Kelat	375	Khooshk Nakhood	383
Kelat-i-Ghiljie	376	Khootpoor	383
Kemang	376	Khopalu	384
Ken	377	Khorzana Kotul	384
Kepra	377	Khowali Syakuk	384
Keris	377	Khozdar	384
Kerku	377	Khund, or Koond	384
Kernasheen	377	Khurbuzy Serai	385
Kettas	377	Khurd Kabool	385
Keypur	377	Khurtoot	385
Keyra Gurrie	377	Khurwar Pass	385
Khairabad	377	Khut-i-Khurga Oona	385
Khairr	377	Khyber Mountains	385
Khisa Ghar	378	Khyber Pass	386
Khajeh Ourieh	378	Khyerpoor	388
Khak-i-Chapan	378	Khyrabad	389
Khanbaila	378	Khyrabad	389
Khandearah	378	Khyree Deree	389
Khangaum	378	Khyrgaon	389

Khyroodden	390	Kohuk	399
Khyrpoor	390	Kohuk	399
Khyrpoor Dahr	390	Kojuk Pass	399
Kidur	390	Kokaran	400
Kijreearee	391	Koker Nag	400
Kila Ameer Khan	391	Kol	400
Kila Budul	391	Kolalgoo	400
Kila Hajee	391	Kolbee	400
Kila Dollah	391	Koleegrum	401
Kilakazee	391	Kolgui	401
Kila Kharzar	391	Kol Narawa	401
Kila Now	391	Kondilan	401
Kilat-i-Ghiljie	391	Koobree	401
Kila Tukuh	392	Koochen	401
Killa Abdalla	392	Koochlak	401
Killa Asseen	392	Koojla	401
Killaee Tilla	392	Kookewaree	401
Killa-i-Azim Khan	392	Kooksheb	401
Killa-i-Bukshee	392	Koolaj	401
Killa-i-Dookter	392	Koolazy	401
Killa-i-Hajee	392	Koolookail	402
Killa-i-Jaffree	393	Kooly Wallee	402
Killa-i-Khalekdad Khan	393	Koond	402
Killa-i-Khurotee	393	Koondeean	402
Killa-i-Lungur	393	Koondul	402
Killa-i-Murgha, or Nowa Murgha	393	Kooner	402
Killa-i-Nadir	393	Koor	402
Killa-i-Ramazan Khan	394	Kooranis	402
Killa-i-Sha Meer	394	Koord	402
Killa-i-Sobha	394	Koorhi Madali	402
Killa Kassim	394	Koorkee Tagrish	402
Killa Rahim Khan	394	Koorum	402
Killawalla	394	Koory	403
Kimbuldai	394	Kooshab	403
Kinjir	394	Kooshak	403
Kinjore	394	Kooshak	403
Kirkunee	395	Kooshk	403
Kirman	395	Kooshk	403
Kirta, or Kista	395	Kooshk-i-Saffeed	403
Kirtarpoor	395	Kopurthelia	404
Kishan	395	Kora	404
Kishanee	395	Koraeen	404
Kishengunga	395	Koraejee Na Gote	404
Kisht	395	Koree	404
Kishtawar	395	Koreh	404
Kista	396	Kosah Nag	404
Kobul	396	Koshaub	405
Koda	396	Kot	405
Kohare	396	Kot	405
Kohat	396	Kotana	405
Kohat	396	Kot Buxada	405
Kohee	397	Kote	406
Kohee Merwitty	397	Kote	406
Koh-i-Baba	397	Kote Belochwala	406
Koh-i-Daman	398	Kote Bhat	406
Koh-i-Doozd	398	Kote Isashah	406
Koh-i-Kharuk	398	Kotell	406
Kohoo, or Kohew	399	Koth	406
		Kotiah	406

Kotkaboo	406	Kulu	413
Kot Kangra	406	Kulul Khan	413
Kotkee	407	Kulung	413
Kot Kumalia	407	Kulutzi, or Khaletse	413
Kotlee	407	Kulyput	414
Kotli	407	Kumaike	414
Kotrdee	407	Kumbur	414
Kotree	407	Kumla Gurh	414
Kotree	407	Kummara	414
Kotree	407	Kummeesa-ka-Gote	414
Kotree	407	Kummur	415
Kottai	408	Kumur	415
Kottanga	408	Kundara	415
Kotul-i-Tucht	408	Kundye, or Kondilan, or Koondelauna	415
Koushan	408		
Kow	409	Kunghal	415
Kowalsir	409	Kunna Khyle	415
Kowranee	409	Kunuk	415
Krishna Gurh	409	Kuraee Killa	415
Kubbur-i-Jubbar	409	Kurazee	415
Kubbur Jabbar	410	Kuri	416
Kuboola	410	Kurjah	416
Kuburmach	410	Kurklekkee	416
Kucheeree	410	Kurkutcha	416
Kuchlak	410	Kurmpoor	417
Kuddeen	410	Kurnee	417
Kudjah	410	Kurpa	417
Kudmeh Ka Tulao	410	Kurramka	417
Kudun	410	Kurrachee	417
Kudunee	410	Kurra Khan	420
Kudur	410	Kurramnoer	420
Kukee	410	Kurreempoor	420
Kukiwaree	410	Kuru	420
Kukur	410	Kurum	420
Kulairee	410	Kusab	420
Kulan Cote, or Kulia Kote	411	Kusmore	421
Kuicha	411	Kusraon	421
Kuleel Khan	411	Kussoor	421
Kuliakote	411	Kutcha	421
Kuligam	411	Kuttajee	421
Kuligam	411	Kuttajee Mukam	421
Kulla Mowr	412	Kye Badanee	421
Kullar	412	Kyodah	421
Kullar Kahar	412	Kyra-ka-Gurree	421
Kulloor	412	Kyree Dera	422
Kullugan	412	Kyree Gurree	422
Kulora	413	Kysur	422
Kulorah	413	Kytoo	422

INDEX TO VOLUME II.

Ladakh, or Middle Tibet	1	Luree	28
Lah	13	Lurge	28
Lah	13	Lurroo, or Durroo	29
Lahore	13	Lus, or Lussa	29
Lahoree Bunder	16	Luttabund Pass	30
Lahoul, or Lawur	16	Lyaree	30
Laigpoor	17		
Lakahurrah	18		
Laka-ka-Turr	18	Machee	31
Lakoora	18	Maddehjee	31
Lal Kanyo	18	Magar Talao	31
Lalabeg	18	Maghribee	32
Lallee	18	Maher Peer	32
Lalloo	19	Mahomed Aga	32
Lalpoor	19	Mahomed Ali	33
Landee Khana	19	Mahomed Amroo	33
Laram Mountains	19	Mahomed Khan Ka Tanda	33
Largebur Kahreez	19	Mahomed Khan Nohur	33
Largee	19	Mahomed Khan Tanda	33
Larkhana	20	Mahomed Sayud-Ja-Gote	33
Larkhara	20	Maidan	33
Laspissor Mountains	20	Maimoke Ghat, or Ferry	33
Laush	20	Maimoodda	34
Lavor	21	Maimund	34
Le	21	Majgurra	34
Lehree	22	Majinda	34
Leia	22	Maju	34
Lidur	23	Makam	34
Lilleah	23	Mal	34
Lodhu	23	Maleea	34
Logurh	23	Malekpur	34
Logurh	23	Malekra	34
Lolab	23	Malgeerk	35
Lolum	24	Malla-Ja-Gote	35
Loodhun	24	Malloodie	35
Loonee	24	Mamadpoor	35
Lora	24	Mamoo Khail	35
Lora	24	Manasa Bul	35
Lorgurkara	25	Manchar	35
Losur	25	Manga	36
Losur	25	Mangeegura	36
Luggaree	25	Mangeegurd	36
Lughman	26	Manihala	36
Luk Bawun	26	Manikyala	36
Luka	26	Manja	38
Lukh	26	Manjai	38
Lukhoki	26	Manjawal	38
Lukhsur	26	Manjawal	38
Lukkee Mountains	26	Mansa	38
Lukkee, Northern	27	Mapa	39
Lukkee, Southern	28	Maragond	39
Lulleeana	28	Maree	39
Lundye, or River of Panjkora	28	Maree	39
Lungur	28	Marchi	39
Lur	28	Maroof	39

Maroojabur	39	Metrie	53
Maroot	39	Meylmunj	53
Marow	40	Mhela-Maunda	53
Marreh	40	Mianee	53
Marsilla	40	Mihee	53
Martee Khan Ka Tanda	40	Millee	53
Mastuch	40	Minkravora	53
Mastung	41	Mir Allah	53
Matan	41	Mirbul	53
Matchie	44	Mir Daoud	54
Matinee	44	Mirza Awlung	54
Matistan	44	Mirzapoor	54
Matum	44	Mishkinya	54
Maunkaira, or Munkere	44	Miskhel	54
Mayar	44	Mitenda Kat	54
Mazeena	44	Mittani	54
Mazufurabad	44	Mittun Kote	54
Mazye	45	Mochara	55
Meealee	45	Modra	55
Meeanee	45	Moghumdee	55
Meeanee	45	Mohavee	55
Meeanee	45	Mohumbah	55
Meeanee	45	Mohunkot	55
Meeanee	45	Mohunkote	55
Meeanee	46	Mohunsa	55
Meean Pooshteh	46	Mojgurh	55
Meea Rozan	46	Mokulmusseed	56
Meeawul	46	Monsur	56
Meemuna	46	Monze Cape, or Ras Mooaree	56
Meengana	46	Moobarekpoor	56
Meenismajera	46	Mookashruk	56
Meer Ali	47	Mookhta	56
Meeranpoor	47	Mookr	57
Meerbur	47	Mookur	57
Meer Doud Serai	47	Moola	57
Meergurh	47	Moola, or Gundava Pass	57
Meerjee	47	Moola Goori	59
Meerkan	47	Moolakadee	59
Meerkhan	47	Moola Khan	59
Meerkhan Tana	47	Moola Kurme	59
Meerpoor	47	Moolana	59
Meerpoor	48	Moolanoh	59
Meerpoor	48	Mooleanee River	59
Meerpoor	48	Mooltan	59
Meerpoor	48	Moondeeshehur	61
Meetee	48	Moonder, or Moondra	61
Meetla	48	Moonee	61
Mehr	48	Moongwud	61
Mehy Bondee	48	Moorghan Kehehur	61
Meighra	48	Moorghaub	61
Meimuna	48	Moosa Koreshee	62
Mekran	49	Mooshakee	62
Melemanda	52	Moostung	62
Meneeka	52	Mootakhala	62
Menotee	52	Mootiah	62
Mer and Ser	52	Mooradpoor	62
Meraub Lukia	53	Morah	62
Metaee	53	Moreed Ka Kote	62
Metrao	53	Mori	62

Morodanee	62	Mutta	69
Moroo	62	Muttaree	69
Morul	63	Mutteh	69
Mota Mar	63	Muzaree	69
Motch	63	Muzifferabad	69
Moujdurria	63	Mydan	69
Mourdalie	63	Mye Otta	69
Moutnee	63	Myesur	69
Moyumbub	63	Mymuauh	69
Mritteh	63		
Muchnee	63		
Mud	64	Naa Bala	69
Mudaree	64	Naaghi	69
Mududa	64	Nabog Nyh, or Nabog Nye	70
Mugdoom	64	Nadali	70
Muggeo Peer	64	Nadaun	70
Mugger Peerke	64	Nadir Deh	71
Muggur Talao	64	Naeewalla	71
Muhar	64	Nagar, or Nagyr	71
Muhidpoor	64	Naggar	71
Muhotai	64	Nagrolah	72
Mukali	64	Nakodur	72
Mukam	64	Nal	72
Mukdamram	64	Naljee Maenee	72
Mukkud	64	Namoosa	72
Mukur	65	Namutzye	72
Mukwar	65	Nandan Sar	72
Mukwul	65	Nanee	72
Mulka	65	Nanga Purbut, or Parwut	73
Mulkabad	65	Nanundur Kot	73
Mull	65	Nao Deh	73
Mulleeree River	65	Narang	73
Mulloh River	65	Narch	73
Mullahpoor	65	Nari	73
Mullyan	65	Narra (Eastern)	73
Mummoo	65	Narra (Western)	74
Mumsee	66	Nasserabad	74
Mumuke	66	Nasumon	74
Mundi	66	Natho Salimke Chistee	74
Mundui	66	Naushera	75
Muneeara	66	Nawa Sun	75
Munejah	67	Nawdree	75
Munkere	67	Nawula-jo-Gote	75
Munoora	67	Nechara	75
Munsoor Kareez	67	Neegaree	75
Munsoor Khan Goondee	67	Neelaub	75
Munsur	67	Neeloo	75
Muree	67	Neembuj	75
Murr	67	Neemla	75
Murraie	67	Neemra	76
Murraie Mukam	67	Nelaee	76
Murra Kharra, properly Murra Khail	67	Nenkur	76
		Nesh	76
Murrow Koostuk	67	Newar Beloochwala	76
Muru Wurdwun	68	Niazpur	76
Murwut	68	Nicetta	76
Mustoee	68	Nihung	76
Mustung	68	Nijrow	76
Muton	69	Nilab	77

Nil Nag	77	Oba	84
Ningana	77	Obeh, or Oba	84
Nishowra	77	Oihman	84
Nobra, or Nubra	77	Oin	84
Nograma	78	Oleera	84
Nohgira	78	Olipore	84
Nohur	78	Omarkote	85
Noogong	78	Omercote	85
Noondroo	78	Oobowrah	85
Noon Mianee	78	Ooch	85
Noorja	78	Oochlan	86
Noor Jumal	78	Oodana	86
Noorpoor	78	Oodar	86
Noorzye	78	Oodeenuggur	86
Nooshky	79	Oodoo-Da-Kote	86
Noshara	79	Oomeepoor	87
Noshurh	79	Oomur	87
Nourak	79	Oonapootla	87
Noushera	79	Oonerpoor	87
Noushera	79	Oonkaee	87
Noushera	79	Oonna	87
Noushera	79	Ooplaun	87
Noushuhr	79	Oorghoon	87
Nowa Dherra	80	Oormool	88
Nowa Gote	80	Oornach	88
Nowagye	80	Oornach	88
Nowa Murgoh	80	Oornach	88
Nowchara	80	Oorudanee	88
Nowneas	80	Oot	88
Nowrut	80	Ootch	88
Nowsharra	80	Ootorahgote	88
Nowsharra	80	Ootpalana	88
Nowshur	80	Ootuk	89
Nowzer	80	Ootul	89
Nubeesur	80	Osanpoor	89
Nufoosk Pass	80	Osman	89
Null	81	Otman	89
Nulhikh	81	Oubazedeh	89
Nummul	81	Outche	89
Nundansur	81	Ouzbin	89
Nundawadagar	81		
Nundel	81		
Nundeweedagur	81	Pacence	90
Nungnehar	81	Pachlawe	90
Nungul	82	Padee Zhur	90
Nunmenwarre	82	Padra	90
Nunuks Durrumsala	82	Padree	90
Nunwarry	82	Paeesht Khana	90
Nur	82	Paharpoor	90
Nurd	83	Paharpoor	90
Nurpur	83	Paien-i-Duras, or Pain Dras	91
Nurrah	83	Pak Pattan	91
Nuryoob	83	Pakba Sidharo	92
Nusseerabad	83	Pakrun	92
Nusseerpoor	83	Palalu	92
Nutyan	83	Pallia	92
Nuzzerpoor	83	Pambur	92
Nyaz Muhumud	84	Pamghan, or Pamghaan	92
		Pampur	92

Panalia	93	Phurrah	103
Panch-Gerai	93	Pind Dadun Khan	103
Pandrenton	93	Pindee Battianka	104
Panduran	93	Pindee Mulik Oulea	104
Paneewan	93	Piniaree River	104
Panjgadgerh	94	Pinjaree Daree	104
Panjkora	94	Pinteeanee	105
Pannoh-Ca-Par	94	Pinyaree	105
Pantur Chuk	94	Pir Jelalpoor	105
Parar	94	Pir Panjal	105
Pareewallah	94	Pisheen	106
Parkoo	94	Pitmutee	106
Parkuta	95	Pittee	106
Parna	95	Piwar	107
Partur	95	Podsheh	107
Parwan	95	Poghuara	107
Parwan Pass	95	Pokrun	107
Passeenoe, or Pacenee	95	Poolajee	107
Pastan	95	Poolkee	108
Patan	95	Poolsingee	108
Patan Kot	96	Poora	108
Pattee	96	Poorally	108
Patten	96	Pooranah	109
Pauk Pattan	96	Pooranuh	109
Paurik	96	Poorur	109
Pa Yech	96	Poranadera	109
Peedur Kussur	97	Porewala	109
Peelinjabad	97	Poshiana	109
Peepree	97	Pota	109
Peepul	97	Potee	109
Peepulwarie Mukam	97	Poulaund	109
Peer Adal	97	Powar Gote	109
Peer Buksh	97	Powar Gote	110
Peer Chutta	97	Powhur	110
Peerka	97	Pubb Mountains	110
Peer Lukkee	97	Pubberwalee	110
Peer Punjah	97	Puchkooa	110
Peer Putta	97	Pudu Davi	110
Peer Radan	98	Pughman, Pemghan, or Pamghan	110
Peer Ukra Gote	98	Pugman, or Pemghan	111
Peesee Bhent	98	Pukatangee	111
Pehie	98	Pukli	111
Peijhour	98	Pulaluk	111
Pemghan	98	Pul-i-Malan	112
Penjhur	98	Pulleeja	112
Pere Pye	98	Pulleeja	112
Pesh Bolak	98	Pulung	112
Peshawer, or Peshawur	98	Pumja Gote	112
Peshawer, or Peshawur	101	Punch	112
Pettee	102	Punch River	112
Peyhour	102	Punchshir, or Punjshir	113
Thagwara	102	Punchshir River	114
Phaliah	102	Pundee	114
Pheloka	102	Pungria	114
Phoogan Garra Koond	102	Punj Deen, or Punj Deh	114
Phoolera	103	Punjab, The	115
Phor River	103	Punjan Goosht	141
Phuluda	103	Pungoor	141
Phumara	103	Punjand	142
Phurano	103		

Punjook	143	Regan	153
Punjshir	143	Reg Rowan	153
Punna	143	Rejla	154
Punnailah	144	Remmuk	154
Purani Deria	144	Retta Sooltan	154
Purean	144	Richel	154
Purwan	144	Rihursi	155
Purwana	145	Rilu	155
Puttee	145	Rimbiara River	155
Puttehpoor	145	Rindan	155
Puttoola Killa	145	Robat	155
Pyrghowla	145	Roda	155
		Rod Bahar	155
		Rodbar	156
Quetta	146	Rogalin	156
		Rogani	156
		Roghan	156
Rabaht	146	Roh	157
Rabat	146	Rokree	157
Radhwarree	146	Rokun	157
Rado	146	Rondu, or Royal	157
Raepoor	146	Rood-i-Adruscund	157
Rageree	146	Rood-i-Guz	157
Rahim Dad	146	Roodinjo	157
Rahmuk	147	Rookenwala	158
Raj	147	Rookun	158
Rajadarah	147	Rookunpoor	158
Raja Gote	147	Roomra River	158
Rajak	147	Roree	158
Rajapoor	147	Roree, or Lohuree	158
Rajarie	147	Rotas	160
Raja Sanse	147	Row	161
Rajawur	147	Rozan	161
Rajh	148	Rozeh	161
Rajoora	148	Rozeh-Bagh	161
Rajtulla	148	Rozur	161
Rajunpoor	148	Ruhul	161
Rajunpoor	148	Rumzan Khan	162
Rajur	148	Rungpoor	162
Raknee	148	Runna	162
Ramnagur	148	Runnie-ka-Kote	162
Ramneghur, or Ramnuggur	149	Rupshu	162
Ramtereth	149	Ruree	162
Raneepoor	149	Rusoolpoor	162
Ranjunpoor	149	Rustom	162
Ras Arubah, or Oremarrah	149		
Rashnn Bustee	150		
Ras Koppah	150	Saadat	163
Ras Malan	150	Sadan	163
Ras Mooarree	150	Sadaut	163
Ras Noo	150	Sadi Khyle	163
Ras Passeenoe	150	Saheewall	163
Ras Pishk	150	Sahoo	163
Ras Seeunney	150	Said Khan	163
Ras Sheid	150	Saidan	163
Ras Shemaul Bunder	150	Saiyadabad	164
Ravee, or Ravi	150	Saiyadwala	164
Rawdon	152	Sakhee Sawar Pass	164
Rawil Pinde	152	Sakhee Surwar	165
Reepree	153	Sakhir	165

Sakree	165	Shah Mushud	185
Sakul	165	Shahpoor	185
Salat	165	Shahpoor	185
Salehkeh	165	Shaik Ka Raj	185
Saliki Serai	165	Shakapore	186
Sallarah	165	Shakhur, or Shenkhur	186
Salulang Pass	165	Shakr Dara	186
Salt Range	166	Shalkot	186
Sandwalle	169	Shargullee	186
Sangad, or Buzdar Pass	169	Sharkee	186
Sang Ghar	170	Sharuk	186
Sangrar	170	Shawl	187
Sarawan	170	Shawl	188
Sarawan	171	Shawpoor	189
Sarn	171	Sheaul	189
Sarungkol	171	Sheer	189
Sata, or Setta	171	Sheerkail	189
Satgharra	171	Sheheruk	189
Satpur	172	Shek	189
Saugra	172	Shekabad	189
Saul	172	Shekwan	190
Scinde	172	Shelghur	190
Seah Khana	172	Shelly Sola	190
Sealkee	172	Sheranow	190
Seaoul	172	Sher Dundan	190
Sebee, or Sewee	172	Sheri	190
Seer	172	Sher-Mahomed-Killa	190
Seerannee	173	Sher-i-Safa	190
Seetaree	173	Sheroo	190
Sehama	173	Shesha Nag	191
Sehkoh	173	Shighur	191
Sehra	173	Shikarpoor	191
Sehwan	173	Shikarpur	194
Seisan	174	Shing	194
Seistan	174	Shinkee	194
Senee	180	Shiniza	194
Serai-i Shah Beg	180	Shoojuabad	194
Seri Gobindpoor	180	Shookrabad	194
Sermih	180	Shorab	194
Sessarah	180	Shorabak	194
Sewestan	180	Shoraee Khojake	195
Sezkoh	181	Shorandan	195
Shadabad	181	Shorawuk	195
Shadadpoor	181	Shorkach	195
Shadaywara	181	Shorkot	195
Shadeezye	181	Shorun	195
Shadehur	181	Shudapoor	195
Shaeewan	182	Shuftul	195
Shagurh	182	Shuhr Roghan	196
Shah Abun	182	Shuhrova	197
Shah Alum	182	Shujabad	197
Shahbad	182	Shujanpoor	198
Shah Billawal	183	Shukur Darah	198
Shah Bunder	183	Shuly Wukyl	198
Shahdazye	183	Shumkool	198
Shahkoogud	184	Shumsabad	198
Shah Kot	184	Shund	198
Shahlimar	184	Shupeyon	198
Shah Mahomed	185	Shurji-Murga	198
Shah Muksood	185	Shutul	199

Shyrkhowi	199	Soormadane	249
Siah Koh	199	Soormasing	249
Sib	199	Soouk Deeval	250
Sickeelale	199	Sopur	250
Sida	199	Sorah	250
Sikunka	199	Sorah	250
Simmasuttee	199	Sorahanee	250
Sineow	199	Soretnee	250
Sinde	199	Soun Lead Mine	250
Sinh-kha-bab	236	Speencha	250
Sinzavee	236	Speenghur	250
Sir Mouth	237	Spinawaree	250
Sira	237	Spundow	250
Sira Durga	237	Subzawur	250
Sirahuh	237	Subzjoo	251
Sir Chusmah, properly Sir Chushmah	237	Subzuleote	251
		Suder Ghur	251
Sidarcote, or Walour	237	Sudoja	251
Sirdar Ghur	237	Sudoo Shaw	251
Siree	237	Suduk River	251
Sirgae	237	Sudur Ghur	251
Sir-i-ab	237	Sufeid Koh	252
Sir-i-asp	238	Suffin Jo Vhan	252
Sirinagur	238	Suhoyum	252
Siringnaghur	244	Sukkerunda	252
Siri Pool	244	Sukkur	253
Sir-i-Sunga	245	Sukyt	253
Sirkany	245	Suldera	253
Sirnawaree	245	Suliman Mountains	253
Sirra Killa	245	Sulleeanee	254
Sir-Ulung	245	Sultanpoor, or Kulu	254
Smalan	245	Sultanpoor	255
Sobarah	245	Sultaree	255
Sodr Wad	245	Sumaboo	255
Soe	245	Sumarakote, or Somanakote	255
Sofahun	246	Sumbi	255
Sohrab	246	Sumbul, Simbul, or Sumbhelpur	255
Soleiman Mountains	246		
Soltanpoor	246	Summa Ka Bustee	255
Sonawarun	246	Summani	256
Sondanwaran	246	Summee	256
Soneaut	246	Sundum	256
Sonmeanee, properly Soumeanee	246	Sungau River	256
		Sunglakhl	256
Sookad	247	Sungrar	256
Sooltan-ka-Kote	248	Sungsa	256
Sooltankhel	248	Sungur	256
Sooltanpoor	248	Sungur	256
Soomerjee Wussee	248	Sunjeree	256
Soona Chanda-ke-Bindee	248	Sunn	257
Soopur	248	Sunnabake Boonga	257
Soorban	248	Sunnee	257
Soorgoorgye	248	Sunneweh	257
Soork Dewar	248	Suntpoor	257
Soorkh-Ab	248	Suranoterano	257
Soorkh-Ab	248	Surdhee	257
Soorkhow	248	Surge	257
Soorkhpoor	249	Surna-kot-killa	257
Soorkh Rood, or Soorkhab	249	Surrukpoor	257
Soorkoon	249	Surtaf	257

Surwod	258	Thoora	270
Sutledge	258	Thullada	270
Sutluj	258	Thutha	270
Sutta Walla	261	Thyreh	270
Suwat	261	Tiba	270
Suyud Bukas	261	Tibbee	270
Swan	261	Tibby	270
Syadabad	262	Tibee	271
Syagard	262	Tigadee	271
Syedad	262	Tira, or Shah Jehanpur	271
Synabad	262	Tissa	271
Syndabad	262	Toba	271
Syndabad	262	Toe	272
Syndan	262	Toga	272
Syudgaum	262	Tohi	272
Syudgote	262	Tokuruk	272
Syud Ka Gote	262	Tolti	272
Syuds Gote	262	Toonea	273
		Toonee	273
		Toorkubar	273
Tab	262	Toot-i-Gussurman	273
Tagon	263	Torbela	273
Tahirbegy	263	Torgad	273
Tag	263	Torgo	273
Takaree	263	Touda Cheena	273
Takeah	263	Trahal	274
Takee	263	Tranee	274
Takht	264	Trankar, or Dankar	274
Takipur	264	Tremou	274
Takkal	264	Triccul	274
Tal	264	Tricota	274
Tal	264	Triloknath (Temple of)	275
Talache	264	Troohawala	275
Talafru	264	Trug	275
Talee	264	Truggar	275
Tameehak	264	Tsok	275
Tamulsir	264	Tubuksir	275
Tandda	265	Tugao Peak	275
Tandi	265	Tukanee	275
Tangee Turkai	265	Tukatoo	275
Tara	265	Tukhtapool	275
Tariana	265	Tukht-i-Sikundur	276
Tatara Pass	265	Tukht-i-Suliman	276
Tatta	265	Tukrow	276
Tawisk	268	Tulkab	276
Tazeen	268	Tull	276
Tebhee	268	Tullar	277
Teendo	269	Tull-i-Kuman	277
Teer Andaz	269	Tulumba, or Toolumba	277
Teeree, or Teera	269	Tulwandee	277
Teeree	269	Tumboo	277
Teeree	269	Tundeh	277
Teher	269	Tuppee	277
Tenghi	269	Tupperah	277
Terie	269	Turahnu	277
Teyaga	270	Turghurree	277
Tezeen	270	Turnak River	277
Thabool	270	Turtee	278
Thana	270	Tushat	278
Thog-ji-Chenmo	270	Tutam Dara	278

www.ingramcontent.com/pod-product-compliance
Lightning Source LLC
Chambersburg PA
CBHW081913170426
43200CB00014B/2717